The Selected Letters of Theodore Roosevelt

The Selected Letters of Theodore Roosevelt

Edited by H. W. Brands

Cooper Square Press

First Cooper Square Press edition 2001

This Cooper Square Press hardcover edition of *The Selected Letters of Theodore Roosevelt* is an original publication. It is published by arrangement with the editor.

Published by Cooper Square Press
An Imprint of the Rowman & Littlefield Publishing Group
150 Fifth Avenue, Suite 817
New York, New York 10011

Distributed by National Book Network

Library of Congress Cataloging-in-Publication Data

Roosevelt, Theodore, 1858–1919.
    [Correspondence. Selections]
    The selected letters of Theodore Roosevelt / [edited by] H. W. Brands.
      p. cm.
    Includes bibliographical references and index.
    ISBN 0-8154-1126-X (alk. paper)
Roosevelt, Theodore, 1858–1919—Correspondence. 2. Presidents—United States—Correspondence. 3. Roosevelt, Theodore, 1858–1919—Family.
4. United States—Politics and government—1901–1909. I. Brands, H. W.
II. Title.

E757 .A4 2001
973.91'1'092—dc21
[B]   2001028178

♾ ™The paper used in this publication meets the minimum requirements of American National Standard for Information Sciences—Permanence of Paper for Printed Library Materials, ANSI/NISO Z39.48–1992.
Manufactured in the United States of America.

Contents

Introduction

Benjamin Franklin's alter ego Poor Richard once prescribed a formula for immortality:

> If you would not be forgotten
> As soon as you are dead and rotten,
> Either write things worth reading
> Or do things worth the writing.

By this standard Theodore Roosevelt was guaranteed a double after-life. Roosevelt was the most literary of American presidents, writing scores of books and countless shorter works. His memoir of the Spanish-American War, *The Rough Riders*, was a bestseller in its day and remains a classic account of what Roosevelt's friend (and secretary of state) John Hay called that "splendid little war." Roosevelt's historical volumes, especially *The Naval War of 1812* (published when he was just twenty-three) and his four-volume *The Winning of the West*, not only retain their dramatic flavor after more than a century but also stand up well to scholarly scrutiny. His hunting and travel pieces, including *Through the Brazilian Wilderness*, have weathered the transition from natural history to history of nature.

If Roosevelt was the most literary of presidents, he was also the most active of American writers. He was, by turns, a New York state assemblyman, a rancher, a candidate for mayor of New York City, a federal civil service commissioner, president of the New York City police board, assistant secretary of the navy, a cavalry officer and military hero, governor of New York, vice president, president, a lion- (and elephant- and rhinoceros-) hunter, the most successful third-party presidential candidate in American history, an Amazon explorer, and the bane of Woodrow Wilson's existence. Few lives encompass more diverse activities, more successfully undertaken. Even if Roosevelt had not written a sentence worth the reading, he did plenty worth the writing.

This much, of course, is common knowledge, appreciated during Roosevelt's time and since. What is less known is that Roosevelt was one of the great letter writers in American history. His output was prodigious, and has been estimated at more than 100,000. (No one has had the energy for a closer count.) He discussed politics with Henry Cabot Lodge, the longtime senator from Massachusetts; international affairs with Cecil Spring-Rice, Jules Jusserand, and Hermann Speck von Steinberg, diplomats respectively from Britain, France, and Germany; naval strategy with Alfred Thayer Mahan, the great naval historian; conservation with John Muir, the father of the environmental movement; higher education with Charles Eliot, president of Harvard, and Nicholas Murray Butler, president of Columbia; literature with Owen Wister and James Brander Matthews; history with Francis Parkman and George Trevelyan; football with Walter Camp, the legendary Yale coach; and innumerable other subjects with authors distinguished and obscure.

He also wrote of personal matters. Roosevelt was the most famous family man in America; the Roosevelt tribe took Washington by storm in 1901 and remained at the center of national attention even after Roosevelt left the presidency. The children were as rambunctious as their father, piling ponies into the White House elevator, sticking spitwads on the portraits on the walls, ambushing one another (and their father) with pillows and weapons slightly more effective, and releasing snakes and other fauna among the eminent guests. Roosevelt's eldest, Alice, was notoriously headstrong. Asked why he didn't rein her in, the president ruefully replied, "I can be president of the United States, or I can attend to Alice. I can't do both."

The reader of Roosevelt's letters watches the children grow; the reader also watches Roosevelt's relationship with the children mature. At first the letters focus on childish matters, but increasingly they include comments on politics and public affairs—comments, in some cases, Roosevelt confided in no one else. The most poignant letters follow the four boys to the front in World War I. The letters reveal a father simultaneously proud of his sons' patriotism and appalled at the danger they face. The letters finally reveal a stricken old man struggling to cope with the death in battle of his youngest child.

The letters reveal much about Roosevelt, but they do not reveal everything. There are very few letters from Roosevelt to his wife of thirty-six years, Edith, for the simple reason that she burned nearly all of them as being none of posterity's business. No feeling person can begrudge this spousal prerogative, but it leaves the student of history unable to fully appreciate a relationship that endured early testing to become one of the great love stories of American public life.

In the present selection, there are no letters *to* Roosevelt. This editorial decision has been made for reasons of space, but it prevents the reader from seeing the give-and-take in Roosevelt's correspondence. Roosevelt had a healthy ego; critics jibed that the publisher of *The Rough Riders* ran out of the capital letter "I" in setting type for the book. Yet in his correspondence Roosevelt was as much the listener as the speaker—a fact that is unfortunately lost in the elimination of all incoming correspondence.

Even regarding the outgoing mail, the culling has been most rigorous. The editors of the eight-volume Harvard University Press collection of Roosevelt letters, Elting E. Morison and John M. Blum, printed approximately one out of ten of the letters Roosevelt wrote; in the present edition, only one out of a hundred letters make the cut. Some of the rejections have been easy: routine acknowledgments, contemporary commentary of no lasting interest or importance, letters that essentially repeat points made in other letters. Yet even allowing for this, a great deal of substance has been left out.

The guiding principle has been to concentrate on letters that illuminate Roosevelt—the man, the public figure, the polymath. In nearly all cases, the letters included are reproduced in their entirety. Although this brings in some material inconsequential of itself, it better enables the reader to follow the working of Roosevelt's mind as he shifted from one topic to another. The letters are also reproduced in their original spelling and syntax. Until he acquired stenographers and secretaries, spelling sometimes presented a challenge to Roosevelt, which doubtless explains his enthusiasm for spelling reform. Such slight inconvenience as his peculiar orthography and sentence construction (his employment of semi-colons outstripped even his use of the first person singular pronoun) cause readers is, in the judgment of the editor, more than offset by the authenticity they afford the letters. Where Roosevelt's handwriting is indecipherable, such has been indicated.

Annotations have been kept to the minimum necessary to render Roosevelt's comments intelligible to readers at the beginning of the twenty-first century. Here again the guiding principle has been to illuminate Roosevelt—and not necessarily the events or persons of which he wrote. The introductions to each section provide a modest amount of additional framing. The reader interested in more detail is referred to the biographies and other sources noted below.

On this point, a reminder may be in order: that a collection of letters, however edited, is no substitute for biography or history per se. Those genres round out the character and the times in a way a collection of letters never can.

Letters do something different. They give us the individual undiluted. Roosevelt speaks here in his own voice, in words of his own choosing. To the extent the long-dead can live again, letters bring them back better than any other medium. Roosevelt was the liveliest person most of his contemporaries knew (one of them remarked, on hearing he had died in his sleep, that death had to take him sleeping because it could never defeat him awake). Even now, eight decades after his passing, Roosevelt's letters capture the verve, the sheer joy in being alive, that was his signature in life and his legacy in death.

A Note on Sources and Additional References

The most important archival collections of Roosevelt's letters are held by the Library of Congress and Harvard University. The Library of Congress collection is available on microfilm; the Harvard collection is not. The most comprehensive published correspondence is *The Letters of Theodore Roosevelt*, edited by Elting E. Morison and published by Harvard University Press (1951–1954). The annotations are extensive, erudite, and often witty; this edition is a model of scholarly editing, and has served as the basis and inspiration for the present volume. Roosevelt's correspondence with Henry Cabot Lodge is covered in *Selections from the Correspondence of Theodore Roosevelt and Henry Cabot Lodge, 1884–1918*, edited by Henry Cabot Lodge and Charles F. Redmond (1925). Other published collections include *Theodore Roosevelt and His Times, Shown in His Own Letters*, by Joseph Bucklin Bishop (1920); *Letters from Theodore Roosevelt to Anna Roosevelt Cowles*, by Anna Roosevelt Cowles (1924); *My Brother Theodore Roosevelt*, by Corinne Roosevelt Robinson (1926); *Theodore Roosevelt's Letters to His Children*, edited by Joseph Bucklin Bishop (1919); and *Letters to Kermit from Theodore Roosevelt*, edited by Will Irwin (1946). Bishop's *Roosevelt's Letters to His Children* has been updated and reissued as *A Bully Father*, edited by Joan Paterson Kerr (1995).

Biographies of Roosevelt are many. A recent one-volume life is *TR: The Last Romantic*, by H. W. Brands (1997). Excellent partial lives are *The Rise of Theodore Roosevelt*, by Edmund Morris (1979); and *Mornings on Horseback*, by David McCullough (1981). Dated and opinionated, but basically sound, is *Theodore Roosevelt*, by Henry F. Pringle (1931). More judicious is *The Life and Times of Theodore Roosevelt*, by William Henry Harbaugh (1961, 1975). These works contain notes and bibliographies identifying additional references to nearly every topic discussed in the letters below.

Acknowledgments

The editor would like to thank Wallace Finley Dailey, curator of the Theodore Roosevelt Collection at Harvard University's Houghton Library, for his gracious and professional assistance over the years. Thanks to the Houghton Library for permission to reproduce letters and photographs from the Theodore Roosevelt Collection, Harvard College Library. Thanks to the Franklin Delano Roosevelt Library for photocopies from its collection. Thanks to the Library of Congress for Roosevelt correspondence and photographs.

PART ONE

Blessed Youth

1858–1881

*T*heodore Roosevelt was born on October 27, 1858, in New York City. His paternal grandfather was Cornelius Van Schaack Roosevelt, one of the handful of wealthiest men in New York, and therefore one of the wealthiest men in America. His father, for whom the boy was named, inherited a quarter of the wealth, being one of four sons. Theodore's mother was the former Martha Bulloch, of a Georgia family distinguished politically and otherwise since the Revolutionary War. This marriage of North and South had an important influence on Theodore's life (beyond the obvious one of his birth): Mittie (as family and friends called Martha; her son sometimes called her "Muffie") could not bear for her husband to take up arms against her Confederate kin, so he did not. Although Theodore Junior never criticized his father on this score, those who knew the boy best felt that his later strong interest in soldiering owed at least in part to a desire to prove that Roosevelts were no slackers.

"Teedie," as Theodore was called, had an older sister, Anna (nicknamed Bamie, short for bambina and pronounced "Bammie"; alternatively "Bye" or "Bysie"), a younger brother, Elliot ("Ellie" or "Nell"), and a younger sister, Corinne ("Conie," "Pussie"). Bamie was several years older than the others, who consequently played more among themselves than with her. Numerous Roosevelt cousins and the occasional Bulloch rounded out the landscape of Teedie's childhood.

During his first decade the boy suffered badly from asthma. Nothing afforded consistent relief, but removal from the soot, smoke, and dust of New York City seemed to help. For this reason the family escaped whenever possible—to Oyster Bay on Long Island, among other summer retreats, and on journeys to Europe and beyond for more extended vacations.

Roosevelt eventually outgrew his asthma. To some extent this probably resulted from simple maturation, but it also reflected a concerted campaign of physical exercise. He took up boxing, wrestling, and other competitive sports; he also engaged in most imaginable outdoor diversions. He hiked, swam, climbed, rowed, sailed, ran, rode horses, hunted, and generally made a point—a religion, almost—of challenging his strength and stamina.

Roosevelt's fondness for the outdoor life also revealed a strong interest in natural history. He collected bugs, birds, and larger beasts—at first with fingers, jars, and nets, later with shotgun and rifle. This armed collecting was often indistinguishable from hunting, which became another passion.

Roosevelt's education was eclectic. He learned to read early, and during his years of ill health, reading provided an outlet for his imagination. Travel—a trip to Europe at ten, to the Middle East at fifteen, followed by a six-month stay in Dresden—broadened him further. Wealthy families in those days often hired tutors for their children; in Roosevelt's case, a Harvard graduate named Arthur Cutler prepared the young man for college, and helped persuade him to choose Harvard.

3

Roosevelt entered Harvard two months before his eighteenth birthday. He quickly became enchanted with his new friends, whom he described admiringly in letters home. He was a good student, but not a standout. Although he enjoyed himself immensely, he gave little indication of special social or political gifts, beyond that which characterized him better than any other: an unquenchable zest for living.

An event of Roosevelt's second year at college briefly challenged that zest. His father developed cancer and died. The death cost Roosevelt both his life model and his best friend, and cast a dark, if temporary, shadow over the young man.

A side effect of his father's passing was Roosevelt's financial independence. As he inherited his share of the family money, the young man enjoyed himself more than ever, becoming quite the gent on campus. Whether this had anything to do with his falling madly in love for the first time is difficult to say. Friends and family had long linked him with Edith Carow, Corinne's best friend. But in Boston another girl, Alice Lee, captured his heart. Following an energetic pursuit he in turn captured hers, and the two were wed not long after his graduation. Their honeymoon took them to Europe, where he showed her what he had learned on previous visits, climbed the Matterhorn, and reflected on what a fortunate young man he was.

April 30, 1868. New York
To Theodore Roosevelt, Senior

My Dear Father

I received your letter yesterday. Your letter was more exciting than Mother's. I have a request to ask of you, will you do it? I hope you will, if you will it will figure greatly in my museum. You know what supple jack's are do you not? Pleas get one for Ellie and two for me. Ask your friend to let you cut off the tiger-cat's tail and get some long moss and have it mated together. One of the supple jack's (I am talking of mine now) must be about as thick as your thumb and finger. The other must be as thick as your thumb. The one which is as thick as your finger and thumb must be four feet long, and the other must be three feet long. One of my mice got crushed. It was the mouse I liked best though it was a common mouse. It's name was Brownie. Nothing particular has happened since you went away for I cannot go out in the country like you can. The trees and the vine on our piazza are buding and the grass is green as can be and no one would dream that it was winter so short a time ago. All send love to all of you.

Yours loveingly

January 1, 1870. Sorrento
To Edith Kermit Carow

My Dear Eidie

We came from Naples today. I have recieved your interesting letter and reply to it on paper recieved on Christmas. Yesterday we made the ascent of Mt. Vesuvius. It was snow covered which heightened our enjoyment. We went first in caraiges for a long while. We then got out and mounted ponies. We mounted now pretty steadily. At first we walked but after a while Papa, Ellie and I galloped ahead with two guides and one strange gentleman. These guides were the only ones mounted. We galloped along untill we came to a gulley coated with ice on which the horses walked with 2 legs on one side and 2 legs on the other side. We got to a house where we dismounted to wait for the others and as Conie came up she gave me a great big snowball on the side. I would have thrown another at her but we had to mount and Ellie and I galloped ahead till we came to the place where we got off our horses. I made a snowball and as Conie came up hit her. We then began the ascent of snow covered Mt. Vesuvius. I went first with one guide with a strap in which I put my hands. One place where the side was steeper than any alp I have been on the guide and I fell. We recovered ourselves right away. Our Alpine stocks went down farther and our guide had to go down to get them. I got up to near the top we went inside of a wall where the snow ceased and it was quite warm. We then went on untill we came to a small hole through which we saw a red flame inside the mountain. I put my alpine stock in and it caught fire right away. The smoke nearly suffacated us. We then went on and saw a larger hole through which I could fall if I liked. We put some pebbles down and they came up with pretty good force. We here sat down to lunch. We ate some of the eggs boiled in Vesuvius sand. Ellie and I played with some soildiers and then we began the decent. This was on the opposite side of the mountain. I was the last, then Mama with Papa on one and a guide on the other side of her and then the rest. We went down the side in loose dirt in which I sunk up to my knees. The decent was verry steep. Mama was so exausted she could hardly walk. When we got to the bottom we mounted our horses and went along a miserable road. There were places where the men who were on foot could hardly walk so it was verry hard for the horses. We then drove to the hotel. But now goodby.

Evere your loving friend,

January 26, 1873. Near Kom Ombos, Egypt
To Anna Bulloch Gracie

Dear Aunt Annie,

My right hand having recovered from the imaginary atack from which it did not suffer, I proceed to thank you for your kind present, which very much delighted me. We are now on the Nile and have been on that great and mysterious river for over a month. I think I have never enjoyed myself so much as in this month. There has always been something to do, for we could always fall back upon shooting when everything else fails us. And then we had those splendid and grand old ruins to see, and one of them will stock you with thoughts for a month. The templ that I enjoyed most was Karnak. We saw it by moonlight. I never was impressed by anything so much. To wander among those great columns under the same moon that had looked down on them for thousands of years was awe-inspiring; it gave rise to thoughts of the in-effable, the unuterable; thoughts which you can not express, which can not be uttered, which can not be answered untill after The Great Sleep.

Feb. 9th

I have had great enjoyment from the shooting here, as I have pro-cured between one and two hundred skins. I expect to procure some more in Syria. Inform Emlen of this. As you are probably aware Father presented me on Christmas with a double barrelled breech loading shot gun, which I never move on shore without, excepting on sundays. The largest bird I have yet killed is a Crane which I shot as it rose from a lagoon near Thebes.

The sporting is injurious to my trousers. Here is a picture of a pair. [sketch]

Now that I am on the subject of dress I may as well mention that the dress of the inhabitants up to ten years of age is—nothing. After that they put on a shirt descended from some remote ancestor and never take it off till the day of their death.

Mother is recovering from an attack of indegestion, but the rest are all well and send love to you and our friends, in which I join sincerely, and remain

Your Most Affectionate Nephew

June 15, 1873. Dresden
To Theodore Roosevelt, Senior

Dear Father,

Last week has been quite full of novelties. Mother stayed here untill yesterday (Saturday) when she went away, at the same time that Corinne moved, bag and baggage over to here to spend the summer. She sleeps in the room with Miss Anna and is not as yet a bit homesick. Last Thursday Anna, Miss Anna Minkvitz, Miss Lina Minkvitz, Elliot and I went out on an excursion, I with a butterfly net, and a case for beetles. We went first of all by boat for an hour and a half, then got off an visited an castle from which we had a beautiful view, and where I got several specimens This afternoon we will go to Aunt Lucy's. This morning we were at the German Reformed Church. The service was very like the Presbyterian. I did not understand much of the Sermon. The German is getting on very well and the French teacher says that if I knew the tenses of the verbs I would have a very good knowledge of the French Language. I can read it just and understand it almost as well as English, and in writing do not make many mistakes in the mere spelling, but am bad in constructing the sentences.

We (Johnie, Ellie, Maud, Corinne and I) have a little club which meets once a week and for which we write pieces. Corinne has "come out strong" in the poetry line.

The boxing gloves are a source of great amusement to us. When ever Johnie comes to see us we have an hours boxing or so. Each round takes one to two minutes.

The best round yet was one yesterday between Johnie and I. I shall describe it briefly. After some striking and warding, I got Johnie into a corner, when he sprung out. We each warded off a right hand blow and brough in a left hander. His took effect behind my ear, and for a minute I saw stars and reeled back to the centre of the room, while Johnie had had his nose and upper lip mashed together and been driven back against the door. I was so weak however that I was driven across the room, simply warding off blows, but then I almost disabled his left arm, and drove him back to the middle where some sharp boxing occurred. I got in one on his forehead which raised a bump, but my eye was made black and blue. At this minute "Up" was called and we had to seperate. Elliott can box better than either of us as he was a winter at a boxing school If you offered rewards for bloody noses you would spend a fortune on me alone. All send love. I send love to all. Tell Aunt Lizzy and Aunt Annie that I will write to them today.

 Your Aff. Son

June 20, 1875. Oyster Bay
To Anna Roosevelt

Dear Bamie,

 At present I am writing in a rather smelly room, as the fresh skins of six night herons are reposing on the table beside me; the said night herons being the product of yesterdays expedition to Loyd's (how do you spell the name?) neck. Elliot and I rowed over there in his little rowboat, although it was pretty rough. We found my old boat that we lost last year,—which alone would have amply (repayed) repaid (!) us for our row.

 My wretched horse has not yet recovered, but in two or three days I hope to be able to ride him. Elliots and Fathers saddle horses are also a little knocked up, but the rest are in fine condition.

 Dr. Swan gave us a very good but rather highflown sermon today. Cousin Corneil was in the qhire choir (I do'n't know what has got into; I can't spell the simplest word), and fell sound asleep with his head on the railing.

 Your Aff. Brother

September 29, 1876. Cambridge
To Martha Bulloch Roosevelt

Darling Motherling,

 When I arrived here on Wednsday night I found a fire burning in the grate, and the room looking just as cosy and comfortable as it could look. The table is almost too handsome, and I do not know whether to admire most the curtains, the paper or the carpet. What would I have done without Bamie! I have placed your photograph on the mantelpiece, where I can always see Motherling, the Babbit, and my "Garrulous Uncle."[1] I do not begin work until Monday, when I shall start with seven or eight hours a day. I rise at 7.15, attend prayers at 7.45 and at 8 take breakfast at common's, where the food is very fair. We have lunch at half past twelve, and dinner at half past five.

Please to send on in the valise, as soon as possible, with the paper and inkstand, my skates. If I can borrow a bag, I intend to spend next Sunday with Mr Minot,[2] who absolutely called on me *the day* after I arrived! With best love to all, I remain

Your Loving Son

October 22, 1876. Cambridge
To Theodore Roosevelt, Senior

Dearest Father

Your letter with the slip of paper containing an account of your speech has only just come to hand. Was Mr Cutlers letter ever so kind? I have also received a letter from Uncle Jimmie Bulloch, which was so sweet and touching that it really almost made me feel like crying. I enclose it to you. I have appreciated greatly the numbers of letters I have received from home and have appreciated still more their contents. I do not think there is a fellow in College who has a family that love him as much as you all do me, and I am sure that there is no one who has a Father who is also his best and most intimate friend, as you are mine. I have kept the first letter you wrote me and shall do my best to deserve your trust. I do not find it nearly so hard as I expected not to drink and smoke, many of the fellows backing me up. For example, out of the eleven other boys at the table where I am, no less than seven do not smoke and four drink nothing stronger than beer.

I wish you would send in a petition for me to attend the Congregational church here. I do not intend to wait until Christmas before taking a mission class, but shall go into some such work as soon as I get settled at the Church.

My expenses have been very heavy hitherto, with paying my room rent in advance, buying my clothing, etc., but at the worst I will not have to draw upon you till about Christmass time, and I may not have to do it then.

With best love to all I am,

Your Loving Son

P.S. Send back Uncle Jimmie's letter when you have finished.

---

[1]The Babbit was Aunt Anna Gracie; the Garrulous Uncle was her husband James Gracie.

[2]Henry Minot would become a close college friend.

November 19, 1876. Cambridge
To Martha Bulloch Roosevelt

Darling Motherling

I shall spend Thanksgiving day with you, coming on Wednsday night. I had hoped to be also able to stay over Friday and Saturday, but owing to examinations occurring at that time I shall have to leave on Friday morning, and even then shall be obliged to cut a recitation. It will be perfectly lovely to see you all again. Although I have enjoyed myself greatly here, very much more, even, than I had expected, yet I do not think I have ever appreciated more the sweetness of home. I have not been atall homesick however, except when I was a little under the weather. I have been in beautiful health, and I do not think I shall have any difficulty atall on that score: except possibly with my eyes, although these seem alright now.

On Friday afternoon I went down to New Haven with seventy or eighty of the rest of the boys to see our foot ball team play the Yale men; in which contest I am sorry to say we were beaten, principally because our opponents played very foul. We stayed at the New Haven house, and were in rather close quarters: I roomed with a sophmore named Pat Grant. My Yale friends, and especially Johny Weeks, were very polite to me and showed me all the principal sights. I am very glad I am not a Yale freshman; the hazing there is pretty bad. The fellows too seem to be a much more scrubby set than ours.

Your Loving Son

P.S. Thank Babbit for sending me letters so regularly.

December 14, 1876. Cambridge
To Corinne Roosevelt

Darling Pussie

I ought to have written you long ago, but I am now having examinations all the time, and am so occupied in studying up for them that I have very little time to myself,—and you know how long it takes me to write a letter. I have had a very monotonous life since I left you, the only excitement being the dancing class which is quite pleasant. Quite a number of my acquaintances will be in New York for part of the vacation, and as I wish to introduce some of them to my swell little sister, I may as well describe a few of my chief friends—principally my table companions. Tom Nickerson is the one who started our table. He is quite handsome with a truly remarkable black moustache. At first he gives one the impression of being effeminate, but is not a bit so in reality, being one of our best football players.

Bob Bacon is the handsomest man in the class, and is as pleasant as he is handsome. He is only sixteen; but is at least as large as Emlen. The two Hoopers are both very pleasant; one of them is really a man, being over twenty one, and acts and feels like one; the other is a great, good-natured awkward boy of eighteen. Three of the best fellows I know here are the three "Harry's," Shaw, Chapin and Jackson.

They are really good fellows and pretty fair students; although I doubt if "dat high-toned pussy-cat" will appreciate them as much as she will some of my other companions. I do not know many New York fellows that I like very much. Pellew and Welling (two of my dig friends) are very nice, and both from New York.

I have just received your postal card. I should like a party very much, if it is perfectly convenient. I should prefer not having it till towards the end of Christmas week as then many of my friends will be on. Will it not be splendid to have dear old John Elliot spend Christmas with us!

Yesterday (Dec 16th) I spent in getting Christmas presents. I did not know what Bamie wished and so got her a pretty edition of Bryants poems. I hope it will please her. I bought most of my presents at Brigs china store.

Ask Bob Clarkson to the party. I come home sometime next Saturday.

Your Loving Brother

February 11, 1877. Cambridge
To Theodore Roosevelt, Senior,
and Martha Bulloch Roosevelt

Dear Father and Mother,

I am going to write such a long, chatty letter that I think it shall be to both of you together. But first a word to Father: not only am I not subsisting on husks, but, to carry out the simile, I still have a good deal of (potted) veal left from the calves so liberally killed for my benefit at Christmas. On the first of next month, however, I shall get you to send me on a hundred dollars, as I told you. Perhaps you would like me to describe completely one day of college life; so I shall take last Monday. At half past seven my scout, having made the fire and blacked the boots calls me, and I get round to breakfast at eight. Only a few of the boys are at breakfast, most having spent the night in Boston. Our quarters now are nice and sunny, and the room is prettily papered and ornamented. For breakfast we have tea or coffee, hot biscuits, toast, chops or beef steak, and buckwheat cakes. After breakfast I study till ten, when the mail arrives and is eagerly inspected. From eleven to twelve there is a latin recitation with a meek-eyed Professor, who calls me Mr. Ruseé-felt (hardly any one can get my name correctly, except as Rosy).

Then I go over to the gymnasium, where I have a set-to with the gloves with "General" Lister, the boxing master—for I am training to box among the lightweights in the approaching match for the championship of Harvard. Then comes lunch, at which all the boys are assembled in an obstreperously joyful condition; a state of mind which brings on a free fight, to the detriment of Harry Jackson, who, with a dutch cheese and some coffee cups is put under the table; which proceeding calls forth dire threats of expulsion from Mrs Morgan. Afterwards studying and recitations took up the time till halfpast four; as I was then going home, suddenly I heard "Hi, Ted! Catch!" and a base ball whizzed by me. Our two "babies," Bob Bacon and Arthur Hooper, were playing ball behind one of the buildings. So I stayed and watched them, until the ball went through a window and a proctor started out to inquire—when we abruptly seperated. That evening I took dinner with Mr and Mrs Tudor, and had a very pleasant homelike time. I like both of them very much. Ask Bamie why she never thanked her for the handkerchiefs. When I returned I studied for an hour, and then, it being halfpast ten, put on my slippers, which are as comfortable as they are pretty, drew the rocking chair up to the fire, and spent the next half hour in toasting my feet and reading Lamb.

Usually there is more study and less play than this, but I generally manage to have my evenings free, except for perhaps an hours work, and there is always something to do; if we do'n't go in to Boston there may be a whist club or coffee party going on. I do not go often to the Theatre, as I do'n't care for it, and it might hurt my eyes. On Friday evening I usually go to the dancing class.

Yesterday (Saturday) I went in town in the afternoon to pay several party calls—among them one on Miss Madeleine Mixter who unfortunately was out. I dined with one of my friends, and in the evening went round to the Andrews where there was quite a little party; and where I had a very pleasant time. I have lately met a very sweet girl, Miss Elsie Burnett, whose brother owns the Deerfoot Farm. I think you know him.

I have been going out a good deal lately, but in two or three weeks we will have a spell of examinations, so we will now have to begin to grind again. I have had two examinations since Christmass, and I passed one fairly (over 50 percent) and one very well. I have so much to do that I am not all homesick. I have been very much astonished at this, and also at my good health. Excepting a little asthma in November, I have not been sick atall.

During the Spring I expect to do a good deal of collecting work with Harry Minot and Fred Gardiner, both of whom have similar tastes to mine. By the way, as the time when birds are beginning to come back is approaching, I wish you would send on my gun, with all the cartridges you can find and my various apparatus for cleaning, loading it etc. Also send on a dozen glass jars, with their rubbers and stoppers (which you will find in my museum) and a German Dictionary, if you have one. Our lessons will be over by the twentieth of June, and then Harry Minot and I intend leaving immediately for the Adirondacs, so as to get the birds in as good plumage as possible, and in two or three weeks we will get down to Oyster Bay, where I should like to have him spend a few days with us. He is a very quiet fellow and would not be the least trouble for you can put him anywhere.

I am having a very nice time with my Sunday-School class, and like my scholars very much, although I do not atall approve of the plan the school is conducted on, which makes the poor little children stay all through the afternoon service, so that they have to remain for an hour and a half, which is of course an awful trial to them. My library has been the greatest possible pleasure to me, as whenever I have any spare time I can immediately take up a book. Aunt Annie's present, the "History of the Civil War," is extremely interesting.

Lately I have been round at the boys houses quite often, and have seen a good deal of their home life; they have all been so kind that it makes it very pleasant for me. I can't help being more and more struck by the fact that if the parents are good and wise, the son generally does pretty fairly too, although of course this does not always hold.

With best love to Bamie, Pussie, Aunt Annie and Uncle Jimmie, I am
Your Loving Son

December 16, 1877. Cambridge
To Anna Roosevelt

Darling Bamie,

I am very uneasy about Father. Does the Doctor think it anything serious? I think that a travelling trip would be the best thing for him; he always has too much work on hand. Thank fortune, my own health is excellent, and so, when I get home, I can with a clear conscience give him a rowing up for not taking better care of himself. The trouble is the dear old fellow never does think of himself in anything. We have been very fortunate, Bamie, in having a father whom we can love and respect more than any other man in the world.

I got 90 in two other examinations recently—Rhetoric and History. I shall probably reach New York Friday morning. Remember me to Miss Jennie Hooper.
Your Loving Brother

February 28, 1878. New York
To Henry Minot

Dear Old Hal,

Many, many thanks both to you and Mrs. Howe, but I think I should prefer to go to my own room, which seems almost like home to me. I shall return next Saturday evening. Dear old boy, your sweet letter cheered us up a great deal. As yet it is almost impossible to realize I shall never see Father again; these last few days seem like a hideous dream. Father had always been so much with me that it seems as if part of my life had been taken away; but it is much worse for Mother and my sisters. After all, it is a purely selfish sorrow, for it was best that Father's terrible sufferings should end. Mother sends her best love, and so does my sister.

Your Loving Friend

December 6, 1878. Cambridge
To Alice Lee

Dear Alice,

I have been anxiously expecting a letter from you and Rose for the last two or three days; but none has become. You must not forget our tintype spree; I have been dextrously avoiding forming any engagements for Saturday. I send this by Minot Weld—who knows nothing of the contents, whatever he may say. Tell Rose that I never passed a pleasanter Thanksgiving than at her house.

Judging from the accounts I have received the new dress for the party at New Bedford must have been a complete success.

Your Fellow-conspirator

March 16, 1879. Cambridge
To Martha Bulloch Roosevelt

Darling Muffie,

I got home this morning at 11 o'clock, too late for church, the cars being delayed six hours; and have just returned from Sunday School. How did darling Bysie enjoy her trip to Boston? The only thing I minded was missing her. I never have passed a pleasanter two weeks than those just gone by; I enjoyed every moment. The first two or three days I had asthma, but, funnily enough, this left me entirely as soon as I went into camp. The thermometer was below zero pretty often, but I was not bothered by the cold atall, except one night when I camped out oil the trail of a caribou (which we followed two days without getting more than a glimpse of the animal). Out in the opens when there was any wind it was very disagreable but in the woods the wind never blows and as long as we were moving about it made little difference how low the temperature was, but sitting still for lunch we felt it immediately. I learned how to manage snowshoes very quickly, and enjoyed going on them greatly. I have never seen a grander or more beautiful sight than the northern woods in winter. The evergreens laden with snow make the most beautiful contrast of green and white, and when it freezes after a rain all the trees look as though they were made of crystal. The snow under foot being about three feet deep, and drifting to twice that depth in places, completely changes the aspect of things. I visited two lumber camps, staying at one four days; it was great fun to see such a perfectly unique type of life. I shot a buck, a coon and some rabbits and partridges and trapped a lynx and a fox—so my trip was a success in every way.

There seems to be a general feeling among the family that I have not done my duty in writing of late, which makes me think you did not get some I sent. Did Elliott get the three sheet letter I sent him about six weeks ago? It was the longest letter I ever wrote.

Love to the trio, and especially to my own sweet Motherling herself.
Your Loving Son

September 29, 1879. Cambridge
To Anna Roosevelt

Darling Bysie,
I have been in Cambridge four days now, and the senior year has opened most auspiciously. The cart and horse, with whip, rug &c, came to hand in fine condition; and I really think I have as swell a turnout as any man. I am perfectly delighted with it. It will be the greatest pleasure to me all this winter. The horse goes beautifully, very much better than I had any expectation that he would. He hardly breaks atall; in fact never, unless he is frightened by a locomotive or something.

I spent Sunday at the Saltonstalls', who were just too sweet to me for anything. There I met Mr. and Mrs. Peabody, who invited me down to visit them.

Dear old Charles Dickey has just dropped in to say good night, so no more at present from
Your Loving Brother

February 13, 1880. Cambridge
To Henry Minot

Deal Hal,
I write to you to announce my engagement to Miss Alice Lee; but do not speak of it till Monday. I have been in love with her for nearly two years now; and have made everything subordinate to winning her; so you can perhaps understand a change in my ideas as regards science &c.
Your Aff Friend

September 12, 1880. Chicago
To Corinne Roosevelt

Darling Pussie,

We have come back here after a weeks hunting in Iowa. Elliott revels in the change to civilization—and epicurean pleasures. As soon as we got here he took some ale to get the dust out of his throat; then a milkpunch because he was thirsty; a mint julep because it was hot; a brandy smash "to keep the cold out of his stomach"; and then sherry and bitters to give him an appetite. He took a very simple dinner—soup, fish, salmi de grouse, sweetbread, mutton, venison, corn, maccaroni, various vegetables and some puddings and pies, together with beer, later claret and in the evening shandigaff. I confined myself to roast beef and potatoes; when I took a second help he marvelled at my appetite—and at bed time wondered why in thunder he felt "stuffy" and I did'n't. The good living also reached his brain, and he tried to lure me into a discussion about the intellectual development of the Hindoos, coupled with some rather discursive and scarcely logical digressions about the Infinity of the Infinate, the Sunday School system and the planet Mars—together with some irrelevant remarks about Texan "Jack Rabbits" which are apparently about as large as good sized cows. Elliott says that these remarks are incorrect and malevolent; but I say they pay him off for his last letter about my eating manners.

We have had very good fun so far, in spite of a succession of untoward accidents and delays. I broke both my guns, Elliott dented his, and the shooting was not as good as we had expected; I got bitten by a snake and chucked headforemost out of the wagon.

Your Seedy Brother

October 17, 1880. Oyster Bay
To Alice Lee

My Dearest Love,

You are too good to write me so often, when you have so much to do; I hope you are not all tired out with the work. But at any rate you will have two weeks complete rest at Oyster Bay, and then you shall do just as you please in everything. Oh, my darling, I do so hope and pray I can make you happy. I shall try very hard to be as unselfish and sunny tempered as you are, and I shall save you from every care I can. My own true love, you have made my happiness almost too great; and I feel I can do so little for you in return. I worship you so that it seems almost desecration to touch you; and yet when I am with you I can hardly let you a moment out of my arms. My purest queen, no man was worthy of your love; but I shall try very hard to deserve it, at least in part.

Goodbye, my own heart's darling.

Your Loving Thee

November 21, 1880. New York
To Elliott Roosevelt

Dear Old Nell,

The little wife and I had the most absolutely ideal time at Oyster Bay; we had the most lovely rows, walks and drives and plenty of lawn tennis, in which, by the way, we came out just even. Davis, Mary Ann, Dare and the calf were all very sociable and very funny. Saturday, a week ago yesterday, we drove in town in fine style; our rooms looked just too pretty for anything. Emlen and Mr. Leavitt both sent Alice boukets; next day she received several others. Hilly gave us his opera box for Monday; so we matronized Bamie and Willie Beekman! Every afternoon I go out in the cart which looks ever so well; the horse goes beautifully. Last Wednesday I went to a meeting of the St. Andrews Society at Mr. Kennedy's and had great fun; I had long conversations with Whitlaw Reid and scotch laird, Sir Evan McKenzie; all the old fellows sang scotch songs and told scotch stories. We are going to revive the whist club; Ike is to give the first meeting; Uncle Jim has purchased the land round Yellowbanks; Doc has taken 10 acres. I had a very pleasant time at the News boys[1]; as soon as they saw me they mistook me for you, and shouted and stamped applause. I thought it pretty nice of them; they were evidently very fond of you. Dear old boy, we all miss you dreadfully; but I know you are having a good time; remember me to Minot, if you are still with him. Alice sends her best love.

Ever your loving Brother

May 22, 1881. Cork
To Rose Lee

Dear little Rosy,

We had a beautiful passage; very nearly as gay as a funeral. If ever a person heartily enjoyed a sea trip, Alice did. She enjoyed it so much that she stayed in bed about all the time; the stewardess and myself being her devoted attendants. I fed her at every blessed meal she ate; and held her head when, about 20 minutes later, the meal came galloping up into the outer world again. I only rebelled once; that was when she requested me to wear a mustard plaster first, to see if it hurt. About every half hour during the night I turned out to superindent matters while Alice went through a kind of stomachic earthquake. After each one of these internal convulsions Alice would conclude she was going to die, and we would have a mental circus for a few minutes; finally after I had implored,

---

[1]The newspaper boys of New York—typically homeless lads—were a favorite cause of the Roosevelt family.

prayed and sworn with equal fervency she would again compose herself for a few minutes. Our chief consolation was the doctor, an Irishman and a very good fellow. Alice was really awfully sick.

Here we are as comfortable as possible. Today we took a most lovely drive in a jaunting car to Blarney castle—a very picturesque old ruin, all over grown with ivy and wild flowers. The country looks too beautiful for anything and it is great fun to go in the curious jaunting cars; the seats run the wrong way. Best love to all from Your Aff.

June 16, 1881. Paris
To Corinne Roosevelt

Darling Pussie,

Your respectable brother and his austere wife turned up at Paris in a happy-go-lucky kind of way, after a voyage that was not so difficult, considering that I know next to nothing of french, and Alice resents it as an impertinence if she is addressed in any language but english. Really, Alice is an excellent traveller; when I reach a station I leave her in a chair with the parcels, and there she stays, round eyed and solemn, but perfectly happy, till I have extricated my luggage, had it put on a hack and arranged everything. We left one trunk in Liverpool; another in London; and when we leave here for Venice (which we do tomorrow) shall dispense with one of our two remaining ones, and the confounded hat box, which has clung to us only too faithfully; it is just large enough to tumble out of any rack it may be put in, in the cars. Being aware of this peculiarity I always arrange it so as to fall on somebody else, and not ourselves.

We are at the Hotel Bellevue, Avenue de l'Opera; it's very comfortable. Our bedroom and parlor are very pretty, and only one flight up. We breakfast (delicious butter and french rolls, with coffee and chocolate) at about ten, and then are off; we lunch at some one of the innumerable restaurants—and how delicious the food is. Hitherto we have enjoyed the Louvre more than anything else. I did not admire any of the French painters much—except Greuze. Rubens three wives are represented in about fifty different ways, which I think a mistake; no painter can make the same face serve for Venus, the Virgin and a flemish lady. Murillo represents the holy family far better to my mind, with his softness of outline and purity of expression, than almost any of the great Italian painters. Altogether it would be difficult to imagine any two people enjoying a trip more than do [The rest of the letter is missing.

August 5, 1881. Zermatt
To Anna Roosevelt

Darling Bysie,

Day before yesterday, at nine in the morning, I started off, accompanied by two guides, to make the ascent of the Matterhorn. I was anxious to go up it because it is reputed very difficult and a man who has been up it can fairly claim to have taken his degree as, at any rate, a subordinate kind of mountaineer. At 6 o'clock in the evening we reached the small hut, half a cavern, where we spent the night; it was on the face of a cliff, up which we climbed by a rope forty feet long, and the floor was covered with ice a foot deep. The mountain is so steep that snow will not remain on the crumbling, jagged rocks, and possesses a certain sombre interest from the number of people that have lost their lives on it. Accidents, however, are generally due either to rashness, or else to a combination of timidity and fatigue; a fairly hardy man, cautious but not cowardly, with good guides, has little to fear. Still, there is enough peril to make it exciting, and the work is very laborious being as much with the hands as the feet, and (very unlike the Jungfrau) as hard coming down as going up. We left the hut at three-forty and, after seeing a most glorious sunrise which crowned the countless snow peaks and billowy, white clouds with a strange crimson irradescence, reached the summit at seven, and were down at the foot of the Matterhorn proper by one. It was like going up and down enormous stairs on your hands and knees for nine hours. We then literally ran down the foot hills to Zermatt, reaching it at half past three. It had been excessively laborious and during the journey I was nearer giving out than on the Jungfrau, but I was not nearly so tired afterwards, and in fact felt as fresh as ever after a cup of tea and a warm bath; went to table d'hote as usual and afterwards over to see the Gardiners, and coming back we spent the rest of the evening with Mrs Baylies, Miss Cornelia & Edmund.

Your Loving Brother

August 21, 1881. The Hague
To Anna Roosevelt

Darling Bysie,

We came down the Rhine in a steamboat. The scenery was lovely, but no more so than the Hudson except for the castles. These "robber knight" castles are so close together that I alway wonder where there was mom for the other people whom the Robber Knights robbed. The Age of Chivalry was lovely for the knights; but it must have at times been inexpressibly gloomy for the gentlemen who had to occasionally act in the capacity of daily bread for their betters. It is like the purely traditional "Merry England" of the Stuarts; where the merriment existed only for the Stuarts, who were about the worst dynasty that ever sat on a throne.

At Cologne we met General and Mrs. Cullum. The latter was cordial and jocose, if you can imagine her being so undignified, and I really like her; but I think that her much-battered old spouse is rather a bore. But he introduced me to a pleasant Commodore Baldwin; and they offered to make me a member of the International Law Congress—for five dollars. I had'n't a dress coat; and refused; I was rather sorry, for they were going to a dinner to meet a Prince Karl of Prussia. However I think the Commodore may do me a good turn at the Navy Department, in getting me access to records for that favourite chateau-en-espagne of mine, the Naval History. You would be amused to see me writing it here. I have plenty of information now, but I can't get it into words; I am afraid it is too big a task for me. I wonder if I wo'n't find everything in life too big for my abilities. Well, time will tell.

You asked me how I liked Kingsford's friend on the Ocean. I liked him very much; and he gave me some very polite invitations, which I unluckily could not accept. If I were not going to London so late I should be able to present some very good letters there, to Swinburne, Tennyson &c, from a half-congenial scallawag I rather fraternised with in Zermatt. He had married a Boston girl whom Alice knew.

Alice having just killed a flea is eying with horror what she calls "his little giblets."

Your Loving and Shadey Brother

August 24, 1881. Brussels
To Corinne Roosevelt

Darling Pussie,

Our trip through the Netherlands has been of necessity short, but very pleasant. What we have chiefly enjoyed, I think, has been looking at the country, the towns and the people themselves; and our regular "sightseeing" time has been devoted mainly to pictures. I know nothing atall, in reality, of art, I regret to say, but I do know what pictures I like. I am not atall fond of Rubens. He is eminently a fleshly, sensuous painter; and yet his most famous pictures are those relating to the Divinity. Above all, he fails in his female figures. Ruben's women are, handsome animals, excellent as pictures of rich flemish housewifes; but they are either ludicrous or revolting when meant to represent either the Virgin or a saint. I think they are not much better as heathen goddesses; I do'n't like a chubby Minerva, a corpulent Venus and a Diana who is so fat that I know she could never overtake a cow, let alone a deer.

Rembrandt is by all odds my favourite. I am very much attracted by his strongly contrasted colouring, and I could sit for hours examining his heads, they are so lifelike and expressive. Van Helst I like for the sake of the sake of the realism with which he presents to you the bold, rich, turbulent dutchmen of his time. Vandykes heads are wonderful; they are very lifelike and powerful—but if the originals were like them I should hardly have admired one. Perhaps the pictures I really get most enjoyment out of are the landscapes, the homely little dutch and flemish interiors, the faithful representations of how the people of those times lived and made merry and died, which are given us by Jan Steen, Van Ostade, Teniers and Ruysdaal. They bring out the life of that period in a way no written history could, and interest me far more than pictures of saints and madonnas. I suppose this sounds heretical, but it is true. This time, I have really tried to like the Holy pictures but I ca'n't; even the Italian masters seem to me to represent good men, and insipidly good women, but rarely anything saintly or divine. The only pictures I have seen with these attributes are Gustav Doree's! He alone represents the Christ so that your pity for him is lost in intense admiration and reverence.

Your Loving Brother

September 5, 1881. London
To Anna Roosevelt

Darling Bysie,

Our stay in Paris was mainly devoted to the intricacies of dress buying: but we did manage to stow in a visit to the famous Cluny (see Personal Charades) and, what I enjoyed even more, to the tomb of Napoleon. I do not think there is a more impressive sepulchre on earth than that tomb; it is grandly simple. I am not very easily awestruck, but it certainly gave me a solemn feeling to look at the plain, red stone bier which contained what had once been the mightiest conqueror the world ever saw. He was a great fighter, at least, though otherwise I suppose an almost unmixed evil. Hannibal alone is his equal in military genius; and Caesar in cruel power and ambition. What a child such a mere butcher as Tamerlane, Genghis Khan or Attila would have been in his hands!

The weather was fairly rough crossing the channel, and poor baby-wife was reduced to a condition of pink and round eyed misery. Until she has been worn out seasickness only makes her look peculiarly bright and healthy. I managed to keep in good trim by vigorous walking up and down the deck in the spray.

Here we have been completing our stock of modest presents for those at home, and today we were overjoyed by finding one for mother after a long hunt; it is just the very thing for her. I'm going to bring you back three soup tickets and a Perpetual Motion machine, and (do'n't read this part aloud) Corinne a flirtation fan and a scotch lachrymatory, if such an instrument exists.

Best love to all, and much from

Your Devoted Brother

PART TWO

Making His Way

1881–1889

*R*oosevelt's inheritance freed him from most monetary concerns in choosing a career, but he had to find something to fill his time. He considered law, and attended Columbia Law School briefly. Yet his heart wasn't in it, and when politics beckoned he abandoned the bar for the stump. Republicans of the Twenty-first District in Manhattan needed someone with energy and money to mount a campaign for the state Assembly against the Tammany Hall Democrats; Roosevelt accepted their invitation, and won.

He took to the political life at once. In Albany he formed alliances with such fellow reformers as William O'Neil. Together they hammered away at the link between the corporate interests of the likes of Jay Gould and the political machines that controlled both parties. The machines struck back—in 1882 Tammany Hall drove most Republicans from the state legislature—but Roosevelt held on, loving every minute. Or almost every minute: The one thing he didn't like about legislating was the separation it required from Alice. Sometimes she accompanied him to Albany, but their home was in New York City, and quite often they spent weeks apart. He made his absence up to her (and to himself) during summers, when the legislature was not in session. They traveled the state, visiting Corinne and her husband, Douglas Robinson, on their estate near Albany, and spending time at such social watering holes as Richfield Springs. The spa life being rather more to Alice's taste than Roosevelt's, he also found time for hunting. During the summer of 1883 he traveled west to Dakota Territory to pursue buffalo, by far the biggest game he had ever gone after. While there he fell in love with the Badlands, and purchased a ranch.

He returned to New York, where Alice was expecting their first child. The legislative session of 1884 kept him away during the final weeks of her pregnancy; in Albany he received the joyous news that she had borne him a baby girl. But the next telegram told that the mother had contracted an infection; he raced south to find her on her deathbed. (Fate doubled the blow by taking Roosevelt's mother the same day.)

He was grief-stricken. Mechanically he completed his term in Albany, but he planned his departure from politics and his escape to Dakota. En route he attended the Republican National Convention in Chicago, where he joined Henry Cabot Lodge of Massachusetts in supporting reformer George Edmunds against James G. Blaine, the candidate of the Republican regulars. Blaine won the nomination, leaving Roosevelt to decide whether to stick with the reformers (derisively called "mugwumps") or throw his lot in with the national party leadership. He left Chicago for Dakota with his intentions unclear—in his own mind and in the interviews he gave inquiring reporters.

That summer afforded the escape he desired. He spent weeks riding across the range, hunting in the mountains, and generally trying to forget about Alice and the life they had led together. (Their daughter, Alice Lee Roosevelt— "Baby Lee"—he left in the care of his sister Bamie.) He considered whether he *might make ranching his career. He hired William Sewall and Will Dow to run his ranch; he himself joined the roundup and other chores of range life, including the pursuit and apprehension of three thieves who stole a boat to make what they hoped would be their getaway down the Little Missouri River.*

Yet he kept in touch with affairs back east. He visited New York regularly, and eventually completed construction of the house he and Alice had intended to occupy at Oyster Bay. He corresponded with Lodge regarding the future of the Republican Party. He accepted Lodge's offer to write a biography of the Missouri statesman Thomas Hart Benton; after an earlier book, The Naval War of 1812, *this suggested a future in literature. With Lodge and others, he discussed the merits and demerits of such authors as Tolstoy and Henry James. He began to sketch out for Lodge and others, including historian Francis Parkman, what he called his "magnum opus"—a multivolume treatise on the settlement of the West. He commented on politics for the* North American Review *and other journals; civil service reform was a topic of his particular interest. When he heard of trouble between the United States and Mexico, he prepared to volunteer for military service.*

On a visit to New York in 1886 he received an invitation from reformers to run for mayor. He accepted, even while realizing that his chances of victory were very slim. And in fact he lost, although by a respectably narrow margin. At about the same time he reencountered Edith Carow, his childhood sweetheart. To his surprise—indeed, to his mortification, since he still considered himself in mourning for Alice—the old flame rekindled. The two courted quietly, then agreed to marry out of the public light. Roosevelt followed Edith to London, where they were wed in a simple ceremony. The best man was a young British diplomat named Cecil Spring Rice, whom Roosevelt met on the ship going over, and who became a lifelong friend. Roosevelt thoroughly enjoyed himself in England, circulating among the clubs and meeting such worthies as historian James Bryce and political leader Randolph Churchill.

While he was gone, Dakota suffered its worst winter in living memory; he returned in the spring of 1887 to find his ranch devastated, with most of the stock dead and most of his investment lost. He abandoned hopes of making a living from the range, and decided to return to politics. The summer and autumn of 1888 found him on the campaign trail, speaking on behalf of state and national Republican candidates, including Benjamin Harrison. When Harrison won the presidency, Roosevelt was in line for a federal appointment. Lodge tried to get him a post in the State Department; when this effort failed, Roosevelt accepted a job with the federal Civil Service Commission.

November 1, 1881. New York
To Voters of the Twenty-first Assembly District

Dear Sir,

Having been nominated as a candidate for member of Assembly for this District, I would esteem it a compliment if you honor me with your vote and personal influence on Election day.

Very respectfully

November 10, 1881. New York
To Charles Washburn

Dear Charley,

Too True! Too True! I have become a "political hack." Finding it would not interfere much with my law I accepted the nomination to the assembly, and was elected by 1500 majority, heading the ticket by 600 votes. But don't think I am going to go into politics after this year, for I am not.

With warmest regards to your mother and father, and from Mrs. R. I am

Your True Friend

November 12, 1882. New York
To William O'Neil

My Dear O'Neil,

All Hail, fellow survivor of the late Democratic Deluge! I see you ran way ahead of your ticket. Down here such voting was never seen before. I carried my Assembly district by 2200 majority, the Republican Congressman by 700, and the Democratic Governor carried it by 1800 the other way! Sprague, in his district, got but 16 majority, and may be counted out. Robb, in the strongest Republican District in the city, was defeated by but 69 votes.

As far as I can judge the next House will contain a rare set of scoundrels, and we Republicans will be in such a hopeless minority that I do not see very clearly what we can accomplish, even in checking bad legislation. But at least we will do our best.

I have a bone to pick with Erwin, over his having nominated Smyth as Chairman of the State Committee; his nomination was an insult to honest men.

Trusting all is well with you, I am,

Very Truly Yours

July 1, 1883. Richfield Springs, New York
To Corinne Roosevelt Robinson

Wee Pussie, proprietress of a still more wee kitten,

The drive up was very pleasant—in spots. In spots it was'n't. On the first day about half way up Overlook Mountain (3200 feet high, the ascent made in 4 miles) which was so steep I had to walk, I was struck by the extraordinary breathing of the horse, and then I for the first time remembered that a year ago he had been, as Burke said "uncommon bad with the heaves"; and the heaves he had, with a vengeance, thanks chiefly to his persisting in trotting up all the mountains, until I had to adopt the plan of leading him up each hill. When he recovered the jolting of the buggy made Alice sick; and when she got well the wheels began to squeak in a way that was simply soul harrowing. I had them oiled, and the horse immediately "hove" again, and then, as we left civilization, Alice mildly but firmly refused to touch the decidedly primitive food of the aborigines, and led a starvling existence on crackers which I toasted for her in the greasy kitchens of the grimy inns. But, on the other hand, the scenery was superb; I have never seen grander views than among the Catskills, or a more lovely country than that we went through afterwards; the horse, inspite of his heaves, throve wonderfully, and nearly ate his head off; and Alice, who reached Cooperstown very limp indeed, displayed her usual marvellous powers of forgetting past woe, and in two hours time, after having eaten till she looked like a little pink boa constrictor, was completely herself again. By the way, having listened with round eyed interest to one man advising me to "wet the feed and hay" of Lightfoot, for his heaves, at the next place she paralyzed the ostler by a direction to "wet his feet and hair" for the same benevolent object. Personally, I enjoyed the trip immensely, in spite of tile mishaps to spouse and steed, and came in to Richfield Springs feeling superbly. But, under the direction of the heavy jowled idiot of a medical man to whose tender mercies Doctor Polk has intrusted me, I am rapidly relapsing. I do'n't so much mind drinking the stuff—you can get an idea of the taste by steeping a box of sulphur matches in dish water and drinking the delectable compound tepid from an old kerosene oil can—and at first the boiling baths were rather pleasant; but, for the first time in my life I came within an ace of fainting when I got out of the bath this morning, I have a bad headache, a general feeling of lassitude, and am bored out of my life by having nothing whatever to do, and being placed in that quintessence of abomination, a large summer hotel at a watering place for underbred and overdressed girls, fat old female scandal mongers, and a select collection of assorted cripples and consumptives.

Now to the great subject of interest. I really can not *write* about it; I am just longing to have a chat with you. I am honestly delighted, however, for I think the dear old boy has won a lovely girl for his wife, and I am greatly mistaken if it does not do him all the good in the world to have something to work for in life. I am very anxious to see her and know her. I am sure I shall like her very much. But it is of no use trying to *write* on such a subject.[1]

Your darling Pussie, I am so sorry you were sick, I do hope you are better. Give my best love to the sweet little motherling, to the Driving Wheel of Destiny and Superintendent-in-Chief of the Workings of Providence, otherwise known as Bysie, the sweetest sister that ever lived, and to that dear old embodiment of energy, Doug (I am so sorry he did'n't win the tennis prize). Alice sends many kisses.

Ever Your Loving Brother

P.S. Fifty kisses for the wee, wee baby boy.

November 20, 1883. New York
To Jonas Van Duzer

My dear Sir,

I was very glad to get your letter; permit me to say that it was the most interesting and practical one I have received.

In answer to your questions I would state that, after having passed through Harvard College, I studied for the bar; but going into politics shortly after leaving college, and finding the work in Albany, if conscientiously done, very harassing, I was forced to take up some out-of-doors occupation for the summer, and now have a cattle ranch in Dakotah. I am a Republican, pure and simple, neither a "half breed" nor a "stalwart"; and certainly no man, nor yet any ring or clique, can do my thinking for me. As you say, I believe in treating all our business interests equitably and alike; in favoring no one interest or set of interests at the expense of others. In making up the committees I should pay attention, first, to the absolute integrity of the men, second, to their capacity to deal intelligently with the matters likely to come before them—for in our present anything but ideal condition of public affairs, honesty and common sense are the two prime requisites for a legislator.

As writing is, at best, unsatisfactory work, I shall try to see you in person before the session begins.

With great regard, I am

Very truly yours

February 6, 1884. Albany
To Alice Lee Roosevelt

Darling Wifie,

How I did hate to leave my bright, sunny little love yesterday afternoon! I love you and long for you all the time, and oh so tenderly;

---

[1]Elliott Roosevelt had become engaged to Anna Hall.

doubly tenderly now, my sweetest little wife. I just long for Friday evening when I shall be with you again. Today I sparred as usual; my teacher is a small man and in the set-to today I bloodied his nose by an upper cut, and knocked him out of time.

In the House we had a most exciting debate on my Reform Charter bill, and I won a victory, having it ordered to a third reading. Tomorrow evening I am to dine at the Rathbones, at half past seven; it was very kind to ask me, but I do not anticipate much fun.

Goodbye, sweetheart.

Your Ever Loving Thee

February 13, 1884. New York
To Dora Watkins

(Telegram)

Dear Dolly

We have a little daughter. The mother only fairly well.

Yours ever

February 18, 1884. New York
To Andrew White

Dear Mr. White:

Many thanks or your kind sympathy and remembrance of me. I shall come back to my work at once; there is now nothing left for me except to try to so live as not to dishonor the memory of those I loved who have gone before me.

Your friend

April 30, 1884. Albany
To Simon North

Dear Mr. North:

I wish to write you a few words just to thank you for your kindness towards me, and to assure you that my head will not be turned by what I well know was a mainly accidental success. Although not a very old man, I have yet lived a great deal in my life, and I have known sorrow too bitter and joy too keen to allow me to become either cast down or elated for more than a very brief period over any success or defeat.[1]

I have very little expectation of being able to keep on in politics; my success so far has only been won by absolute indifference to my future career; for I doubt if any man can realise the bitter and venomous hatred

---

[1]Roosevelt had orchestrated the selection of a delegation to the Republican National Convention pledged to support George Edmunds.

with which I am regarded by the very politicians who at Utica supported me, under dictation from masters who were influenced by political considerations that were national and not local in their scope. I realize very thoroughly the absolutely ephemeral nature of the hold I have upon the people, and a very real and positive hostility I have excited among the politicians. I will not stay in public life unless I can do so on my own terms; and my ideal, whether lived up to or not is rather a high one.

For very many reasons I will not mind going back into private for a few years. My work this winter has been very harassing, and I feel both tired and restless; for the next few months I shall probably be in Dakota, and I think I shall spend the next two or three years in making shooting trips, either in the far West or in the Northern Woods—and there will be plenty of work to do writing.

Very truly yours

**May 1, 1884. Albany
Recipient unknown**

Dear Sir,

I do not know where you would find a sketch of my life. I will give you an outline myself. Do you wish me to send you a photograph of myself? Some are much worse than others. I will send you one if you wish.

I was born in New York, Oct 27th 1858; my father of old dutch knickerbocker stock; my mother was a Georgian, descended from the revolutionary Governor Bulloch. I graduated at Harvard in 1880; in college did fairly in my studies, taking honors in Natural History and Political Economy; and was very fond of sparring, being champion light weight at one time. Have published sundry papers on ornithology, either on my trips to the north woods, or around my summer home on the wooded, broken shore of northern Long Island. I published also a "History of the Naval War of 1812 with an account of the Battle of New Orleans," which-is now a text book in several colleges, and has gone through three editions. I married Miss Alice Lee of Boston on leaving college in 1880. My father died in 1878; my wife and mother died in February 1884; I have a little daughter living.

I am very fond of both horse and rifle, and spend my summers either on the great plains after buffalo and antelope or in the northern woods, after deer and caribou.

Am connected with various charitable organizations, such as the Childrens Aid Society, Orthopaedic Hospital, National Prison Association, and others, in which my father took a leading part.

I was elected to the Assembly from the 21st district of New York in the autumn of 1881; in 1882 I served on the Committee on Cities. My chief work was endeavouring to get Judge Westbrook impeached on the ground of malfeasance in office and collusion with Mr. Jay Gould, in connection with railroad litigation.

Was reelected and in 1883 when the Republicans were in a minority was their candidate for speaker, thus becoming their titular leader on the floor. My main speech was on the report of the democratic committee giving Sprague (Republican) the seat wrongly held by Bliss (Democrat), which report was reversed by the action of the Democratic house. Was again reelected. The republicans were in the majority; was a candidate for the speakership, and in the caucus received 30 votes to the 42 received by the successful candidate Mr Sheard, who was backed by both the halfbreeds who followed Senator Miller, and the stalwarts of President Arthurs train. This winter my main work has been pushing the Municipal Reform bills for New York City; in connection with which I have conducted a series of investigations into its various departments. Most of my bills have been passed and signed.

In the primaries before the Utica Convention, I led the independents in my district, who, for the first time in the history of New York City Politics, won against the machine men, though the latter were backed up by all the Federal and municipal patronage. At Utica, I led the Edmunds men, who held the balance of power between the followers of Blaine and of Arthur; we used our position to such good effect as to procure the election of all four delegates as Edmunds men, though we were numerically not over 70 strong, barely a seventh of the total number of men at the convention. Am fairly well off; my recreations are reading, riding and shooting.

Very Respy

May 5, 1884. Albany
To Henry Cabot Lodge

My dear Mr. Lodge,

Curiously enough I had just begun a letter to you when I received yours. I wish to, in turn, congratulate you upon your success, which, by the way, is of a far more solid and enduring kind than is mine. The result of the Utica convention was largely an accident; chance threw in our way an opportunity such as will never occur again; and I determined to use it for every ounce it was worth.

Unquestionably, Blaine is our greatest danger; for I fear lest, if he come too near success, the bread-and-butter brigade from the south will leave Arthur and go over to him. We who stand against both *must* be organized, and, moreover, must select our candidate with the greatest care. I have a plan which I would like to talk to you about. I do not believe New York can by any possibility be held solid; our delegation will split into three, and we will do more than I believe we can if we unite any two of the parts.

Can you not come to New York on Saturday the 16th; and stay with me, at 6 West 57th St? We are breaking up house, so you will have to excuse very barren accommodations. On Saturday I hope to have a number of the independent delegates meet, and should like you to see them. I will then go on with you to Washington with pleasure. On Thursday I go down to New York to stay till Monday; so write me there (6 West 57th St.)

Very truly yours

June 8, 1884. St. Paul, Minnesota
To Anna Roosevelt

Darling Bysie,

Many thanks for your sweet note. Can you tell Douglass to get me files of the "Times" and "Sun" for the week ending June 7th? Also of the "Post." I would like to see them. I am now on my way to the Little Missouri; I shall probably be back about July 4th, but will write or telegraph to you before; perhaps I shall be back much earlier, as I intend to take quite a long hunting trip this fall, there being now no necessity of my taking part in the political campaign.

Well, the fight has been fought and lost, and moreover our defeat is an overwhelming rout. Of all the men presented to the convention as presidential candidates, I consider Blaine as by far the most objectionable, because his personal honesty, as well as his faithfulness as a public servant, are both open to question; yet beyond a doubt he was opposed by many, if not most, of the politicians and was the free choice of the great majority of the Republican voters of the northern states. That such should be the fact speaks badly for the intelligence of the mass of my party, as well as for their sensitiveness to the honesty and uprightness of a public official, and bodes no good for the future of the nation—though I am far from thinking that any very serious harm can result even from either of the two evils to which our choice is now limited viz:—a democratic administration or four years of Blaine in the White House. The country has stood a great deal in the past and can stand a great deal more in the future. It is by no means the first time that a vast popular majority has been on the side of wrong. It may be that "the voice of the people is the voice of God" in fifty one cases out of a hundred; but in the remaining forty nine it is quite as likely to be the voice of the devil, or, what is still worse, the voice of a fool.

I am glad to have been present at the convention, and to have taken part in its proceedings; it was a historic scene, and one of great, even if of somewhat sad, interest. Speaking roughly the forces were divided as follows: Blaine 340, Arthur 280, Edmunds 95, Logan 60, Sherman 30, Hawley 15. But second choice of all of the Logan and Sherman and of nearly half the Arthur men, was Blaine, which made it absolutely impossible to form a combination against him. Arthurs vote was almost entirely from office holders, coming mainly from the south, and from the great cities of the north. Except among a few of the conservative business men he had absolutely no strength at all with the people. The votes for Logan, Sherman and Hawley represented nothing but the fact that Illinois, Ohio and Connecticut each had a "favorite son." The Edmunds vote represented the majority of the Republicans of New England, and a very respectable minority in New York, New Jersey, and the three states of Wisconsin, Michigan and Minnesota. It included all the men of the broadest culture and highest character that there were in the convention; all those who were prominent in the professions or eminent as private citizens; and it included almost all the "plain people," the farmers and others, who were above the average, who were possessed of a keen sense of personal and official honesty, and who were accustomed to think for themselves.

Blaines adherents included the remainder, the vast majority of those from the middle and eastern states, and some from New England. These were the men who make up the mass of the party. Their ranks included many scoundrels, adroit and clever, who intend to further their own ends by supporting the popular candidate, or who know Mr Blaine so well that they expect under him to be able to develope their schemes to the fullest extent; but for the most part these Republicans were good, ordinary men, who do not do very much thinking, who are pretty honest themselves, but who are callous to any but very flagrant wrongdoing in others, unless it is brought home to them most forcibly, who "do'n't think Blaine any worse than the rest of them," and who are captivated by the man's force, originality and brilliant demagoguery.

About all the work in the convention that was done against him was done by Cabot Lodge and myself, who pulled together and went in for all we were worth. We achieved a victory in getting up a combination to beat the Blaine nominee for temporary chairman, who was also supported by the Logan men. To do this needed a mixture of skill, boldness and energy, and we were up all night in arranging our forces so as to get the different factions to come in to line together to defeat the common foe. Many of our men were very timid; so we finally took the matter into our own hands and forced the fighting, when of course our allies had to come into line behind us. White, Curtis and Wadsworth were among the weak kneed ones; but when we got in Curtis made a good speech for us. I also made a short speech, which was listened to very attentively and was very well received by the delegates, as well as the outsiders; it was the first time I had ever had the chance of speaking to ten thousand people assembled together.

Some of the nominating speeches were very fine, notably that of Governor Long of Massachusetts, which was the most masterly and scholarly effort I have ever listened to. Blaine was nominated by Judge West, the blind orator of Ohio. It was a most impressive scene. The speaker, a feeble old man of shrunk but gigantic frame, stood looking with his sightless eyes towards the vast throng that filled the huge hall. As he became excited his voice rang like a trumpet, and the audience became worked up to a condition of absolutely uncontrollable excitement and enthusiasm. For a quarter of an hour at a time they cheered and shouted so that the brass bands could not be heard at all, and we were nearly deafened by the noise.

Tell Uncle Jimmie that I may write to him to send me out money for my cattle ranche to the German American Bank, St. Paul; and if Chas. P. Miller wishes two thousand dollars he is to have it.

Yours always

June 17, 1884. Little Missouri, Dakota
To Anna Roosevelt

Darling Bysie,

I hope you got my letter about the convention; it was a long one for me. Here my opportunities for writing are limited; so show this to Elliott and Douglass, both of whom have written me. I was very glad to get your letters. The "interview" in the St Pauls despatch was made up out of the whole cloth; it was very annoying; I had not spoken a dozen words to any reporter.[1]

Well, I have been having a glorious time here, and am well hardened now (I have just conic in from spending *thirteen* hours in the saddle). For every day I have been here I have had my hands full. First and foremost, the cattle have done well, and I regard the outlook for making the business a success as being *very* hopeful. This winter I lost about 25 head, from wolves, cold etc; the others are in admirable shape, and I have about a hundred and fifty five calves. I shall put on a thousand more cattle and shall make it my regular business. In the autumn I shall bring out Seawall and Dow and put then on a ranche with very few cat-

---

[1]Roosevelt was quoted as supporting Blaine's candidacy.

tle to start with, and in the course of a couple of years give them quite a little herd also.

I have never been in better health than on this trip. I am in the saddle all day long either taking part in the round up of the cattle, or else hunting antelope (I got one the other day; another good head for our famous hall at Leeholm[1]). I am really attached to my two "factors," Ferris and Merrificld; they are very fine men.

The country is growing on me, more and more; it has a curious, fantastic beauty of its own; and as I own six or eight horses I have a fresh one every day and ride on a lope all day long. How sound I do sleep at night now! There is not much game however; the cattle men have crowded it out and only a few antelope and deer remain. I have shot a few jackrabbits and curlews, with the rifle; and I also killed eight rattlesnakes.

Tomorrow my two men go east for the cattle; and I will start out alone to try my hand at finding my way over the prairie by myself. I intend to take a two months trip in the Fall, for hunting, and may, as politics look now, stay away over Election day; so I shall return now very soon, probably leaving here in a week. I shall go on to Chestnut Hill at once, as the latter part of my stay I would rather spend in New York; if I telegraph to you can you not have Douglass send on my cart, (your) horse and man to the Hill, so as to get there before me? Give my best love to all; and especially to your own dear self.

Your loving brother

P.S. Tell Nell I am delighted to hear that he has settled so well in business.

June 18, 1884. Little Missouri
To Henry Cabot Lodge

My dear Lodge,

I have just received your long and welcome letter; my brief note of yesterday was sent before I had received it. I am now writing under difficulties, being in the cattlemen's hut, and having just spent thirteen hours in the saddle.

The St. Paul "Interview" was absolutely without foundation in fact; I had not spoken a dozen words to any reporter; my telegrams to the "Post" merely contained an explicit denial of its authenticity.

I allowed myself to be interviewed in St. Paul for the purpose of giving a rap to the *Post*; but to my regret the cream of the interview does not seem to have been copied in the Eastern papers. I thought I would touch up Godkin[2] and Sedgwick a little.

---

[1]Leeholm was the house Roosevelt had been building for Alice.

[2]Reformist editor E. L. Godkin.

You are pursuing precisely the proper course; do not answer any assaults unless it is imperatively necessary; keep on good terms with the machine, and put in every ounce, to win. Certainly the Independents have little cause to congratulate themselves on a candidate of Cleveland's moral character; with Barnum to manage his canvass, and Hendricks to carry behind. The veto of the Tenure-of-Office Bill was inexcusable; I have written a letter to a fellow Assemblyman (Hubbell) about it, which I think will be published shortly in the *Tribune*. I shall be east about a week after you get this letter, and shall write you immediately, as I wish to see you at once; I am very anxious you should take no steps hastily, for I do not know a man in the country whose future I regard as so promising as is yours; and I would not for anything have you do a single thing that could hurt it, unless it was a question of principle, when of course I should not advise you to hesitate for a moment.

With warmest regards to Mrs. Lodge, believe me,

Always yours

P.S.—I have not seen a newspaper since I left Chicago.

July 28, 1884. New York
To Henry Cabot Lodge

My dear Lodge,

I was very glad indeed to hear from you; Mrs. Lodge and yourself *must* make us a visit next winter; my sister is as anxious as I am to have you.

I did not have a chance to see either Sedgwick or Godkin; I wrote Putnam and incidentally asked him to give my compliments to either or both of the gentlemen named, and to tell them from me that I thought they were suffering just at present from a species of moral myopia, complicated with intellectual strabismus. Most of my friends seem surprised to find that I have not developed, hoofs and horns; the independents are rapidly cultivating the belief that the Utica Convention was really gotten up in the interest of Blaine; and that you and I are, with Elkins, his chief advisers.

I have received shoals of letters, pathetic and abusive, to which I have replied with vivacity or ferocity, according to the circumstances of the case.

The bolt is very large among the dudes and the Germans; how large the corresponding bolt among the labouring men is I can not now tell.

Keep straight on; get out of the committee as soon as it is in decent working order; don't answer any attacks, and work every line for success.

Remember me most warmly to Mrs. Lodge.

Always your friend

August 24, 1884. Powder River, Montana
To Henry Cabot Lodge

My dear Lodge,

You must pardon the paper and general appearance of this letter, as I am writing out in camp, a hundred miles or so from any house; and indeed whether this letter is, or is not, ever delivered depends partly on Providence, and partly on the good will of an equally inscrutable personage, either a cowboy or a horse thief, whom we have just met, and who has volunteered to post it—my men are watching him with anything but friendly eyes, as they think he is going to try to steal our ponies. (To guard against this possibility he is to sleep between my foreman and myself—delectable bed-fellow he'll prove, doubtless.)

I have no particular excuse for writing, beyond the fact that I would give a good deal to have a talk with you over political matters, just now. I heartily enjoy this life, with its perfect freedom, for I am very fond of hunting, and there are few sensations I prefer to that of galloping over these rolling, limitless prairies, rifle in hand, or winding my way among the barren, fantastic and grimly picturesque deserts of the so-called Bad Lands; and yet I can not help wishing I could be battling along with you, and I can not regret enough the unfortunate turn in political affairs that has practically debarred me from taking any part in the fray. I have received fifty different requests to speak in various places—among others, to open the campaign in Vermont and Minnesota. I am glad I am not at home; I get so angry with the "mugwumps," and get to have such scorn and contempt for them, that I know I would soon be betrayed into taking some step against them, and in favor of Blaine, much more decided than I really ought to take. At any rate I can oppose Cleveland with a very clear conscience. I wonder what he will do about Davidson.

By the way, did I tell you about my cowboys reading and in large part comprehending, your "Studies in History"? My foreman handed the book back to me today, after reading the "Puritan Pepys," remarking meditatively, and with, certainly, very great justice, that early Puritanism "must have been darned rough on the kids." He evidently sympathized keenly with the feelings of the poor little "examples of original sin."

I do not at all agree with *The Atlantic Monthly* critic in thinking that the volume would have been better if you had omitted the three essays dealing more especially with English subjects. Puritanism left if anything a more lasting impress upon America than upon England; the history of its rise, and especially of its fall, has quite as direct a bearing upon the development of New England as a province, and afterwards of the United States as a nation, as it has upon the development of latter-day Britain. Cobbett's visit to America gives us a vivid glimpse of a very curious phase of our early national existence, while a close and accurate knowledge of the England in which the younger Fox played so prominent a part is absolutely essential to the students of American affairs. Your view of George III is certainly a novel one; I think it very true, as regards the moral side of his character; but do you not think he was a stupid man, in spite of his low, treacherous cunning? Have you had time yet to read Lecky's History of England in the 18th Century? (You've been pretty busy in politics for the last year or two, or I would not ask the question.) I have a good deal of admiration for his account of the Revolutionary war.

Now, for a little criticism on a wholly trivial point. Do you not think you do Cornwallis a great injustice in lumping him with the British imbeciles who commanded with him in that war? His long campaign in the southern states, in which he marched and countermarched from Virginia to Georgia through the midst of a bitterly hostile population, and in the course of which he again and again defeated in the open field superior forces of American troops, led by our best commanders, and often largely composed of the excellent continental soldiery—this campaign, I think, was certainly creditable to him; and his being hemmed in and forced to surrender to greatly superior forces at Yorktown was entirely Clinton's fault, and not at all his own. I believe Washington was, not even excepting Lincoln, the very greatest man of modern times; and a great general, of the Fabian order, too, but on the battle field I doubt if he equalled any one of half a dozen of the Union and Rebel chiefs who fought in the great Civil War.

Sometimes I think that your diagnosis of the Whig party under Walpole would apply pretty well to the Republican party, and to the condition of public opinion that rendered Blaine's nomination possible; but I regard reformation as being quite as impossible to expect from the Democrats as it would have been in England to expect it from the Jacobites; all the good elements have their greatly preponderant representation in the Republican Party. Excuse this rambling scrawl. Remember me to Mrs. Lodge.

Always Yours

September 20, 1884. Fort McKinney, Wyoming
To Anna Roosevelt

Darling Bysie,

For once I have made a very successful hunting trip; I have just come out of the mountains and will start at once for the Little Missouri, which I expect to reach in a fortnight, and a week afterwards will be on my way home. I hope to hear from you there.

It took sixteen days travelling (during which I only killed a few bucks) before I reached the foot of the snow capped Bighorn range; we then left our wagon and went into the mountains with pack ponies, and as I soon shot all the kinds of game the mountains afforded, I came out after two weeks, during which time I killed three grizzly bear, six elk (three of them have magnificent heads and will look well in the "house on the hill") and as many deer, grouse and trout as we needed for the table; after the first day I did not shoot any cow or calf elk, or any deer at all, except one buck that had unusual antlers;—for I was more anxious for the quality than for the quantity of my bag. I have now a dozen good heads for the hall. Merrifield killed two bears and three elk; he has been an invaluable guide for game, and of course the real credit for the bag rests with him, for he found most of the animals. But I really shot well this time.

We met a heard of a dozen parties either of English or Eastern amateurs, or of professional hunters, who were on the mountain at the same time we were; but not one of them had half the success I had. This was mainly because they hunted on horseback, much the easiest and least laborious way, while Merrifield and I, in our moccasins and buckskin suits hunted almost every day on foot, following the game into the deepest and most inaccessible ravines. Then again, most of them would only venture to attack the grizzly bears if they found them in the open, or if there were several men together, while we followed them into their own chosen haunts, and never but one of us shot at a bear. Merrifield, indeed, who is a perfectly fearless and reckless man, has no more regard for a grizzly than he has for a jack rabbit; the last one we killed he wished to merely break his leg with the first shot "so as to see what he'd do." I had not atall this feeling, and fully realized that we were hunting dangerous game; still I never made steadier shooting than at the grizzlies. I shall not soon forget the first one I killed. We had found where he had been feeding on the carcass of an elk; and followed his trail into a dense pine forest, fairly choked with fallen timber. While noiselessly and slowly threading our way through the thickest part of it I saw Merrifield, who was directly ahead of me, sink suddenly to his knees and turn half round, his face fairly ablaze with excitement. Cocking my rifle and stepping quickly forward, I found myself face to face with the great bear, who was less than twenty five feet off—not eight steps. He had been roused from his sleep by our approach; he sat up in his lair, and turned his huge head slowly towards us. At that distance and in such a place it was very necessary to kill or disable him at the first fire; doubtless my face was pretty white, but the blue barrel was as steady as a rock as I glanced along it until I could see the top of the bead fairly between his two sinister looking eyes; as I pulled the trigger I jumped aside out of the smoke, to be ready if he charged; but it was needless, for the great brute was struggling in the death agony, and, as you will see when I bring home his skin, the bullet hole in his skull was as exactly between his eyes as if I had measured the distance with a carpenters rule. This bear was nearly nine feet long and weighed over a thousand pounds. Each of my other bears, which were smaller, needed two bullets apiece; Merrifield killed each of his with a single shot.

I had grand sport with the elk too, and the woods fairly rang with my shouting when I brought down my first lordly bull, with great branching antlers; but after I had begun bear killing other sport seemed tame.

So I have had good sport; and enough excitement and fatigue to prevent over much thought; and moreover I have at last been able to sleep well at night. But unless I was bear hunting all the time I am afraid I should soon get as restless with this life was with the life at home.

I shall be very, very glad to see you all again. I hope Mousiekins will be very cunning; I shall dearly love her.

I suppose all of our friends the unco' good are as angry as ever with me; they had best not express their discontent to my face unless they wish to hear very plain English. I am sorry my political career should be over, but after all it makes very little difference.

If any Englishman named Farquahr, Lee or Grenfell calls get Douglass or Elliott to do anything they can for them; I met them hunting. Tell Douglass to write me when the last day of registry comes.

Your Loving Brother

November 11, 1884. New York
To Henry Cabot Lodge

Dear Cabot,

I am awfully sorry, but I shall in all probability be unable to get back the west until Xmas; can you not appoint some time in January or February when Mrs. Lodge and yourself can come to stay with us? Any time will suit us; but you *must* come. I really long to have a chance of talking with you.

I was very glad to receive your letter; and I can not say how glad I have been to hear from all sides of the gallant front you showed in defeat. That the blow is a serious one I do not pretend to deny; that it is necessarily fatal however I am far from admitting. The Republican party in Massachusetts will not break up; it will remain the dominant party of the State; and it will feel thoroughly that it owes its success in the immediate past more to you than to any other man, and that you have sacrificed yourself to save it; your hold upon it—a hold gained not by one service, but by a long course of services performed during a considerable space of time—is very strong; and the party will, I think, next put you in a position where you can receive its vote throughout the State.

Of course it may be that we have had our day; it is far more likely that this is true in my case than in yours, for I have no hold on the party managers in New York. Blaine's nomination meant to me pretty sure political death if I supported him; this I realized entirely, and went in with my eyes open. I have won again and again; finally chance placed me where I was sure to lose whatever I did; and I will balance the last against the first. I have stood a great deal; and now that the throw has been against me, I shall certainly not complain. I have not believed and do not believe that I shall ever be likely to come back into political life; we fought a good winning fight when our friends the Independents were backing us; and we have both of us, when circumstances turned them against us, fought the losing fight grimly out to the end. What we have been cannot be taken from us; what we are is due to the folly of others and to no fault of ours. By the way, R. R. Bowker tackled me the other day; and I think I made mince meat of him. Last night I lectured before the 19th Century Club. Now, old fellow, I think the end with you is not yet reached; at least you have done the right thing, and have done it manfully and bravely and in spite of the pressure brought to bear on you; you have been really independent.

With warmest regards to Mrs. Lodge, I am, as ever

Your friend

December 14, 1884. Chimney Butte Ranch, Dakota
To Anna Roosevelt

Darling Bysie,

I have just received your telegram. I suppose that now the article is too much a thing of the past to need an answer; but I am sorry I could not have countered on the hypocritical liars of the Post while the thing was fresh.

I have just returned from a three days trip in the Bad Lands after mountain sheep; and after tramping over the most awful country that can be imagined I finally shot a young ram with a fine head; I have now killed every kind of plains game. I have to stay here till after next Friday to attend a meeting of the Little Missouri stockmen; on Saturday the 20th I start home, and shall be in New York the evening of the 23d. I have just had 52 ponies brought in by Ferris, and Seawall and Dow started down the river with their share yesterday. The latter have lost two horses; I am afraid they have been stolen.

Best love to Baby Lee,

Your Aff Brother

P.S. Will you get me some Xmas present for Pussie? The others are all right.

May 15, 1885. Medora, Dakota
To Henry Cabot Lodge

Dear Cabot:

I was delighted to see your familiar handwriting again; many thanks for the newspaper clipping; there is no need to remind me of my promised visit to you, for you may be sure I shall not forget it. As yet, however, I cannot tell the exact date when I will be in Boston. By the way, some kind friend sent me a criticism from *Life* on my *Century* article, and on myself, which was marked by all the broad intelligence and good humor so preeminently characteristic of the latter day mugwump. In fact it was quite Godkinesque—two parts imbecility and one part bad temper.

I have had hard work, and a good deal of fun since I came out here. Tomorrow I start for the roundup; and I have just come in from taking a thousand head of cattle up on the trail. The weather was very bad and I had my hands full, working night and day, and being able to take off my clothes but once during the week I was out.

The river has been very high recently and I have had on two or three occasions to swim my horse across it; a new experience to me. Otherwise I have done little that is exciting in the way of horsemanship; as you know I am no horseman, and I can not ride an unbroken horse with any comfort. The other day I lunched with the Marquis de Mores, a French cavalry officer; he had hunted all through France, but he told me he never saw in Europe such stiff jumping as we have on the Meadowbrook hunt.

Cleveland is "spindling" wonderfully; Higgins has been repeated *ad nauseam*. I am afraid Evarts is too old; I doubt if we are able to do much with him.

Remember me most warmly to Mrs. Lodge.

Yours

(Writ in a cowcamp; I fear that my caligraphy harmonizes with the environment.)

October 8, 1885. New York
To Jefferson Davis

Mr. Theodore Roosevelt is in receipt of a letter purporting to come from Mr. Jefferson Davis, and denying that the character of Mr. Davis compares unfavorably with that of Benedict Arnold. Assuming the letter to be genuine Mr. Roosevelt has only to say that he would indeed be surprised to find that his views of the character of Mr. Davis did not differ radically from that apparently entertained in relation thereto by Mr. Davis himself. Mr. Roosevelt begs leave to add that he does not deem it necessary that there should be any further communication whatever between himself and Mr. Davis.

March 27, 1886. Medora, Dakota
To Henry Cabot Lodge

Dear Cabot,

I thought the article on [Gouverneur] Morris admirable in every way; one of your crack pieces. Some of the sentences were so thoroughly characteristic of you that I laughed aloud when I read them. One of my men, Sewall (a descendant of the Judge, by the way) read it with as much interest as I did, and talked it over afterwards as intelligently as any one could.

I have written the first chapter of the Benton; so at any rate I have made a start. Writing is horribly hard work to me; and I make slow progress. I have got some good ideas in the first chapter, but I am not sure they are worked up rightly; my style is very rough and I do not like a certain lack of sequitur that I do not seem able to get rid of.

At present we are all snowed up by a blizzard; as soon as it lightens up I shall start down the river with two of my men in a boat we have built while indoors, after some horsethieves who took our boat the other night to get out of the county with; but they have such a start we have very little chance of catching them. I shall take Matthew Arnold along; I have had no chance at all to read it as yet.

Have you begun on your Washington yet? And do you really intend to run for Congress this fall?

Give my warmest love to Nannie; and remember me to everybody else, including "Commander" Luce; I hope he has forgiven me for having dubbed him by that infernal title.

Goodbye, old fellow.

Yours

April 6, 1886. Medora, Dakota
To Henry Cabot Lodge

Dear Cabot,

I think the Harvard speech a first rate one (bar the allusion to me; did you see the N. Y. *Herald* on this latter point?); and was also greatly pleased with the editorials on Dawes and Indiana Civil Service Reform—especially the latter. Black must be quite a pill for the civil service people, by the way; what perverse lunatics the mugwumps are any-way. The St. Paul *Pioneer Press,* a very liberal paper, had a stinging ar-ticle on them the other day. Your Hamilton is a work which was most assuredly well worth doing.

I got the three horsethieves in fine style. My two Maine men and I ran down the river three days in our boat and then came on their camp by surprise. As they knew there was no other boat on the river but the one they had taken and as they had not thought of our build-ing another they were taken completely unawares, one with his rifle on the ground, and the others with theirs on their shoulders; so there was no fight, nor any need of pluck on our part. We simply crept noiselessly up and rising when only a few yards distant covered them with the cocked rifles while I told them to throw up their hands. They saw that we had the drop on them completely and I guess they also saw that we surely meant shooting if they hesitated, and so their hands went up at once. We kept them with us nearly a week, being caught in an ice jam; then we came to a ranch where I got a wagon, and I sent my two men on down stream with the boat, while I took the three captives overland a two days journey to a town where I could give them to the Sheriff. I was pretty sleepy when I got there as I had to keep awake at night a good deal in guarding, and we had gotten out of food, and the cold had been intense.

The other day I presided over the meeting of the Little Missouri Stockmen here, preserving the most rigid parliamentary decorum; I go as our representative to the great Montana Stockmeeting in a day or two.

Can you tell me if President Harrison was born in Virginia? I have no means of finding out here. I hope he was; it gives me a good sen-tence for Benton.

I am as brown and as tough as a hickory nut now.

Yours always

May 15, 1886. Medora, Dakota
To Anna Roosevelt

Darling Bysie,

The enclosed bills are correct; if you can I should greatly like to have them paid.

You were very sweet to send me the newspaper cuttings. I was greatly amused to find I had unknowingly won a political victory, but I would much rather not have been made President of the Association.[1] If I am going to do anything at all I like to give my time to it; and that I

---

[1]The Twenty-first District Association.

can not do in this instance. How did you like my Civil Service piece in the Princeton Review?

Mrs. Dodd's article was very bright and clever; I wish you would tell her how much I enjoyed it. Also I particularly ask to have my very warmest well-wishes given to Miss Swan; I would write myself if I had decent paper (I have just ridden up to Medora, and may not get a chance to write again for some little time; until after the roundup you may not hear very much from me). Tell her it is a sincere pleasure to me to have two people happy for both of whom I genuinely care; they will be another one of our few couples who are good on both sides.

Now, can you, without bother, do me a favor? The poor little mite of a Seawall girl, just baby Lee's age, has neither playmates nor play toys. I do'n't appreciate it as a table companion, especially when fed on, or rather feeding itself on, a mixture of syrup and strawberry jam (giving it the look of a dirty little yellow haired gnome in war paint); but I wish the poor forlorn little morsel had some playtoys. If you go in town ever; or if you do not, could Uncle Jimmie or Aunt Annie, get and send out to me a box with the following toys, all stout and cheap; a big colored ball, some picture blocks, some letter blocks, a little horse and wagon and a rag doll. Mrs. Seawall and Mrs. Dow are very nice; they will do all they can to make you comfortable next summer if we can arrange a visit; though I rather dread seeing you at table, for we have of course no social distinctions, and the cowboys sit down in their shirt sleeves.

My men here are hardworking, labouring men, who work longer hours for no greater wages than many of the strikers; but they are Americans through and through; I believe nothing would give them greater pleasure than a chance with their rifles at one of the mobs. When we get the papers, especially in relation to the dynamite business they become more furiously angry and excited than I do. I wish I had them with me, and a fair show at ten times our number of rioters; my men shoot well and fear very little.[1]

I miss both you and darling Baby Lee dreadfully; kiss her many times for me; I am really hungry to see her. She must be just too cunning for anything. Yet I enjoy my life at present. I have my time fully occupied with work of which I am fond; and so have none of my usual restless, caged wolf feeling. I work two days out of three at my book or papers; and I hunt, ride and lead the wild, half adventurous life of a ranchman all through it. The elements are combined well. Goodbye, dearest Bysie.

Your loving brother

---

[1]The Haymarket riot had convulsed Chicago.

June 19, 1886. Medora, Dakota
To Anna Roosevelt

Darling Bysie,

The round up has stopped for a day or two, and on riding into town I was delighted to find your two letters; they told me just what I wanted to hear, about the jolly parties at Sagamore,[1] and all the rest of it. I have never considered myself a very social personage; but I do wish I could have been present at some of the sprees; and I simply can not say how much I wish to see you and to kiss and pet darling baby. Did you,ever receive my letter in which I asked if you could conveniently send me some toys (blocks, a ball, a woolly dog, a rag doll etc) for the forlorn little mite of a Seawall child? I shall probably be home about October 1st; perhaps a fortnight sooner, perhaps not until two or three weeks later; make all your plans without reference to me, and I will fit into them somehow.

I enclose a letter which I wish you could get Mrs. Butler to answer. I can't make out the signature, nor the sex of the writer nor whether a friend or a stranger.

I am very glad you had Mrs. Lee to stay with you—I can say darling martyr Bi and the interminable grabage—and that she enjoyed herself so much, as she says in a long sweet letter to me.

La Guerre et La Paix, like all Tolstoi's work, is very strong and very interesting. The descriptions of the battles are excellent, but though with one or two good ideas underneath them, the criticisms of the commanders, especially of Napoléon, and of wars in general, are absurd. Moreover when he criticises battles (and the iniquity of war) in his capacity of author, he deprives himself of all excuse for the failure to criticise the various other immoralities he portrays. In Anna Karénine he let each character, good or bad, speak for itself; and while he might better have shown some reprobation of evil, at least it could be alleged in answer that he simply narrated, putting the facts before us that we ourselves might judge them. But when he again and again spends pages in descanting on the wickedness and folly of war, and passes over other vices without a word of reproach he certainly in so far acts as the apologist for the latter, and the general tone of the book does not seem to me to be in the least conducive to morality. Natacha is a bundle of contradictions, and her fickleness is portrayed as truly marvellous; how Pierre could ever have ventured to leave her alone for six weeks after he was married I can not imagine. Marie as portrayed by him is a girl that we can hardly conceive of as fascinating Rostow. Sonia is another variety of the patient Griselda

---

[1]The rechristened Leeholm.

type. The two men André and Pierre are wonderfully well drawn; and all through the book there are touches and descriptions that are simply masterpieces.

The round up has been great fun. If I did not miss all at home so much, and also my beautiful house, I should say that this free, open air life, without any worry, was perfection, and I write steadily three or four days, and then hunt (I killed two elk and some antelope recently) or ride on the round up for as many more.

I send the enclose slip from a criticism of my book on account of the awful irony of the lines I have underscored; send it to Douglass when you write him.

Ever your loving brother

August 10, 1886. Medora, Dakota
To Henry Cabot Lodge

Dear Cabot,

Just a line, to make a request.

I have written on to Secretary Endicott offering to try to raise some companies of horse riflemen out here in the event of trouble with Mexico. Will you telegraph me at once if war becomes inevitable? Out here things are so much behind hand that I might not hear the news for a week. I haven't the least idea there will be any trouble; but as my chance of doing anything in the future worth doing seems to grow continually smaller I intend to grasp at every opportunity that turns up.

I think there is some good fighting stuff among these harum-scarum roughriders out here; whether I can bring it out is another matter. All the boys were delighted with your photographs—except the one in which you left the saddle, which they spotted at once. They send a very cordial invitation to come out here; though they don't approve of bobtailed horses.

I sent the Benton ms. on to Morse yesterday; I hope it is decent, but lately I have been troubled with dreadful misgivings.

Remember me particularly to Nannie and tell her that the opening lines of "Childe Harold to the dark tower came" (in Browning, I mean) now always excite pensive memories in my gentle soul.

Always yours

September 20, 1886. Medora, Dakota
To Anna Roosevelt

Darling Bamie,

On returning from the mountains I was savagely irritated by seeing in the papers the statement that I was engaged to Edith Carow; from what source it could have originated I can not possibly conceive.

But the statement itself is true. I am engaged to Edith and before Christmas I shall cross the ocean and marry her. You are the first person to whom I have breathed one word on the subject; I am absolutely sure that I have never betrayed myself in any way, unless some servant has seen the address on the letters I wrote. When it finally became impossible to keep it longer from them, Edith told her mother and sister, but under such conditions (especially as they are abroad) that I can scarcely believe either of them told anyone else. When I was back in July I would have told you, but at that time I was uncertain whether it would not be a year before we were married, for reasons which I will give you in full when we meet. On returning to Medora I received letters giving definite shape to my plans; I did not write you at once because a letter is such a miserably poor substitute for talking face to face; and I should not write you now, had it not been for this report; for I will see you before you have time to answer me.

I utterly disbelieve in and disapprove of second marriages; I have always considered that they argued weakness in a man's character. You could not reproach me one half as bitterly for my inconstancy and unfaithfulness, as I reproach myself. Were I sure there were a heaven my own prayer would be I might never go there, lest I should meet those I loved on earth who are dead. No matter what your judgement about myself I shall most assuredly enter no plea against it. But I do very earnestly ask you not to visit my sins upon poor little Edith. It is certainly not her fault; the entire blame rests on my shoulders. Eight years ago she and I had very intimate relations; one day there came a break, for we both of us had, and I suppose have, tempers that were far from being of the best. To no soul now living have either of us ever since spoken a word of this.

As regards yourself, my dearest sister, I can only say you will be giving me the greatest happiness in your power if you will continue to pass your summers with me. We ourselves will have to live in the country almost the entire year; I thoroughly understand the change I will have to make in my life. As I already told you, if you wish to you shall keep Baby Lee, I of course paying the expense.

I will write to Elliott and Anna, Corinne and Douglas, and Aunt Annie and Uncle Jimmie. No other person is to be told a word about it.

I will explain everything in full when I see you.

Forever your loving brother,

As I do not care to see Rosy Lee I shall return about Oct 6th 86.

October 17, 1886. Oyster Bay
To Henry Cabot Lodge

Dear Cabot,

Just two hours after writing you my last card, I was visited by a succession of the influential Republicans of the city to entreat me to take the nomination for Mayor. With the most genuine reluctance I finally accepted. It is of course a perfectly hopeless contest, the chance for success being so very small that it may be left out of account. But they want to get a united Republican party in this city and to make a good record before the people. I am at the head of an unexceptionable ticket. They seemed to think that my name would be the strongest they could get, and were most urgent for me to run; and I did not well see how I could refuse.

If I make a good run it will not hurt me; but it will if I make a bad one, as is very likely. Many of the decent Republicans are panicky over George,[1] whose canvass is not at all dangerous, being mainly wind; if the panic grows thousands of my supporters will go to Hewitt[2] for fear George may be elected—a perfectly groundless emotion. The *Evening Post* is for Hewitt and is harping vigorously on this string. So it is quite on the cards that I will be most hopelessly defeated. All that I hope for, at the best, is to make a good run and get out the Republican vote; you see I have over forty thousand majority against me. If I could have kept out I would never have been in the contest.

We have the horse show here on the 3rd, 4th and 5th of November; can not you come on to me then? I will be in hopeless confusion; but I would like to see you for twenty-four hours at any rate—and as much more as you can give. I hate to give up my visit to you.

Always yours

Write me a line how your own private contest is progressing.

November 22, 1886. London
To Henry Cabot Lodge

Dear Cabot,

I have had very good fun here. I brought no letters and wrote no one I was coming, holding myself stiffly aloof; and, perhaps in consequence, I have been treated like a prince. I have been put down at the Athenaeum and the other swell clubs, have been dined and lunched every day, and have had countless invitations to go down into the country and hunt or

---

[1]Reformer Henry George.
[2]Democrat Abram Hewitt.

shoot. I have really enjoyed meeting some of the men—as Goschen, Shaw-Lefevre, John Morley, Bryce (who wished to be remembered to you, and was especially complimentary about your Hamilton) and others, Lord North and Lord Carnarven were also pleasant.

I had one very good day with the Essex hounds, including an hour's sharp run. It was totally different from our Long Island draghunting; there was infinitely more head work needed by the men and more cleverness by the horses, but there was not any of our high jumping or breakneck galloping. My horse was a good one but his wind gave out and we came two tremendous croppers; but the ground was so soft I was hardly even jarred and I kept my reins tight, so as to be over again as soon as the horse was up. The field was a couple of hundred strong. But the country was so blind that I could not ride my own line at all, and followed the master or one of the two or three in the first flight all the time. The horses I saw would not, I believe, face our high timber at all; but ours would do quite as badly at first here; they would go straight into the ditches on the far sides of the hedges. I hate jumping through bull-finches.

I am to be married on Dec. 2d. Edith sends her warmest remembrance to you and Nannie, and says that you two at any rate must try to like her.

Remember to send me a copy of the Benton, if not too much trouble.

Yours always

January 24, 1887. Sorrento
To Cecil Spring Rice

My dear Spring Rice,

My sister has just written me that you are again in New York, and I hardly know whether to be most pleased that you are once more on our side of the water, or sorry that you are not to be in London when we get back there; for I owe you all the very pleasant times I had last November. At any rate, Mrs. Roosevelt and I are looking forward to seeing you, for just as long as you can stay, at Sagamore Hill; and you are to come whenever you can.

Indeed you can hardly realize how much your kindness and thoughtfulness added to the pleasure of my stay in London. We have had a most delightful trip in Italy, making our leisurely way from Hyéres—where I was greatly interested in the queer Provençal tongue and traits of the people—to Pisa, by carriage. We made but short visits to Rome and Florence, and have now been for some little time here and at Capri; by the way, I wish Italians did not so evidently regard a pedestrian as a lunatic.

I should have given a good deal to see the faces of some of my good

Tory friends when Lord Randolph Churchill resigned. I am glad to have met Goschen; but I doubt if he can construct as well as he can criticise.

With warm regards from Mrs. Roosevelt, I am

Ever faithfully yours

February 15, 1887. Paris
To Henry Cabot Lodge

Dear Cabot,

I am delighted that you are pleased with the Benton; you can easily imagine how pleased I was with your letter. If I write another historical work of any kind—and my dream is to make one such that will be my magnum opus—I shall certainly take more time and do it carefully and thoroughly, so as to avoid the roughness and interruption of the Benton. Of course from its very nature if it attracts criticism at all it will be savagely attacked. It was not written to please those political and literary hermaphrodites the mugwumps.

I wish them joy of Dawes. Hiscock is a good man—and a politician too.

By the way, don't you think Lowell has rather fallen off? Of course he is a great writer; but there seemed to me to be a good deal of rather thin matter, or else of wrong headedness; in certain of his "Essays" just out. But of course there was much that was admirable; and I especially liked the address on Wordsworth; and, saving your presence, don't you think that much of it might apply to Browning? Not that I would compare the two.

A former friend and political supporter of mine, Harold Frederic, is writing a serial in the *Scribner's* which I like very much; it is worth reading"—"Seth's Brother's Wife" is the name. Thank Heaven Henry James is now an avowedly British novelist.

I have regarded with much dispassionate enjoyment the the Corrigan-McGlynn-George-Davitt-Papal controversy. May each vanquish all the others! It is one of those few contests in which *any* result is for the good.

When will the Washington be ready?

Was the Senate wise in rejecting that amiable colored Democrat Matthews?

Yours always

April 20, 1887. Medora, Dakota
To Henry Cabot Lodge

Dear Cabot,

I was delighted to receive your two letters. Your speech was admirable. Massachusetts is *the* important State; and with the present infernal mugwumpian squint in the public eye you must organize from now on to carry it. You were right in beginning the campaign now. I am not on the ground; but after Rhode Island I feel nervous? I hope Andrew may be buried out of sight.

I hate speech making and never feel confident of my ability to do more than make a few pointed remarks in debate. However, I suppose I shall have to do my best at the Federal Club; I shall certainly take a hack at the estimable Godkin.

Well, we have had a perfect smashup all through the cattle country of the northwest. The losses are crippling. For the first time I have been utterly unable to enjoy a visit to my ranch. I shall be glad to get home.

The scrap of paper you enclosed me contains some excellent ideas, which I shall try to use.

Give my love to Nannie and remember we are looking forward to seeing you both in June.

I must be off, now, down the river; so goodbye.

Yours ever

September 13, 1887. Oyster Bay
To Anna Roosevelt

Darling Bysie,

Things came with a rush even sooner than any one had expected.

Edith was taken ill last evening at nine, and the small son and heir was born at 2.15 this morning. Edith is getting on very well; she was extremely plucky all through. The boy is a fine little fellow about 8 1/2 pounds.

We were pretty nearly caught badly. Of course the nurse is not here yet. Aunt Annie spent the night here and took charge of Baby.

Little Alice is too good and cunning for anything, and devoted to "my own little brother;" she will not allow her rocking chair to be moved from alongside him.

I am heartily glad it is all over so quickly and safely.

Yours ever

January 6, 1888. Oyster Bay
To James Bryce

My dear Mr. Bryce,

You must by this time be tired of hearing your book compared to De Tocquevilles; yet you must allow me one brief allusion to the two together. When I looked over the proofs you sent me I ranked your book and his together; now that I see your book as a whole I feel that the comparison did it great injustice. It has all of De Tocqueville's really great merits; and has not got, as his book has, two or three serious and damaging faults. No one can help admiring the depth of your insight into our peculiar conditions, and the absolute fairness of your criticisms. Of course there are one or two minor points on which I disagree with you; but I think the fact that you give a good view of all sides is rather funnily shown by the way in which each man who refuses to see any but one side quotes your book as supporting him. I was rather amused to see that the Spectator considered that the facts you gave told heavily against Home Rule—because our state legislatures were not ideal bodies and that similarly the Saturday Review had its worst suspicions of democracy amply confirmed.

I was especially pleased at the way in which you pricked certain hoary bubbles; notably the "tyranny of the majority" theory. You have also thoroughly understood that instead of the old American stock being "swamped" by immigration, it has absorbed the immigrants and remained nearly unchanged. Carl Schurz, even, has'n't imported a German idea into our politics; Albert Gallatin had something of the Swiss in his theories; our present Mayor Grant, of Irish blood, will serve New York, whether well or ill, solely by American principles.

But I do not think that the Irishman as a rule loses his active hatred of England till the third generation; and I fear that a good deal of feeling against England—mind you, none whatever against an Englishman—still foolishly exists in certain quarters of our purely American communities. But they are perfectly ready to elect Englishmen to office; relatively to the total number of immigrants many more English than Irish are sent to Congress, for instance.

Did you notice that this fall we, for the first time in five years, beat the Irish candidate for Mayor in Boston, because the Irish were suspected of hostility to the public schools? though they warmly protested that the accusation was untrue.

It is very difficult for an outsider to tell how your politics are trending, nowadays.

Very sincerely yours

January 15, 1888. New York
To Jonas Van Duzer

My dear Van,

I was, as always, very glad indeed to hear from you. I wish we could have a meeting of our old set—O'Neil, Hunt, Home, Hubbell, Kruse, you and myself. I do not think our legislative work was wasted in the least; I think we have a right to look at the years we spent in the New York Legislature as honorable ones; I shall always be glad to think of them.

Like yourself, I shall probably never be in politics again. I hope the Republican party does not get into the habit of becoming a mere party of reaction; I never had much sympathy with the Dependent Pensions bill. Do you not think it would be dangerous to take the internal revenue tax off whisky?

Ranching has been even less profitable than farming of late. But I am very sorry you have suffered so much from illness, old fellow. My own health has been excellent.

I have a small son now; and am settling down more and more to country life for all but a couple of months of the year. My literary work occupies a good deal of my time; and I have on the whole done fairly well at it; I should like to write some book that would really take rank as in the very first class, but I suppose this is a mere dream.

Blaine will be our next candidate, will he not? Do you not think that Cleveland will be re-elected anyhow? I fear so.

Be sure and let me see you if you come to New York.

Your friend always

April 23, 1888. Oyster Bay
To Francis Parkman

My dear Sir,

I suppose that every American who cares at all for the history of his own country feels a certain personal pride in your work—it is as if Motley had written about American instead of European subjects, and so was doubly our own; but those of us who have a taste for history, and yet have spent much of our time on the frontier, perhaps realize even more keenly than our fellows, that your works stand alone, and that they must be models for all historical treatment of the founding of new communities and the growth of the frontier, here in the wilderness.

This—even more than the many pleasant hours I owe you—must be my excuse for writing.

I am engaged on a work of which the first part treats of the extension to our frontier westward and southwestward during the twenty odd years from 1774 to 1796—the years of uninterrupted Indian warfare during which Kentucky and Tennessee were founded and grew to statehood, under such men as Daniel Boone and George Rogers Clark, John Sevier, James Robertson and Isaac Shelby. I have gathered a good deal of hitherto unused material, both from the unpublished mss. of the State Department, and from the old diaries, letters and memoranda in various private libraries at Louisville, Nashville, Lexington &c.

This first part I have promised the Putnams for some time in 1889; it will be in two volumes, with such title as "The Winning of the West and Southwest," and perhaps as a subtitle "From the Alleghenies to the Mississippi."

I should like to dedicate this to you. Of course I know that you would not wish your name to be connected in even the most indirect way with any but good work; and I can only say that I will do my best to make the work creditable. William Everett, John Morse or Cabot Lodge can tell you who I am.

I do not know if you have ever seen a little series published in Boston, the "American Statesmen"; if so, the first chapter in the "Benton" will give you an idea of the outline I intend to fill up.

Yours very truly

August 8, 1888. Oyster Bay
To Anna Roosevelt

Darling Bysie,

Your telegram was characteristic of you, you darling sister; it was just like you to send it.

Unfortunately, we will not have to take advantage of it; for Edith has just had a miscarriage. She is getting on all right now. The mischief of course came from my infernal tumble at the polo match. The tumble was nothing in itself; I have had twenty worse; but it *looked* bad, because I was knocked perfectly limp and senseless, and though I was I all right in an hour, the mischief had been done to Edith, though we did not know it for over a week. So I shall not go out west for a fortnight, and perhaps not then.

Dora is out here now, and is having a great time; she loves being with the children. We had a terrible storm a couple of days ago, and among other feats it took the roof clean off the bathing houses.

Your aff brother

November 18, 1888. Oyster Bay
To Cecil Spring Rice

Dear Cecil,

It was very good of you, and just like you, to send us those rare prints; indeed we appreciate them very highly, and we appreciate even more your thoughtfulness in sending them to us.

I am now recuperating from the Presidential campaign—our quadrennial Presidential riot being an interesting and exciting, but somewhat exhausting, pastime. I always genuinely enjoy it and act as target and marksman alternately with immense zest; but it is a trifle wearing.

I have adopted polo this summer. We have an aboriginal polo club at O. B.[1] now, and this summer played a match with a third-rate Meadowbrook team and beat them—I getting knocked senseless at the end of the match. I went to the Kootenai country this fall and shot a bear and a bull caribou I am hard at work at a volume of history, to be published next spring; and Freeman (your man) has asked me to write a volume for his "historic towns" series. So I have plenty to do, and though my ranch almost burst me, I am as happy as a king—to use a Republican simile. My wife and babies are well.

Goodbye and good luck, old fellow; when are you coming here again? I wonder if I shall ever get to London.

Yours ever

You were awfully good to my sister in London.

March 25, 1889. New York
To Henry Cabot Lodge

Dear old Cabot,

You are certainly the most loyal friend that ever breathed. Edith and I were more touched than I can say over your letter; all the more so from its absolutely unexpected nature. I hope you will tell Blaine how much I appreciate his kind expressions.

I would have particularly liked to have been in Washington, in an official position, while you were in Congress; we would have had a very good time; and so I would have been glad to have been appointed.[2] But aside from this feeling—and of course the pleasure one feels in having one's services recognized—it is a good deal better for me to stay where I am. I would like above all things to go into politics; but in this part of the State that seems impossible, especially with such a number of very wealthy competitors. So I have made up my mind that I will go in especially for literature, simply taking the part in politics that a decent man should. I am going to keep my residence in the city because I have more hold here.

I was much amused the other day at an editorial in the *Times* about your Winchester system; it was fairly complimentary though of course it's mugwump mind felt a certain suspicion of the affair. Whitridge, by the way, has apparently suffered a change of heart; he spoke with bitter contempt of the futility of the average reformer, the other evening, and casually mentioned that he regarded you as the most promising young man in America! I fairly gaped at him.

---

[1]Oyster Bay.

[2]Lodge was trying to get Roosevelt a State Department position.

Give my best love to Nannie, from both Edith and myself, and with the very heartiest thanks, old fellow, I am

Ever your friend

April [ ], 1889. New York
To Henry Cabot Lodge

Dear Cabot,

I hope you will be here on Saturday the 27th; Ernest Crosby, our "high license" man, and a first rate fellow, will be here to dinner, and perhaps Choate; do come; I want to see and talk with you dreadfully. I do hope the President will appoint good civil service commissioners; I am very much discontented with him so far; in this state he has deliberately built up a Platt machine.

Yours

PART THREE

Public Servant

1889–1898

*T*he job of Civil Service Commissioner was hardly the most sought after in the federal government. The pay was modest, and power was shared with two other commissioners. The task of the commission was to implement recent regulations regarding federal employees, the general thrust of the regulations being that merit, rather than patronage, should determine who was hired and who retained. The trouble was that patronage had long been the glue that held political parties together, and party leaders were reluctant to relinquish that perquisite of office. Almost at once Roosevelt found himself butting heads with Postmaster General John Wanamaker and others in the Harrison administration who considered civil service reform a nuisance.

But the Civil Service job had the singular advantage of transporting Roosevelt to Washington. He stayed at the Lodge home while looking for a house for his own family, and he got to know the leading members of the national Republican Party. Thomas Reed of Maine struck Roosevelt as particularly able, but other figures were scarcely less impressive. Roosevelt realized that he had landed in the seat of power, and he found the experience most exciting.

Washington also afforded the opportunity to mingle with a literary crowd. Roosevelt got to know Henry and Brooks Adams. He met Rudyard Kipling. He maintained contact with Francis Parkman and introduced himself to Frederick Jackson Turner, a young historian who put forward a provocative theory about the role of the frontier in shaping American history. He discussed Hamlin Garland, Tolstoy, Shakespeare, and other authors with old and new friends. He extended earlier discussions of practical and theoretical issues of natural history.

Roosevelt's family continued to grow. Daughter Ethel and sons Archie and Quentin joined Alice, Ted, and Kermit to make an even half dozen. The full house occasionally strained the family budget, especially after the Dakota debacle. Edith managed most of the finances, but occasionally Roosevelt discovered debts he had managed to overlook. Yet their lifestyle did not noticeably suffer. They still summered at Oyster Bay, in the big house they called Sagamore Hill. And he and Edith took occasional trips, as to the Columbian Exposition in Chicago in 1893. Most family news during this period was good; one exception was the death of Roosevelt's brother, Elliott, following a tragic and scandalous personal disintegration.

Following the return of the Democrats to the White House in 1893, Roosevelt expected to be removed from the Civil Service Commission. To his surprise President Grover Cleveland kept him on. But by 1895 Roosevelt realized that his political future, if any, lay with the Republican Party, and that too-long association with Democrats could only cast that future into doubt. He passed up an invitation to run for mayor of New York City—and quickly regretted his decision. When the new mayor offered him a job on the city's police commission, he accepted.

Roosevelt's tenure as president of the police board was tumultuous and *brief. He generated headlines (and political cartoons) by prowling the streets at night looking for corrupt coppers. He attempted to enforce a law against liquor on Sundays, in the face of much adverse public opinion. He made friends of such urban reformers as Lincoln Steffens and Jacob Riis, but enemies of such powerful figures as Thomas Platt, the head boss of New York Republican politics.*

Appreciating that Platt could have him fired at will, Roosevelt paid increasing attention to national and international affairs. The rise of populism in the West and South seemed to him a threat to reason and law, and at every opportunity he lambasted the populists, starting with William Jennings Bryan and working down. Events in Hawaii and Venezuela provided the opportunity for Roosevelt to reveal his vigorously expansionist ideas on foreign policy. An insurrection in Cuba had him itching for war to eject imperial Spain from the Western Hemisphere.

The election campaign of 1896 found Roosevelt backing Thomas Reed for the Republican nomination, but when Reed lost to William McKinley, Roosevelt took to the trail for the latter. His good service once more put him in line for a federal appointment. This time Cabot Lodge found him a post in the Navy Department, as assistant secretary. Roosevelt reveled in the work, not least since his superior, John D. Long, was often sick and absent. Roosevelt prepared the navy for war, which he tried to talk McKinley into declaring against Spain. For months his arguments fell on deaf ears, but finally, in April 1898, McKinley came round to Roosevelt's bellicose way of thinking.

June 12, 1889. Washington
To Anna Lodge and Henry Cabot Lodge

Dear Nannie and Cabot,

When I reached here Tuesday morning I found my room all ready, and a very nice breakfast waiting for me. Martha seems a very good woman; she cooks well, keeps my room in order and doesn't bother me. (By the way, I gave her Nannie's note.) Everything is as comfortable as possible; you have no idea of the difference it makes, coming here instead of to a hotel; and I *am* fully aware of what I owe you, Edith to the contrary notwithstanding.

Of course I feel a little homesick at being away from Edith and the children; but I have my hands fairly full of work. On Sunday we leave for a ten days' trip through some western post offices; I guess there is a Cleveland hold-over at Milwaukee who will stand some overhauling.

I called on the Blaines, and on Quay; then my (two) visiting cards gave out, and I must wait until Edith sends me some more. I also called on Billy Wharton, and we arranged to dine together for the next two or three evenings, until I go west—tonight I dine at the Thompsons.

Tell Bay[1] to brace up and study all he knows how, and we'll have a great trip to the Little Missouri. If there is any point of his equipment about which he needs information let him write me at once. I called on Walker Blaine to see about Butterfield, and I think he will be all right. Let Cabot be sure to write some time to Governor Merriam of Minnesota about Tom Reed; I will do so too—or rather I will see him when I go out in the fall.

Goodbye; I shall keep you informed from time to time how things are going on.

Yours ever

P.S. To Cabot; don't write about Bishop Potter until you have read his piece; it was really not what he said, but what the mugwumps interpreted it to mean, together with a certain lack of wisdom in choosing the time and place for utterance that made the remarks unfortunate. They were unwise in part; but they also contained some truth; and there are far more serious offenders than Bishop Potter.

June 24, 1889. Washington
To Henry Cabot Lodge

Dear Cabot,

Well, here I am back again, to routine work, and heat, and, as a relief, pleasant dinners with the equally lonely Wharton.

---

[1]George Cabot Lodge, son of Henry Cabot and Anna Lodge.

We had only a week's trip but we stirred things up well; the President has made a great mistake in appointing a well-meaning, weak old fellow in Indianapolis, but I think we have administered a galvanic shock that will reinforce his virtue for the future. Cleveland's postmaster at Milwaukee is about as thorough paced a scoundrel as I ever saw—an oily-Gammon, church-going specimen. We gave him a neat hoist. The Chicago postmaster is a trump; a really good fellow (Republican). At Grand Rapids, the redoubtable Congressman Belknap turned up as meek as a lamb and we fraternized most amicably. The West knows much less about civil service reform than the East, and there will be a row next winter; nevertheless some of their papers are very strong on the subject. I enclose an editorial from the Chicago *Tribune.*

I haven't seen my book at all; but I know yours is out for I saw a three column review, of the most appreciative order, in the N.Y. *Tribune.* It was written very intelligently and really seemed to appreciate pretty well the magnitude of the work you had accomplished. All that it needed to make it perfectly truthful was to have summed up by stating that it was *the* life of the greatest of all Americans. It is no small triumph to have written such a book as that.

Best love to Nannie.

Yours

June 29, 1889. Washington
To Henry Cabot Lodge

Dear Cabot,

Tell Nannie I have called on all the people whose names she gave me, and virtue has had its reward. The Hitts had me to dinner (where I met Blaine and Phelps), Linden Kent drives me out to the country club this evening and last evening I dined with the Herberts, who were very pleasant; I am sworn friends with Billy Wharton and usually dine with him at Welckers. There we usually growl over our respective griefs. Blaine, and Walker B. do not treat him with the consideration that is his due; Walker usurps all the most pleasant and honorable part of his duties. As for me, I am having a hard row to hoe. I have made this Commission a living force, and in consequence the outcry among the spoilsmen has become furious; it has evidently frightened both the President and Halford a little. They have shown symptoms of telling me that the law should be rigidly enforced where people will stand it, and gingerly handled elsewhere. But I answered militantly; that as long as I was responsible the law should be enforced up to the handle *every where;* fearlessly and honestly. I am a great believer in practical politics; but when my duty is to enforce a law, that law is surely going to be enforced, without fear or favor. I am perfectly willing to be turned out—or legislated out—but while in I mean business. As a matter of fact I believe I have strengthened the administration by showing, in striking contrast to the facts under Cleveland, that there was no humbug in the law now. All the Chicago and Milwaukee papers are backing me up heartily. The Indiana men are very angry—even Browne has gone back on his previous record. It is disheartening to see such folly; but its only effect on me personally is to make me more doggedly resolute than ever to insist on exact and full justice.

I still have not seen your Washington; it must be awaiting me at Sagamore Hill.

Yours

July 1, 1889. Oyster Bay
To Henry Cabot Lodge

Dear Cabot,

I was delighted to receive your letter, and need hardly say how much pleased I was with your opinion of my book. You must certainly see the *Tribune* review; it is written with real appreciation; it is headed "A Brilliant Work." I have now read your book carefully through, and can only reiterate what I have already said as to its worth. It is head and shoulders above what you have already done; and it is *the* life of Washington. You have now reached what I am still struggling for; a *uniformly* excellent style. The contrast between your description of Virginian society in this book and in your "History of the Colonies," is so great as to be almost amusing. Moreover, though you have no absolutely new material, your chapter on "Washington as a party man" (I am thankful you took that exact title; it acts as a mordant to set the picture) is in reality as absolutely new as if based on mss. never before unearthed. It is a great work.

I was glad to hear from you in approval of my western trip, when I made "a slam among the post offices." I have been seriously annoyed at the mugwump praises, for fear they would discredit me with well-meaning but narrow Republicans; and for the last week my party friends in Washington have evidently felt a little shakey. This has no effect on me whatever; I took the first opportunity to make a slash at the Port Huron man especially to show that I was resolutely bent on following out my course to the very end. Even Halford, however, says he is alarmed at the feeling against the law in the West; but as I told him, it had far better be repealed than allowed to remain as under Cleveland a non-enforced humbug. If you get the chance do dwell on the fact that it is to Harrison's credit, all that we are doing in enforcing the law. I am part of the Administration; if I do good work it redounds to the credit of the Administration. This needs to be insisted on, both for the sake of the mugwumps and for the sake of Harrison himself.

How fortunate it is that I did not get the Assistant Secy'ship of State! I could have done nothing there; whereas now I have been a real force, and think I have helped the cause of good government and of the party.

Best love to Nannie.

July 11, 1889. Washington
To Henry Cabot Lodge

Dear Cabot,

I read your speech with great care; I did not write you about it before because I wished to write a little at length. I think it so good as to be worth keeping in permanent form. Keep an accurate copy; it must go in, if it ever becomes necessary to publish a volume of "letters and speeches" of a distinguished, etc., etc. You took Bishop Potter's sermon exactly right, laying stress on just the proper points—the time chosen to deliver it, the application made by the mugwumps, and the failure to see that one has as much right to use Benedict Arnold as Washington as a sample public man of a century back; and yet you did not rebel at proper criticism. Moreover your whole speech was in tone and style that of a trained scholar who was also a trained politician—using the word in its proper meaning. I wonder whether it did not occur to our mugwump friends that it was an honor to the community to have in Congress a man capable of making such a speech.

Your remarks about indiscriminate, abusive criticism of course go to my heart; I am going to try to drag in something of the sort into my volume on N. Y. for Freeman's series if I ever write it. I regard this dishonest jealousy of decent men on the part of people who claim to be good, and this wholesale abuse, as two of the most potent forces for evil now existent in our nation. The foul and coarse abuse of an avowed partisan, willing to hurt the nation for the sake of personal or party gain, is bad enough; but it receives the final touch when steeped in the mendacious hypocrisy of the mugwump, the miscalled Independent. If the Civil Service Reform papers do not make much of your address, it can only be because they care less for reforming civil service than for gratifying their malignant personal jealousies and animosities, at any cost to good government. I do not know when I have read a clearer, stronger, terser argument on behalf of the reform than that in your speech. It was in all ways admirable.

I am glad your Washington sold so well; but I have never had a doubt as to the reception. In fact, in both literature and policies, you hate attained a really wonderful position; in literature you have won it both with educated critics and with the general reading public, and in politics you have the confidence of the great body of decent American citizens who are neither silly nor vicious, who form part of neither the mugwumps nor the snob.

As for me, I have come back to my work. I saw Wharton for a moment; and the Commission had a very satisfactory interview with the President. The old boy is with us,—which was rather a relief to learn definitely. Wanamaker[1] has been as outrageously disagreeable as he could possibly be; and he hinted at so much that when the President telegraphed for us yesterday we thought it looked like a row. But as a matter of fact he has, if not supported us against Wanamaker, at least not supported Wanamaker against us; and when we are guaranteed a fair field I am quite able to handle [him] by myself. We have done our best to get on smoothly with him; but he is an ill-conditioned creature. He seems to be the only one of the Cabinet who wants to pitch into us; Porter (who will keep his census out of our grip) is the best of friends with me; and I get along well with the absurd Tanner. It has been a great and genuine satisfaction to feel that the President is with us. The Indianapolis business gave him an awful wrench, but he has swallowed the medicine, and in his talk with us today did not express the least dissatisfaction with any of our deeds or utterances.

By the way, about interviewing, I really say very little; but I can't help answering a question now and then, and it promptly comes out as an interview. I was rather glad that Puck pitched into me; the chorus of mugwump praise was growing too loud. The attack was purely by innuendo and indirection, and was therefore in true mugwump style.

How about Bay? I hope he will come out with me whether he passes or not; it will do him good and it would be a great disappointment to him not to go.

During the hot weather we shall have comparatively little to do; it is pretty dreary to sizzle here, day after day, doing routine work that the good Lyman is quite competent to attend to by himself; and I shall take my six weeks in the West with a light heart and a clear conscience. I shall start about August 6th.

Give my best love to Nannie, and tell her it is everything for me to have 1211 as a home.

Yours ever

---

[1]Postmaster General John Wanamaker (also the Philadelphia department store magnate), who was Roosevelt's bete noire on civil service reform.

I guess from what the Prex says I will stay in unless knocked on the head by Congress—but I do wish he would give us a *little* more active support; in this Milwaukee case Wanamaker from pure spite will not interfere to prevent the (Democratic) Postmaster from turning out the subordinate who gave us the information.

July 13, 1889. Washington
To Francis Parkman

My dear Mr. Parkman,

I am much pleased that you like the book.

I have always had a special admiration for you as the only one—and I may very sincerely say, the greatest—of our two or three first class historians who devoted himself to American history; and made a classic work—not merely an excellent book of references like Bancroft or Hildreth. I have always intended to devote myself to essentially American work; and literature must be my mistress perforce, for though I really enjoy politics I appreciate perfectly the exceedingly short nature of my tenure. I much prefer to really accomplish something good in public life, no matter at what cost of enmity from even my political friends than to enjoy a longer term of service, fettered by endless fear, always trying to compromise, and doing nothing in the end.

I thought it really necessary to hit Gilmore a rap; his work is very dishonest. I am not quite sure how the Kentuckians and Tenneseeans will take my book; they have the dreadful habit of always writing of themselves in the superlative tense.

Mr. Draper unfortunately thinks one bit of old ms. just exactly as good as any other.

Very sincerely yours

July 31, 1889. Washington
To James Brander Matthews

Dear Matthews,

O, you Mugwumps! The way you go and arrogate all virtue to yourselves is enough to exasperate an humble party man like myself. Here am I, feebly trying to do my duty, threatened with overwhelming disaster by my own party men, who, as the last bitterest term of reproach, accuse me of being a mugwump; and now you want to join in and help foster the delusion. By the way, if you see our good friend Bunner, give him the love of the "Bob-tailed" statesman. Seriously, I have pretty hard work, and work of rather an irritating kind; but I am delighted to be engaged in it. For the last few years politics with me has been largely a balancing of evils, and I am delighted to go in on a side where I have no doubt whatever, and feel absolutely certain that my efforts are wholly for the good; and you can guarantee I intend to hew to the line, and let the chips fly where they will. Just yesterday, in a brief interval of battling with the spoilsmen, I strolled into a club-room here—glad to get anywhere out of the sizzling heat of the Washington streets—and picked up a copy of *Scribner's*. As soon as I saw your article, I knew that you had written the piece about which you spoke to me two years ago. On reading it, I was electrified when I struck the name of the fort. It may be prejudice on my part, but I really think it is one of the best of your stories, and I am very glad to have my name connected with it in no matter how small a way. I congratulate you on it very sincerely. Much obliged for the information about Emmett's book. It has been wholly impossible for me to work at the volume on New York this summer as I had intended, but in the fall I shall take it up, and then I will get you to put me in the way of getting Emmett's volume of illustrations and documents.

I am going to spend six weeks after the 5th of August out West among the bears and cowboys, as I think I have fairly earned a holiday.

Faithfully yours

October 30, 1889. New York
To Henry Cabot Lodge

Dear Cabot,

Last evening the Crugers invited me over to dine with Hiscock; and tonight I dine with ex-Senator Miller. Hiscock remarked that the New York delegation were "practically solid" for Reed; and he said that he thought we stood an excellent chance of electing our State ticket—he is the first politican who has told me so. Miller is, naturally, in a bitterly angry and contemptuous mood towards the Administration; as for the election he says that no human being can forecast the result; if the Cleveland men are not curs they will stand aloof, and if [they] do we may very well win.

The man who criticised me in *The Atlantic* knew a good deal of the subject; I don't suppose any author sets a true value on his work; but I felt that he did not give me sufficient credit for the many things I had done, while he made one or two points—and failed signally in trying to make one or two others against me. On the whole I thought he was a hostile critic; and therefore the grudging praise that was unwillingly extorted from him was all the more valuable. I have finished my controversy with Kirke; in my last letter I put the knife into him up to the hilt.

What funnily varied lives we do lead, Cabot! We touch two or three little worlds, each profoundly ignorant of the others. Our literary friends have but a vague knowledge of our actual political work; and a goodly number of our sporting and social acquaintances know us only as men of good family, one of whom rides hard to hounds, while the other hunts big game in the Rockies.

Can I come pretty often to dinner while in Washington before Edith comes?

You *must* beat Russell. It would be gall and wormwood to have him elected.

Love to Nannie.

Yours

January 13, 1890. Washington
To George Haven Putnam

Dear Haven:

I never, never, never dreamed of writing a Life of Nelson, and unless I was drunk or crazy I could not have told Bishop so. I wish you would get him to send you on my letter. He must have misunderstood me somehow or other. I think you are absolutely right about the western history. As I told you last winter, I was foolish enough to promise 18 months ago Professor Freeman, of England, a volume on New York for his Historic Town Series, and that promise I shall have to keep. It has been weighing over me like a nightmare for the past eighteen months, but I do not believe it will take much time when I can get down to it. Outside of this I shall not go into any literary work excepting the *Winning of the West*. I have already collected most of the material for my third and fourth volumes, and have outlined the first few chapters. I realize perfectly that my chance of making a permanent literary reputation depends on how I do this big work, not on doing a lot of little booklets, and I need hardly say that I infinitely prefer all my books to come from your press, and that you will always hereafter have first chance at any book I may write. I was led into the Freeman matter in a moment of weakness, not at the time understanding the consequences of my promise, and now I cannot honorably back out. I want to ask you however about what you say as to magazine articles. The only magazine articles I care to write are a couple of papers on civil service reform and some hunting articles for the *Century*. The civil service reform pieces I regard as in the way of my present business. It is no pleasure to me to write them, but I feel it more or less a duty to do so. The hunting articles take up no time, for I do them in odd moments, when I am out west, for instance, or now and then in the evening. Being merely narrative, they are perfectly easy to do. They do not interfere in the slightest with my work on the *Winning of the West*, whereas my history of New York does very materially interfere. I wish you would write me a little at length as to whether you think these hunting articles ought to be dropped too. If you do, of course I will drop them after simply finishing the three or four I have already partially completed. I wish to reiterate that my great work to which I intend steadily to devote myself is the *Winning of the West*, and that hereafter you shall always have the refusal of anything I do. Of course you understand that while I am at work at this civil service Commission business I cannot do very much, or very satisfactory, work on the *Winning of the West*, whereas I can write off a magazine article without any difficulty. For the *Winning of the West* I have got to have all my books and papers around me and devote myself steadily to it. This winter, for instance, I could not well work at it anyhow, even if I had not a line of other work to write; moreover I must first visit and explore two or three out-of-the-way places for documents I need.

I am delighted to hear that your health has improved so much. Do take good care of yourself and take an ample holiday before coming back, and you shall ride every variety of pony I have at Oyster Bay. Let me hear from you in response to this letter. Best luck old man.

Yours ever

P.S. I half wish I was out of this Civil Service Commission work, for I can't do satisfactorily with the Winning of the West until I am; but I suppose I really ought to stand by it for at least a couple of years.

February 10, 1890. Washington
To James Brander Matthews

Dear Matthews,

You evidently touched friend Andrew on the raw; but I wish your counter stroke had not been suppressed. I was looking forward to it.

Work is progressing slowly but steadily on the "New York." It is about a quarter through. I find that I have got to make it sketchy to get it into the limits; and really so far I have done more rejecting than accepting material. There is some original matter which I should like to use, but can't, because it would make the book lopsided. Do'n't you find it harder to write when you have to condense? I knew about Adam's "Chapter of Erie," but I am much obliged to you for the hints about Parton and the Mag. of Am. Hist for '82. I am not altogether satisfied with my work on the book. I have to do it at odd times, in the midst of the press of this civil service business; and so I do'n't feel at all that I can do the subject justice.

Can't you get down here some time this winter? I would like you to see some of our "men of action" in congress. They are not always polished, but they are strong, and as a whole I think them pretty good fellows. I swear by Tom Reed[1]; and I tell you what, all copyright men ought to stand by him. No one man can filibuster and beat a bill now. A house may do well or ill; but at least it can do *something* under the new dispensation. Besides, I am tired of flabbiness, and I am glad to see a Republican of virility, who really does something! There is no great hardship in refusing to entertain purely filibustering and dilatory motions and in counting a man as present when he is present, even if he is at the moment howling out that he is "constructively" absent.

Warm regards to Madame.

Yrs. Faithfully

May 12, 1890. Washington
To Alfred Thayer Mahan

My dear Captain Mahan,

During the last two days I have spent half my time, busy as I am; in reading your book[2]; and that I found it interesting is shown by the fact that having taken it up I have gone straight through and finished it.

I can say with perfect sincerity that I think it very much the clearest and most instructive general work of the kind with which I am acquainted. It is a *very* good book—admirable; and I am greatly in error if it does not become a naval classic. It shows the faculty of grasping the meaning of events and their relations to one another and of taking in the whole situation. I wish the portions dealing with commerce destroying could be put in the hands of some of the friends of a navy, and that the whole book could be placed where it could be read by the navy's foes, especially in congress. You must read the two volumes of Henry Adams history dealing with the war of 1812 when they come out. He is a man of infinite research, and his ideas are usually (with some very marked exceptions) excellent.

With sincere congratulations I am

Very cordially yours

August 23, 1890. Washington
To Henry Cabot Lodge

Dear Cabot,

From all I can glean in the papers you did well in Maine, and I congratulate you. But I really regret much that you were not here while

---

[1]Thomas B. Reed, Republican Maine congressman, currently (and later) speaker of the House, and for years Roosevelt's model of a political leader.

[2]*The Influence of Sea Power upon History.*

Bryce was. It was only for two days, but I contrived to let him see a good deal in that time. Each morning I breakfasted alone with him and his wife—a bright, pleasant woman. One day we lunched in the Speaker's room, with the Hitts; the next day he lunched with John Andrew to meet a number of the House Democrats—including Rogers and others of the ilk. One evening the Hitts gave them a dinner, asking among others Ingalls, Carlisle, Gibson, Wheeler, Bingham and Adams—mixed.

The next night I had Bryce to dinner of representative Republicans—Hoar, Hawley, Saunders, Jones of Nevada, who is the most amusing storyteller I ever met, Reed, McKinley, Butterworth, Cannon, Hitt and McKenna of California. They are an able set of men, and Bryce thoroughly appreciated them. He grasped at once the distinction between these men who *do* things, and the others who only think or talk about how they ought to be done. I think his visit here will be a needed antiseptic; for he now goes to visit Godkin and Eliot! He ended his letter of thanks, when he left, "I won't let myself be captured by excessive mugwumpery after your warnings." So you see I did good missionary work.

I hate to leave my work here now. The P. M. G. [Postmaster General] has refused us any detail of clerks and it is almost—indeed quite—impossible to get the papers marked for the new places without them; so we shall fall behind, and there will be a row which I hate to leave Lyman to face. Oh, Heaven, if the President had a little backbone, and if the Senators did not have flannel legs!

Write me to O. B.

Love to Nannie.

Yours

September 23, 1890. Medora, Dakota
To Henry Cabot Lodge

Dear Cabot,

Just after writing you my letter, five minutes ago, the mail came in with yours of the 19th, and the paper containing Greenhalge's speech and the platform. Both of them are admirable. Massachusetts is certainly well to the front. Heavens, how I wish we could win this year! The great point is, shall our Congress legislate or not—shall our Congress be a real legislative body, or an assembly on the Polish order. This is even a more important question than that of any particular piece of legislation, vital though the latter may be. I would give a great deal to be allowed to make just one speech about it. I see that Kilgore, Cummings and others violently forced their way out the other day; I think it very unfortunate they are not fined as least five hundred dollars a head.

I think I shall have to skin Grosvenor again.

To my amusement Bay's hunter, an old Buffalo hunter named Mason, turns out to be an intense Republican and warm admirer of yours; a very staunch supporter of the election bill. He is a really intelligent old fellow. Bay likes him; is enjoying himself thoroughly, and is growing continually more hardy.

Thank you greatly for what you did in the Grosvenor matter.

Yours ever

October 18, 1890. Washington
To Gertrude Carow[1]

My dear Mrs. Carow,

I have rarely seen Edith enjoy anything more than she did the six days at my ranch, and the trip through the Yellowstone Park; and she looks just as well and young and pretty and happy as she did four years ago when I married her—indeed I sometimes almost think she looks if possible even sweeter and prettier, and she is as healthy as possible, and so young looking and slender to be the mother of those two sturdy little scamps, Ted and Kermit. We have had a lovely year, though we have minded being away from Sagamore so much; but we greatly enjoyed our winter at Washington, and our months trip out west was the crowning touch of all. Edith particularly enjoyed the riding at the ranch, where she had an excellent little horse, named wire fence, and the strange, wild, beautiful scenery, and the loneliness and freedom of the life fascinated and appealed to her as it did to me. Did she write to you that I shot a deer once while we were riding together? Are not you and Emily coming over here next summer? It will be over two years since you have seen Edith; and Kermit will be older than Ted was when you left. Of course I do not know what your plans are, nor how you find it necessary to shape them; but I should think that any extra expense entailed by the voyage over and back would be made up by the fact that you would be at Sagamore pretty much all the time you were here. Edith does want to see you both very much. If there are two ponies here she and Emily could ride together while I was away.

The children are darlings. Alice has grown more and more affectionate, and is devoted to, and worshipped by, both the boys; Kermie holds out his little arms to her whenever she comes near, and she really takes care of him like a little mother. Ted eyes him with some suspicion; and when I take the wee fellow up in my arms Ted clings tightly to one of my legs, so that I can hardly walk. Kermie crawls with the utmost rapidity; and when he is getting towards some forbidden spot and we call to him to stop Ted always joins in officiously and

---

[1]Roosevelt's mother-in-law.

overtaking the small yellow-haired wanderer seizes him with his chubby hands round the neck and trys to drag him back—while the enraged Kermie endeavours in vain to retaliate. Kermie is a darling little fellow, so soft and sweet. As for blessed Ted he is just as much of a comfort as he ever was. I think he really loves me, and when I come back after an absence he greets me with wild enthusiasm, due however, I fear, in great part to knowledge that I am sure to have a large paper bundle of toys—which produces the query of "Fats in de bag," while he dances like an expectant little bear. When I come in to afternoon tea he and Alice sidle hastily round to my chair, knowing that I will surreptitiously give them all the icing off the cake, if I can get Edith's attention attracted elsewhere; and every evening I have a wild romp with them, usually assuming the role of "a very big bear" while they are either little bears, or "a raccoon and a badger, papa." Ted has a most warm, tender, loving little heart; but I think he is a manly little fellow too. In fact I take the utmost possible enjoyment out of my three children; and so does Edith.

I really enjoy my work as Civil Service Commissioner; but of course it has broken up all my literary work.

Faithfully yours

October 22, 1890. Washington
To Henry Cabot Lodge

Dear Cabot,

Just after sending you my note yesterday I received your letter enclosed in one from Edith. It contained just what I wished to hear about you. Of course take just as much care as if Everett were a formidable foe; but I can not help believing you will even increase your majority against him. Your reception in Music Hall must indeed have pleased you.

Foulke is here. He is going to pitch into Wanamaker strong in a few days—my withers are unwrung. Foulke is a very good fellow. I find he is with us on the election bill; and I will relate to you an amusing dialogue he had with one of your opponents in Boston, in which, to the unspeakable horror of the mugwump, he admitted that you had faults, but called on your foe, as an honest man, to admit that Cleveland's were much worse, and his good qualities less conspicuous. Foulke also thinks Reed all sound. He is weak on the McKinley bill—but I can easily forgive him that. If I can get my article on the Bennett law I'll send it to you.

Here things are much as usual. I had a very short and cold interview with the President. His one anxiety is *not* to have anything [to do] with us or the Civil Service Law.

Love to Nannie.

Yours

November 10, 1890. Washington
To Henry Cabot Lodge

Dear Cabot,

I have felt too down hearted over the election to write you since; and besides there seemed really nothing to say. Well, at any rate you showed yourself stronger than your party by running ahead of your ticket, as far as I can judge by the return. The overwhelming nature of the disaster is due entirely to the McKinley bill; as you know I never liked that measure. There were some other features of the election which I wish to discuss with you; especially some insight I got during the last two months into the way things were looked at at home.

The Democratic majority will run wild; and Andrew, Hoar & Co. will have a fine time keeping pace with the capers of the Alliance men of the West and Southwest.

Now, finish your "Boston" and get it off your hands; and let me know the day and train you arrive.

Love to Nannie.

Yours

June 17, 1891. Washington
To Anna Roosevelt

Dearest Bysie,

Your long letter containing the account of Elliott's hopeless mis-conduct and outrageous behaviour and the final decision that he should live alone, came day before yesterday. I await your next with painful eagerness.

He is evidently a maniac, morally no less than mentally. How glad I am I got his authorization to compromise the Katy Mann affair![1]

You must leave just as soon as Anna[2] is convalescent. You have no business to submit to such a life one day longer than is absolutely nec-essary.

But Anna ought to leave at once herself, taking the children. As soon as she can travel let her come home with the children. If Elliott raises a row why slip away anyhow. If he can not be confined, disregard him utterly; let Anna take her children and come home. Pay no heed to his threats. Let him make a scandal if he so wishes; I do'n't like a scan-dal, but there are things infinitely worse. If he threatens to go off alone,

---

[1]Katy Mann, a former servant in Elliott's house, claimed that Elliott was the father of her child.

[2]Elliott's wife. She and Elliott were the parents of Eleanor Roosevelt.

let him go. He is evidently a dangerous maniac. Let Anna come home with the children *at once;* then we can proceed against him to have some provision made for all their support. It makes little difference about her taking the first step rather than him, compared to the importance of her getting away from him; and coming back here with the children, where we can protect her and them. Read her this, and tell her from me again that it is no less criminal than foolish for her to go on living with him. She must come home at once. Let him plainly know that he has no hold over her. He has'n't any, if she will only act with moderate spirit and sense. On yours and my testimony alone any court would decide in her favor. Do'n't yield an ounce to his threats; keep a look out that he does'n't try to kidnap one of the children. Refuse point blank to let him have them; let Anna slip away with them if necessary, having engaged her passage on a French line steamer. If he can't be confined for Heaven's sake let him go off alone; the sooner the better.

Yours ever

June 19, 1891. Washington
To Henry Cabot Lodge

Dear Cabot,

Your two letters reached me almost together. It was funny our copies of Reed's amusing letters crossing one another.

Springy has been paying your "Boston" an evidently sincere meed of praise by reading it all through in two days, from beginning to end; he considers it very interesting and called my attention to various points as he read. Sensible, appreciative boy, Springy—very. He is much worked up at present over the excessive iniquity of American diplomacy. By the way, there *has* been some queer work of some sort over the Behring [Bering] Sea matter; but we seem to have come out of it very well. Wharton has had his suspicions, and he talks very freely at rare intervals; but he is not in the confidence of the Administration and really knows very little more about it than every one does.

Beard's letter was very good. I shall devote a little spare time to him in our next annual report, showing the small number of dismissals and resignations, and saying that this is clear proof of honest enforcement of the law. Can you not have copies sent me of the extracts from Saltonstall's letters. I particularly wish them.

I am glad Hayes advised you not to run for Governor. You don't wish that position. Washington is your place; and let it get abroad quietly, that you are to make the run for United States Senator.

Now, for a piece of social news, which will be of interest to Nannie, as she ought to know of the more noted entertainments in high diplomatic and administrative circles. On Wednesday and Thursday evenings of this week I gave two dinners, assisted by Springy, with nice colored Millie as cook and waitress. First dinner. Guests, the British Minister and the Secretary of War. Bill of fare, crabs, chicken and rice, cherries, claret and tea. (Neither guest died; and I think Proctor, who is a good native American, hungered for pie, in addition). Springy nervous and fidgety; I, with my best air of oriental courtesy, and a tendency to orate only held in check by the memory of the jeers of my wife and intimate friend. 2nd Dinner. Guests, the Secretary of the Navy and the British Minister, who was laboriously polite and good but somewhat heavy in grappling with the novelty of the situation. Bill of fare, chops and rice, *pâté de foie gras*, raspberries, claret and tea. (Guests still survive.) Springy still nervous. Tracy in great form, very amusing and entertaining.

I'll bet they were dinners new to Sir Julian's experience, but both the Secretaries enjoyed them.

Yours

July 22, 1891. Washington
To Henry Cabot Lodge

Dear Cabot:

Here I am back again at work, and there is mighty little work to do. I am now at work on the annual report. I am going to put in a good deal of matter that I cannot relieve myself of in any other way.

I wrote to both Clapp and O'Meara, as you requested, and received exceedingly nice letters in return. I am very glad you gave me a hint in the matter.

Our polo team did very much better than I had any idea they would. Having a heavy handicap they beat Essex, making three goals which stood them six to the good, and in the finals with Morristown were only beaten by a quarter of a goal,—that is, by a knockout for safety. Next year, Heaven willing I intend to be on the team myself, and do my own part.

Here I have been greeted warmly by Springy, still lame but no longer on crutches. Martha takes excellent care of me, as usual. Please tell Nannie this.

I need scarcely tell you what a great comfort it is to me that I am in your house, and not staying around at some dreary hotel in this hot weather. Naturally I am a little homesick for Oyster Bay, and as there seems to be very little to be done here I shall soon go back to it. I do not object in the least to staying here to work just as hard as can possibly be, but when there is nothing to be done, literally, then I hate to stay. However, I am getting off most of my report,—my annual report, and my Baltimore report is pretty nearly ready. In fact, all the work that can be done has been done. If the President would only act a little differently there is a whole raft of work which we could do, and which I should very much like to do. However, I cannot complain.

Best love to Nannie.

Yours very cordially

P.S. The President actually refuses to consider the changes in the rules which are necessary to enable us to do our work effectively. He has never given us one ounce of real backing. He won't see us, or consider any method for improving the service, even when it in no way touches a politician. It is horribly disheartening to work under such a Chief. However, the very fact that he takes so little interest gives me a free hand to do some things; and I know well that in life one must do the best one can with the implements at hand, and not bemoan the lack of ideal ones.

Foster is doing his best in the Keystone Bank affair. Foster has also chosen two admirable men to investigate the seal fisheries. On the other hand, in truckling to the foreign vote he has chosen pretty poor sticks to investigate the all important problem of the immigrants who come here from Europe.

January 25, 1892. Washington
To Cecil Spring Rice

Dear Cecil,

When I was in Paris my wife wrote me "Springy has been in to see me several times; he always comes at once, the moment he thinks we are in any trouble." This is not a bad reputation to have, old fellow; and it may help explain the very real sense of loss I felt when I found that you had gone. Edith and I miss you greatly, and we and all your other friends talk of you continually and wish very much you were back here. I am sure you *will* be back sometime; I hope as minister—but anyhow, come back. You have left many very warm friends behind.

Henry Adams and John Hay have gone south on a trip with the Camerons. Bob was here the other day, staying with the Lodges. He and Cabot, on Cabot's two horses, and I on old Dick from the riding school, took a long ride last Sunday morning. Dick pulls a bit, but he is certainly a big jumper; he larked over better than four feet of timber with perfect light-heartedness. I guess he would be rather hot-headed for hunting in cramped country with a big field, however.

I am now steeped in what Mark Twain would call "a profound French calm" as regards the Civil Service commission; that is, I have only three or four active difficulties on hand, and one of these, thank

Heaven, is with democrats. The mugwumps are now having catalepsy over the strong possibility of Cleveland's defeat for the nomination.

Cabot and his wife are very well; the former often lends me his horse Egypt, a very nice horse, and we ride around the country together. Of course we are going out to dinner a good deal now; if Washington can be said to have a season it is now at it's height. I see a great deal of Tom Reed, and also of the nice Herberts.

Mrs. Roosevelt, and Ted, send you their best love. With warm regards

Always faithfully your friend

May 3, 1892. Washington
To Cecil Spring Rice

Very nice, but very bad, Springy, what will become of you if you waste your substance on gorgeous gifts to riotous American friends? Seriously, we think your present one of the handsomest we have ever received; it is beautiful; I like it even more than the Lodges cranes. It will hold the place of honor at Sagamore Hill; may it not be too long e'er the donor sees it there! Of course the children are enthralled with it. Last evening Ted, after gazing silently at it, suddenly remarked of his own accord that he wanted to send you a kiss because you brought him flowers when he was sick, and that he wanted you to come back very soon and stay with us—a wish in which we all heartily join.

I have been passing a good deal of my time—a third—away from Washington this winter, on investigations etc. One of them took me down to Texas, and I then got off for six days, went down to some ranches in the semi tropical country round the Nueces, and hunted peccaries. I killed two. It was great fun, for we followed them on horseback, with hounds—such hounds!—and the little beasts fought with the usual stupid courage of pigs when brought to bay. They ought to be killed with a spear; the country is so thick, with huge cactus and thorny mesquite trees, that the riding is hard; but they are small, and it would be safe to go at them on foot—at any rate for two men.

Cabot and I have been riding a good deal, on his two horses. The woods are now in the first flush of their beauty; the leaves a tender green, the dog-woods and Judas Trees in bloom.

Did you see Joel Chandler Harris's new book "On the Plantation"? It is very good. I am also very much pleased with Kiplings new edition of his poems; it contains several favorites of mine which I had never before seen except in the newspapers. I have been reading Chaucer with industry lately, and as I gradually become used to his language I get to enjoy him and more; but I must say I think he is altogether needlessly filthy—such a tale as the "Sompnours" for instance is unpardonable, and indeed unreadable.

Henry Adams is exactly the same as ever; we dine with him to-morrow night. John Hay still has for his idols James G. Blaine and Henry James Jr—a combination which indicates a wide range of appreciation. Cabot is in great form, and I begin to think there really is some chance of his making the Senatorship. As for me I am involved in rely usual array of struggles, Wannamaker officiating with his customary obliging readiness as head devil and awful object lesson.

Good bye, old fellow! I'll let you know from time to time how we're getting on. Good luck to you!

Your friend

May 22, 1892. Washington
To Francis Parkman

My dear Mr Parkman,

I thank you sincerely for the two volumes. It is difficult, my dear sir, to say anything about them without seeming to use over-strained language. It must have been rather hard for any one to whom Gibbon, for instance, sent his work to find perfectly fit words to use in acknowledging the gift.

Looking over the recent census figures for New England it is curious, and rather melancholy, to see the strange revenge which time is bringing to the French of Canada. They are swarming into New England with ominous rapidity. Of course they will conform to and keep our laws, and in most places our language, though I should not be surprised to see French become the tongue of occasional counties in the north, and possibly even of one or two manufacturing towns. But their race will in many places supplant the old American stock; and I am inclined to believe that in a generation or two more, Catholicism, though in a liberalized form, will become the predominant creed in several of the Puritan commonwealths. Yet I am a firm believer that the future will somehow bring things right in the end for our land.

Again thanking you, I am

Very cordially yours

May 31, 1892. Washington
To James Brander Matthews

Dear Brander,

I am very sorry you should be having such trouble about the measles. I suppose it does knock our lunch on the head; but at least I shall see you later on. When do you leave New York? I want to see if I can't arrange to meet you.

I have just finished, with sweat and tears, my article for Howells dealing with Repplier and others.

I hope it is true that Kipling is not to be admitted to the Players. There is no earthly reason he should not call New York a pig trough; but there is also no reason why he should be allowed to associate with the pigs. I fear he is at bottom a cad.

Remember me warmly to Mrs. Matthews. I liked both the Page and the Jewett articles you refer to very much.

Yours always

July 27, 1892. Washington
To Henry Cabot Lodge

Dear Cabot,

I had seen Adams' ridiculous article. I enclose the data you request; also the 7th Report which deals with the removals in the classified service. We have no means of knowing what they are in the unclassified— where however the amount is that both sides have removed about everybody.

Frankly I think the record pretty bad for both Cleveland and Harrison, and it is rather Walrus and Carpenter work choosing between the records of the two parties, as far as civil service reform is concerned. In the classified service Cleveland made more extensions than Harrison; but on the other hand Tracy has made an admirable start in the Navy Yards—but it is only a start, not permanent, and can not be until put under us. Cleveland had a much worse Commission; but Harrison has not sustained his Commission at all, and has allowed Wanamaker to put a premium upon the clearest violations of the law—in which the Republican members of the C. S. Committee have sustained him. So I really think it about a stand off here. We have put much more of a stop to political assessments; but the offices have been used for political purposes more shamefully and openly than even under the last Administration. In the first term of the 51st Congress we did better, and in the second worse, than in any term of the 49th or 50th.

Altogether I am by no means pleased with what our party, at both the White House and the Capitol, has done about Civil Service Reform. You are the one conspicuous Republican leader who has done his whole duty—and very much more than his whole duty—by the reform in the last three years.

I leave Washington tomorrow and start west from Oyster Bay on August 1st or 2nd. I have just written an article on the foreign policy of this Administration, where it is much sounder than on Civil Service Reform.

Edith and I have really had a pleasant time here in spite of the heat.

I play tennis with Wharton at the Legation, on most afternoons; hitherto we have come out exactly even on sets, so it is good fun.

Best love to Nannie.

Yours ever

September 25, 1892. Oyster Bay
To Henry Cabot Lodge

Dear Cabot,

Even in the West I saw by the occasional notices in the papers that you were getting the Republican machine into fine condition in Massachusetts, and that everyone recognized the fact that *your* hand was on the throttle. I can not help believing that you will win the Senatorship this time; if for any cause you fail, why it merely puts you in better shape for the struggle two years hence. Of course you are looking with double care after your congressional fences.

Although I had read your Homeric article in ms., I have actually reread it twice since it appeared in print. I think it one of the very best essays, both in style and matter, I have ever read, by anyone on any subject.

Here, on my return after a month's tedious but important tour among the Indian reservations and schools, I find all very well; Edith and I have been taking long rides on the polo ponies. Bamie is absorbed in her World's Fair work; Elliot F. Shepard has just made a most scurrilous and indecent attack, in his paper, on her and her associates, by name. She, and my uncles, are very desirous I should not respond, for fear he will go on attacking her; and I am in a perfect quandary over the matter. He ought, by rights, to be horsewhipped.

The Farmers' Alliance is giving our people serious concern in Kansas. Nebraska and South Dakota; and ditto, the Germans in Illinois and Wisconsin. I feel like making a crusade against the latter. I wish the cholera would result in a permanent quarantine against most immigrants!

I passed a very pleasant three weeks on my ranch, arid on the trip south to Deadwood, shooting three or four deer and antelope—one deer from the ranch verandah! In Deadwood I was enthusiastically received, and opened the Republican campaign by speaking to a really large audience in the fearful local opera house. Did you see my article on our Foreign Policy in the *Independent?* I enclose a very nice letter from Admiral Brown, thanking me for it. Please return this.

I have now got to plunge into the very disagreeable business of fighting political assessments.

Give my best love to Nannie. How is Constance?

Yours always

April 22, 1893. Washington
To James S. Clarkson

My Dear General Clarkson:

It was, as always, a great pleasure to me to hear from you. As you say, though you and I may differ, I think we always keep our respect and liking for each other, and are likely to do so as long as we both continue to speak frankly and openly. Be sure and let me know if you come to Washington.

Now, I am sorry to say it will be out of the question for me to be at Louisville. I already have an engagement for the 11th and on the 9th must be in New York; but even if this were not so I question whether it would be well for me to be present now. It has always been hard drawing the line at exactly what I was and what I was not at liberty to do. My idea has been to take a sufficiently active part in the elections, both by speech and contribution, to make it evident that I was a thoroughgoing Republican, and yet not seem to do too much political work, or of a kind that my office forbade; so I am going to ask you not to quote this letter, but to consider it as private and for your own use only.

Of course as yet matters haven't gone very far, and it is hard to make very much of an issue; but there is one thing that I personally feel very strong about, and that is about hauling down the flag at Hawaii. I am a bit of believer in the manifest destiny doctrine. I believe in more ships; I believe in ultimately driving every European power off of this continent, and I don't want to see our flag hauled down where it has been hauled up.

I have thought a good deal over your suggestion of the election of postmasters by the people, and I hardly know what to say to it. I don't think it ought to be done in the larger offices, but I should think that in the fourth class post offices the plan might perhaps be a good one, if other methods failed of getting security of tenure. Have you looked over Lodge's Fourth Class Postmasters bill? It might be worth your while to do so.

On the general subject of civil service reform my advice now would be the same as it was to the National Convention one year ago; don't promise more than we can perform. State that we believe in the principles of civil service reform; that we believe the civil service law should be executed with rigid impartiality in letter and spirit, and that the classified service should be extended as rapidly as the conditions of good administration warrant. It would have been much better for us to have said simply this five years ago rather than go into the sweeping declarations in which we actually indulged, for we made statements to which we could not live up, and then did not live up even on points which we might have. If we had simply said that the law would be enforced rigidly and its application extended as fast as it became practicable we would have promised what we could have performed, and would not have committed ourselves to statements which could be quoted against us whenever there was a change in the unclassified service. Personally, as you know, I hold extreme views on the question, but I have never advocated the party's committing itself to more of these views than it was willing to live up to.

Thanking you most cordially for your kindness in writing me, I am,
Sincerely yours

June 8, 1893. Washington
To James Brander Matthews

Dear Brander,

I am really pleased that you liked my Century article, for I felt very doubtful over it; and the Wholly Innocent Man had to have all the snap taken out of his speech.

I saw Kipling's article and thought it quite good; I certainly can not hazard any guess concerning your Trombone—Frog. By the way, without altogether agreeing with all of Boyeson's positions, I most emphatically do agree with what he said about your reviewing; we have hardly any good reviewers, and I do hope you will keep up your work of this sort. And the Essays too! It will be long before I read other essays as good as those in Americanisms and Briticisms.

Indeed Chicago *was* worth while. The buildings make, I verily believe, the most beautiful architectural exhibit the world has ever seen. If they were only permanent! That south lagoon, with the peristyle cutting it off from the lake, the great terraces, the grandeur and beauty of the huge white buildings, the statue, the fine fountains, the dome of the administration building, the bridges guarded by the colossal animals— well, there is simply nothing to say about it. And the landscape effects are so wonderful. In the fine-arts building, by the way, did you not like the "Death arresting the hand of the sculptor," and the "Peace Sign," the quiet pose of the naked warrior on the naked horse?

In a week or so you will receive my "Wilderness Hunter." Just glance at the fourth chapter, because I know you like out-of-doors things, and at the last, for the sake of the allusions to Washington.

Warm regards to Mrs. M.
Yours

December 17, 1893. Washington
To Anna Roosevelt

Darling Bye,

Edith cut out the enclosed for Rosy; I was pleased with it; it does pay, after all, to be a courteous gentleman and to appreciate that a representative of our Government has a duty to *all* travellers of his own nationality, whether they are of importance or not.

Even my Micawber-like temperament has been unable to withstand a shock it received this week. Douglas blandly wrote me that there had been a mistake as to my income & expenditure, and that I was $2500 behind! We are going to do everything possible to cut down expenses this year; if we again run behind I see nothing to do save to leave Sagamore; and I think we will have to do this anyhow in a few years when we begin to educate the children. The trouble is that my career has been a very pleasant, honorable and useful career for a man of means; but not the right career for a man without the means. If I can I shall hold this position another winter; about that time I shall publish my next two volumes of the Winning of the West; I am all at sea as to what I shall do afterwards.

We had the Hagues to dinner; she is so much pleasanter than she was. We also had the Thorons. One evening this week we went to the Pellews, which was rather pleasant as they had my friend Rockhill the Thibetan explorer. Another evening we dined with the Storers, to meet divers Mick ecclesiastics; among others Bishop Keane whom I like, and with whom I had a long and very plainspoken argument over the public schools. The Catholics show a little restiveness over these, and are helped by the bigots on our own side; but the public school system can not be overthrown here.

This evening we dine with Henry Adams. I took a walk with Cabot this morning; and am now about starting for a scramble up Rock Creek with the three elder children. Ted sends you many kisses and also several "bear waves".

Your aff brother

February 10, 1894. Washington
To Frederick Jackson Turner

My Dear Sir:

I have been greatly interested in your pamphlet on the Frontier.[1] It comes at *the* right time for me, for I intend to make use of it in writing the third volume of my "Winning of the West," of course making full

---

[1] "The Significance of the Frontier in American History."

acknowledgment. I think you have struck some first class ideas, and have put into definite shape a good deal of thought which has been floating around rather loosely.

Very sincerely yours

February 11, 1894. Washington
To Anna Roosevelt

Darling Bye,

I hope you will be presented at court; in your position you ought to be. What snobs the Hays are! they have no business to bring out their daughter abroad. If you see Gussie Jay give him a hint that if he educates his children abroad he will lose all chance of being returned to our diplomatic service, and ought to lose it.

Uncle Jim wishes to buy only my ten acre lot. Do you know who surveyed it, or where I can find out? I want to start it for Uncle Jim as soon as possible. Edith is well; and Kermit has remained unstricken, while all the others are recovering and at this moment are playing upstairs with furious energy.

I am so glad you are having this winter in London; it is everything for Rosy in the first place, and in the next I am glad for your own sake.

London is such a world in itself (do you realize that it is far more populous than the entire empire of Queen Elizabeth and Shakespeare?) that I suppose you get your own little set, besides a general knowledge of all sets, and no human being counts for enough to be of real importance in the maelstrom. I wish that I could be over with you for a fortnight; I would enjoy it so much; and there are a number of people whom I would greatly like to see.

Washington is just a big village, but it is a very pleasant big village. Edith and I meet just the people we like to see. This winter we have had a most pleasant time, socially and officially. All I have minded is that, though my work is pleasant, I have had to keep at it so closely that I never get any exercise save an occasional ride with Cabot. We dine out three or four times a week, and have people to dinner once or twice; so that we hail the two or three evenings when we are alone at home, and can talk and read, or Edith sew while I made ineffective bolts at my third volume. The people we meet are mostly those who stand high in the political world, and who are therefore interested in the same subjects that interest us; while there are enough who are men of letters or of science to give a pleasant and needed variety. Then besides our formal dinners, we are on terms of informal intimacy in houses like the Caboty's, the Storers, the Wolcotts and Henry Adams. It is pleasant to meet people from whom one really gets something; people from all over the Union, with different pasts and varying interests, trained, able, powerful men, though often narrow minded enough.

This is like a spring day, and Cabot and I have just returned from a three hours ride over the fields and beside the Potomac. I am writing in great difficulties, for Ted is lying on my back, having climbed up on the chair behind me; he says (at the top of his voice in my ear, his paddy-paws round my neck) "Give Auntie Bye a hundred bear-waves, first; we wish she was here; I know I love her very much."

Your loving brother

March 3, 1894. Washington
To Madison Grant

My Dear Grant:

Many thanks for your letter. I am at present at work on the third and fourth volumes of my *Winning of the West*, but they will only take me down through Wayne's victory and the treaties of Jay and Pinckney. The next volumes I take up I hope will be the Texan struggle and the Mexican War. I quite agree with your estimate of these conflicts, and am surprised that they have not received more attention.

I think your suggestion for an article for our next volume just the thing, and I am almost sorry I have you on the moose article now, for I would like to start you at it; but don't you think you and I and Grinnell could get the article on the names of our game up together and have it put in unsigned as editorial matter?

Our species certainly are distinct from those of Europe as a rule; but speaking scientifically, I think you will find I am correct in what I say of their close relationship. The best zoologists nowadays put North America in with North Asia and Europe as one arctogeal province, separate from the South American, Indian, Australasian, and South African provinces, which have equal rank. Our moose, Wapiti, bear, beaver, wolf, etc., differ more or less from those of the Old World but the difference sinks into insignificance when compared with the differences between all these forms, Old World and New, from the tropical forms south of them. The wapiti is undoubtedly entirely distinct from the European red deer; but I don't think the difference is as great as between the black-tail and white-tail deer. It's normal form of antler is, as you describe, six points, all on the same plan, without any cup on top, and the fourth or dagger point having a prominence which it does not have at all in the European red deer; but occasionally, especially in Oregon and Washington, elk are found with this cup, and when a rather undersized Oregon elk possessing this cup is compared with one of the big red deer of Asia Minor, which are considerably larger than those of Europe, the difference is less by a good deal than the difference between the black-tail and white-tail. But all of these points can very interestingly be treated in the article to which you refer; and, as I say, I think it would be admirable, and we must certainly adopt it and put it into execution. Do send me your moose piece as soon as you can.

Cordially yours

[Handwritten.] P.S. The moose, caribou and wapiti, for instance are very close indeed to their old-world relatives, when either are compared with the South American or Indian deer.

April 1, 1894. Washington
To Anna Roosevelt

Darling Bye,

Your letters are just dear. Do tell us about all the funny people you meet; and do you see anything of the Fergies? Last Monday the Kiplings came to dinner, with the Brooks Adams, Langley, Miss Pauncefote, Willie Phillips & Emily Tuckerman. It was very pleasant. Kipling is an underbred little fellow, with a tendency to criticise America to which I put a stop by giving him a very rough handling, since which he has not repeated the offence; but he is a genius, and is very entertaining. His wife is fearful however.

I had to go to Philadelphia for a couple of days, on a fruitless investigation. My 4th volume is making laboriously painful progress.

Yesterday, Sunday, Edith and I, with Ted, Alice, John Lodge, and various assorted friends took a long scramble up Rock Creek. Edith walked so well, and felt so well, that it was a pleasure to see her. Over some of the worst rocks I let down the children with a rope; and did much climbing myself. The spring is later than I have ever seen it in Washington.

Tell Helen how we all look forward to seeing her for a good long visit at Sagamore.

Your loving brother

May 5, 1894. Washington
To James Brander Matthews

Dear Brander:

I am awfully afraid I am not going to be able to get on to New York before you leave. I am very sorry, as there were some things I particularly wished to talk over with you. Lodge regretted so much failing to find you while in New York.

Yes, we have a small boy. I begin to think that this particular branch of the Roosevelt family is getting to be numerous enough. Mrs.

Roosevelt is very well. She was out for a two hours' drive with me yesterday through this beautiful country. Are you so fond of New York
that you don't care for the country? If not, I do wish you could come on
to Washington sometime in the spring, that I may show you Rock
Creek when the trees are budding and the flowers are out. Do you
know I don't believe our people half appreciate how picturesque and
beautiful our landscapes are.

I decidedly envy you your reputation as being the champion of
American methods and ways in literature, in spelling, and in all other
directions.

I reinclose your cowboy article. I like it. I began to be a little doubtful about my own dialect accuracy. The things I have been trained to
observe I can observe all right, but it is astonishing how difficult it is to
record even what one is familiar with if one is not accustomed to
recording it.

If on the other side you see Andrew Lang give him my love.

Faithfully yours

[Handwritten] P.S. Apropos of your article on bookbinding I have
just seen a very beautiful specimen from Philadelphia; a book written
by Henry Adams on Samoa, but not yet published. Warm regards to
the Madam.

I am glad the Harvard boys did so well; I had been supplying them
with some arguments.

June 24, 1894. Washington
To Anna Roosevelt

Darling Bye,

You saw the Derby under very exceptional circumstances; it was a
great spectacle, and well worth seeing.

I wrote to Rosy last week, asking him to come to Sagamore, or
down here. Did'n't I tell you about Jack Astor's book? It is astounding
that he could have written it; it is a rather wooden, but florid adapta-
tion of Jules Verne; not wholly bad.

Edith writes me that she sent you the Sun, with an account of my
counter stroke on Godkin; so I enclose you his last effort in return. I had
him on the hip!

It is pretty hot here now, but not really oppressive. I am having my
usual rows over Civil Service matters. Not even Wanamaker was a
meaner, smaller cur than Carlisle; he is dishonest, untruthful and cowardly. In fact (but this is *not* for publication) Cleavland's second administration is a lamentable falling off from the first; and the Democrats have given an exhibition of fairly colossal incompetence. If I read
the signs aright they will meet with humiliating disaster next fall.

Rosy turned up on Friday evening to spend the night, and was a dear good fellow—minding the heat dreadfully. It was a real pleasure to see him and have a long talk; about you, and his own affairs, and everything. I like him so much.

Bye, how is your ear? I wish you would go to a first rate London specialist about it; the London specialists are the best in the world; and it is too serious a thing to take any chances with.

Edith has had a hard week; Kermit has a trouble with his knee, for which he has had to be taken to see Dr. Schaafer.

Your loving brother

June 29, 1894. Washington
To James Brander Matthews

Dear Brander:

I think the cutting about Mahan's book was one of the most delicious things I have ever read. It circulated freely throughout Washington, from Lodge on. Sometime or other I shall write an article on James Stuart, the Hanoverian Pretender, or on the Duke of Cumberland, the well-known Jacobin leader who fell at Culloden.

I am very glad the immigration has come to a standstill for the last year. We are getting some very undesirable elements now, and I wish that a check could be put to it.

I shall be ranching in September. Up to that time I shall alternate between Sagamore Hill and this hot city. I shall get back from the West early in October and report at 121 promptly.

After receiving your letter I got Hamlin Garland's book and read it. I think you are right about Garland, excepting that I should lay a little more stress upon the extreme wrong-headedness of his reasoning. For instance, he is entirely wrong in thinking that Shakespeare, Homer and Milton are not permanent. Of course they are; and he is entirely in error in thinking that Shakespeare is not read, in the aggregate, during a term of years, more than any ephemeral author of the day. Of course every year there are dozens of novels each one of which will have many more readers than Shakespeare will have in the year; but the readers only stay for about a year or two, whereas in Shakespeare's case they have lasted, and will last quite a time! I think that his ignorance, crudity, and utter lack of cultivation make him entirely unfit to understand the effect of the great masters of thought upon the language and upon literature. Nevertheless, in his main thought, as you say, he is entirely right. We must strike out for ourselves; we must work according to our own ideas, and must free ourselves from the shackles of conventionality, before we can do anything. As for the literary center of the country being New York, I personally never had any patience with the talk of a literary center. I don't care a rap whether it is New York, Chicago, or any place else, so long as the work is done. I like or dislike pieces in the *Atlantic Monthly* and the *Overland Monthly* because of what they contain, not because of one's being published in San Francisco or the other in Boston. I don't like Edgar Fawcett any more because he lives in New York, nor Joel Chandler Harris any the less because he lives at Atlanta; and I read Mark Twain with just as much delight, but with no more, whether he resides in Connecticut or in Missouri. Garland is to me a rather irritating man, because I can't help thinking he has the possibility of so much, and he seems just to fail to realize this possibility. He has seen and drawn certain phases of the western prairie life with astonishing truth and force; but he now seems inclined to let certain crude theories warp his mind out of all proper proportion, and I think his creative work is suffering much in consequence. I hate to see this, because he ought to be a force on the right side.

By the way, have you seen that London *Yellow Book?* I think it represents the last stage of degradation. What a miserable little snob Henry James is. His polished, pointless, uninteresting stories about the upper social classes of England make one blush to think that he was once an American. The rest of the book is simply diseased. I turned to a story of Kipling's with the feeling of getting into fresh, healthy, out-of-doors life.

I think your vignettes are really admirable, and I am much pleased that in your last you allowed a more cheerful ending than you sometimes do, and that when the bullet struck the young lady it should have only made a flesh wound in her arm. There is more than one particular in which that vignette struck a high note. I think that Dan Wister has been doing some very good work.

Give my warm regards to Mrs. Matthews.

Faithfully yours

July 29, 1894. Washington
To Anna Roosevelt

Darling Bye,

All the early part of the week I was at Sagamore. On Monday I took blessed little Kermit in to see Dr. Schaeffer, who is yet unable to say whether, as he hopes, the affair is one of the knee cap merely, or whether it is in the bone itself, in which case the poor little fellow may have to wear the instrument a couple of years. It tells on him, and makes him peevish. Ethel, who is a perfect scamp, and as cunning as she can be, and who does everything and manages everybody, has fearful fights with Kermit; they celebrated my homecoming by a row in which Ethel bit him, and he then stood on his head and thumped her with his steel leg. Alice and Ted have been revelling in Corinne's children, with whom they are now devoted friends. We have found a large hollow tree, the hollow starting from a huge opening twenty feet up; the other day, with much labor I got up the tree, and let each child in turn down the hollow by a rope. Ted is such a blessing! he is very manly and very bright—but he is clumsy in spite of his quickness. How impossible it is to tell how any of them will turn out! Archie is such a wee, merry baby, and lies on his back on the bed waving his little arms.

Corinne is so dear; and also Douglass. But I do wish Corinne could get a little of my hard heart about Elliott; she can do, and ought to do, nothing for him. He can't be helped, and he must simply be let go his own gait. He is now laid up from a serious fall; while drunk he drove into a lamp post and went out on his head. Poor fellow! if only he could have died instead of Anna!

On Friday I left with Springy, who for four weeks has led the life of a Sagamore Hill Trappist, and with Trent, the University of Sewanee man, for whom I have much regard. I made an address in Philadelphia that evening, and came on to this sweltering place yesterday. I am now practically, living with the ever-delightful Caboty.

Darling Bye, I know how dreadfully you feel about dear Alice Lippencott's death; I feel it much for myself too; I valued greatly her loyalty and straightforward honesty.

Your loving brother

August 12, 1894. Washington
To Anna Roosevelt

Darling Bye,

Another week has passed, and the tariff wrangle in the Democratic party still continues; but I think the end *must* come soon. Well, it has been to my advantage, at any rate, for it has kept Cabot here, and I have been virtually living at his house.

Every afternoon I have been playing tennis with funny, gruff old Olney. Cabot and I breakfast together, and dine together, alone, or with some congressman; Tom Reed, or Dolliver of Iowa, who has suddenly developed a distinct literary sense, or Quigg, who always shakes his head mournfully over the fact that, together with my many admirable qualities I also possess such a variety of indiscretions, fads and animosities that it is impossible to run me for Mayor. To which I answer him that I have run once!

It has been cool and pleasant. Once or twice we have dined at the Hitts. Procter is a great comfort to me in my work.

I am very homesick for Edith and the children. Edie has been very much worried about poor little Kermit, all the time; it is heartbreaking to see the poor little fellow sitting still and looking at the other children play.

Elliott is up and about again; and I hear is already drinking heavily; if so he must break down soon. It has been as hideous a tragedy all through as one often sees.

I fear I shall be in the west when you arrive; I suppose I can not send you more than a couple of letters more.

Give my love to Rosy and little Helen.

Your loving brother

August 18, 1894. Oyster Bay
To Anna Roosevelt

Darling Bye:

On Monday William, who has been so loyal and faithful to Elliott, telegraphed that he was really sick. I was off in Washington; but Uncle Jimmie went in Tuesday morning, and found him much as he has been for the last year, so he thought there was nothing unusual the matter; yet that evening late he died. It was well so for he would have been in a straight jacket had he lived forty eight hours longer. It was his fall, aggravated by frightful drinking, that was the immediate cause; he had been drinking whole bottles of anisette and green mint, besides whole bottles of raw brandy and of champagne, sometimes half a dozen a morning. But when dead the poor fellow looked very peaceful, and so like his old, generous, gallant self of fifteen years ago. The horror, and the terrible mixture of sadness and grotesque, grim evil continued to the very end; and the dreadful flashes of his old sweetness, which made it all even more hopeless. I suppose he has been doomed from the beginning; the absolute contradiction of all his actions, and of all his moral even more than his mental qualities, is utterly impossible to explain. For the last few days he had dumbly felt the awful night closing on him; he would not let us come to his house, nor part with the woman, nor cease drinking for a moment, but he wandered ceaselessly everywhere, never still, and he wrote again and again to us all, sending to me two telegrams and three notes. He was like some stricken, hunted creature; and indeed he was hunted by the most terrible demons that ever entered into man's body and soul.

His house was so neat and well kept, with his bible and religious books, and Anna's pictures everywhere, even in the room of himself and his mistress. Poor woman, she had taken the utmost care of him, and was broken down at his death. Her relations with him have been just as strange as everything else. Very foolishly, it had been arranged that he should be taken to be buried beside Anna; but I promptly vetoed this hideous plan, Corinne, who has acted better than I can possibly say throughout, cordially backing me up; and he was buried in Greenwood beside those who are associated with only his sweet innocent youth, when no more loyal, generous, brave, disinterested fellow lived.

All his old friends came to the funeral; the church was filled. It was very, very sad; and behind it followed the usual touch of the grotesque and terrible, for in one of the four carriages that followed to the grave, went the woman Mrs. Evans and two of her and his friends, the host and hostess of the Woodbine inn. They behaved perfectly well, and their grief seemed entirely sincere. Fred took charge of her; Rome went out to the grave, and West and Frank.

Katy Mann came in to Douglas' office with the child which she swears was his; I have no idea whether it was or not; she was a bad woman, but her story *may* have been partly true. But we can not know. Well, it is over, and we need only think of his bright youth.

Corinne and I went through his letters; those from Aunt Ella made my blood boil. They were really fitted to do him all the harm possible. I don't suppose they made any difference; but they were just suited to destroy him and to destroy wretched Anna. Poor Anna, and poor Elliott!

Yours

August 29, 1894. Washington
To Corinne Roosevelt Robinson

My darling little sister,

My thoughts keep hovering round you now, and I love you so. There is one great comfort I already feel; I only need to have pleasant thoughts of Elliott now. He is just the gallant, generous, manly boy and young man whom everyone loved. I can think of him when you and I and he used to go round "exploring" the hotels, the time we were first in Europe; do you remember how we used to do it? and then in the days of the dancing class, when he was distinctly the polished man-of-the-world from outside, and all the girls, from Helen White and Fanny Dana to May Wigham used to be so flattered by any attentions from him. Or when we were off on his little sailing boat for a two or three days trip on the Sound; or when he first hunted; and when he visited me at Harvard.

I enclose Uncle Jimmie Bulloch's letter—rather solemn and turbid—because I think he would like me to.

Give my love to all.

Your loving brother

October 22, 1894. Washington
To Anna Roosevelt

Darling Bye,

It has been the greatest pleasure to me to think of blessed Edie and the bunnies up with you in the high, clear air of Vermont; they—and especially Edith—needed the change.

Here, I have had much work, of the ordinary kind, in connection with the Civil Service Commission; in the evenings there is of course little to do.

I made a mistake in not trying my luck in the mayoralty race. The prize was very great; the expense would have been trivial; and the chances of success were good. I would have run better than Strong; yet Strong has an even chance of beating Grant. But it is hard to decide when one has the interests of a wife and children to consider first; and now it is over, and it is best not to talk of it; above all, no outsider should know that I think my decision was a mistake.

I have written to darling Pussie. The Sherman letters seemed to me unusually good.

Your loving brother

October 24, 1894. Washington
To Henry Cabot Lodge

Dear Cabot,

I'll tell you all about the mayoralty business when we meet. The last four weeks, ever since I decided not to run, have been pretty bitter ones for me; I would literally have given my right arm to have made the race, win or lose. It was the one golden chance, which never returns; and I had no illusions about ever having another opportunity; I knew it meant the definite abandonment of any hope of going on in the work and life for which I care far more than any other. You may guess that these weeks have not been particularly pleasant ones; but outside of my immediate family nobody but you knows this. At the time, with Edith feeling as intensely as she did, I did not see how I could well go in; though I have grown to feel more and more that in this instance I should have gone counter to her wishes and made the race anyhow. It is not necessary to say to you that the fault was mine, not Edith's; I should have realized that she could not see the matter as it really was, or realize my feelings. But it is one of the matters just as well dropped.

Reed's New York speech was a marvel; it was a well-earned compliment to ask you to be the chief speaker at another such meeting. Tell Nannie that Harry dined with me last evening, and was delightful.

My civil service work here, now, seems to me a little like starting to go through Harvard again after graduating.

Yours

October 27, 1894. Washington
To Henry Cabot Lodge

Dear Cabot:

I thought Sewall's [speech] more than good. It fired my blood to read it. I am not very keen about the tariff business myself, having, as you know, a tinge of economic agnosticism in me, but our foreign policy is, to me, of an importance which is difficult to overestimate. There is one comfort about my not being in the mayoralty race this year. I could not talk against the Democracy on the subject on which I feel deepest, our foreign relations, while I was running for mayor. I am surprised all the time to receive new proofs that every man even every Southerner who lives outside the country, has gotten to have a perfect hatred and contempt for Cleveland's administration because of its base betrayal of our interests abroad. I do wish our Republicans would go in avowedly to annex Hawaii and build an oceanic canal with the money of Uncle Sam.

Harry Davis is just leaving. He was with me again the other day, and I read him a couple of pages of an article I am trying to compose for *The Forum*, these pages having reference to Edward Atkinson. I have a large vocabulary I should like to use on that person, and I have only used about half. Harry, who is of a ferocious temperament, much approved of my expressions. I shall show them to you to see if you think them too strong. One of the mildest of them is a pet sentence in which I state that he combines the imagination of a green grocer with the heart of a Bengalee baboo.

Always yours

P. S.—I am writing a note to the editor of the *Atlantic* about a piece by Henry Childs Merwin defence of Tammany, in which he says the Civil Service Law in the departments at Washington was under Harrison and is now under Cleveland "a mere mockery," quoting Carlisle and you as authorities. If not too much trouble send me what you really said, as I am going to rap him.

December 7, 1894. Washington
To James Brander Matthews

Dear Brander:

Being laid up in the house with a slight attack of bronchitis I have just got your book. I feel a little ashamed of having you send it to me; but there is one comfort when I receive books from you, and that is that

I have always read them before, and have always liked them. I feel about your books like the traditional Kentuckian about whiskey; some of them are better than others, but they are all good. I think the "Royal Marine," however, one of the best of your stories.

By the way did you see Hamlin Garland's piece in the last *Harper's Weekly?* It is very good, and is much less morbid than his pieces have grown to be. It looks to me as though he were going to, in a somewhat different way, suffer as Howells has done, by taking a jaundiced view of life. This is not an uncommon development of the reform spirit, unfortunately. Even in this piece I am amused at one thing. He often predicates the unhappiness of people accustomed to entirely different surroundings from his because he, or because cultivated men brought up in ease, would mind such surroundings. I really doubt whether he has seen from the inside the life he describes nearly as much as I have, and he certainly must mind it far more. For instance, I have been a great deal in logging camps such as the one he describes in this last article in *Harper's,* and I know that the men in them regard a good logging camp as a first-rate place, very comfortable, very warm, with an abundance of good food, and often pleasant company. I have thoroughly enjoyed such camps myself. He speaks of the greasy quilts, etc. Well, they are distressing to an overcivilized man; but for my own pleasure this year when I was out on the antelope plains I got into a country where I didn't take my clothes off for ten days. I had two cowpunchers along, and the quilts and bedding, including the pillows which they had, were quite as bad as those Garland describes in his logging camp; yet they both felt they were off on a holiday and having a lovely time. Our food on this ten days' trip was precisely like that he describes in the logging camp, except that we had venison instead of beef, and we ate it under less comfortable surroundings as a whole, or at least under what my men regarded as less comfortable surroundings. I have worked hard in cow camps for weeks at a time, doing precisely such work as the cowpunchers, and I know what I am talking about. I didn't play; I *worked,* while on my ranch. There is a great deal of toil and hardship about the out-of-door life of lumbermen & cowboys, and especially about some phases which he doesn't touch, such as driving logs in the springtime and handling cattle from a line camp in bitter winter weather; but the life as a whole is a decidedly healthy and attractive one to men who do not feel the need of mental recreation and stimulus—and few of them do.

However, this story of Garland's is a good one, and I am glad that he should go back to writing good stories, and not try to evolve some little school of literary philosophy, where the propriety of his purpose is marred by the utter crudity of his half-baked ideas, and where he is not tempted to group himself and one or two friends under some such absurd heading as "veritists."

I shall see you in mid-January when I come on to New York. Meanwhile I wish you would come on here.

March 11, 1895. Washington
To Walter C. Camp

My dear Mr. Camp:

I was genuinely pleased to receive your note and the *Football Facts and Figures*. I am ashamed to say that I had never had time to examine the latter before though of course I often saw it quoted. I was particularly delighted with your putting in the extracts from the *Yale Courant* and *Scribner's Monthly*, especially the latter, with its reprobation of brutal baseball, and its championship of croquet as the national game. I read it with delight to my colleague on the Civil Service Commission, Mr. Proctor, a Kentuckian. One of Mr. Proctor's sons is a midshipman. He was on the Annapolis team, and put out his knee just before the game with West Point. Neither the boy nor his father cared a rap about the injury, except because it prevented the boy from playing in the great game. His other son is a freshman at Harvard. Last year he was trying for the team there and broke a bone in his arm; and of course all that either father or son cared about the accident was the fact that it barred the boy from the team.

I am very glad to have a chance of expressing to you the obligation which I feel all Americans are under to you for your championship of athletics. The man on the farm and in the workshop here, as in other countries, is apt to get enough physical work; but we were tending steadily in America to produce in our leisure and sedentary classes a type of man not much above the Bengalee baboo, and from this the athletic spirit has saved us. Of all games I personally like football best, and I would rather see my boys play it than see them play any other. I have no patience with the people who declaim against it because it necessitates rough play and occasional injuries. The rough play, if confined within manly and honorable limits, is an advantage. It is a good thing to have the personal contact about which the New York *Evening Post* snarls so much, and no fellow is worth his salt if he minds an occasional bruise or cut. Being nearsighted I was not able to play football in college, and I never cared for rowing or baseball, so that I did all my work in boxing and wrestling. They are both good exercises, but they are not up to football. Since I left college I have worked hard in a good many different ways, and sport has always been a mere accessory to my other business; yet I managed to ride across country a good deal, to play polo, and to shoot, and the like. I was knocked senseless at polo once, and it was a couple of hours before I came to. I broke an arm once riding to hounds, and I broke my nose another time; and out on the roundup in the West I once broke a rib, and at another time the point of my shoulder. I got these injuries when I was father of a family, and while of course they caused more or less inconvenience, and my left arm is not as strong as it might be now, nothing would persuade me to surrender the fun and the health which I could not have had save at the risk; and it seems to me that when I can afford to run these slight risks college boys can afford to take their chances on the football field. A couple of years ago a man was killed at Harvard in a friendly boxing bout, and during the time that I rode to hounds with the Meadowbrook Hunt Club on Long Island two men were killed; while if you collect the coasting accidents I think you will find that the double runner sled is about twenty times as dangerous as the gridiron field.

I am utterly disgusted with the attitude of President Eliot and the Harvard faculty about football, though I must also say I feel very strongly in favor of altering the rules, so far as practicable, to do away with needless roughness in playing, and, above all, in favor of severe umpiring, and the expulsion from the field of any player who is needlessly rough, even if he doesn't come quite within the mark of any specific rule. I do not know anything about umpiring football games, but I have had a good deal of experience in umpiring polo games. However, personally though I would like to see the rules changed and to see the needless brutality abolished, I would a hundredfold rather keep the game as it is now, with the brutality, than give it up. The other day I spoke at a civil service reform meeting in Cincinnati and was introduced by an old Yale man of the class of '75, Judge Taft, one of the best fellows and most useful public men it has ever been my good fortune to meet. He put the thing in a nutshell when he said he wanted reformers who ate roast beef, and who were able to make their blows felt in the world. I have always been greatly interested in the purification of politics; and in the struggle to attain this I do not give a snap for a good man who can't fight and hold his own in the world. A citizen has got to be decent of course. That is the first requisite; but the second, and just as important, is that he shall be efficient, and he can't be efficient unless he is manly. Nothing has impressed me more in meeting college graduates during the fifteen years I have been out of college than the fact that on the average the men who have counted most have been those who had sound bodies. Among the Harvard men whom I have known for the last six years here in Washington, Lodge, the Senator, was a great swimmer in college, winning a championship, and is a great horseman now. Storer, a Congressman from Cincinnati, played first base on our nine. Hamlin, the Assistant Secretary of the Treasury, also played on the nine. Sherman Hoar, another Congressman, was on our class crew; and so on and so on; and I am inclined to think that even more good than comes to the top men from athletics comes to men like myself, who were never more than second-rate in the sports, but who were strengthened in every way by them. The Latin I learned in college has helped me a little in after life in various ways, but boxing has helped me more.

Now, my dear sir, you see what you brought on yourself by sending me the book. I had no idea of inflicting this tirade on you when I began to write.

Faithfully yours

April 3, 1895. Washington
To Henry Cabot Lodge

Dear Cabot:

I received a strong appeal from Douglas to take the Police Commissionership if offered me. I do not know that there is much need of discussing the matter now, for I suppose the Mayor has settled on somebody else. A week ago he would have offered it to me if I had been willing to take it. Still, I wish you would see Douglas and tally the matter over with him and talk the matter over with Strong too. The average New Yorker of course wishes me to take it very much. I don't feel much like it myself, but of course I realize that it is a different kind of position from that of Street Cleaning Commissioner, and one I could perhaps afford to be identified with.

Murray writes me that there is nothing in the tally of my being Chairman of the Commission. You know as well as I do, and indeed I think you feel as much as I do, the arguments for and against my being Police Commissioner. You are on the ground, and do talk it over with Douglas and the Mayor; it is an important thing for me and if I ought to take it I must do so soon. It is very puzzling!

Faithfully yours

April 7, 1895. Washington
To Anna Roosevelt

Darling Bye,

The cold weather lasted until the end of this week, but now it really seems that Spring has come. Cabot and Nannie have been in New York; and we have missed them much. The Brooks Adams have been here, both very pleasant; we dined with them last evening.

On Friday Dan Wister was in town, and I gave him a dinner; the other guests were Kipling, Tom Page, John Hay, Austin Wadsworth, Merriam, Rockhill and Proctor. It was the pleasantest dinner of the winter, if I was the host, and they stayed until one. All got on beautifully, and the stories, discussions and all were as entertaining as possible. Wister and Kipling were at their best; Kipling in particular, who is certainly a genius, and who has been exceptionally well behaved ever since our rough-and-tumble the first night.

This afternoon we are going to take the children out for their weekly scramble up Rock Creek; which has become quite a feature, as divers other children usually turn up to take part in it. I'll drag Kermit and Ethel on the buckboard, and leave them to pick flowers with Edie, while I clamber over the rocks with the others; I have a rope for the steeper cliffs!

I have been working like a beaver in my office and at my books; my work is very attractive, but it does keep me busy.

Your own brother

May 18, 1895. New York
To Henry Cabot Lodge

Dear Cabot:

I should have written you earlier, but I have had more work on my hands than you can imagine; on an average I have not left this office until after six, and once I left it after eight. I hope in a fortnight when I have grown warm in the collar I shall be able to get through my work quicker.[1]

It is absorbingly interesting; but you need not have the slightest fear about my losing my interest in National Politics. If the Re-organization Bill had only gone through, I would have had this force completely remodeled in six months; and after that time, though I should have been interested in it, and would have been very glad to have the work in default of any other, yet its great interest for me would have gone. As it is now, I shall have a lively and far from pleasant interest in the work all summer, for the difficulties in getting a good force are immeasurably increased and the result will necessarily be far more imperfect and the process much slower.

We shall have to try to get this legislation next year, which again will keep me interested through the winter. If we don't get it next year the chances are we shall not get it at all, and in any event by the time

---

[1]Roosevelt had accepted appointment to the New York City Police Commission.

we do get it, if it is two years hence, most of the work will be done in some shape or other; if we do get it, three months at that time will enable us to finish the whole affair. So that in a couple of years or less I shall have finished the work here for which I am specially fitted, and in which I take a special interest. After that there will remain only the ordinary problems of decent administration in the Department, which will be already in good running order. I shall then be quite ready to take up a new job, if I think I can do it better, or can accomplish more in it. While, if nothing offers itself, I shall continue to do my work here; by that time all the big problems here will be disposed of one way or the other, and I can put my hand on other things.

For the next six months I am going to be absorbed in the work here and under a terrific strain; I have got to move against the scandals in this Department, if my work is to be at all thorough; but my hands have been tied in a large measure, thanks to the action of the legislature.

I shall not neglect the political side, you may be sure. With Quigg, Brookfield and some of the others, I shall keep in close touch. I shall do my best to keep out of faction fighting, but it will be difficult, for its perfectly astounding to see how Platt succeeds in identifying himself with the worst men and the worst forces in every struggle, so that a decent man *must* oppose him.

I wrote to Ainsworth in a very hearty and friendly way. I won't be able to do as much on the political side as I should wish, because I am so completely absorbed by the work and struggle here, but I shall do what I can, you may rest assured.

Edith is distinctly better; the children are well.

Give my best love to Nannie. You cannot imagine how I miss her and you; and Edith is as homesick for you both as I am. Really, I have hardly seen her and the children, I have been so busy.

Ever yours

P.S. I think I shall move against Byrnes at once. I thoroughly distrust him, and cannot do any thorough work while he remains. It will be a very hard fight, and I have no idea how it will come out.

May 19, 1895. New York
To Anna Roosevelt

Darling Bye,

You are too good, to have written Chamberlain that I can stay here when in town this summer, as I so often must be; it will be a great convenience to me; I'll get my meals at the club, but it is much more comfortable to be able to leave my clothes here.

I have never worked harder than during the last two weeks; I am down town at nine, and leave the office at six—once at eight. The actual work is hard; but far harder is the intense strain. I have the most important, and the most corrupt, department in New York on my hands. I shall speedily assail some of the ablest, shrewdest men in this city, who will be fighting for their lives, and I know well how hard the task ahead of me is. Yet, in spite of the nervous strain and worry, I am glad I undertook it; for it is a man's work. But I have had to stop my fourth volume for the time.

Love to Rosy and Helen.

Yours

June 16, 1895. Oyster Bay
To Anna Roosevelt

Darling Bye,

Twice I have spent the night in patrolling New York on my own account, to see exactly what the men were doing. My experiences were interesting, and the trips did good, though each meant my going forty hours at a stretch without any sleep. But in spite of my work I really doubt whether I have often been in better health. It is very interesting; and I feel as though it was so eminently practical; it has not a touch of the academic. Indeed anything more practical it would be hard to imagine. I am dealing with the most important, and yet most elementary, problems of our municipal life. The work has absorbed me. I have not tried to write a line of my book since I took the office; and a rather melancholy feature of it is that I do'n't see very much of the children. In the morning I get little more than a glimpse of them. In the evening I always take a romp with Archie, who loves me with all his small silly heart; the two little boys usually look over what they call my "jewel box" while I am dressing; I then play with cunning Ethel in her crib; and Alice takes dinner with us.

Emily's visit has made a very great difference to Edith.

Lovingly yours

July 14, 1895. Oyster Bay
To Henry Cabot Lodge

Dear Cabot,

For good or ill I have made an upset in New York politics; and, with true parochialism, the average New Yorker regards the tariff, silver, and presidential nominees as all secondary to the Excise question.

It is an awkward and ugly fight; yet I am sure I am right in my position, and I think there is an even chance of our winning on it. Hill has written a long letter, with a labored attack on me and on my position, picturing me as "indulging in a champagne dinner at the Union League Club" while I deny the poor man his beer. Clarkson, quite needlessly, came to Hill's assistance, in an interview in which he assailed me for aiding the democrats by my "puritanism," and compared me to the Iowa Prohibitionists. The Goo-Goos, and all the German leaders, backed ferociously by the *Staats-Zeitung*, the *World* and the *Morning Journal*, and also by Platt's paper, the *Advertiser*, have attacked me. The *Evening Post* flinched characteristically; but has finally been driven to support me. All the churches however have rallied round me enthusiastically. I am going to assail Hill with heart and soul at a German City Reform Club Tuesday; and I shall not flinch one handsbreadth from my position. Their last move, and a momentarily embarrassing one has been, through various lawyers, to revive various obsolete blue laws, and bring the cases before the magistrates. Parker is proving an invaluable ally; and we shall win on the main point. The blue law business is puzzling; but I think I am working out even a solution to that. Meanwhile I have, for once, absolutely enforced the law in New York, which has always been deemed impossible.

I receive all kinds of clippings from outside papers, among them one from a paper of yours, the Springfield *Union*, with an editorial on me as a scholar and statesman, in which it says I am like Salisbury and Rosebury in England, or Lodge and *Everett* in America! Intelligent editor; very.

Cornell made a very poor showing at Henley.

I am at work as hard as ever, or harder, and see no chance of a let up: and my own work is so absorbing that I don't keep as well posted as I should in outside matters. The silver craze is certainly subsiding.

Give my warmest love to Nannie; and remember me to Bay and John.

One comic feature of the situation here is that recently several persons supposed to look like me have been followed at night by very unfriendly mobs! However I've never encountered anything unpleasant myself on my midnight patrols.

Yours always

P.S. The other day there was an Irish riot against the Orange parade in Boston. Friday was the anniversary of the Boyne battle, and the Orange-men paraded here. There had been some uneasiness because of the Boston riot; so I had all the reserves in the stations with their night sticks, and sent a double number with the parade, under Inspector McCullough, who is of protestant Irish blood; and instructed him that the word was to be "clubs" if there was the slightest disturbance or attempt to interfere with the procession. It went off as quietly as a Sunday school meeting!

This has been a very egoistic letter. Edith sends you both her love, and says she wishes she were with you. I should wish it too, if I had time enough to wish anything. Do write me all about the people you meet, and particularly the Whites; to whom remember me very warmly. They are among the few people whom I really wish to see again.

Edith is well; she is going to ride Diamond soon; that veteran polo pony is now a saddle horse for her sister Emily Carow. I shall write Harry as soon as the *Montgomery* comes to harbor, and try to get him out here.

The children are in fine health. Archie crawls up to Jessie and kisses her muddy nose, and Jessie licks his face; which seems symptomatic of rather untidy affection. I have bought Ted a Flobert rifle and am teaching him how to shoot. The Boone and Crockett gave Willie Chanler and Von Höhnel a dinner, which was one of the pleasantest I ever went to.

The only exercise I get is to ride to and from the station on a bicycle when I don't pass the night in Town.

Have you met Bryce and Balfour, Morley and Lang?

Yours

July 20, 1895. New York
To Henry Cabot Lodge

Dear Cabot:

While you are engaged in a round of reckless dissipation with the English aristocracy, I intend, from time to time, to inflict on you accounts of the work we hot and groveling practical politicians of the baser sort are doing as our summer work in New York.

Two or three nights a week I have to stay in town; Sunday I spend in the country; the other days I ride to and from the station on my bicycle, leaving my house at half past seven in the morning, spending a perfect whirl of eight hours in New York, and returning just in time for a short play with the children before I get dressed for supper.

I have never been engaged in a more savage fight. Senator Hill thinks he sees in my actions a chance to strike the keynote for the Democratic campaign this fall. He has accordingly written a long letter against me and my conduct to the Local Democracy. I responded in a speech, of which I enclose a copy from a hostile paper; will you send it back to me? It produced me the following telegram from Senator Hoar:

"WORCESTER, MASS.,
July 18, 1895.

Your speech is the best speech that has been made on this continent for thirty years. I am glad to know that there is a man behind it worthy of the speech.

GEORGE F. HOAR."

That was pretty good for the old man, was it not? I was really greatly flattered. I have had letters from all over the country backing me up, and even in New York City here, I believe there is a very strong feeling for me; but of course the outcry against me at the moment is tremendous. The *World, Herald, Sun, Journal* and *Advertiser* are shrieking with rage; and the *Staats-Zeitung* is fairly epileptic; the *Press* stands by me nobly. The *Tribune* and *Times* more tepidly; the *Evening Post* has been afraid of its life, and has taken refuge in editorials that are so colorless as to be comical.

P. S. The *Post* has now suddenly changed and is howling in my favor; and the *Tribune* is strengthening considerably. However, I don't care a snap of my finger; my position is impregnable; and I am going to fight no matter what the opposition is.

Parker is proving himself an exceedingly efficient ally, and I get on well with both my other colleagues.

Carl Schurz has written me an agonizing letter to enforce the law against soda-water as much as beer. I wrote him back that I would tackle the soda-water in time, but nothing could make me relax my grip on the liquor sellers. Tell me about the Whites; and the different people whom you have met. Give my best love to Nannie.

Yours always

August 3, 1895. New York
To Charles A. Dana

Sir:

In your list of Indian words adopted into our language I did not notice that you included "cayuse," in use for small Indian horses in the far Northwest, nor "whisky-jack," which is derived from the Indian, and is the most common of the various names applied by the hunters and trappers of the northern woods and Rocky Mountains to that drab-colored haunter of wilderness camps, the Canada jay. Besides "wangan," the Maine and Minnesota lumbermen use "wanigan" as a name for the big chest in which the men keep their spare clothes and a few personal belongings.

Out on my ranch on the Little Missouri there was once a huge German whose first experience of American life had been gained in a logging camp. When he came out to our little town of Medora, in the cow country, he had with him a trunk, which he called his wanigan. Somebody "rustled" it, and his perpetual inquiries after it resulted in his receiving the name of "Dutch Wanigan." He finally adopted this name himself, and gradually every one grew to forget that he had any other name. Even his few letters came addressed "D. Wanigan, Esq."

By the way, I was surprised to see your correspondent put down "bronco" as a Spanish word. It is hardly ever used on the Mexican border, while it is in universal use on the northern cattle plains.

August 6, 1895. New York
To Horace E. Scudder

My dear Mr. Scudder:

Permit me to introduce to you Mr. J. L. Steffens[1] who has an admirable article on the Police Department, which I thought might possibly be of interest to you.

Mr. Steffens represents the *Evening Post*. He is a graduate of the University of California, and has studied abroad in Germany and Paris. He is a personal friend of mine; and he has seen all of our work at close quarters. He and Mr. Jacob Riis have been the two members of the Press who have most intimately seen almost all that went on here in the Police Department; so he speaks at first hand as an expert.

You are, of course, the best judge as to whether or not the article is suitable for the *Atlantic*; but as to Mr. Steffens' competency as an expert I can, myself, vouch.

Very truly yours

September, 1895. New York
To Henry Cabot Lodge

Dear Cabot:

I have just received your two letters from France. Yes, I received the clippings right after I sent you the letter asking you to get them for me.

Edith and I have enjoyed your letters immensely. I am sorry to say she seems to sympathize with your view as to my probable failure to appreciate the splendid architecture of the Norman Cathedral towns. In this she is wrong. The great Cathedrals have always possessed as much fascination for me as for those who know far more about architecture than I do.

I envy you your trip both in England and in France. How I wish we could have been abroad at the same time.

Like yourself, I was a little nervous about the *Defender*. Edith and I went down to see the first race on the Police Patrol Boat; and at its finish I was not nervous in the least. In a very low wind and in smooth waters the two boats were nearly equal; but when there was a sea on the

---

[1]The investigative journalist better known as Lincoln Steffens.

Defender was the better boat; and as soon as the wind rose her superiority became very marked. Her second race was a really wonderful feat, thanks to Dunraven's fouling her (when he tried a piece of sharp practice and attempted to bluff the Yankee Captain, who would not be bluffed), the *Defender* was never able to make use of her large head sails at all; but although crippled she was beaten by only forty-seven seconds. This second race proved that the *Valkyrie* had not a chance. Dunraven then funked; it was a clear case of showing the white feather. His talk about the excursion boats was all nonsense; they bothered one boat as much as the other. They did not interfere seriously with either of the boats. And in the third race, which he abandoned, they did not interfere at all. They had no effect whatever on the result of either race.

He has shown himself a poor sportsman; he has sulked and flinched.

I am very much touched by your persistence in far overestimating the position I hold; but you really make me a little uneasy for I do not want you to get false ideas of my standing. I undoubtedly have a strong hold on the imagination of decent people; and I have the courageous and enthusiastic support of the men who make up the back-bone of the Republican party; but I have no hold whatever on the people who run the Republican machine.

Platt's influence is simply poisonous. I cannot go in with him; no honest man of sincerity can. Yet, his influence is very great; he has completely overthrown the Brookfield people. At the Primaries, my own Assembly District we held, although after a close vote; but elsewhere throughout the city the Platt people generally triumphed. He can gain victories over Republicans in Primaries and Conventions; but he cannot gain victories against Democrats; and he has no hold on the rank and file of the Republican party. On the contrary they are reluctant to vote for any man whom he controls. The Platt men carry the other Assembly Districts in my Congressional District.

At present, I do not see how I can get to the National Convention as a delegate. The Platt people will probably control the District. Moreover, in my own Assembly District there are:

Chauncey Depew,	Gen'l. Sam Thomas,
Joseph Choate,	Mayor Strong, and
Anson G. McCook,	Brookfield.

All of these are men of note; and all of them, excepting probably Choate and Strong, will be among the many candidates for Delegates for the presidential Convention. The shrewdest among them are, I think, McKinley men; and the decent people are all embittered against Platt so that it would be very difficult to make them join with his people, even merely to send two Reed Delegates. I shall try to fix up some arrangement by which I can go with another Reed man, whether the latter be for Platt or Brookfield; but just at this moment I don't see my way clear to success.

The absolute cowardice and dishonesty of the Platt people who now control our Republican State politics, was shown at the Republican State Convention.

This summer, I have, as you know, been careful to identify myself in every way with the Republicans. Hill has attacked me violently as a Republican; and I have made an equally savage counter-attack upon him. He has made me the arch foe of the Democracy. The Clergy of all denominations are standing by me with the utmost enthusiasm.

Hill has committed the Democracy to attacking me and my course; and also to attacking the principle of closing the saloons on Sunday. Not only common honesty; but every consideration of expediency, indicated to the Republicans to follow the opposite policy to the one pursued by the Democrats; yet, the Platt people prepared a platform from which every allusion to the Excise matter was struck out, and in the Committee on Resolutions they voted down even a resolution endorsing our course in honestly enforcing the law. If the platform had gone through in this shape I would have been absolutely debarred from saying a word for the party; and what is much more important, we would have been beaten overwhelmingly, for the excise issue is the main issue in our State. Warner Miller, however, made a bold fight in open convention and got in a plank, which while not very satisfactory, still does give us a chance of success and enables me to support the party. This was done in spite of every effort of the Platt people; but the union of the Brookfield people with the country Republicans who are afraid of church-going voters proved irresistible on this one point.

I bore you with this account of our rather parochial politics just so that you may understand that I seriously mean what I say when I tell you that I have no real hold on the party machinery here, and cannot under the present circumstances get such a hold without sacrificing my self-respect. The chance for future political preference for me is just about such a chance as that of lightning striking. In the meanwhile, however, I have certainly accomplished a great deal in my present position; and I have what is, perhaps, as great a satisfaction as any man can have, the knowledge of having performed a difficult and important work well. It would be mock modesty for me not to say this. But it would be self-deception if I thought that I had gained a permanent position, or opened any future career. However, I have had a thoroughly enjoyable time, and I am over-joyed that I took the position.

Give my warm love to Nannie. Tell me a little about Bay's plans.

Yours always

November 29, 1895. New York
To Frederic Remington

My dear Remington:

I never so wished to be a millionaire or indeed any person other than a literary man with a large family of small children and a taste for practical politics and bear hunting, as when you have pictures to sell. It seems to me that you in your line, and Wister in his, are doing the best work in America today.

In your last *Harper's* article you used the adjective "gangling"; where did you get it? It was a word of my childhood that I once used in a book myself, and everybody assured me it did not have any real existence beyond my imagination.

Faithfully yours

December 2, 1895. New York
To Henry Cabot Lodge

Dear Cabot:

I enclose a clipping from the *Evening Post* which really pleases me. I wish you would show it to Reed, and then send it back again. The *Post*, in view of my attitude on Reed and our foreign policy, has been obliged to give up all attempt to support me in my police work.

This is comic rather than serious; but the attitude of the Platt people here in New York *is* serious. Nothing ever done by Tammany or by the Southern Democrats in the way of fraudulent management of primaries and of stuffing and padding the district associations, has surpassed what Platt bas been doing recently. The decent Republicans are getting savage, and there is very ugly talk of establishing a separate county organization and of sending a rival set of delegates to the National Convention. These delegates will represent the best element in the party here, the element without which the party will be in a hopeless minority, and will in point of character stand not much above Tammany; but the evil feature of it is that many of them will not be Reed men. I am getting seriously alarmed lest Platt's utter unscrupulousness and cynical indifference to the wellfare of the party, unless it redounds to his own personal benefit, should make the decent people here indifferent on the Presidential question and muddle everything in a desire to beat Platt. I wish Quigg could have gotten me a chance to see Platt, talk with him, and sound him on the Reed matter.

I now see two rocks ahead; first that Platt may decide to throw over Reed; and second, that the anti-Platt people, many of whom are for McKinley or Harrison, may be thrown by Platt into a combination against him and whomever he supports. The minute I find out anything of importance I shall communicate at once with either you or Reed. Don't think that I am gloomy as to the outlook, it is only that I wish to keep the dangers in mind.

Always yours

December 22, 1895. Oyster Bay
To William Cowles[1]

Dear Will,

Your letter to Ted was awfully nice; you were a trump to think of writing it. I have really greatly enjoyed all four of the Hakluyt volumes.

We are much interested in the outcome of the Venezuelan matter.[2] I earnestly hope our government do'n't back down. If there is a muss I shall try to have a hand in it myself! They'll have to employ a lot of men just as green as I am even for the conquest of Canada; our regular army is'n't big enough.

It seems to me that if England were wise she would fight now; we could'n't get at Canada until May, and meanwhile she could play havoc with our coast cities and shipping.

Always yours

December 27, 1895. New York
To Henry Cabot Lodge

Dear Cabot:

Your two letters were a great comfort and pleasure. Don't imagine that I really get very blue. Every now and then I feel sullen for an hour or two when everybody seems to join against me here; but I would not for anything give up my experience of the last eight months; I prize them more than any other eight months in all my official career. You were more than wise in advising me to come here.

I am deeply interested in what you say about Harrison. It looks now as if Platt was going to make a serious effort on behalf of Morton, and if that proves useless to go in for Reed. I must say it irks me a little to have to be for Morton. I like the old gentleman well enough; but my

---

[1]Anna Roosevelt's new husband.

[2]The Cleveland administration took the side of Venezuela in a boundary dispute with the British colony of Guiana.

whole heart is in the Reed canvass and I feel all the time that very uncomfortable sensation of sailing under false colors. However, I suppose that by what I have written and spoken about him I have really given him more help—slight though this help was—than I could give him by an attempt to get a Reed delegate in some one New York district. I doubt if I can get to St. Louis myself, and may have to limit my exertions to get in two delegates from our district who will be straight out Reed men for second choice.

It seems to me that our action on the tariff under Reed's leadership was admirable; we have countered on Cleveland most effectively.

I most earnestly hope that our people won't weaken in any way on the Venezuela matter. The antics of the bankers, brokers and anglomaniacs generally are humiliating to a degree; but the bulk of the American people will I think surely stand behind the man who boldly and without flinching takes the American view.

As you say, thank God I am not a free-trader. In this country pernicious indulgence in the doctrine of free trade seems inevitably to produce fatty degeneration of the moral fibre. Did you read the *Sun's* admirable editorial upon the damage done to England by American correspondents of the British Press, who utterly misrepresented the whole tone of American thought?

Smalley's whole attitude is contemptible beyond words. As for the Editors of the *Evening Post* and *World* it would give me great pleasure to have them put in prison the minute hostilities began. I felt I must give utterance to my feelings. I am more indignant than I can say at the action of the Harvard people. Do you think there would be any harm in my writing to the *Crimson* a smashing letter as per enclosed giving my views and saying a word for Patriotism and Americanism; unless I hear from you to the contrary I think I shall send this on. I wish to at least do what I can to save Harvard from degredation. Our peace at any price men, if they only knew it, are rendering war likely, because they will encourage England to persist; in the long run this means a fight. Personally I rather hope the fight will come soon. The clamor of the peace faction has convinced me that this country needs a war.

Give my best love to Nannie.

Always yours

If you like what I say to the *Crimson*, return it, and I will send it.

January 2, 1896. New York
To the Editors of the *Harvard Crimson*

I have seen a newspaper statement that various professors and students of Harvard have urged through your columns the Harvard graduates and undergraduates to bring such pressure as they could upon Senators and Congressmen in order to prevent their upholding the honor and dignity of the United States by supporting the President and the Secretary of State in their entirely proper attitude on the Venezuelan question. I do not believe that any considerable number either of Senators or Congressmen would consent to betray the American cause, the cause not only of national honor but in reality of international peace, by abandoning our position in the peace, by abandoning our position in the Venezuelan matter; but I earnestly hope that Harvard will be saved from the discredit of advising such a course.

The Monroe Doctrine had for its first exponent Washington. In its present shape it was in reality formulated by a Harvard man, afterwards President of the United States, John Quincy Adams. John Quincy Adams did much to earn the gratitude of all Americans. Not the least of his services was his positive refusal to side with the majority of the cultivated people of New England and the Northeast in the period just before the war of 1812 when these cultivated people advised the same spiritless submission to improper English demands that some of their intellectual descendants are now advising.

The Monroe Doctrine forbids us to acquiesce in any territorial aggrandizement by a European power on American soil at the expense of an American state. If people wish to reject the Monroe Doctrine in its entirety, their attitude, though discreditable to their farsighted patriotism, is illogical; but let no one pretend that the present Venezuelan case does not come within the strictest view of the Monroe Doctrine. If we permit a European nation in each case itself to decide whether or not the territory which it wishes to seize is its own, then the Monroe Doctrine has no real existence; and if the European power refuses to submit the question to proper arbitration, then all we can do is to find out the facts for ourselves and act accordingly. England's pretentions in this case are wholly inadmissible and the President and Secretary of State and the Senate and House deserve the highest honor for the course they have followed.

Nothing will tend more to preserve peace on this continent than the resolute assertion of the Monroe Doctrine; let us make this present case serve as an object lesson, once for all. Nothing will more certainly in the end produce war than to invite European aggressions on American states by abject surrender of our principles. By a combination of indifference on the part of most of our people, a spirit of eager servility toward England in another smaller portion, and a base desire to avoid the slightest financial loss even at the cost of the loss of national honor by yet another portion, we may be led into a course of action which will for the moment avoid trouble by the simple process of tame submission to wrong. If this is done it will surely invite a repetition of the wrong; and in the end the American people are certain to resent this. Make no mistake. When our people as a whole finally understand the question they will insist on a course of conduct which will uphold the honor of the American flag; and we can in no way more effectively invite ultimate war than by deceiving foreign powers into taking a position which will make us certain to clash with them once our people have been fully aroused.

The stock-jobbing timidity, the Baboo kind of statesmanship, which is clamored for at this moment by the men who put monetary gain before national honor, or who are still intellectually in a state of colonial dependence on England, would in the end most assuredly invite war. A temperate but resolute insistence upon our rights is the surest way to secure peace. If Harvard men wish peace with honor they will heartily support the national executive and national legislature in the Venezuela matter; will demand that our representatives insist upon the strictest application of the Monroe Doctrine, and will farther demand that immediate preparation be made to build a really first-class Navy.

Yours truly '

March 9, 1896. New York
To Anna Roosevelt Cowles

Darling Bye:

Late Saturday evening Cabot turned up unexpectedly, on his way to the funeral of poor Governor Greenhalge. He was in fine form, though very indignant with me because I had to be at the Monthly Meeting of the Century Club that night and because next morning I had to breakfast out to meet the Chief Justice of New South Wales. He also felt decidedly injured because we had to take him down to lunch at Mrs. Fred. Jones's. At lunch, by the way, I sat by Dr. Weir Mitchell and found him particularly interesting.

Cabot is far from pleased at the way things have gone on at Washington and, in strict confidence, he, as well as I, feel that Tom Reed has missed his opportunity this winter. He is trying to make a reputation as a conservative economist, and has merely succeeded in giving the idea that he has turned timid. He has given us no support whatever, save in the most perfunctory manner, for coast defences and a good Navy and while I think we shall get both in the end, and that he will help us, he really has not done so with any vigor. Moreover, I think he ought to have taken the chance given by the Silver Senators when they smashed the tariff, and have declared outright against free silver and have ruled the freesilver men who bolted the tariff out of the Republican Party.

Smalley dined with us the other evening; he is more British than the British. He is the kind of man who makes me a ferocious jingo. To my immense amusement LaFarge, who was present, blossomed out as a jingo; and to my still greater surprise, so, in somewhat modified fashion, did Maggie Perkins.

Things are beginning to look a little brighter for me. The screeching mendacity of the *Herald* and *World* and the other newspapers is beginning to wear through in places, and the fact that our Police Department is far more efficient than ever before is gradually growing evident even to the dull public mind. Platt and his people remain resolute to try to turn us out of office, but affairs in Albany are shaping themselves so that it seems on the whole most probable that we shall stay in. There is nothing certain about it, and it may be that we shall be turned out, but I think now that the odds are at least slightly in our favor.

I am busy correcting the proof of the fourth volume of *The Winning the West,* and by the middle of May or June I shall be through the hardest part of my work both literary and official; I shall then have finished a year of as hard work and of as much worry and responsibility as a man could well have; yet, I have enjoyed it extremely, and am in excellent health. I don't mind work; the only thing I am afraid of is that by and by I will have nothing to do, and I should hate to have the children grow up and see me having nothing to do. If I am turned out it can hardly be until sometime in May, so I will have had my year here, and I will have earned six months rest. If I am not turned out I will have finished my most wearing and disagreeable work and will have a much easier time in the future.

Tell Will that it is very difficult for me not to wish for a war with Spain, for such a war would result at once in getting us a proper Navy and a good system of coast defence.

Your loving brother

March 30, 1896. New York
To Anna Roosevelt Cowles

Darling Bye,

During the last week we have had two visits from Cabot, on his way to and from his State Convention, where he scored a great triumph. On his return he spent a couple of nights with us, and was as delightful as ever, on everything, from politics to literature.

I wish our people would really interfere in Cuba; but the President (who by the way has just written me a rather long letter, for no particular reason) shies off from anything except Venezuela. We ought to drive the Spaniards out of Cuba; and it would be a good thing, in more ways than one, to do it. Congress ought to take more decisive action; I always hate words unless they mean blows. But Cabot and his followers *do* mean blows; though I doubt if anything comes of it.

Your friend Mrs. Kroub is *very* nice about me indeed. I have had rather a hard row to hoe here; I hope I have accomplished something, but I am not over-sure.

I went on to speak to the boys at Harvard one evening last week, on athletics, and on the proper Harvard spirit generally, and was a good deal touched by the warmth with which I was received.

Bob spent a couple of days with us, and then went back to Canada, looking rather seedy.

Ted the other day was walking back from dancing school alone, practicing his steps on the pavement, according to his custom. Passing by two ladies, one in mourning, he overheard them discussing how to raise mushrooms in a green house; whereupon he beamed on them through his spectacles, and joined affably in the conversation, remarking that where he lived the mushrooms grew in Smith's field! After which they walked on together in conversation until he got home. From Grant Le Farge we found afterwards that they were Emily Lardenberg and a Miss Benedict.

Yours

April 29, 1896. New York
To Henry Cabot Lodge

Dear Cabot:

It was very good of you to send that letter to Laura, and she was deeply touched.

Did you see in *Scribner's* of this month the opening sentences in reference to yourself by the man who was writing about the Consulates? Such a purely incidental tribute speaks more than all the resolutions of the Civil Service Reform Association for the good work you have done.

I was deeply interested in both the volumes by Gustave LeBon. He is really a thinker—not the kind of "thinker" whom the Mugwumps designate by that title—and his books are most suggestive. At the same time I think he falls into fundamental errors quite as vicious in their way as Brooks Adams', especially when he states positively and without qualification a general law which he afterwards himself qualifies in a way that shows that his first general statement was incorrect. I was rather amused at seeing that while his last summing up contained a sweeping prophecy of evil quite as gloomy as Brooks', it was based on exactly the opposite view. One believes that the mass, the proletariat, will swallow up everything and grind capital and learning alike into powder beneath the wheels of socialism. The other believes that the few men on top, the capitalists, will swallow up everything, and will reduce all below them to practical vassalage. But what LeBon says of race is very fine and true.

I see that President Eliot attacked you and myself as "degenerated sons of Harvard." It is a fine alliance, that between the anglo-maniac mugwumps, the socialist working men, and corrupt politicians like Gorman, to prevent the increase of our Navy and coast defenses. The moneyed and semi-cultivated classes, especially of the Northeast, are doing their best to bring this country down to the Chinese level. If we ever come to nothing as a nation it will be because the teaching of Carl Schurz, President Eliot, the *Evening Post* and the futile sentimentalists of the international arbitration type, bears its legitimate fruit in producing a flabby, timid type of character, which eats away the great fighting features of our race. Hand in hand with the Chinese timidity and inefficiency of such a character would go the Chinese corruption; for men of such a stamp are utterly unable to war against the Tammany stripe of politicians. There is nothing that provokes me more than the unintelligent, cowardly chatter for "peace at any price" in which all of those gentlemen indulge.

Give my best love to Nannie.

Always yours

June 20, 1896. Oyster Bay
To Anna Roosevelt Cowles

Darling Bye,

While I greatly regret the defeat of Reed, who was in every way McKinley's superior, I am pretty well satisfied with the outcome at St. Louis. We have an excellent platform on almost every point: finance, civil service reform, foreign policy. Only the pension plank is bad. McKinley himself is an upright and honorable man, of very considerable ability & good record as a soldier & in congress; he is not a strong man, however; and unless he is well backed I should feel rather uneasy about him in a serious crisis, whether it took the form of a soft-money craze, a gigantic labor riot, or danger of foreign conflict.

Grace Potter is spending Sunday with us; she is very much as she always was. Corinne's last relapse seems to have made our darling reckless sister think seriously of trying to take care of herself; she now meditates spending two really quiet months at some little seaport in Maine.

The children are passing their usual heavenly summer. Archie is the sweetest thing imaginable, and such fun to play with. Alice is as good as gold; Edith is giving her and Ted as well a genuine taste for good literature. Kermit is improving in health all the time; and Ethel is the best of rosy, chubby little girls. Yesterday we all had our first swim; and after Edith came back from her ride I put Alice on Diamond for a mile's trot & canter.

Mrs. Bliss—who was never especially attractive to me—is spending a few days at Uncle Jimmie's; her fixity of purpose is evident.

Yours always

July 12, 1896. Oyster Bay
To Anna Roosevelt Cowles

Darling Bye,

The trial—which was really very nearly as much a trial of me as of Parker—is over, I am glad to say, though the Mayor has not yet given his decision; and though I fear the courts, when they review this decision, may reverse it even if it is all right. I have quite forgiven Tracey, for in his effort to break me down, by a six hour cross examination, he gave me just the chance I wished; and I had the satisfaction of telling under oath, with Parker not six feet distant, just what I thought of him, and of his mendacity, treachery and duplicity.[1]

I could'n't get out here at all until Friday afternoon; but I am now passing three days of delightful rest, and enjoyment of the children. They are such darlings! Archie tries to make his skin horse say it's prayers.

Nellie Tyler is here; today we all lunched on Austin Wadsworth's yacht. I have been trying to get started on that naval matter for Cowles; but have not yet succeeded.

Love to Will.

Yours always

P.S. I have been able to do one nice thing; I got Nellie Nick's son Latrobe appointed at Annapolis, through Congressman Low.

July 26, 1896. Oyster Bay
To Anna Roosevelt Cowles

Darling Bye,

Last week went by much as usual. I spent three nights in town, and the others out here; a Professor Smith, a friend of Bob's turned up, and dined with me—also Jacob Riis & Stephen Crane—and we dropped in afterwards to discuss a girl's library in the Jewish quarter with that

---

[1]The trial involved the police corruption Roosevelt was trying to root out.

entertaining but untrustworthy Mrs. Van Rennselaer; yesterday I stayed here, rode with Edith, played with the children, and tried the new military rifle at a target. Hallett Phillips, who is a dear, and my colleague Andrews, are passing Sunday with us.

Not since the Civil War has there been a Presidential election fraught with so much consequence to the country. The silver craze surpasses belief. The populists, populist-democrats, and silver- or populist-Republicans who are behind Bryan are impelled by a wave of genuine fanaticism; not only do they wish to repudiate their debts, but they really believe that somehow they are executing righteous justice on the moneyed oppressor; they feel the eternal and inevitable injustice of life, they do not realize, and will not realize, how that injustice is aggravated by their own extraordinary folly, and they wish, if they cannot lift themselves, at least to strike down those who are more fortunate or more prosperous. At present they are on the crest, and were the election held now they would carry the country; but I hope that before November the sober common sense of the great central western states, the pivotal states, will assert itself. McKinley's position is very hard; the main fight must be for sound finance; but he must stand by protection also, under penalty if he does, of making his new democratic allies lukewarm, and if he does not, of making a much larger number of his old followers hostile. Matters are very doubtful; Bryan's election would be a great calamity, though we should in the end recover from it.

Love to Will. Your last letter was most interesting.

Yours always

August 5, 1896. New York
To Cecil Spring Rice

Dear Cecil:

You would have been well repaid for your trouble in writing if you had seen the eagerness with which Mrs. Roosevelt and I read and reread your letter, and repeated parts of it to the children. As you know we are not fond of many people, and we are very fond of you; and if you don't come back to America for ten years, yet, whenever you do, you will find us just as anxious to see you as we always were in the old days at Washington. Funnily enough just about four days prior to the arrival of your letter we were talking you over, apropos of Willie Phillips, who was spending a week with us in the house, and were saying that he, Bob Ferguson and perhaps Grant LaFarge, were the only people who approached you in our minds as being guests whom we really liked to have stay for no matter how long a time in the house. Mrs.

Roosevelt always refers to your last visit as one during which she got steadily to be more and more glad that you were in the house, so that she felt as if one of the family had gone when you left.

Ted has been learning to shoot with a Flobert rifle. We have a Scotch terrier, an offspring of the Lodge's Peter, with two beautifully forked & pointed ears, and an exceedingly stiff tail; the other day she stood end-on at some little distance looking at us, so that the tail appeared like a bar between the forked ears, and Ted remarked with pleased interest "doesn't Jessie look just exactly like a rifle sight." He rides on pony Grant, when that aldermanic little beast seems less foundered than usual. Alice is as tall as Mrs. Roosevelt now, and just as good as she can be. Archibald, the Cracker, is a darling, although I suppose that to all people but his parents, both his temper and his intelligence would seem to leave much to be desired. Kermit has his brace off, and the little fellow is very happy. He fights with Ethel a good deal, but they are rather more peaceful than formerly. I think I wrote you that both the little boys, in the interest of economy, were clad, over their regular clothes, in the beautiful and simple national garb of the American hired man, that is, blue overhauls with a waist under the armpits.

Ted is as much at home in the water as a duck. Mrs. Roosevelt and I ride a good deal on the two black ponies and we also row now and then, sometimes for a whole day on the water.

Did I tell you that Speck spent three days at our house last winter? One of his duties was to get up a report as to America's strength and weakness in the event of his Government finding it necessary to take a smash at us; he was going about it, and discussed it with me, with his usual delightfully cold-blooded impartiality.

The bulk of my work here is over; the worry will not be over until I leave. The fight has been against terrific odds, and it has been made up of innumerable petty conflicts in which I have lost about as often as I have won; and I could not begin to express the wearing anxiety of the incessant battles now against the Tammany Comptroller, now against the press, now against the machine Republican legislature, now against the dishonesty and scoundrelism of one of my colleagues, with, the whole time, the ingrained and cynical corruption of the Force we inherited from Tammany, as a ground on which all these influences can act. Nevertheless, while I have come very far short of doing what I would like to do, and what I am sure I could have done, had the conditions rendered it possible for any man to do it, yet, I think I can say that we have done a good deal, and that the standard of efficiency and honesty has been immeasurably raised so far as the administration of this Force is concerned.

If Bryan wins, we have before us some years of social misery, not markedly different from that of any South American Republic. The movement behind him is most formidable, and it may well be that he will win. Still, I cannot help believing that the sound common sense of our people will assert itself prior to the election, and that he will lose. One thing that would shock our good friends who do not really study history is the fact that Bryan closely resembles Thomas Jefferson; whose accession to the Presidency was a terrible blow to this nation. Cabot has been one of the men who was instrumental in forcing the gold plank into the Republican platform.

I quite agree with what you say as to the effect that the military training: of a whole nation must in the end have on that nation's character; and I also entirely agree with what you say as to Brooks Adams' book, & of these threadbare comparisons of modern nations with the Roman Empire. As long as the birth rate exceeds the death rate, and as long as the people of a nation will fight, and show some capacity of self-restraint and self-guidance in political affairs, it is idle to compare that nation with the dying empire which fell because there sprang from its loins no children to defend it against the barbarians.

On this side the real danger is either that we shall stop increasing, as is true now of parts of New England, exactly as it is true of France, or else that we shall become so isolated from the struggles of the rest of the world, and so immersed in our own mere material prosperity, or lack of prosperity, so that we shall become genuinely effete, and shall lose that moral spring, which no matter how bent will straighten out a really great people in adversity, if it exists in them.

But there is one inexplicable thing about military training and its effect as instanced by the immigrants we see here. I am entirely unable to detect any improvement in the Germans as fighting policemen because of the military training that their fathers for the last generation have been receiving in the old world. I cannot on any philosophical ground explain why the average Irishman certainly makes a better policeman in an emergency than the average German. We appoint hundreds of both races, and while there are scores of exceptions on both sides, yet as a general rule the fact remains as I have said. It is so in the Police of Chicago and Minneapolis; likewise, it was so with our soldiers of the Civil War. After one, or at most two generations the difference dies out. The children and grandchildren of the German and Irish immigrants, whom we appoint on our Force, are scarcely distinguishable from one another, and the best of them are not distinguishable from the best of the appointees of old American stock. But it certainly does seem to take a generation to make the German, in point of fighting capacity, come up to the Irish, or native American.

The other side of the Police Force amuses me much, and I shall have lots to tell you about it when, if ever, we meet.

Bob Ferguson spent a day with us before going abroad. I think he is coming back to New York next winter.

You will remember Captain Robert Evans? He was in here with the *Indiana*, which is a splendid ship. Kipling, by the way, went all over it, and he and Evans got on capitally together. Harry Davis was here with the *Montgomery*. He spent a day with us in the country. He has the *Montgomery* at a very high pitch of efficiency, especially in the drill of her guns; and when questioned about her, I was much amused to see the struggle in his mind between his ingrained tendency to state that everything was and must be wrong everywhere, and as bad as could possibly be; and his deep-seated pride and belief that nothing of her size really could be better than his own vessel.

Good bye, old man! Mrs. Roosevelt sends you her love, so do Alice and Ted. Do write us now and then for your letters are always very welcome.

Faithfully yours

P.S. Indeed Russia is a problem very appalling. All other nations of European blood, if they develop at all, seem inclined to develop on much the same lines; but Russia seems bound to develop in her own way, and on lines that run directly counter to what we are accustomed to consider as progress. If she ever does take possession of Northern China and drill the Northern Chinese to serve as her Army, she will indeed be a formidable power. It has always seemed to me that the Germans showed shortsightedness in not making some alliance that will enable them to crush Russia. Even if in the dim future Russia should take India and become the preponderant power of Asia, England would merely be injured in one great dependency; but when Russia grows so as to crush Germany, the crushing will be once for all. The growth of the great Russian state in Siberia is portentious; but it is stranger still nowadays to see the rulers of the nation deliberately keeping it under a despotism, deliberately setting their faces against any increase of the share of the people in government.

Well, just at this moment, my country does not offer a very inspiriting defense of democracy. This free silver, semianarchistic, political revolutionary movement has the native American farmer as its backbone; it is not the foreign-born people of the great cities; who work for wages and have no property, but the great mass of farmers who own their freeholds, and are of old American stock, that form a menace to the country in the present election; and the Immigrants who back them are the Scandinavians, Scotch & English, not the Irish; while the Germans are among the chief props of sound money.

October 8, 1896. New York
To Cecil Spring Rice

Dear Cecil:

Just a line to tell you in the first place, how greatly we both enjoyed your delightful letter; and in the second place I think the tide has turned here as regards Bryan.

Your descriptions were simply enchanting. How I should love to see the country and to ramble about over the hills; but I could not climb those hills well now without undergoing a good deal of training. Excepting twelve days on my ranch this fall, during which I merely rode a good deal, (shooting five antelope) I have not taken any exercise for two years.

The change of feeling about free silver has been very great. I have never seen a campaign carried along on a higher plane. The appeal has been made straight out on the grounds of morality and patriotism; and the people generally are responding well. I think we shall carry the East by unprecedented majorities, and the middle west by large majorities; the Rocky Mountain States and the South will be against us; and along the border line between; Maryland, West Virginia, Kentucky, Nebraska, the Dakotas, and possibly the Pacific coast States will be close, and we probably shall carry some of them.

The Bryanites have more and more dropped free silver as the issue of the campaign; the fight has nothing to do with bimetallism; it is simply a gathering of the forces of social unrest. All the men who pray for anarchy, or who believe in socialism, and all the much larger number who have not formulated their thoughts sufficiently to believe in either, but who want to strike down the well-to-do, and who have been inflamed against the rich until they feel that they are willing to sacrifice their own welfare, if only they can make others less happy, are banded against us. Organized labor in the lowest Unions is hot for Bryan, although the workingman would suffer more than anyone else by free silver; but the higher class, including the immense mass of the railroad employees, are for us.

Ted has begun his career at the Cove school, and accepts his new experience with happy philosophy.

I shall be on the stump in Illinois and Michigan next week. Cabot and I have just concluded a week's stumping tour.

This and my work at the office here, which is especially onerous before an election, take up all my time and more.

In great haste, I am
Ever faithfully yours

November 8, 1896. Oyster Bay
To Anna Roosevelt Cowles

Darling Bye,

You may easily imagine our relief over the election. It is not pleasant to feel that such a candidate as Bryan should have received such a vote. Still, we have beaten him by the largest majority ever recorded against a presidential candidate, at any rate for the last half century; a majority much larger than is indicated even by the decisive vote in the electoral college. In the east the majorities were almost incredible; in the middle west they were not so overwhelming, and yet were larger than had ever before been given. We also carried the Pacific coast, and the northernmost tier of southern states.

It was the greatest crisis in our national fate, save only the civil war; and I am more than glad I was able to do my part in the contest. I enclose a very pleasant article from the Sun; please send it back.

As for my own police work, we have the force at a very high point of efficiency, and we gave the city the most honest and orderly election it has ever had. I have done nearly all I can do with the police under the present law; and now I should rather welcome being legislated out of office. So I can await events with an equal heart.

Love to Will. I am having a delightful three days at Sagamore with Edith and the children.

Yours always

December 4, 1896. New York
To Henry Cabot Lodge

Dear Cabot:

I need hardly say with what intense interest I read your letter. I am delighted at what you say about McKinley. I do hope he will take a strong stand both about Hawaii and Cuba. I do not think a war with Spain would be serious enough to cause much strain on the country, or much interruption to the revival of prosperity; but I certainly wish the matter could be settled this winter. Nothing could be better than the attitude you describe him as having on the tariff, and on civil service reform.

Now, old man, as to what you say about myself, I shall not try to express any gratitude, for I don't suppose that between you and me it is necessary for me to say what I feel. Of course I have no preconceived policy of any kind which I wish to push through, and I think he would find that I would not be in any way a marplot or agitator; but I really look upon the matter with philosophical equanimity. The main reason why I would care to go to Washington is to be near you. If you were not in Washington, I should certainly prefer to stay here, even under the present unsatisfactory law, and I am so absorbed in this work that I would not leave it if I had the proper power, or if I did not feel that I had about come to the end of what I could accomplish that was worth accomplishing. Rather to my amusement today General Wilson—"Cavalry" Wilson, of Delaware—turned up, and I lunched with him and Charles A. Dana. Wilson had been writing to me hoping to have me made Secretary of the Navy. I told him that was all nonsense, and he then earnestly begged me *not* to take the Assistant Secretaryship. I did not say anything to him, because I thought it better not. Dana evidently did not share his views, but wanted me to call on Platt, and see if I could not get him to give us proper police legislation. Of course I did not give either of them a hint that you or anyone else had approached McKinley (Storer has just written me that he went to see him, and evidently Mrs. Storer spoke to him about me at that time).

I wish I could call on Platt and see Governor Black. I have nothing to ask for myself, but I would like them not to do anything, or permit the legislature to do anything, which will damage the Republican Party. I wonder if Platt would misinterpret my calling on him? What do you think?

Now old fellow! you must not mind in the least if McKinley does not offer it to me. I think Storer will write him, but I don't suppose there is anyone else that would, and I hate to ask anyone to, for I don't like to appear in the position of a supplicant—for I am not a supplicant. I think I could do honorable work as Assistant Secretary. If I am not offered it, then I shall try to do honorable work here as long as I can, and then I shall turn to any work that comes up.

Give my best love to Nannie and Bay.

Always yours

January 2, 1897. Oyster Bay
To Anna Roosevelt Cowles

Darling Bye,

On Xmas the ever-delightful Captain Stoots arrived, looking like a queer sea-growth from among his own clams, and sent in an envelope with the outside "merry Xmas" and inside, his bill!

I am a quietly rampant "Cuba Libre" man. I doubt whether the Cubans would do very well in the line of self-government; but anything would be better than continuance of Spanish rule. I believe that Cleveland ought now to recognize Cuba's independence and interfere; sending our fleet promptly to Havanna. There would not in my opinion be very serious fighting; and what loss we encountered would be thrice over repaid by the ultimate results of our action.

Xmas week here was lovely; heavy snow, bright, cold weather, and out of door sport from morning to night. It is now mild, with everything thawing. We can go up and down both the front and back roads, and wheels are supplanting runners. Ted and I yesterday found we could no longer use skis, and have gone back to chopping. I hate to leave the country; but for the next two or three months it will be better for me to be in town, because of my work. In the Police Department we make progress at the cost of the same ceaseless worry and interminable wrangling. I shall have about five million things to talk over with you and Will when I see you.

Yours always

March 8, 1897. New York
To Henry White

My dear White:

You are very good to have written me. In view of John Hay's selection, I hope I may regard your matter as settled; at least it seems perfectly incredible to me that there should be any other possible solution than your reappointment.

As for myself, I have been so absorbed in the fight here that I have had little time to think of my chances of Assistant Secretary of the Navy; and during the last month or so, I have become convinced that they are very small, because neither the Platt nor the anti-Platt people of New York feel that I am a useful ally, and in this feeling they are quite right. I know they have industriously sought to persuade the President and Secretary Long that I would be headstrong, impractical and insubordinate. As a matter of fact, were I appointed, the very qualities that have made me insist on the obedience of my subordinates, would also render me prompt in carrying out the policy of my superior officer. It ought not to be necessary to say that I would take the position understanding thoroughly that I was there, not to carry out my own course, but to help to the best of my ability Secretary Long to carry out his, and to make his administration a success, and this I should certainly try to do.

However, as I said, the intolerable nature of the situation here has completely absorbed my attention. I rather think that Grant and Parker have been partly acting under orders with a view to giving the machine an excuse for passing a bill to legislate us out, and thereby getting control of the patronage. I do not mind an open fight, but with two such men as colleagues, the struggle lacks all of the exhilaration of actual combat. It is like watching somebody to see that he does not put poison in your coffee.

Lodge is not only my dearest friend, but is also the most faithful and loyal man I have ever known. I am deeply touched by what he is doing.

Give my warm regards to Mrs. White; Mrs. Roosevelt and I hated not having had a chance to see you both.

Always faithfully yours

March 23, 1897. New York
To Henry Cabot Lodge

Dear Cabot:

Just a line to tell you that the machine people here evidently have it in their heads that I am to be made Assistant Secretary of the Navy, and evidently approve of it as a means of getting me out of New York. I rather wonder whether some of what Platt told Doty and Olcott was not merely said with the hope of making me give him something in connection with this office, or else to establish a ground for holding off, so as to get something for the Administration.

Always yours

P.S. Harry White has just turned up: and he was really touching in describing how you have worked for me. There is nothing I can say except that I am well aware of it, old man.

April 11, 1897. New York
To Anna Roosevelt Cowles

Darling Bye,

This is probably the last letter I shall write you; and your cable, which it was so sweet of you to send, shows that you know the news. I was even more pleased than I was astonished at the appointment; for I had come to look upon it as very improbable. McKinley rather distrusted me, and Platt actively hated me; it was Cabot's untiring energy and devotion which put me in; and Long really wanted me. Of course until next Wednesday the Senate, where I have very bitter enemies, may reconsider the confirmation; but there is only a very small chance of this.

One crumpled rose leaf is that it is going to prevent my meeting you. On May 1st and just around it, there will be so much to do that it would be wrong for me at once to bolt away from Sec'y Long. I hate not meeting you, Bye; it is only the sheer impossibility that prevents me.

Now the Lodges and we ourselves are hoping you'll live at Washington next winter!

Will is off on the Fern, and has just written me an enthusiastic letter of congratulation. He is such a good fellow! The children adopted him at once in the most matter-of-course manner.

Yours always

April 18, 1897. New York
To Jacob Riis

Dear Mr. Riis,

I shall always keep your letter, to show to my children, as that of the most loyal and disinterested man I ever knew; and I can not tell you highly I prize what you say of me. For these two years you have been my main prop and comfort. May the Unseen and Unknown Powers be ever with you and yours!

Give our love to Mrs. Riis; and let me hear from you now and then, if only to tell me how your boy likes the west.

Faithfully yours

April 26, 1897. Washington
To William McKinley

To the President:

It seems to me inadvisable to send a battleship to the Mediterranean unless we intend to make a demonstration in force, in which case we should send certainly three or four armored vessels, and not one. At the moment the only 1st-class battleship which could be sent to the Mediterranean is the *Indiana,* and as she rolls heavily in a sea-way it would not be advisable to send her, unless absolutely necessary, until she has bilge keels fitted. The *Massachusetts* is having them fitted. She will be ready in June. The *Iowa* could be pressed into the service at that date were there an emergency. The armored cruiser *Brooklyn* could be sent off now, but she will not be in entirely good shape until about the first of June. The 2nd-class battleship *Texas* needs repairs, and should not be sent from our coast unless necessary. The *Maine* is only a 2nd-class battleship. If any additional ships are sent to the Mediterranean, therefore, I should advise that they be either *New York* or the *Columbia.* The *Columbia* was to have been laid up. She is the one of our cruisers that could best be spared. The *New York* is a powerful armored cruiser, although less powerful than the *Brooklyn,* but unless we intend to send a formidable fighting squadron to Turkish waters the *Columbia* could do about as much as the *New York* in the way of protecting the missionaries, and keeping in check mob outbreaks; while to fight the Turks, even if such a plan were entertained, it would be useless to send out less than a formidable squadron.

If there is need of another cruiser in the Mediterranean I should suggest either that the *Columbia* be sent there, and not laid up, or that the *Brooklyn,* after going to the Queen's jubilee, be sent there.

We should keep the battleships on our own coast, and in readiness for action should any complications arise in Cuba. The *Massachusetts* will have her bilge keels and be all ready early in June. The *Indiana* should then be put in dock and have bilge keels fitted. The *Texas* also needs various repairs. The *Maine* is in good condition. The *New York* is in good condition. Neither of them is fit to oppose a 1st-class battleship such as the Spanish *Pelayo*. The *Iowa* will be in commission early in June, but it will probably take a month before all her weak points are discovered and remedied, even after she has gone into commission.

In other words if the *Columbia* or *Brooklyn,* or both of them, are sent to the eastern Mediterranean we should have on our shores available for action in the event of trouble in Cuba, three 1st-class battleships, the *Massachusetts, Indiana* and *Iowa,* two 2nd-class battleships, the *Texas* and *Maine,* and one armored cruiser, the *New York.* After June I, the *Massachusetts, Maine* and *New York* will be available at any time. The *Indiana* will he in dock having her bilge keels fitted. This would probably mean that she would not be available until early in August. The *Texas* also needs repairs, although such repairs would probably not keep her as long, but at present she is not in trustworthy shape. The *Iowa* could be used at once, but until a month was past would be liable to break down on one point or another. It does not seem to me that we could afford to lay up any of these ships. Even docking and repairing them as needed would make it impossible to call upon more than four at twenty-four hours' notice, and all these four would certainly be useful in the event of any trouble over Cuba. We could not afford to do with less, and we should have to do with less if any one of the armored battleships or cruisers were laid up.

In addition to the above we have the four monitors, of which three, the *Amphitrite,* the *Terror* and the *Puritan,* are in commission, and even if laid up could be made ready very soon. The *Miantonomoh* is now at League Island, and probably it would be a month before she could be put in fighting trim. If these monitors are laid up it is probable that until by actual test, and the scheme perfected it would mean at least three weeks before they could be put in commission, and in consequence they would not be available for any sudden crisis.

In other words if the *Brooklyn* is allowed to go to the eastern Mediterranean we shall have on the coast available for any crisis in Cuba four armored vessels instantly ready. There would be four more which could be turned in, in say three weeks, and two which might need a longer time. Should, however, there be warning given in advance the entire ten could be ready at any time during the summer.

Very respectfully

P. S. The *Cincinnati,* though under orders to return when relieved by tile *Raleigh,* could be detained on the station if necessary.

April 26, 1897. Washington
To John D. Long

My dear Mr. Secretary:

I was much pleased at receiving your note this morning. All right, I will look into the matter at once and give you the results of my investigation, to aid you in your decision when you come on.

I went on to New York after finishing my morning's work on Saturday and came back yesterday afternoon, and I wasn't easy a single hour I was away, and never again shall I leave this city when you are not here, unless you expressly order me to. I told Mrs. Roosevelt that I guessed I should have to give up even the thing I care for most—seeing her and the children at all until next fall when they come on here; this because I don't wish again to be away when there is the slightest chance that anything may turn up.

By the way, remember that I don't need any thirty or even twenty days' holiday.

I shall have made out against your and the President's return a full list of the ships which are now available to be sent to the East, and what one or two could be sent, which would be a formidable force, and yet leave a force which would be available at twenty-four hours' notice in the event of things in Cuba taking an unexpected turn. I do this in obedience to a request made to me by the President this morning.

Very sincerely yours

April 28, 1897. Washington
To Hermann Speck von Sternberg

My dear Sternberg:

Yesterday, to my great concern, I learned for the first time, through Miss Pauncefote, of your sickness. I am very sorry indeed, but am glad to hear that the latest news was that you were getting better. I only wish you would come over here for your health. I am sure you know how warmly your American friends would greet you.

Two or three months ago I sent you a letter containing a report by Sergeant Petty of the pistol practice with the new police revolver. I am afraid you may not have gotten it, as I fear you had left your post on account of your sickness before the letter got over there.

As you see, I am now back in Washington, as Assistant Secretary of the Navy. I had done about all I could do with the New York Police Force, and as you know I am immensely interested in the Navy. I earnestly wish I could see you and have a long talk over various matters, especially about your new battleships. I don't know whether your quick-fire guns are behind armor or not. Personally, I regret that in our latest ships we have discarded the 8-inch guns. I see you have reduced the calibres of your large guns on the 1st-class battleships. I suppose the fact of it is that only the final test of war will really settle the comparative merits of the different types, and even then we shall have to make allowance for the comparative merits of the men who handle the different types. No perfection of material will atone for shortcomings in the personnel.

I am now staying with Senator Lodge. Spring here in Washington is as beautiful as ever. I only wish you were here to take a run through the country.

Faithfully yours

May 3, 1897. Washington
To Alfred Thayer Mahan

Personal and Private

My dear Captain Mahan:

This letter must, of course, be considered as entirely confidential, because in my position I am merely carrying out the policy of the Secretary and the President. I suppose I need not tell you that as regards Hawaii I take your views absolutely, as indeed I do on foreign policy generally. If I had my way we would annex those islands tomorrow. If that is impossible I would establish a protectorate over them. I believe we should build the Nicaraguan canal at once, and in the meantime that we should build a dozen new battleships, half of them on the Pacific Coast; and these battleships should have large coal capacity and a consequent increased radius of action. I am fully alive to the danger from Japan, and I know that it is idle to rely on any sentimental good will towards us. I think President Cleveland's action was a colossal crime, and we should be guilty of aiding him after the fact if we do not reverse what he did. I earnestly hope we can make the President look at things our way. Last Saturday night Lodge pressed his views upon him with all his strength. I have been getting matters in shape on the Pacific coast just as fast as I have been allowed. My own belief is that we should act instantly before the two new Japanese warships leave England. I would send the *Oregon*, and, if necessary, also the *Monterey* (either with a deck load of coal or accompanied by a coaling ship) to Hawaii, and would hoist our flag over the island, leaving all details for after action. I shall press these views upon my chief just so far as he will let me; more I cannot do.

As regards what you say in your letter, there is only one point to which I would take exception. I fully realize the immense importance of the Pacific coast. Strictly between ourselves, I do not think Admiral

Beardslee quite the man for the situation out there, but Captain Barker, of the *Oregon*, is, I believe, excellent in point of decisions, willingness to accept responsibility, and thorough knowledge of the situation. But there are big problems in the West Indies also. Until we definitely turn Spain out of those islands (and if I had my way that would be done tomorrow), we will always be menaced by trouble there. We should acquire the Danish Islands, and by turning Spain out should serve notice that no strong European power, and especially not Germany, should be allowed to gain a foothold by supplanting some weak European power. I do not fear England; Canada, is a hostage for her good behavior; but I do fear some of the other powers. I am extremely sorry to say that there is some slight appearance here of the desire to stop building up the Navy until our finances are better. Tom Reed, to my astonishment and indignation, takes this view, and even my chief, who is one of the most high-minded, honorable and upright gentlemen I have ever had the good fortune to serve under, is a little inclined toward it.

I need not say that this letter must be strictly private. I speak to you with the greatest freedom, for I sympathize with your views, and I have precisely, the same idea of patriotism, and of belief in and love for our country. But to no one else excepting Lodge do I talk like this.

As regards Hawaii I am delighted to be able to tell you that Secretary Long shares our views. He believes we should take the islands, and I have just been preparing some memoranda for him to use at the Cabinet meeting tomorrow. If only we had some good man in the place of John Sherman as Secretary of State there would not be a hitch, and even as it is I hope for favorable action. I have been pressing upon the Secretary, and through him on the President, that we ought to act now without delay, before Japan gets her two new battleships which are now ready for delivery to her in England. Even a fortnight may make a difference. With Hawaii once in our hands most of the danger of friction with Japan would disappear.

The Secretary also believes in building the Nicaraguan canal as a military measure, although I don't know that he is as decided on this point as you and I are; and he believes in building battleships on the Pacific slope.

Faithfully yours

**May 3, 1897. Washington
To John Hay**

My dear Mr. Ambassador:

Even without your letter I should have done, and as a matter of fact did, all I could for Paul Dashiell, but I am sorry to say I failed. He is just the man who should have been given the position. He puts ginger into those boys in every way, morally, mentally and physically, and I fought for him as hard as I knew how; but the President and Secretary Long thought there should be an astronomer in the place, and all that I could say amounted to nothing. I am very sorry. I have been battling for Rockhill also.

We have been watching your doings in the papers with great interest. The Delaware Lorelei seems to have kept up his zeal to the very end, albeit his voice grew a trifle raucous. I see that, with a splendid lack of sense of the fitness of things, he kept a tight grip on the log of the *Mayflower*. Really his conduct has been most extraordinary. However, it is a fitting climax to his career as Ambassador, after all.

I am glad to hear you had such a pleasant voyage. I feel dreadfully blue over the way Washington is deserted. To have you and Mrs. Cameron and Herodotus Adams,[1] and the Endicotts and the Rockhills all going, is pretty melancholy. I am staying with the Lodges, and Mistress Nannie is as charming as I have ever seen her, and in excellent spirits. She has had great fun recently with the amiable Walter Berry, whom we have christened "the ball of worsted," because he is such a nice thing for a kitten to play with. The suggestion implied in the name made Cabot a little suspicious at first, but not for long, as he now rates the good Walter at his proper level of harmlessness. P. S. This should be merely for family information.

I lunch almost every day with Adams not Herodotus.[2] He is having a delightful time here, and simply revelling in gloom over the appalling social and civic disasters which he sees impending.

I was of course astonished at the engagement between Chandler Hale and Rachel Cameron.

Remember me warmly to Mrs. Hay and all of my friends. I must close, as I am expecting Cabot for a walk, and Cabot is not a man who has patience with such a trifling detail as correspondence when the time has come for exercise.

Faithfully yours

May 18, 1897. Washington
To Henry F. Osborn

Sir:

I have been greatly interested in Dr. Merriam's article as to discriminating between species and subspecies. With his main thesis I entirely

---

[1]Brooks Adams.
[2]Henry Adams.

agree. I think that the word "species" should express degree of differentiation rather than intergradation. I am not quite at one with Dr. Merriam, however, on the question as to how great the degree of differentiation should be in order to establish specific rank. I understand entirely that in some groups the species may be far more closely related than in others; and I suppose I may as well confess that I have certain conservative instincts which are jarred when an old familiar friend is suddenly cut up into eleven brand new acquaintances. I think he misunderstands my position, however, when he says, "Why should we try to unite different species under common names?" He here assumes, just as if he were a naturalist of eighty years ago, that a "species" is always something different by its very nature from all other species; whereas the facts are that species, according to his own showing in the beginning of his article, are merely more or less arbitrary divisions, established for convenience's sake by ourselves, between one form and its ancestral and related forms.

I believe that with fuller material Dr. Merriam could go on creating new "species" in groups like the bears, wolves and coyotes until he would himself find that he would have to begin to group them together after the manner of the abhorred "Campers." His tendency to discover a new species is shown by the allusion in the last part of his article to the "unknown form of wapiti" which has been exterminated from the Allegheny country. The wapiti was formerly found in the Allegheny regions; there it was beyond a doubt essentially the same animal that is now found in the Rockies. Probably it agreed more closely with the wapiti of Minnesota, which still here and there survives, than the latter does with those of Oregon. It may have been slightly different, just as very possibly a minute study of wapiti from the far South, the far North, the dry plains, the high mountains, and the wet Pacific forests might show that there were a number of what Dr. Merriam would call "species" of wapiti. If this showing were made, the fact would be very interesting and important; but I think it would be merely cumbrous to lumber up our zoological works by giving names to all as "new species." It is not the minor differences among wapiti, but their essential likenesses, that is important.

So with the wolves. Dr. Merriam has shown that there are different forms of wolf and coyote in many different parts of the country. When he gets a fuller collection I am quite sure he will find, a still larger number of differences and he can add to the already extensive assortment of new species. Now, as I have said before, it is a very important and useful work to show that these differences exist, but I think it is only a darkening of wisdom to insist upon treating them all as a new species. Among ordinary American bipeds, the Kentuckian, the New Englander of the sea coast, the Oregonian, the Arizonian, all have characteristics which separate them quite as markedly from one another as some of Dr. Merriam's bears and coyotes are separated; I should just as soon think of establishing a species in the one case as in the other.

Some of the big wolves and some of the coyotes which Dr. Merriam describes may be entitled to specific rank, but if he bases separate species upon characters no more important than those he employs, I firmly believe that he will find that with every new locality which his collectors visit, he will get new "species," until he has a snarl of forty or fifty for North America alone; and when we have reached such a point we had much better rearrange our terminology, if we intend to keep the binomial system at all, and treat as a genus what we have been used to consider as a species. It would be more convenient and less cumbersome; and it would be no more misleading.

Dr. Merriam states that the coyotes do not essentially resemble each other, or essentially differ from the wolves. It seems to me, however, that he does, himself, admit their essential difference from the wolves by the fact that he treats them all together even when he splits them up into three supra-specific groups and eight to eleven species. He goes on to say that there is an enormous gap between the large northern coyote and the small southern coyote of the Rio Grande, and another great gap between the big gray wolf of the north and the big red wolf of the south, while the northern coyote and the southern wolf approach one another. Now I happen to have hunted over the habitats of the four animals in question. I have shot and poisoned them, and hunted them with dogs, and noticed their ways of life. In each case the animal decreases greatly in size, according to its habitat, so that in each case we have a pair of wolves, one big and one small, which, as they go south, keep relatively as far apart as ever, the one from the other. At any part of their habitat they remain entirely distinct; but as they grow smaller toward the south a point is of course reached when the southern representative of the big wolf begins to approach the northern representative of the small wolf. In voice and habits the differences remain the same. As they grow smaller they of course grow less formidable. The northern wolf will hamstring a horse, the southern carry off a sheep; the northern coyote will tackle a sheep, when the southern will only rob a hen-roost. In each place the two animals have two different voices, and as far as I could tell, the voices were not much changed from north to south. Now, it seems to me that in using a term of convenience, which is all that the term species is, it is more convenient and essentially more true to speak of this pair of varying animals as wolf and coyote rather than by a score of different names which serve to indicate a score of different sets of rather minute characteristics.

Once again let me point out that I have no quarrel with Dr. Merriam's facts, but only with the names by which he thinks these facts can best be expressed and emphasized. Wolves and coyotes, grizzly bears and black bears, split up into all kinds of forms; and I well know how difficult it will be, and how much time and study will be needed, to group all these various forms naturally and properly into two or three or more species. Only a man of Dr. Merriam's remarkable knowledge and attainments and ability can ever make such groupings. But I think he will do his work, if not in better shape, at least in a manner which will make it more readily understood by outsiders, if he proceeds on the theory that he is going to try to establish different species only when there are real fundamental differences, instead of cumbering up the books with hundreds of specific titles which will always be meaningless to any but a limited number of technical experts, and which, even to them, will often serve chiefly to obscure the relationships of the different animals by overemphasis on minute points of variation. It is not a good thing to let the houses obscure the city.

May 28, 1897. Washington
To Caspar Goodrich

My dear Captain Goodrich:

Your letter of the 22nd instant to the Secretary was referred to me to think up a special problem for the Staff and Class at the War College. I enclose one which will, I think, be of interest and importance in certain contingencies.

Very sincerely yours

Special Confidential Problem for War College:

Japan makes demands on Hawaiian Islands.

This country intervenes.

What force will be necessary to uphold the intervention, and how shall it be employed?

Keeping in mind possible complication with another Power on the Atlantic Coast (Cuba).

May 29, 1897. Washington
To Cecil Spring Rice

Dear Cecil:

Your letter made amends for all your silence.

First, as to myself and my belongings. I have been a month in office now, and I heartily enjoy the work. I was very sorry to leave the New York Police Force for some reasons, because it was such eminently practical work, and I very strongly feel that if there is going to be any solution of the big social problems of the day, it will come, not through a vague sentimental philanthropy, and still less through a sentimental parlor socialism, but through actually taking hold of what is to be done and working, right in the mire. We have got to take hold of the very things which give Tammany its success, and show ourselves just as efficient as Tammany; only, efficient for decency. During my two years on the Police Force I felt I accomplished a substantial amount of good. It was nothing like what I would have liked to accomplish, but it was something, after all. However, I came to about the end of what I could do, and this was an opening for four years at something in which I was extremely interested, and in which I believe with all my heart. I think that in this country especially we want to encourage, so far as we can, the fighting virtues, and it is a relief to be dealing with men who are simple and straightforward, and want to do well, and strive more or less successfully to live up to an honorable ideal. There is a great deal of work to be done here, and though my position is of course an entirely subordinate one, still I can accomplish something. I have been busy enough so far, for the Secretary, who is a delightful man to work under, has been sending me around to various navy yards, and during the hot weather I am expecting to stay here steadily.

By the way, I have just sent Laird Clowes my contribution to his history of the British Navy. It deals with the War of 1812. Mahan does the Revolutionary War for him. I don't suppose my part will be out for a year.

For the last five weeks I have been staying with the dear Lodges, as my house won't be ready until June, and my family are not coming on until the fall. The Lodges are just the same as ever, but Mrs. Lodge is very much depressed at the moment because poor Willie Phillips was drowned two weeks ago. You know him a little when you were here. He was a man of whom we became steadily fonder and fonder, and I hardly know any one who would have left so real a gap in so many households. Mrs. Roosevelt always used to say that he and you were the two guests whom she would like to have stay any length of time at her house.

Mrs. Roosevelt herself is well. I have never seen her so well as she was this winter, in looks, in health, in spirits and everything. Alice is taller than she is now, and has become a very sweet girl indeed. Ted is an excessively active and normally grimy small boy of nine. He is devoted to Kipling's stories and poems, and has learned to swim, ride and chop quite well. He and Kermit go to the Cove School, where they are taught by the daughter of Captain Nelse Hawkshurst, one of the old-time baymen. Ethel is a cunning, chubby, sturdy little thing of five, and

Archie is just three, and is treated by the entire family as a play-toy. I can't say much for either his temper or his intelligence; but he is very bright and cunning, and we love him dearly. The one thing I mind about this place is being absent from my wife and children and my lovely home at Sagamore.

Poor little Speck! The day after I received your letter I got one from him, a pathetic, wooden letter, just like the little man himself. I am awfully sorry about it.

What you say about Brooks Adams' book[1] is essentially true. I would have written my review very much more brutally than I did, but really I think the trouble is largely that his mind is a little unhinged. All his thoughts show extraordinary intellectual and literary dishonesty; but I don't think it is due to moral shortcomings. I think it really is the fact that he isn't quite straight in his head. For Heaven's sake don't quote this, as I am very fond of all the family. His fundamental thesis is absolutely false. Indeed, the great majority of the facts from which he draws his false deductions are themselves false. Like the Roman Empire in the Second Century—like the Greek dominions in the Third Century before Christ—our civilization shows very unhealthy symptoms; but they are entirely different symptoms, and the conditions are not only different, but in many important respects directly opposite to those which formerly obtained. There seems good ground for believing that France is decadent. In France, as in the later Roman world, population is decreasing, and there is gross sensuality and licentiousness. France is following Spain in her downward course, and yet from entirely different causes, and along an entirely different path of descent. The bulk of the French people exist under economic conditions the direct reverse of those which obtained in Rome, for in France the country is held by an immense class of small, peasant propriexors instead of being divided among the great slave-tilled farms of later Rome; and in France there is no such tendency to abnormal city growth as in the English-speaking countries.

I quite agree with you that the main cause of Rome's fall was a failure of population which was accompanied by a change in the population itself, caused by the immense importation of slaves, usually of inferior races. Our civilization is far more widely extended than the early civilizations, and in consequence, there is much less chance for evil tendencies to work universally through all its parts. The evils which afflict Russia are not the same as those which afflict Australia. There are very unhealthy sides to the concentration of power, at least of a certain kind

---

[1]*The Law of Civilization and Decay.*

of power, in the hands of the great capitalists; but in our country at any rate, I am convinced that there is no real oppression of the mass of the people by these capitalists. The condition of the workman and the man of small means has been improved. The diminishing rate of increase of the population is of course the feature fraught with most evil. In New England and France the population is decreasing; in Germany, England and the Southern United States it is increasing much less fast than formerly. Probably some time in the Twentieth Century the English-speaking peoples will become stationary, whereas the Slavs as yet show no signs of this tendency, and though they may show it, and doubtless will in the next century, it certainly seems as if they would beat us in the warfare of the cradle. However, there are still great waste spaces which the English speaking peoples undoubtedly have the vigor to till. America north of the Rio Grande, and Australia, and perhaps Africa south of the Zambesi, all possess a comparatively dense civilized population, English in law, tongue, government and culture, and with English the dominant strain in the blood. When the population becomes stationary I shall myself feel that evil days are probably at hand; but we need to remember that extreme fecundity does not itself imply any quality of social greatness. For several centuries the South Italians have been the most fecund and the least desirable population of Europe.

It certainly is extraordinary that just at this time there seems to be a gradual failure of vitality in the qualities, whatever they may be, that make men fight well and write well. I have a very uneasy feeling that this may mean some permanent deterioration. On the other hand, it may be merely a phase through which we are passing. There certainly have been long stretches of time prior to this when both writers and fighters have been few in number. The forty years following the close of the first decade of the Eighteenth Century is a case in point.

Proctor, whom you remember, sends you his regards. He is listening to me as I dictate these closing sentences. He is a confirmed optimist. I am not quite so much of a one, but I am not a pessimist by any means.

Always yours

June 9, 1897. Washington
To Alfred Thayer Mahan

Personal

My dear Mahan:

I have shown that very remarkable letter to the Secretary. Yesterday I urged immediate action by the President as regards Hawaii. Entirely between ourselves, I believe he will act very shortly. If we take Hawaii now, we shall avoid trouble with Japan, but I get very despondent at times over the blindness of our people, especially of the best-educated classes.

In strict confidence I want to tell you that Secretary Long is only lukewarm about building up our Navy, at any rate as regards battleships. Indeed, he is against adding to our battleships. This is, to me, a matter of the most profound concern. I feel that you ought to write to him—not immediately, but sometime not far in the future—at some length, explaining to him the vital need of more battleships now, and the vital need of continuity in our naval policy. Make the plea that this is a measure of peace and not of war. I cannot but think your words would carry weight with him.

He didn't like the address I made to the War College at Newport the other day. I shall send it to you when I get a copy.

I do not congratulate you upon the extraordinary compliment paid you by the Japanese, only because I know you care more for what we are doing with the Navy than for any compliment.

Sincerely yours

June 11, 1897. Washington
To Franklin Delano Roosevelt

Dear Franklin:

We shall be very glad to see you at Sagamore Hill on either the 2d or 3d of July, for as long as you can stay. One train leaves Long Island City for Oyster Bay (our station) at 11 o'clock, and another at 2. You take the East Thirty-fourth Street Ferry about 15 minutes earlier. Let us know the day before which train you are coming on.

Sincerely yours

August 13, 1897. Washington
To Cecil Spring Rice

Dear Cecil:

Your letter was very interesting. I find the typewriter a comfort, and indeed when I have to carry on so much official correspondence it is the only way I have to write at all at length. I don't know whether I sent you a copy of my address at Newport, so I send one to you now. I don't think that even you can complain of the way I speak of England, and with a change of names it seems to me to be just the kind of doctrine that you preach to your people. I am very certain that both of our peoples need to have this kind of view impressed upon them.

I have not seen Bay. If he has sufficiently recovered from the Brooks

Adams influence to be rational I should much like to talk with him, for he is an able young fellow.

You happen to have a mind which is interested in precisely the things which interest me, and which I believe are of more vital consequence than any other to the future of the race and of the world; so naturally I am delighted to hear from you, and I always want to answer your letters at length.

Did I tell you that I met such a nice Englishman here, named Spencer Walpole? He also is interested in the same problems.

In a couple of months I shall send you the collection of my essays, simply because I want you to read my reviews of Pearson's book, and of Kidd's *Social Evolution*. I have not heard from Laird Clowes since I sent him my piece on the War of 1812 for his book, so I don't know whether he thought it satisfactory or not. *I* did! or I would not have sent it.

Before speaking of the Russians and of their attitude toward us, a word about the Germans. I am by no means sure that I heartily respect the little Kaiser, but in his colonial plans I think he is entirely right from the standpoint of the German race. International law, and above all interracial law, are still in a fluid condition, and two nations with violently conflicting interests may each be entirely right from its own standpoint. If I were a German I should want the German race to expand. I should be glad to see it begin to expand in the only two places left for the ethnic, as distinguished from the political, expansion of the European peoples; that is, in South Africa and temperate South America. Therefore, as a German I should be delighted to upset the English in South Africa, and to defy the Americans and their Monroe Doctrine in South America. As an Englishman, I should seize the first opportunity to crush the German Navy and the German commercial marine out of existence, and take possession of both the German and Portuguese possessions in South Africa, leaving the Boers absolutely isolated. As an American I should advocate—and as a matter of fact do advocate—keeping our Navy at a pitch that will enable us to interfere promptly if Germany ventures to touch a foot of American soil. I would not go into the abstract rights or wrongs of it; I would simply say that we did not intend to have the Germans on this continent, excepting as immigrants whose children would become Americans of one sort or another, and if Germany intended to extend her empire here she would have to whip us first.

I am by no means sure that either your people or mine have the nerve to follow this course; but I am absolutely sure that it is the proper course to follow, and I should adopt it without in the least feeling that the Germans who advocated German colonial expansion were doing anything save what was right and proper from the standpoint of their own people. Nations may, and often must, have conflicting interests, and in the present age patriotism stands a good deal ahead of cosmopolitanism.

Now, the reason why I don't think so much of the Kaiser is that it seems to me Germany ought not to try to expand colonially at our expense when she has Russia against her flank and year by year increasing in relative power. Of course if Germany has definitely adopted the views which some of the Greek States, like the Achaean League, adopted toward Rome after the second Punic War, I have nothing to say. These Greek States made up their mind that Rome had the future and could not be striven against, but they decided to take advantage of whatever breathing space was given them by warring on any power which Rome did not choose to befriend, hoping that Rome might perhaps spare them, and that meanwhile they would stand high compared to all the States but Rome. If Germany feels this way toward Russia, well and good; but if she does not feel this way, then every year she waits to strike is just so much against her. If the Kaiser were a Frederick the Great or a Gustavus Adolphus; if he were a Cromwell, a Pitt, or, like Andrew Jackson, had the "instinct for the jugular," he would recognize his real foe and strike savagely at the point where danger threatens.

A few years ago Germany could certainly have whipped Russia, even if, in conjunction with Austria and Italy, she had had to master France also. Of course it would be useless to whip her without trying to make the whipping possibly permanent by building up a great Polish buffer State, making Finland independent or Swedish, taking the Baltic Provinces, etc. *This* would have been something worth doing; but to run about imprisoning private citizens of all ages who do not speak of "Majesty" with bated breath seems to me foolish, at this period of the world's progress. That the Germans should dislike and look down upon the Americans is natural. Americans don't dislike the Germans, but so far as they think of them at all they look upon them with humorous contempt. The English-speaking races may or may not be growing effete, and may or may not ultimately succumb to the Slav; but whatever may happen in any single war they will not ultimately succumb to the German, and a century hence he will be of very small consequence compared to them.

Of course the Kaiser objects to liberalism in his country. Liberalism has some great vices, and the virtues which in our opinion outweigh these vices might not be of weight in Germany.

Now, about the Russians, who offer a very much more serious problem than the Germans, if not to our generation, at least to the generations which will succeed us. Russia and the United States are friendly, but Russians and Americans, in their individual capacity, have nothing whatever in common. That they despise Americans in a way is doubtless true. I rather doubt if they despise Europeans. Socially, the upper classes feel themselves akin to the other European upper classes, while they have no one to feel akin to in America. Our political corruption certainly cannot shock them, but our political institutions they doubtless both despise and fear. As for our attitude toward them, I don't quite take your view, which seems to be, after all, merely a reflection of theirs. Evidently you look upon them as they think they should be looked upon—that is as huge, powerful barbarians, cynically confident that they will in the end inherit the fruits of our civilization, firmly believing that the future belongs to them, and resolute to develop their own form of government, literature and art; despising as effete all of Europe and especially America. I look upon them as a people to whom we can give points, and a beating; a people with a great future, as we have; but a people with poisons working in it, as other poisons, of similar character on the whole, work in us.

Well, there is a certain justification for your view, but the people who have least to fear from the Russians are the people who can speak English. They may overrun the continent of Europe, but they cannot touch your people or mine, unless perhaps in India. There is no such difference between them and us as there was between the Goths and Byzantines; it will be many a long year before we lose our capacity to lay out those Goths. They are below the Germans just as the Germans are below us; the space beween the German and the Russian may be greater than that between the Englishman and the German, but that is all. We are all treading the same path, some faster, some slower; and though the Russian started far behind, yet he has traveled that path very much farther and faster since the days of Ivan the Terrible than our people have traveled it since the days of Elizabeth. He is several centuries behind us still, but he was a thousand years behind us then. He may develop his own art and his own literature, but most assuredly they will be developed on European models and along European lines, and they will differ from those of other European nations no more than Macaulay and Turner differ from Ariosto and Botticelli—nor will his government escape the same fate. While he can keep absolutism, no matter how corrupt, he will himself possess infinite possibilities of menace to his neighbors; but as sure as fate, in the end, when Russia becomes more thickly populated, when Siberia fills with cities and settled districts, the problems which in different forms exist in the free republic of the United States, the free monarchy of England, the free commonwealths of Australia, the unfree monarchy of Prussia, the unfree

Republic of France and the heterogeneous empire of Austria, will also have to be faced by the Russian. The nihilist is the socialist or communist in an aggravated form. He makes but a small class; he may temporarily disappear; but his principles will slowly spread. If Russia chooses to develop purely on her own line and to resist the growth of liberalism, then she may put off the day of reckoning; but she cannot ultimately avert it, and instead of occasionally having to go through what Kansas has gone through with the populists she will sometime experience a red terror which will make the French Revolution pale. Meanwhile one curious fact is forgotten: The English-speaking people have never gone back before the Slav, and the Slav has never gone back before them save once. Three-quarters of a century ago the Russians meant that Northwestern America should be Russian, and our Monroe Doctrine was formulated as much against them as against the other reactionaries of continental Europe. Now the American has dispossessed the Russian. Thirty years ago there were thirty thousand people speaking more or less Russian in Alaska. Now there are but a few hundreds. The American—the man of the effete English-speaking races—has driven the Slav from the eastern coast of the North Pacific.

What the Russian thinks of us—or indeed what any European thinks of us—is of small consequence. What we are is of great consequence; and I wish I could answer you with confidence. Sometimes I do feel inclined to believe that the Russian is the one man with enough barbarous blood in him to be the hope of a world that is growing effete. But I think that this thought comes only when I am unreasonably dispirited.

The one ugly fact all over the world is the diminution of the birth rate among the highest races. It must be remembered, however, that Ireland has shown conclusively, as Italy still shows, that a very large birth rate may mean nothing whatever for a race; and looking at the English-speaking people I am confident that as yet any decadence is purely local.

The growth of liberalism undoubtedly unfits us for certain work. I don't like the look of things in India for instance. It seems to me the English position there is essentially false, unless they say they are there as masters who intend to rule justly, but who do not intend to have their rule questioned. If the English in India would suppress promptly any native newspaper that was seditious; arrest instantly any seditious agitator; put down the slightest outbreak ruthlessly; cease to protect usurers, and encourage the warlike races so long as they were absolutely devoted to British rule, I believe things would be much more healthy than they are now.

As for my own country, it is hard to say. We are barbarians of a certain kind, and what is most unpleasant we are barbarians with a certain middle-class, Philistine quality of ugliness and pettiness, raw conceit, and raw sensitiveness. Where we get highly civilized, as in the northeast, we seem to become civilized in an unoriginal and ineffective way, and tend to die out. Nevertheless, thanks to the men we adopt, as well as to the children we beget, it must be remembered that actually we keep increasing at about twice the rate of the Russians; and though the commercial and cheap altruistic spirit, the spirit of the Birmingham school, the spirit of the banker, the broker, the mere manufacturer, and mere merchant, is unpleasantly prominent, I cannot see that we have lost vigor compared to what we were a century ago. If anything I think we have gained it. In politicial matters we are often very dull mentally, and especially morally; but even in political matters there is plenty of rude strength and I don't think we are as badly off as we were in the days of Jefferson, for instance. We are certainly better off than we were in the days of Buchanan. During recent years I have a great deal of the New York Police Force, which is a very powerful, efficient and corrupt body, and of our Navy, which is a powerful, efficient and honorable body. I have incidentally seen a great deal of the constructors who build the ships, and the public works, of the civil engineers, the dock builders, the sailors, the workmen in the iron foundries and shipyards. These represent, all told, a very great number of men, and the impression left upon my mind, after intimate association with the hundreds of naval officers, naval constructors, and civil engineers, and the tens of thousands of seamen and mechanics and policemen, is primarily an impression of abounding force, of energy, resolution and decision. These men are not effete, and if you compare the Russians with them (and of course exactly the same thing would be true if you compared the Russians with corresponding Englishmen) I think you would become convinced that the analogy of the Goth and the Byzantine is forced. These men would outbuild, out administer and outfight any Russians you could find from St. Petersburg to Sebastopol or Vladivostock—if that's the way you spell it. I doubt if our Presidents are as effete as the average Czar or Russian minister. I believe our Generals and Admirals are better; and so, with all their hideous faults, our public administrators. Of course both the English and the Americans are less ruthless, and have the disadvantages of civilization. It may be that we are going the way of France, but just at present I doubt it, and I still think that though the people of the English-speaking races may have to divide the future with the Slav, yet they will get rather more than their fair share.

To drop from questions of empire to those of immediate personal interest, I am immensely interested in my work here. I think on the whole I enjoy it rather more than anything I have ever done. It is a cool summer. We have a very nice house just opposite the British Embassy. Mrs. Roosevelt has been spending ten days here furnishing it with fragments fifty or sixty years old from our ancestral houses—said fragments representing the haircloth furniture (or unpolished stone) period of New York semicivilization.

Aside from my work I have been able to do two or three things which gratify me immensely, for I was mainly instrumental in getting Proctor retained as Civil Service Commissioner, and in having Rockhill kept in the diplomatic service as Minister to Greece.

I spent three weeks at Oyster Bay and had a lovely time. Counting my own children and their little cousins, there are now sixteen small Roosevelts there, and one day I took the twelve eldest on a picnic.

Always yours

[Handwritten] P. S. Mrs. Roosevelt sends you her love, and wishes to know whether you would be very good and write out the lovely ballad of "Hurry my Johnny, the jungle's afire" for her? The children are always asking for it.

August 14, 1897. Washington
To James Alfred Roosevelt

Dear Uncle Jim:

I am very much obliged to you. As for the property tax, you know about it as well as I do. I am assessed, however, as much again as the property and buildings cost me and I could not begin to get that amount in open market.

Now, as to my personal tax: That again is put on me much heavier than it used to be in New York, and I adhere to New York as my place of abode, so I shan't pay any in Oyster Bay. I have been voting in New York for the past two years, and that has been my residence. I am very much obliged to you for taking this trouble.

By the way, did you see the photographs of all the children which were taken that day you and I and Emlen were up around the old barn? They seemed to me very good and very funny.

Faithfully yours

August 17, 1897. Washington
To Russell A. Alger

My dear General Alger:

For what I am about to write you I think I should have the backing of my fellow-Harvard man, your son. I should like very much to revive the football games between Annapolis and West Point. I think the Superintendent of Annapolis, and I dare say Colonel Ernst, the Superintendent of West Point, will feel a little shaky because undoubtedly formerly the academic routine was cast to the winds when it came to these matches, and a good deal of disorganization followed. But it seems to me that if we would let Colonel Ernst and Captain Cooper come to an agreement that the match should be played just as either eleven plays outside teams; that no cadet should be permitted to enter or join the training table if he was unsatisfactory in any study or conduct, and should be removed if during the season he becomes unsatisfactory; if they were marked without regard to their places on the team; if no drills, exercises or recitations were omitted to give opportunities for football practice; and if the authorities of both institutions agreed to take measures to prevent any excesses such as betting and the like, and to prevent any manifestations of an improper character—if as I say all this were done—and it certainly could be done without difficulty—then I don't see why it would not be a good thing to have a game this year.

If you think favorably of the idea, will you be willing to write Colonel Ernst about it?

Faithfully yours

August 19, 1897. Washington
To Bellamy Storer

Dear Bellamy:

It was delightful to catch a glimpse of your familiar handwriting, but it makes me a little melancholy to think that you are away from Washington in all probability for the entire time we shall be here, and we shall miss you both all the time; and when I say "we" I mean not only Mrs. Roosevelt and myself, but the children.

I will try to get you that report at once and have it sent out. I do not think there will be any trouble about the matter.

I don't wonder that foreigners should giggle at our having to send our battleship to be docked abroad. It is highly discreditable. I have a board on docks busily at work now; of course dry docks take time. Incidentally it would be quite like our people, having provided us battleships with no dry docks, to now, in a burst of patriotism, provide a lot of dry docks and stop building battleships. Why this nation ever does live at all sometimes seems puzzling.

The Secretary is away, and I am having immense fun running the Navy. I am absorbed in my work. It is delightful to be dealing with matters of real moment and of great interest, and at the same time with men who are not unadulterated scoundrels.

Mrs. Roosevelt spent ten days here getting the house in order. Now she has gone back to a home which possesses the modified happiness compatible with the existence of whooping cough among my infernal children.

Give my love to Mrs. Storer, and with warm regards, I am, as ever, Yours

[Handwritten] P. S. I called on Bishop Keane yesterday; I think I shall have some photos of the children to send you soon.

September 11, 1897. Washington
To Henry Cabot Lodge

Dear Cabot:

Many thanks for sending me the editorial from the *Journal*. By the way, after thinking it over I came to the conclusion you were right, and, before making my piece public, I sent a copy to the President. I didn't ask his approval, because I thought that might look as if I wanted something more than the Secretary's, so I merely sent it to him with a statement that I wished him to see it in advance; and that the words "in my own opinion" had been put in by direction of the Secretary. Apparently it has done good.

I have never enjoyed three days more than my three days with the fleet, and I think I have profited by it. In fact I know I have, for there are a lot of things I am doing now because of what I saw there. I was very fortunate in the weather, which was wonderfully calm. Think of it, on the Atlantic Ocean, out of sight of land, going out to dinner to a battleship in evening dress without an overcoat! I saw for myself the working of the different gear for turning turrets—electric, hydraulic, steam, and pneumatic. I was aboard the *Iowa* and the *Puritan* throughout their practice under service conditions at the targets, and was able to satisfy myself definitely of the great superiority of the battleship as a gun platform. I was on the *New York* during the practice at night with searchlights and rapid fire guns at a drifting target, the location of which was unknown. I saw the maneuvers of the squadron as a whole, and met every captain and went over with him, on the ground, what was needed.

Harry has come back; I shall see him today. We are having a spell of hot weather now, but I don't mind it. When the Secretary will return I haven't the slightest idea. I hope the President gets back next week, as there are a number of things I should like to talk to him about.

With warm love to Nannie.

Yours ever

The London *Morning Post* has an article on me as "a Jingo of the Lodge and Morgan school"; and the *Evening Post* of N. Y. is filled with wrath and contempt at my visiting the squadron because I am a "civilian."

September 15, 1897. Washington
To Henry Cabot Lodge

My dear Cabot:

Murray Crane was in yesterday with a couple of Massachusetts men, whose business I was able to attend to. I then got him to tell me about you and the Senatorship. He says there is absolutely no danger whatever. All he wants is that you and your friends should do nothing, and stay quiet; that there mustn't be the slightest acknowledgment that there is so much as a contest. It must all be taken for granted that your renomination is a matter of course.

The President has returned, and yesterday I went out driving with him. He was very much pleased with your letter to him some little time ago in reference to his civil service order and the course of the administration generally; and laughed heartily when I told him how you had written me at once to send my pamphlet to him before publishing it. He had previously told me that he hadn't had time to read the pamphlet when it came, but seeing how much attention it attracted in the newspapers he had afterwards read every word of it, and was exceedingly glad that I had put it out. Somewhat to my astonishment he also said that I was quite right in my speech to the Naval Militia, in which I mentioned Japan; that it was only the headlines that were wrong; and, in fact, generally expressed great satisfaction with what I had done, especially during the last seven weeks that I have been in charge of the Department. Of course the President is a bit of a jollier, but I think his words did represent a substratum of satisfaction.

He is evidently by no means sure that we shall not have trouble with either Spain or Japan; and, though he wants to avoid both, yet I think he could be depended upon to deal thoroughly and well with any difficulty that arises. I told him that I thought we ought to have some warning in the Navy Department, and that we ought not to be kept ready all the time. We can get ready for any time set us, just as you can get horses ready for any particular time; but you can't keep horses ready minute after minute for 24 hours and have them worth much at the end of the period. I also told him that I would guarantee that the Department would be in the best possible shape that our means would permit when war began; and that, as he knew, I myself would go to the war. He asked me what Mrs. Roosevelt would think of it, and I said that both you and she would regret it, but that this was one case where I would consult neither. He laughed, and said that he would do all he could, and thought he could guarantee that I should have the opportunity I sought if war by any chance arose.

To my great pleasure he also told me that he intended we should go on building up the Navy, with battleships and torpedo boats, and that he did not think the Secretary would recommend anything he (the President) did not approve. Altogether I had a very satisfactory talk.

We have had a very hot spell this month.

As I wrote you, I had three delightful days with the squadron. It was a wonderful and beautiful sight, and did me a lot of good, and the squadron some good.

I lunched with Harry on Sunday, and we then took a long bicycle ride. With best love to Nannie, and all,

Faithfully yours

September 15, 1897. Washington
To Frederic Remington

My dear Remington:

I wish I were with you out among the sage brush, the great brittle cottonwoods, and the sharply-channeled, barren buttes; but I am very glad at any rate to have had you along with the squadron; and I can't help looking upon you as an ally from henceforth on in trying to make the American people see the beauty and the majesty of our ships, and the heroic quality which lurks somewhere in all those who man and handle them.

Be sure to let me know whenever you come anywhere in my neighborhood.

Faithfully yours

September 21, 1897. Washington
To Henry Cabot Lodge

Dear Cabot:

I shall not reply again to the journal. Curiously enough, I did it this time on a hint from the President, who I found to my astonishment had taken the statements about the *Indiana* with entire seriousness and felt much worried, and was correspondingly relieved when I told him that the story was an absolute fake; that the damage done was a dent: at its deepest point an inch and a half in depth, which in a battleship 350 feet long no one but a trained expert would be able even to discover, and which, during the month the vessel had been at sea, had not caused even the tiniest leak. However, I shan't have another interview.

The President has been most kind. I dined with him Friday evening, and yesterday he sent over and took me out to drive again. I gave him a paper showing exactly where all our ships are, and I also sketched in outline what I thought ought to be done if things looked menacing about Spain, urging the necessity of taking an immediate and prompt initiative if we wished to avoid the chance of some serious trouble, & of the Japs chipping in. If we get Walker with our main fleet on the Cuban coast within forty-eight hours after war is declared—which we can readily do if just before the declaration we gather the entire fleet at Key West; and if we put four big; fast, heavily armed cruisers under, say, Evans, as a flying squadron to harass the coast of Spain until some of the battleships are able to leave Cuba and go there; and if at the same time we throw, as quickly as possible, an expeditionary force into Cuba, I doubt if the war would last six weeks so far as the acute phase of it was concerned. Meanwhile, our Asiatic squadron should blockade, and if possible take, Manila. But if we hesitate and let the Spaniards take the initiative, they could give us great temporary annoyance by sending a squadron off our coast, not to speak of the fact that if they were given time, when once it was evident that war had to come, there would be plenty of German and English, and possibly French, officers instructing them how to lay mines and use torpedoes for the defense of the Cuban ports. Besides we would have the Japs on our backs. However, I haven't the slightest idea that there will be a war.

I am very much obliged to you for sending me Long's speech, and I shall write to him at once about it. His allusions to me were most kind and generous.

Yesterday I saw for the first time your new volume of essays, and I read it all through again from beginning to end. I think they make as good work of the kind as was ever done on this side of the water, and so far as I know, the only work of the kind that has been done here by a man who was a doer as well as a writer. I am particularly pleased that you put in your article about our foreign policy. It was timely, and it all goes to build up the body of public sentiment on the subject. I don't think the cover up to the seriousness & weight of the essays.

Give my best love to Nannie.

Faithfully yours

September 29, 1897. Washington
To Arlo Bates

My dear Mr. Bates:

Just a line to say how very much I have enjoyed your volume of essays just out. Cabot Lodge wrote me calling my attention to it, and I owe him a debt of gratitude. Having numerous small children of my own I am pleased to find that we are doing just what you advise in the way of giving them reading matter. They read every one of the books you enumerate, and like yourself, I take just as much enjoyment in them as they do—though I have always had a dreadful mental limitation about the first and most popular part of *Robinson Crusoe,* and about a good deal of the *Arabian Nights.* I am happy to say that this is not shared by either Mrs. Roosevelt or the children.

It did me good to see the straightforward fashion in which you dealt with Maeterlinck, Ibsen, Verlaine, Tolstoi and the decadents generally. I wish Howells could be persuaded to read and profit by what you have written!

It seems to me, however, that both Meredith and Hardy in his latter books, beginning with *Tess* show distinct symptoms of the same disease, although it takes very different forms in the two cases. Moreover, I always feel like putting in a plea for Longfellow. I think there will be a revival of appreciation for Longfellow sometime. He is more than simply sweet and wholesome. His ballad-like poetry, such as "The Saga of King Olaf," "The Discovery of the North Cape," "Belisarius," and others, especially of the sea have it seems to me the strength as well as the simplicity that marks Walter Scott and the old English ballad writers. However, I may be a crank about this, for I am extremely fond of a great deal of Macaulay's ballad poetry, in spite of all the fustian that there is in parts of it.

I must really thank you for a number of most pleasant hours.

Very sincerely yours

September 30, 1897. Washington
To John D. Long

Sir:

The steady growth of our country in wealth and population, and its extension by the acquisition of non-contiguous territory in Alaska, and at the same time the steady growth of the old naval powers of the world, and the appearance of new ones, such as Germany and Japan, with which it is possible that one day we may be brought into contact, make me feel that I should respectfully, and with all possible earnestness, urge the advisability the Navy Department doing all it can to further a steady and rapid upbuilding of our Navy. We cannot hope to rival England. It is probably not desirable that we should rival France; while Russia's three-fold sea front, and Italy's peculiar position, render it to the last degree improbable that we shall be cast into hostile contact with either of them. But Japan is steadily becoming a great naval power in the

Pacific, where her fleet already surpasses ours in strength; and Germany shows a tendency to stretch out for colonial possessions which may at any moment cause a conflict with us. In my opinion our Pacific fleet should constantly be kept above that of Japan, and our naval strength as a whole superior to that of Germany. It does not seem to me that we can afford to invite responsibility and shirk the burden that we thus incur; we cannot justify ourselves for retaining Alaska and annexing Hawaii unless we provide a Navy sufficient to prevent all chance of either being taken by a hostile power; still less have we any right to assert the Monroe Doctrine in the American hemisphere unless we are ready to make good our assertion with our warships. A great navy does not make for war, but for peace. It is the cheapest kind of insurance. No coast fortifications can really protect our coasts; they can only be protected by a formidable fighting navy. If through any supineness or false economy on our part, we fail to provide plenty of ships of the best type, thoroughly fitted in every way, we run the risk of causing the nation to suffer some disaster more serious than it has ever before encountered—a disaster which would warp and stunt our whole national life, for the moral effect would be infintely worse than the material. We invite such a disaster if we fail to have a sufficiency of the best ships, and fail to keep both our materiel and personnel up to the highest conditions.

I believe that Congress should at once give us six (6) new battleships, two (2) to be built on the Pacific and four (4) on the Atlantic; six (6) large cruisers, of the size of the *Brooklyn,* but in armament more nearly approaching the Argentine vessel *San Martin;* and seventy-five (75) torpedo boats, twenty-five (25) for the Pacific and fifty (50) for the Atlantic. I believe that we should set about building all these craft now, and that each one should be, if possible, the most formidable of its kind afloat.

We should at once build new dry docks. With the additions which are outlined above we should need to have one more dry dock for the largest battleships on the Pacific coast, and three more on the Atlantic coast; that is, four extra, although we probably could get along with only two extra.

Many of our cruisers and battleships are armed, in part, with the slowfire six-inch gun, a weapon which is now obsolete. It would be cruel to pit these vessels against hostile vessels nominally of the same type, but armed with modern rapid-fire guns. The vessels could be doubled in effectiveness by substituting the converted rapid-fire six-inch guns for the old style guns as rapidly as possible. There are ninety-five of these old style guns in the service. The conversion would cost about $1,000 per gun. We should have guns for all auxiliary cruisers; we now have almost none. The greatest need at the moment is smokeless powder. Smokeless powder would greatly increase the power and rapidity of the fire, and would be of great tactical advantage. We should get two million pounds at once, in order to completely outfit our ships. This would probably cost $1,500,000. For $100,000 all our armor-piercing shell should be capped, loaded and fused. We should provide a reasonable reserve supply of projectiles (about nine thousand in all) so as to permit a complete refill of all the ships.

If we stop building up the Navy now it will put us at a great disadvantage when we go on. The greatest difficulty was experienced when we began our work on the new Navy in 1883. We had to train the workmen and the designers; we had to build factories, and make tools. The difference between such a vessel as the *Texas* and such a vessel as the *Indiana* will illustrate the cost to the country of carrying on such an experiment. We are now in a situation to build up a navy commensurate with our needs, provided the work is carried on continuously, for the era of experiment has passed, and we possess designs suitable for our own use, with types of vessels equal to those of any other power. But if the work is interrupted, and new vessels are not begun, we shall soon find it necessary to start all over again, as we did in 1883, and to reinstruct the men and manufacturers and re-educate the officers and designers and re-experiment with the designs. It would be difficult to calculate the course we should incur by such a proceeding; and meanwhile we should be exposing the country to the possibility of the bitterest humiliation.

Very respectfully

October 25, 1897. Washington
To Jacob Riis

Private

My dear Mr. Riis:

As usual you have acted just right. Mrs. Lowell has been very unreasonable—extremely so. I asked permission of the President to take part in this campaign, and he told me with the greatest emphasis that I must not interfere, and that he himself would keep neutral. When Bliss came out for Tracy I asked permission again to come out for Low, and again the President told me I must not. I spoke to Carl Schurz and John Kennedy Todd about it, and both said it would be foolish in the highest degree for me to resign my position here when it doesn't seem as if I could do an amount of work that would be worth the sacrifice. All that I could do quietly I of course have done.

Indeed the story you tell me touches me deeply. My beloved friend, does not even your modesty see that those two little mites came to Police Headquarters because of what you had done, and not I? When

I went to the Police Department it was on your book that I had built, and it was on you yourself that I continued to build. Whatever else I did there was done because I was trying, with much stumbling and ill success, but with genuine effort, to put into practice the principles you had set forth, and to live up to the standard you had established. And all the trials and everything else count for nothing compared with the fact that we were able to do a little.

I am sorry you couldn't join me at lunch, but am consoled in knowing that you and Mrs. Riis will be in Washington this winter. I shall have Senator and Mrs. Lodge to meet you, and probably my chief, Secretary Long, too.

Let me know about your boy from time to time; and do write me occasionally, for I prize your letters more than I can say.

Faithfully yours

October 28, 1897. Washington
To Anna Roosevelt Cowles

Darling Bye,

You were just too good to send me for my birthday the very thing I wished; indeed the only thing I wished; and in such handsome binding. I am so glad to get it! If I had bought it I would never have got it in such a handsome covering.

Edith and all the family reached here safely. This morning I took the two little boys round and put them in the Public School, where they both seem to have started well. Tomorrow, for my sins, I start on a dusty jaunt to Ohio, at the President's request, to speak for Hanna.

The Secretary has been a dear, as he always is; I only wish I could poison his mind so as to make him a shade more truculent in international matters.

I shall be coming to New York about the 12th; shall I find you at home?

Yours ever

November 4, 1897. Washington
To John Hay

Dear Mr. Ambassador,

Well, we've met the enemy with disastrous results in New York; but elsewhere I think the outcome has been fairly satisfactory.

We've elected Hanna and beaten Gorman, and these were the two main objects from the national standpoint. We had to expect a certain reaction. In New York the astounding defeat was simply a revolt against the intolerable tyranny, (as vicious as Tammany's, and more stupid) of Platt. For two years there the Republican Machine has cut antics worthy of Hill and Croker[1] at their best; and as for the Citizens Union, you know the kind of cattle the reformers of that brand are. I was on the stump for Hanna. I kept out of the New York fight; conduct of which the President much approved.

I quite agree with what you say of attacks on England. I sent your letter to Cabot. I am a bit of a jingo—I wish we would turn Spain out of Cuba before Congress meets—but I have a horror of bluster which does not result in fight; it is both weak and undignified.

By the way, while in Cleveland I spent a charming afternoon at the Mathers, who were most kind. Do tell Mrs. Hay; and give her my warm regards. My family are all here now.

Always yours

In the December Scribners Kipling has a fine, strong poem, dedicated to the memory of good Willie Phillips; I was touched by his thought of the dear fellow, whom we all miss so continually.

Is'n't "Captains Courageous" good?

November 19, 1897. Washington
To William W. Kimball

My dear Mr. Kimball:

When will you be at Savannah or at Brunswick, Georgia? I am afraid I am not going to be able to make it, but if I can I shall. If I fail, then I shall join you at one of the gulf ports later. I don't think it will be possible for me to get to Charleston.

I will sound Captain Crowninshield to find out what the intentions are as to that submarine boat, but I don't want to interfere unless I see a fair opening.

Now, about the Spanish war. In the first place it is always a pleasure to hear from you. In the next place to speak with a frankness which our timid friends would call brutal, I would regard a war with Spain from two standpoints: first, the advisability on the grounds both of humanity and self-interest of interfering on behalf of the Cubans, and of taking one more step toward the complete freeing of America from European dominion; second, the benefit done our people by giving them something to think of which isn't material gain, and especially the benefit done our military forces by trying both the Navy and Army in actual practice. I should be very sorry not to see us make the experiment of trying to land, and therefore feed and clothe, an expeditionary force, if only for the sake of learning from our own blunders. I should hope that the force would have some fighting to do. It would be a great

---

[1] New York Democratic boss Richard Croker.

lesson, and we would profit much by it. I expressed myself a little clumsily about the transport question. Of course if we drift into the war butt end foremost, and go at it in higgledy-piggledy fashion we shall meet with occasional difficulties. I am not the boss of this Government; (and I want to say that I do think President McKinley, who is naturally desirous of keeping the peace, has combined firmness and temperateness very happily in his treatment of Spain); from my own standpoint, however, and speaking purely privately, I believe that war will have to, or at least ought to, come sooner or later; and I think we should prepare for it well in advance. I should have the Asiatic squadron in shape to move on Manila at once. I would have our squadron in European waters consist merely of the *Brooklyn, New York, Columbia* and *Minneapolis;* and of course I should have this, as well as the Asiatic squadron, under the men whom I thought ought to take it into action. All the other ships in the Atlantic I would gather around Key West before the war broke out. I should expect it would take at least a fortnight before the Army could get at Tampa or Pensacola the thirty or forty thousand men who should land at Matanzas. During that fortnight I should expect that our Navy would have put a stop to the importation of food to Cuba and would have picked up most of the Spanish vessels round about. At the end of that time I believe it would be safe to gather an ample number of vessels for the transport of the army. This ought not to take them more than a week or ten days from their legitimate duties. Meanwhile I believe that plenty of arms and a considerable number of men would go over to Cuba on private ventures, and that the Cuban insurrection would be infinitely more formidable than it is now. With thirty or forty thousand men at Matanzas, re-enforced from time to time, I believe that the Navy could for the most part resume its duties, and that, while it would be the main factor in producing the downfall of the Spaniards, the result would be much hastened by the Army.

I didn't think the Cosmopolitan article worth paying much heed to. A writer who knows so little of naval affairs as to think that the *Columbia* would be unable to get her men to quarters or fire a gun before she was sunk by Spanish cruisers which she had previously descried, is hardly to be taken seriously.

Let me hear from you at any time. It is always a pleasure.

Very sincerely yours

November 19, 1897. Washington
To Anna Roosevelt Cowles

Darling Bye,

Very unexpectedly Quentin Roosevelt appeared just two hours

ago. Edith is doing well. By the aid of my bicycle I just got the Doctor & Nurse in time! We are very glad, and much relieved.

Yours

November 30, 1897. Washington
To Frederic C. Selous

Dear Mr. Selous:

Your letter made me quite melancholy—first, to think I wasn't to see you after all; and, next, to realize so vividly how almost the last real hunting grounds in America have gone. Thirteen years ago I had splendid sport on the Big Horn Mountains which you crossed. Six years ago I saw elk in bands of one and two hundred on Buffalo Fork; and met but one hunting expedition while I was out. A very few more years will do away with all the really wild hunting, at least so far as bear and elk are concerned, in the Rocky Mountains and the West generally; one of the last places will be on the Olympic peninsula of Oregon, where there is a very peculiar elk, a different species, quite as big in body, but with smaller horns which are more like those of the European red deer, and with a black head. Goat, sheep and bear will for along time abound in British Columbia and Alaska.

Well, I am glad you enjoyed yourself anyhow, and that you did get a sufficient number of fair heads—wapiti, prongbuck, blacktail and whitetail. Of course I am very sorry that you didn't get a good sheep and a bear or two. In the northeastern part of the Park there is some wintering ground for the elk; and I doubt if they will ever be entirely killed out in the Park; but in a very short while shooting in the West, where it exists, will simply be the kind that can now be obtained in Maine and New York; that is, the game will be scarce, and the game laws fairly observed in consequence of the existence of a class of professional guides; and a hunter who gets one good head for a trip will feel he has done pretty well. You were in luck to get so fine a prongbuck head.

Do tell Mrs. Selous how sorry I am to miss her, as well as you. I feel rather melancholy to think that my own four small boys will practically see no hunting on this side at all, and indeed no hunting anywhere unless they have the adventurous temper that will make them start out into wild regions to find their fortunes. I was just in time to see the last of the real wilderness life and real wilderness hunting. How I wish I could have been with you this year! but, as I wrote you before, during the last three seasons I have been able to get out West but once, and then only for a fortnight on my ranch, where I shot a few antelope for meat.

You ought to have Hough's *Story of the Cowboy* and VanDyke's *Still Hunter*. Also, I think you might possibly enjoy small portions of the three volumes of the Boone and Crockett Club's publications. They could be obtained from the *Forest and Stream* people at 346 Broadway, New York, by writing. Have you ever seen Washington Irving's *Trip on the Prairie* and Lewis and Clark's Expedition? And there are two very good volumes about [words missing] now out of print, by a lieutenant in the British Army named Ruxton, the titles of which for the moment I can't think of, but I will look them up and send them to you. He describes the game less than the trappers and hunters of the period; men who must have been somewhat like your elephant hunters. When I was first on the plains there were a few of them left; and the best hunting trip I ever made was in the company of one of them, though he was not a particularly pleasant old fellow to work with.

Now, to answer your question about ranching; and of course you are at liberty to quote me. I know a good deal of ranching in western North Dakota, eastern Montana, and northeastern Wyoming. My ranch is in the Bad Lands of the Little Missouri, a good cattle country, with shelter, traversed by a river, into which run here and there perennial streams. It is a dry country, but not in any sense a desert. Year in and year out we found that it took about 25 acres to support a steer or cow. When less than that was allowed the ranch became overstocked, and loss was certain to follow. Of course where hay is put up, and cultivation with irrigation attempted, the amount of land can be reduced; but any country in that part of the West which could support a steer or cow on 5 acres would be country which it would pay to attempt to cultivate, and it would, therefore, cease to be merely pastoral country.

Is this about what you wish? I have made but a short trip to Texas. There are parts of it near the coast which are well watered, and support a large number of cattle. Elsewhere I do not believe that it supports more cattle to the square mile than the northwestern country, and where there are more they get terribly thinned out by occasional droughts. In Hough's book you will see some description of this very ranching in Texas and elsewhere.

Do give my warm regards to Buxton when you meet him. I am very sorry that it has been so long since I have seen him; and I really grudge the fact that you and Mrs. Selous got away from this side without my even getting a glimpse of you.

Faithfully yours

December 23, 1897. Washington
To John A. Merritt

My dear Sir:

I am very much pleased indeed at your courtesy in writing me. I don't know that my suggestions will do the least good, but it seems to me that there are certain subjects which would lend themselves to treatment that would make very handsome and very typical postage stamps. Thus a picture of one of the horse Indians in full war dress with his bonnet of eagle feathers; such a picture as that of a Cheyenne warrior in Frederic Remington's recently published book of illustrations. Again, take a picture of an old-time plains or Rocky Mountain hunter and trapper, which could also be reproduced from Remington; an old fellow with the full beard, the belted hunting shirt and long rifle. Then again, one of Remington's cowboys would be an appropriate figure. I mention all these three because from Remington's drawings they could be obtained readily; and these drawings have great artistic merit aside from their wonderful fidelity to nature. I suppose that an emigrant wagon, an old-style prairie schooner, would take up rather too much room. It would be a thoroughly characteristic subject, but I appreciate that on a postage stamp one does not wish to have the figures too small or the subject too complicated. Thus in the Columbian postage stamps the most effective were those where a single ship or a single figure was used. Too much detail on a small space fails to produce a marked effect.

If single portraits are to be used I could suggest no one better than old Kit Carson. On the other hand Custer riding at the head of his cavalry would be a most picturesque picture, and would typify the very great influence the Army had in opening the West. By all means have one of those postage stamps with a buffalo on it. The vanished buffalo is typical of almost all the old-time life on the plains, the life of wild chase, wild warfare and wild pioneering. If any bit of scenery were taken I should suggest your going up to the Cosmos Club here or to the Geological Survey and examine three or four of their photographs of the boldest canon walls, or of Pike's Peak.

With great regard, believe me,
Very sincerely yours

December 23, 1897. Washington
To William Astor Chanler

Private and Confidential
Dear Willie:

Your letter pleased me very much, and it will delight Cabot. I will now say what I did not write before, because I feared you might misunderstand it, namely, that Cabot and two or three of the other Hawaiians have been getting so irritated at the attitude of the pro-Cuban men that there has been serious danger of their antagonizing Cuba.

My feeling about these matters is just this: I wish we had a perfectly consistent foreign policy, and that this policy was that ultimately every European power should be driven out of America, and every foot of American soil, including the nearest islands in both the Pacific and the Atlantic, should be in the hands of independent American states, and so far as possible in the possession of the United States or under its protection. With this end in view I should take every opportunity to oust each European power in turn from this continent, and to acquire for ourselves every military coign of vantage; and I would treat as cause for war any effort by a European power to get so much as a fresh foothold of any kind on American soil. Now, our people are not up as yet to following out this line of policy in its entirety, and the thing to be done is to get whatever portion of it is possible at the moment. One year ago it was manifestly impossible to annex Hawaii; but Cleveland came near being willing to interfere on behalf of Cuba. In such case, though I think for military reasons Hawaii is almost more important to us, I should have gone in heartily to do what was possible at the moment, and should have tried to take Cuba. At present, owing mainly to the change in the Spanish policy, it is not possible at the moment to do anything about Cuba, but it is possible to get Hawaii. In consequence it is obviously the proper thing for men who feel as you and I do to take what is possible, that is, to take Hawaii. Nothing would please anti-Americans of the *Evening Post* stamp so much as to see us always refusing to do what we *can*, in pursuance of a proper foreign policy, on the excuse that we ought first to do what we *can't*. Moreover, Hawaii is of more pressing and immediate importance than Cuba. If we don't take Hawaii it will pass into the hands of some strong nation, and the chance of our taking it will be gone forever. If we fail to take Cuba it will remain in the hands of a weak and decadent nation, and the chance to take it will be just as good as ever. As you know, our squadron is going down to gulf waters this year. I do not believe that the administration will admit even to themselves that this is due to the fact that they are recognizing that our hand may be forced in the Cuban matter; yet I firmly believe such to be the fact. I do not believe that Cuba can be pacified by autonomy and I earnestly hope that events will so shape themselves that we must interfere some time in the not distant future; but if we do not take Hawaii now we may find to our bitter regret that we have let pass the golden moment, forever. So that I believe you have done a wise and patriotic action, and I congratulate you and thank you with all my heart. Your letter is a good Christmas gift to both Cabot and myself. You ought to get Mahan's last book on America's interest in Sea Power.

Faithfully yours

January 14, 1898. Washington
To John D. Long

Sir:

In one way it is of course proper that the military and naval branches of the Government should have no say as regards our foreign policy. The function of the military army is merely to carry out the policy determined upon by the civil authorities.

Nevertheless, sir, it will be absolutely impossible to get the best results out of any military policy unless the military authorities are given time well in advance to prepare for such policy. At present the trouble with Spain seems a little less acute, but I feel sir, that I ought to bring to your attention the very serious consequences to the Government as a whole, and especially to the Navy Department (upon which would be visited the national indignation for any check, no matter how little the Department was really responsible for the check) if we should drift into a war with Spain and suddenly find ourselves obliged to begin it without preparation, instead of having at least a month's warning, during which we could actively prepare to strike. Some preparation can and should be undertaken now, on the mere chance of having to strike. In addition to this, when the blow has been determined upon we should defer delivering it until we have had at least three weeks or a month in which to make ready. The saving in life, money, and reputation by such a course will be very great.

Certain things should be done at once if there is any reasonable chance of trouble with Spain during the next six months. For instance the disposition of the fleet on foreign stations should be radically altered, and altered without delay. For the past six or eight months we have been sending small cruisers and gunboats off to various ports of the world with a total disregard of the fact that in the event of war this would be the worst possible policy to have pursued. These smaller cruisers in the event of war would be of use only on one or two points. If scattered about the high seas they would be worse than merely useless; for they would inevitably run the risk of being snapped up by the powerful ships of the enemy which they cannot fight, and from which they are too slow to run; and every such loss would be an item of humiliation for the Department and for the nation. If we have war with Spain there will be immediate need for every gunboat and cruiser that we can possibly get together to blockade Cuba, threaten or take the less protected ports, and ferret out the scores of small Spanish cruisers and gunboats which form practically the entire Spanish naval force around the Island. Probably a certain number of our smaller cruisers could be used with advantage in the Asiatic Squadron for similar work around the Philippines. In these two places the unarmored cruisers would be very valuable. Everywhere else they would simply add an element of risk and weakness to our situation.

We have now in home waters on the Atlantic Coast, the *Marblehead, Montgomery* and *Detroit,* three thoroughly efficient ships for the work we would need around Cuba. We also have the *Vesuvius,* which could be used for the same purpose, although its field of usefulness would be limited. We also have ready the *Nashville, Annapolis, Newport* and *Vicksburg,* and the *Princeton is* almost ready. These four vessels are of the so-called gunboat class, and if used instantly on the outbreak of war, together with others of their kind, they would practically root out the small Spanish vessels in the Cuban waters. If there was a delay of two or three weeks some of these small Spanish vessels might inflict serious depredations in the way of attacks on our merchant marine or on our transports, especially if the Army was sent to Cuba. The *Princeton* should be pushed to immediate completion. The *Nashville* should not be allowed to leave our shores, the *Newport* should be recalled to Key West; and the *Vicksburg* sent there.

On the South Atlantic Station we have the *Cincinnati,* a very efficient fighting cruiser of small coal capacity, and two gunboats the *Wilmington* and *Castine.* If we have a war now these ships should all be recalled. It will take them thirty days to get home, and they will reach here without any coal. In other words for the first five or six most important weeks of the war these vessels will be absolutely useless, and might as well not be in existence. In my opinion they should tomorrow be ordered to Pernambuco. When they get there a week or two hence, we can then tell whether to bring them back to Key West or not. They should be at Key West and filled with coal and in readiness for action before the outbreak of hostilities. The presence of the *Cincinnati* might make the difference of being able to reduce Matanzas at the same time we blockade Havana. The presence of the two gunboats might make the difference of destroying a Spanish flotilla, or of driving out the Spanish garrison from one end of the Island.

More urgent still is it to take action with regard to the vessels in Europe. These include the *San Francisco,* a good cruiser, of not very great coal capacity, and with slow-fire six-inch guns; the *Helena,* a small gunboat, and the *Bancroft,* a still smaller gunboat. The *Helena* and *Bancroft* should be brought back from Europe today if there is the slightest chance of war with Spain. Against any fair-sized cruiser they could make no fight, and they are too slow to escape. The best that could happen in the event of war, would be that they would be shut up in a European port, if they stay where they now are. They would run great risk of capture, which, aside from the loss, would mean humiliation. If brought back however, they would aid materially in the reduction of Cuba for the reasons given above. I should also bring the *San Francisco* immediately back the minute a chance of war came. The *San Francisco* is a respectable fighting ship. She could aid not merely in the blockade of Cuba, but in the attack on some of the less protected towns; but, like the *Philadelphia*, she is not fit to oppose a first-class modern cruiser, thoroughly well armed. Her coal capacity, although respectable, is not very great, and she is probably not swift enough to insure her escape if pursued. For these reasons I do not think that she should form a part of the flying squadron, the sending out of which into Spanish home waters. I regard as one of the most essential elements in the plan of campaign yesterday submitted to you. Accordingly she should be brought home.

On the Asiatic station Commodore Dewey will have the *Olympia, Boston, Concord* and *Petrel*. This will probably be enough to warrant his making a demonstration against the Philippines, because he could overmaster the Spanish squadron around those islands. At the same time the margin of force in his favor is uncomfortably close, and I should advise in the event of trouble with Spain that the *Baltimore, Bennington, Marietta,* and possibly the *Wheeling* be sent to him in advance. If we had trouble with any power but Spain I should not advise Hawaii being left unprotected, but with Spain I do not think we need consider this point.

One of the most important points in our scheme of operations should be the flying squadron. This should especially be the case if we are not able to bombard Havana. To my mind the chief objection to bombarding Havana is to be found in the lack of ammunition, of which we are so painfully short. I believe we could reduce Havana, but it might be at the cost of some serious loss, and, above all, at the cost of exhausting our supply of ammunition. If we bombard Havana we must make it a success at any cost for the sake of the effect upon the people. If we do not bombard it, then we must do something else, for effect on the people, and upon the Navy itself. This something else can partly take the shape of the capture of Matanzas and other towns and the rooting out of the Spanish cruisers around Cuba; but we especially want to keep the Spanish cruisers at home to prevent depredations on our own coast. In fighting efficiency the Spanish fleet is about double what it was so late as last April. They now have seven battleships, which, in average strength, are about equal to the *Maine* and *Texas*. We could beat these seven battleships if we could get at them, but they could cause us trouble if we allowed them to choose the time and place of attack. If, however, we send a flying squadron, composed of powerful ships of speed and great coal capacity, to the Spanish coasts we can give the Spaniards all they want to do at home, and will gain the inestimable moral advantage of the aggressive. The ships to be sent in this squadron should be the *New York* and *Brooklyn*, the *Minneapolis* and Columbia, and two of the auxiliary steamers like the *St. Paul* and *New York* of the American line, which steamers could be fitted in about ten days. The squadron should start the hour that hostilities began; it should go straight to the Grand Canary, accompanied by colliers. At the Grand Canary they should coal to their limit and leave coal there, if possible under some small guard. They should then go straight up, say through Gibraltar by night and destroy the shipping in Barcelona, returning immediately to the Grand Canary. If the Spaniards had occupied the Grand Canary in force, they could then go home. If not, they could replenish with coal, and strike Cadiz; then go off the coast and strike one of the northern seaports on the Bay of Biscay. Probably after this they would have to return home. Such an enterprise would, in all human probability, demoralize the Spaniards, and would certainly keep their fleet in Spanish waters, for they would be "kept guessing" all the time. Only the vessels I have named above would be fit to take part in the enterprise. The *Columbia* and *Minneapolis* are now laid up. It would take them three weeks to get ready. They are only valuable for just such an operation, and the operation would itself be of most value at the very outset of the war. They should therefore be got ready at once and kept in readiness so long as there is the least danger of war with Spain. Their captains should be assigned them, not because it is any man's turn to be assigned, but with a view to the fact that we will need for this flying squadron the very best men in the Navy. I should strongly advise, in the event of war, your substituting one or two men who now have no ships in the place of one or two of those who have ships; but in any event when the *Columbia* and *Minneapolis* are commissioned they should be sent to sea under a couple of the very best men whom you now have ashore.

Our most urgent need is ammunition. If there is any prospect of war, steps should be taken in advance to get this ammunition. We should have to accept a less high grade of powder than we now demand, and should have to get the companies to work night and day.

We also need more men. The battleships left on the Pacific could perhaps be depleted of most of their men, who should be sent east; and we could fill their places, temporarily at least, by the naval militia on the California coast. At the same time we should draw on the best of the naval militia on the Atlantic coast, and on any force that we can get from the Revenue Marine and Coast Survey; and this in addition to the extra men who should be immediately provided for by Congress. Our best ships are now undermanned. In the event of war I wish to reiterate what I have said in two or three former reports, that we should increase the number of officers on the battleships.

The work should be pushed with the utmost energy on the *Puritan* and *Brooklyn*. If war came tomorrow we should have no ships ready to put in this flying squadron except the *New York*.

Well in advance we should get every vessel we may possibly need, and especially an ample supply of colliers. It is extraordinary how many of these vessels would be needed under the conditions of actual sea service in time of war with a modern fleet, and lack of coal will reduce the Navy to immediate impotence. As soon as war broke out we could of course no longer get coal in foreign ports.

Some of the steps above advised should be taken at once if there is so much as a reasonable chance of war with Spain. The others it is not necessary to take now, but they should be taken well in advance of any declaration of war. In short, when the war comes it should come finally on our initiative, and after we had had time to prepare. If we drift into it, if we do not prepare in advance, and suddenly have to go into hostilities without taking the necessary steps beforehand, we may have to encounter one or two bitter humiliations, and we shall certainly be forced to spend the first three or four most important weeks not in striking, but in making those preparations to strike which we should have made long before.

Very respectfully

January 17, 1898. Washington
To Hermann Speck von Sternberg

My dear Sternberg:

It was delightful to hear from you again, especially as I gather that your health must be very nearly restored. We miss you and Springie all the time. There is no one to take your place. I have had two of the members of your Embassy here—Count von Gotzen and Baron Hermann—on my walks. But they can't walk like you, and of course even if they could walk they wouldn't in any way take your place otherwise. I have, however, developed a great companion in the shape of one of our Army Surgeons.[1] He is a graduate of Harvard, and he took part in the most severe of the Apache campaigns, and was one of the three men in our troops who could march as well as the Apaches, week in and week out, over the deserts. He is a splendid fellow. Every Sunday we take our children out for a scramble up Rock Creek, and we get away alone whenever we can on a weekday afternoon. There is also an Army captain here

---

[1]Col. Leonard Wood.

who goes with me occasionally, and so does a young Harvard fellow, both of whom you would like.

Between ourselves I have been hoping and working ardently to bring about our interference in Cuba. If we could get the seven Spanish ironclads together against our seven seagoing ironclads on this coast we would have a very pretty fight; and I think more could be learned from it than from the Yalu; but unless their ironclads came across I think that the war at sea would mainly take the shape of a blockade of the Cuban coast, although I have a couple of plans which, if I can persuade the Department to adopt them, will be sure to produce interesting results of some kind. I wish I could get you over here if there were any trouble.

Mrs. Roosevelt is not very well at present, as she has a severe attack of grippe. She has a little baby two months old, so we now have six children,—four sons and two daughters. She often speaks of you, and she sends you her warm love. The Lodges also join in; they are as delightful as ever.

I am glad Mahan is having such influence with your people, but I wish he had more influence with his own. It is very difficult to make this nation wake up. Individually the people are very different from the Chinese, of course, but nationally our policy is almost as foolish. I sometimes question whether anything but a great military disaster will ever make us feel our responsibilities and our possible dangers; and of course in the event of such disaster, instead of blaming themselves they will blame the officers to whom they have refused to give the means which would have averted the disaster. I do not believe we shall make very much advance with our navy in point of numbers this session. In the Pacific we are now inferior to Japan, and we shall continue to be inferior. The Japs are going ahead wonderfully. I do not know whether they can stand the strain financially, but if they can they will be a formidable counterpoise to Russia in the Far East. Just at present it is very doubtful whether we will take Hawaii when offered to us. Such folly, in refusing it, would seem incredible; but there is great danger of our committing it. Moreover, if we did refuse it it would be quite on the cards that with utter lack of logic we would go to war with some other power for having taken it. Of course I feel that we ought to have interfered in Cuba long ago.

Our new navy rifle is not yet satisfactory. Sometimes it does not shoot very accurately, and the machinery is a little apt to get out of order. I supposed with all these weapons time has to be taken before they can really be put in very good trim. I got no shooting this year. That is a wonderful ram's head of Littledales.

It was a great pleasure to hear from you. Do drop me a line now and then.

Faithfully yours

February 5, 1898. Washington
To Francis C. Moore

My dear Sir:

Many thanks for your letter. I must say, however, that of all the nations of Europe it seems to me Germany is by far the most hostile to us. With Russia I don't believe we are in any danger of coming into hostile contact; but with Germany, under the Kaiser, we may at any time have trouble if she seeks to acquire territory in South America.

Of course treat this letter as entirely confidential.

Very truly yours

P.S. For over a century France has been no more friendly to us than England. Under Napoleon she was quite as unfriendly as England was under Pitt, and during our Civil War, though England behaved badly, France behaved worse. When England goes wrong, as was the case in the Venezuelan incident, I should favor this nation taking the most emphatic attitude against her, but I should be heartily against attacking her when she did right; and still less would I submit to anything from Germany, France or Russia which was aimed at the interests of this country.

February 7, 1898. Washington
To Thomas R. Woodrow

My dear Sir:

I feel very strongly that every college man should enter politics. I don't mean by this that he should strive for political position, for I don't think it wise for a man to try to make politics his sole career unless he possesses ample means, in which case I should strongly advocate his going into public life, staying in as long as he conscientiously can, and going out with cheerful philosophy whenever he finds he cannot consistently with his own self-respect stay in—always remembering, however, that he must not mistake mortified vanity, or the pet projects either of himself or of a small clique of friends who are unused to politics, for the demands of self-respect. Other college men should, of course, work either in the primaries or independently and with both disinterestedness and common sense for decent politics.

I venture to refer you to my article on the college man in politics in the little book called *American Ideals*, which I have just published, for my further views in the matter.

Yours truly

February 9, 1898. Washington
To Francis C. Moore

My dear Mr. Moore:

I agree with you so heartily on almost all questions of real importance, whether affecting our foreign policy or anything else, that I hate
to disagree with you, and I don't think that fundamentally I do. I quite
agree with you that naturally our alliance should be with a republic, and
I entirely agree with you that there cannot be a fundamental agreement
between us of America and the tory aristocracy of Great Britain. With
Englishmen of the sort who stood by us during our Civil War—that is,
with Englishmen like Lord Spenser, John Bright, and the Lancashire cotton spinners of your correspondent—I could have on most questions a
hearty sympathy. The only reason I asked you to treat my letters as confidential is that I have of course no right to publish opinions in which
my chiefs of the administration very possibly do not share.

I should myself like to shape our foreign policy with the purpose
ultimately of driving off this continent every European power. I would
begin with Spain, and in the end would take all other European nations, including England. It is even more important to prevent any new
nation from getting a foothold. Germany as a republic would very possibly be a friendly nation, but under the present despotism she is much
more bitterly and outspokenly hostile to us than is England; and even
as a republic there is of course always the possibility of repeating what
the French republic did a century ago, when she forced us to administer a sound drubbing to her, taking her frigates and sloops in pitched
battle, and smashing her West Indian privateers.

What I want to see our people avoid is the attitude taken by the
great bulk of Americans at the beginning of this century, and the end
of the last, when the mass of the Jeffersonians put the interests of
France above the interest and honor of America, and the mass of the
Federalists did the same thing in England. I am not hostile to any European power in the abstract. I am simply an American first and last,
and therefore hostile to any power which wrongs us. If Germany
wronged us I would fight Germany; if England, I would fight England.

I should like very much to have a chance of meeting you and talking all this over at length sometime.

Faithfully yours

February 25, 1898. Washington
To George Dewey

(Cablegram)

Dewey, Hong Kong:

Order the squadron, except the *Monocacy,* to Hong Kong. Keep full of coal. In the event of declaration of war Spain, your duty will be to see that the Spanish squadron does not leave the Asiatic coast, and then offensive operations in Philippine Islands. Keep Olympia until further orders.

March 3, 1898. Washington
To Douglas Robinson

Dear Douglas:

Edith certainly seems a little stronger during the last two days; but her fever continues, and puzzles us greatly. The Baltimore expert did no good. Ted is very decidedly better.

I don't know what to do about my taxes. You see, last August I got off from my personal taxes in Oyster Bay on the ground that I was not a resident of Oyster Bay, and had not yet given up my residence in New York. Of course, as a matter of fact, on November 1st my last interest in 689 lapsed. I did not vote in New York, and could not have voted, and abandoned my residence there, and had no intention whatever of resuming it. Could I not make an affidavit that on November 1st my interest in New York ceased; that I did not vote there and have no residence there; and that I then intended, and now intend, to (keep) make my residence at Oyster Bay, where I shall vote and pay all my taxes this year? I don't want to bother you, but it would be a great favor if you would have someone look it up for me, and find out if this can be done; and would you also look up and find out whether I have under you the $50,000 worth of taxable property? I wish you would consult Uncle Jim.

Faithfully yours

P.S. Rather than have the least suspicion attach to me, I would of course pay the taxes, and I don't think it makes much difference this year anyhow, for everything seems to be going with a jump, and I might as well be resigned to it.

By the way, will you please find out from the Life Insurance Company if my policy would be vitiated if I should go to Cuba in the event of war?

March 21, 1898. Washington
To Brooks Adams

My dear Adams:

Your letters pleased me deeply; and they touched both Mrs. Roosevelt and myself still more deeply. I showed them to Lodge, and he told me that what you said of me should be ample reward for any work and worry I have had in this office; and I told him that I quite agreed with him, and so I do.

Like you, I breathed more freely and held my head higher when the President and Congress rose to the level of the emergency. I don't understand how John Hay was willing to be away from England at this time. Harry White has done excellently there. I entirely agree with you that England's attitude was very important to us; and I also entirely agree with you that having taken the position we did it will indeed be ill for us if we fail to carry out the responsibilities we have assumed. Personally, I feel that it is not too late to intervene in Cuba. What the administration will do I know not. In some points it has followed too closely in Cleveland's footsteps to please me, excellently though it has done on the whole. In the name of humanity and of national self-interest alike, we should have interfered in Cuba two years ago, a year and a half ago, last April, and again last December. The defective imaginations of many good people here, the limited mental horizon of others, and the craven fear and brutal selfishness of the mere money-getters, have combined to prevent us from doing our duty. It has been a case of the offer of the sibylline books over again. Month by month has gone by, each leaving less for us to interfere on behalf of, and increasing the danger that would result from our interference; and yet interfere we must sooner or later. The blood of the Cubans, the blood of women and children who have perished by the hundred thousand in hideous misery, lies at our door; and the blood of the murdered men of the *Maine* calls not for indemnity but for the full measure of atonement which can only come by driving the Spaniard from the New World. I have said this to the President before his Cabinet; I have said it to Judge Day, the real head of the State Department; and to my own chief. I cannot say it publicly, for I am of course merely a minor official in the administration. At least, however, I have borne testimony where I thought it would do good.

Incidentally, our Navy is in much better shape than it was a year ago. We are lamentably weak in certain particulars, thanks to the unwisdom of Congress; and the Spanish torpedo-boat destroyers may cause us serious trouble; but our men have in them the stuff of those who fought in 1812, and in 1861, and they handle their ships and their guns as American seamen should.

Remember me most warmly to Mrs. Adams.

Faithfully yours

[Handwritten] P. S. Mrs. Roosevelt has been very, very sick all winter; for weeks we could not tell whether she would live or die. At last she was put under the knife; and now, very slowly, she is crawling back to life. I hope never to see another such winter. We have had to send all the children away from the house. Nannie has been more than kind, and Cabot; and indeed all our friends. You can hardly know how often Mrs. Roosevelt and I think and talk of you both.

March 30, 1898. Washington
To William Cowles

Dear Will:

Many thanks for your letter, and for that very interesting testimony of Powelson's. Of course I cannot speak in public, but I have advised the President in the presence of his Cabinet, as well as Judge Day and Senator Hanna, as strongly as I knew how, to settle this matter instantly by armed intervention; and I told the President in the plainest language that no other course was compatible with our national honor, or with the claims of humanity on behalf of the wretched women and children of Cuba. I am more grieved and indignant than I can say at there being any delay on our part in a matter like this. A great crisis is upon us, and if we do not rise level to it, we shall have spotted the pages of our history with a dark blot of shame.

Now, write me in full, and definitely, what you want in the event of trouble—whether it is a change of ship or an additional armament on the *Fern*, or anything else. I don't know whether I can get anything for you or not, but I shall most certainly try. Meanwhile, let me say that it seems to me you would do well to keep the *Fern*, simply putting more guns aboard of her; but whatever you decide I will try to have carried out. Remember; however, how limited my power is; all the more so, as I am now suspected by the administration because of my entire dissent from their views about what our honor and dignity demand in the settlement of this Cuban question.

Faithfully yours

March 31, 1898. Washington
To James Bryce

My dear Mr. Bryce:

It will give me great pleasure to meet Mr. Trevelyan, not only because he is a friend of yours, but because of my admiration for his father; and I shall like much to meet the Webbs also.

I have had a very busy time, but anxious only in the sense that I fear this nation will not do its duty. I feel that we have been derelict in not interfering on behalf of Cuba for precisely the same reason that I felt you were derelict in not interfering on behalf of Armenia—and I never preach for others what I don't, when I have the power, advocate doing myself. We should drive Spain from the Western World. For the last three years in Cuba she has revived the policy and most of the methods of Alva and Torquemada. I know you are not interested in Hawaii; and I am afraid that our people, with supine indifference, will let the place slip from their grasp. I cordially sympathize with England's attitude in China, and I am glad to say that there seems to be a gradual coming together of the two peoples. They certainly ought to come together.

In great haste,
Faithfully yours

April 8, 1898. Washington
To Robert Bacon

Dear Bob:

In the main I thoroughly agree with your views. If it is in any way possible, the President and Congress must act together. But I do not feel that there is any honorable escape from war. We should not haggle over matters separately. Let us treat the whole question as an entirety and put Spain out of the western hemisphere. I am perfectly willing to follow the policy of intervening without recognizing independence, although I think it a mistake; for I should be very doubtful about annexing Cuba in any event, arid should most emphatically oppose it unless the Cubans wished it. I care nothing about recognizing the present government if only we emphatically state that we will recognize the independence of Cuba. I don't want it to seem that we are engaged merely in a land-grabbing war. Let us fight on the broad grounds of securing the independence of a people who, whether they amount to much or not, have been treated with hideous brutality by their oppressors; upon the further ground of putting a medieval power once for all out of the western world; and, finally, with the determination to get the only satisfaction we can for our murdered men,[1] not by taking blood money for them, but by securing the two objects outlined above.

Faithfully yours

---

[1]Roosevelt was referring to the deaths of the 266 Americans aboard the *Maine,* destroyed in Havana harbor.

PART FOUR

Hero

1898–1901

As soon as the war began, Roosevelt resigned his post at the Navy Department to volunteer for the army. He explained his views to various correspondents; what sometimes went unsaid was his desire to discover if he was the man he hoped he was.

With Colonel Leonard Wood he raised the First Volunteer Cavalry Regiment, labeled by some anonymous alliterist the Rough Riders. Roosevelt took great pride in these western cowboys and eastern athletes, who seemed to him the essence of America. He took considerably less pride in the bureaucracy of the War Department, which seemed inept and unwilling to let his men get to the front. During the course of the summer, Roosevelt's disdain for such regular officers as Nelson Miles and William Shafter would grow to the point of insubordination.

All was forgotten, at least temporarily, in the thrill of the fighting. After landing at Daquirí, Roosevelt took part in two actions. A brief battle at Las Guasimas was followed by a more serious encounter on the San Juan Heights in front of Santiago. In the latter clash Roosevelt conducted himself with what, by his own account and that of eyewitnesses, constituted conspicuous bravery. Then and ever after, he considered Santiago the great day of his life.

Having proved his courage under fire, Roosevelt was outraged at what seemed to him the cavalier treatment of his men following their victory. Disease set in, decimating their ranks while Shafter and the other general officers dithered. Roosevelt wrote bitterly in private to Lodge about the plight of his men; in public he moderated his tone only slightly, sponsoring a round-robin letter to Shafter telling the commanding general what a poor job he was doing.

The letter probably spoiled Roosevelt's chances of wining the Medal of Honor, which he dearly sought (he received it only a century later, in January 2001). But it didn't hurt his chances of political preferment. No one emerged from the war more heroically than Roosevelt, who accordingly became the darling of New York Republicans. Boss Platt engineered his nomination for governor; following a campaign characterized by bugle calls and testimonials from Rough Riders, Roosevelt entered the governor's mansion in Albany.

He took himself more seriously as governor than Platt did. Roosevelt accommodated his style to Platt, meeting regularly with the boss to discuss matters of party and state business. But his independence of mind struck Platt as ungrateful, and before long the boss was plotting to get rid of him.

The vice presidency seemed the perfect exile, especially after the incumbent died suddenly. Roosevelt resisted, fully aware of the impotence of the office. He wrote McKinley's manager and friend, Marcus A. Hanna, explaining how much greater benefit he would be to the party as New York governor than as vice president. Hanna required no convincing, for he distrusted Roosevelt as much as Platt did. But Platt was better organized than Hanna, and managed to have his way at the convention in the summer of 1900.

Roosevelt bowed to fate—and even engaged in some ex post facto ration-
alizing that all was for the best. He campaigned with his usual verve, and as-
sumed the nation's second office upon McKinley's reelection. The vice presi-
dency left him plenty of time to catch up on correspondence, to go hunting, to
play with his growing children, and to plot with Lodge and a few others how
he might succeed McKinley in 1904.

April 18, 1898. Washington
To Paul Dana

My dear Dana:

Will you read this letter, and then hand it to whoever wrote the more than kind editorial upon me in today's *Sun?*

I do not want you to believe that if I go with the Army in the event of war I shall be acting in a mere spirit of levity or recklessness, or without having carefully thought out my duty according to my convictions. It has been very hard for me to keep to this decision, for my family and friends are all against it, and the Secretary and President are good enough to express great reluctance at my going. But I am influenced to disregard their advice by two or three considerations.

In the first place my work here has been mainly one of preparation. In time of peace military men cannot speak to the civilian heads of the administration as I could, and did, speak, and I have been able to accomplish a good deal in getting the Navy ready. It is not of course in exactly the shape I should like to see it, but still it is in very good shape indeed, and will respond nobly to any demand made upon it. Now, as I say, I have been useful in this work of preparation; but when the clash of arms comes the work of preparation will, for the most part, be done, and the task will be shifted to those whose duty it is to use aright the materials already prepared. I have been urging the Secretary to appoint some first-class man like Admiral Walker as his chief of staff here, because the military element must be predominant during the time of war; and I have been urging this, although the appointment of such a man would necessarily greatly contract my sphere of usefulness, and therefore my importance. The case of Assistant Secretary Fox is not parallel, because Fox was a naval officer who spoke with an authority in warlike matters to which no civilian could pretend. In time of peace a civilian can do very much in building up the Navy, but in time of war it is too late to build up; it is then a matter of using aright the weapons ready furnished. Moreover, in time of war military men no longer fear to speak, and their words no longer pass unheeded. Very much of my usefuless during the past year has been due to the fact that I gave persistent expressions to the views of the best officers of the Department who could not otherwise have made themselves heard. In time of war these men will be heard without difficulty.

Secondly, I want to go because I wouldn't feel that I had been entirely true to my beliefs and convictions, and to the ideal I had set for myself if I didn't go. I don't want you to think that I am talking like a prig, for I know perfectly well that one never is able to analyze with entire accuracy all of one's motives. But I am entirely certain that I don't expect any military glory out of this Cuban war, more than what is implied in the honorable performance of duty. For two years I have consistently preached the doctrine of a resolute foreign policy, and of readiness to accept the arbitrament of the sword if necessary; and I have alway intended to act up to my preaching if occasion arose. Now the occasion has arisen, and I ought to meet it. I have had, as you know, a perfect horror of the ideas which are perhaps most clearly crystalized in the editorials of papers like the *Evening Post*; that is, of the ideas of the peace-at-any-price theorists on the one side, the timid and scholarly men in whom refinement and culture have been developed at the expense of all the virile qualities; and a horror even greater of the big moneyed men in whose minds money and material prosperity have finally dwarfed everything else. I don't think this nation needs any incitement to development on the money-making side, and if we who have preached the doctrine fail to put our words into effect when the time comes, our preaching will lose much of its force. For two years I have been urging that we put Spain out of Cuba, and if there ever was a righteous war it will be this; and if, owing to the unfortunate delay in beginning it, we see our men dying of yellow fever in Cuba I should hate to be comfortably at home in Washington, although I have as much dislike of death as anyone could have, and take as keen enjoyment in life.

Moreover, an additional reason for my going is the fact that though I have a wife and six children, they are not dependent upon my exertions for support. I am not a rich man, and my children will have to work; but they will be well educated and comfortably brought up, and inasmuch as I have never been in a money-making pursuit my loss would not very materially affect their income.

I have written you thus at length, and with what may seem too great frankness, because I was really very much touched by the editorial, and because I want you to believe that whether I am right or not, I am at least acting conscientiously and in pursuance of convictions which I have held for many years, and which I should feel rather ashamed to abandon at this time.

Faithfully yours

April 28, 1898. Washington
To John Moore

My dear Mr. Moore:

My regiment of mounted riflemen will probably be mustered in at San Antonio. Will you do me a great favor? I would like a couple of good, stout, quiet horses for my own use. They must not be gun shy;

they must be trained and bridlewise—and of course no bucking or anything of the kind—for I will have no time to fool with anything but a
broke horse. If you think you can get a couple of animals of this type
for me to look at when I come down, do so, and if necessary, I would
be very much obliged if you would pay a small amount of purchase
money just to bind the bargain, so that I can get them when I wish—in
other words give me an option on them.

Pray present my regards to Mrs. Moore.

With best regards, I am,

Very sincerely yours

May 2, 1898. Washington
To Brooks Brothers

(Telegram)
Ordinary cavalry lieutenant colonel's uniform in blue Cravenette.

May 10, 1898. Washington
To Leonard Wood

My dear Col. Wood:

In the first place there are two more recruits whom we will have to
take, as we have extra men allowed us now. The first is the son of the
Hon. John Russell Young, the Librarian of Congress, a warm personal
friend of Secretary Alger's,[1] for whom I should do anything anyhow,
and for whom Secretary Alger wishes us to do what we can. The boy's
name is Howard Young. He will turn up about the time this letter does.
The other is young Crowninshield, a nephew of Captain Crowninshield, Chief of the Bureau of Navigation; the champion pistol shot of
the Mass. artillery.

Very sincerely yours

P.S. I spent a good deal of yesterday and today fussing with the
Ordnance and Quartermaster General's Department. They have sent
out tracers, and tell me that by day after tomorrow the rifles and most
of the supplies will be at San Antonio. I hope you have got your horses
pretty well purchased by this time. The enclosed letter shows that you
are allowed to purchase over the number if necessary. I suppose we
shall have to establish a recruiting depot and have men sent after us;
and I only hope you are able to get your twelve companies organized
at once with regular officers at the head of three. I have telegraphed
Capron to send me the number of men he will have to start down on
Thursday, and I will get the transportation and provisions for them

---

[1] War Secretary Russell Alger.

here. When this is done, and having sent out the tracers and seeing that the orders are given for us to go from Galveston, I really don't see that there is much left for me to do; and this afternoon I shall wire you hoping that you will allow me to start tomorrow (Thursday). I hate to be hanging around here with you in all the turmoil of bringing order out of chaos. I appreciate of course that it was absolutely necessary for me to stay until we got these things started, for sending out the tracers undoubtedly hurried them, but now it seems as if everything was being done, and if you start early next week I should be cutting connections pretty closely if I waited here later than Thursday. I do hope we can get our troops down with the first expedition, drill or no drill. They are an unusually fine lot of men, and at the very beginning we can use them for scouting and outpost duty, and they could be speedily drilled into shape on the field. I suppose you are drilling them now.

Faithfully yours

P.S. I enclose a recommendation for a young fellow named Hervey who has been in Cuba, and who seems rather fresh, but who is certainly a good shot and out-of-doors man. If you think well of him I wish you would try to enlist him.

P.S. Jack Astor has offered us his mountain battery, and the Secretary seems to think we had better accept it. It may have to go in in lieu of one of the extra companies. I suppose you have your men in process of forming the three new companies. Capron's men are delayed by washouts, and will not get to you until Saturday. The Secretary told me that we should have our steamer and be hurried over to join the regulars just as soon as we are ready.

I don't want to be unpatriotic, but I feel like saying "Thank heaven," for I hear that the four Spanish cruisers are back in Cadiz. If true this means that instead of Sampson ending the war we will be put in to end it in Cuba.

May 19, 1898. San Antonio
To Henry Cabot Lodge

Dear Cabot:

Will you tell Gussie that I know he will pardon me for not writing. I am told that he is with Wilson's staff, and much appreciate his sending me the note. Here we are working like beavers and we are getting the regiment into shape. It has all the faults incident to an organization whose members have elected their own officers—some good and more very bad—and who have been recruited largely from among classes who putting it mildly, do not look at life in the spirit of decorum and conventionality that obtains in the East. Nevertheless many of our offi-

cers have in them the making of first rate men, and the troopers, I believe, are on the average finer than are to be found in any other regiment in the whole country. It would do your heart good to see some of
the riding. The Eastern men are getting along very well. You would be
amused to see three Knickerbocker club men cooking and washing
dishes for one of the New Mexico companies. We have a number of Indians, who are excellent riders and seem to be pretty good fellows. The
bulk of the men are quiet and self-respecting, often men of very considerable education and I think generally men of some property. The
order has been excellent; we have had but one fight and one case of
drunkenness. [Name omitted] is turning out only fairly well as a major.
I have been drilling his squadron and one of the others this afternoon.
The dust, heat and mosquitoes prevent existence being at all sybaritic.
I am heartily enjoying it nevertheless, and as the Spanish squadron has
so far eluded our people, I think this regiment will be in trim to move
whenever the advance on Cuba is to be made; but you can have no conception of the interminable delays of the Ordnance and Quartermaster's Departments.

I have a couple of scrawny horses, which they say are tough. I hope
so, as otherwise I shall probably have to eat them and continue my career on foot.

I feel pretty homesick, of course. If it were not for that, I should really be enjoying myself thoroughly.

Wood is doing splendidly and the amount of work he has accomplished is incredible.

Give my best love to Nannie, and do not make peace until we get
Porto Rico, while Cuba is made independent and the Philippines at any
rate taken from the Spaniards.

I have given a note of introduction to you to a big stockman from
Texas, Simpson, formerly of Forrest's cavalry, who went with us last
trip on the gold issue.

Yours ever

May 25, 1898. San Antonio
To Henry Cabot Lodge

Dear Cabot:

Just a line to tell you how we are getting on. I really doubt if there ever
has been a regiment quite like this. I know you will believe that more than
ever I fail to get the relations of this regiment and the universe straight,
but I cannot help being a little enthusiastic about it. It is as typical an
American regiment as ever marched or fought. I suppose about 95 per
cent of the men are of native birth, but we have a few from everywhere,

including a score of Indians, and about as many of Mexican origin from New Mexico; then there are some fifty Easterners—almost all graduates of Harvard, Yale, Princeton, etc.,—and almost as many Southerners; the rest are men of the plains and the Rocky Mountains. Three fourths of our men have at one time or another been cowboys or else are small stockmen; certainly two thirds have fathers who fought on one side or the other in the civil war. Of course, a regiment cannot be made in a week, but these men are in it because they want to be in it. They are intelligent as well as game, and they study the tactics, talking all the movements over among themselves; in consequence we have made really remarkable progress. You would enjoy seeing the mounted drill, for the way these men have got their wild half-broken horses into order is something marvellous. I am surprised at the orderly manner in which they have behaved; now and then a small squad goes to town and proceeds to paint things red, and then we get hold of them and put them into the guardhouse, but the great bulk of the men are as quiet and straight as possible. I am very confident there has been much less disturbance than there would have been with the ordinary National Guard or the ordinary regular regiment. I have been both astonished and pleased at my own ability in the line of tactics. I thoroughly enjoy handling these men, and I get them on the jump so that they execute their movements at a gallop.

Wood is the ideal man for Colonel. Woody Kane has risen to be first lieutenant, and Goodrich, the captain of the Harvard crew, a second lieutenant. The First Major is a dandy—Major Brodie, of Arizona—a grizzled old frontier soldier, who was in the regular army—is a pitiful failure, between ourselves; and some of the other officers are very poor.

We most earnestly hope we can be sent to Cuba, and if for any reason Cuba should fail, then to the Philippines—anywhere so that we can see active service. Of course, if we do not see active service, I am left, but if we do, I shall feel amply repaid for the loss of what I liked to make myself believe was a career in the Navy Department.

Give my best love to Nannie. I wonder how Bay is enjoying himself? I do not suppose either he or I will see much fighting.

If they begin to send troops to Cuba, I shall wire you to see that we go. We are all ready now to move, and will render a good account of ourselves. I earnestly hope that no truce will be granted and that peace will only be made on consideration of Cuba being independent, Porto Rico ours and the Philippines taken away from Spain.

Give my respects to the members of the Senate Committee on Foreign Relations and tell them I pin my faith to them; and will you give my love to Secretary Long when you see him?

Faithfully yours

June 6, 1898. Tampa
To the Roosevelt children

Blessed Bunnies,

It has been a real holiday to have darling mother here. Yesterday I brought her out to the camp, and she saw it all—the men drilling, the tents in long company streets, the horses being taken to water, my little horse Texas, the colonel and the majors, and finally the mountain lion and the jolly little dog Cuba, who had several fights while she looked on. The mountain lion is not much more than a kitten as yet, but it is very cross and treacherous.

I was very much interested in Kermit's and Ethel's letters to-day.

We were all, horses and men, four days and four nights on the cars coming here from San Antonio, and were very tired and very dirty when we arrived. I was up almost all of each night, for it happened always to be at night when we took the horses out of the cars to feed and water them.

Mother stays at a big hotel about a mile from camp. There are nearly thirty thousand troops here now, besides the sailors from the war-ships in the bay. At night the corridors and piazzas are thronged with officers of the army and navy; the older ones fought in the Civil War, a third of a century ago, and now they are all going to Cuba to war against the Spaniards. Most of them are in blue, but our rough-riders are in brown. Our camp is on a great flat, on sandy soil without a tree, though round about are pines and palmettos. It is very hot, indeed, but there are no mosquitoes. Marshall is very well, and he takes care of my things and of the two horses. A general was out to inspect us when we were drilling to-day.

June 10, 1898. Port Tampa
To Henry Cabot Lodge

Dear Cabot:

No words could describe to you the confusion and lack of system and the general mismanagement of affairs here; a good deal of it is the inevitable accompaniment of a sudden war where people have resolutely refused to make the needed preparations, but a very great deal could be avoided. For a month the troops have been gathering here in a country where lines of temporary railroad could be laid down for miles in 24 hours, yet to this day, while the troops are at Tampa there is but a single line connecting them with the point of debarkation 9 miles off and there are no switches to speak of and no facilities whatever for unloading freight or troops. There are hundreds of freight cars containing stores of all kinds which nobody knows anything about, and the single line is so jammed that it is impossible to move over it as fast as the muletrains go alongside. When we unloaded our regiment at Tampa we had to go 24 hours without food and not a human being met us to show us our camp or tell us anything about what we were to do. When we were ordered to embark here it took us twelve hours to make the nine miles of railroad, and on the wharf not one shadow of preparation had been made to receive any regiment; no transports had been assigned in advance, and there was actually no office for either the commissary or Quartermaster. We had to hunt all over the dock among ten thousand people before, by chance we ran across first one and then the other, and each regiment had to seize its transport and hold it against all comers; nothing but the most vigorous, and rather lawless, work got us our transport. Under these circumstances it, of course, took over three days to embark the troops. No sooner were they embarked than we received word from Washington not to start. We have been here two days now; the troops jammed together under the tropical sun on these crowded troop ships. We are in a sewer; a canal which is festering as if it were Havana harbor. The steamer on which we are contains nearly one thousand men, there being room for about five hundred comfortably. We have given up the entire deck to the men, so that the officers have to sit in the cabin, and even so several companies are down in the lower hold, which is unpleasantly suggestive of the Black Hole of Calcutta. We are apparently to be kept here three or four days more, for they say we are to start on Monday. The officers' horses were embarked last Sunday with the artillery horses; they have had to disembark them for the simple reason that they began to die. Of course there was no shadow of a reason for putting them aboard until the last moment.

If the people at Washington understood the fearful danger to health that lies in keeping these troops on the transports, and understood further that they cannot be disembarked and reembarked under five days' time, they would surely make up their minds in advance whether they intended to start or not, and when they once did put us on would let us go. Four or five days of this will reduce the efficiency of the landing force just about ten percent, and must inevitably shake the morale of the men. Our men are behaving peculiarly well, as they have behaved all along; we have a remarkably fine set; they never complain; but surely they should be put into action as soon as possible before letting some malignant disease break out in the crowds here on shipboard. They won't even let us put out into the bay, where we should all swim in spite of the sharks, and we stay crowded in this fetid ditch, the men not allowed to swim or go ashore, where indeed there is nothing to do in the thick sand. Last night Gen. Young, who is our brigade commander, together with Gen. Sumner and Gen. Wheeler, spoke to me and said they wished that the people at Washington could know how hard it is upon the cavalry to leave behind their horses. We do not complain of this, for we would go on all fours rather than not get there at all, and if we are to rush Santiago of course we must do it on foot; but I do most earnestly hope (and they wish me to write you this) that, without bringing my name in, you will try to see that our horses are forwarded to us as soon as possible. With two brigades of cavalry we can do a tremendous amount of work in Cuba; we can drive the Spanish foragers from the fields and take the small towns and close the larger ones—and it is a shame to dismount all our men.

Do, old man, try to see that the expedition is not longer deferred, because the bad effects of so deferring it are evident to everyone, and do see that our horses are sent after us at the earliest moment. But above all, let us get over now, to Cuba or Porto Rico; and have neither peace nor armistice until the job is thoroughly done.

Count von Goetzen and Captain Lee[1] told Wood and myself the other day that the two things that astonished them most were, first: the rapidity with which this regiment had been raised, armed and put into so fairly efficient a state, and, second, the utter lack of system and organization in the way matters as a whole are managed. They got quite confidential and I think said more than they intended. Still I am having genuine soldiering even if we have not seen the enemy, and oh how I hope we shall soon see him.

Let me know about Bay and John and Gus, and give my warm love to Nannie and Constance.

Ever yours

P. S.—One man should be in absolute control here, with autocratic authority, especially over the railroad people who have behaved very badly.

June 12, 1898. Port Tampa (On board U.S. Transport *Yucatan*)
To Henry Cabot Lodge

Dear Cabot:

I wonder if it would be possible for you to tell the Administration, that is, the President, and if necessary the Secretary of War, just what is going on here and the damage that is being done. Of course, I cannot speak publicly in any way; I should be courtmartialed if I did, but this letter I shall show to Wood, my Colonel, and it is written after consultation with Gen. Young, my brigade commander. I shall not show this first

---

[1]British military observer Arthur Lee would become a fast friend.

paragraph to Wood or to Young, for I want to say that it would be impossible to get a better man for Colonel than Wood has shown himself to be, and so far as I am concerned I am entirely content with Young as a Brigade General, but otherwise the mismanagement here is frightful. Wood thinks that if Miles could be given absolute control he would straighten things out and I most earnestly wish the experiment could be tried, though personally I cannot help feeling that Miles might have remedied a great deal that has gone wrong if only he had chosen or had known how. Think of embarking troops by sending their regiments higgledy-piggledly from their camp to the port ten miles away on a one-line railroad without ever assigning to each regiment its transport and without having a single officer detailed to meet the regiment its transport and without having a single officer detailed to meet the regiment and show them where to go or what they were to do. Our experience was that of every other regiment. We were up the entire night standing by the railway track at Tampa, hoping for trains that did not come. At dawn we were shifted to another railway track, and then owing to some energetic work of Wood and myself succeeded in getting the troops on empty coal cars, in which we came down to the wharf. At the wharf we could find no human being who could tell us what our transport was. Gen. Miles and Gen. Shafter both told us that if we did not find out soon we would not be able to go, and said they knew nothing more about it. The Quartermaster General and the Commissary General were allotting the boats. Neither had an office nor any place where he was to be found. The wharf was over a mile long, jammed with trains, with boats everywhere alongside, ten thousand troops embarking. Through this crowd Wood and I had to hunt until almost at the same time we both found the Quartermaster General. He allotted us a transport and advised us to seize her instantly if we hoped to keep her. The advice was good, for it proved she had been allotted to another regiment—the 71st N.Y. While Wood went out into the stream in a boat which he had seized for the purpose and got aboard the transport and brought her in, I brought up my four hundred men at a double and took possession in the very nick of tine to head off the 71st regiment, which was also advancing for the purpose. Meanwhile they unloaded our stores about a mile off and we had to bring them up by hand. However, all this we could stand, but just as soon as we were all loaded and ready work came that there had been a complete change of plans and that the expedition was indefinitely postponed. As it had taken three days to load all the troops and would take six to unload them and load them again, it was obviously unwise to do anything but keep them on board until there was definite information from Washington. So, thanks to this vacillation of purpose at

Washington this is the fifth day we have spent (and the eighth day some of the troops have spent) packed and sweltering on these troop ships in Tampa bay under the semi-tropical June sun. In spite of the sharks, we let the men bathe morning and evening, as it is too hot during the rest of the day. The shore is mere sand, but fortunately we have been moved out of the fetid ditch beside the wharf where we first lay, so that the men can be very rarely sent ashore. We have given them the entire deck and they are packed so close that they can get no exercise and no drill, while the officers, except when inspecting the ship or attending a disembarkation, have to keep to their own cabins.

Now, if this were necessary no one would complain for a moment, and the men are perfectly cheerful as it is; but it is absolutely unnecessary; the five days' great heat and crowded confinement are telling visibly upon the spirits and health of the troops. It seems incredible that a place like Tampa should have been chosen without previous inspection, that no improvements should have been made in the railroad facilities at the place during the last month and that the Ordinance and Quartermaster Departments should have fallen into such inextricable confusion; a confusion partly due to their own dilatory inefficiency and partly due to the utter incompetence of the railway managers here and the inadequacy of their system. Finally, it was in excusable to get the troops to Tampa unless it was intended to embark them, while it seems literally incredible that they could have been embarked before it was intended to use them.

All this is in the past now, but at least it may be possible to prevent such blunders in the future. It should be well determined in advance, before sending troops, that they are to sail, and when they are once sent aboard they should sail forthwith. Agents of the Government, men of push and intelligence, and above all men of youth, should be sent to every point of debarkation to tell exactly the difficulties and the needs and how they can be met. It, of course, goes without saying, that men should be appointed as Generals of Divisions and Brigades who are physically fit, as well as morally and mentally. The Ordnance Dept. in particular needs a thorough shaking up; and there should in every port like this be one responsible head who would be held to a rigid accountability. Some of the regular army officers were saying today that every day we had remained on these transports had reduced the efficiency of the force just about five percent, while to disembark the men now would mean a serious harm to the morale. They will get over it, of course, just as they would get over the effects of a repulse by the Spaniards, but it would be about as serious as a repulse.

I did not feel that I was fit to be Colonel of this regiment and I was certainly much less fit than Wood, who has done better with it than I possibly could have done, but I am more fit to command a Brigade or a Division or attend to this whole matter of embarking and sending the army than many of those whose business it is to do the work. I do not know whether the circumstances at Tampa were exceptional; if not, there is need of an immediate and radical change or the inefficiency of our Government in 1812 will be more than paralleled.

Naturally this is not a letter that can be shown to anyone, but I am going to keep you informed as to the facts, and for the credit of the country and administration I wish you would try to straighten things out. I know what a fight you have on strictly the line of your own duties, old man, and of course you must not neglect that, no matter what happens to the Administration. You must get Manila and Hawaii; you must prevent any talk of peace until we get Porto Rico and the Philippines as well as secure the independence of Cuba. These jobs are big enough, but if besides doing them you can make the Administration realize that we have to go into this thing with a good heart and have to put the best men into the important positions and insist upon efficiency as the one vital requisite, you will add enormously to the debt the country already owes you.

I see Bronson and my old aid Sharp both got into the fight at Santiago. Lucky fellows! Harry and I are left, so far, but I do most sincerely hope we shall yet be able to get in. We are already in the yellow fever zone and at the beginning of the yellow fever season, and I only hope that no weakness or vacillation will prevent our being put where we can do some service inasmuch as we are already running the risk. I doubt if Cuba is much more unhealthy than the low coast of Florida now.

Give my love to Nannie.

Faithfully yours

June 15, 1898. In the Gulf of Mexico (on board the *Yucatan*) To Corinne Roosevelt Robinson

Today we are steaming southward through a sapphire sea, wind-rippled, under an almost cloudless sky. There are some forty-eight craft in all, in three columns, the black hulls of the transports setting off the gray hulls of the men-of-war. Last evening we stood up on the bridge and watched the red sun sink and the lights blaze up on the ships, for miles ahead and astern, while the band played piece after piece, from the "Star Spangled Banner" at which we all rose and stood uncovered, to "The Girl I Left Behind Me."—But it is a great historical expedition, and I thrill to feel that I am part of it. If we fail, of course we share the fate of all who do fail, but if we are allowed to succeed (for we certainly shall succeed, if allowed) we have scored the first great triumph in what will be a world movement. All the young fellows here dimly feel what this means; though the only articulate soul and imagination among them belong rather curiously, to ex-sheriff Captain "Buckey" O'Neil of Arizona. We have school for the officers and underofficers, and the drill the men a couple of hours in the manual, especially for firing. Everyone seems happy, now that we are going; though our progress is so slow that we may be a week before we reach Santiago, if we are going there. Thanks to the folly of having kept us a needless six days on board there will probably be some sickness among the men.

Monday, June 20th '98, Troop Ship nearing Santiago.

We didn't stop anywhere after all, so you'll get this letter with my last one, I suppose. Until yesterday we sailed slowly but steadily south of east, against the trade wind that blew all the time in our faces. The weather was always fine; there were vexatious delays, thanks to a schooner, which, by an act of utter folly at Washington, or here, is being towed, stopping the whole fleet, and by an act of further folly our steamer, which has no tow rope, was sent back to bear it company and all the rest of the fleet are out of sight ahead. If the Spaniards had any enterprise they would somewhere or other have cut into this straggling convoy especially when Gen. Shafter left us as stragglers in the rear; but they haven't any and so we are safe and nearly in sight of Santiago; wondering very much whether that city has fallen, in which case our expedition is wasted, or whether it will fight, and if so how hard. All day we have steamed close to the Cuban Coast, high barren looking mountains rising abruptly from the shore, and at this distance looking much like those of Montana. We are well within the tropics, and at night the Southern Cross shows low above the horizon; it seems strange to see it in the same sky with the friendly Dipper. There has been very little to do, but we drill the men in the manual of arms each day, and hold officers' school in the evening. On Sundays I "support" the chaplain at church.

Las Guasimas, June 25th '98.

Yesterday we struck the Spaniards and had a brisk fight for 2 1/2 hours before we drove them out of their position. We lost a dozen men killed or mortally wounded, and sixty severely or slightly wounded. Brodie was wounded; poor Capron and Ham. Fish were killed. Will you send this note to Fish's father? One man was killed as he stood beside a tree with me. Another bullet went through a tree behind which I stood and filled my eyes with bark. The last charge I led on the left using a rifle I took from a wounded man; and I kept three of the empty cartridges we got from a dead Spaniard at this point, for the children. Every man behaved well; there was no flinching. The fire was very hot at one or two points where the men around me went down like ninepins. We have been ashore three days and were moved at once to the front without our baggage. I have been sleeping on the ground in the mackintosh, and so drenched with sweat that I haven't been dry a minute, day or night. The marches have been very severe. One of my horses was drowned swimming through the surf. I haven't seen Marshall. My bag has never turned up, like most of our baggage, and it is very doubtful if it ever does turn up, and I have nothing with me, no soap, toothbrush, razor, brandy, medicine chest, socks or underclothes. Will you ask Douglas to get me the articles as by enclosed list, and express them to my regiment at Tampa at once? I shan't be very comfortable until I get them. Richard Harding Davis was with me in the fight and behaved capitally. The Spaniards shot well; but they did not stand when we rushed. It was a good fight. I am in good health.

June 27th '98 Camp 5 miles from Santiago.

The day after our skirmish we stayed in camp, and to my great relief, my bundle came up. A number of our officers never got theirs at all. Also poor Marshall turned up, too sick to be any use to me. I am personally in excellent health, in spite of having been obliged for the week since I landed, to violate all the rules for health which I was told I must observe. I've had to sleep steadily on the ground; for four days I never took off my clothes, which were always drenched with rain, dew or perspiration, and we had no chance to boil the water we drank. We had hardtack, bacon and coffee without sugar; now we haven't even salt; but last evening we got some beans, and oh! what a feast we had, and how we enjoyed it. We have a lovely camp here, by a beautiful stream which runs through jungle-lined banks. So far the country is lovely; plenty of grass and great open woods of palms both sago and [indecipherable], with mango trees and many others; but most of the land is covered with a dense tropical jungle. This was what made it so hard for us in the fight. It was very trying to stand, or advance slowly, while the men fell dead or wounded, shot down from we knew not whence; for smokeless powder renders it almost impossible to place a hidden foe. The morning after the fight we buried our dead in a great big trench, reading the solemn burial service over them, and all the regiment joining in singing "Rock of Ages." The vultures were wheeling overhead by hundreds. They plucked out the eyes and tore the faces and the wounds of the dead Spaniards before we got to them, and even of one of our own men who lay in the open. The wounded lay in the path, a ghastly group; there were no supplies for them; our doctors did all they could, but had little with which to do it; a couple died in the night, and the others we took back on improvised litters to the landing place. One of them, a

Mexican cowpuncher, named Rowland, shot through the side, who had returned to the firing line after his wound caused him to fall out, refused to go aboard the hospital ship, and yesterday toiled out here to rejoin us. I really don't see how he ever walked with such a wound. One of the mortally wounded, Heffner, got me to prop him against a tree, and give him his water canteen and rifle, and continued firing until we left him as we went forward. The woods are full of land crabs, some of which are almost as big as rabbits; when things grew quiet they slowly gathered in gruesome rings around the fallen.

I am glad I asked for Douglas to send me those things, though my own have now turned up; for I shall need them anyhow.

July 3, 1898. Outside Santiago
To Henry Cabot Lodge

Dear Cabot:

Tell the President for Heaven's sake to send us every regiment and above all every battery possible. We have won so far at a heavy cost; but the Spaniards fight very hard and charging these intrenchments against modern rifles is terrible. We are within measureable distance of a terrible military disaster; we *must* have help—thousands of men, batteries, and *food* and ammunition. The other volunteers are at a hideous disadvantage owing to their not having smokeless powder. Our General is poor; he is too unwieldy to get to the front. I commanded my regiment, I think I may say, with honor. We lost a quarter of our men. For three days I have been at the extreme front of the firing line; how I have escaped I know not; I have not blanket or coat; I have not taken off my shoes even; I sleep in the drenching rain, and drink putrid water. Best love to Nannie.

Yours ever

July 4, 1898. Outside Santiago
To Leonard Wood

Sir:

On July 1 the regiment, with myself in command, was moved out by your orders directly following the First Brigade. Before leaving the camping ground several of our men were wounded by shrapnel. After crossing the river at the ford we were moved along and up its right bank under fire and were held in reserve at a sunken road. Here we lost a good many men, including Captain O'Neil, killed, and Lieutenant Haskell, wounded. We then received your order to advance and support the regular cavalry in the attack on the intrenchments and blockhouses on the hills to the left. The regiment was deployed on both sides of the road, and

moved forward until we came to the rearmost lines of the regulars. We
continued to move forward until I ordered a charge, and the men rushed
the blockhouse and rifle pits on the hill to the right of our advance. They
did the work in fine shape, though suffering severely. The guidons of
Troops E and G were first planted on the summit, though the first men
up were some A and B troopers, who were with me.

We then opened fire on the intrenchments on a hill to our left which
some of the other regiments were assailing and which they carried a few
minutes later. Meanwhile we were under a heavy rifle fire from the intrenchments along the hills to our front, from whence they also shelled
us with a piece of field artillery until some of our marksmen silenced it.
When the men got their wind we charged again and carried the second
line of intrenchments with a rush. Swinging to the left, we then drove the
Spaniards over the brow of the chain of hills fronting Santiago. By this
time the regiments were much mixed, and we were under a very heavy
fire, both of shrapnel and from rifles from the batteries, intrenchments,
and forts immediately in front of the city. On the extreme front I now
found myself in command with fragments of the six cavalry regiments of
the two brigades under me. The Spaniards made one or two efforts to re-
take the line, but were promptly driven back.

Both General Sumner and you sent me word to hold the line at all
hazards, and that night we dug a line of intrenchments across our front,
using the captured Spaniards' intrenching tools. We had nothing to eat
except what we captured from the Spaniards; but their dinners had fortunately been cooked, and we ate them with relish, having been fighting
all day. We had no blankets and coats, and lay by the trenches all night.
The Spaniards attacked us once in the night, and at dawn they opposed
a heavy artillery and rifle fire. Very great assistance was rendered us by
Lieutenant Parker's Gatling battery at critical moments; he fought his
guns at the extreme front of the firing line in a way that repeatedly called
forth the cheers of my men. One of the Spanish batteries which was used
against us was directly in front of the hospital so that the Red Cross flag
flew over the battery, saving it from our fire for a considerable period.
The Spanish Mauser bullets made clean wounds; but they also used a
copper-jacketed or brass-jacketed bullet which exploded, making very
bad wounds indeed.

Since then we have continued to hold the ground; the food has
been short; and until to-day we could not get our blankets, coats, or
shelter tents, while the men lay all day under the fire from the Spanish
batteries, intrenchments, and guerrillas in trees, and worked all night
in the trenches, never even taking off their shoes. But they are in excellent spirits, and ready and anxious to carry out any orders they receive.

At the end of the first day the eight troops were commanded, two by captains, three by first lieutenants, two by second lieutenants, and one by the sergeant whom you made acting lieutenant.

We went into the fight about 490 strong, 86 were killed or wounded, and there are about half a dozen missing. The great heat prostrated nearly 40 men, some of them among the best in the regiment. Besides Captain O'Neil and Lieutenant Haskell, Lieutenants Leahy, Devereux, and Carr were wounded. All behaved with great gallantry. As for Captain O'Neil, his loss is one of the severest that could have befallen the regiment. He was a man of cool head, great executive capacity, and literally dauntless courage.

The guerrillas in trees not only fired at our troops, but seemed to devote themselves especially to shooting at the surgeons, the hospital assistants with Red Cross bandages on their arms, the wounded who were being carried in litters, and the burying parties. Many of the guerrillas were dressed in green uniforms. We sent out a detail of sharpshooters among those in our rear, along the line where they had been shooting the wounded, and killed thirteen.

To attempt to give a list of the men who showed signal valor would necessitate sending in an almost complete roster of the regiment. Many of the cases which I mention stand merely as examples of the rest, not as exceptions. Captain Jenkins acted as major, and showed such conspicuous gallantry and efficiency that I earnestly hope he may be promoted to major as soon as a vacancy occurs. Captains Lewellen, Muller, and Luna led their troops throughout the charges, handling them admirably. At the end of the battle Lieutenants Kane, Greenwood, and Goodrich were in charge of their troops, immediately under my eye, and I wish particularly to commend their conduct throughout. Lieutenant Franz, who commanded his troop, also did well.

Corporals Waller and Fortesque and Trooper McKinley, of Troop E; Corporal Rhoads, of Troop D; Troopers Allerton, Winter, MacGregor, and Ray Clark, of Troop F; Troopers Bugbee, Jackson, and Waller, of Troop A; Trumpeter MacDonald, of Troop L; Sergeant Hughes, of Troop B, and Trooper Geiven, of Troop G, all continued to fight after being wounded, some very severely. Most of them fought until the end of the day.

Trooper Oliver B. Norton, of B, with his brother, was by my side throughout the charging, was killed while fighting with marked gallantry. Sergeant Ferguson, Corporal Lee, and Troopers Bell and Carroll, of Troop K; Sergeant Daine, of Troop E; Troopers Goodwin, Campbell, and Dudley Dean, and Trumpeter Foster, of B, and Troopers Greenwald and Bardelas, of A, are all worthy of special mention for coolness and gallantry. They merit promotion when the opportunity comes. But the most conspicuous gallantry was shown by Trooper Rowland. He was wounded in the side in our first fight, but kept in the firing line. He was sent to the hospital next day, but left it and marched out to us, overtaking us, and fought all through this battle with such indifference to danger that I was forced again and again to rate and threaten him for running needless risk.

Great gallantry was also shown by four troopers whom I cannot identify, and by Trooper Winslow Clark, of G. It was after we had taken the first hill—I had called out to rush the second, and, having by that time lost my horse, climbed a wire fence and started toward it. After going a couple of hundred yards, under a heavy fire, I found that no one else had come; as I discovered later, it was simply because in the confusion, with men shooting and being shot, they had not noticed me start. I told the five men to wait a moment, as it might be misunderstood if we all ran back, while I ran back and started the regiment; and as soon as I did so the regiment came with a rush. But meanwhile the five men coolly lay down in the open, returning the fire from the trenches. It is to be wondered at that only Clark was seriously wounded, and he called out, as we parted again, to lay his canteen where he could reach it, but to continue the charge and leave him where he was. All the wounded had to be left until after the fight, for we could spare no men from the firing line.

Very respectfully

July 7, 1898. Outside Santiago
To Henry Cabot Lodge

Dear Cabot,

As I only write you and Edith you must pardon my persistent jeremiads. First, the unimportant, which is personal. Wood has commanded his brigade, and I my regiment, in the hardest battle of the war; they lost a heavier percentage than any other regiment or brigade; and we feel we are entitled to the promotions rather than outsiders. If it is judged that other men in the field have shown greater efficiency, why we have nothing to say; but we ought to receive the promotions rather than men who have not been in the fight. Gen. Wheeler says he intends to recommend me for the medal of honor; naturally I should like to have it. And, when we take Santiago, do try to see that we are sent to the front again, and not kept as garrison. I think we have shown we can fight.

Next, as to the important. It is criminal to keep Shafter in command. He is utterly inefficient; and now he is panic struck. Wheeler is an old dear; but he is very little more fit than Shafter to command. Our part of the battle fought itself under the brigade and regimental commanders. Sumner deserves more credit than Wheeler for it—but as I say the regiments themselves really fought it. The mismanagement has been beyond belief. We have a prize fool—who handled a balloon so as to cause us very great loss. We are half starved; and our men are sickening daily. The lack of transportation, food and artillery has brought us to the very verge of disaster; but above all the lack of any leadership, of any system or any executive capacity.

Best love to Nannie. Do go and see Edith. I wish I could hear about Harry and Bay.

Yours ever

July 18, 1898. Santiago
To Alice Roosevelt

Darling Alice,

I was very glad to get your letter, and to hear of all you had done. I have had a very hard and dangerous month. I have enjoyed it, too, in a way; but war is a grim and fearful thing. It is strange to see "Nicanor lie dead in his harness," when Nicanor and you have that morning spoken together with eager longing of glory and honor to be won or lost, and of the loved ones who will be thrilled or struck down according as the event of the day goes. Worse still is the awful agony of the field hospital where the wounded lie day and night in the mud, drenched with rain and scorched with the terrible sun; while the sky overhead is darkened by the whirling vultures and the stream of staring fugitives, the poor emaciated women and the little tots of children, some like Archie and Quentin. One poor little mite still carried a canary in a little cage. My men are not well fed, and they are fierce and terrible in battle; but they [gave] half they had to the poor women and children. I suppose a good many of them thought, as I did, of their own wives or sisters and little ones. War is often, as this one is, necessary and righteous; but it is terrible.

Your loving father

July 19, 1898. Santiago
To Henry Cabot Lodge

Dear Cabot:

It was the greatest pleasure to receive your two letters of the 24th and 25th, which came in inverse order, a couple of days ago. Wood was immensely flattered at your sending him your regards in so kind a way, and I was, naturally, deeply touched, old man, by the whole tone of your note and especially by your thinking now that I was justified in coming. Somehow or other I always knew that if I did not go I never

would forgive myself; and I really have been of use. I do not want to be
vain, but I do not think that anyone else could have handled this regiment quite as I have handled it during the last three weeks and during
these weeks it has done as well as any of the regular regiments and infinitely better than any of the volunteer regiments, and indeed, frankly,
I think it has done better than the regulars with the exception of one or
two of the best regular regiments. We have moved up to the foothills,
but fever is making perfect ravages among us. I now have left less than
half of the six hundred men with whom I landed; but the gallant fellows struggle back to me from the hospital just as soon as their wounds
are healed or the fever or dysentery lets up a little.

Well, the fight is over now and we have won a big triumph, so there
is no use in washing dirty linen, except that surely we ought to profit by
our bitter experiences in the next expeditions. Even now with Santiago
taken and our ships in the bay and with a month in which to have gotten
ample transportation, food and medical supplies, our condition is horrible in every respect. I have over one hundred men down with fever in
my own camp out of my regiment of four hundred, 200 having previously died or having been sent to the rear hospitals. The mismanagement
of the hospital service in the rear has been such that my men will not
leave the regiment if they can possibly help it; yet here we have nothing
for them but hardtack, bacon and generally coffee without sugar. I cannot get even oatmeal and rice except occasionally, by paying for it myself, which seems a little needless in as rich a government as ours. I have
to buy the men canned tomatoes and tobacco. The regiment was moved
yesterday and I was given one wagon in which to transport everything,
which simply meant a night of exposure for the men and a couple of very
scanty meals, while as Gen. Shafter made us move at midday we had
fifty cases of heat prostration, the tropical sun working its will upon men
weakened by poor food, constant exposure and the grinding hardship of
labor in the trenches. Curiously enough the part in which we have broken down has been the administrative and business part, and to a less extent in the mechanical part, while we have been saved by the dogged
fighting of the individual regiments. The engineers and artillery have
done poorly and the hospital division worse. But the prime difficulty has
been lack of transportation, including lack of means to land from the
ships. We should have had a great number of barges, lighters and small
steam craft as a matter of course. During the month that has passed, Gen.
Shafter should have insisted upon having a sufficiency of wagons, mule
trains and small craft of the kind mentioned above. Even now we keep
the wagons idle while the ships are in the bay, and our men half starved
and in tatters. If only I could get decent food for my men!—rice, corn-

meal, canned fruit, dried meat. I hope you will not think I grumble too much or am too much worried; it is not in the least for myself; I am more than satisfied even though I die of yellow fever tomorrow, for at least I feel that I have done something which enables me to leave a name to the children of which they can rightly be proud and which will serve in some sense as a substitute for not leaving them more money. But, as any honorable man must, I feel very keenly my share of the responsibility for this army and especially my responsibility for this regiment. I am deeply touched by the way the men of the regiment trust me and follow me. I think they know I would do anything for them, and when we got into the darkest days I fared precisely as they did. Certainly in battle or in the march or in the trenches I never went anywhere but I found them eager to follow me. I was not reckless; but with a regiment like this, and indeed I think with most regiments, the man in command must take all the risks which he asks his men to take if he is going to get the best work out of them. On the day of the big fight I had to ask my men to do a deed that European military writers consider utterly impossible of performance, that is, to attack over open ground unshaken infantry armed with the best modern repeating rifles behind a formidable system of entrenchments. The only way to get them to do it in the way it had to be done was to lead them myself. Now, naturally, I feel terribly to see them suffering for lack of plain food, to see my sick men in high fever lying in the mud on their soggy blankets without even so cheap a comfort as a little rice or even sugar for their tea or coffee.

Lt. Day was promoted for conspicuous gallantry. He was sent to the rear wounded with some of our men. They were kept in the hospital 48 hours before they were given a mouthful of food, and as for water they had to depend upon those of their number who could walk. My men's shoes are worn through; two of them went into the last battle barefooted. Their clothes are in tatters. They have not changed their underclothes since they landed a month ago; yet do what I can I cannot get them spare clothing.

However, enough of grumbling. Did I tell you that I killed a Spaniard with my own hand when I led the storm of the first redoubt? Probably I did. For some time, for your sins, you will hear from me a great many "grouse in the gunroom" anecdotes of this war. I am just wild to see you and spend an evening telling you various things. For the first hour of the last battle we had a very uncomfortable time. We were lying in reserve under orders, where the bullets of the enemy reached us, and man after man was killed or wounded. I lay on the bank by Lieut. Haskell, talking with him. Finally he did not answer some question of mine; I turned to find that he had been shot through the stomach. I gave an order to one of my men, who stood up and saluted and then fell over my knees with a bullet through his brain. But then came the order to advance, and with it my "crowded hour"; for there followed the day of my active life. I got my men moving forward, and when the 9th regiment of regulars halted too long firing, I took my men clean through it, and their men and younger officers joined me. At the head of the two commands I rode forward (being much helped because I was the only man on horseback) and we carried the first hill (this was the first entrenchment carried by any of our troops; the first break in the Spanish line; and I was the first man in) in gallant shape and then the next and then the third. On the last I was halted and for 24 hours I was in command, on the extreme front of the line, of the fragments of the six cavalry regiments, I being the highest officer left there.

Two of my men have died of yellow fever, but we hope to keep it out of the camp, and if we succeed we also hope we shall soon be ordered to Porto Rico.

Remember that I do not hear any news and do write me about anything, especially about Bay, Harry and Gus. You have done everything where you are. You have been more useful than any General, for you occupy the larger field; it would have been criminal for you to leave your task.

Warm love to Nannie.

Ever yours

July 19, 1898. Santiago
To Douglas Robinson

Dear Douglas:

The box of medicines and underclothes came and was just what I needed; it was most useful. May I bother you yet once more? Will you find out if Brooks has sent to me my extra pair of breeches and gaiters to the regiment at Tampa, or if he still has it will you have it sent to me if I cable; I cannot tell you how to send it for I do not know what our plans will be or what means there may be of sending things to us. I think I shall just have to be extravagant and run risks in the way of having things sent to me—I shall get Edith to order another pair of stout shoes for me, as my own are rotting, and have you send them to me at the first chance.

I made Bob a lieutenant for gallant service at the time of the big fight. Poor Kenneth I never saw after he was wounded, but they tell me in the hospital he showed himself to be a real hero by his cheerfulness, which had the greatest possible good effect on the others. That he did well in battle, I was an eyewitness. I had the whole regiment on my hands and I could not stop to go to the rear for any human being, no matter how dear to me.

Two of our men have died of yellow fever—we hope to keep it out of camp, and if we succeed I trust we shall soon get to Porto Rico. Whatever comes, I cannot say how glad I am to have been in this—I feel I now leave the children a memory that will partly offset the fact that I do not leave them much money. I have been recommended for the colonelcy of this regiment and for the medal of honor. Of course, I hope I get both, but I really do not care very much for the thing itself is more important than the reward; and I have led this regiment during the last three weeks—the crowning weeks of its life. There is nothing I would have exchanged for having led it on horseback where first of all our army we broke through the enemy's entrenchments. By the way, I then killed a Spaniard myself with the pistol Will gave me which was raked up from the *Maine*. One gets curiously philosophic here, not only about bullets but about yellow fever. I think I shall probably come through all right now unless we get some fearful epidemic of disease, for I believe this is the hardest fighting any of our armies will have. The mismanagement has been something beyond belief, and the sufferings of the troops great, in consequence. We have no adequate transportation or hospital facilities nor a proper supply of food. I cannot get even rice and oatmeal for the sick, who lie on the muddy ground in their soggy blankets raging with fever. My men are in tatters and their shoes like those of tramps, yet I can get neither footgear nor clothing for them. The few delicacies—if beans and tomatoes can be called such—which they have had I have had to purchase myself; and all this weighs on me a good deal, for I am proud of them beyond measure and I hate to see them needlessly suffer, all the more because they never grumble. Of the six hundred with whom I landed, less than three hundred are left; the others are dead or are in the hospital from wounds, fever and dysentery. Many of those with me are wrecks of what they were, and many crawl back to rejoin the colors as soon as the fever lets up or their wounds are partially healed. By the way, young Fortescue has shown himself to be a particularly good man.

I have not yet had time to wonder what I shall do when or if I get out of this or even to wonder whether you have done anything with the ranch.

I enclose a brief note for Corinne.

With many thanks again old fellow, I am,

Always yours

**July 20, 1898. Santiago
To Leonard Wood**

Sir:

In obedience to your directions, I herewith report on the operations of my regiment from the 1st to the 17th inst., inclusive.

As I have already made you two reports about the first days' operations, I shall pass them over rather briefly. On the morning of the 1st my regiment was formed at the head of the Second Brigade, by the El Poso sugar mill. When the batteries opened the Spaniards replied to us with shrapnel, which killed and wounded several of the men of my regiment. We then marched toward the right and my regiment crossed the ford before the balloon came down there and attracted the fire of the enemy, so that at that point we lost no one. My orders had been to march forward until I joined Gen'l Lawtons left wing, but after going about three quarters of a mile I was halted and told to remain in reserve near the creek by a deep line. The bullets dropped thick among us for the next hour while we lay there and many of my men were killed or wounded; among the former was Capt. O'Neill, whose loss was a very heavy blow to the regiment, for he was a singularly gallant and efficient officer. Acting Lieutenant Haskell was also shot at this time. He showed the utmost courage and had been of great use during the fighting and marching. It seems to me some action should be taken about him. You then sent me word to move forward in support of the regular cavalry and I advanced the regiment in columns of companies, each company deployed as skirmishers. We moved through several skirmish lines of the regiment ahead of us, as it seemed to me that our only chance was in rushing the entrenchments in front instead of firing at them from a distance. Accordingly we charged the blockhouse and entrenchments on the hill to our right against a heavy fire. It was taken in good style, the men of my regiment thus being the first to capture any fortified position and to break through the Spanish lines. The guidons of G and E troops were first at this point, but some of the men of A and B troops who were with me personally got in ahead of them. At the last wire fence up this hill I was obliged to abandon my horse and after that went on foot. After capturing this hill we first of all directed a heavy fire upon the San Juan hill to our left, which was at the time being assailed by the regular infantry and cavalry, supported by Captain Parker's gatling guns. By the time San Juan was taken a large force had assembled on the hill we had previously captured, consisting not only of my own regiment but of the 9th and of portions of other cavalry regiments. We then charged forward under a heavy fire across the valley against the Spanish entrenchments on the hill in the rear of the San Juan hill.

This we also took, capturing several prisoners. We then formed in what order we could and moved forward driving the Spaniards before us to the crest of the hills in our front which were immediately opposite the city of Santiago itself. Here I received orders to halt and hold the line of hill crest. I had at that time fragments of the six cavalry regiments and an occasional Infantry man under me—three or four hundred men all told. As I was the highest there, I took command of all of them and so continued until next morning.

The Spanish attempted a counterattack that afternoon, but were easily driven back, and then and until dark we remained under a heavy fire from their rifles and great guns lying flat on our faces, on the gentle slope just behind the crest. Captain Parker's gatling battery was run up to the right of my regiment and did most excellent and gallant service. In order to charge the men had, of course, been obliged to throw away their packs, and we had nothing to sleep in and nothing to eat. We were lucky enough, however, to find in the last blockhouse captured the Spanish dinner still cooking, which we ate with relish. It consisted chiefly of rice and peas, with a big pot containing a stew of fresh meat, probably for the officers. We also distributed the captured Spanish blankets, as far as they would go, among our men, and gathered a good deal of the Mauser ammunition for use in the Colt's rapid-fire guns which were being brought up. That night we dug entrenchments across our front. At 3 o'clock in the morning the Spaniards made another attack upon us, which was easily repelled, and at 4 they opened the day with a heavy rifle and shrapnel fire. All day long we lay under this, replying whenever we got the chance. In the evening at about 8 o'clock the Spaniards fired their guns and then opened a heavy rifle fire, their skirmishers coming well forward. I got all my men down into the trenches, as did the other commands near me, and we opened a heavy return fire. The Spanish advance was at once stopped and after an hour their fire died away. This night we completed most of our trenches and began to build bomb proofs. The protection afforded to our men was good and next morning had but one man wounded from the rifle and shell fire until 12 o'clock, when the truce came.

I do not mention the officers and men who particularly distinguished themselves, as I have nothing to add in this respect to what was contained in my two former letters. There were numerous Red Cross flags flying in various parts of the city, two of them so arranged that they directly covered batteries in our front and for some time were the cause of our not firing at them. The Spanish guerillas were very active, especially in our rear, where they seemed by preference to attack the wounded men who were being carried on litters, the doctors and medical attendants with Red Cross bandages on their arms and the burial

parties. I organized a detail of sharpshooters and sent them out after
these guerillas, of whom they killed 13. Two of the men thus killed were
shot several hours after the truce had been in operation, because in spite
of this fact they kept firing upon our men as they went to draw water.
They were stationed in trees (as the guerillas were generally) and owing
to the density of the foliage and to the use of smokeless powder rifles it
was an exceedingly difficult matter to locate them. For the next seven
days, until the 10th, we lay in our lines while the truce continued. We
had continually to work at additional bomb proofs and at the trenches,
and as we had no proper supply of food and utterly inadequate medical
facilities the men suffered a good deal. The officers clubbed together to
purchase beans, tomatoes and sugar for the men, so that they might
have some relief from the bacon and hard tack. With a great deal of difficulty we got them coffee.

As for the sick and wounded they suffered so in the hospitals when
sent to the rear from lack of food and attention that we found it best to
keep them at the front and give them such care as our own doctors
could. As I mentioned in my previous letter, thirteen of our wounded
men continued to fight through the battle in spite of their wounds, and
of those sent to the rear many, both of the sick and wounded, came up
to rejoin us as soon as their condition allowed them to walk; most of the
worst cases were ultimately sent to the States.

On the 10th the truce was at an end and the bombardment re-
opened. As far as our lines were concerned, it was on the Spanish part
very feeble. We suffered no losses and speedily got the fire from their
trenches in our front completely under. On the 11th we were moved
3/4 of a mile to the right, the truce again being on. Nothing happened
here, except we continued to watch and do our best to get the men, especially the sick, properly fed, and having no transportation and being
unable to get hardly any through the regular channels, we used anything we could find—captured Spanish cavalry horses, abandoned
mules, which had been shot, but which our men took and cured,
diminutive skinny ponies purchased from the Cubans, etc. By these
means and by the exertions of the officers we were able from time to
time to get supplies of beans, sugar, tomatoes, and even oatmeal, while
from the Red Cross people we got one invaluable load of rice, corn
meal, etc. All of this was of the utmost consequence, not only for the
sick normically [sic] well, as the lack of proper food was telling terribly
on the men. It was utterly impossible to get them clothes and shoes;
those they had were, in many cases literally dropping to pieces.

On the 17th the city surrendered. On the 18th we shifted camp to
here, the best camp we have had, but the march hither under the noon-

day sun told very heavily on our men weakened by underfeeding and overwork, and next morning 123 cases were reported to the doctors, and I now have but half of the 600 men with which I landed four weeks ago, fit for duty, and these are not fit to do anything like the work they could do then. As we had but one wagon, the change necessitated leaving much of the stuff behind, with a night of discomfort, with scanty shelter and scanty food, for most of the officers and many of the men. Only the possession of the improvised pack train alluded to above saved this from being worse. Yesterday I sent in a detail of six officers and men to see if they could not purchase or make arrangements for a supply of proper food and proper clothing for the men, even if we had to pay for it out of our own pockets. Our suffering has been due primarily to lack of transportation and of proper food and sufficient clothing and of medical supplies. We should now have wagon sheets for tentage.

Very respectfully

July 27, 1898. Santiago
To Douglas Robinson

Dear Douglas:

I was delighted to get your letter, and as I am told there are various packages awaiting me, I suppose some of them are probably from you. We had a bully fight at Santiago, and though there was an immense amount that I did not exactly enjoy, the charge itself was great fun. Frankly, it did not enter my head that I could get through without being hit, but I judged that even if hit the chances would be about three to one against my being killed; that has been the proportion of dead to wounded here.

As for the political effect of my actions; in the first place, I never can get on in politics, and in the second, I would rather have led that charge and earned my colonelcy than served three terms in the United States Senate. It makes me feel as though I could now leave something to my children which will serve as an apology for my having existed. In spite of the strain and the anything but hygienic conditions under which we have lived, I am in very good health, so far having been the only officer in my regiment, excepting one, who has escaped the fever; even Wood has been down with it. If we stay here all summer we shall have yellow fever among us, of course, but I rather think I will pull through that too. I wish they would let us go to Porto Rico, or, if not, then let me get all my regiment together in Maine or somewhere like that and get them in trim for the great campaign against Havana in the fall. I wish you could see these men. I am as proud of them as I can be, and I verily believe they would go anywhere with me. Just now we have plenty of food—in fact have been living high the past three days—and if it was not for the way they are being knocked down right and left with the fever I would not have an objection to make to this camp so long as we had to be inactive.

I hope Kenneth is doing well. Bob is in pretty fair health. He and I went over Morro Castle yesterday.

Give my warmest love to Corinne and tell her not to be nervous. I shan't take any risks unless I really think I ought to, and now I begin to believe I am going to get home safely.

Always yours

July 31, 1898. Santiago
To Henry Cabot Lodge

Dear Cabot:

I was delighted to get your letter from New York; and with it came my commission as Colonel, which resulted in my now being in command of the Brigade, for bullets and disease have worked havoc among the higher officers.

I suppose Gussie is now in Porto Rico. I wish him all possible luck.

It is part of the grotesque mismanagement of our campaign that half of this army has not been sent there.

During the past fortnight the yellow fever cases have been very few and have been confined to Siboney, a port 15 miles away. If we had been shipped a week ago there would have been absolutely no danger; if we were shipped now there would be practically no danger; but it is simply infamous to keep us here during the sickly months that are now on and which will last until October, to serve no possible object, but merely because the authorities to whom the United States has entrusted the lives of the men as well as the honor of the flag are helplessly unable to do their duty. We have had at Siboney a few cases of yellow fever; two of my men who were sent to the hospital there caught this yellow fever and died, as did a few others from different regiments. Here at the front we have had no yellow fever whatever but any amount of malarial fever, probably 1500 cases in the Cavalry Division alone; not a death has resulted, and the men all go back to their work after a few days, but very much shattered and weakened and in fine shape to catch yellow fever or anything. The malarial fever is no more contagious or infectious than a cut finger; yet Alger in his message to us absolutely seems to treat the yellow fever and the malarial fever as if they were alike; he says that he will take the troops back when the fever shows signs of lessening. Of course, the malarial fever won't lessen; it will increase, and if he does as he says he will simply keep us here, growing weaker and weaker, until Yellow Jack does come in and we die like rotten sheep, and this for absolutely no end whatever and with absolutely no excuse. Among the doctors here the name of this fever is the Five-day Fever; and because the Secretary cannot distinguish between this Five-day Fever and the Yellow Jack, he actually proposes to keep us here until we catch the latter. I am determined that my skirts shall be clear of this particular form of murder, and so I have written the enclosed letter.

I am not in the least alarmed about myself; in the first place I don't think I should die if I caught it, and in the next place should the worse come to the worst I am quite content to go now and to leave my children at least an honorable name (and, old man, if I do go, I do wish you would get that medal of honor for me anyhow, as I should awfully like the children to have it, and I think I earned it). But these men under me, who have fought and worked and marched and endured hardship and exposure and semi-starvation without complaint, and whose fellows have met death bravely and quietly, are entitled at least to just treatment. I have spent their blood like water myself when there seemed an object and have flung them straight against entrenchments and kept them hour after hour, dropping under rifle and shrapnel fire, and now if there was need of our holding a town against any foe, I would care not one jot more for yellow fever than for Spanish bullets and would not mind sacrificing the lives of my entire command; but to sacrifice them pointlessly from mere stupidity and inefficiency is cruel.

I do not suppose you can do anything, and when you receive this it may be too late anyhow, but if the army is not brought away from here with all possible expedition and if an epidemic does really break out, the President and the Secretary of War will have incurred a debt as heavy as Walpole incurred when he wasted the lives of Admiral Hozier's 3000 men in these same West Indian waters against this same Spanish foe. Perhaps you think I write too bitterly. I can only say, old man, that what I have seen during the last five weeks has been enough to make one bitter.

But, Oh, how well the Navy has done. The courage and fighting capacity of our soldiers on shore cannot be surpassed by their brethren on the sea, but Oh, the difference in the Departments and in the men in the higher ranks.

I know just how you feel about Harry and Bay. You cannot help being nervous and yet you would not for anything in the world have them elsewhere than where they are. Mark my words, however, that they will not suffer any more than the Navy has hitherto suffered. The remaining war vessels of the Spaniards will fight less effectively than those which we have captured or have sunk have fought, and Bay and Harry, and any other officer, will off Spain do as they have done off Cuba and the Philippines, that is, win undying honor and glory at a cost that we may disregard.

Oh, how I wish I were in Porto Rico with Gussie and under General Wilson. He'd be proud of this command. Frankly, I think anyone would be.

Do write me again, old man, and don't think I am not having a good time, for I am; this has been, aside from Edith, *the* time of my life; but there have been a good many grim features to it, and you're the only man to whom I can write of them.

As for politics, I am not really able to take any steps about them now, because while this war lasts the only thing I want to do is to command this regiment and get it into all the fighting I can. As I told you, I am at present in command of the Brigade, and I enjoy handling that, too, for I feel perfectly competent to handle a Brigade in the field now. Of course, if I can possibly get out of it I do not intend to stay in the army merely for police work; I only want to be in while there is actual fighting on a fairly big scale. If I could get down to National politics instead of dealing with sewers and police boards in New York, I should greatly prefer it, but I haven't any real knack of getting on in politics, and the favor of the multitude (especially when extended about equally to our regiment, which has an almost unequalled record, and the 71st New York, which did very badly) is a matter of about ten days. The good people in New York at present seem to be crazy over me; it is not very long since on the whole they felt I compared unfavorably with Caligula. By the time election day comes round they may have reverted to their former feeling; and in any event I don't know how to get on with the New York politicians. If I had money enough to keep in National politics it would not be difficult, because the average New York boss is quite willing to allow you to do what you wish in such trivial matters as war and the acquisition of Porto Rico and Hawaii, provided you don't interfere with the really vital questions, such as giving out contracts for cartage in the Custom House and interfering with the appointment of street sweepers.

Warmest love to Nannie, John and Sturgis Bigelow.

Faithfully yours

Our regiment ranks with the regulars; aside from us, it was purely the regulars who did the real fighting. The National Guard regiments, with their black powder muskets, were nearly worthless.

August 3, 1898. Santiago
To William R. Shafter

Sir:

In a meeting of the general and medical officers called by you at the Palace this morning we were all, as you know, unanimous in our views of what should be done with the army. To keep us here, in the opinion of every officer commanding a division or a brigade, will simply involve the destruction of thousands. There is no possible reason for not shipping practically the entire command North at once.

Yellow-fever cases are very few in the cavalry division, where I command one of the two brigades, and not one true case of yellow fever has occurred in this division, except among the men sent to the hospital at Siboney, where they have, I believe, contracted it.

But in this division there have been 1,500 cases of malarial fever. Hardly a man has yet died from it, but the whole command is so weakened and shattered as to be ripe for dying like rotten sheep, when a real yellow-fever epidemic instead of a fake epidemic, like the present one, strikes us, as it is bound to do if we stay here at the height of the sickness season, August and the beginning of September. Quarantine against malarial fever is much like quarantining against the toothache.

All of us are certain that as soon as the authorities at Washington fully appreciate the condition of the army, we shall be sent home. If we are kept here it will in all human possibility mean an appalling disaster, for the surgeons here estimate that over half the army, if kept here during the sickly season, will die.

This is not only terrible from the standpoint of the individual lives lost, but it means ruin from the standpoint of military efficiency of the flower of the American army, for the great bulk of the regulars are here with you. The sick-list, large though it is, exceeding four thousand, affords but a faint index of the debilitation of the army. Not twenty per cent are fit for active work.

Six weeks on the North Maine coast, for instance, or elsewhere where the yellow-fever germ cannot possibly propagate, would make us all as fit as fighting-cocks, as able as we are eager to take a leading part in the great campaign against Havana in the fall, even if we are not allowed to try Porto Rico.

We can be moved North, if moved at once, with absolute safety to the country, although, of course, it would have been infinitely better if we had been moved North or to Porto Rico two weeks ago. If there were any object in keeping us here, we would face yellow fever with as much indifference as we faced bullets. But there is no object.

The four immune regiments ordered here are sufficient to garrison the city and surrounding towns, and there is absolutely nothing for us to do here, and there has not been since the city surrendered. It is impossible to move into the interior. Every shifting of camp doubles the sick-rate in our present weakened conditions, and, anyhow, the interior is rather worse than the coast, as I have found by actual reconnoissance. Our present camps are as healthy as any camps at this end of the island can be.

I write only because I cannot see our men, who have fought so bravely and who have endured extreme hardship and danger so uncomplainingly, go to destruction without striving so far as lies in me to avert a doom as fearful as it is unnecessary and undeserved.

Yours respectfully

August 3, 1898. Santiago
To William R. Shafter

We, the undersigned officers commanding the various brigades, divisions, etc., of the Army of Occupation in Cuba, are of the unanimous opinion that this army should be at once taken out of the island of Cuba and sent to some point on the Northern seacoast of the United States; that can be done without danger to the people of the United States; that yellow fever in the army at present is not epidemic; that there are only a few sporadic cases; but that the army is disabled by malarial fever to the extent that its efficiency is destroyed, and that it is in a condition to be practically entirely destroyed by an epidemic of yellow fever, which is sure to come in the near future.

We know from the reports of competent officers and from personal observations that the army is unable to move into the interior, and that there are no facilities for such a move if attempted; and that it could not be attempted until too late. Moreover, the best medical authorities of the island say that with our present equipment we could not live in the interior during the rainy season without losses from malarial fever, which is almost as deadly as yellow fever.

This army must be moved at once, or perish. As the army can be safely moved now, the persons responsible for preventing such a move will be responsible for the unnecessary loss of many thousands of lives.

Our opinions are the result of careful personal observation, and they are also based on the unanimous opinion of our medical officers with the army, who understand the situation absolutely.

J. Ford Kent,

Major-General Volunteers Commanding First Divisions, Fifth Corps.

J. C. Bates,

Major-General Volunteers Commanding Provisional Division.

Adnah R. Chaffee,

Major-General Commanding Third Brigade, Second Division.

Samuel S. Summer,

Brigadier-General Volunteers Commanding First Brigade, Cavalry.

Will Ludlow,

Brigadier-General Volunteers Commanding First Brigade, Second Division.

Adelbert Ames,
Brigadier-General Volunteers Commanding Third Brigade, First Division
Leonard Wood,
Brigadier-General Volunteers Commanding the City of Santiago.
Theodore Roosevelt,
Colonel Commanding Second Cavalry Brigade.

August 27, 1898. Montauk, Long Island
To Seth Low

My dear President,
   You are more than kind and I deeply appreciate your constant thoughtfulness. I am "running" in the same kind of way that you did. I am just letting events take their course. There is a great deal I have to tell you about; like you I have a fire on both flanks.
   Very Cordially Yours

September 19, 1898. Oyster Bay
To Henry Cabot Lodge

Dear Cabot:
   Will you tell the men of the Middlesex Club that, while I cannot promise, yet if I possibly can come to their dinner, I most certainly shall. You know the peculiar feeling I have for Massachusetts and for the Republican Party in Massachusetts.
   If I can get away at the time they give their dinner, I certainly will. As to the Republican Club, tell them that there is nothing I should like more than to speak for them, but that if I am nominated, I *cannot* leave the State. My managers would not permit it.
   Will you also tell Hayes that I telegraphed right and left to try to get Turner, but never heard from him or saw him.
   That letter of Wilson's, I think, is something that should be kept as an invaluable heirloom for Gussie's descendants. It is as different as possible from the ordinary letter of commendation; in fact, I have never known any letter precisely like it, except one which Gen. Lawton wrote about Wood. I wish I could see Gus and Bay.
   Apparently, I am going to be nominated. I saw Platt the other day, and had an entirely satisfactory talk. Of course, I shall have great trouble in the governorship, but there is no use in shirking responsibilities. The first installment of trouble is already on hand, for I cannot accept the so-called independent nomination and keep good faith with the other men on the Republican ticket, against whom the independent ticket is really put up. I would give a great deal were you where I could talk over things

with you now and then, but I am being as circumspect as possible and am trying to commit as few mistakes as possible.

Give my best love to Nannie.

Faithfully yours

P. S.—I wish, if you are willing, that you would write a line to the President for Wood for one of the vacant Brigadier Generalships in the Regular Army. It would be rather revolutionary to put him in over the heads of the elder men, but it would be one of the best things that could happen to the Army. We want young Generals of Wood's capacity, sound good sense and extraordinary energy.

November 25, 1898. Oyster Bay
To Cecil Spring Rice

Dear Cecil:

Of course, I was delighted to get your cable, and I knew you would be pleased with my success. I have played it in bull luck this summer. First, to get into the war; then to get out of it; then to get elected. I have worked hard all my life, and have never been particularly lucky, but this summer I was lucky, and I am enjoying it to the full. I know perfectly well that the luck will not continue, and it is not necessary that it should. I am more than contented to be Governor of New York, and shall not care if I never hold another office; and I am very proud of my regiment, which was really a noteworthy volunteer organization.

Mrs. Roosevelt is now almost as well as ever she was and the children are well too. I am up to my ears in work and have time only to send you a line.

Isn't it nice to think how closely our two nations have come together this year? We must make every effort to see that they stay together. Do you recollect a letter I wrote you last year about Germany and especially Russia?

Mrs. Roosevelt sends you her love. Did you know that my sister Anna Cowles had a baby?

Faithfully yours

December 6, 1898. New York
To Henry Cabot Lodge

Dear Cabot:

Hearty thanks! The attitude of the Secretary of course simply means that the War Department does not intend that I shall have the Medal of Honor. If I didn't earn it, then no commissioned officer ever can earn it. I was not acting in accordance with orders. I had been told to *support* the attack of the Regulars with my regiment. I moved through the 9th Regiment, of my own accord, and gave the order to charge, and led in person that portion of the line on horseback, being the first man on the Hill, and killing a Spaniard with my own hand. I led in person the next charge on the second line of block-houses; I led in person the third charge; and then at the extreme front commanded the fragments of the six cavalry regiments and brigade until the next morning. I don't ask this as a favor—I ask it as a right. Wood, Wheeler, and Shafter joined in making the request for me; Miles has told me it certainly should be granted as a matter of course; and General Sumner, and Captain Stevens of the 9th, Captain Steele and Captain Howze of General Sumner's staff, and Captains McBlaine and McAnee, of the Ninth, and Captain Ayres of the Tenth, could all be summoned as eyewitnesses—not to speak of my own men. I have stood, without making a counter attack, the Secretary's publication of my private letter, and the President's failure to interfere with it. I do not feel much like standing the refusal to give me the only reward they possibly can give me. Remember that though I had commanded a brigade, and though I had been singled out in reports for special commendation, I was given no brevet rank. For this I don't care, but I am entitled to the Medal of Honor, and I want it.

The Daly matter has rather complicated matters, and may result in my appointing Hendricks. I will tell you about it when we meet.

Faithfully yours

P. S.—I have seen that Spanish report. Do get me a copy of the Wood-Wheeler-Shafter recommendation. I feel rather ugly on this medal of honor business; and the President and War Dept. may as well understand it. If they want fighting, they shall have it.

December 12, 1898. Oyster Bay
To Susan B. Anthony

My Dear Madam:

Your letter really pleased me. I have always favored allowing women to vote, but I will say frankly, that I do not attach the importance to it that you do. I want to fight for what there is the most need of and the most chance of getting, at the moment. I think that, under the present laws, woman can get all the rights she will take; while she is in many cases oppressed, the trouble is in her own attitude, which laws cannot alter.

Very sincerely yours

January 10, 1899. Albany, New York
To Helen Kendrick Johnson

My dear madam:

I had already read your book and was much interested in it. If you will pardon me for saying so, I think you confound two phases of the struggle for what are rather vaguely called "Woman's rights." I do not wonder at this at all, for the advocates of the movement not only do the same thing, but the noisiest of them usually lay all the stress on the very undesirable side; in other words, the professional Woman's rights people contain in their number altogether too many representatives of the same intellectual and moral type as the bulk of the professional abolitionists. The antislavery cause was eminently just, and even the professional abolitionists probably on the whole did good; but the more one reads of these professional abolitionists (I do not mean men like Birney, but the men who advocated disunion or anarchy and who betrayed a foolish and feeble violence in dealing with all practical questions),—the more one feels that they were about as undesirable a class of people as the country ever saw. But it would have been literally criminal folly to wish to perpetuate slavery because so many of the extreme professional antislavery champaions were noxious members of the body politic, or because most of their ideas were wrong, or even because the slaves would not do as well when free as was hoped.

The extreme advocates of any cause always include fanatics, and often fools, and they generally number a considerable proportion of those people whose mind is so warped as to make them combine in a very curious degree a queer kind of disinterested zeal with a queer kind of immorality. A great many self-styled woman's champions revolt, not against the laws of man, but against the laws of nature. It certainly seems to our finite minds a great injustice of nature that the hardest lot in life should fall to the weakest half of the human race. On the average the woman has a harder time than the man, and must have, from the mere fact that she must bear, nurse and largely rear her children. There is no use in blinking this fact. It must simply be accepted as war or any necessarily hazardous profession must be accepted. The first duty of woman is the duty of motherhood, just as the first duty of the man is breadwinning—homemaking. Marriage is, of course, just as much the duty of one as of the other. There are exceptional men and women who need not or ought not to marry, just as there are exceptional men and women who need not or ought not to work, or to go to war; but these are exceptions, sometimes to be honored and sometimes to be pitied. The normal, healthy man should always count upon working hard and should hold himself ready at any time to go to war, or to go into any occupation, no matter how hazardous—like that of a miner, a deep-sea fisherman, a railroad man or a fireman,—while the normal, healthy woman should be a mother. Our race is unfit to cumber the earth, if its men do not work hard, and are not always ready, if there is need, to fight, and, of course, a race is neither fit to cumber the earth nor able to do so, unless its women breed. Work—fight—breed—a race may do all these things, and yet be worthless; but unless it does them, it certainly *must* be worthless.

So far then as the movement for woman's rights represents a revolt against either common sense or morality, it should be smashed. But we are no more justified in opposing it because there is this element in it, than we would have been in championing slavery because there was a similar element in the abolition movement. It is not necessary to say that I entirely agree with you about the home and its all-importance. Remember that the very evils which the opponents of the present movement most dread exist to their fullest extent in societies where that movement has absolutely no footing. In France the race has begun to decrease and the nation is decaying mainly because of the way in which men and women look upon the relations between the sexes, upon family life and upon having children. But France is the very country where the legal and social attitude of the body politic on questions like divorce, the property of women, headship of the man, the different standards of morality for the man and the woman, political rights of the woman etc. is the least progressive and is the most medieval and most divergent from the views taken by the advocates of the betterment of woman's condition. The worst results that could follow the adoption of the ideas of the new champions of woman, could no more than equal the results that have happened in France, where those ideas have never gained the least foothold.

Sane advocates of woman's rights would bring about, I am confident, a great betterment in her status, while at the same time simply causing her better to perform every duty she now performs. Just the same arguments that were advanced against giving women the suffrage are or were advanced in favor of keeping the man the absolute tyrant of the household. As a rule the headship of the man is most complete the lower we go in the social and ethnic scale (heroic Greece to the contrary notwithstanding), and the higher and nobler the race is, the more nearly the marriage relation becomes a partnership on equal terms—the equality, of course, consisting not in the performance of the same duties by the two parties, but in the admirable performance of utterly different duties, and in mutual forbearance and respect.

I do not for a moment believe that the suffrage will do all that is claimed for it, whether for women or for men, and I should always introduce it tentatively in new groups of either sex. There are great bodies of women who are unfit for it, just as unquestionably, taking the world as a whole, (including Asia and Africa for instance), the great majority of men are unfit to exercise it. Only in the highest country, like our own, is it wise to try universal suffrage. In our own country the gradual betterment of woman's condition has been due to the working of forces which may or may not ultimately find expression through the suffrage. But I think the suffrage would accomplish something. If you will read such a story as Mary E. Wilkins's "The Revolt of Mother," you will appreciate how even in our country there are enormous bodies of, on the whole, pretty good people, where women are shamefully wronged because they are not treated as equals. What we need is to teach the woman self-respect, and the man to respect the woman; for in the last resort I hardly know whether to despise most the being who neglects his or her duties, or the being who fails to assert his or her rights. If the woman were a voter, if the woman were in the eye of the law a citizen with full rights of citizenship, it would undoubtedly on the whole have a tendency to increase her self-respect and to wring a measure of reluctant respect for her from man. There never was an extension of the suffrage yet which was not accompanied by some evil results, but on the whole, in the present state of society, the only way to ensure the proper regard for the rights of any particular section of a community like ours seems to be to let that section have a voice in the general affairs. Practically I may mention that in my own little school district admission of women to the franchise for school matters has resulted distinctly well. I should like by degrees to increase the sphere in which the women of New York State can exercise the suffrage, doing it very cautiously and by degrees, and seeing how each extension practically works.

Very truly yours

February 8, 1899. Albany
To Jacob Riis

Dear Friend:

I have your letter of the 6th instant and will support the bill you refer to. Now as to the case of Mrs. Place. I have not yet heard from her lawyers who together with certain other of her champions are to argue before me. Remember this is not my first case. I have already refused to pardon a negro convicted of wife murder. This is a woman convicted of a very cruel murder of another woman. I have exactly the same feeling that you have about womanhood and about the burdens which nature has placed upon women and the duty of man to make them as light as possible. For instance, where a poor seduced girl kills her child to hide her shame, I would infinitely rather punish the man who seduced her than the poor creature who actually committed the murder. But there are some fiends among women, and I hardly think, old man, that we help womanhood by helping these exceptions. However, I shall go into it with the utmost care and with the very highest sense of my own responsibility.

Am I to see Mrs. Kelley and Miss Addams on the afternoon of the 17th?

Faithfully yours

February 14, 1899. Albany
To Cecil Spring Rice

Dear Cecil:

I am very glad you are in Persia, because I know it is interesting; but I do wish there was some chance of getting you over here while I am Governor. The chances, of course, are very small that I shall again hold any important position, for New York politics, as you know, are of a very kaleidoscopic nature, and now during my hour of triumph, I should like very much to have around me the few people for whom I really care.

By the way, the change of tone in this country may perhaps be illustrated by a letter I have this morning received from an applicant for appointment, who bases his claims partly upon the fact that in a public speech he answered Bourke Cockran's attack upon England and explained the debt the world owes England and the way that the English and American should work hand in hand! Of course, there will be differences between the nations and the present fervor of feeling will probably cool off a little, but I do not believe it will ever cool off entirely. I do not believe that we shall ever go back to the old unfortunate ways. A curious thing is that I think those Americans who were Anglo-Saxon by adoption, as it were, are quite as strong about the unity of the two peoples as any others. The applicant before spoken of is like your humble servant, of Holland ancestry. The third generation of Germans feel far more akin to England as a rule than they do to Germany.

So far I have gotten along very well in this position, and I think I can conscientiously say that I have managed it on a pretty high plane. I do not intend to be impractical and I carefully refrain from breaking with the machine, and indeed so far they have been decidedly friendly in their attitude. But neither do I intend doing anything that is out of the way. There has not been an appointment that I have made, where the appointee has not been a man of good character, whose ability to fill the position has been the first question as to which I have satisfied myself; and in every matter, legislative or executive, with which I have had to deal, I have been as careful to steer clear of demagogism as I am to see that the largest possible measure of good is done for the men who most need it.

That I can get on permanently without trouble is not to be expected, but I do firmly intend that after my two years' term, the whole governmental service in this State shall be a little better off because of it.

Mrs. Roosevelt is really enjoying herself. We have a great big house which is very comfortable, although in appearance and furnishing, painfully suggestive of that kind of elegance which one sees in a swell Chicago hotel or in the board room of the directors of some big railway. The children are perfectly happy and on the whole well.

Always yours

March 1, 1899. Albany
To G. P. Putnam's Sons

Gentlemen:

I have your letter of the 28th ult.

I certainly did not understand from the terms of the agreement that the publication of the new volume (which of course will mean the falling off in sales of the old volume) was to prevent my getting the royalty on the first 1500 copies of the *Wilderness Hunter*, when the total sale had reached 3000 copies. What section of the memorandum of agreement do you regard as providing for this?

Very truly yours

March 15, 1899. Albany
To Thomas C. Platt

My Dear Senator Platt:

I have just received your telegram and I am exceedingly sorry that I cannot get down for Sunday. But some friends will pay us a visit then that I have once before had to defer, and I do not see how I can possibly get away. I enclose an invitation from Mrs. Roosevelt, who hopes that Mrs. Platt and yourself can come here for two or three days next week. I do wish you could come; but I shall at any rate see you Friday of next week, when I shall come down to New York. Can you breakfast with me on Saturday morning at 689 Madison Avenue, 8:30 o'clock? There are many things I wish to talk over with you. Since you left I have had one exceedingly painful and disagreeable duty to perform, in the case of the convicted murderess, Mrs. Place. I am also much puzzled over two or three bills; the Astoria Gas Bill, the Rapid Transit bill, and the Tunnel bill. Ought there not to be some arrangement by which, if the franchises prove very valuable, a portion of the gross earnings should be paid to the public treasury? The bills seem to me proper in their general purposes, but I do think that something should be done to secure the payment of a certain percentage of the gross earnings after some point is reached.

My slate of appointments being now definitely fixed, you see that I promptly begin to bother you about legislation! I shall be *very* glad to see you back.

Very sincerely yours

**April 27, 1899. Albany
To Henry Cabot Lodge**

Dear Cabot:

I enclose you a Chicago speech of mine. It seems to have attracted attention of an adverse sort in Massachusetts as I have been continually receiving marked copies of the *Transcript, Herald* and Springfield *Republican* containing editorials and letters by thoughtful publicists which take a very black view of my character, antecedents and prospects. I made another speech in which I said that we had equally to dread the corrupt machine politician and the fool reformer. A large number of gentlemen, seemingly recognizing the fact that they came under the latter head, have written me in indignant denunciation, and the *Evening Post* is especially bitter about it.

I have just finished your chapter in the May *Harper's*, and I think it altogether admirable. The end really stirred my blood! You seem to have struck your "note" in style once for all. You did more than justice to the Rough Riders. Before publishing in book form I should like to submit one or two minor corrections to you, but nothing of the least importance.

Well, the legislature has just ended, and the heavy work, so far as I am concerned, is over for the year 1899. I think I may say that I have come out of it all right. I am on excellent terms with Senator Platt. He has treated me admirably in every way and is I believe equally satisfied with the way I have treated him, except that I have not been able to back up some of his views about corporations. Frank Platt like Elihu Root[1] has occasionally appeared before me on behalf of corporation measures. It has happened that I have decided against both of them in every case. I mentioned this to the Senator, saying that I was really sorry for it, but of course, I felt that they should appear before me exactly as they would appear before the Supreme Court, when any corporation measure for which they had a retainer was concerned. He told me he absolutely agreed with me.

I have had great success with my appointments. I do not believe there is a single one that I have made that was open to any serious criticism, and on the whole I believe they average better than those made

---

[1]Elihu Root, Secretary of War from 1899 to 1904, and Secretary of State from 1905 to 1909, would support Roosevelt loyally but not unskeptically.

by any Governor during as long a time as I can remember. I got an excellent Civil Service Law passed, a first-class rapid transit bill, a first-class measure for taxing franchises—or rather for laying the foundation in the matter of taxing franchises; together with a sweatshop bill, the factory inspector's bills, a good banking law, etc., etc.

All together I am pretty well satisfied with what I have accomplished. I do not misunderstand in the least what it means—or rather, how little it may mean. New York politics are kaleidoscopic and 18 months hence I may be so much out of kilter with the machine that there will be no possibility of my renomination, and if renominated, my own conduct, or merely the general drift of events, may make it impossible to re-elect me; but at least I have a substantial sum of achievement to my credit in the Governorship already, and I have kept every pledge, expressed or implied, that I made on the stump or anywhere else.

So much for my own parochial politics. As regards the nation at large, I do wish that President McKinley would get rid of Alger! Bryan is I believe a good deal stronger than he was three years ago, and it looks now, as though it was going to be a serious struggle in 1900. Of course, McKinley must be renominated; so the success of the Republican party depends upon him. I believe that we shall carry him through, even with Alger, but when one has to make a hard fight there is no use of handicapping one's self. I told all this to Postmaster General Smith and to Judge Kohlsaat while in Chicago.

We have had a rather disagreeable experience with Captain Coghlan. He talked too much, but I confess that if I had been the President I should have told Germany that until they apologized for what Admiral Von Diederichs *did,* they need not worry themselves about what Captain Coghlan *said.* The attitude of the *Staats-Zeitung* has been infamous; also that of some of the professional Irish leaders.

While Alger is in the Cabinet I always have a feeling of uneasiness about Cuba and the Philippines. We need to exercise much care in the former and to show unyielding resolution in the latter. There are symptoms apparently of a breakup among the Philippine insurgents, but if it does not come soon, I wish that McKinley would mobilize the 35,000 volunteers, and send a large force to the Islands.

Brooks and Mrs. Adams are passing a couple of days with us. Brooks is fairly revelling in his belief of our utter and absolute administrative breakdown and is firm in his conviction that the government is corrupt from top to bottom.

If you see Sir George Trevelyan give him my warm regards, and with best love to Nannie and the boys from both myself and Edith, I am,
    Ever yours

May 8, 1899. Albany
To Thomas C. Platt

My dear Senator:

I received your letter yesterday afternoon, and have taken 24 hours to consider it deeply before replying.

In the first place, my dear Senator, let me express my sense of the frankness, courtesy and delicacy with which you write and with which you have invariably treated me ever since my nomination. The very keen sense that I have of this makes it more unpleasant than I can say to have to disagree with you. As I have told you, and as I have told very many others, you have treated me so well and shown such entire willingness to meet me half way, that it has been the greatest possible pleasure for me to agree with you and to try to carry out your ideas, and it has caused me real pain when I have had to disagree with you. I am peculiarly sorry that the most serious cause of disagreement should come in this way right at the end of the session.

I remember well all the incidents of our meeting which you describe; and I knew that you had just the feelings that you mention; that is, apart from my "impulsiveness," you felt that there was a justifiable anxiety among men of means, and especially men representing large corporate interests, lest I might feel too strongly on what you term the "altruistic" side in matters of labor and capital and as regards the relations of the State to great corporations. I very earnestly desired to show that this was not to any improper degree the case. My dear Senator, I cannot help feeling that I *have* shown it. Now, I do not like to say this when you think I *have not*, because you have infinitely more experience than I have in matters of this sort, and in most of such cases your judgment is far better than mine; but pray do not believe that I have gone off halfcocked in this matter. I should have been delighted to have escaped the need of taking action at all, and I only did take action when it was forced upon me, after an immense amount of thought and worry.

I appreciate all you say about what Bryanism means, and I also know that when parties divide on such issues, the tendency is to force everybody into one of two camps, and to throw out entirely men like myself, who are as strongly opposed to populism in every stage as the greatest representative of corporate wealth, but who also feel strongly that masses of these representatives of enormous corporate wealth have themselves been responsible for a portion of the conditions against which Bryanism is in ignorant, and sometimes wicked, revolt. I do not believe that it is wise or safe for us as a party to take refuge in mere negation and to say that there are no evils to be corrected. It seems to me that our attitude should be one of correcting the evils and thereby showing that, whereas the populists, socialists and others really do not correct the evils at all, or else only do so at the expense of producing others in aggravated form, on the contrary the Republicans hold the just balance and set our faces as resolutely against improper corporate influence on the one hand as against demagogy and mob rule on the other. I understand perfectly that such an attitude of moderation is apt to be misunderstood when passions are greatly excited and when victory is apt to rest with the extremists on one side or the other; yet I think it is in the long run the only wise attitude. I believe that in the long run here in this State we should be beaten, and badly beaten, if we took the attitude of saying that corporations should not, when they receive great benefits and make a great deal of money, pay their share of the public burdens; and that on the other hand, if we do take this attitude we shall be all the stronger when we declare that the laborers shall commit no disorder and that we are utterly against any attack on the lawful use of wealth. For instance, when trouble was anticipated just now in Buffalo, I at once sent Major General Roe out there and got the whole brigade of National Militia in the neighborhood in shape to be used immediately. The labor men came up to protest. I told them instantly that I should entertain no protest; that the militia would not be called out unless the local authorities stated that they needed them; but that the minute this condition was found to exist, they would be called out, and that I should not consider for a moment the protest that this was "intimidating the laboring men," because it would intimidate no one unless he was anxious to commit lawlessness, and that in that case it would be my especial care to see that he *was* intimidated.

Now, let me take up this particular franchise tax bill. I wish that its opponents would recollect that it is by no means a revolutionary measure. Franchises are taxed in very much the same way in Connecticut and have been for many years. They are taxed in a somewhat different way in Pennsylvania. They are taxed much more severely in many parts of Great Britain. Where they have escaped taxation the result has been as in Detroit, Toledo and Chicago, to make the citizens generally join in such a revolt that they have swung to the opposite extreme of municipal ownership and have forbidden the granting of any franchises. I think we wish to be careful about taking a position which will produce such a revolt. And as regards the effect on the party, I believe that the killing of this bill would come a great deal nearer than its passage to making New York democratic a year from next fall. If we run McKinley against Bryan the big corporate influences must in self-defense go for the former; and on the other hand, we shall have strengthened the former by strengthening the republican party among the mass of our people and making them believe that we do stand squarely for the interests of all of the people, whether they are or are not connected in any way with corporations. When I sent in my first taxation message to the Legislature it did not seem as if any bill could be passed or agreed upon by the legislature; and was then told that this Committee would be appointed and that a serious effort would be made to tax franchises. In the message itself you will remember I took the most positive ground in favor of thus taxing them. Without any notification to me the Senate suddenly took up and passed the Ford bill. I then began to study it pretty carefully and the more I studied it, the more convinced I became that it was along the right lines; that is, that franchises should be taxed as realty, according to the Connecticut plan.

Now, as to the inference about my yielding to the yellow journals and public clamor. I have not this year to my knowledge seen a copy of the *Journal*. I doubt very much if I have seen a copy of the *World* twice and certainly I have never looked at its editorial page; and it would be an overestimate to say that I have seen a dozen editions of the *Herald*. I have, however, read the *Tribune* quite often and the *Sun* very often. These are almost the only papers I have seen except the Albany *Evening Journal*. I feel the most profound indifference to the clamor of the yellow papers. I think I showed it in my attitude on the Mrs. Place matter; in my veto of the World's labor bill; in putting the militia in readiness in Buffalo to meet the strike; also in my attitude on the 71st Regiment business. I appreciate absolutely that any applause I get from any such source too evanescent for a moment's consideration. I appreciate absolutely that the people who now loudly approve of my action in the Franchise Tax bill will forget all about it in a fortnight, and that on the other hand, the very powerful interests adversely affected will always remember it— certainly to my disadvantage, which is unimportant, and not impossibly to the disadvantage of the party, which *is* important. But I feel that we should be put in the wrong if the bill failed to become a law.

However, to return to the thread of the narrative of the bill. It got into the House and everybody agreed that some action in reference to taxation would have to be taken this session; that is, that the principle of taxing franchises would have to be recognized in some shape or form so as to give the Committee something to work on. As I told you that morning at breakfast, and as I have reiterated to Odell[1] on his last visit here, I was anxious to accept any bill, whether I approved of it in all its details or not, provided it met your approval, and recognized substantially the principles sought to be attained. When Odell was up here the Monday and

---

[1]Platt protégé Benjamin Odell.

Tuesday before the legislature adjourned, I went over this matter with him. He agreed with me in the most unequivocal manner that some measure taxing franchises must be passed—indeed treated this as a matter of course. At first on looking over the Rodenbeck and Ford bills, he said he preferred the Ford bill, but that an amendment should be inserted giving the taxing power to the State authorities. I think he said the State Assessors, but otherwise the Comptroller. To this I cordially agreed. That same afternoon he told me he preferred the Rodenbeck bill. I said, very well; that although I did not think it much of a measure, I would cordially back it if that was what the Organization wanted. Accordingly I summoned the different senators, Ellsworth, Raines, Higgins, Stranahan and others and asked them whether they would take up the Rodenbeck bill. They positively refused to do so and said that the Ford bill was what everyone wanted. I then saw Nixon and Allds and found that they were bent upon the Rodenbeck bill. I asked the leaders of the two houses to consult together and come to an agreement. They failed to reach any agreement; in my presence Ellsworth told Nixon that they must pass the Ford bill. I then wrote to Ellsworth and Nixon personal letters explaining that something ought to be passed; that though I did not like the Rodenbeck bill, I was entirely content to take it, but that the two houses ought to agree on some measure. Finally the day before adjournment Nixon and Allds called upon me and said they could no longer withstand the pressure; the people wanted the Ford bill (Allds used the words that he had "received orders not to pass it,") and they could not withstand the pressure any longer and would have to pass it, but wished it to be understood that they were not solely responsible for it—that is, I understood that they wished that I would share the responsibility. They explained that they knew they could not get the Rodenbeck bill through the Senate and did not think they could get it through the House. The senators had also told me by this time that they could not pass the Rodenbeck bill, and that if any amendment was made to the Ford bill, they thought that at that late day in the session it simply meant its death. Accordingly after Nixon and Allds went out and after Fallows had come in to state that without an emergency message they could not pass the bill, I sent them down the emergency message. Nixon says, and then said, that it was absolutely necessary for us to pass the bill; Ellsworth said it had to be passed, Nixon said my message was needless, and my message was never read. Exactly what became of it after it left my messenger's hands and passed into the custody of the Assembly, I do not know; I believe it was torn up. At any rate, the course was followed of refusing to entertain it; the objection being frankly made to the passage of the bill by Mr. Kelly, among others, that it could not be passed because Mr. Brady (he who deluged these counties last year with the money to beat our ticket) was against it. The representatives of the corporations here were perfectly frank in stating that they did not intend to have any legislative recognition of the principle that franchises should be taxed; that they were against it in any and every shape; that they were perfectly willing to have a committee appointed, because they would take care that that committee made its report in such shape as to prevent franchises being interfered with, but that no substantial action recognizing their taxation should be taken. They also urged upon me that I personally could not afford to take this action for under no circumstances could I ever again be nominated for any public office, as no corporation would subscribe to a campaign fund if I was on the ticket and that they would subscribe most heavily to beat me, and when I asked if this was true of republican corporations, the cynical answer was made that the corporations that subscribed most heavily to the campaign funds subscribed impartially to both party organizations. Under all these circumstances it seemed to me there was no alternative but to do what I could to secure the passage of the Ford Bill without amendment—not that I altogether liked it, but that I thought it a great deal better than inaction under these conditions. I accordingly sent in my second message.

The serious objection to this bill is that the levying and assessing of the tax is made by the local authorities. It seems to me right that the payment should be to the local authorities, but the levying and assessing should be done by the State authorities. In its essence the tax is right. It should be a tax as realty and not as personalty. I question very much if we could by law secure at the outset the right method of getting at the exact money value of these franchises. It seems to me that it would be wiser to leave that question to a board of assessors. Nevertheless if the opposite course is deemed desirable I am perfectly willing to acquiesce. If the Mazet Committee brings out, as you tell me it will, the utter corruption of Tammany in laying these taxes, my own idea would be, subject to your approval, that we should use that as a justification for requesting speedy action by the joint Committee of the two Houses in preparing a proper tax bill, and I am then entirely willing if it is deemed best to call together the legislature and have the present bill amended, or have it repealed by the passage of a full and proper tax bill; it being always understood, of course, that this tax bill shall contain provisions under which these franchises will be taxed in reality and genuinely and not nominally, so that they shall pay their full share of the public burdens.

I have just received a telegram from Odell saying that he cannot come up here to spend the night with me. I shall ask him up for tomorrow night and will submit my memorandum on the bill to him.

I would come down to see you but it is simply impossible to leave the thirty-day bills at this time.

Faithfully yours

July 1, 1899. Oyster Bay
To Henry Cabot Lodge

Dear Cabot:

On receiving your first letter about the Duffield incident, I looked up the official reports, and so was very glad to get your second. What you said was known by everybody to be the exact truth. I doubt if there was a man in the army who did not know that Duffield and his Michigan regiments let themselves be stopped by a resistance so trivial as to be contemptible. He had the greatest chance of the war, for if he had chosen to have pushed home, I verily believe he could have taken Morro, or at least could have put himself in shape to guarantee a detachment of the army taking it. But he and Shafter arranged matters so that the official report holds Duffield blameless.

Incidentally, let me say that I think your last chapter on the war is almost the best. Everyone has agreed that yours is the only good history of the war that has yet come out.

I have just come back from a week in the west where I went to attend my regimental reunion at Las Vegas. It would really be difficult to express my surprise at the way I was greeted. At every station at which the train stopped in Indiana, Illinois, Wisconsin, Iowa, Missouri, Kansas, Colorado and New Mexico, I was received by dense throngs exactly as if I had been a presidential candidate. My reception caused some talk, so I thought it better to come out in an interview stating, that of course I was for President McKinley's renomination, and that everyone should be for it, and giving the reasons. Equally of course I am for Hobart's renomination, if he will take it.

Now as to what you say about the Vice-Presidency. Curiously enough Edith is against your view and I am inclined to be for it. I am for it on the perfectly simple ground that I regard my position as utterly unstable and that I appreciate as well as anyone can how entirely ephemeral is the hold I have for a moment on the voters. I am not taken in by the crowds in the west or by anything else in the way of vociferous enthusiasm for the moment. It would be five years before it would materialize and I have never yet known a hurrah to endure five years; so I should be inclined to accept any honorable position; that the Vice-Presidency is. As a matter of fact, I have not the slightest idea that I could get it, if I did decide to take it, and I should feel like taking any honorable position that offered itself. On the other hand, I confess I should like a position with more work in it. If I were a serious possibility for 1904, I should feel there was very much in what you say, but I do not think we need concern ourselves over the chances of the lightning striking me at that time rather than any other one of a thousand men. Meanwhile I could do more work in two years of the governorship, although I might get myself in a tangle. What I should really most like would be to be re-elected governor with a first-class lieutenant governor, and then be offered the secretaryship of war for four years. Of course it would be even better if I could become United States Senator, but of that I do not see any chance. Of all the work that I would like to undertake, that of Secretary of War appeals to me most. There I think I really could do something, but of course I have no idea that McKinley will put me in the position.

Last night I dined with Wood and Greene and we went over at length the problems in Cuba and the Philippines. I have been growing seriously concerned about both, and this morning I decided to send to John Hay a letter of which I enclose a copy. Having just come out in an interview for the President's renomination, I thought he might tolerate a little advice. I do not suppose it will do the least good, but I wrote on the off chance.

The President's civil service order was justifiable in part, and in part very unjustifiable. More than the matter, it was the manner of doing it that hurt, and especially the way in which it was trumpeted by Kerr, Grosvenor and similar cattle.

By the way, I particularly liked what you said about the attitude of the Germans and French in the last war. It is just as well those gentry should have a reminder now and then as to the effect of their conduct. Did I tell you that Captain Coghlan came out and took lunch here the other day? He was most amusing. I told him that there were no reporters present and that like the old Chancellor with Mr. Pell, he might "damn himself in confidence."

My week's railroading in the west put the finishing touch and I am now feeling completely tired out. I hope to have six weeks of practically solid rest before me, for I have worked pretty hard during the last four years.

Give my best love to Nannie and the boys. Occasionally we see cables in the papers about you.

Ever yours

August 11, 1899. Oyster Bay
To Cecil Spring Rice

Dear Cecil:

Your letter was delightful. Mrs. Roosevelt has read it and Grant La-Farge and Bob Ferguson—but not the Lodges! Mrs. Roosevelt was as amused as I was over Bay's remark; but good Lord man, you must not take a thing like that too seriously. I have just received an English review of my *Rough Riders* in *Literature,* which says that there is in the book an American twang, that cuts the air like the whistle of a Mauser bullet, but I do not on that account jump to the conclusion that the best English literary papers regard my literary breeding as hopeless! On the contrary, the very review in question really shows the most kindly and appreciative spirit; and so you would find that Bay, though he has a habit not wholly unknown to other members of his race on both sides of the Atlantic, of saying unpleasant things, would cordially support England against any foreign power.

I appreciate all you say as to the causes which tend to undermine the friendship between America and England, nor do I minimize the professional German and professional Irish vote which is at the present moment so hostile to the republican party because of the party's record of sincere good feeling for England, as to add a very real element of danger to the campaign next year. Nevertheless, remember that year by year the class of professional Irishmen and professional Germans becomes smaller, and not only the Germans, but even the Irish in a couple of generations tend to become absolutely Americanized and become part of the great English-speaking race and to regard America's friends as their friends, her foes as their foes. Remember that though I am Dutch and Irish myself, I am not only a good American, but as sincere a well-wisher of, admirer of and believer in England as you would wish to see. The German is of our blood, our principles and our ideas. As a rule in one generation he becomes absolutely indistinguishable in any way from his fellow Americans, unless of course he settles in what may be called congestive German districts. I could name to you German after German among my close friends and associates on the bench, in Congress, in the State legislature, in the army and in the navy, whose parents were born in Germany, and who possibly were born there themselves, who are absolutely indistinguishable in habit, feeling and ideals from the great native American stock. (For instance, this letter is being dictated to my specially trusted stenographer who is himself of German parentage). These men are not Germans. They are Americans. The Secretary of our Peace Delegation at The Hague, Frederick W. Holls, a particular friend of mine, is of pure German parentage. As you have seen, he, like the other delegates, including Mahan the Irishman, acted in absolute unison with the English delegates. Holls has a very wide and intimate acquaintance with the New York Germans, and he was of particular service in telling the Kaiser whom he knows personally, that he was absolutely in error if he believed that the bulk of the men of German ori-

gin in the United States would do anything save for the United States
enthusiastically if it clashed with Germany. About the straightest man I
knew in the legislature, Kruse, was a German, and I have been trying in
vain to have him elected Judge. About the best executive officer in
Sampson's fleet was Haesler of the Texas. He has charge of the Texas big
guns, and he remarked to me, patting them lovingly after the war was
ended, that he had hoped before peace came to turn them on Von
Diederich's fleet. Our Admiral at tea, Kautz, is of German parentage,
and he is the especial bugbear of the Germans next to Captain Coghlan
who is of Irish blood. The delightful Coghlan was out here to lunch the
other day and was great fun. The navy is a unit in wanting to smash
Germany. The professional Irishman is losing his grip and the bulk of
the Irish are becoming Americans. The feeling of hostility to England is
continually softening. One of our best Captains in the navy, for whom I
got a ship in the war, is Delehanty, Senator Murphy's brother-in-law.
He casually mentioned to me the other day that until a year and a half
ago he always hated England, but that now he was for England and expected to remain so. Laffan of the *Sun* said the same thing to me. The
feeling here in favor of England is deeper than you would think. The
other day I addressed thirteen thousand Methodists at Asbury Park,
and the program included a song by two girls, descendants of Carroll of
Carrollton, in which one carried an American and the other a British
flag, the first singing "Columbia" and the other "Rule Britannia," and
then crossing the flags. The taste of the manifestation might possibly be
criticised, but the sentiment it stood for was excellent, and the audience
boiled with enthusiasm and demanded two encores. This could not
have occurred a couple of years ago. Again, take what the Canadians
have recently been doing. As you know, the Canadians do not like the
United States. I do not know whether you have studied the Alaska
boundary question. Without going into the technicalities of the case, it
is perhaps sufficient to point out that the Canadian maps until less than
twenty years ago gave the same boundaries that ours did, and that
American towns have grown up in the disputed territory and have for
years been administered as under the American flag. Because of the
hitch in the negotiations over this, the Canadian prime ministers and the
other prominent Canadians of the Opposition and the Government
both recently indulged in public threats in which they used the word
war, as being one of the alternatives. Two years ago this would have
provoked frantic retaliatory denunciation on our part and action in the
State legislatures and Congress, which really might have endangered
the peace. Now it is for the most part dismissed by our papers and by
all of our public officers with the good-humored remark that there is to

be no interruption of the friendship between England and America, and that to talk of any rupture in their relations is mere nonsense.

Now, all of this may not last, and it probably won't last quite in its present good shape, but I am greatly mistaken if we ever slide back into the old condition of bickering and angry distrust, and there will always be at least a chance that in a great emergency, the nation of the two which vitally needs it, may get more than moral aid from the other.

I understand all that you feel about Russia, and of course Asia is the very place where America could least help you. As I said in one of my former letters, you feel as the Greeks of the time of Demosthenes felt toward Macedon. That there is ground for your apprehension I fully admit, but historical analogies must always be carefully guarded, and I am not at all sure that the Macedon analogy will hold. As you know I have always regretted that the nations of Western Europe could not themselves put an end to the rule of the Turk, and supplant it with that of some nationality, whether Rouman or South Slav, which would itself inevitably be hostile to Russia; and I agree with Vanbery who certainly cannot be accused of pro-Russian sympathies, that Russia's march over barbarous Asia does represent a real and great advance for civilization. But I feel that to have England's power curtailed even by this Russian advance would be a great calamity. If Germany were wise she would recognize in Russia the real menace to her power, and would strike her down while it is yet time. Russia could never be conquered in the sense of being enslaved, but I do not believe it is all of the question thoroughly to whip her, and Germany could create in Finland and the Baltic provinces, and possibly in old Poland, new states which could be independent, or else an alliance with the Germans against the orthodox Slav. However, Germany does not seem inclined to make the experiment, and the steady ethnic growth of Russia in Asia as opposed to Great Britain's purely administrative and political growth, does make the Asian problem look serious. I have never been on the ground and know nothing save what I have read, but I want to point out one or two chances. In the first place, if the worst come to the worst and Great Britain were driven from Asia, I cannot help thinking that the blow instead of cowing the English-speaking race would serve thoroughly to arouse and anger all their communities. To you India seems larger than Australia. In the life history of the English-speaking people I think it will show very much smaller. The Australians are building up a giant commonwealth, the very existence of which, like the existence of the United States, an alteration in the balance of the world and goes a long way towards ensuring the supremacy of the men who speak our tongue and have our ideas of social, political and religious freedom and morality. If only you can send enough settlers to Africa and let some men like Kitchener deal in his own way with the Boers, if it is absolutely necessary, I think that the future of the African continent will lie in your hands and be under your direction. And what a splendid work this will be! It is enough of itself to establish a race for all time.

Moreover, mind you, that this is taking the gloomiest view and supposing that Russia sometime knocks the English-speaking people out of their domination in southern and South East Asia. I never have seen how this domination could last through the ages. It has always seemed to me from its very nature, that in the end (though I hope not until many centuries have passed) it would probably vanish as the Greek Bactrian kingdom vanished, or as the Greek empire of the Seleucids passed away. Yet here again I am by no means sure. You have done such marvelous things in India that it may be you will gradually, as century succeeds century, by keeping your hold, transform the Indian population, not in blood, probably not in speech, but in government and in culture, and thus leave your impress as Rome did hers on Western Europe. If our race becomes effete, if we become decadent, then of course this cannot happen, and you and I and all our peoples will go down, as Spain has gone down, but I do not see the slightest symptoms of its decadence as yet, whether in military, in administrative or in business and social matters. I should not envy the Russian General who clashed with Kitchener! Moreover, it may well be that Russia will tend to grow less formidable from the very causes that seem to make her most formidable. She is from two to eight hundred years behind the rest of Europe in social organization, but she is travelling the path that the rest of Europe has travelled. The factory system is now growing up within her borders, and in a couple of generations she will be a manufacturing as well as an agricultural population, a country in which there will be an urban as well as a rural population, a great commercial as well as a great land-owning caste. All this will bring about profound social changes, and it may be that when she has filled out her present territories Russia will have all she can do to solve her own internal problems instead of trying to menace her neighbors. The two great fiction writers of today with a serious purpose are Tolstoi and Kipling, and each stands as typical for something in his own race and nationality. Which do you think the most healthy product for a nation, the author of the *Kreutzer Sonata* and *My Religion,* or the author of the "Recessional" and the Mulvaney stories? There are parts of Tolstoi I do like and there are parts of Kipling I do not. But after all it is the Slav, not the Englishman, who shows decadence.

Do not misunderstand me; do not think me a mere optimist. I do not pretend to be able to see into the future. I feel so perfectly healthy myself and the Americans and English for whom I care, with whom I have been thrown, seem so healthy, so vigorous, and on the whole so decent, that I rather incline to the view of my beloved friend Lt. Parker of the Gatlings whom I overheard telling the Russian Naval Attaché at Santiago that "the two branches of the Anglo-Saxon race had come together, and that together we can whip the world, Prince, we can whip the world"! But it may be that in the future disaster may overcome you in Asia and most certainly there are evil forces at work among us in America. The diminishing birth rate among the old native American stock, especially in the north east, with all that that implies, I should consider the worst. But we have also tremendous problems in the way of the relations of labor and capital to solve. My own belief is that we shall have to pay far more attention to this than to any question of expansion for the next fifty years, and this although I am an expansionist and believe that we can go on and take our place among the nations of the world, by dealing with the outside problems without in any way neglecting those of our internal administration.

All of which, old man, when condensed amounts to saying that while the future is dim and uncertain, there is no more reason for saying that it is black than for saying that it is all light, and in any event we have all of us got to face it and do the best we can, with conditions as they actually arc.

Give my warm regards to your chief. I wish I could meet him. Everyone here sends you warm love. Col. Lee, the British Military Attaché, who is a trump, has been visiting us and will visit us again this fall, and so will beloved Speck.

Ever yours

November 27, 1899. Albany
To Hermann Speck von Sternberg

My dear Speck:

I have just received yours of the 3rd on my return to Albany after several days' absence. I send this to the German Embassy at Washington as you say you will be there so soon. I am perfectly delighted that you are to be on this side. We are not in the country this year, so I do not suppose you would care to come to us for Christmas; but we would be delighted to have you if you could come up here to Albany.

What you say about the Kaiser is most interesting. He is far and away the greatest crowned head of the present day. He is a Monarch— a King in deed as well as in name, which some other Kings are not. He is a fit successor to the Ottos, the Henrys, and the Fredericks of the past.

I take just the view you do of the Boer war. I have great sympathy for the Boers and great respect and liking for them, but I think they are battling on the wrong side in the fight of civilization and will have to go under. I have not been a bit surprised at the English defeats. You had told me what you thought of their practical military knowledge of the present day, and in reading of their Indian campaigns by their own best critics, I had been struck by the fact that they nearly encountered disaster again and again under circumstances which would have meant, if pitted against a formidable foe, just exactly the disasters that actually happened. Their victories seem to me to have been won by their disciplined courage, their numbers, and perhaps their artillery, in spite of the superior individual fighting, and for the matter of that, fighting as a whole, of the Boer riflemen. I had been told, moreover, that their military organization was only a little better than ours, and though this was an exaggeration, it had in it an element of truth. At Santiago the courage of our enlisted men and the good conduct of the junior officers could not be surpassed, but after what I saw of the higher officers, and the utter breakdown in administration, I am most heartily thankful that we did not have against us formidable an enemy as General White has encountered at Ladysmith.

In great haste,
Ever faithfully yours

November 28, 1899. Albany
To Finley Peter Dunne

My dear Mr. Dunne:

I regret to state that my family and intimate friends are delighted with your review of my book.[1] Now I think you owe me one; and I shall exact that when you next come east you pay me a visit. I have long wanted the chance of making your acquaintance.

Sincerely yours

December 11, 1899. Albany
To Henry Cabot Lodge

Dear Cabot:

I have yours of the 7th inst. In the first place, do you not think that Beveridge would be a good man on the Committee on Foreign Affairs? He seems to be sound on those matters.

Now, about the Vice-Presidency. It seems to me that the chance of my being a presidential candidate is too small to warrant very serious consideration at present. To have been a good Colonel, a good Governor and a good Assistant Secretary of the Navy is not enough to last

---

[1]*The Rough Riders.*

four years. If McKinley were to die tomorrow I would be one of the men seriously *considered* as his successor—I mean that and just no more. But four years hence the Spanish War will be in the very remote past and what I have done as Governor will not be very recent. Nobody can tell who will be up by that time. Of course, I should like to feel that I would still be in the running, but I do not regard it as sufficiently probable to be worth receiving very much weight.

There therefore remains the question of what each office is by itself. The Vice-Presidency is a most honorable office, but for a young man there is not much to do. It is infinitely better than many other positions, but it hardly seems to me as good as being Governor of this State, which is a pretty important State. Then while it is very unlikely that I could be President, there is a chance of my being something else—Governor General of the Philippines, or a Cabinet Officer, or perchance in the remote future, Senator. Mind you, I do not think that any of these things are likely, but at least there is sufficient chance to warrant my taking them seriously, while I do not think the chance for the presidency *is* sufficient to warrant our taking it seriously. If I am Vice-President I am "planted" for four years. Here I can turn around. Platt told me definitely that of course he was for me for a renomination—that everybody was—and though we shall have a good deal of friction from time to time, I do not believe it very likely that he will come to a definite break with me, because I like him personally, I always tell him the truth, and I genuinely endeavor to help him, if I can, with proper regard for the interest of the State and party.

The upshot of it is that it seems to me that I had better stay where I am. The great argument on the other side is, as I have said before, your judgment, which on the whole I have found better than my own. Some of the Western men are wild to have me go on to strengthen the ticket, but it scarcely seems to me that the ticket needs strengthening. Root would be an admirable man.

Give my best love to Nannie.

Ever yours

January 22, 1900. Albany
To Theodore Douglas Robinson

Dear Teddy,

I have your note of the 18th. All right, I am down for the 6th and 7th. I am very much obliged to you for writing and giving me the information.

By the way, I was awfully pleased to bear indirectly the other day of the good influence you had on the younger boys. Ted came home in his soldier suit with a puffed eye, which he explained to me was due to a battle with a "Mick" who had sneeringly referred to him as a toy soldier. I am afraid Ted did not fight wholly in accordance with the rules of the prize ring, for he explained that when he got the Mick down, he sat on his chest and pounded his head until the Celt agreed that he had had enough. His own attire looked somewhat dishevelled in consequence.

Your affectionate uncle

January 30, 1900. Albany
To Henry Cabot Lodge

Dear Cabot:

I have just received your letter and it has given me much food for thought. I shall have to see Senator Platt before I can say anything. There is an amusing, new complication in the fact that Woodruff may have already gotten all the delegates from New York, so that Platt cannot get them away from him, in which case Platt will certainly not want me to stand. Moreover, if Woodruff is to be the Governor, that may again cause a grave question whether I ought to stand, as it is by no means certain that he could carry the State. Woodruff is a most good-humored, friendly fellow, wild to have me nominate him for Vice-President, which I suppose for my sins I might have to do (not if I can help it!), and he is amusingly and absolutely certain that nothing can prevent his nomination. He is a great worker, and he has had rather a remarkable success in getting nominations and handling the machine here, and he is absolutely confident that he can get the Vice-Presidency. He had a long and frank talk with me the other day, though I told him I could not speak as frankly in return. He explained that he did not want the Governorship; that he had seen Black cut his own throat from ear to ear, and seen me keep the machine from cutting its throat (and mine too) by main force, and at the constant peril of a break which would have been just as fatal and which could only be averted by the incessant exercise of resolution and sleepless judgment; and that he did not want the Governorship, while he did very much want the Vice-Presidency, chiefly because he had plenty of money and could entertain, and he knew he could act as Presiding Officer of the Senate. The money question is a serious one with me. As you know, my means are very moderate, and as my children have grown up and their education has become more and more a matter of pressing importance, I have felt a very keen regret that I did not have some money-making occupation, for I am never certain when it may be necessary for me to try to sell Sagamore and completely alter my whole style of life. As Governor, I am comparatively well paid, having not only a salary but a house which is

practically kept up during the winter, and thanks to the fact that the idiots of the magazines now wish to pay me very large prices for writing,
on account of my temporary notoriety, I was enabled to save hand-
somely last year and will be enabled to do so again this year. But great
pressure would come upon me if I went in as Vice-President. I could
only live simply. Of course, I could not begin to entertain as Morton
and Hobart have; and even to live simply as a Vice-President would
have to live would be a serious drain upon me, and would cause me,
and especially would cause Edith, continual anxiety about money. If
the place held out a chance of doing really good work, I should not
mind this, for I must try to carry out my scheme of life, and as I am not
to leave the children money, I am in honor bound to leave them a
record of honorable achievement; but of course the chance for a Vice-
President to do much of anything is infinitesimal. I suppose I should
have leisure to take up my historical work again, but that is about all.
If the Vice-Presidency led to the Governor Generalship of the Philippines, then the question would be entirely altered, but I have a very uncomfortable feeling that there will be a strong although entirely unreasonable feeling against my resigning. Of course, there should not be, as
the succession is arranged in the Secretaryship of State.

   I am extremely pleased at the conversation you report with the President. President Schurman[1] had spoken to me about his intention to speak
to the President concerning the Governor Generalship, but I had not
thought over the matter one way or the other in connection with him and
had not the slightest idea whether he had carried out his intention. It is
quite needless to say that I absolutely agree with the theory that until the
war is over, we want to have the military authority not merely supreme
but alone. It would never do to have a divided authority, and it would not
be worth while for a really good man to go out there with divided authority. In public life it seems to me the blue ribbon part is of very small
value. The point is to get hold of some job really worth doing and then to
do it well. The Governor Generalship of the Philippines, especially the
first Governor Generalship, would be exactly such a piece of work. I
should approach it with a very serious sense, not only of its importance,
but of its difficulty; but as far as I can see among those who are likely to
be considered as candidates, I would be quite as apt to do well as any.

   As soon as I can I will see Senator Platt and then will let you know.

   It would be idle for me to thank you, old man. As I have said before, if I began to thank you I should have to take up so much time that

---

   [1]Jacob Schurman, president of Cornell University and former president of
the U.S. Philippine Commission.

there would be very little time left for anything else. You are the only man whom, in all my life, I have met who has repeatedly and in every way done for me what I could not do for myself, and what nobody else could do, and done it in a way that merely makes me glad to be under the obligation to you. I have never been able to do, and never shall be able to do, anything in return, I suppose, but that is part of the irony of life in this world.

I am glad you like the canal report. I came to the conclusion that the position had to be taken boldly. I doubt if anything comes of it at the moment; but it will ultimately.

As for the Payn matter, seemingly I have won out; by dint of combining inflexible determination with extreme good nature, and resolutely refusing the advice of Godkin, Parkhurst and of the various small-fry Chapmans, Villards etc., who wanted me to quarrel with the machine, in which case I should have had about six votes out of the fifty in the Senate. Of course, these gentlemen are not only unwise but dishonest. Their opponents are too fond of calling them impracticable and omitting their dishonesty. Heaven knows they *are* impracticable! but they are also eaten up by vanity, hypocrisy, mendacity and mean envy. In fact, they combine with great meety the qualities of the knave and the qualities of the fool.

How I have gone over them! Whatever comes hereafter it is a great pleasure to feel how I have trodden them down.

And on the other hand, I have made the machine act with absolute decency and have never yielded one hair's breadth to it on a question of morality or principle. I can say quite conscientiously that during my term the Governorship of New York has been managed on as high a plane as the Governorship of Massachusetts!

What a terrible tine the English are having! There is no question that the Boers outfight them. I am heartily ashamed of Mason, Hale and the other men of their stamp who show the particularly mean attribute of jumping on England when she is down. But of course those scoundrels who have been entirely against their own nation cannot be expected to have any sense of propriety in dealing with another nation which was friendly during the war with Spain when they were traitors.

With best love to Nannie.

Ever yours

February 3, 1900. Albany
To Henry Cabot Lodge

Dear Cabot:

Now this letter is to be strictly secret.

I have found out one reason why Senator Platt wants me nominated for the Vice-Presidency. He is I am convinced, genuinely friendly, and indeed I think I may say really fond of me, and is personally satisfied with the way I have conducted politics; but the big-monied men with whom he is in close touch and whose campaign contributions have certainly been no inconsiderable factor in his strength, have been pressing him very strongly to get me put in the Vice-Presidency, so as to get me out of the State. It was the big insurance companies, possessing enormous wealth, that gave Payn his formidable strength, and they to a man want me out. The great corporations affected by the franchise tax have also been at the Senator. In fact, all the big-monied interests that make campaign contributions of large size and feel that they should have favors in return, are extremely anxious to get me out of the State. I find that they have been at Platt for the last two or three months and he has finally begun to yield to them and to take their view. Outside of that the feeling here is very strong indeed against my going. In fact, all of my friends in the State would feel that I was deserting them, and are simply unable to understand my considering it. I appreciate entirely the danger of this position, but after all I suppose there is no work without an attendant risk, and it does not seem to me that I am ready to leave a real piece of work for a position in which there is not any work at all and where I really do not think there is anything for me to do and no reputation to make.

I earnestly hope the Philippine business can wait a couple of years. Ever yours

April 3, 1900. Albany
To Marcus A. Hanna

My dear Senator Hanna:

About the tenth of May I shall be on to Washington at which time I want to see you about various matters. Meanwhile, let me point out that I am convinced that I can do most good to the national ticket by running as Governor in this State. There will be in New York a very curious feeling of resentment both against myself and against the party leaders if I ran as Vice-President, and this will affect our vote I believe; whereas if I ran as Governor I can strengthen the national ticket in this State more than in any other way. I do not think we can afford to take liberties in this State.

However, this is all aside. What I want to do now is to get you to have a box reserved for Mrs. Roosevelt and her party at the National Convention. She takes the entirely rational view which I share that during these two years of my Governorship we ought both of us to have all the fun that there is. Accordingly she has been to Cuba and now she wants to go to the National Convention.

Sincerely yours

April 30, 1900. Albany
To Anna Roosevelt Cowles

Darling Bye:

You may have seen that when I was in Chicago I took the opportunity of saying that I would rather be in private life than to be vice-president. I thought that this was putting it as emphatically as I could put it, and much less offensively than to say that I would not accept the position even if nominated; because the latter is an attitude which a man in active politics, who is sincerely devoted to his party, ought to be very wary about taking.

The qualities that make Cabot invaluable as a friend and invaluable as a public servant also make him quite unchangeable when he has determined that a certain course is right. There is no possible use in trying to make him see the affair as I look at it, because our points of view are different. He regards me as a man with a political career. If I felt that I really had any great chance of such a career I might very possibly take his view. The reason I do not take his view is that I am thoroughly convinced that American politics in general, but above all New York State politics, are of such a kaleidoscopic character, that it is worse than useless for a man of my means and my methods in political life to think of politics as a career. This year we shall probably carry the Presidency, and because there is a presidential election, with Bryan against us, and only because of this, there is a chance of our carrying New York. Therefore, there is a chance of my being either vice-president or Governor. Personally, I regard the election of the republican candidate for the former position as more likely than for the latter. But there is nothing to do as vice-president and there is a great deal to do as Governor, and as I believe the swing of the pendulum will inevitably take me out of public life at the next election after the one this year, even if not at this one, it therefore seems to me wise to try for the position where I can really accomplish something; for the only point to my mind in holding a position is to accomplish something in it.

Cabot feels that I have a career. The dear old goose actually regards me as a presidential possibility of the future, which always makes me thoroughly exasperated, because sooner or later it will have the effect of making other people think that I so regard myself and that therefore I am a ridiculous personage. He thinks that at any rate I could legitimately aspire to some such position as a cabinet officer, or—the one position I should really like—that of Governor General of the Philippines. Now he realizes that when I come a cropper in New York, it means in all probability the end of any outside ambition, and he realizes that this cropper is perfectly certain to arrive sooner or later. There is, at least an even chance

of my being beaten for Governor this fall. Two years ago when I was in
the first flush of my war honors I carried the State by less than 18,000
votes. This year a change of 9,000 votes would beat me. Now I have certainly alienated more than that number who voted for me, from the simple fact that with such a constituency as mine, and facing such difficulties
as I have to face, I continually *have* to alienate men. The pharmacists want
the regimental pharmacists to be made first lieutenants, which cannot be
done without disorganizing all the grades; therefore, I have to alienate a
number of good people who arc generally for me. The labor unions want
a certain course followed about the manufacture of school furniture; it is
impossible to follow it without demoralizing the work in our prisons, and
this costs me more votes. And so it goes with bill after bill. The wealthy
corporations object to the franchise tax and are bitter against me in consequence. The federation of labor grows angry because I have out the
militia with great promptness to prevent rioting in the strike at Croton
Dam. The Machine men are with difficulty kept in line at all, and the more
extreme among them mutter that they might as well have a democrat, because I show no mercy to incompetence and less than mercy to dishonesty; while on the other hand, the well-meaning impracticables get disgusted because I consult with the Machine at all. So it goes, all the time,
and I continually alienate little interests, while so far as I can see there is
no one who voted against me before whom I should have a right to expect
would change his vote now. My chance of success therefore depends
solely upon whether or not the feeling against Bryan is so strong that,
among the democrats who will vote against him, there will be a sufficient
number who will vote against the whole ticket, to offset any losses due to
disaffection with me personally. Understand me. I think I am stronger
probably than any other republican would be, but this is a democratic
State, and we have against us the great sodden democratic mass and in
addition scores of thousands of men who because they are goo-goos or
mugwumps, or anti-expansionists, or mere impracticables at large, cannot be depended upon to back up a rational effort to do good work. The
New York Democrats this year wish to win the Governorship at all hazards, because of the effect it will have for them in the councils of the party.
They will put up the best candidate they can find and dropping the presidency will devote their whole attention to electing the Governor. I certainly think the chances are about even, if not in their favor.

This being so, Cabot from his standpoint is entirely right in not
wishing to see me exposed to these chances. Moreover, he feels that if I
am re-elected the same old trouble will begin of trying to keep the elements together, and that no matter how well I do, the mere swing of the
pendulum will bring the democracy to the front two years hence; so
that in the middle of McKinley's second term this State will be turned

against me, or rather, against the local republican organization; and this, even if I am able to avoid a split with the Machine or a smashup with the independents prior to that time.

I myself realize all these chances, but am not only willing, but anxious, to take them, as to my mind the final and conclusive consideration is that I do not want the vice-presidency and that I would like to be Governor again because of the work there is in it.

Of course, you will arrange so that I shall see a good deal of Cabot or rather you need not arrange it, because I shall make my morning and afternoon hours conform to his. I am particularly anxious to see Arthur Lee and go over some of the military problems of this Boer War. I cannot understand Long's choice of an Assistant Secretary.

With love to Will.

Ever yours

May 16, 1900. Albany
To William Allen White[1]

My dear Mr. White:

I have your letter of the 9th inst. about my going to Ottawa. I do not want to accept another invitation to speak if it can be avoided. Of course, if Funston is to be there I will come. Do you think I ought to come if Funston is not there? Would it do instead of my going out later in the campaign—that is, could this be accepted as a substitute for campaign work there, even though I did not mention politics?

I think I have got things fixed so that I shall be free of the vice-presidency. It is the last office I want. I should like to be Governor of New York again.

Faithfully yours

June 21, 1900. New York
To William McKinley

(Telegram)

I appreciate deeply your congratulations and am proud to be associated with you on the ticket.

June 25, 1900. Oyster Bay
To Anna Roosevelt Cowles

Dear Bye:

The thing could not be helped. There were two entirely different forces at work. The first was the desire to get me out of New York, partly because the machine naturally prefers someone more pliable, but

---

[1]Republican editor from Kansas.

mainly because of the corporations' or rather the big speculative corporations' unhealthy attitude toward me. This desire was absolutely unoperative as regards results for I stood Mr. Platt and the machine on their heads when the trial of strength came and forced the entire New York delegation to declare for someone else. It was the feeling of the great bulk of the Republicans that I would strengthen the National ticket and they wanted me on it at all hazards. Mr. Hanna was quite as much opposed to my going on as Mr. Platt was to my staying off, but both were absolutely and utterly powerless. While, of course, I should have preferred to stay where there was more work I would be both ungrateful and a fool not to be deeply touched by the way in which I was nominated. The vital thing in this election is to re-elect President McKinley and to this I shall bend all my energies. If we succeed, well and good, and as regards myself I shall try most earnestly, and I most humbly hope not to forfeit the respect and good will of the people who put me in as vice-president. If we are beaten, my own disappointment will not be a drop in the ocean to my bitter regret and alarm for the Nation.

Give my warm love to Will. I hope he is getting better.

June 25, 1900. Oyster Bay
To Marcus A. Hanna

My dear Senator Hanna:

I must hear from you as to what course I should follow on certain points. I must go to Oklahoma. My intention is not to make that a political campaign at all and get through with as little notoriety as possible. It would cause more heart burning for me to go back on the matter now than it would do good, or else I should go back on it.

Now, as to my other engagements. I most emphatically do not wish to appear like a second-class Bryan. I take it for granted from what was said to me that it was desired that I should go over the country and make a certain number of speeches in the doubtful Western states as well as in my own. Of course you understand that whatever the leaders in the campaign have thoughtfully considered best I will do but I must avoid at all hazards giving the belief that I am going to do anything undignified. Now, do you think I ought to go out to the meeting of the Republican National League at St. Paul? If my not going will give bitterness, of course I will go but I want you to think it over carefully and see whether it would or would not be wise. Meanwhile, I shall make no other engagements of any sort or kind but keep myself ready for the national committee's direction. I have told the people in South Dakota that if the national committee wished me to speak I certainly would do so.

Sincerely yours

June 25, 1900. Oyster Bay
To Henry Cabot Lodge

Dear Cabot:

The enclosed explains itself. I think from every standpoint that the appointment of Daly will be a master stroke. I know the little fellow and he is a corker. I should be only too glad to have him as an officer under me.

Well, old man, I am completely reconciled and I believe it all for the best as regards my own personal interests and it is a great load of personal anxiety off me. Instead of having to fight single-handed against the trusts and corporations I now must take pot luck with the whole ticket and my anxiety on behalf of the nation is so great that I can say with all honesty there is none left. As regards my own personal election on one thing you may rest assured, I am most deeply sensible of the honor conferred upon me by the way the nomination came. I shall do my best to deserve it and not to disappoint those who trusted me and think well of me. I should be a conceited fool if I was discontented with the nomination when it came in such a fashion, and according to my lights I shall endeavor to act not only fearlessly and with integrity but with good judgment. Edith is becoming somewhat reconciled.

Nannie's letter was just dear. Give her my warm love and say to her I do wish she could have seen my hour of triumph.

As for you, old trump, I shall never forget how, as I mounted the platform, you met me with a face of almost agonized anxiety and put your head down on the table as I began to speak, and, as I turned for a glass of water in the middle of the speech, you whispered with a face of delight that I was doing splendidly. It certainly is odd to look back sixteen years when you and I sat in the Blaine convention on the beaten side while the mugwumps foretold our utter ruin, and then in this convention, over which you presided to think how you recognized me to second McKinley's nomination and afterwards declared me myself nominated in the second place on the ticket.

Give my love to Bay and John.

Faithfully yours

August 6, 1900. Oyster Bay
To William Howard Taft

My dear Will:

Your letter gave me very great pleasure. I would have particularly liked to have stayed as Governor, not so much because of any one specific piece of policy, though there were several I should like to have pressed to a successful conclusion, but because of the general policy for which I thought I stood, that is, the policy of being practical and yet decent; by working with the machine and yet steadfastly refusing to be servile to it, and by seeking to put an end to that most unfortunate of divisions, the division between men who actually do the work in public life and men who theorize as to how that work should be done. Godkin is without doubt flatfooted for Bryan on the ground that never before in our history has any man been surrounded by such corrupt scoundrels as McKinley is. I suppose the scoundrels to whom he especially alludes are yourself, Leonard Wood, Hay, Long, Root and of course myself. Carl Schurz has not openly come out for Bryan but continues the most ferocious attacks on McKinley. The feeling for my nomination was practically unanimous and I could not refuse without giving the ticket a black eye. I had a great deal rather be your assistant in the Philippines or even Root's assistant in the War Department than be vice-president. The kaleidoscope will be shaken, however, before 1904 some new man will come to the front. I am entirely content if I have been of any help to the ticket this year.

Mrs. Roosevelt wants to be remembered to you. Give my warmest regards to your wife when you write.

Faithfully yours

November 9, 1900. Oyster Bay
To Henry Cabot Lodge

Dear Cabot:

Just a line to say how glad I was to get your telegram. I have any amount to tell you about the canvass. If political conditions were normal in the South, Bryanism would have received scarcely a score of votes in the electoral college. Well, I am delighted to have been on the national ticket in this great historic contest, for after McKinley and Hanna, I feel that I did as much as anyone in bringing about the result—though after all it was Bryan himself who did most.

Do tell Nannie that I have got to give her full information about certain of my ardent backers, the Mulhalls of Oklahoma Territory. The members of the family whom I know are Colonel Mulhall, his son and two daughters, one of whom is named Miss Bossie. There are also several gentlemen friends with sporting proclivities, occasional homicidal tastes and immense resourcefulness in every emergency. No ordinary novelist would venture to portray such types, because he would regard them as hopelessly exaggerated. They have a large and very prosperous ranch some sixty miles from Oklahoma City, and they all came in to see me at the regimental reunion last July, together with a dozen of the Mulhall cowboys. The Colonel is a solidly built person with chin whiskers and an iron jaw. One daughter drove the buckboard; the other rode a horse man fashion, the latter being Miss Bossie. She took her part with the cowboys in a steer-roping contest in the afternoon, and afterwards, together with the rest of her family, dined with me in evening dress, not particularly different from that of more conventional regions. They have many greyhounds and wanted me to come out for a wolf hunt, which I could not do, so Miss Bossie sent me a stuffed wolf as a mascot. During my campaign I came upon the entire family at St. Louis where they had come in to race some of their horses. They were democrats but were backing McKinley chiefly because I was on the ticket. I came upon the entire family including their gentlemen friends perfectly at home in the barroom of the Planters Hotel sitting around a table eating lunch and drinking whiskey in the shape known as "high-balls." They were all very glad to see me, but especially the Colonel and Miss Bossie, both of whom had bet heavily upon me, Miss Bossie telling me that unless I won I must never venture to come near their ranch, as she had bet all her ponies and race horses on the result. She has written Edith to congratulate her and the Colonel has wired me. I assured Edith she would find Bossie a distinct addition to our social circle should she ever come here on a visit, but I regret to state that Edith has betrayed an unexpected narrow-mindedness and seems apprehensive as to exactly how the young lady would get on in the new environment.

I hope you noticed how I called down Croker, Van Wyck and Devery when there threatened to be trouble in New York. I was glad that Croker gave me the chance through his man Devcry.

Harry Davis has written us such a characteristic note of congratulation upon our victory over what he calls the "combined idiocy and evil of the country."

Ever yours

November 10, 1900. Oyster Bay
To John Hay

My dear Mr. Secretary:

In the first place, I wish you would always call me Theodore as you used to do. In the next place, this letter of yours joined with very many others from you I shall always keep. I feel that I should like to have my children know that I was on intimate terms with you.

I was really grateful to Croker for making Devery commit an overt act which put the whole gang in my power. I immediately took some secret steps which have never come out, getting into communication with the Adjutant General instantly, so that in the event of need I could have any regiment of the National Guard out at once. I believed that

they would take water as they actually did. If they had not, I would
have taken off the heads of the mayor, sheriff and district attorney
within forty-eight hours—that is just long enough for the legal formal-
ities of a trial to be complied with, and if by any possible construction
I could have gotten at Croker and Hearst,[1] I should have done all that
was within my power to make them pay to the last cent for any misconduct which really would have been due to them. However, it all
went off without any difficulties.

The President and all his cabinet have indeed reason to be profoundly grateful and extremely proud about the result. I do not think I
am wrong in my historic judgment of contemporary matters when I say
that President McKinley's administration will rank next to Lincoln's
during the whole nineteenth century in point of great work worthily
done. Other Presidents, such as Jefferson, Madison and Polk met great
crises, but they did not meet them in as fine a spirit—they did not do
the great work as well.

With warm regards to Mrs. Hay,

Always yours

**November 26, 1900. Albany
To Edward Sanford Martin**

Dear Dan:

I shall write to Bangs and thank him.

Now, about small Ted's fighting. I believe you will find that he is
not quarrelsome, and that above all, he is not a bully. I think it has been
in amicable wrestling and boxing bouts that in your boy's words he has
"licked all the boys in his form." In a measure, I am responsible for some
of his fighting proclivities, but most of them came naturally. For instance, my two youngest small boys are not in the least fighters like Ted,
although I think I have succeeded in instilling into them the theory that
they ought not to shirk any quarrel forced upon them.

Now, do you want to know the real underlying feeling which has
made me fight myself and want Ted to fight? Well, I summed it up to
Ted once or twice when I told him, apropos of lessons of virtue, that he
could be just as virtuous as he wished *if only he was prepared to fight*. Fundamentally this has been my own theory. I am not naturally at all a
fighter. So far as any man is capable of analyzing his own impulses and
desires, mine incline me to amiable domesticity and the avoidance of effort and struggle and any kind of roughness and to the practice of home
virtues. Now, I believe that these are good traits, not bad ones. But I also

---

[1]Yellow journalist and later politician William Randolph Hearst

believe that if unsupported by something more virile, they may tend to evil rather than good. The man who merely possesses these traits, and in addition is timid and shirks effort, attracts and deserves a good deal of contempt. He attracts more, though he deserves less, contempt than the powerful, efficient man who is not at all virtuous, but is merely a strong, selfish, self-indulgent brute; the latter being the type [indecipherable]. I was fortunate enough in having a father whom I have always been able to regard as an ideal man. It sounds a little like cant to say what I am going to say, but he really did combine the strength and courage and will and energy of the strongest man with the tenderness, cleanness and purity of a woman. I was a sickly and timid boy. He not only took great and loving care of me—some of my earliest remembrances are of nights when he would walk up and down with me for an hour at a time in his arms when I was a wretched mite suffering acutely with asthma—but he also most wisely refused to coddle me, and made me feel that I must force myself to hold my own with other boys and prepare to do the rough work of the world. I cannot say that he ever put it into words, but he certainly gave me the feeling that I was always to be both decent and manly, and that if I were manly nobody would long laugh at my being decent. In all my childhood he never laid hand on me but once, but I always knew perfectly well that in case it became necessary he would not have the slightest hesitancy to do so again, and alike from my love and respect, and in a certain sense, from my fear of him, I would have hated and dreaded beyond measure to have him know that I had been guilty of a lie, or of cruelty, or of bullying, or of uncleanness, or of cowardice. Gradually I grew to have the feeling on my own account, and not merely on his. There were many things I tried to do because he did them, which I found afterwards were not in my line. For instance, I taught Sunday school all through college, but afterwards gave it up, just as on experiment I could not do the charitable work which he had done. In doing my Sunday school work I was very much struck by the fact that the other men who did it only possessed one side of his character; [indecipherable] My ordinary companions in college would I think have had a tendency to look down upon me for doing Sunday school work if I had not also been a corking boxer, a good runner, and a genial member of the Porcellian Club. I went in for boxing and wrestling a good deal, and I really think that while this was partly because I liked them as sports, it was even more because I intended to be a middling decent fellow, and I did not intend that anyone should laugh at me with impunity because I was decent. It is exactly the same thing with history. In most countries the "Bourgeoisie"—the moral, respectable, commercial, middle class—is looked upon with a certain contempt which is justified by their timidity and unwarlikeness. But the minute a middle class produces men like Hawkins and Frobisher on the seas, or men such as the average Union soldier in the civil war, it acquires the hearty respect of others which it merits.

Well, I have wanted to pass on to my boys some of what I got from my own father. I loathe cruelty and injustice. To see a boy or man torture something helpless whether in the shape of a small boy or little girl or dumb animal makes me rage. So far as I know my children have never been cruel, though I have had to check a certain amount of bullying. Ted is a little fellow, under the usual size, and wears spectacles, so that strange boys are rather inclined to jump on him at first. When in addition to this I have trained him so that he objects strongly to torturing cats or hurting little girls, you can see that there are chances for life to be unpleasant for him when among other boys. Now I have striven to make him feel that if he only fights hard enough he is perfectly certain to secure the respect of all his associates for his virtues. I do not believe he is quarrelsome. I do not think your little boy has found him so. I do not think he oppresses smaller boys, but he does hold his own. When his aunt goes to see him at school, he flings his arms around her neck and is overjoyed with her companionship and has the greatest difficulty to keep from crying when she goes away. Now there are certain of his companions who would be inclined to think him a mollycoddle for betraying such emotion over a female relative; but they won't think him a mollycoddle if he shows an instantaneous readiness to resent hostile criticism on the subject.

Of course, there are dangers in any such training. Every now and then Ted gets an attack of the big head and has to have it reduced, usually by his own associates, occasionally by his affectionate father. Moreover, I know perfectly well that all my training him will only amount to one element out of the many which will go to determine what he is in the future. As you say in your last article, the mother has much more to do than the father with the children's future.

By the way, Mrs. Roosevelt and I laughed all the way down in the cars the other day over that article. I suppose "Jonas" is Ted's school fellow. Your account of the father's function in sickness so exactly reproduced our experience that it made me feel guilty and Mrs. Roosevelt decorously exultant. So with my tendency to be a little late at meals, and the tuition of my wife towards the children on the subject.

There I have written you much longer than I had any idea I was going to. With hearty regards,

Faithfully yours

P. S. I have just received your second note. I have rarely read a more touching letter than Mrs. Moore's. What a fine woman she must be and what a fine son she must have had! I return her letter herewith. If you think she would not mind it, I wish you would give her my most respectful and sincere sympathy.

December 3, 1900. Albany
To Andrew Dickson White

My dear Mr. White:

Your letter of November 16th pleased me greatly. But for Heaven's sake do not think of me as a possible Presidential candidate. In the first place, the possibility is merely that of lightning striking; and in the next place, with the examples of Tom Reed and Dewey fresh before me, it seems to me there can be no more awful fate than for a man to get a Presidential bee in his bonnet.

Moreover, when I think of the kind of life I have led, the marvel is that I have gotten as far as I have. I have always expressed my opinions with great freedom, and though I think I have grown fairly judicious now, this was certainly not the case ten or a dozen years ago. There are plenty of printed statements I have made, some of them absolutely true, some of them true from my standpoint, but expressed in such a shape as legitimately to give offense and which would operate against me at any rate among politicians and perhaps among some who are not politicians. While I did not want the Vice-Presidency I am now entirely content to have taken it, for it enabled me to be of considerable use in a great campaign. Now all that there is for me to do is to perform with regularity and dignity the duty of presiding over the Senate, and to remember the fact that the duty not being very important is no excuse for shirking it.

I shall do just as you suggest and wait on events for some little time before speaking about expansion or anything of the kind.

Let me heartily congratulate you upon your speech which I have just been reading.

Faithfully yours

January 14, 1901. Keystone Ranch, Colorado
To Theodore Roosevelt, Jr.

Blessed Ted,

From the railroad we drove fifty miles to the little frontier town of Meeker. There we were met by the hunter Goff, a fine, quiet, hardy fellow, who knows his business thoroughly. Next morning we started on horseback, while our luggage went by wagon to Goff's ranch. We started soon after sunrise; and made our way, hunting as we went, across the high, exceedingly rugged hills, until sunset. We were hunting cougar and lynx or, as they are called out here, "lion" and "cat." The first cat we put up gave the dogs a two hours' chase, and got away among some high cliffs. In the afternoon we put up another, and had a very good hour's run, the dogs baying until the glens rang again to the echoes, as they worked hither and thither through the ravines. We walked our ponies up and down steep, rockstrewn, and tree-clad slopes, where it did not seem possible a horse could climb, and on the level places we got one or two smart gallops. At last the lynx went up a tree. Then I saw a really funny sight. Seven hounds had been doing the trailing, while a large brindled bloodhound and two half-breeds between collie and bull stayed behind Goff, running so close to his horse's heels that they continually bumped into them, which he accepted with philosophic composure. Then the dogs proceeded literally to *climb the tree*, which was a many-forked pinon; one of the half-breeds, named Tony, got up certainly sixteen feet, until the lynx, which looked like a huge and exceedingly malevolent pussy-cat, made vicious dabs at him. I shot the lynx low, so as not to hurt his skin.

Yesterday we were in the saddle for ten hours. The dogs ran one lynx down and killed it among the rocks after a vigorous scuffle. It was in a hole and only two of them could get at it.

This morning, soon after starting out, we struck the cold trail of a mountain lion. The hounds puzzled about for nearly two hours, going up and down the great gorges, until we sometimes absolutely lost even the sound of the baying. Then they struck the fresh trail, where the cougar had killed a deer overnight. In half an hour a clamorous yelling told us they had overtaken the quarry; for we had been riding up the slopes and along the crests, wherever it was possible for the horses to get footing. As we plunged and scrambled down towards the noise, one of my companions, Phil Stewart, stopped us while he took a kodak of a rabbit which sat unconcernedly right beside our path. Soon we saw the lion in a treetop, with two of the dogs so high up among the branches that he was striking at them. He was more afraid of us than of the dogs, and as soon as he saw us he took a great flying leap and was off, the pack close behind. In a few hundred yards they had him up another tree. Here I could have shot him (Tony climbed almost up to him, and then fell twenty feet out of the tree), but waited for Stewart to get a photo; and he jumped again. This time, after a couple of hundred yards, the dogs caught him, and a great fight followed. They could have killed him by themselves, but he bit or clawed four of them, and for fear he might kill one I ran in and stabbed him behind the shoulder, thrusting the knife you loaned me right into his heart. I have always wished to kill a cougar as I did this one, with dogs and the knife.

March 21, 1901. Oyster Bay
To Booker T. Washington

My dear Mr. Washington:

Mrs. Roosevelt is as much pleased as I am with your book. I shall not try to tell you what I think about it, my dear sir, for I do not want to seem to flatter you too much. You know I have always been afraid that you might succumb to the flattery you have received; and that would be a great misfortune, for I do not know who could take your place in the work you are doing. I wish I could see you to talk with you more at length than I was able to at the Century.

With hearty regards and many thanks,

Very sincerely yours

April 26, 1901. Oyster Bay
To William Howard Taft

Dear Will:

I write the inclosed letter with all my heart. Prof. Jenks is a fine fellow. He is not a mere theorist, is always entirely reasonable and wants to tell the truth. I believe he could do good work, and I feel that it is an excellent thing whenever we can get a competent observer whose word will carry weight to go out and make a study of Philippine conditions. Of course, when such an observer reports as he is bound to report, the *Evening Post* will state pleasantly, as it did of President Schurman and Bishop Potter, that he has been bought by the Government; but we cannot help that.

I am rather ashamed to say that I am enjoying the perfect ease of my life at present. I am just living out in the country, doing nothing but ride and row with Mrs. Roosevelt, and walk and play with the children; chop trees in the afternoon and read books by a wood fire in the evening. Mrs. Roosevelt is as fond of the woods and fields as I am, and now that the spring is well on, we are reveling in the fresh green sprouts on tree and bush; in the red of the blossoming maples and the sweet scent and coloring of the May flowers. Do you care for birds? The robins, meadow larks, song sparrows, field sparrows, vesper finches, bluebirds and redwings are all in full note now. I have ugly feelings now and then that I am leading a life of unwarrantable idleness, and very soon I intend to take up the study of law. But though I am inclined to be melancholy at times at not having any work, I always console myself by remembering that my work really came in the campaign, and that it counted.

Leonard Wood has just come north for a visit. Recently he has had a rougher time than you have had, and the mugwump press has been denouncing him almost as savagely as Funston.

By the way, give my regards to the latter energetic gentleman when you happen to see him.

With warm love to any of your family whom you are able to reach, I am,

Always yours

May 15, 1901. Oyster Bay
To George B. Aiton

My dear sir:

I have your letter of the 13th inst. and thank you cordially for your courtesy.

It would not be possible for me to have another picture taken in my uniform, but I take pleasure in sending you the one I already have, which I like.

Now, about my relations with my fellow Americans of Jewish faith. Really, my dear sir, all that I have done is to treat them precisely and exactly as I treat other Americans. I have rather prided myself on one point: As I told Zangwill when he was over here, I made up my mind it would be a particularly good thing for men of the Jewish race to develop that side of them which I might call the Maccabee or fighting Jewish type. I was confident that nothing would do more to put a stop to the unreasoning prejudice against them than to have it understood that not only were they successful and thrifty businessmen and high-minded philanthropists, but also able to do their part in the rough, manly work which is no less necessary. Accordingly, when I was police commissioner I made a point of encouraging Jews to enter the force on exactly the same footing as Gentiles. When Rector Alward came over here to preach an anti-Jewish crusade, after some thought I decided that the best thing to do was to have him protected by forty Jewish policemen. Of course it was my duty to see that he was not molested, and it struck me to have him protected by the very members of the race he was denouncing was the most effective answer to that denunciation. When I went into the Rough Riders a certain number of Jews also enlisted. All of them did well. One was promoted to a lieutenancy by me for gallantry. Another after being wounded had his wounds dressed and returned immediately to the regiment, continuing to serve as before. I may add that I did not promote the one I made lieutenant because he was a Jew, any more than I promoted his four companions at the same time because they were Christians. I just took the five men because they were the most gallant and able men, those best entitled to the promotions. So it was while I was Governor. When I appointed Judge Hirschberg of Newburg on the Appellate Division of the Supreme Court I did so not because he was a Jew, but because I thought he was the best Judge for promotion. On the State Board of Charities I thought it was right to see that the different creeds had representation, and I think that the Jews whom I appointed, beginning with ex-Attorney General Rosendale were as fine a body of American citizens as have ever been put on such a Board. When I made Jastrow Alexander of New York City the State Gas Meter Inspector I did not appoint him because he was a Jew. Indeed I doubt if I knew it at the time. I simply knew that he was a very able and upright man who had served with distinguished gallantry in the United States army, and such being the case I did not care a snap of my fingers whether he was born here or abroad, whether he was Jew or Gentile or Protestant or Catholic. I may mention that the Republican State Senator with whom I was on particularly close relations, he coming from the great City of New York,—Senator Nathaniel A. Elsberg,—is a Jew.

I trust that this is the information you desire. If you care to you are at liberty to mention that I should prefer not to have it used as coming from me; for then I should promptly be flooded by requests for similar information from all kinds of people.

Sincerely yours

June 13, 1901. Oyster Bay
To Arthur E. Brown

My dear Mr. Brown:

I thank you for both the pamphlets. I was particularly interested in your view of the descent of the anthropomorpha. It has always seemed to me that we should ultimately have to put the branching off of man's direct ancestors from the mass of the other primates to a remote tertiary period, and I am interested in your view that the parent stem branched off directly from the early lemuroid forms, instead of from some monkeylike form after the latter had itself branched off. As I understand it, the belief now is that the existing species even of the sharply defined and small rhinoceros family represent three stems which have remained wholly distinct since eocene times.

Sincerely yours

July 3, 1901. Oyster Bay
To Cecil Spring Rice

Dear Cecil:

Your letter of the 15th ult. from Geneva received.

Somebody told me the other day that they had seen you looking fairly offensively plutocratic, and upon hearing the news we dolefully shook our heads and said that we did not believe you would now write us. So that we were very much pleased to get your letter. We were delighted to hear about the beloved Winty Chanlers and were both of us greatly interested in what you said as to social conditions at the top in England, and as to Russia and Germany.

I have a feeling of contempt and of anger for our socially leading people on this side, and our special apostles to culture irritate me almost as much. No more unhealthy developments can be imagined than the two which culminate in the New York four hundred and the New York *Evening Post*. But the classes represented here have no such leadership as they have with you, and so are not nearly as dangerous. The *Evening Post* stands for the bitter, sour, ineffective men who possess much refinement, culture, knowledge and scholarship of a wholly unproductive type. They always speak in the name of virtue, but they usually act against decency and almost invariably against manliness. They hate a good man who is strong so much, that they will even try to build up against him a bad man. They contribute nothing useful to our intellectual, civic or social life. At the best they stand aside. At the worst they get in the way, or help the forces of evil. As for the social people,—the four hundred, the men and women who at this moment find their most typical expression at Newport—they lead lives which vary from rotten frivolity to rotten vice. There are exceptions, of course, and plenty of them, but as a whole they are not serious people even when they are not immoral, and thanks to the yellow press, and indeed to the newspapers generally, they exercise a very unwholesome influence on the community at large by the false and unworthy standards which they set up.

Nevertheless, there is plenty of cause for hopefulness. Curiously enough, while the four hundred as a whole has rather grown worse, I believe that the colleges are constantly producing a rather better type. Harvard, Yale, Princeton and many others like them have grown tremendously during the last quarter of a century, and they not only turn out a far larger number of students, but they turn out better men. A cleaner, sturdier, more high-minded set than are these young fellows as a rule, it would be most difficult to find. Moreover, there is a very earnest set of men who do work at politics and civics [indecipherable] in our great cities and who work exceedingly well. Finally, and what is far more important, although there are very uncomfortable and ugly developments in our people as a whole—notably in the diminishing birth rate—yet there is an immense amount of sturdy self-respect and manhood among them. I do not want to say anything that sounds cheap or demagogic, but I have much more trust in the man of moderate means,—in the mechanic, the [indecipherable], the skilled handicraftsman, the farmer,—than I have in the big millionaire. Recently I joined the Masons, and in our lodge here in this village, for instance, I meet a set of men whom one can thoroughly and heartily respect, and with whom one can work with a clear conscience.

While there are very uncomfortable analogies between society now and Greek society in the period succeeding Alexander, and Roman society in the days of Augustus, and even to French society just before the Revolution, yet the analogy could readily be pushed too far. The women to whom you allude who are dowdy, but who live in the country, raise large families of healthy children, and with dull respectability fulfill their various duties, had but few representatives, comparatively speaking, in any of the societies above named. I earnestly wish there were more of them here.

I entirely agree with you about the very rich. Unfortunately, with me personally the lack of appreciation of riches has always taken too acute a form. I am so entirely satisfied with what I have got, and so thoroughly realize that I have had a thousand times as happy a life as any of the very rich men whom I know, that it has resulted in my following a career which will make my children do the drudgery from which I was free. I do not see very much of the big-moneyed men in New York, simply because very few of them possess the traits which would make them companionable to me, or would make me feel that it was worth while dealing with them. To spend the day with them at Newport, or on one of their yachts, or even to dine with them save under exceptional circumstances, fills me with frank horror. Money is undoubtedly one form of power and I appreciate this fact in them and acknowledge it; but I would rather have had the career of Dewey or of Tom Reed, though both ended in a failure (I say "a failure" and not "failure" for the latter would not be true) than the career of Pierpont Morgan. I have known a few men of wealth who use their wealth to full advantage. I have known plenty of men who are only able to do their work because they have inherited means. This is absolutely true of both Cabot and myself, for instance. Cabot is quite a rich man, but I am not; but each of us has been able to do what he has actually done because his father left him in such shape that he did not have to earn his own living. My own children will not be so left, and of course I regret the fact; but I shall try to bring them up—or to speak more accurately—I shall try to assist my wife to bring them up, so that they shall be fit to support themselves and to do good work as the occasion arises.

The more I have heard of the Kaiser the more my respect for him has grown, and though I do not think the Czar is as much of a man, still I think he is a good fellow in his way too. The German press at times makes me so angry that I feel a cordial desire to try a fall with Germany. But as a matter of fact I think it would be most unfortunate if Germany could not continue to get along well with both the United States and England. I have had a very interesting talk with the German Ambassador explaining to him in full my views on the Monroe Doctrine—a doctrine about which I feel so deeply that I should take my stand on it even without regard to the attitude of the administration.

By the way, that exceedingly pernicious idiot, Smalley, has simply infected the London *Times* and other English papers with the theory that when I speak of the Monroe doctrine I have especial reference to England. I should suppose that even Smalley's guinea-pig brain would take in the fact that as things are now the Monroe Doctrine does not touch England in any shape or way, and that the only power that needs to be reminded of its existence is Germany. I explained to the German Ambassador that I did not want to see America get a foot of territory at the expense of any one of the South American states, and that I did not want her to get a single commercial advantage over Germany or any other European power save as it was obtained by fair competition by the merchants or by the ordinary form of treaty; but that I most emphatically protested against either Germany or any other power getting new territory in America—just as I am certain England would object to seeing Delagoa Bay becoming German or French instead of Portuguese.

I have felt more and more melancholy over the South African business. A good many of the Boer leaders have called upon me, most of them with a certain dignified sorrow that though I was of Dutch blood, I seemed to have no sympathy with them when they so earnestly believed in the righteousness of their cause. As a matter of fact, I had and have the warmest personal sympathy with them, and yet I have always felt that by far the best possible result would be to have South Africa all united, with English as its common speech; and I believe that at present it cannot stand alone and that it can do infinitely better under Great Britain than under any other great power. I confess I am wholly puzzled by the duration of the war and the bitter and stubborn determination with which the Boers continue to fight. I have far too keen an appreciation of our own national shortcomings and blunders to feel the slightest inclination to criticize; but I do wish I knew the facts more accurately.

With love from all,
Ever yours

July 15, 1901. Oyster Bay
To William Howard Taft

My dear Will:
I hope your wife and family have stood the Philippine climate all right. It seems idle to keep repeating to you what a lively appreciation

not only I but all the rest of us here have of what you are doing. But when you are so far away and are engaged in a work which though of intense interest entails much that is so irksome and indeed worse than irksome, both for you and your family, I do want you to understand that you are constantly in the thoughts of very many people, and that I have never seen a more widespread recognition of service among men of character than the recognition of the debt we owe you. My good friend, Bishop, of the *Commercial Advertiser*, is a particularly staunch adherent of yours, and your letters, or portions of them, have been laid both by him and by me before a number of men like Seth Low & Lyman Abbot whom we thought ought to know what you are doing.

Here everything is at slack water politically. Let, me at the outset say one thing about myself at the risk of seeming even to you of being in the position of the lady who doth protest too much. Of course, I should like to be President, and feel I could do the work well; but as I think, I wrote you, I have seen too many men, beginning with Tom Reed and Dewey, at close quarters when they were suffering from the effects of the presidential bee, ever to get it into my head. Moreover, it would be simply foolish for me to think seriously of my chances of getting the office, when the only certain feature of the situation is that my own State will be against me. Just at the moment, when the effects of my part in last year's campaign have not worn off, I undoubtedly have a good deal of nebulous popularity in the west and in New England. But in New York Odell will have both the Machine and the mugwumps; the Machine because he will do for them all kinds of things, politically and financially, which they would never even dream of asking me to do; and the mugwumps because their motives are those which you so admirably describe in your letter to Bishop as being inherent in the extremist from the days of the Fifth Monarchy to those of the modern prohibitionists. Exactly as the fanatical temperance people have always opposed me, while the saloon element has recognized in me an infinitely more dreaded foe than any prohibitionists, so all the *Evening Post* mugwumps and those affiliated with them hate me so that they really spend a large part of their time even now in explaining that I am a very bad character; and they champion Odell heartily merely to break down me. Odell has been a good Governor; but he has done things which if I had done them would have caused me to have been branded from one end of the State to the other as not merely a servile but a corrupt tool of Platt. Platt has gotten more from Odell by a good deal than he got from me, and though there is a break between them at present, I am inclined to think that in the long run they will come together because they have fundamentally more in common than either has with me. Nevertheless, Platt now remembers regretfully that though I often went against him, I always treated him squarely, never went back on my word and never deceived him; while Odell did deceive him, deliberately going back on his word, and thereby brought him to shame and humiliation.

All this means that in all human probability Odell will have the Machine when the next nomination comes around, and that all the professional independents will also back him simply because they will want to down me. Now this may not result in the nomination of Odell, for very possibly under such circumstances the West will take the view that if it is not to choose its own man in New York it will take a western man. But the conditions in this State, especially the demoralization in the democratic party here, render it probable that Odell will be re-elected, and of course I shall do everything in my power to help re-elect him. If he is re-elected he will have a very good chance of the nomination for the presidency, and if the west refuses to take New York's candidate, I think it unlikely that it will take any but a western man. If the convention were held now; my hold is still so strong both in the west and in New England that I might very well get the nomination without regard to New York. But my present position is one in which I can do absolutely nothing to shape policies, and so looked at dispassionately, I cannot see that there is any but the very smallest chance of my keeping enough hold even to make me seriously spoken of as a candidate.

There is another thing to be considered. I said above that I should like to be President. But I want you to understand that I should throw up my hat for the chance of nominating one or two outside men for President. For instance, I believe Root would make a most admirable President. I am inclined to think that Spooner would. But if I had the naming either of President or Chief Justice, I should feel in honor bound to name you. Sometime I want to get the chance to say this in public. As far as I know you are the only man of whom it can be truthfully said. In all seriousness, as a mere bit of judgment on contemporary politics, I mean that I think that you are of all the men in this country the one best fitted to give the nation the highest possible service as president, and yet also best fitted to give it the highest possible service as Chief Justice. The Supreme Court has not helped itself by the loose and confused way in which by a narrow majority it rendered its recent decision in the Porto Rico cases. I feel that if any one of the judges had possessed your clear judgment, your sound common sense *and your knowledge of men as well as of law*, together with your power, the court would have stood very differently in the estimation of our people today.

Before leaving merely personal matters, I find that the judge whom

I appointed when your brother refused to accept the position, was an old classmate of yours, John Proctor Clarke. He has made an admirable judge, and is just the salt of the earth.

The Ohio democratic convention has interested us all. The old conservative wing, which was uppermost when Cleveland was in power, has again assumed control. They turned down Bryan and silver with a smash. Their opposition to what has been done in the Philippines has a perfunctory ring to it. They make a ferocious onslaught on trusts, and demand a revision of the tariff in the interests of making it for revenue only. On such a platform the national democracy can I think make a very formidable fight. The protective tariff has vindicated itself in a most astonishing way, but our own people now acknowledge—or at least some of them do—that in some way or shape the reciprocal principle should be introduced in our tariff dealings with other nations; and when we admit that there should be any change in the tariff the inevitable result is to strengthen those who agitate for a disruption of the tariff. It is not easy to make any change in the tariff without opening the door for all sorts of changes. Personally I should think that the nation would understand the need of continuity and steadiness of tariff policy as far more important than all else. But when people are very prosperous they always think they can take liberties with their prosperity, and they never pay any heed to benefits that have accrued in the past as compared with any real or seeming trouble in the present. So it is with trusts. Trusts have prospered because every form of business has prospered. But the man who earns his wages regularly, or who gets his small profits regularly, is apt to forget this fact in his envy, partly justifiable, and in large part unjustifiable, of the great business man who has of course prospered far more, for the simple reason that he is a great business man. I myself believe very strongly in both the State and the Nation taking ample powers for the supervision, and if need be, of the regulation of "trusts," and indeed of all corporations; but I believe even more strongly in exercising this power with the utmost caution and self-restraint. I do not think that most people can point out exactly the evils that are caused by corporations at least where there is any remedy. I know I cannot. But there are evils, and in dealing with them we are hampered by those who refuse to admit their existence, or who desire their continuance, and also by those who oppose them on demagogic grounds, or in a spirit of mere emotional unreason, and who will not support any rational plan, and who advocate measures so destructive that they would create far worse evils than they would prevent.

Nevertheless if the democrats make no attempt really to upset what has been done in our outlying possessions, or to reverse the course the nation has followed the last three years in reference thereto, and abandon all effort to unsettle the currency, they can undoubtedly make a formidable fight if they denounce trusts and contend for a change in the tariff. They will ultimately get back practically all the old democratic strength and they will attract the discontented of every grade from the Cleveland mugwump to the man of ordinary type who always suspects the powers that be. There will be little chance to see exactly the strength of the reformed or partially reformed democracy this fall except in Ohio. We shall have our usual fight against Tammany in New York, but unless there is a great change in public feeling there will be no such awakening of the popular conscience as to give us a chance of success.

I do not know whether I told you that Yale is to give me an LL.D. on her 200th Anniversary. I really appreciate the compliment, and I only wish they would give me a chance to speak and let me take you as my subject.

Always yours

[Handwritten] Warm regards to Mrs. Taft. I wish I had a photo of you.

August 20, 1901. Oyster Bay
To Henry Cabot Lodge

Dear Cabot:

From the domestic standpoint July should be called "Little Rosamond's month of misfortunes" in our family. All the children have awful colds; I had to make a fortnight's whooping western trip with an attack of bronchitis which naturally got no better and threatened to turn into something worse; Ted and Quentin had to have slight surgical operations; and finally Alice got an abscess under one tooth which threatened to be very serious indeed, though I think the ugly possibilities of the case have now pretty well vanished. She had to be sent to the Roosevelt Hospital in New York where Edith and I have been for the last four days and nights with her. I am now out at Oyster Bay for forty-eight hours when I shall rejoin Edith at the hospital and take Quentin there if necessary.

I may be a mere prophet of evil, but I do not anticipate any good out of the belated action in the Sampson-Schley case.[1] The trouble is that Sampson originally absolutely right has elaborately done the wrong thing again and again, and that their superiors have committed the fatal error of striking soft. It has just been one of the cases where the effort to

---

[1]A controversy originating in a dispute regarding credit for victory over the Spanish fleet off Santiago.

weave in and out around the trouble has proved a failure. Either the President and Secretary ought to have stood by Schley straight out from the beginning, or if they shared the belief of ninety-five per cent of the navy, including all the best officers, they should have hit him hard at the very beginning. In the course they have pursued they have elaborately combined all possible disadvantages. As regards the Board, Dewey, I suppose, will take the lead. During the the the past two years I have lost every vestige of confidence I once had in Dewey's moral courage in a case like this. He has got the same thirst for notoriety that has helped to ruin Miles, and in his soreness at the result of his own folly, he has become very bitter against the administration. The popular feeling is overwhelmingly for Schley, and I think that Dewey now cares very little for the navy people or for the real interests of the navy. In consequence I thoroughly believe that he will yield to the popular clamor and to his feeling against the administration and whitewash Schley. Of course, he may be true to his old naval traditions, in which case, he will be very severe upon him. But I do not regard the outlook as promising.

My fortnight's trip west was to attend the quarter-centennial celebration of statehood in Colorado at Colorado Springs. I have been greatly astonished at the feeling displayed for me, not only in Colorado and Kansas, but in Missouri and even in Illinois. All the Colorado people, and all their leaders are a unit, and are perfectly straight out in their declarations. In Kansas and Missouri there have been genuine popular movements started on my behalf, and if there is any real strength at all in the movement for me those two States will be in it. In Illinois, at the moment the bulk of the leaders on both sides are heartily for me, and all took particular pains to call upon me and assure me of the fact. I could not understand their action at first; but it appears that just at this time the Illinois people genuinely want me, and therefore the politicians feel they can strengthen themselves by coming out for me. However, I do not feel that the play of the forces are by any means as simple in Illinois as in Kansas and Colorado, and I am not prepared to say how much substance there is in the movement for me. The trip was a revelation to me. I know with what extreme caution one must accept what one hears on such a trip. But the men who spoke to me were not nobodies. They were national committeemen, chairmen of state committees, Congressmen, and the like. Many of them spoke with as little reserve and as much emphasis as you and Murray Crane and George Lyman that night at dinner. I told them all they must be prepared to have New York against me. To some this came as a surprise, but most of them had already discovered it.

Did I ever tell you that just before I left for the west when I met

Platt, he volunteered the statement that he should support me for the presidential nomination when the time came? I do not put much confidence in this, because I think he is growing very feeble and will be ousted definitely from his leadership during the next three years by Odell; and because he and Odell down at bottom are politicians of the same stripe who have more in common than either can ever really have with me. Platt's reason for announcing that he would support me was that I had always behaved in a strictly honorable manner towards him, and though I had often not done what he wished, I had never lied to him or deceived him. Of course, Odell has; but equally of course in the last resort Odell will often do things for him which Platt would not even ask me to do, and Platt knows this perfectly well, and I am rather inclined to think that when he acts in cold blood he will probably remember it as the decisive factor.

I write you this so that you may know exactly how things stand. I hope I need not say that I do not write because my nomination seems at all likely. Looked at dispassionately it is of course very nearly out of the question that a man can be nominated with his own State against him, and it is practically certain that my State will be against me. But at the moment there is undoubtedly a feeling for me especially in the west, and to a certain extent also in New England and in those parts of the south where there is a genuine republican party of so strong a character that it must be taken into consideration as a factor of possible weight in the nomination.

Give my warm love to Nannie and to Bay and his wife and Henry Adams.

Ever yours

PART FIVE

President

1901–1909

In September 1901 Roosevelt's vice presidential leisure abruptly ended. An assassin felled McKinley, and Roosevelt became president. Although he appreciated that the circumstances of his accession were less than ideal, he set about making the most of his opportunity. He reassured his inherited cabinet (including Secretary of State John Hay, Secretary of War Elihu Root, and Attorney General Philander Knox) and Republican leaders in Congress (notably Senators John Spooner, Orville Platt, Nelson Aldrich, and Joseph Foraker) that he was not the wild man Mark Hanna said he was. He also sought to convince Hanna of the same thing.

Wild or not, Roosevelt certainly could be provocative. Within weeks of taking office he enraged the white South by having African-American leader Booker T. Washington to dinner. He antagonized Wall Street by ordering an antitrust prosecution against J. P. Morgan's Northern Securities railroad trust. He additionally upset the captains of industry by thrusting himself into the middle of an anthracite coal strike that threatened to freeze the Northeast and paralyze the country. He elicited charges of imperialist high-handedness by sponsoring a coup in Panama, guaranteeing the new government against Colombian intervention, and negotiating American control of a canal zone. He outraged liberal opinion by drumming dozens of black soldiers out of the army for failing to testify against their fellows after a violent altercation in Brownsville, Texas. He occasioned howls and hoots by attempting to simplify the system of American spelling.

Other initiatives were less provocative. He brought the Philippine war to an end. He warned Germany away from Venezuela and asserted American hegemony in the Western Hemisphere. He mediated a settlement of the Russo-Japanese War and helped defuse a European crisis regarding Morocco (winning the Nobel Peace Prize for his pains). He extended federal control over forests and grazing lands and made conservation a national priority for the first time. He shepherded consumer-protection laws and railroad regulation through Congress. He appointed Oliver Wendell Holmes, Jr., to the Supreme Court. He expanded the American battle fleet and sent it on a round-the-world cruise. He orchestrated the government's response to financial panics in 1903 and 1907. He became the first president to leave the country while in office, traveling to Panama to observe the canal construction.

Through it all he maintained his outside interests. Alice and Ted experienced close scrutiny as First Daughter and First Son; Roosevelt tried to help Ted enjoy the scrutiny more and Alice to enjoy it less. He discussed birds with John Burroughs and went camping at Yosemite with John Muir. He revisited his old stomping grounds in Dakota, hunted in Colorado and Mississippi, and vacationed in Virginia. He wrestled and boxed in the White House. He discussed medieval literature with French ambassador Jusserand, poetry with Brander Matthews, and modern literature with Owen Wister. He tramped with his sons and nephews about Oyster Bay. He urged Walter Camp to reform the rules of football.

And he never missed a political beat. He deftly neutralized Mark Hanna and those party regulars who would have denied him nomination in his own right in 1904, and swept to victory over Alton Parker in the general election by a historic margin. On the night of his victory he swore off trying for a third term in 1908—but then left enough doubt regarding a recant that potential successors were frozen until he had dictated the nomination of William Howard Taft. He counseled Taft on policy and appearances, and congratulated him—and himself—on Taft's election in November 1908. He left office in March 1909 for an African safari, convinced that Taft would carry on the progressive work so well begun.

September 9, 1901. Buffalo, New York
To Henry Cabot Lodge

Dear Cabot:

I answered your cable to Hotel Brighton, Paris, and hope it reached you. There is no use in telling you of the stunned amazement of the people over the attempted assassination of the President. You know all about it, because you know your own feelings. I was with Senator Proctor in Vermont at the time, and at first the news seemed literally incredible. You and I have lived too long, and have seen human nature from too many different sides to be astounded at ordinary folly or ordinary wickedness, but it did not seem possible that just at this time in just this country, and in the case of this particular President, any human being could be so infamous a scoundrel, so crazy a fool as to attempt to assassinate him. It was in the most naked way an assault not on power, not on wealth, but simply and solely upon free government, government by the common people, because it was government, and because though in the highest sense a free and representative government, it yet stood for order as well as for liberty. McKinley is a man hardly even of moderate means. He is about as well off say as a division superintendent of the New York Central railroad. He lives in a little house at Canton just as such a division superintendent who had retired would live in a little house in Auburn or some other small New York city or big country town. He comes from the typical hard-working farmer stock of our country. In every instinct and feeling he is closely in touch with and the absolute representative of the men who make up the immense bulk of our Nation—the small merchants, clerks, farmers and mechanics who formed the backbone of the patriotic party under Washington in the Revolution; of the Republican Party under Lincoln at the time of the Civil War. His one great anxiety while President has been to keep in touch with this body of people and to give expression to their desires and sentiments. He has been so successful that within a year he has been re-elected by an overwhelming majority, a majority including the bulk of the wage-workers and the very great bulk of the farmers. He has been to a high degree accessible to everyone. At his home in Canton anyone could see him just as easily as anyone else could be seen. All that was necessary was, if he was engaged, to wait until his engagement was over. More than almost any public man I have ever met, he has avoided exciting personal enmities. I have never heard him denounce or assail any man or any body of men. There is in the country at this time the most widespread confidence in and satisfaction with his policies. The occasion chosen by the assassin was one when the President was meeting great masses of his fellow-citizens in accordance with the old American idea of the relations between the President and the people. That there might be no measure of Judas-like infamy lacking, the dog approached him under pretense of shaking hands.

Under these conditions of National prosperity, of popular content, of democratic simplicity and of the absolutely representative character of the President, it does seem utterly impossible to fathom the mind of the man who would do such a deed. Moreover, the surgeons who have in all probability saved the President's life, have thereby saved the life of his assailant. If he is only indicted for assault with intent to kill, and behaves well while in jail, he will be a free man seven years hence, and this, after having committed a crime against free government, a thousand times worse than any murder of a private individual could be. Of course I feel as I always have felt, that we should war with relentless efficiency not only against anarchists, but against all active and passive sympathizers with anarchists. Moreover, every scoundrel like Hearst and his satellites who for whatever purposes appeals to and inflames evil human passion, has made himself accessory before the fact to every crime of this nature, and every soft fool who extends a maudlin sympathy to criminals has done likewise. Hearst and Altgeld, and to an only less degree, Tolstoi and the feeble apostles of Tolstoi, like Ernest Howard Crosby and William Dean Howells, who unite in petitions for the pardon of anarchists, have a heavy share in the burden of responsibility for crimes of this kind.

As soon as I heard the news I came straight to Buffalo. My position was of course most delicate, but I felt that the only course to follow was that which was natural, and that the natural thing was to come at once to Buffalo, where I might see how the President was getting on; and to stay here until he was on the highroad to recovery. As soon as I had seen and talked at length with the doctors, I cabled you. After my talk with them I became very confident of the President's recovery. I found that they would have felt this entire confidence if it had been an ordinary case of some stranger in a hospital, and that it was only the magnitude of the stake that caused their anxiety. Long before you receive this letter I believe the last particle of danger will have vanished; nor do I anticipate even a long convalescence.

The President's splendid inherited strength, the temperate life he has led, and his singularly calm and equable temper of mind all count immensely in his favor.

Of course, I have stayed absolutely quiet here, seeing a great deal of Root, of whom I am very fond. We have had our own troubles during the past month. Curiously enough, Alice and Quentin at the same time had to be taken to the Roosevelt Hospital, although the trouble of neither was in any way connected with the trouble of the other. Alice was as brave and cheerful as possible. Quentin's trouble was in his ear and after the operation, during which he had been chloroformed, his ear had to be dressed every two hours for some days, and the poor little fellow suffered the most exquisite agony. I spent five or six days and nights at the hospital, and Edith was there steadily for a fortnight, and I was almost as glad for her sake as for the sake of the children when she was able to take them all, well and sick, up to the Adirondacks. I was about to join them when I was summoned to Buffalo.

I suppose you were as much astonished as we were at Austin Wadsworth's marriage, and of course you are as pleased as we are. I have always felt it very nearly a crime for Austin to leave no heirs for that beautiful Geneseo Valley estate.

In Vermont and just previously in Minnesota and Illinois I had a most interesting time. In each state I was received with wild enthusiasm, and the Governor of Illinois and Senator Knute Nelson in Minnesota and Senator Proctor in Vermont at the dinners to me proceeded to nominate me for President. I understand entirely that in the case of a promise where no consideration passes from the party on the other side, the promise is in no wise binding, and simply expresses present intentions. If I had been able I should have liked to defer the expression of feeling for some time to come, because in the next three years all may change utterly, and indeed probably will change; but just at present Illinois and Minnesota, like Vermont, are heartily for me, because there is a genuine popular sentiment for me. As yet, Odell has no hold whatever outside of New York. Fairbanks' has gone to Illinois, Minnesota and Kansas, and in every place the leaders had told him they could not support him, because they were going to support me, as that was what the popular feeling demanded. All of this may absolutely change, and I do not want you to think that I attach any special importance to it; but I wanted you to know exactly how things stood. I am going to speak in the campaign both in Ohio and in Iowa. In New York Odell is absolutely in the saddle at the moment.

Give my warm love to Nannie and to all.

Ever yours

September 23, 1901. Washington
To Henry Cabot Lodge

Dear Cabot:

I must just send you a line, hoping it will catch you before you leave, for naturally you have been in my thoughts almost every hour of the last fortnight. It is a dreadful thing to come into the Presidency this way; but it would be a far worse thing to be morbid about it. Here is the task, and I have got to do it to the best of my ability; and that is all there is about it. I believe you will approve of what I have done and of the way I have handled myself so far. It is only a beginning, but it is better to make a beginning good than bad.

I shall not try to give you even in barest outline the history of the last two weeks, and still less to talk of the policies that press for immediate consideration. I hope you can make it convenient to come and see me soon after your return.

I had a very nice talk with Murray Crane. Give my love to Nannie and all.

Ever yours

September 30, 1901. Washington
To Joseph B. Foraker

My dear Senator:

It is a matter of regret to me that I am now unable to take part in your campaign.

I do not suppose it is possible for me to see you until after it is over, but then I particularly want to have a talk with you on several subjects.

Faithfully yours

September 30, 1901. Washington
To John C. Spooner

My dear Senator:

I suppose it is hardly necessary for me to say that during the coming three years I hope to keep in closest touch with you and to profit by your advice in the future as I have profited by it in the past.

You helped me a year ago in the campaign, and at our lunch at the Century Club last spring you outlined a course which I substantially followed in my addresses this summer.

Now, before writing my message, I want much to consult with you on certain points. In the course of the next two or three weeks could you make it convenient to come to Washington? Of course, do not think of coming if it is inconvenient; but I should like greatly to see you before, say, November first.

Faithfully yours

October 5, 1901. Washington
To John Hay

Dear John,

This seems very disrespectful, and I only use the address because I am afraid you would not use "Theodore" if I did not. Edith and I have held a solemn conclave over the matter, and we hope this was the right conclusion.

I read her your letter, and pronounced the last sentence, about your age "affectation," whereupon she answered severely "Not at all! I know just what he means, and I feel exactly the same way myself!" She is forty, and I do not think I deceive myself when I say that she neither looks nor acts nor feels as if she was thirty. As for me, on the whole I have continued all my life to have a better time year after year.

The treaty does seem to be in fine shape; one can never prophesy with the Senate, but I think we can get it through. In my judgement we should get it in as soon as the session begins; delay will give time for quarrels which will lessen our chances.

Do'n't come back until after the Yale celebration.

Love to Mrs Hay,

Yours always

October 9, 1901. Washington
To John Burroughs

Dear Mr. Burroughs.

Mrs. Roosevelt and I were so pleased to read your account of the trip you took with Ted. He had described to us the bluebird incident exactly as it occurred and as you set it forth. The little fellow killed his first buck this year, shooting it with his rifle at a distance of over a hundred yards. It was about a week before his fourteenth birthday; and I suppose life in the future will rarely hold such bright moments for him.

Have you seen my account of my cougar hunt, in *Scribner's,* or rather the first half of it, which was published this month? If not, I shall send you the two *Scribner's* containing the account.

Faithfully yours

October 11, 1901. Washington
To Hermann Speck von Sternberg

Personal

My dear Speck:

I thank you very much for your letter. How could I properly and with discretion try to have you brought back to Washington? Would it do for me to sound Holleben about it? I think you would be of great assistance to me here and would be a help to your country and to mine. I most earnestly desire to have Germany and the United States work hand in hand. I regard the Monroe Doctrine as being equivalent to the open door in South America. That is, I do not want the United States or any European power to get territorial possessions in South America but to let

South America gradually develop on its own lines, with an open door to all outside nations, save as the individual countries enter into individual treaties with one another. Of course this would not anywhere interfere with transitory intervention on the part of any State outside of South America, when there was a row with some State in South America. I wish that the same policy could be pursued in China. That is, if the Chinese could be forced to behave themselves—not permitted to do anything atrocious, but not partitioned, and with the ports kept open to all comers, as well as having the vexatious trade restrictions which prevent inter-Chinese trade in the interior, abolished.

What you tell me about England's decay makes me feel rather sad, but is in exact accord with my own observations and with what I hear from other sources. I wonder if the presence of Russia and Germany face to face, and with their commercial frontiers overlapping alike in Asia Minor and in China, will have any effect upon future affairs! France seems to be still at a good point of military and political efficiency, though her policy is stationary, and she is therefore not a nation which can spread on a safe commercial and industrial basis. I wonder whether her present alliance with Russia is permanent or not?

I am told that the Marquis Ito is coming here and I am looking forward to seeing him, as he is said to be a very remarkable man.

Faithfully yours

October 19, 1901. Washington
To Theodore Roosevelt, Jr.

Blessed Ted:

I was very sorry to learn that you had broken your collarbone; but I am glad you played right through the game, and that you seem to have minded it so little. It is hard luck to lose the rest of the football season, but still you have had four good weeks and you must have improved a great deal. I understand you have played steadily at "end," which I should think would be exactly your right position.

I hope you are getting on all right with your studies. You know how I like you to enjoy your play; but I want you to do your work first.

I am having any amount of work myself. It is no easy job to be President. But I am thoroughly enjoying it and I think so far I have done pretty well. My play consists in riding Bleistein, who has turned out a capital horse. Mother rides Yagenka with me, and looks so young and pretty that I heard the other day that someone had said "she must be his daughter, for she is only a girl." Archie and Quentin are just as cunning as can be. This evening I had a "bear" play with them in their room and Kermit and Ethel could not resist the temptation and came in also, and we had a terrific romp on the bed.

Both Mr. Horace Devereux and Mr. Philip Stewart have been here, and I treated them as playmates and took rides and scrambles with them.

Your loving father

October 24, 1901. Washington
To Lucius L. Littauer

Personal

Dear Lucius:

I cannot write that message, though I should like to.

As to the Booker T. Washington incident, I had no thought whatever of anything save of having a chance of showing some little respect to a man whom I cordially esteem as a good citizen and good American. The outburst of feeling in the South about it is to me literally inexplicable. It does not anger me. As far as I am personally concerned I regard their attacks with the most contemptuous indifference, but I am very melancholy that such feeling should exist in such bitterly aggravated form in any part of our country.

There are certain points where I would not swerve from my views if the entire people was a unit against me, and this is one of them. I would not lose my self-respect by fearing to have a man like Booker T. Washington to dinner if it cost me every political friend I have got. Nevertheless it is very gratifying to have you write as you do.

By the way, I want Odell to tell you all about our meeting the other day. It was most satisfactory and I don't think there is the least chance of any future misunderstanding.

Faithfully yours

October 28, 1901. Washington
To Curtis Guild

Personal

Dear Curtis:

I would rather have you do that than anyone. I would not have the faintest idea what reminiscences to dictate. I have not seen Wister's article, but I have seen unfavorable comments on it.

I am confident I am all right in my Southern policy, which is to insist upon good men and take the best man white or black. The negroes and Republicans all were fearful when this policy seemed to imply that a great majority of the present negro appointees would be cut out; and now I am sorry to say that the idiot or vicious Bourbon element of the South is crazy because I have had Booker T. Washington to dine. I shall have him to dine just as often as I please, exactly as I should have Eliot or Hadley.

Faithfully yours

November 8, 1901. Washington
To Albion W. Tourgée

Personal & Private

My dear Mr. Tourgée:

Your letter pleases and touches me. I too have been at my wits' ends in dealing with the black man. In this incident I deserve no particular credit. When I asked Booker T. Washington to dinner I did not devote very much thought to the matter one way or the other. I respect him greatly and believe in the work he has done. I have consulted so much with him it seemed to me that it was natural to ask him to dinner to talk over this work, and the very fact that I felt a moment's qualm on inviting him because of his color made me ashamed of myself and made me hasten to send the invitation. I did not think of its bearing one way or the other, either on my own future or on anything else. As things have turned out, I am very glad that I asked him, for the clamor aroused by the act makes me feel as if the act was necessary.

I have not been able to think out any solution of the terrible problem offered by the presence of the negro on this continent, but of one thing I am sure, and that is that inasmuch as he is here and can neither be killed nor driven away, the only wise and honorable and Christian thing to do is to treat each black man and each white man strictly on his merits as a man, giving him no more and no less than he shows himself worthy to have. I say I am "sure" that this is the right solution. Of course I know that we see through a glass dimly, and, after all, it may be that I am wrong; but if I am, then all my thoughts and beliefs are wrong, and my whole way of looking at life is wrong. At any rate, while I am in public life, however short a time that may be, I am in honor bound to act up to my beliefs and convictions. I do not intend to offend the prejudices of anyone else, but neither do I intend to allow their prejudices to make me false to my principles.

Faithfully yours

November 15, 1901. Washington
To Orville H. Platt

Personal

My dear Senator Platt:

I have had that matter up with the Attorney General, and my view was this: that we can pass the law. Mr. Knox believes that a law that can stand could be devised. I have asked that such a law be passed, unless Congress in its judgment believes that it is unconstitutional, in which case a constitutional amendment should be passed. I shall get you together with the Attorney General as soon as you come on here to see if we can devise such a law.[1]

With hearty thanks,

Faithfully yours

November 18, 1901
To Nelson W. Aldrich

Personal

My dear Senator Aldrich:

Hearty thanks for your letter. I will follow exactly the course outlined therein and in my conversation with you. I have kept what I have said about reciprocity entirely unchanged since I saw you—that is, after putting in the amendments you suggested. All I shall do about the treaties will be to say I call the attention of the Senate to them. I think that if I did not make any allusion to them, some unfavorable comment would be excited.

I hate to be a nuisance, but if on Monday of next week you are able to be here, I should much like to submit my whole message to you for a last looking over of certain parts.

Faithfully yours

December 12, 1901. Washington
To Booker T. Washington

Personal

My dear Mr. Washington:

Upon my word, it is very difficult to know what to do. I receive a number of letters like that which you enclose. For instance, the gentleman of whom you spoke to me, Mr. Wright, makes the most violent charges against Lyons and especially Rucker and Deveaux, in Georgia. Various colored men assure me that all the colored men in office are against me personally, and what is much more important that they do no good to the race and are not satisfactory officials. On the other hand, each and every one of these statements is specifically contradicted. I am at my wits' end to know what to do. As for the "delegations" from the southern states, I simply shall not consider them in making any appointment, for I believe if I once began to try to consider them or the effect my appointments would have on them, there would be an end to all effort to put in a fit and decent set of officeholders.

---

[1]Roosevelt was trying to decide how to regulate the trusts. This initial foray would facilitate government oversight of corporate activities.

I wish I could cast off all my burdens as easily as I cast off the consideration about the delegations. What gives me real concern is the impossibility of being sure as to the character of the men, particularly the colored men, who are in office in the south or apply for office from the south.

Faithfully yours

December 17, 1901. Washington
To Edward Everett Hale

Personal

My dear Mr. Hale:

I value Mr. Cummings' sermon. If you meet him I wish you would tell him so. I thank you for sending it to me.

The great difficulty that I find is not to do harm to our brother by pretending to help him. The easy thing to do in international matters, for instance, is to follow those amiable but very far from wise philanthropists who think we can help our brother by doing nothing whatever, who think, for example, that we can benefit the Filipino by getting out of the Philippines and letting him wallow back into savagery. Unfortunately, the most difficult task is that which has been so conscientiously undertaken by Root and Taft in trying to bring the Filipinos forward in the path of orderly self-governing liberty.

Again, in South America it is positively difficult to know just how far it is best to leave the nations alone and how far there must be interference, and also how far we can with justice prevent interference by others; because in each case the equities vary.

Faithfully yours

December 26, 1901. Washington
To Marcus A. Hanna

To *The* Senator!

Many thanks, old man; your note gave me real pleasure. All good wishes to you and yours.

Yours always

December 31, 1901. Washington
To Andrew Carnegie

Personal

My dear Mr. Carnegie:

I will serve with the greatest pleasure. Let me congratulate you upon the very high character—indeed I may say the extraordinary character—of the men whom you have secured as trustees; and I con-

gratulate the nation upon your purpose to found such an institution.[1]
It seems to me to be precisely the institution most needed to help and
crown our educational system by providing for and stimulating original research. A happy new year to you!

Sincerely yours

January 4, 1902. Washington
To Endicott Peabody

Dear Cotty:

Pray do not think me grown timid in my old age until you read this
note through. Ted would have a fit if he knew I were writing it, as I found
that by having written you about his collarbone he was rendered very
uncomfortable. In addition to Ted's collarbone, the dentist tells me that
he has killed one front tooth in football, and that tooth will get black.
Now I don't care a rap for either accident in itself; but Ted is only fourteen and I am afraid if he goes on like this he will get battered out before
he can play in college. Last night a Groton graduate, one of the Harvard
substitutes, told me of his own accord that he thought it had been a mistake for Ted to play against heavy boys so much this year. I do not know
whether he knows anything about it or not; but De Saulles, the Yale quar-
terback, who was there, added that he thought it was a pity a young boy
should get so battered up, if it came from playing larger ones, as it might
interfere with other playing later. Now all this may be merely a rumor,
and Ted may not have been playing against heavier boys, but I thought
I would write you about it anyway.

I am very glad he got to be 2d in his class in studies.

Faithfully yours

June 16, 1902. Washington
To George F. Hoar

Personal

My dear Senator Hoar:

It would be but a poor-spirited man who would resent such a letter
as yours or fail to be moved as I am moved both by the spirit which
prompts it and by its references to me individually.

Mr. Andrew Carnegie has just written me in terms not wholly unlike the sentences you quote.

When I used the sentence containing the word independence I was
thinking of our conversation. As you know, I went carefully over with
Judge Taft the advisability of definitely stating what you desire. I told

[1]The Carnegie Institution of Washington.

Judge Taft that I was entirely willing to take the position which as I understood you wished—that is, that when and if the Filipinos attained a
degree and capacity for self-government which in our judgment made it
reasonably probable they could stand by themselves, then we should
leave it to them to decide whether or not they would be independent of
us or continue knit to us by some form less of dependence than of interdependence. Governor Taft earnestly advised me not to make such an
announcement. He said that it would in its effects simply produce a feeling of unrest among the Filipinos, that it would change their attitude
from that of desiring to secure peaceful self-government under our laws
into one of agitation for immediate independence and would inevitably
do great and serious damage, encouraging our enemies to work for independence in the immediate future and making our friends afraid that
we would desert them, and thereby checking and perhaps reversing the
present steady movement towards orderly liberty. Now, my dear Senator, you are the last man who would ask me to do something which
might be fraught with disaster to the people of the Philippines, with the
idea of straightening my own record in the future. I do not think that the
people of the Philippines would believe in or would care for a promise
which might very well apply not to them but to their descendants a generation or two generations hence.

You speak of the Mexican war and of what followed, and you
please me by saying that you have read my life of Benton. You doubtless remember that I all along took a different view of the Mexican war
from that taken by most Republicans of inherited antislavery feeling. It
seems to me that my present position should be compared rather with
the attitude of the early Republican leaders towards slavery, in con-
tradistinction to the attitude of the Wendell Phillips and Garrison abolitionists. Lincoln absolutely declined to announce that he was an abo-
litionist or that slavery should be destroyed in the States where it
existed. He even declined to announce that he favored its abolition in
the District of Columbia, saying merely that he believed that Congress
had the right to abolish it, but should exercise that right only when the
people of the District were altogether willing. His great effort was to
prevent the extension of slavery; not to abolish it. Now, it seems to me
that Lincoln in these matters showed not abandonment of a high ideal,
but great common sense. I do not think he was less moral than Wendell
Phillips or Garrison; I believe he was more practical.

I am striving my best, doubtless with many shortcomings, but, as I
am sure you believe, with sincerity and earnestness, to hasten the day
when we shall need no more force in the Philippines than is needed in
New York. I am encouraging in every way the growth of the conditions

which now make for self-government in the Philippines and which, if the Filipino people can take advantage of them, will assuredly put them where some day we shall say that if they desire independence they shall have it. But I cannot be certain when that day will be, and of course there is always the possibility that they may themselves behave in such fashion as to put it off indefinitely. Now I do not want to make a promise which may not be kept. Above all things, I want for myself and for the nation that there shall be good faith. Senator Hoar, I honor you and revere you. I think you are animated by as lofty a spirit of patriotism and of devotion to and belief in mankind as any man I have ever met in public life. I hate to seem in your eyes to be falling short of my duty on a great question. I ask you to believe that after much painful thought, after much groping and some uncertainty as to where my duty lay, I am now doing it as light has been given me to see it.

Faithfully yours

July 10, 1902. Oyster Bay
To Henry Cabot Lodge

Dear Cabot:

I have received your letter. We were overjoyed by the arrival of your young namesake. I wrote to Bay that we were so glad to know that Bessie was doing well.

Now as to Holmes: If it becomes necessary you can show him this letter. First of all, I wish to go over the reasons why I am in his favor. He possesses the high character and the high reputation both of which should if possible attach to any man who is to go upon the highest court of the entire civilized world. His father's name entitles the son to honor; and if the father had been an utterly unknown man the son would nevertheless now have won the highest honor. The position of Chief Justice of Massachusetts is in itself a guarantee of the highest professional standing. Moreover, Judge Holmes has behind him the kind of career and possesses the kind of personality which make a good American proud of him as a representative of our country. He has been a most gallant soldier, a most able and upright public servant, and in public and private life alike a citizen whom we like to think of as typical of the American character at its best. The labor decisions which have been criticized by some of the big railroad men and other members of large corporations constitute to my mind a strong point in Judge Holmes' favor. The ablest lawyers and greatest judges are men whose past has naturally brought them into close relationship with the wealthiest and most powerful clients, and I am glad when I can find a judge who has been able to preserve his aloofness of mind so as to keep his broad humanity of feeling and his sympathy for the class from which he has not drawn his clients. I think it eminently desirable that our Supreme Court should show in unmistakable fashion their entire sympathy with all proper effort to secure the most favorable possible consideration for the men who most need that consideration.

Finally, Judge Holmes' whole mental attitude, as shown for instance by his great Phi Beta Kappa speech at Harvard is such that I should naturally expect him to be in favor of those principles in which I so earnestly believe.

Now a word as to the other side. It may seem to be, but it is not really, a small matter that his speech on Marshall should be unworthy of the subject, and above all should show a total incapacity to grasp what Marshall did. In the ordinary and low sense which we attach to the words "partisan" and "politician," a judge of the Supreme Court should be neither. But in the higher sense, in the proper sense, he is not in my judgment fitted for the position unless he is a party man, a constructive statesman, constantly keeping in mind his adherence to the principles and policies under which this nation has been built up and in accordance with which it must go on; and keeping in mind also his relations with his fellow statesmen who in other branches of the government are striving in cooperation with him to advance the ends of government. Marshall rendered such invaluable service because he was a statesman of the national type, like Adams who appointed him, like Washington whose mantle fell upon him. Taney was a curse to our national life because he belonged to the wrong party and faithfully carried out the criminal and foolish views of the party which stood for such a construction of the Constitution as would have rendered it impossible even to preserve the national life. The Supreme Court of the sixties was good exactly in so far as its members fitly represented the spirit of Lincoln.

This is true at the present day. The majority of the present Court who have, although without satisfactory unanimity, upheld the policies of President McKinley and the Republican party in Congress, have rendered a great service to mankind and to this nation. The minority— a minority so large as to lack but one vote of being a majority—have stood for such reactionary folly as would have hampered well-nigh hopelessly this people in doing efficient and honorable work for the national welfare, and for the welfare of the islands themselves, in Porto Rico and the Philippines. No doubt they have possessed excellent motives and without doubt they are men of excellent personal character; but this no more excuses them than the same conditions excused the various upright and honorable men who took part in the wicked folly of secession in 1860 and 1861.

Now I should like to know that Judge Holmes was in entire sympathy with our views, that is with your views and mine and Judge Gray's, for instance, just as we know that ex-Attorney General Knowlton is, before I would feel justified in appointing him. Judge Gray has been one of the most valuable members of the Court. I should hold myself as guilty of an irreparable wrong to the nation if I should put in his place any man who was not absolutely sane and sound on the great national policies for which we stand in public life.

Faithfully yours

July 12, 1902. Oyster Bay
To Elihu Root

To the Secretary of War:

I am informed that the Board on Uniforms recommended a turndown collar on the field blouse, but that this has been changed in the War Department to a standing collar. Before this is done I would like to go over the matter with the proper people. I am convinced that a standing collar for field work is foolish and undesirable. When we get into field work the loosest and freest garments must be given the soldier. With my *present* knowledge I desire the recommendation of the Board for a turndown collar to prevail.

August 19, 1902. Oyster Bay
To Oliver Wendell Holmes, Jr.

My dear Judge:

I have your letter of the 17th. Pettigrew said that South Carolina was too small for an independent republic and too large for a lunatic asylum. The Senate is not too large for a lunatic asylum, and if there is any opposition whatever to your confirmation, I shall certainly feel that it fulfills all the conditions of one. Seriously, I do not for one moment believe that a single vote will be cast against your confirmation. I have never known a nomination to be better received, but I shall write to Lodge and get his advice on the point you raise. Then if necessary I shall withdraw my official tender of the place to you and wait until the Senate convenes.

Sincerely yours

August 21, 1902. Oyster Bay
To Philander Knox

Personal
My dear Mr. Attorney General:

What is the reason we cannot proceed against the coal operators as being engaged in a trust? I ask because it is a question continually being asked of me.

If you have to go to Paris, good luck go with you.

Faithfully yours

September 25, 1902. Washington
To Theodore Roosevelt, Jr.

Blessed Ted:

The bruise on my leg[1] developed into a small abscess and I had to give up my western trip and come home and go to bed. Mother is just too pretty for anything, and has something of the air of triumph in attending me that she had when you were under her charge at the White House and all danger in your case had passed.

Don't bother yourself about writing me too much, but let mother or me know now and then how you are getting on with your studies, whether you have begun football, and anything else you think of interest. Evidently you have taken good care of Kermit and have been a great comfort to him, and I am much pleased about it. Let me know how he seems to be getting on both in his studies and among his classmates, and whether he has tried his hand at football.

All of the White House people received us with great enthusiasm here, although of course we are not yet in the White House. One of the policemen came over last night especially to find out if Archie had come too. My western trip, as far as it went, was a great success: I was received with rather noteworthy enthusiasm and was able to make two or three speeches which I deemed of importance. Thank Heaven an abscess did not come from the bruise on my face which still remains swollen slightly, although the accident took place over three weeks ago.

Your loving father

September 27, 1902. Washington
To Marcus A. Hanna

My dear Senator:

For more reasons than one I am very sorry that I am not to be with you a week from Sunday at Cleveland. I am a good deal puzzled over the tariff situation, especially as I find the feeling in the Northwest. But what gives me the greatest concern at the moment is the coal famine. Of course, we have nothing whatever to do with this coal strike and no earthly responsibility for it. But the public at large will tend to visit upon our heads

---

[1]Roosevelt had been involved in a streetcar accident that killed one person and badly bruised Roosevelt.

responsibility for the shortage in coal precisely as Kansas and Nebraska visited upon our heads their failure to raise good crops in the arid belt, eight, ten or a dozen years ago. I do not see what I can do, and I know the coal operators are especially distrustful of anything which they regard as in the nature of political interference. But I do most earnestly feel that from every consideration of public policy and of good morals they should make some slight concession. I do not suppose there is the least chance of your being able to get down to Washington, but if you are anywhere in my neighborhood, do let me see you, and at any rate, do write me and tell me if you have anything in the world to suggest.

I had a great time in Cincinnati, and also in Detroit.

I read with interest your speech in the pamphlet "Peace and Plenty," which you kindly sent to me.

With warm regards to you all, I am,

Faithfully yours

September 27, 1902. Washington
To Henry Cabot Lodge

Dear Cabot:

First, let me say how pleased I was to know that Gussie had practically won his nomination. I forgot to mention it before because everything had been swallowed up in the anxiety about Constance.

Now, as to what you say about the situation. I entirely agree with you that it is alarming, and chiefly from the cause you mention. There is a further cause. Now that there is complaint of high prices at home, people are being very much worried at the way in which articles are sold at a lower price abroad than they are sold here. The fact is undoubted. It is of course due to the further fact that in every business the surplus is disposed of at below the regular prices. The popular way of expressing the fact is that the trusts sell goods lower abroad than at home, because of the way they are pampered by the tariff; yet the type example being used, for instance, in Kansas is the price of a pair of American shoes in Kansas and in London respectively; and of course there is no shoe trust. This is a tariff question pure and simple, and has no relation whatever to the trusts. Yet I think it has a good deal of a hold on the popular mind. Moreover, in the Northwest there is a good deal of formless and vague uneasiness about the trusts in favor of tariff revision.

But the real concrete trouble is in connection with the coal strike. The tariff of course has nothing whatever to do with the matter, as there is no tariff on anthracite coal. The coal operators are not combined so as to enable us legally to call them a trust; and if they were, all that we could do would be to proceed against them under the law against trusts, and

whatever might be the effect as between them and the consumers in ordinary times, such a proceeding would damage, slightly at least, both
them and the working miners, and would therefore have no possible effect of a favorable nature upon the present strike even if it were not improper to take it. There is literally nothing, so far as I have yet been able
to find out, which the national government has any power to do in the
matter. Nor can I even imagine any remedial measure of immediate benefit that could be taken in Congress. That it would be a good thing to
have national control, or at least supervision, over these big coal corporations, I am sure; but that would simply have to come as an incident of
the general movement to exercise control over such corporations.

All this is aside from the immediate political effect. The same unreasoning feeling which made the farmer in Kansas hold the government responsible because he himself had tried in vain to carry on an
impossible agriculture in the arid regions, will now make the people
hold the government responsible if they do not get enough coal. I have
been in consultation with Quay, on the one hand, and with Sargent on
the other, as to what I can do, each of them having been in touch, both
with representatives of the operators and with Mitchell.[1] One of the
great troubles in dealing with the operators is that their avowed determination in connection with the present matter is to do away with what
they regard as the damage done to them by submitting to interference
for political reasons in 1900. From the outset they have said that they
are never going to submit again to having their laborers given a triumph over them for political purposes, as Senator Hanna secured the
triumph in 1900. They are now repeating with great bitterness that they
do not intend to allow Quay to bully them into making any concession
for his political ends, any more than they would allow Hanna to do it
for his. I shall soon see Quay again, and I may see Hanna. I shall see Sargent and Wright. Unfortunately, the strength of my public position before the country is also its weakness. I am genuinely independent of the
big monied men in all matters where I think the interests of the public
are concerned, and probably I am the first President of recent times of
whom this could be truthfully said. I think it right and desirable that
this should be true of the President. But where I do not grant any favors
to these big monied men which I do not think the country requires that
they should have, it is out of the question for me to expect them to grant
favors to me in return. I treat them precisely as I treat other citizens;
that is, I consider their interests so far as my duty requires and so far as

[1]John Mitchell, president of the United Mine Workers.

I think the needs of the country warrant. In return, they will support me, in so far as they are actuated purely by public spirit, simply accordingly as they think I am or am not doing well; and so far as they are actuated solely by their private interests they will support me only on points where they think it is to their interest to do so. The sum of this is that I can make no private or special appeal to them, and I am at my wits' end how to proceed. I shall consult Root in the matter.

Ever yours

P. S. I shall make no more tours this year, and no speeches until after election; then only three or four special ones in November. I have delivered my message, and hope you will like what I said about the tariff.

October 3, 1902. Washington
To Marcus A. Hanna

Personal

My dear Senator Hanna:

Well, I have tried and failed. I feel downhearted over the result both because of the great misery made necessary for the mass of our people, and because the attitude of the operators will beyond a doubt double the burden on us who stand between them and socialistic action. But I am glad I tried anyhow. I should have hated to feel that I had failed to make any effort. What my next move will be I cannot yet say. I feel most strongly that the attitude of the operators is one which accentuates the need of the Government having some power of supervision and regulation over such corporations. I would like to make a fairly radical experiment on the anthracite coal business to start with! At the meeting today the operators assumed a fairly hopeless attitude. None of them appeared to such advantage as Mitchell whom most of them denounced with such violence and rancor that I felt he did very well to keep his temper. Between times they insulted me for not preserving order (and they evidently ignored such a trifling detail as the United States Constitution) and attacked Knox for not having brought suit against the miners' union as violating the Sherman Antitrust Law. You have probably seen my statement and Mitchell's proposition. I regarded the latter as entirely fair and reasonable. Now it is over, I may mention that if the operators had acceded to it I intended to put you on the commission or board of arbitration. But the operators declined to accede to the proposition or to make any proposition that amounted to anything in return; and as I say I must now think very seriously of what the next move shall be. A coal famine in the winter is an awful ugly thing, and I fear we shall see terrible suffering and grave disaster.

Faithfully yours

October 13, 1902. Washington
To Joseph B. Bishop[1]

Personal

My dear Bishop:

Do you think you are fully alive to the gross blindness of the operators? They fail absolutely to understand that they have any duty toward the public. Most emphatically I shall not compromise with lawlessness. But with a hundred and forty thousand workmen idle there is certain to be some disorder. I have been told, on excellent authority, that this disorder has been very great in the present instance and of a very evil kind. On equally good authority I am told the exact contrary. I shall speedily find out for myself. But in any event what has been done so far in no wise justifies a refusal to have some dispassionate body settle the respective rights and wrongs of the two parties. The coal operators and their friends and their allies of the type of the *Sun* have been attacking me, just as they attacked me about the trust business. Do they find much comfort, not only in the speeches of Bryan and Tom Johnson, but of David Hill and of Olney? Do they not realize that they are putting a very heavy burden on us who stand against socialism; against anarchic disorder?

A word as to the interference of politicians. Quay and Hanna are Senators; Odell is Governor; I am President. If any one of us interferes in a spirit of mere political trickery, or to gain political ends of an unworthy kind in an unworthy manner, if he threatens or hectors, why he should be condemned without stint. But the heaviest weight of condemnation should be reserved for any one of us who represents the people and who yet fails to do all in his power in the interest of the people to bring to an end a situation fraught with such infinite danger to the whole commonwealth. If during the ensuing week there comes some heavy riot on the East Side in New York, in my judgment the operators, more than the miners, are responsible for it.

Meanwhile I am sure that you know that I shall take no step which I do not think can be justified by the sound common sense of both of us six months or a year hence. I shall do whatever I can to meet the present emergency, but I shall not meet it in a way that will invite future disaster.

Come on here at any time. You know I will always be more than glad to see you.

Faithfully yours

---

[1] One of Roosevelt's favorite journalists.

October 15, 1902. Washington
To J. Pierpont Morgan

Personal

My dear Mr. Morgan:

After thinking all over the matter I got Root to telephone you this morning, as you know, expressing my desire to appoint two extra men, that is, seven in all for the commission, and to substitute ex-President Cleveland for the proposed military or naval member of the commission. After making this proposition, Mr. Mitchell, whom I had summoned to meet me here but who had not indicated to me any of his plans, arrived and I went over the situation with him. On behalf of the miners he protested in the strongest terms against any limitation as to my choice of men. He said that the miners would agree to abide by my choice because they believed that I would in a matter so vital to them be sure to see that a fair and impartial tribunal was chosen, but that in their judgment the terms presented by the operators were such as to eliminate the possibility of putting upon the commission men who might be supposed to know the miners' side of the controversy. He insisted very strongly that I should be given an absolutely free hand in making the nominations and that if the miners were willing to trust me the operators ought to be willing to do so. I told him that before seeing him I had asked Mr. Root to telephone you as to my views, and went over at length the reasons why, in view of the very great urgency of the case, I thought he should defer to the operators' views. I do not attempt to conceal from you the fact that I would have preferred to be left unhampered in my choice. If I am fit to choose such a commission of inquiry at all, it does not seem to me right and proper to hamper me in the choice. If I intended to appoint a commission unfavorable to the operators or biased against them, why under the proposed terms by a very little ingenuity I could make at least four of the five members of the commission demagogic opponents of the operators and of capital generally—and this while still keeping strictly within the letter of the proposal. In such a case, as the limitation does not prevent me from doing harm, and merely hampers me in doing good, I am sorry it was put on.

But the thing that I most desire to do is to bring to an end the dreadful situation now existing; and I finally got Mr. Mitchell to agree to the proposition which I had made you. I now repeat this proposition in detail, with the names of those whom I would like to appoint.

I accept the suggestions of the operators as to my five appointees of the commission, except that I do not believe it is wise to put a member of the army or navy on, and in place of this member of the army or navy I will nominate Hon. Grover Cleveland, ex-President of the United States.

As the Judge, I will name Judge Gray, whose name you submitted to me and whose appointment I feel will, like that of Mr. Cleveland himself, command universal confidence. As sociologist, I nominate my official adviser, the Commissioner of Labor, Mr. Carroll D. Wright. As the man of practical experience in anthracite mining and selling, I will appoint Mr. Thomas H. Watkins, whose name you gave me and of whom I hear most excellent reports. As the practical mining engineer I will appoint either Mr. Edward W. Parker, the editor of the *Engineering and Mining Journal,* or Professor Henry Smith Munroe, the head of the Department of Mining in Columbia University, whichever the operators desire. As regards these five men I thus take four in accordance with the proposition of the operators, and for the fifth I substitute the ex-President of the United States. None of the men thus indicated, with the possible exception of Mr. Wright, are in any way representative of the wageworkers or miners. I believe them all to be fair and upright men; but for the same reason that I think it right to have such men as Mr. Watkins and Mr. Parker or Mr. Munroe on the commission as in a certain sense peculiarly understanding the interests of the operators, so I think it a matter of mere equity that there should be on the commission men familiar with the interests of the wageworkers. I nominate for this purpose Bishop Spalding of Illinois and Mr. E. E. Clark, Grand Chief, Order of Railway Conductors. I should not put on either Bishop Spalding or Mr. Clark if I did not believe that they were incapable of doing injustice to any capitalist, exactly as I believe that Mr. Watkins and either Mr. Parker or Mr. Munroe would be incapable of doing injustice to any wageworker; but I think it very important that there should be on the commission men capable of understanding and of presenting the viewpoint of both parties in interest.

The commission then would consist of Hon. Grover Cleveland, Judge George Gray, Bishop Spalding, Hon. Carroll D. Wright, Mr. Thomas H. Watkins, Mr. Parker or Mr. Munroe, and Mr. E. E. Clark. I feel that it would be well-nigh impossible to get a commission of abler men more certain to approach the whole subject in a spirit of fearlessness and sober good sense and of resolute purpose to do evenhanded justice.

Let me say again with all the earnestness at my command that I feel this crisis is one which does not warrant standing on any punctilio or prejudice. Mr. Mitchell finally accepted my proposition and has told me that if the operators accept it he will do all in his power to persuade the miners to agree to abide by the decision of the commission and immediately to resume work. A refusal to come to terms means the possibility of dreadful disaster to our whole people—a disaster of far more than temporary results. With whatever of earnestness there is in me I urge for the sake of the welfare of our nation and our people that this proposition be agreed to. The miners desire that I should appoint a commission unhampered by any conditions. The operators desire that I should appoint a commission of five, all five selected under certain given conditions. I have appointed a commission of seven, four of them selected under the conditions laid down by the operators, the fifth being the ex-President of the United States, while the sixth and seventh I have chosen of my own free will. Surely there can be no good reason for refusing such a commission.

Faithfully yours

October 16, 1902. Washington
To Marcus A. Hanna

My dear Senator:

Late last night when it became evident that we were going to get a commission which would be accepted by both sides I remarked "Well, Uncle Mark's work has borne fruit" and everybody said "Yes." The solution came because so many of us have for so long hammered at the matter and gained a little here and a little there until at last things got into shape which made the present outcome possible. I hardly suppose the miners will go back on Mitchell. If they do, they put themselves wholly in the wrong.

I earnestly hope you are now in good shape physically.

Faithfully yours

November 26, 1902. Washington
To James A. Smyth

Personal

My dear Sir:

I am in receipt of your letter of November 10 and of one from Mr. Hemphill, the editor of the *News and Courier*, under date of November 11, in reference to the appointment of Dr. Crum as collector of the port of Charleston.

In your letter you make certain specific charges against Dr. Crum, tending to show his unfitness in several respects for the office sought. These charges are entitled to the utmost consideration from me and I shall go over them carefully before taking any action. After making these charges you add, as a further reason for opposition to him, that he is a colored man, and after reciting the misdeeds that followed carpetbag rule and negro domination in South Carolina, you say that "we have sworn never again to submit to the rule of the African, and such an appointment as that of Dr. Crum to any such office forces us to protest unanimously against this insult to the white blood"; and you add that you understood me to say that I would never force a negro on such a

community as yours. Mr. Hemphill puts the objection of color first, saying—"First, he is a colored man, and that of itself ought to bar him from
the office." In view of these last statements, I think I ought to make clear
to you why I am concerned and pained by your making them and what
my attitude is as regards all such appointments. How anyone could
have gained the idea that I had said I would not appoint reputable and
upright colored men to office, when objection was made to them solely
on account of their color, I confess I am wholly unable to understand. At
the time of my visit to Charleston last year I had made, and since that
time I have made, a number of such appointments from several States
in which there is a considerable colored population. For example, I
made one such appointment in Mississippi, and another in Alabama,
shortly before my visit to Charleston. I had at that time appointed two
colored men as judicial magistrates in the District of Columbia. I have
recently announced another such appointment for New Orleans, and
have just made one from Pennsylvania. The great majority of my appointments in every State have been of white men. North and south
alike it has been my sedulous endeavor to appoint only men of high
character and good capacity, whether white or black. But it has been my
consistent policy in every State where their numbers warranted it to recognize colored men of good repute and standing in making appointments to office. These appointments of colored men have in no State
made more than a small proportion of the total number of appointments. I am unable to see how I can legitimately be asked to make an exception for South Carolina. In South Carolina to the four most important
positions in the State I have appointed three men and continued in office a fourth, all of them white men—three of them originally gold Democrats—two of them, as I am informed, the sons of Confederate soldiers. I have been informed by the citizens of Charleston whom I have
met that these four men represent a high grade of public service.

I do not intend to appoint any unfit man to office. So far as I legitimately can I shall always endeavor to pay regard to the wishes and feelings of the people of each locality; but I cannot consent to take the position that the door of hope—the door of opportunity—is to be shut upon
any man, no matter how worthy, purely upon the grounds of race or
color. Such an attitude would, according to my convictions, be fundamentally wrong. If, as you hold, the great bulk of the colored people are
not yet fit in point of character and influence to hold such positions, it
seems to me that it is worth while putting a premium upon the effort
among them to achieve the character and standing which will fit them.

The question of "negro domination" does not enter into the matter
at all. It might as well be asserted that when I was Governor of New
York I sought to bring about negro domination in that State because I

appointed two colored men of good character and standing to responsible positions—one of them to a position paying a salary twice as large as that paid in the office now under consideration—one of them as a director of the Buffalo exposition. The question raised by you and Mr. Hemphill in the statements to which I refer, is simply whether it is to be declared that under no circumstances shall any man of color, no matter how upright and honest, no matter how good a citizen, no matter how fair in his dealings with all his fellows, be permitted to hold any office under our government. I certainly cannot assume such an attitude, and you must permit me to say that in my view it is an attitude no man should assume, whether he looks at it from the standpoint of the true interest of the white men of the south or of the colored men of the south—not to speak of any other section of the Union. It seems to me that it is a good thing from every standpoint to let the colored man know that if he shows in marked degree the qualities of good citizenship—the qualities which in a white man we feel are entitled to reward—then he will not be cut off from all hope of similar reward.

Without any regard as to what my decision may be on the merits of this particular applicant for this particular place, I feel that I ought to let you know clearly my attitude on the far broader question raised by you and Mr. Hemphill; an attitude from which I have not varied during my term of office.

Faithfully yours

December 6, 1902. Washington
To Woodrow Wilson

My dear President Wilson[1]:

I have just finished your really notable address which I read for the first time in the *Atlantic Monthly*. As a decent American I want to thank you for it.

Is there any chance of your getting down to Washington to spend a night with me at the White House this winter? There are many things I would like to talk over with you.

Faithfully yours

December 26, 1902. Washington
To Grover Cleveland

My dear Mr. Cleveland:

It is just six years since you took action in the Venezuela case. I have always been proud of the fact that I heartily backed up what you then did; and reading over in a little volume I published, called *American*

---

[1]Wilson was president of Princeton University.

Ideals, my views on the Monroe Doctrine written in support of your position, I am pleased to see how closely what I therein said foreshadowed what I have said about the Monroe Doctrine in my two messages to Congress and in my note to Germany about the Venezuela case. It seems to me that you have special cause for satisfaction in what we have succeeded in accomplishing this time in connection with getting England and Germany explicitly to recognize the Monroe Doctrine in reference to their controversy with Venezuela and in getting all of the parties in interest to accept arbitration by the Hague court. I congratulate you heartily on the rounding out of your policy.

With best wishes to Mrs. Cleveland and to you personally, I am,

Sincerely yours

March 7, 1903. Washington
To John Burroughs

My dear Mr. Burroughs:

I was delighted with your *Atlantic* article. I have long wished that something of the kind should be written. The fashion of the books you are criticizing was of course set in Kipling's jungle stories, but equally of course the latter are frankly fairy tales, and so they can do only good—though Kipling makes one or two blunders as when he takes it for granted that the great wild beasts like the song birds mate in spring. But when the people like those you criticize solemnly assert that they are relating exact facts they do positive harm. By the way, I wonder why they seem to select the porcupine for some of their most absurd misstatements.

Don't you think that you perhaps scarcely allow sufficiently for the extraordinary change made in the habits of the wild animals by experience with man, especially experience continued through generations? I do not believe that there is any instinct whatever that teaches them to be afraid of him in regions where he is wholly unknown. On Pacific islands that have never been visited by ships the birds at first have not the slightest fear of man, nor do they fear either cats, dogs or pigs. Proverbially cute though the fox is, the Falkland Island fox and in most of the Arctic regions that Arctic fox were both found by the first explorer to be as bold, stupid and helplessly fearless as these Pacific island birds. A very little experience makes the polar bear as afraid of man as our small black bear, but the first travelers that came across these polar bears in hitherto unvisited places have always found them very bold, evidently regarding man as their natural prey like seals. On the Upper Missouri the grizzly is today, as I have found personally, one of the wariest of animals—a century ago Lewis and Clark found it one of the most ferocious, fearless and least shy. I believe that inherited instinct must be supplemented by some means of communication among animals. Otherwise I do not know how to account for the fact that even the unhunted fox in all settled regions, where foxes pass their lives in danger, is so shy and wary, while in a region where all foxes are unhunted and do not know man as an enemy none of them are particularly wary. The "wolfers" in the west always told me that in a given locality the wolves would after a while become accustomed to some particular means of getting at them, and that good frequently occurred from changing these means.

By the way, as even Homer nods, do not object to my saying that I think you praise overmuch for its fidelity to life Charles Dudley Warner's admirable little tract on deer hunting. You recollect that at the very end he makes the buck come up to the fawn and lead it off? Of course in real life the buck is never found associating with the doe or fawn when the latter is young, then as a matter of fact he has not been associated with the doe since the preceding fall. Charles Dudley Warner's story was an excellent little tract against summer hunting and the killing of does when the fawns are young. It is not an argument against hunting generally, for as Nature is organized, to remove all checks to the multiplication of a species merely means that that very multiplication itself in a few years operates as a most disastrous check by producing an epidemic of disease or starvation.

If the Senate will permit, and unless it proves impossible to dodge the infernal yellow papers, I would like to visit the Yellowstone Park for a fortnight this spring. I want to see the elk, deer, sheep and antelope there, for the Superintendent of the Park, Major Pitcher, tells me they are just as tame as domestic animals. I wonder whether you could not come along? I would see that you endured neither fatigue nor hardship. With regards,

Sincerely yours

May 19, 1903. Sacramento, California
To John Muir

My dear Mr. Muir:

I enclose the three letters. I trust I need not tell you, my dear sir, how happy were the days in the Yosemite I owed to you, and how greatly I appreciated them. I shall never forget our three camps; the first in the solemn temple of the giant sequoias; the next in the snowstorm among the silver firs near the brink of the cliff; and the third on the floor of the Yosemite, in the open valley, fronting the stupendous rocky mass of El Capitan, with the falls thundering in the distance on either hand.

Good luck go with you always.

Faithfully yours

May 27, 1903. Helena, Montana
To Henry Cabot Lodge

Strictly personal

Dear Cabot:

For your private information I would like you to know that the following three telegrams passed between myself and Senator Hanna:

Cleveland, Ohio, May 23, 1903

The President, Seattle, Washington.

The issue which has been forced upon me in the matter of our State Convention this year endorsing you for the Republican nomination next year has come in a way which makes it necessary for me to oppose such a resolution. When you know all the facts I am sure you will approve my course.

M. A. Hanna

May 25, 1903

Hon. M. A. Hanna, Cleveland, Ohio.

Your telegram received. I have not asked any man for his support. I have had nothing whatever to do with raising this issue. Inasmuch as it has been raised of course those who favor my administration and my nomination will favor endorsing both and those who do not will oppose.

Theodore Roosevelt

Cleveland, Ohio, May 26, 1903

The President.

Your telegram of the 25th. In view of the sentiment expressed I shall not oppose the endorsement of your administration and candidacy by our State Convention. I have given the substance of this to the Associated Press.

M. A. Hanna

May 27, 1903

Hon. M. A. Hanna, Cleveland, Ohio.

I thank you for your telegram and appreciate your action.

Theodore Roosevelt

After the receipt of the first I thought over the matter a full 24 hours, consulting with Mellen, Byrnes and Moody, and decided that the time had come to stop shilly-shallying, and let Hanna know definitely that I did not intend to assume the position, at least passively, of a suppliant to whom he might give the nomination as a boon. I accordingly sent him my answer, and as you doubtless saw, made a similar statement for the public press, of course not alluding to the fact that Hanna had sent me the telegram—my statement simply going as one made necessary by Hanna's long interview in which he announced that he would oppose my endorsement by the Ohio Convention. I rather expected Hanna to fight, but made up my mind that it was better to have a fight in the open at once than to run the risk of being knifed secretly. Mellen and also Loeb were confident that he would not fight. The result proved that they were right, as his last telegram shows.

I am pleased at the outcome as it simplified things all around, for in my judgment Hanna was my only formidable opponent so far as the nomination is concerned. I have had a great reception here in the West, and yesterday at Spokane made what I consider my best speech, which I think will be given out perhaps under a Butte headline in the papers tomorrow. If so, I would like you to read it. I made it particularly with reference to having a knockdown and dragout fight with Hanna and the whole Wall Street crowd, and I wanted them to understand that if they so desire they shall have all the fighting they wish. At the same time I wished the labor people absolutely to understand that I set my face like flint against violence and lawlessness of any kind on their part, just as much as against arrogant greed by the rich, and that I would be as quick to move against one as the other. I think I made my position clear. The big New York and Chicago capitalists—and both the criminal rich and the fool rich—will do all they can to beat me.

This whole incident has served one temporarily useful purpose, for it has entirely revived me. I was feeling jaded and tired. The trip has been very severe and I have gotten so I cannot sleep well—which always tells on one. But this last business gave me a new and vivid interest in life. Now, thank heavens, I have little more than a week left. The last three days in Iowa and Illinois will be the worst.

Give my love to Nannie.

Faithfully yours

P.S.—Tell Murray Crane that early in July I may want to see him, perhaps to have him meet President Mellen of the Northern Pacific, and one or two other friends, so as to begin taking measures concerning New York. That is the State which I think needs most looking after.

May 27, 1903. Butte, Montana
To Alice Roosevelt

Darling Alice:

I was really delighted with your letter, and before I received it I had been very much pleased with all I had heard of how you had acted in Porto Rico. I am very much pleased that you found the visit so interesting; and it was a good thing in more ways than one. You were of real service down there because you made those people feel that you liked them and took an interest in them, and your presence was accepted as a great compliment.

Tell mother that you and I will leave for Cleveland about five o'clock on the 9th. It is probable we shall simply stay the day and on the evening of the 10th at eleven o'clock start back. We may stay over the 10th.

I am feeling pretty well tired, but the trip has been a useful one; indeed I think it has been of service in more ways than one. I have been literally loaded down with gifts of every kind and description. I fear there are only a very few of them to which mother will consent to give house room, although I shall have to preserve most, as many of them are of great value, as far as expense goes, and as I suppose the donors will be inquiring after them. There are a number of minor ones, however, which can be distributed among my offspring. I rather think you will like Josiah the badger. So far he is very good tempered and waddles around everywhere like a little bear submitting with perfect equanimity to being picked up, and spending much of his time in worrying the ends of anybody's trousers.

Ask Dave Goodrich if he got my letter.

Good-bye blessed girl. I like your letter very much indeed.

Your loving father

May 27, 1903. Butte, Montana
To Joseph B. Bishop

My dear Bishop:

For your private information I send you the four telegrams that passed between Hanna and myself. Also, did you see my speech made at Spokane, but substantially repeated at Butte and sent out by the Associated Press under that headline? I want to call your especial attention to the absolute clearness and the unqualified way in which I struck alike at the crimes of the criminal rich and the crimes of the criminal poor—crimes of greed and cunning on the one hand, and crimes of violence on the other.

I hope to see you as soon as I get back.

Faithfully yours

June 15, 1903. Washington
To Pierre De Coubertin

My dear Baron Coubertin:

I was much interested in your letter and the accompanying newspaper clipping. The idea you suggest is to me new, at least to the extent that you have for the first time formulated it. I agree with you entirely. If a growing boy, a young fellow up to the time that he attains manhood, achieves a certain degree of mastery in such exercises as those you enumerate—walking, running, riding, shooting, swimming, skating, etc. I fully believe that he does, through what you so aptly describe as muscular memory, acquire the capacity to retain a large degree of his powers through their comparatively infrequent use.

There are just two suggestions, both of which you have doubtless developed in your book. The first is that it is impossible to put all boys and young men on the same Procrustean bed, whether of body or of mind; and the second is that so far as possible, if only for the effect on the mind, the boy's own tastes should be consulted as to the sports in which he is chiefly exercised.

For example, I have four boys. The youngest is five and therefore can be left out of account for our purpose. The next oldest is nine. He is a sweet-tempered little fellow, not at all combative. He runs, walks, and climbs well, and has learned to swim fairly well. He is most fond of his bicycle and his pony. The latter, like all of my boys when young, he rides with a small Mexican or "cow" saddle. This summer I intend to teach him to shoot with a small calibre rifle.

The next oldest, Kermit, is thirteen. He had water on the knee when young and it kept him back and has prevented his ever becoming really proficient in sports. He is not at all combative but seems to hold his own well with boys. I have been utterly unable to teach him to box, but he wrestles pretty well for his weight and age. He does not take to horseback riding at all but is very fond of his bicycle. In running he is no good at all for the sprints, but has a good deal of endurance and comes in well for the long distances. I am utterly unable to make him care for shooting. He skates rather poorly. At last I have got him so that he swims fairly.

The oldest, Ted, is fifteen. He is a regular bull terrier and though devoted to his mother and sisters, and although I don't believe he is quarrelsome among his friends he is everlastingly having sanguinary battles with outsiders. In most branches of sport he has already completely passed me by. He can outwalk and outrun me with ease, and perhaps could outswim me—although I think not yet; I am inclined to think him a better rider than I am, and owing to his weight he can certainly take my horses over jumps which I would not care to put them at unless there was necessity. On account of my weight I could probably still beat him at boxing and wrestling, but in another year he will have passed me in these. I do not shoot at all with the shotgun, whereas he has already become a good wing shot. I can still beat him with the rifle. He plays football well. In a game last year he broke his collar bone, but finished the game without letting anyone know what had happened. . . .

Now with all these boys I have been able to do a certain amount in guiding them, but their own instincts have decided the very marked differences among them. Personally I have always felt that I might serve as an object lesson as to the benefit of good hard bodily exercise to the ordinary man. I never was a champion at anything. I have never fenced, although this winter I have done a good deal of broadsword and singlestick work with my friend, General Leonard Wood, and other Army officers. I was fond of boxing and fairly good at it. I was a fair rider, a fair rifle shot, and possessing the ordinary hardihood and endurance of an out-of-door man I have done a good deal of work in the wilderness after big game. Of late years, since I have been Governor of New York and afterwards President, my life has necessarily been very sedentary; but I have certain playmates among my friends here in Washington and with them I occasionally take long walks, or rather scrambles, through the woods and over the rocks.

Mrs. Roosevelt is very fond of riding and we ride a good deal together. In summer at my home on Long Island Sound I often take her for long rows. Like the average married man of domestic habits, my ability to take violent exercise has been much diminished by the fact that when I have leisure I like, so far as possible, to spend it in doing something in company with my wife or children. Of late years I have gone back very much in physical prowess, tending to grow both fat and stiff. I could not begin to walk or run for the length of time or at the speed of the old days, and I could not successfully ride the kind of horses I used to ride on my ranch, or in the hunting field across a country so stiff as to insure my having bad falls, for I should shake myself up too much. But I have kept up just exactly the kind of exercise you describe and with exactly the same effect. I can ride fifty miles on horseback or walk twenty on foot, if I am allowed to choose my own gait. I can enjoy a day's hunting as much as ever. I have had to abandon wrestling because I found that in such violent work I tended to lay myself up; and I do but little boxing because it seems rather absurd for a President to appear with a black eye or a swollen nose or a cut lip. Four times I have broken bones in falls with horses.

I think that you preach just the right form of the gospel of physical development. You are well aware of the mistake that so many of my English friends have made, that is of treating physical development as the be-all and the end-all—in other words as the serious business—of life. I have met English officers to whom polo and racing, football and baseball were far more absorbing than their professional duties. In such a case athleticism becomes a mere harmful disease. Nevertheless the fact remains that in our modern highly artificial, and on the whole congested, civilization, no boon to the race could be greater than the acquisition by the average man of that bodily habit which you describe— a habit based upon the having in youth possessed a thorough knowledge of such sports as those you outline, and then of keeping up a reasonable acquaintance with them in later years.

When are you coming over here? I would like you to pay me a visit here in Washington and we will take some walks and rides together. If you come when I am in the country we will row or chop trees or shoot at a target, as well as ride and swim.

Sincerely yours

June 22, 1903. Washington
To Lyman Abbott

Private and confidential
My dear Dr. Abbott:

I desire to write you about two things. In the first place I am having great trouble with Russia, simply because of the extraordinary mendacity with which we are being treated by the Russian authorities. In this Manchurian matter we are not striving for any political control or to help any nation acquire any political control or to prevent Russia from acquiring any political control of the territory in question. All that we ask is that Russia shall do what over and over again she has agreed to do and shall not prevent the Chinese from giving us the rights for which we have fought in connection with the open-door policy. We wish for our people the commercial privileges which Russia again and again has said we shall have which all the powers in the world have said we shall have, but which China refuses to give because Russia threatens her with dire consequences if she gives them. Almost worse than the offenses is the planner of committing them. Russia to our Ambassador in St. Petersburg and through her Ambassador here assures us that she is favorable and not hostile to our contention, and at the same time her representative in Peking emphatically forbids the Chinese Government to act as China desires. When we call the attention of the Russian authorities to this state of affairs we are met by perfectly vague and inconclusive answers, and while reiterating their assurances to us they decline to instruct their Pelting representative to go around with our representative to the Chinese authorities and make these assurances good. It is very irritating. I do not know what action may be necessary in the future, but I wish you to be acquainted with some of the inside facts of the situation so as to be prepared for whatever comes up in the way of a new phase.

Second. I enclose you a letter from Judge Jones. You can hardly realize the immense service rendered by him in his recent peonage decisions, or the great moral courage he showed in rendering them. Unfortunately there is in the south a very large element which because of the very fact that they have been let alone by the north as regards dealing with the Negro have been resolute in their intention practically to reintroduce some form of serfage or slavery. This large white element in the south is not in the least concerned about those bugaboos, "social equality," "negro domination," and "miscegenation," all three of which are the merest phantoms. It hates and despises the Negro but is bent upon his continuing in the land. It is this element which in the black belt controls the towns and ran out the emigration agents who sought to get the Negroes to go to Oklahoma. This element strives to prevent the Negro's rising in any way and seeks to drive him from every trade in which he can be a rival to a white, and at the same time to force him to work on the white's terms wherever the white does not want to work. The absence of protest from the north has undoubtedly, whatever may have been its good effects in certain lines, had a bad effect in encouraging this white element; and the bold action of Judge Jones is therefore all the more valuable. Of course it is far better that such action should come from a Southerner, but the north ought in every way to uphold the hands of the Southerner brave and wise enough to take it. When I last saw Mr. Kennan he spoke of going south to look into the Negro business. If he could be put in touch with Judge Jones and do as the Judge suggests he might render incalculable service.

Sincerely yours

July 7, 1903. Oyster Bay
To Seth Bullock

My dear Captain:

On August 20th Ted will reach Deadwood. His cousin George Roosevelt will be with him. You know Ted. George is of the same age but a bigger boy, being six feet tall. They are both of them hardy, and, as easterners go, they are fair riders and can shoot 'a little. If it comes to walking you need not have the least uneasiness about either of them,—they can walk twice as far as I can, and I guess they can ride twice as far, too. They will bring their own guns and clothes, but unless you say to the contrary I would rather that you would get bedding, slickers, and if necessary, saddles and bridles for them. Will this bother you too much? Of course send on all the bills to me.

I am very much obliged to you for your kindness in taking these boys out. It will be everything for them to have two or three weeks in the Black

Hills and in the ranch country. I hope they can see a roundup, or at least a good big ranch. If they can get any shooting they will naturally be very much pleased, and so will I; but if they don't get any shooting, why it is all right anyhow if they are able to live in the open and ride or walk all day. I earnestly hope you will be able to go with them yourself. If you find you cannot, may I bother you to hire a couple of good men who will give them a chance to shoot if there is any shooting to be done, and who will take them over the country anyhow? I do not know whether you will take along a wagon or just a pack pony or two. The boys, as I said, are hardy, and you need not be in the least afraid of letting them rough it. As soon as they get used to the country I believe they will be of very little bother.

Now, Captain, I hope you will be able to see that they are treated just like any two boys who go off for a spree, just as if I was not President. If possible I should like to have everything ready for them to start from Deadwood as soon as they arrive. It will be a good thing for them to get into the open country as soon as possible, and when they once get out among the cowboys there will be no further trouble about anyone treating them as if there was such a being as a president in existence. Moreover, in any city there is sure to be some fool who will think it a smart thing to try to get them into saloons, etc., to which naturally I should strongly object.

May I ask you to write me when you receive this letter and tell me if it is all right?

Give my warm regards to Mrs. Bullock and tell her how greatly I appreciated your being able to be with me on part of my trip.

Faithfully yours

July 24, 1903. Oyster Bay
To Philander Chase Knox

Personal

My dear Mr. Knox:

After as careful, and I may add as solemn, thought as I have devoted to anything, I have decided not to interfere in the case of Benjamin Hill. I should like to write you why it seems to me that this is a case I cannot treat by itself. We are now passing through an era of lawlessness in this country. Lynching has become very common, and where the victims are colored men it takes the inhuman aspect of putting to death by torture—usually by burning alive. Among the causes that have produced this outbreak of lynching—I say only "among them," for I do not know how prominent it should be put among them—is, in my judgment, unquestionably the delays of the law, and the way in which clever criminal lawyers are able ofttimes to secure the acquittal, and almost always to secure long delay in the conviction, of men accused of offenses for which the penalty should be absolutely certain and the punishment as quick as possible. Every pardon of a murderer who should have been executed is to my mind just so much encouragement to lynching, just so much putting of a premium upon lawlessness. In this case of Hill's, if, instead of being a white man killing his wife, he had been a negro killing a white woman with whom he had quarreled, he would in all probability have been lynched out of hand, and very possibly have been burnt alive.

The only portion of the affidavits to which I thought the slightest attention should have been paid was that in reference to the alleged insanity of the man. Now, this alleged insanity was never brought up prior to or during the trial. It is to my mind inconceivable that such should have been the case, if it really existed in a degree that warranted my paying any heed to it whatever. Have you ever read Weir Mitchell's very interesting article on the responsibility of the insane? There are undoubtedly insane people who are entirely irresponsible; but most of the people on whose behalf the insanity plea is entered after they have committed some crime, are not one whit more insane than tens of thousands of others whom no one would dream of shutting up in an asylum, and who, if their insanity takes the form of the development of immoral tendencies, are controlled only as many putative criminals are controlled, that is, by fear of the consequences.

Sincerely yours

July 30, 1903. Oyster Bay
To Edward Sandford Martin

My dear Martin:

In your last article there is one thing that specially struck Mrs. Roosevelt and myself—the point you make as to its being really a wise choice, from the standpoint of pleasure even, to select home life instead of some alternative. Every now and then I meet friends of my youth who incline to praise me for having gone into politics, or for living in the country in very simple manner with a fair-sized family of small children, instead of whirling about in that social life of New York which in recent years has had its summer center at Newport. I always explain to these good people that they might just as well praise me for having cared to ride horseback and go hunting in the Rocky Mountains, instead of sitting in a corner and knitting. Personally, the life of the Four Hundred, in its typical form, strikes me as being as flat as stale champagne. Upon my word, I think that for mere enjoyment I would a great deal rather hold my own in any congenial political society—even in Tammany—than in a circle where Harry Lehr is deemed a prominent and rather fascinating person.

I used to hunt at Hempstead. The members of the Four Hundred who were out there rode hard and well, and I enjoyed riding to hounds with them. But their companionship before and afterwards grew so intolerable that toward the end I would take a polo pony and ride him fourteen miles over before the hunt and fourteen miles back after the hunt, rather than stay overnight at the club. It seems to me that you and I, and those like us, who have in many different ways and with many failures and shortcomings, endeavored in some fashion or other to do our duty and to lead self-respecting lives, and to whom Fortune has granted the inestimable happiness of good wives and good children, stand on a plane which, even from the viewpoint of mere enjoyment, is immeasurably above that of the unfortunate creatures who, however well groomed and well cared for, and however luxurious their surroundings may be, yet lead essentially mean, petty and ignoble lives.

I suppose young girls and even young men naturally like a year or two of such a life as the Four Hundred lead; and it has its pretty, attractive, and not unwholesome sides. But I do not think anyone can permanently lead his or her life amid such surroundings and with such objects, save at the cost of degeneration in character. I have not a doubt that they would mortally object to associating with me—but they could not possibly object one one-hundredth part as much as I should to associating with them—and this not as a matter of virtue but as a matter of preference.

I hope "Jonas" is well. Tell him I have just had three of my offspring and six cousins off on an all-night's expedition to camp out, not far from where we picnicked that day he was here. We rowed in three boats, and as there was a heavy wind against us coming home next day, we had plenty of exercise. My own children and their cousins have the fond belief, which I would not for anything unsettle, that there is a peculiarly delicious flavor in the beefsteaks and sliced potatoes which I fry in bacon fat over a camp fire.

Sincerely yours

August 6, 1903. Oyster Bay
To Henry Cabot Lodge

Personal

Dear Cabot:

I sent the additional information to Knox as you suggested.

Another effort at delay, of which of course you know, has been made by the British and has been met by Foster and Loomis in excellent shape. By the way, I have had as thoroughly satisfactory talks with both Root and Turner as anyone could desire. I think you will find them in absolute harmony with you.

What an adroit creature Gorman is! He has just started an intrigue which if successful may cause us considerable annoyance. The Maryland delegation to the Grand Army meeting is taking out General Miles as its special guest for the purpose of making him commander of the Grand Army. The further object is to have him the Vice-Presidential candidate on the Democratic ticket. Merely qua Miles, I do not think he would add any strength to the ticket; but as commander in chief of the Grand Army he will of course spend his time this winter in making impossible demands upon the Pension Office and posing as the friend of the soldier, and he may very possibly cause a great deal of irritation among the soldiers against the Republican party and make them inclined to attack the Republican party, by way of giving it a lesson, next year.

The financial situation here looks ugly. What the outcome will be no one can prophesy. Secretary Shaw feels that as yet things are not really threatening. Root is inclined to think the danger much greater. At present there is nothing I or anyone else can do. The panic is due chiefly, almost solely, to the speculative watering of stocks on a giant scale in which Pierpont Morgan and so many of his kind have indulged during the last few years. Of course, if the panic spreads so as to affect the business world I shall have to pay for it.

By the way, day before yesterday I went off with Ted for an hour and a half's ride bareback; he on Renown and I on Bleistein. I found I sat not only at the gallop but the trot without difficulty—and the trot of a big hunter is not easy—but I succeeded in taking the skin off the inside of my legs and rather wished I had not gone.

Give my love to Nannie.

Always yours

August 9, 1903. Oyster Bay
To John Hay

Dear John:

Now I shall sit down and endeavor to keep my promise to write you something of what happened on the western trip. But I do not believe I can put it down as with Moody's assistance I told it when we were dining at your house. You see there was much of it about which I would not have thought at all if Moody had not been along during most of the time that Seth Bullock, for instance, was with me. It was Moody's intense interest in what he called the "neighborhood gossip" between Seth Bullock and myself that first made me think that there really was an interesting side to this gossip—chiefly because of the side lights it cast on our ways and methods of life in the golden days when the men of the vanishing frontier still lived in the Viking age. I looked up my books the other day to see if I had written down any of these anecdotes, but I could not find them. At the time they seemed to me very much less important than my various feats of adventure and misadventure in the hunting field. So it is really to Moody that I owe having thought of the matter at all.

Of course my whole trip was interesting anyhow. Although politics is at present my business I cannot stand more than a certain amount of uninterrupted association with men who are nothing but politicians, contractors, financiers, etc. Unadulterated Congress, like unadulterated Wall Street, though very good for a change, would drive me quite crazy as a steady thing. And there are only a certain limited number of politicians who have other sides to them. So on this trip I showed sedulous forethought in preparing cases for myself in the shape both of traveling companions and of places to visit. I went to the Yellowstone Park with John Burroughs, and to the Yosemite with John Muir, and to the Canyon of the Colorado with an assorted collection of Rough Riders, most of them with homicidal pasts. I had President Nicholas Murray Butler of Columbia University with me for three weeks, President Wheeler of the University of California for nearly a fortnight; Root was with me for a day or two and Moody for nearly a month. Stewart White, the author of *The Blazed Trail*, which among recent novels I like next to *The Virginian*, was also with me for a fortnight.

Much of the trip of course was of the conventional kind with which you are so well acquainted; and this part I shall skip through hurriedly. For four days after leaving Washington I was in the thick of civilization. I left on Wednesday. Thursday I spent in Chicago. I went to the University of Chicago and the Northwestern University; made such addresses as I would have made to college men anywhere and spoke that night in the Auditorium on the Monroe Doctrine—a speech calculated to avoid jarring even the sensitive nerves of Carter Harrison, who as Mayor had to greet me, and who was just in the final days of a contest for re-election in which I fondly and vainly hoped he would be beaten. The next day I struck Wisconsin and the day after Minnesota. In both States I was greeted with bellowing enthusiasm. Wherever I stopped at a small city or country town I was greeted by the usual shy, self-conscious, awkward body of local committeemen, and spoke to the usual audience of thoroughly good American citizens—a term I can use in a private letter to you without being thought demagogic! That is the audience consisted partly of the townspeople, but even more largely of rough-coated, hard-headed, gaunt, sinewy farmers and hired hands from all the neighborhood, who had driven in with their wives and daughters and often with their children, from ten or twenty or even thirty miles round about. For all the superficial differences between us, down at bottom these men and I think a good deal alike, or at least have the same ideals, and I am always sure of reaching, them in speeches which many of my Harvard friends would think not only homely, but commonplace. There were two bodies which were always gathered to greet me—the veterans and the school children. The veterans felt that I had fought too, and they claimed a certain right of comradeship with me which really touched me deeply; and to them I could invariably appeal with the certainty of meeting an instant response. Whatever their faults and shortcomings, and however much in practice they had failed to come up to their ideal, yet they had this ideal, and they had fought for it in their youth of long ago, in the times when they knew "how good was life the mere living," and yet when they were willing lightly to hazard the loss of life itself for the sake of being true to the purposes, half hidden often from themselves, which spurred them onward to victory. I have trouble enough, heaven knows, with the unreasonable demands which the veterans make on me all the time—and it is quite possible that they will suddenly champion some scoundrel like Miles as their especial hero and representative—but after all it is because of what they did that I am President at all, or that we have a country at all; and whenever I see in an audience a grim-featured old fellow with a hickory shirt and no collar or cravat and only one gallus to keep up his trousers, but with a Grand Army button in his buttonhole, there is a man to whom, if I am only able to strike the right note, I can surely appeal in the name of something loftier and better than his mere material well-being or advantage. As for the school children, I found to my utter astonishment that my letter to those Van Vorst women about their excellent book had gone everywhere, and the population of each place invariably took the greatest pride in showing off the children. Children always interest me—I am very fond of my own!—I have always cherished the way in which yours, when little, treated me with hail—fellow comradeship, when I spent the night with you at Cleveland, and it touches me to see a hard-working father, evidently in his holiday best, carrying one child, also in its holiday best, with three or four others tagging after him to "see the President," while for the woman, who in most cases cannot go out at all unless she takes her entire brood with her I have the liveliest sympathy and respect. I hope you won't think it absurd, but it was a real satisfaction to me to feel that the hard-worked mother of a large family felt aglow of pride and comfort when she showed that family to the President and felt that he deemed her worthy of respect and thanks as having done her part well by the Republic. If only we can make the man or the woman who, in the home or out of the home, does well his or her hard duty, feel that at least there is a recognition of respect because of that duty being well performed, we shall be by just so much ahead as a nation.

In Milwaukee, in St. Paul and in Minneapolis the crowds were something extraordinary. In Milwaukee there was a distant touch of novelty in the reception at the Deutscher Club, whose inmates received me at first with somewhat formal courtesy, having a lively memory of the fact that I was steadily engaged in the business of teaching the Kaiser to "shinny on his own side of the line"; but as I was heartily glad to see them they soon began to believe, possibly mistakenly, that they were also glad to see me, and we enjoyed our meeting to the full, and ended singing "Hoch soll er leben" with much enthusiasm.

On Sunday I struck Sioux Falls and began to get into the real West, the Far West, the country where I had worked and played for many years, and with whose people I felt a bond of sympathy which could not be broken by very manifest shortcomings on either part. Senator Kittredge was on hand to receive me. Not being himself a church-going man he had naturally fallen helpless when faced with the church problem, and I found he had committed me to a morning and an evening service. But I enjoyed both, contrary to my expectations. The morning service was in a little German Lutheran church of very humble folk, where the women, in primitive fashion, sat on one side of the aisle and the men on the other. They had imported a first-class preacher, the head of a Lutheran seminary in Iowa, and so clearly did he speak, though in German, that I was able to follow without effort his admirable sermon. It was on the Faith, Hope and Charity text, and I am rather ashamed to say that it was owing to this German Lutheran sermon that I for the first time realized the real meaning—"love"—of the word that we in the authorized version have translated "charity." The Dutch Reformed service in the evening was more canonical but it interested me much because so many good homely people were there, many of them with their babies, and all feeling such a kindly interest in having the President at their church. Between services, by the way, I took an afternoon ride of twenty miles with Seth Bullock and Dr. Rixey, Seth having turned up to see me safe through to the Yellowstone Park. From this time on I was able to get good long rides each Sunday, and I am sure that they did much toward keeping me in good trim throughout the trip.

Next day I went north through South Dakota, stopping at place after place, sometimes speaking from the end of the train, sometimes going in solemn procession with the local notables to a stand specially erected for the occasion, the procession being headed by the town brass band, which usually played "Hail to the Chief" as a brilliant novelty when I stepped off the train. The following day I went west along the Northern Pacific through North Dakota. In the forenoon it was just as it had been in South Dakota, except that at Bismarck they had a barbecue which I had to attend; where, by the way, the ox, which had been roasted whole, tasted deliciously. At each stop there were the usual audiences of grizzled, bearded, elderly men; of smooth-faced, shy, hulking young men; of older women either faded and dragged or exceedingly brisk and capable; and of robust, healthy, high-spirited young girls. Most of these people habitually led rather gray lives, and they came in to see the President much as they would have come in to see a circus. It was something to talk over and remember and tell their children about. But I think that besides the mere curiosity there was a good feeling behind it all, a feeling that the President was their man and symbolized their government, and that they had a proprietary interest in him and wished to see him, and that they hoped he embodied their aspirations and their best thought.

As soon as I got west of the Missouri I came into my own former stamping ground. At every station there was somebody who remembered my riding in there when the Little Missouri roundup went down to the Indian reservation and then worked north across the Cannon Ball and up Knife and Green Rivers; or who had been an interested and possibly malevolent spectator when I had ridden east with other representatives of the cow men to hold a solemn council with the leading grangers on the vexed subject of mavericks; or who had been hired as a train hand when I had been taking a load of cattle to Chicago, and who remembered well how he and I at the stoppages had run frantically down the line of the cars and with our poles jabbed the unfortunate cattle who had lain down until they again stood up and thereby gave themselves a chance for their lives; and who remembered how when the train started we had to clamber hurriedly aboard and make our way back to the caboose along the tops of the cattle cars. At Mandan two of my old cow hands, Sylvane and Joe Ferris, joined me. At Dickinson all of the older people had known me and the whole town turned out with wild and not entirely sober enthusiasm. It was difficult to make them much of a speech as there were dozens of men each earnestly desirous of recalling to my mind some special incident. One man, how he helped me bring in my cattle to ship, and how a blue roan steer broke away leading a bunch which it took him and me three hours to round up and bring back; another, how seventeen years before I had come in a freight train from Medora to deliver the Fourth of July oration; another, a gray-eyed individual named Paddock, who during my early years at Medora had shot and killed an equally objectionable individual named Livingstone, reminded me how just twenty years before, when I was on my first buffalo hunt, he loaned me the hammer off his Sharp's rifle to replace the broken hammer of mine; another, recalled the time when he and I worked on the roundup as partners, going with the Little Missouri outfit from the head of the Box Alder to the mouth of the Big Beaver, and then striking over to represent the Little Missouri brands on the Yellowstone roundup; yet another recalled the time when I as deputy sheriff of Billings County had brought in three cattle thieves named Red Finnigan, Dutch Chris, and the Half Breed to his keeping, he being then sheriff in Dickinson, etc., etc., etc. At Medora, which we reached after dark, the entire population of the Bad Lands down to the smallest baby had gathered to meet me. This was formerly my home station. The older men and women I knew well; the younger ones had been wild towheaded children when I lived and worked along the Little Missouri. I had spent nights in their ranches. I still remembered meals which the women had given me when I had come from some hard expedition, half famished and sharpset as a wolf. I had killed buffalo and elk, deer and antelope with some of the men. With others I had worked on the trail, on the calf roundup, on the beef roundup. We had been together on occasions which we still remembered when some bold rider met his death in trying to stop a stampede, in riding a mean horse, or in the quicksands of some swollen river which he sought to swim. They all felt I was their man, their old friend; and even if they had been hostile to me in the old days when we were divided by the sinister bickering and jealousies and hatreds of all frontier communities, they now firmly believed they had always been my staunch friends and admirers. They had all gathered in the town hall, which was draped for a dance—young children, babies, everybody being present. I shook hands with them all and almost each one had some memory of special association with me which he or she wished to discuss. I only regretted that I could not spend three hours with them. When I left them they were starting to finish the celebration by a dance.

Next day I reached the Yellowstone and went into it for a fortnight with John Burroughs.

When I got out I struck down by the Burlington across northwestern Wyoming, which I had known so well in the old days. Except for the railroad it seemed very little changed. The plains rivers, winding in thin streams through their broad sandy beds fringed with cottonwoods, the barren hills, and great sage brush plains, all looked just as they did when I had crossed them looking for lost horses, or hunting game, or driving the branded herds to market or to new pastures. Each little town, however, was in gala attire, the ranchmen having driven or ridden in clad in their rough coats, often of wolf skin; the chief citizens of the town always stiff and stern in their very best clothing; the little boys marshaled by their teachers without having any very clear idea why; and the little girls, each in her Sunday best, and most of them with some gift of wild flowers for me. Seth Bullock, with Alec Mackenzie, another former sheriff whom I had known in the old days, was along, and at Edgemont, where a contingent of Black Hills miners joined us, we had the orthodox cowboy sports.

When I reached the Yellowstone Park Major Pitcher said to me, "By the way, Mr. President, an old friend of yours named Bill Jones has been very anxious to see you, but I am sorry to say he has got so drunk that we had to take him out into the sage brush. I will try to have him meet you before we leave the Park." Sure enough when I was leaving the Park Bill Jones turned up. He had been sheriff of Billings County when I was on the ranch and I had been deputy under him. Our positions relatively to one another had crisscrossed in public and private life. As a private citizen I was the owner of the ranch and he was one of my hired hands, but in public position he was the sheriff and I his deputy. His real name was not Bill Jones, and there were in the county at that tire two other Bill Joneses—the name in each case being assumed because the owner did not think it advisable to go under his rightful title. To distinguish the Sheriff from the other two Bill Joneses, one of whom was known as Texas Bill and the other as Three-Seven Bill, he (the sheriff) was always called Hell-Roaring Bill Jones. He was a very good official when sober, and a trustworthy, hard-working man while in my employ; but on his occasional sprees he got very drunk indeed and then he swore a great deal and shot occasionally. The first time I ever saw Seth Bullock I had gone south with a wagon from Medora to the Belle Fourche. Bill Jones was driving the wagon. Sylvane Ferris and I were riding. We looked pretty rough when we struck the Belle Fourche—as Bill Jones expressed it, we looked exactly like an outfit of tinhorn gamblers; and when somebody asked Seth Bullock to meet us he at first expressed disinclination. Then he was told that I was the Civil Service Commissioner, upon which he remarked genially, "Well, anything civil goes with me," and strolled over to be introduced.

On this trip down the casual conversation between Sylvane and Bill cast some sidelights on Bill's past career. Happening to learn that he had been a constable in Bismarck but had resigned, I asked him why, whereupon he answered, "Well, I beat the mayor over the head with my gun one day. The mayor he didn't mind it, but the superintendent of police he said he guessed I'd better resign"—his evident feeling being that the superintendent of police had shown himself a mere martinet.

There was also a good deal of talk about a lunatic, and some cross-questioning brought out a story which cast light on the frontier theory of care for the insane. Sylvane began—"Well, the way of it was this. That lunatic he was on the train and he up and he shot the newsboy, and at first they wasn't going to do anything to him because they just thought he had it in for the newsboy. But someone said 'Why, he's plumb crazy and is liable to shoot one of us'—and then they threw him off the train." It was at Medora where this incident occurred, and it appeared that on demand being made for some official to take charge of the murderer Sheriff Jones came forward. Here he took up the tale himself: "The more fool I! Why, that lunatic didn't have his right senses. At first he wouldn't eat, till me and Snyder got him down in the shavings and *made* him eat!" (Snyder was a huge, happy-go-lucky cowpuncher, at that time Bill Jones' deputy.) Jones continued: "You know Snyder, don't you? Well, he's plumb stuck on his running and he's soft-hearted, too. He'd think that lunatic looked peaked and he'd take him out on the prairie for an airing and the boys they'd josh him as to how much start he could give the lunatic and then catch him again." According to the size of the "josh" Snyder would give the lunatic a greater or less start and then run him down. I asked what would have happened if Snyder had failed to catch him. This was evidently a new idea to Bill who responded, "Well, he always did catch him." "But supposing he hadn't caught him," I insisted. "Well," said Bill Jones thoughtfully, "if Snyder hadn't ketched the lunatic I'd have whaled hell out of Snyder." Under the circumstances Snyder naturally ran his best and always got his game.

The temple of justice in Medora was a low building with two rooms in one of which Bill Jones slept and in the other the lunatic. Bill continued: "You know Bixby? Well, Bixby thinks he's funny (with deep disfavor). He used to come and wake that lunatic up when I had gone to bed and then I'd have to get up and soothe him. But I fixed Bixby! I rigged a rope to the door and the next time Bixby came there to wake the lunatic I let the lunatic out on him and he most bit his nose off. I learned Bixby!" With which specimen of rather full-bodied humor the story closed.

My next three days after leaving Wyoming were very hard and rather monotonous. I went through Nebraska, Iowa and northeastern Missouri. I spoke at dozens of prosperous towns, in each case to many thousands of most friendly and often enthusiastic citizens. I genuinely liked and respected them all. I admired the thrift and indeed the beauty both of the country and the towns—and I could not to save my neck differentiate one town from another or one crowd from another. Moreover, much though I liked them and glad though I was to see them, it was inevitable that I should begin repeating myself unless I wished to become merely fatuous; and I was glad on the evening of the 29th to get to St. Louis. The next day, April 30th, I solemnly opened the World's Fair. The city was filled with enormous crowds. Everybody was enthusiastic and friendly; and the arrangements at the Fair itself represented confusion worse confounded. The drive through the multitudes; the review of the procession; the scrambling, pushing, shoving lunch in a densely packed tent; the shouting address in the great hall to forty thousand people, at least twenty thousand of whom could not hear one word I said—all this was of a kind with which you are thoroughly familiar. The next two days in Kansas City, Missouri, and then westward through Kansas, were but repetitions of those in Nebraska and Iowa.

Sunday, May 2d we spent in a little ranch town in the extreme western part of the Kansas plains. Like Medora it was a regular town of the cow country; but it rejoiced in a church, although not in a preacher. The lack was supplied by draining the country for a hundred miles east and producing a Presbyterian, a Methodist and a dear old German Lutheran. I think every ranch within a radius of forty or fifty miles sent its occupants to church that day, and the church was jammed. My own pew was the only one that did not bulge with occupants. There were two very nice little girls standing in the aisle beside me. I invited them in and we all three sang out of the same hymn book. They were in their Sunday best and their brown sunburned little arms and faces had been scrubbed till they almost shone. It was a very kindly, homely country congregation, all the people of a type I knew well and all of them looking well-to-do and prosperous in a way hardly warranted as it seemed to me by the eaten-off, wire-fence-enclosed, shortgrass ranges of the dry plains roundabout. When church was over I shook hands with the three preachers and all the congregation, whose buggies, ranch wagons, and dispirited-looking saddle ponies were tied to everything available in the village. I got a ride myself in the afternoon and on returning found that all the population that had not left was gathered solemnly around the train. Among the rest there was a little girl who asked me if I would like a baby badger which she said her brother Josiah had just caught. I said I would, and an hour or two later the badger turned up from the little girl's father's ranch some three miles out of town. The little girl had several other little girls with her, all in clean starched Sunday clothes and ribbon-tied pigtails. One of them was the sheriff's daughter, and I saw her nudging the sheriff, trying to get him to make some request, which he refused. So I asked what it was and found that the seven little girls were exceedingly anxious to see the inside of my car, and accordingly I took them all in. The interior arrangements struck them as being literally palatial—magnificent. The whole population of the plains now looks upon the Pullman sleepers and dining cars just as Mark Twain describes the people along the banks of the Mississippi as formerly looking at the Mississippi steamers, and for the same reasons. I liked the little girls so much that I regretted having nothing to give them but flowers; and they reciprocated my liking with warm western enthusiasm, for they hung about the car until it grew dark, either waving their hands to me or kissing their hands to me whenever I appeared at the window. The badger was christened Josiah, and became from that time an inmate of the train until my return home, when he received a somewhat stormy welcome from the children, and is now one of the household. The numerous gifts I received on the trip, by the way, included not only the badger but two bears, a lizard, a horned toad and a horse.

Next day we entered Colorado, and at the first stopping place (where the Governor joined me together with his Adjutant General, Sherman Bell, who had been one of the best men in my regiment) the riders of a roundup had come in to greet me, bringing the chuck wagon. They had kindled a fire and cooked breakfast in expectation of my arrival. It seemed absurd to get off and eat at the tail end of a chuck wagon in a top hat and a frock coat, but they were so heartbroken by my refusal that I finally did. The rest of the day was of the ordinary type. Denver, Colorado Springs and Pueblo showed the usual features—enormous crowds, processions, masses of school children, local Grand Army posts; sweating, bustling, self-conscious local committees; universal kindliness and friendliness; little girls dressed up as Goddesses of Liberty; misguided enthusiasts who nearly drove the horses mad by dumping huge baskets of flowers over them and us as we drove by favorable windows; other misguided enthusiasts who endeavored to head stampedes to shake my hand and felt deeply injured when repulsed by the secret service men and local policemen, etc., etc., etc. But in the evening when I reached Trinidad I struck into the wild country once more. Do you remember that letter from Captain Llewellyn, which ran as follows?

My dear Colonel:

I have the honor to report that comrade Ritchie late of Troop G is in jail at Trinidad, Colo. on a charge of murder. It seems that our comrade was out at a small town some twelve miles from Trinidad, Aguillar, when he became involved in a controversy and said controversy terminated in his killing his man. I have just received a long letter from our comrade giving his version of the little affair, and it appears from said version that the fellow he killed called him very bad names, even going as far as to cast reflections on the legitimacy of our comrade's birth. He killed the fellow instantly, shooting him in the heart.

Ritchie was one of the boys in Troop G and was a splendid soldier and I am going to see that he has a first-class defense.

Also have to report that comrade Webb late of Troop D
has just killed two men at Bisbee, Ariz. Have not yet received the detail of our comrade's trouble in this instance,
but understand that he was employed as a ranger in Arizona and that the killing occurred in a saloon and that he
was entirely justified in the transaction.

This is about all the news regarding the comrades in this
neck of the woods. Was out at the Penitentiary yesterday, and
had a very pleasant visit with comrade Frank Brito whom you
will remember was sent to the Penitentiary from Silver City
for killing his sister-in-law and he is very anxious to get out.
The sentiment in Grant County is very strongly in his favor.
You will doubtless recall the fact that he was shooting at his
wife at the time he killed his sister-in-law. Since he has been in
the Penitentiary his wife has ran off with Comrade Coyne of
Troop H, going to Mexico. This incident has tended to turn
popular sentiment strongly in Brito's favor.

Well, two days later I was joined by the hero of the Arizona killing,
who it appears had been doing his duty, and on this evening at Trinidad
Ritchie joined me. He explained to me how he had happened to kill his
man. It appears that Ritchie, who is a justice of the peace, had, as he expressed it, "sat into a poker game" with several friends and a stranger.
The stranger had bad luck and grew very abusive. Ritchie appears to
tend bar as well as to be a justice of the peace, and when the stranger became too abusive he got up and walked behind the bar to get his gun. His
friends appreciated the situation and either got outside the room or lay
down. But the stranger leaped after him, endeavoring to wrench his pistol from his hip pocket, with much foul language, and Ritchie shot him.
"Had he drawn his gun, Ritchie?" said I. "He didn't have time, Colonel,"
answered Ritchie simply. Ritchie was acquitted.

Next day we spent in New Mexico, stopping at Santa Fe and Albu-
querque. Of course scores of my former regiment joined me, headed by
Captain Llewellyn. The excellent captain is a large, jovial, frontier Mi-
cawber kind of personage, with a varied past which includes considerable man-killing. He had four bullets in him when he joined my regiment, and after the war when we had to have him operated on in the
hospital for something or other, the surgeons who conducted the operation incidentally ran across two of these bullets. He was up in the
Black Hills at one time, where Seth Bullock knew him, and Seth did not
wholly approve of him. Seth has killed a good many men himself, but
is at bottom a very tender-hearted man; whereas Llewellyn, for all his

geniality, and although in a tight place where desperate fighting was needed I would (hardly) not trust him as I would Seth Bullock, or Pat Garrett, or Ben Daniels, nevertheless has a ruthless streak which the others lack. Seth had explained to me, apropos of one man whom Llewellyn had killed in the Black Hills, that he had had great difficulty in getting the jury to acquit Llewellyn, and added, "Under the circumstances, Colonel, I wouldn't have killed that man, and you wouldn't either, Colonel"—which I thought was very likely true. I was much amused to see Llewellyn's face change when he heard I had been with Seth Bullock; and he asked with nervous eagerness what Seth had said of him—a curiosity I did not gratify.

As for the rest of my men, most of them were busy, hard-working fellows. Three or four were engineers or brakemen, others were at work on ranches or in the mines, or in the little frontier towns. For the most part they were entirely orderly and had lived decent lives; but death by violence had entered into their scheme of existence in a matter-of-course way which would doubtless seem alien to the minds of Boston anti-imperialists. The conversation would continually come back to this man or the other man who had "up and killed a man down in El Paso," or who had "skipped the country because the sheriff wanted him for stealing horses," or who "got killed when he went up against a faro game at Phoenix."

Santa Fe interested me particularly. One of my men, of pure Mexican origin, Sergeant Amigo, had been blessed by the arrival of a baby shortly before I came to Santa Fe, and nothing would do but that I must stand sponsor for it. He was a Catholic, but the Bishop made no objections, and accordingly, lighted taper in hand, I stood solemnly behind the father and mother while the baby was christened in the old adobe mission cathedral. His ancestors and mine had doubtless fought in The Netherlands in the days of Alva and Parma, just about the time this mission was built and before a Dutch or English colonist had set foot on American soil.

That evening the train went through the waterless desert country of New Mexico, a desolate land but always attractive with its strange coloring and outline. Next day we spent at the Canyon of the Colorado, to me the most impressive piece of scenery I have ever looked at. I don't exactly know what words to use in describing it. It is beautiful and terrible and unearthly. It made me feel as if I were gazing at a sunset of strange and awful splendor. When I was not looking at the canyon I was riding some forty miles with assorted members of my regiment, from the Governor of Arizona down including Ben Daniels, he whose ear was bitten off when he was marshal of Dodge City, and whose appointment as marshal of Arizona, a proper recognition for his excellent fighting record in my regiment, had been revoked because it turned out he had been three years in the penitentiary for robbery under arms.

The Pacific Coast trip I shall not try to describe. After we got out of the Mojave Desert, with its burning plains and waterless mountains, its cactus and fantastic yucca trees, we crossed the Cascades and came at once into that wonderful paradise of southern California—a veritable hotbed of fruits and flowers. The people were wildly enthusiastic of course, and I have literally never seen anything like the flowers. Wherever I went the roads were strewn with them, and generally a large proportion of the men, women and children were festooned with them. It is an interesting country and I think will produce a new type. I felt as if I was seeing Provence in the making—that is, Provence being changed by, and in its turn changing, a northern race. The missions interested me greatly, and of course the people most of all.

I was very greatly impressed by the two universities also. The University of California is the greatest, but Leland Stanford was singularly beautiful in architecture and surroundings and climate—in every way. What an influence these two great universities will have on the Pacific Slope of our own country, and perhaps on all the countries around the Pacific!

In San Francisco I was received with bellowing hospitality and passed three wild days. There was not much to distinguish it from a visit to any other of our big cities except the way in which here, and from this time on, I was given gifts—a gold goblet by the Board of Trade of San Francisco; a gold ash receiver from the Arctic Brotherhood at Seattle (a collection of exceedingly well-dressed men and women who had come down from the Klondike), a gold vase, silver and copper vases, and drinking cups, etc., etc.

After visiting the Yosemite I went northward to Oregon and Washington. Their coast regions, including a territory about as large as England, have the English climate. And here again I think the people in the end will be different—will in the end represent a new type on this continent. Puget Sound impressed me greatly. I suppose our children will see some city thereon, probably Seattle, containing a million inhabitants.

From Washington I turned eastward and when I struck northern Montana again came to my old stamping grounds and among my old friends. I met all kinds of queer characters with whom I had hunted and worked and slept and sometimes fought. From Helena I went southward to Butte, reaching that city in the afternoon of May 27th. By this time Seth Bullock had joined us, together with an old hunting friend, John Willis,— A Donatello of the Rocky Mountains—wholly lacking, however, the morbid self-consciousness which made Hawthorne's faun go out of his head because he had killed a man. Willis and I had been in Butte some seventeen years before at the end of a hunting trip in which we got dead broke, so that when we struck Butte we slept in an outhouse and breakfasted heartily in a two-bit Chinese restaurant. Since then I had gone through Butte in the campaign of 1900 the major part of the inhabitants receiving me with frank hostility and enthusiastic cheers for Bryan. However, Butte is mercurial and its feelings had changed. The wicked, wealthy, hospitable, full-blooded little city welcomed me with wild enthusiasm of the most disorderly kind.

The mayor, Pat Mullins, was a huge, good-humored creature, wearing for the first time in his life a top hat and a frock coat, the better to do honor to the President. National party lines count very little in Butte, where the fight was Heinze and anti-Heinze, ex-Senator Carter and Senator Clark being in the opposition. Neither side was willing to let the other have anything to do with the celebration, and they drove me wild with their appeals until I settled that the afternoon parade and speech was to be managed by the Heinze people and the evening speech by the anti-Heinze people; and that the dinner should contain fifty of each faction and be presided over in his official capacity by the mayor. The ordinary procession in barouches was rather more exhilarating than usual and reduced the faithful secret service men very nearly to the condition of Bedlamites. The crowd was filled with whooping enthusiasm and every kind of whiskey, and in their desire to be sociable broke the lines and jammed right up to the carriage. There were a lot of the so-called "rednecks" or dynamiters, the men who had taken part in the murderous Coeur d'Alene strike, who had been indulging in threats as to what they would do to me, and of course the city is a hotbed of violent anarchy. Seth Bullock accordingly had gone down three days in advance and had organized for my personal protection a bodyguard composed of old friends of his on whom he could rely, for the most part tough citizens and all of them very quick with a gun. By occupation they were, as he casually mentioned, for the major part gamblers and "sure thing" men. But they had no sympathy whatever with anarchy in any form. They thoroughly believed in men of wealth, for they wished to prey on them. These men kept a close watch over all who approached me, and I was far less nervous about being shot myself than about their shooting some exuberant enthusiast with peaceful intentions. Seth Bullock rode close beside the rear wheel of the carriage, a splendid—looking fellow with his size and supple strength, his strongly marked aquiline face with its big mustache, and the broad brim of his soft hat drawn down over his hawk eyes. However, nobody made a motion to attack me. At one point the carriage was brought to a stop while a dozen large burly men fought their way through the crowd till they got to it. I stood up while a bullthroated man with a red face and a foghorn voice bellowed an address of welcome on behalf of the citizens of Anaconda, and presented me from them a really handsome copper and silver vase. When we reached one hotel I made an address to the entire population of Butte, which was gathered in the cross streets below; and then the mayor presented me with a large silver loving cup in behalf of the Butte people. Immediately afterwards I was genuinely touched by a representative of the colored citizens of Butte giving me as a present from them a miniature set of scales with a design of Justice holding them even.

My address was felt to be honor enough for one hotel, and the dinner was given in the other. When the dinner was announced the mayor led me in or to speak more accurately, tucked me under one arm and lifted me partially off the ground, so that I felt as if I looked like one of those limp dolls with dangling legs carried around by small children, like Mary Jane in "The Golliwoggs," for instance. As soon as we got in the banquet hall and sat at the head of the table the mayor hammered lustily with the handle of his knife and announced, "Waiter, bring on the feed!" Then in a spirit of pure kindliness he added, "Waiter, pull up the curtains and let the people see the President eat!"—but to this I objected. The dinner was soon in full swing and it was interesting in many regards. Besides my own party, including Seth Bullock and Willis, there were fifty men from each of the Butte factions. In Butte every prominent man is a millionaire, a professional gambler, or a labor leader; and generally he has been all three. Of the hundred men who were my hosts I suppose at least half had killed their man in private war, or had striven to compass the assassination of an enemy. They had fought one another with reckless ferocity. They had been allies and enemies in every kind of business scheme, and companions in brutal revelry. As they drank great goblets of wine the sweat glistened on their hard, strong, crafty faces. They looked as if they had come out of the pictures in Aubrey Beardslee's *Yellow Book*. The millionaires had been laboring men once; the labor leaders intended to be millionaires in their turn or else to pull down all who were. They had made money in mines; they had spent it on the races, in other mines, or in gambling and every form of vicious luxury. But they were strong men for all that. They had worked and striven and pushed and trampled, and had always been ready, and were ready now, to fight to the death in many different kinds of conflict. They had built up their part of the West. They were men with whom one had to reckon if thrown in contact with them. There was Senator Clark with his Iscariot face; goat-bearded Carter with his cold gray eyes; Heinze, heavy-jowled, his cheeks flushed, his eyes glittering—he regarded the dinner as a triumph for him because the mayor was his man, and in pure joy he had lost twenty thousand dollars in reckless betting on horse races that afternoon. In Butte proper at the moment he was the wealthiest and most powerful man. There were plenty of those at the table who would stop at no measure to injure him in fortune, in limb or in life; and as he looked at them he would lean over and tell me the evil things he intended in turn to do to them. But though most of them hated each other, they were accustomed to taking their pleasure when they could get it, and they took it fast and hard with the meats and wines.

Old Con Kohrs, a fine old boy and old friend of mine, a member of the Legislature, and an absolutely honest man, was there. He repeated stories of hunting and Indian fighting and prospecting in the early days, and then told the company how he and I some twenty years previously had worked on the cattle ranges together, and been fellow delegates at the stockmen's meetings in the roaring little cattle town of Miles City. This started Willis upon our feats when we had hunted bear and elk and caribou together in the great mountain forests; and many a man spoke up to recall some incident when he and I had met in the past on a roundup, or in the rush to a new mining town, or out hunting. To my horror I found that Seth Bullock had drunk too much. I wanted him to go back to the train and go to bed. This he felt was ignominious. But he took off his gun, a long forty-four, and solemnly handed it to Loeb as a compromise.

Before the dinner could get too far under way I left to attend my meeting held under the auspices of the labor unions. At ten o'clock when the train pulled out, I stood on the rear platform while numerous friends howled and fired their guns in the air. From the shouting and the popping of guns Butte evidently intended to continue the celebration through the night.

Next day we went through Idaho, and at Boise City as at Walla Walla and Spokane and so many other of these far western towns, I was struck by the growing beauty of the town, by the trees, the well-built public library, the good taste and refinement evident in the dress, the bearing, and the homes of so many of the men and women.

Utah was much like the other States, although the lunch at Senator Tom Kearns' had its points of merit. He had a Catholic bishop and an Episcopal bishop and a Mormon apostle all at the lunch, together with various men and women of prominence. Among the latter was one of the plural wives of the Mormon elder. Most of the women were just such as one would meet at Washington, and some of them just such as one would meet at Boston. We discussed *The Virginian*, and the Passion Play, and Wagner, and the flora of the Rocky Mountains, and John Burroughs' writings, and Senator Ankeny's fondness for Bacon's Essays; and there at the table were the two bishops and the apostle, the plural wife, one Gentile who had done battle with the Danites in the long past; and in short every combination of beliefs and systems of thought and civilizations that were ages apart. In many of the leading men in Utah I was particularly struck by a queer combination of the fanaticism of the ages of faith, with in non-religious matters the shrewdest and most materialistic common sense.

All this while Moody was delighting in the conversations of Seth Bullock, especially when Seth happened to be touching upon incidents in the past in which he and I had both taken part. These would usually come from his dwelling upon some story which would in some way lead up to a mutual friend and that mutual friend's career. Often, however, it would merely be Seth's way of looking at things. Thus he explained the reluctance he had felt as to certain features of his professional duty, remarking, "You see, when I was sheriff first there was a good deal of shooting, and right at the outset I had to kill two men. Moody, I felt like getting out of politics!"

When we got into Wyoming we now and then came across individuals whom he had arrested but who had now reformed, or men for or against whom he had fought. Among them were occasional people I had had some connection with. Thus he suddenly asked me if I knew what had become of Lippy Slim, a half-breed horse thief whom I had caught at one time and handed over to Granville Stewart who was then acting on behalf of the Montana cattle men (he was afterwards Cleveland's minister to the Argentine). I said "No," whereupon he responded, "Well, Stewart he hung him." I had also arrested a rather well-meaning but worthless young fellow named Calamity Joe who had become involved in horse stealing. I took him down to Mandan, and the night before the trial he and I and the judge all slept in one room with two beds; and as the judge felt it undignified to sleep with a horse thief he slept with me instead. It proved afterwards that Calamity was a nephew of Senator Dietrich.

Seth was telling of an Indian fight in which one of his companions was named—Bill Hamilton. I asked if this was the father of the Bill Hamilton who, under the name of Three-Seven Bill Jones, had been foreman of a cow outfit in the Little Missouri country. It proved that the latter was his son. I knew the son well. He had on one occasion stopped a mail train by shooting at the conductor's feet to make him dance. Two or three days after, I had been over at Mingersville, and in the wretched little hotel had been put in a room with two beds and three other men, one of them Bill Jones. He and I had slept in the same bed. In the middle of the night there was a crash, the door was burst in, a lantern was flashed in my face, and as I waked up I found a gun had been thrust in my face too. But I was dropped at once, a man saying "He ain't the man. Here—here he is. Now Bill, come along quietly." Bill responded, "All right, don't sweat yourselves. I'm coming quietly"; and they walked out of the room. We lit a light. I tried to find out from my companions the reason of what had happened, but they possessed the alkali etiquette in such matters, the chief features of which are silence, wooden impassiveness, and uncommunicativeness. So we blew out the light and went to sleep again.

In this same hotel, by the way, I had more than one odd experience. It was the place where I was shot at by the fellow who had been on a spree and had shot up the face of the clock. By watching my chance I was able to knock him down, his head hitting the corner of the bar as he went down, so that he was knocked senseless. Upon another occasion I had a small room with one bed to myself upstairs, and had sat up to read, for I usually carried a book in my saddle pocket. Everyone had gone to sleep; when a cowboy arrived very drunk, yelling and shooting as he galloped through the darkness. When the host finally opened the door in response to repeated thumps the sounds below told that he at first had cause to regret having done so. Evidently the puncher seized him, half in play and half in enmity, jammed his gun against him, and then started to waltz around the room with him. The agonized appeals of the host came upward. "Jim, don't! Don't, Jim! It'll go off!, Jim, It'll go off!" Jim's response was not reassuring. "Yes, damn you, it'll go off. I'll learn you! Who in hell cares if it does go off? Oh, I'll learn you!" Finally the host reduced his guest to a condition of comparative quiet, which was announced by loud demands for a bed, which was promised immediately. Then I heard steps in the hall, a knock at the door, and when I opened it there stood the host announcing that he was sorry but that he had to put a man in with me for the night. I explained that he was not as sorry as I was—and that the man could not come in. He reiterated his regret and said that the man was drunk and on the shoot and *had* to come in. This description did not add to the attractiveness of the proposal and I explained that I should lock my door again, put out my light, and shoot any man who tried to break in. Where the puncher slept that night I do not know, but I was left free.

From Laramie to Cheyenne we took a sixty-five mile ride, going around by Van Tassel's ranch. We had five relays of horses and most of the time we went like the wind. Before getting on my first horse I had to make half an hour's talk at Laramie. When we got within three miles of Cheyenne I stopped to review the troops of the post, and in Cheyenne I got off my horse to ascend a stand and make a three-quarters of an hour speech under the auspices of the veterans, as it was Decoration Day. I had very good horses and thoroughly enjoyed the ride. The marshal was with me, an excellent fellow; also a deputy marshal whose name I wish I could remember. He was a gentle, kindly little fellow, a Texan who looked much like Alf in one of Stewart White's stories; very soft-spoken, and had killed a large number of men. He knew all about me, as one of his brothers had been in my regiment and another brother was foreman of the Hash-knife outfit and had worked on the Box Alder roundup with me in the spring of '85.

The following Monday we saw some first-class steer roping and riding of mean horses out at the Cheyenne fair grounds. After that the way home through Nebraska, Iowa, Illinois, and Indiana, though important and irksome, offered nothing of special interest in the telling. We stopped at many towns and little cities; were greeted by enormous crowds of thoroughly good people; were escorted by Senators and Congressmen, by Uncle Joe Cannon and Secretary Wilson; visited Lincoln's tomb at Springfield, dedicated a monument to Lincoln at Freeport, and a hall to the old soldiers somewhere else; and on Friday, the 6th, I reached Washington on the minute, having made the two months and over trip without a hitch—which I think speaks well for the railroads.

Faithfully yours

August 19, 1903. Oyster Bay
To John Hay

Personal

My dear John:

Loomis sent me the enclosed paper from John Bassett Moore. It seems to me important.

On your way back cannot you stop here, and we will go over the canal situation? The one thing evident is to do nothing at present. If under the treaty of 1846 we have a color of right to start in and build the canal, my off hand judgment would favor such proceeding. It seems that the great bulk of the best engineers are agreed that that route is the best; and I do not think that the Bogota lot of jack rabbits should be allowed permanently to bar one of the future highways of civilization. Of course under the terms of the Act we could now go ahead with Nicaragua and perhaps would technically be required to do so. But what we do now will be of consequence, not merely decades, but centuries hence, and we must be sure that we are taking the right step before we act.

Ever yours

September 5, 1903. Oyster Bay
To Lyman Abbott

Personal

My dear Dr. Abbott:

I have read your editorial with the greatest interest. As regards the Indian agencies, I agree with you absolutely. I am very reluctant to divert the army from its legitimate duties, but I believe that we could get enough agents among retired army officers, and among those officers on the active list who, for one reason or another are temporarily unfitted for other duties. At present the difficulty of getting thoroughly good Indian agents is greater than you would believe. If vacancies come in New Mexico or Arizona I have a fairly free hand in filling them; but if they come in any *state*, I simply cannot get a man confirmed unless the senators from that state approve of him, and their approval is well-nigh certain to be conditioned upon the man's possessing qualities which have no relation whatever to the position for which I wish him. They may also make, and often do make, an effort to see that he has those qualities in addition; but the temptation is very great for a man in active politics, who has to deal with vigorous but not oversensitive frontiersmen, to try to get in the nominee certain qualities which may really interfere with his being a good agent. Furthermore I wish to state with all possible emphasis that to take an agent recommended by the average body of professional humanitarians, or by the average religious body, usually results in a worse failure than to take one procured in ordinary fashion. To politicians [he] is, for instance, as poor an adviser as Herbert Welsh.

As regards the proper custodian for the Indian as a ward, I have not thought over the matter sufficiently to be sure that the courts would be more careful than the Interior Department. As regards the public-school system in our territories, etc., I, of course, absolutely agree with you. How far it would be practicable out of hand to change the existing system I cannot say.

Now, to change to something else. The *Sun* and the *Harper's Weekly*, who seem at present to be the recognized exponents of that portion of the capitalistic class which objects to any kind of supervision or control, no matter how limited, over the great corporations and great controllers of corporations, have entered upon a systematic campaign, not merely against me, which is not important, but against the principles for which I stand. Both those papers, and in addition to those, papers like the *Times* and Brooklyn *Eagle*, so far as their financial columns go, have been endeavoring, sometimes by open statements, sometimes by insinuation, to persuade the public that my action in the Northern Securities suit, and in addition, my action in securing the passage of the law creating a Department of Commerce, with in it a Bureau of Corporations to secure publicity, has been mainly responsible for the financial stringency in Wall Street. Of course this is a preposterous falsehood. A promoters', speculators' and overcapitalizers' panic—it is this which we have seen. But any disturbance in the business world, no matter how purely due to the excesses of speculators, is sure to effect great numbers of other people, and when these feel the pinch it is invariably a relief to them to have somebody or something concrete on which to lay the blame; and there are plenty of businessmen, wealthy, venturous and unscrupulous, men of whom the archetype is William C. Whitney, who find it for their advantage to encourage this feeling, as what they most wish is absolute and unfettered freedom to act without regard to law. Such being the case I think it is well to recall that on this labor and capital question the following are the important steps I have taken:

1.   On the advice of Knox I directed the bringing of the Northern Securities case. The court of first resort was unanimously, by a vote of four judges, declared in favor of the Government. The position of the *Sun* and the *Harper's Weekly* in this matter is then baldly that although the law may be clear, yet it must not be invoked against Mr. Pierpont Morgan and Mr. Hill; that is against any people whose financial interests are sufficiently vast. To my view this position is not only profoundly immoral, but quite as profoundly foolish, from the standpoint of property itself. Nothing would so jeopardize the rights of wealthy men in this country as the acceptance by the public of the belief that the laws could not touch these men if they offended against it.

2.   Securing the enactment of the law in reference to a bureau of corporations. This was the law against which the Standard Oil Company so bitterly fought. The creation of this bureau is undoubtedly a very important thing from the standpoint of these big corporations doing an interstate business; for from it can be developed by experiment and trial, an effective method of regulation and supervision over them. But avowedly, in its present form, what is to be done is of tentative character; our first object being merely to get at and publish the facts that ought properly to be made public. The peculiar venom the passage of this law has caused among corporations like the Standard Oil is sufficient to show its need; and moreover, emphasizes how much more may be accomplished by resolute but moderate and practical action than by anything revolutionary. The Standard Oil and similar corporations have never really been frightened by any of the demagogic assaults upon them; they do not mind David B. Hill's empty threats about nationalizing them; and they laugh at the populists and professional labor agitators; but they have been aroused to intense hostility by having put upon the statute books a measure which does mean that a practical step in advance has been taken in reference to their supervision and regulation.

3.   The law making real the requirement that railroads shall give no rebates to favored shippers; in other words, throwing the highways of commerce open on equal terms to all who use them. So fair is this law that the hostility to it dares not openly avow itself; that there is such underhand antagonism.

4.   The settlement of the anthracite coal strike—I was of course not

required by the Constitution to attempt this settlement; and if I had failed to attempt I should have held myself worthy of comparison with Franklin Pierce and James Buchanan, among my predecessors. For the time being, and in vital fashion, this question was that which beyond all others, concerned the entire nation; and, as being for the moment the head of the nation, I obeyed the supreme law of duty to the republic in acting as I did. I think all competent observers agree that if the strike had not been settled there would have been within thirty days the most terrible riots that this country has ever seen, with as their sequence the necessity of drastic, and perhaps revolutionary measures, by the various state governments, or by the national government. The strike certainly would not have been settled if I had not interfered. It was settled in a manner which commanded the asset of both parties to it; and the report of the Commission is of lasting value as a textbook in which the principles of dealing in concrete instances with disputes between labor and capital are set down temperately, sanely, but clearly and forcefully. What I did here was of no more advantage to labor than it was to capital—in fact I think that nothing can be done which is of real advantage to the one without being of real advantage to the other.

5.   The Miller case in the Government Printing Office; here, not by preaching, but by immediate action, I enforced the doctrine that the union man and the nonunion man stand on an exact equality in the eye of the law, and therefore in the Government service. This was simply carrying out what I had said in my last message, that corporate capital and organized labor alike should be protected when they did well, and should not be allowed to do ill; for the fundamental right of each man is to do what he wishes with his own property or his own labor, as long as he does not infringe upon the rights of others.

6.   When the miners' strike in Arizona became a riot and the Acting Governor telegraphed that the territorial authorities could not deal with it and could not restore order, I sent thither instantly some regular troops. At their coming resistance to the civil authority ceased at once, peace was restored and I was able to withdraw them. This was simply putting into practice what I had said over and over again as to putting down of crimes of violence, just as the Northern Securities suit was enforcing what I had said about putting down crimes of greed and cunning.

The above represent as well as I can recall the six affirmative steps I have taken as regards labor and capital. They have carried out exactly what I preached—what for instance I preached in my speeches and my letter of acceptance as Vice-Presidential candidate, when the *Sun* and the *Harper's Weekly* and all their employers who now so bitterly oppose me heartily applauded me, evidently under the impression that what I said was only intended for electioneering purposes, or at least that it did not matter, as I was not to be put where I could turn my words into deeds. Now they hope to use against me, alike the hatred of those labor unions who demand that tyranny shall be connived at by the Government, if it is the tyranny of labor unions; and the hatred of those great corporations who demand that lawbreaking shall be condoned by the executive, if the lawbreaker is so wealthy that his welfare can be said to be essential to the general business welfare. Of course they do not for the most part venture to avow the reasons of their opposition; yet they do avow them often enough and with suffcient bitterness to make them plain. They may win or they may not; but I intend if possible that the true reason of their hostility shall be made clear.

Can you come out to see me sometime within the next two or three weeks?

Faithfully yours

**September 30, 1903. Oyster Bay
To Henry Cabot Lodge**

Dear Cabot:

Well, the summer has come to an end. On Monday, the 28th we came back here. The last three days were very pleasant. It was brilliant fall weather. Grant La Farge and Dan Wister came out on Wednesday night, and Friday morning I took them on a three hours' ride. Dr. Lyman Abbott was at lunch. The afternoon I spent chopping—having practically struck out all official work, attending to my correspondence in the evening. Friday was a delicious day, cool and fresh, and I on Bleistein and Edith on Yagenka had a four hours' ride. It was really delightful. George Bird Grinnell, with' whom I wanted to talk Indian reservations, and incidentally some points on big-game zoology, was out for lunch. In the afternoon I played tennis. Saturday I took Edith off in a rowboat, and we were out all day, rowing down to the great marsh at the end of Lloyd's Neck, where we took our lunch and watched the white sails of the coasters passing up and down the Sound. I had a stiff row home against wind and tide.

Edith thinks that the enclosed clippings describing the woes of my tailor over my taste in dress, may amuse you and Nannie. Send them back to me when you have read them. Do the same with Mrs. Stuyve Fish's "appreciation" of Edith's dress and my social habits.

I have been reading Aristotle's *Politics* and Plutarch's miscellany, and as usual take an immense comfort out of the speeches of Lincoln. I have just run across a speech of his on lynching, delivered, I think, in 1836, which I wish I had remembered when I wrote to Governor Durbin. I should have quoted from it with a free hand.

Dan Wister, by the way, is absorbed in putting *The Virginian* on the stage.

As soon as I got back here I had to take up various bits of work, especially the Miller case with the labor unions, and the post-office scandals. John Mitchell, Gompers, and various other leaders of the unions called upon me about the Miller case, and the announcement that they intended to do so caused one of those curious panics habitual among our friends of the wealthy and cultivated classes. They got it into their fool heads that as I was to hold a "conference" with the labor men, this meant that I intended to weaken. They immediately fell into a panic and screamed that I *had* weakened. It was some time before I discovered that their trouble was with the terminology of the affair. I happened to say to one shrill remonstrant that I certainly could not deny to anybody a hearing, whether it was to the labor people or the trust magnates. He seemed immensely relieved, and said that as long as it was a "hearing" and not a "conference" it was all right. I did not attempt to find out exactly what the distinction was in his mind; but whatever it was it seems to have been widespread, for all my financial and intellectual friends have solemnly agreed that while it would be wicked to hold a conference it would be eminently proper to hold a hearing. The labor leaders who saw me were entirely reasonable, Mitchell of course especially so. Gompers (who is a sleek article) thought it better to be so. The others counted less. When not in my presence they have passed multitudes of denunciatory resolutions, but I had no difficulty with them when face to face. In order that there should be no chance of misinterpreting or misquoting me, I finally read to them my decision as follows:

I thank you and your committee for your courtesy, and I appreciate the opportunity to meet with you. It will always be a pleasure to see you or any representatives of your organizations or of your federation as a whole.

As regards the Miller case, I have little to add to what I have already said. In dealing with it I ask you to remember that I am dealing purely with the relation of the government to its employees. I must govern my action by the laws of the land, which I am sworn to administer, and which differentiate any case in which the government of the United States is a party from all other cases whatsoever. These laws are enacted for the benefit of the whole people, and cannot and must not be construed as permitting discrimination against some of the people. I am President of all the people of the United States, without regard to creed, color, birthplace, occupation, or social condition. My aim is to do equal and exact justice as among them all. In the employment and dismissal of men in the government service I can no more recognize the fact that a man does or does not belong to a union as being for or against him than I can recognize the fact that he is a Protestant or a Catholic, a Jew or a Gentile, as being for or against him.

In the communications sent me by various labor organizations protesting against the retention of Miller in the Government Printing Office, the grounds alleged are twofold: That he is a nonunion man; that he is not personally fit. The question of his personal fitness is one to be settled in the routine of administrative detail, and cannot be allowed to conflict with or to complicate the larger question of governmental discrimination for or against him or any other man because he is or is not a member of a union. This is the only question now before me for decision, and as to this my decision is final.

Mitchell stated he was absolutely satisfied with what I had said. The others appeared to be also. The union controlled by that indicted scoundrel, Sam Parks, the Bridge Builders' Union, has just added its mite of denunciation. Moody has been of the utmost assistance to me throughout this incident; so have Cortelyou, Garfield and Sargent.

In the Post-Office scandal I have had some ugly times. Payne unfortunately became involved in the Delaware row between the Addicks and anti-Addicks people. His position was defensible, but unfortunately, whoever touches Addicks is smirched by him, and it was not well that the thing should have happened just at the time when the Post Office was under fire anyhow. I am making a grand roundup of the people who have gone crooked. In strict secrecy, we have skated unpleasantly near Don Cameron, having had to indict his former private secretary. Fortunately, he himself was just cleared. I had a very ugly time over the indictment of State Senator Green of New York. He is the close personal, political, and business friend of Dunn, the State Chairman, and of the State Comptroller, Miller. Dunn is a heavy stockholder in the concern on behalf of which the crookedness was done, and he is very naturally bitter against me. Whether he himself was cognizant of the wrongdoing or not, I cannot say. It is greatly to be regretted that he is Chairman of the State Committee. Platt was disturbed and angry over the affair, but seemingly Odell was more so. He sent down the Comptroller, Miller, to see me to explain that if Green were indicted it was his judgment that we should certainly lose the State next fall. I was as polite as possible, answering that of course I was more interested in carrying the State than anyone else was, but that in the first place I should certainly not let up on any grafter, no matter what the political effect might be; and that in the second place, my judgment was that whereas we might lose the State if we did make it evident that we intended to prosecute every guilty man, we should certainly lose it if we did not. It has been a worrying and disheartening business. Of course it is perfectly possible that the public at large may simply take the view that as the scandals have been discovered in my administration, I am responsible for them. On the other hand we have a year and may be able to make the public see that I am responsible, not for the evil, but for finding it and rooting it out.

Under the leadership of that vicious body, the American Protective Tariff League, there has been a revival of the crusade against the Cuban reciprocity treaty. The Pennsylvania delegation now show symptoms of being affected by it. It does not seem possible to make some excellent people, including for instance General W. F. Draper, understand that the menace to the protective tariff is greatest from such foolish extremists as those with whom he is associating himself. It now appears, by the way, that some of the bitterest articles circulated by the League against the Cuban Reciprocity Treaty, attacking me specifically for having advocated it, were by Tom Reed. This is of a piece with Tom Reed having tried to do what he could against us on the trust issue and on the Northern Securities suit. The figures of his estate show that he had made immense amounts of money in New York through the Morgan people and certain others. I have no doubt that he kept technically honest; and I have also no doubt that he got the money as the equivalent or consideration for using his name and influence, against me personally, and against all others who were striving to make good the promises given before election. If the man were alive now he would be the rallying point for all the disaffected elements.

Ever yours

[*Handwritten*] Balfour's pamphlet on Free Trade & Protection is a brilliant bit of work.

October 4, 1903. Washington
To Theodore Roosevelt, Jr.

Dear Ted:

In spite of the "Hurry! Hurry!" on the outside of your envelope, I did not like to act until I had consulted Mother and thought the matter over; and to be frank with you, old fellow, I am by no means sure that I am doing right now. If it were not that I feel you would be so bitterly disappointed, I would strongly advocate your acquiescing in the decision to leave you off the second squad this year. I am proud of your pluck, and I greatly admire football—though it was not a game I was ever able to play myself, my qualities resembling Kermit's rather than yours. But the very things that make it a good game make it a rough game, and there is always the chance of your being laid up. Now, I should not in the least object to your being laid up for a season if you were striving for something worth while, to get on the Groton school team, for instance, or on your class team when you entered Harvard— for of course I don't think you will have the weight to entitle you to try for the varsity. But I am by no means sure that it is worth your while to run the risk of being laid up for the sake of playing in the second squad when you áre a fourth former, instead of when you are a fifth former. I do not know that the risk is balanced by the reward. However, I have told the Rector that as you feel so strongly about it, I think that the chance of your damaging yourself in body is outweighed by the possibility of bitterness of spirit if you could not play; and therefore that you are to play. Understand me; I should think mighty little of you if you permitted chagrin to make you bitter on some point where it was evidently right for you to suffer the chagrin. But in this case I am uncertain, and I shall give you the benefit of the doubt. If, however, the coaches at any time come to the conclusion that you ought not to be in the second squad, why you must cope off without grumbling.

As I said, I am delighted to have you play football. I believe in rough, manly sports. But I do not believe in them if they degenerate into the sole end of anyone's existence. I don't want you to sacrifice standing well in your studies to any overathleticism; and above all, I need hardly tell you that character counts for a great deal more than either intellect or body in winning success in life. Athletic proficiency is a mighty good servant, and like so many other good servants, a mighty bad master. Did you ever read Pliny's letter to Trajan in which he speaks of its being advisable to keep the Greeks absorbed in athletics because it distracted their minds from all serious pursuits, including soldiering, and prevented their ever being dangerous to the Romans? I have not a doubt that the British officers in the Boer War had their efficiency gravely reduced because they had sacrificed their legitimate duties to an inordinate and ridiculous love of sports. A man must develop his physical prowess up to a certain point; but after he has reached that point there are other things that count more. In my regiment nine-tenths of the men were better horsemen than I was, and probably two-thirds of them better shots than I was, while on the average they were certainly hardier and more enduring. Yet after I had had them a very short while they all knew, and I knew too, that nobody else could command them as I could. I am glad you should play football; I am glad that you should box; I am glad that you should ride and shoot and walk and row as well as you do. I should be very sorry if you did not do these things and if you lacked the spirit you show in them. But don't ever get into the frame of mind which regards these things as constituting the end to which all your energies must be devoted, or even the major portion of your energies.

Yes, I am to speak at Groton on prize day. I felt that while I was President and while you and Kermit were at Groton I wanted to come up there and see you, and the Rector wished me to speak, and so I was very glad to accept.

By the way, I am working hard to get Renown accustomed to automobiles. He is such a handful now when he meets them that I seriously mind encountering them when Mother is along. Of course I do not care if I am alone, or with another man, but I am uneasy all the time when I am out with Mother. Yesterday I tried Bleistein over the hurdles at Chevy Chase. The first one was new, high and stiff, and the old rascal never rose six inches, going slap through it. I thought he would fall; but he stood up like a house. I took him at it again and he went over all right.

I am very busy now, facing the usual endless worry and discouragement, and trying to keep steadily in mind that I must not only be as resolute as Abraham Lincoln in seeking to achieve decent ends, but as patient, as uncomplaining and as even-tempered in dealing, not only with knaves, but with the well-meaning foolish people, educated and uneducated, who by their unwisdom give the knaves their chance; and that I must show the same spirit in painfully groping to find out the right course. Garfield is a great comfort to me. I see much of him and take him out to walk, and I also play tennis with him; although tennis is not very exciting to him as he is at least as good a player as George, and I do not average more than one game in a set. He is working very hard, and as it is a new department, he actually took no holiday this summer. I shall have to bundle him off for a fortnight to the North Woods, if I can make him go. He has such poise and sanity—he is so fearless, and yet possesses such common sense, that he is a real support to me. He tells me that his father, President Garfield, when he and his brother were at school and only 15 and 13 years of age, used to write them in full about his plans why he went to the Senate instead of staying in the House, etc., etc. The man has the sound body, the sound mind, and above all the sound character, about which I tend to preach until I become prosy!

Your loving father

October 5, 1903. Washington
To Marcus Alonzo Hanna

Personal

My dear Senator:

Many thanks for your letter of the 4th. You may have noticed that I have not said a word in public about the canal. I shall have to allude to it in my message, but I shall go over this part of my message with you before putting it in its final form. I am not as sure as you are that the only virtue we need exercise is patience. I think it is well worth considering whether we had not better warn those cat-rabbits that great though our patience has been, it can be exhausted. This does not mean that we must necessarily go to Nicaragua. I feel we are certainly justified in morals, and [indecipherable] justified in law, under the treaty of 1846, in interfering summarily and saying that the canal is to be built and that they shall not stop it.

From all I can gather things seem to be going well in Ohio.

Faithfully yours

October 13, 1903. Washington
To Roger S. Baldwin

Personal

My dear Mr. Baldwin:

Would it be possible for you to get up something in the nature of a petition that would justify me in saying that there was a genuine movement in the State itself to have the forest rangers made game wardens? I can show you my attitude in the matter by the analogy of the Yosemite. I think the Yosemite should be under national control. A lot of good people in California think so too; but until there is a strong sentiment—if possible a predominant sentiment—to that effect, I should do damage by advocating it, for I should merely arouse hostility. It is just the same thing with these forest reserves. I want to go just as far in preserving the forests and preserving the game and wild creatures as I can *lead* public sentiment. But if I try to *drive* public sentiment I shall fail, save in exceptional cases. Occasionally, where I have deemed the case wholly exceptional, I have gone, and in the future in such cases I shall go, directly contrary to public sentiment, and sometimes I have had public sentiment turn right around and support me; but in a government like ours the wisdom of an extreme step of this kind is directly proportionate to its rarity.

Sincerely yours

October 20, 1903. Washington
To Theodore Roosevelt, Jr.

Dear Ted:

Your letter pleased me very much. I think your decision was wise and right. And oh, Ted! I was so much amused and interested with the description of the way you got to feel because you had won the position for yourself in the football field among the older fellows. I never did well enough in athletics while a boy to get such a position, either at school or college; but immediately after leaving college I went to the legislature. I was the youngest man there, and I rose like a rocket. I was re-elected next year by an enormous majority in a time when the republican party as a whole met with great disaster; and the republican minority in the house, although I was the youngest member, nominated me for speaker, that is, made me the leader of the minority. I immediately proceeded to lose my perspective, also. Unfortunately, I did not recover it as early as you have done in this case, and the result was that I came an awful cropper and had to pick myself up after learning by bitter experience the lesson that I was not all important and that I had to take account of many different elements in life. It took me fully a year before I got back the position I had lost, but I hung steadily at it and achieved my purpose.

I am very much pleased over what has just been accomplished in the Alaska Boundary award. I hesitated sometime before I would consent to a commission to decide the case and I declined absolutely to allow any arbitration of the matter. Finally I made up my mind I would appoint three men of such ability and such firmness that I could be certain there would be no possible outcome disadvantageous to us as a nation; and would trust to the absolute justice of our case, as well as to a straight-out declaration to certain high British officials that I meant business, and that if this commission did not decide the case at issue, I would decline all further negotiations and would have the line run on my own hook. I think that both factors were of importance in bringing about the result. That is, I think that the British Commissioner who voted with our men was entitled to great credit, and I also think that the clear understanding the British Government had as to what would follow a disagreement was very important and probably decisive.

Ever your loving father

October 21, 1903, Washington
To Ray Stanndard Baker

Private and personal
My dear Sir:

I am immensley impressed by your article. While I had know in rather a vague way that there was such a condition you describe, I had not known its extend, and as far as I am aware the facts have never before been brought before the public in such striking fashion. How emphatically this relevlation emphashizes the need of drawing the line on *conduct,* among labor unions, among corporations, among politicians, and among private individuals alike! The organs of the Wall Street men of a certain type are bitter in their denunciations of the labor unions, and have not a word to say against the iniquity of the corporations. The labor leaders of a certain type howl against the corporations, but do not admit that there is any wrong ever perpetrated by labor men. Democrats like Mr. Olney grow indignant at what they call revelations of

Republican rascality, while they are seeking to profit, as Olney's people in Massachusetts are seeking to profit, by the work of McSweeny, who we are now preparing to indict for shamelss corruption and wrongdoing like that of which the Post-Office officials have been guilty. And I regret to say that high Republican policitians come to me and beg me not to expose Republican rascality, lest it may hurt the party; while me standing high in the business circles of New York,—men whom I know socially,—follow a course of conduct which, in its essence, is as immoral as that of any boodle alderman.

I believe in corporations; I believe in trade unions. Both have come to stay, and are necessities in our present industrial system. But where, in either the one or the other, there develops corruption or mere brutal indifference to the rights of others, and shortsighted refusal to look beyond the moment's gain, then the offender, whether union or corporation, must be fought, and if the public sentiment is calloused to the iniquity of either, by just so much the whole public is damaged.

Can you not come here and see me sometime at your convenience?
Sincerely yours

October 29, 1903. Washington
To Lyman Abbott

Personal
My dear Dr. Abbott:

After reading the enclosed paper on the rapid evolution of the Jamaica negro, will you send it to your son if he has already gone South?

I had a most interesting talk with the Archbishop of the West Indies the other day. Not long ago I spoke to the English traveler Colquhoun. Our task is more difficult than that of the English in Jamaica, just as our task with the Indians in the West has been more difficult than that of the English in Canada; yet in each case, on the whole, after making every allowance, we have performed the task worse. On the one hand I know how inadvisable it is merely to scold the South. During the time I have been President I do not recall having uttered a public word of bitterness about the South. On the other hand I think it would be worse to let them think that they were blameless, or to let them cast the blame on anyone else.

Yesterday the Episcopal bishops and clergymen called to see me. The Bishops of Kentucky, Mississippi, Alabama, Georgia, North Carolina, Virginia, etc., etc., were all there. Among them was an archdeacon from North Carolina and a clergyman from Maryland, both of them negroes. They came into the White House in line among the rest of the bishops, deacons, and doctors of divinity. Nobody shrank from them; nobody seemed to think it unnatural that I should receive them in the White House. These high prelates of the Episcopal Church brought their wives and daughters along in their company. They did not sit down at table, but they all were received by Mrs. Roosevelt and myself on the same terms. If any of them took any refreshments the colored men doubtless did so too. I wonder whether these same southern bishops and clergymen were shocked when, two years ago, Booker Washington sat down at my table with me. In South Carolina, at Florence, I have just reappointed a negro postmaster with the approval of the entire community. Why South Carolina should go crazy over the appointment of an equally good negro as Collector of the Port of Charleston, I do not know. Why the southerners should be glad to visit the White House in company with a colored archdeacon, and yet feel furious because I received in only slightly more intimate fashion a great colored educator, I am again at a loss to understand.

Senator Gorman, in Maryland, has been doing something very curious. He is conducting his campaign for the moment largely on the race issue. He gave to a certain banker here in Washington, a friend of mine, the enclosed campaign button showing Booker Washington and myself at dinner, asking the banker at the same time for a subscription. I am told by our republicans that he has been very successful by the use of this button and by his addresses, etc., in stirring up the race feeling in Maryland, although I have not appointed a single colored man to any position whatever in that State—or for the matter of that in Virginia. But I was still more interested in Gorman's denouncing me for my action "against the business interests," "thereby interfering with the prosperity of the country." This attack he did not make very specific, and of course he could only refer to the establishment of the Bureau of Corporations, to the Northern Securities suit, and to the anthracite coal strike—the three matters which, together with the action taken in the Miller labor-union case, I am proudest of as regards my internal administration. I have good reason to believe that the Rockefellers, who you will remember were most bitter in their opposition to the enactment of the legislation creating the Bureau of Corporations, are now behind Gorman as they are now behind McClellan in New York—and this, not because they care for Gorman or McClellan, but because they intend to beat me next year and to elect some democrat whom, consciously or unconsciously, they can control. I say consciously or unconsciously. They would control Mr. Gorman consciously. Mr. Cleveland, whom I like, was more completely controlled by the corporations—largely through Messrs. Whitney and Olney—than any President we have had in our time. But I do not for a moment believe that he was conscious that they were controlling him; his action in the anthracite coal strike last year shows this.

Faithfully yours

November 4, 1903. Washington
To Nicholas Murray Butler

Dear Murray:

Well, the dog has returned to its vomit, as far as New York is concerned. If you noticed the *Sun's* editorial on Low this morning and the fact that the Whitney, Ryan, Lamont and Rockefeller stocks went up as soon as Tammany's victory was assured, it will be unnecessary to waste time in explaining one of the causes of defeat. The wealthy capitalists who practice graft and who believe in graft alike in public and in private life, gave Tammany unlimited money just as they will give my opponent, whoever he may be next year, unlimited money. And their organs, like the *Sun*, do not forgive Low for what they style his improper consideration of labor. With these rich men, who ludicrously enough style themselves conservatives, stood shoulder to shoulder all the corrupt and violent classes—as was natural enough—for the criminal and violent poor and the criminal and corrupt rich are in the essentials of character alike. Of course, I do not mean to say that these capitalists represent the main element in Low's overwhelming defeat, but they represent a big element. The Democratic desire to see a straight Democratic ticket elected counted for more; and the treachery or indifference of certain Republican Machine men counted for something, although I believe not nearly as much as is alleged. The chief element was the fact that Tammany on the whole comes nearer than a reform administration could come to giving New York the kind of administration which, when it is not having a spasm of virtue, it likes.

Outside of New York City and of Maryland, we have every reason to be satisfied with the showing at the polls. And it must be remembered that both New York City and Maryland did better than either did in the election immediately preceding the Presidential campaign of 1900. Up the state the Republicans were victorious everywhere. Cleveland took no stand against Tammany or in favor of Low, but he did try to accomplish something for Rice, the Democratic candidate for Mayor in Albany, who was beaten overwhelmingly. The victories in Ohio and Pennsylvania were truly phenomenal. Iowa and Nebraska, Colorado and Massachusetts, went Republican by very large majorities—phenomenal majorities for an off year. With Massachusetts I am particularly pleased, because the Cleveland-Olney-Gaston crowd made a tremendous effort to win by reviving the old alliance of the mugwumps, the corporation people, and all shades of the Democrats, including those of socialistic leanings.

You remember speaking to me about reading and especially about the kind of books one ought to read. On my way back from Oyster Bay on Election day I tried to jot down the books I have been reading for the last two years, and they run as follows. Of course I have forgotten a great many, especially ephemeral novels which I have happened to take up; and I have also read much in the magazines. Moreover, more than half of the books are books which I have read before. These I did not read through, but simply tool out the parts I liked. Thus, in *Waverley*, I omitted all the opening part; in *Pickwick* I skipped about, going through all my favorite scenes. In Macaulay I read simply the essays that appealed to me, while in Keats and Browning, although I read again and again many of the poems, I think that there must be at least 80 or 90 per cent of the old poetry of each, as far as bulk is concerned, which I have never succeeded in reading at all. The old books I read were not necessarily my favorites; it was largely a matter of chance. All the reading, of course, was purely for enjoyment and of most desultory, character. With this preliminary explanation, here goes!

Parts of Herodotus; the first and seventh books of Thucydides; all of Polybius; a little of Plutarch; Aeschylus' Orestean Trilogy; Sophocles' *Seven Against Thebes*; Euripides' *Hippolytus* and *Bacchae*; and Aristophanes' *Frogs*. Parts of the *Politics* of Aristotle; (all of these were in translation); Ridgeway's *Early Age of Greece*; Wheeler's *Life of Alexander*; and some six volumes of Mahaffey's *Studies of the Greek World*—of which I only read chapters here and there; two of Maspero's volumes on the early Syrian, Chaldean and Egyptian Civilizations—these I read superficially. Several chapters of Froissart. The *Memoirs* of Marbot; Bain's *Life of Charles the Twelfth*; Mahan's *Types of Naval Officers*; some of Macaulay's *Essays*; three or four volumes of Gibbon and three or four chapters of Motley. The Life of Prince Eugene, of Admiral de Ruyter, of Turenne, and of Sobieski (all in French). The battles in Carlyle's *Frederick the Great*; Hay and Nicolay's *Lincoln*, and the two volumes of Lincoln's *Speeches and Writings*—these I have not only read through, but have read parts of them again and again; Bacon's *Essays*—curiously enough, I had never really read these until this year; Mrs. Roosevelt has a volume which belonged to her grandfather, which she always carries around with her, and I got started reading this. *Macbeth; Twelfth Night; Henry the Fourth; Henry the Fifth; Richard the Second*; the first two Cantos of *Paradise Lost*; some of Michael Drayton's *Poems*—there are only three or four I care for; portions of the *Nibelungenlied*; portions of Carlyle's prose translation of Dante's *Inferno*; Church's *Beowulf*; Morris' translation of the *Heimskringla*, and Dasent's translation of the sagas of Gish and Burnt Njal;

Lady Gregory's and Miss Hull's *Cuchulain Saga* together with *The Chil-
dren of Lir, The Children of Turin*, the *Tale of Deirdre*, etc.; *Les Precieuses
Ridicules, Le Barbier de Seville;* most of Jusserand's books—of which I was
most interested in his studies of the *Kingis Quhair;* Holmes' *Over the
Teacups;* Lounsbury's *Shakespeare and Voltaire;* various numbers of the
Edinburgh Review from 1803 to 1850; Tolstoi's *Sebastopol* and *The Cossacks;*
Sienkiewicz's *Fire and Sword*, and parts of his other volumes; *Guy Man-
nering; The Antiquary; Rob Roy; Waverley; Quentin Durward;* parts of
Marmion and the *Lay of the Last Minstrel;* Cooper's *Pilot;* some of the ear-
lier stories and some of the poems of Bret Harte; Mark Twain's *Tom
Sawyer; Pickwick Papers; Nicholas Nickleby; Vanity Fair; Pendennis; The
Newcomes; Adventures of Philip;* Conan Doyle's *White Company;* Lever's
Charles O'Malley; Romances of Brockden Brown (read when I was confined to my room with a game leg, from motives of curiosity and with
no real enjoyment). An occasional half hour's reading in Keats, Browning, Poe, Tennyson, Longfellow, Kipling, Bliss Carmen; also in Poe's
Tales and Lowell's *Essays;* some of Stevenson's stories, and of Alling-
ham's *British Ballads;* Wagner's *Simple Life.* I have read aloud to the children, and often finished afterwards to myself, *The Rose and the Ring;*
Hans Andersen; some of Grimm; some Norse Folk Tales; and stories by
Howard Pyle; *Uncle Remus* and the rest of Joel Chandler Harris' stories
(incidentally, I would be willing to rest all that I have done in the South
as regards the negro on his story "Free Joe"); two or three books by Jacob
Riis; also Mrs. Van Vorst's *Woman Who Toils,* and one or two similar volumes; the nonsense verses of Carolyn Wells, first to the children, and afterwards for Mrs. Roosevelt and myself; Kenneth Grahame's *Golden Age;*
those two delightful books by Somerville' and Ross, *All on the Irish Shore*
and *Experiences of an Irish M. P.;* Townsend's *Europe and Asia;* Conrad's
Youth; Phoenixiana; Artemus Ward; Octave Thanet's stories, which I always like, especially when they deal with labor problems; various books
on the Boer War, of which I liked best Viljoen's, Stevens', and studies by
the writer signing himself Linesman; Pike's *Through the Subarctic Forest,*
and Peer's *Cross Country with Horse and Hound,* together with a number
of books on big-game hunting, mostly in Africa; several volumes on
American outdoor life and natural history, including the rereading of
much of John Burroughs; Swettenham's *Real Malay;* David Gray's *Gallops;* Miss Stewart's *Napoleon Jackson;* Janvier's *Passing of Thomas* and
other stories; the *Benefactress;* the *People of the Whirlpool;* London's *Call of
the Wild;* Fox's *Little Shepherd of Kingdom Come;* Hamlin Garland's *Captain
of the Gray-horse Troop;* Tarkington's *Gentleman from Indiana;* Churchill's
Crisis; Remington's *John Ermine of the Yellowstone;* Wister's *Virginian, Red
Men and White, Philosophy Four, Lin McLean;* White's *Blazed Trail, Con-
juror's House* and *Claim Jumpers;* Trevelyan's *American Revolution.* Often
I would read one book by chance, and it would suggest another.

There! that is the catalogue; about as interesting as Homer's Catalogue of the Ships, and with about as much method in it as there seems in a superficial glance to be in an Irish stew. The great comfort, old man, is that you need not read it and that you need not answer this!

Yours ever

November 4, 1903. Washington
To Kermit Roosevelt

Dear Kermit:

Tonight while I was preparing to dictate a message to Congress concerning the boiling caldron on the Isthmus of Panama, which has now begun to bubble over, up came one of the ushers with a telegram from you and Ted about the football match. Instantly I bolted into the next room to read it aloud to mother and sister, and we all cheered in unison when we came to the Rah! Rah! Rah! part of it. It was a great score. I wish I could have seen the game.

In spite of Tammany's victory in New York and Gorman's in Maryland, I am on the whole well pleased with the results of the elections.

Just at present I am attending to the Panama business. For half a century we have policed that Isthmus in the interest of the little wildcat republic of Colombia. Colombia has behaved infamously about the treaty for the building of the Panama Canal; and I do not intend in the police work that I will have to do in connection with the new insurrection any longer to do for her work which is not merely profitless but brings no gratitude. Any interference I undertake now will be in the interest of the United States and of the people of the Panama Isthmus themselves. There will be some lively times in carrying out this policy. Of course, I may encounter checks, but I think I shall put it through all right.

Ever your loving father

November 6, 1903. Washington
To Albert Shaw

Personal

My dear Dr. Shaw:

You are all right in every way! When people come to compare what has happened in the Isthmus, with what you said in the *Review of Reviews*, they will come to the conclusion that you are the seventh son of a seventh son! I entirely agree with you as to cutting off the dog's tail by inches. I did not foment the revolution on the Isthmus, and as you know from my previous correspondence with you, it is idle folly to speak of there having been a conspiracy with us. The people of the Isthmus are a unit for the Canal, and in favor of separation from the Colombians. The latter signed their death warrant when they acted in such infamous bad faith about the signing of the treaty. Unless Congress overrides me, which I do not think probable, Colombia's grip on Panama is gone forever.

Always yours

November 9, 1903. Washington
To Cecil Spring Rice

Personal
Dear Cecil:

Cabot has told me that he endeavored by every means to get you sent over to this side, and Harry White writes that you may be sent. I do not know whether there is any chance of your coming, and still less whether you would be willing to come; but for selfish reasons I so eagerly hope that you may come that I must send you just a line to say so. It would mean a real difference in Mrs. Roosevelt's and my pleasure to have you on this side.

If you get here I want to show you the maps submitted by the British commission in the Alaskan boundary case. These maps, to my mind, show conclusively that there was literally no Canadian case at all on their main points, and that the two Canadian Commissioners are inexcusable in attacking Lord Alverstone as they have done. He could not have decided otherwise. On the points where there was room for geniune controversy there was, as there should have been, give and take between him and the American Commissioners; but on the points raised by the Canadians there was really no room for controversy, whatever. It has been a very fortunate and happy thing to get the question definitely settled and out of the way.

You have probably seen that events on the Panama Isthmus came to a head. The Colombia people proved absolutely impossible to deal with. They are not merely corrupt. They are governmentally utterly incompetent. They wanted to blackmail us and blackmail the French company; but the main trouble was that they would not or could not act on any terms. The treaty we offered them went further in their interests than we by rights ought to have gone, and it would have given them a stability and power such as no other Spanish-American republic possessed between Mexico and Chile. But in spite of the plainest warnings they persisted in slitting their own throats from ear to ear.

Ever yours

November 17, 1903. Washington
To William Gibbs McAdoo

Personal

My dear Mr. McAdoo:

Your letter pleases me very much.

From what part of the South do you come? Perhaps you know I am half a southerner, my mother having been a Georgian. I have always felt that my southern ancestry was responsible for much of my attitude in foreign politics. I do not intend to do injustice to anyone; but I do not intend to be withheld from doing justice to all, including our own people, by either technicality or sentimentality.

With hearty thanks for your courtesy, I am,

Sincerely yours

November 26, 1903. Washington
To George Haven Putnam

Personal

Dear Haven:

Dr. Albert Shaw was on in connection with certain public matters, and I asked him about the negotiations with Collier for that edition of my books. He tells me that Collier's have now offered to guarantee 50,000 sets sale in two years, at 60 cents royalty, or in other words to guarantee $30,000 royalty. This offer is satisfactory and I desire to have it accepted. I shall also ask that instead of dealing with Collier's direct you deal with them through Albert Shaw. The question of an edition of my works of such a size being gotten out by Collier's at this time is important from several aspects, and I should like the offer closed with at once. I had a very full talk with Shaw on the subject.

Of course treat this letter purely for the use of you and your brothers, and as confidential save as to them.

I should like to arrange with you about the division of this $30,000 royalty. Can you also let me know the details of the sale of the so-called Sagamore Edition? Was it the Sagamore Edition that went to the Siegel Cooper Company?

Sincerely yours

November 28, 1903. Washington
To John Biddle

Personal

My dear Colonel Biddle:

You have charge of Rock Creek Park have you not? If so, I wish to lay before you certain facts. The other day to my surprise and I might almost say to my horror—I found that preparations were being made for flagging one or more of the footpaths through the park; that is, for changing them from woodland footpaths into stone sidewalks. Now, I think that this is a real and serious mistake, and I wish most emphatically to protest against it. When people go into the park to walk, they go to get off the pavements, and it is worse than absurd, carefully and at much expense to see that they are unable to get off. I had noticed for some time those masses of big stone flags at certain places in the creek bottom, but, frankly, it never occurred to me that there could be any intention of using them for so foolish a purpose. But the other evening in walking down I was astounded to find that some flags had already been laid where the path on the west side of the stream crosses the meadow a little above the northern boundary of the Zoological Park. Such a flag path is hideous to look at and will greatly detract from the beauty of the park, and it is uncomfortable to walk on. It has not a single merit. If anyone wants to walk on a pavement, let him keep in the city and not go off into the woods. Personally, I would far rather see a good dirt road in the park than the macadamized roads, but I do not make a point of this. When, however, the question is of doing all that can be done to ruin the park for the only people who care to walk in it, by laying down these flag paths, I feel that the situation at least calls for an explanation.

Sincerely yours

November 30, 1903. Washington
To Otto Gresham

My dear Mr. Gresham:

I thank you for your letter. I confess I am utterly astounded at what you say as to there being any soldiers of '61 who are puzzled over what we have done in the Panama matter. I did not suppose there would be any man of intelligence who would be taken in by such arrant nonsense as that we were "recognizing secession." Such a mental attitude can only come from an invincible determination to look at names instead of things. As you with your knowledge of history are of course aware, one of the stock arguments of Southerners in '61, and of their sympathizers in England, was that Jefferson Davis was simply doing what George Washington had done, and that the secession of the Southern States stood on an exact par with the secession of the thirteen colonies from England. Of course such a comparison was utterly absurd; but it is not one whit more absurd than to make the same comparison now in the case of Panama and Colombia. Each case must be determined by its own rights and equities. The South revolted from a great free republic in which the southerners had always had amplest justice and recognition, because they could not force from the North abject submission to their demands as regards slavery. The American colonies revolted from England because England declined to treat them as freemen with equal rights, but insisted that the American was subject to the Englishman. Panama revolted from Colombia because Colombia, for corrupt and evil purposes or else from complete governmental incompetency, declined to permit the building of the great work which meant everything to Panama. By every law, human and divine, Panama was right in her position.

Now, how anyone can conceive that Colombia has the slightest right in the matter I do not understand. We have been more than just, have been generous to a fault, in our dealings with Colombia. It seems incredible to me that anyone could take the position which you speak of as being taken by some men, provided those men have either red blood or common sense in them. Are these men ignorant of the fact that General Reyes (a clipping concerning whom you enclose) and President Marroquin are now endeavoring to get us to break faith with Panama, just exactly as they themselves broke faith with us, on the specific ground that they will do for us the precise thing which they contemptuously and unanimously refused to do last summer?

The case in a nutshell is this: The government of Colombia was solemnly pledged to give us the right to dig that canal. The government of Colombia now, through Reyes and through their minister, asserts that it will instantly carry out that pledge and ratify the treaty we proposed— or if necessary a treaty even more favorable to us; yet last summer the government refused to ratify this treaty, and said that in view of the unanimous adverse action of the Colombian Congress it had no power to do what we desired. Of course this means that it was guilty of deliberate bad faith. The Colombians have not been badly treated; they have been well treated, and have themselves behaved badly; and if Congress should appropriate money to indemnify them my present feeling is that I should veto the appropriation. If Colombia and Panama should come to an agreement, that is another matter; but the United States owes Colombia nothing in law or in morals. The Colombians need not come here to ask justice from me. They have received exact justice, after I had in vain endeavored to persuade them to accept generosity. In their silly efforts to damage us they cut their own throats. They tried to hold us up; and too late they have discovered their (error) criminal error.

By the way, on the score of morality it seems to me that nothing could be more wicked than to ask us to surrender the Panama people, who are our friends, to the Colombian people, who have shown themselves our foes; and this for no earthly reason save because we have, especially in New York City and parts of the Northeast, a small body of shrill eunuchs who consistently oppose the action of this government whenever that action is to its own interests, even though at the same time it may be immensely to the interest of the world, and in accord with the fundamental laws of righteousness—which is now a synonym for anemic weakness.

Sincerely yours

January 11, 1904. Washington
To Theodore Roosevelt, Jr.

Dear Ted:

This will be a long business letter. I sent to you the examination papers for West Point and Annapolis. I have thought a great deal over the matter, and discussed it at great length with Mother. I feel on the one hand that I ought to give you my best advice, and yet on the other hand I do not wish to seem to constrain you against your wishes. If you have definitely made up your mind that you have an overmastering desire to be in the Navy or the Army, and that such a career is the one in which you will take a really heartfelt interest—far more so than any other—and that your greatest chance for happiness and usefulness will lie in doing this one work to which you feel yourself especially drawn,—why, under such circumstances, I have but little to say. But I am not satisfied that this is really your feeling. It seemed to me more as if you did not feel drawn in any other direction, and, wondered what you were going to do in life or what kind of work you would turn your hand to, and wondered if you could make a success or not; and, that you are therefore inclined to turn to the Navy or Army chiefly because you would then have a definite and settled career in life, and could hope to go on steadily without any great risk of failure. Now, if such is your thought I shall quote to you what Captain Mahan said of his son when asked why he did not send him to West Point or Annapolis. "I have too much confidence in him to make me feel that it is desirable for him to enter either branch of the service."

I have great confidence in you. I believe you have the ability, and above all the energy, the perseverence and the common sense, to win out in civil life. That you will have some hard times and some discouraging times I have no question; but this is merely another way of saying that you will share the common lot. Though you will have to work in different ways from those in which I worked, you will not have to work any harder, nor to face periods of more discouragement. I trust in your ability, and especially your character, and I am confident you will win.

In the Army and the Navy the chance for a man to show great ability and rise above his fellows does not occur on the average more than once in a generation. When I was down at Santiago it was melancholy for me to see now fossilized and lacking in ambition, and generally useless, were most of the men of my age and over who had served their lives in the Army. The Navy for the last few years has been better, but for twenty years after the Civil War there was less chance in the Navy than in the Army to practice, and do, work of real consequence. I have actually known lieutenants in both the Army and the Navy who were grandfathers—men who had seen their children married before they themselves attained the grade of captain. Of course the chance may come at any time when the man of West Point or Annapolis who has stayed in the Army or Navy finds a great war on, and therefore has the opportunity to rise high. Under such circumstances I think that the man of such training who has actually left the Army or the Navy has even more chance of rising than the man who has remained in it. Moreover, often a man can do as I did in the Spanish war, even though not a West Pointer.

This last point raises the question about your going to West Point or Annapolis and leaving the Army or Navy after you have served the regulation four years (I think that is the number) after graduation from the academy. Under this plan you would have an excellent education and a grounding in discipline, and in some ways a testing of your capacity greater than I think you can get in any ordinary college. On the other hand, except for the profession of an engineer, you would have had nothing like special training; and you would be so ordered about, and arranged for, that you would have less independence of character than you would gain from Harvard. You would *have* had fewer temptations; but you would have had less chance to develop the qualities which overcome temptations and show that a man has individual initiative. Supposing you entered at seventeen, with the intention of following this course. The result would be that at twenty-five you would leave the Army or Navy without having gone through any law school or any special technical school of any kind, and would start your life work three or four years later than your school fellows of today, who go to work immediately after leaving college. Of course, under such circumstances, you might study law, for instance, during the four years after graduation; but my own feeling is that a man does good work chiefly when he is in something which he intends to make his permanent work, and in which he is deeply interested. Moreover, there will always be the chance that the number of officers in the Army or Navy will be deficient, and that you would have to stay in the service instead of getting out when you wished.

I want you to think over all these matters very seriously. It would be a great misfortune for you to start into the Army or Navy as a career, and find that you had mistaken your desires and had gone in without really weighing the matter.

Your loving father

[*Handwritten*] You ought not to enter unless you feel genuinely drawn to the life as a lifework. If so, go in; but not otherwise.

Mr. Loeb told me today that at 17 he tried for the army, but failed. The competitor who beat him is now a captain; Mr. Loeb has passed him by, although meanwhile a war has been fought. Mr. Loeb says he wished to enter the army because he did not know what to do, could not foresee whether he would succeed or fail in life, and felt the army would give him "a living and a career." Now if this is at bottom your feeling I should advise you not to go in; I should say yes to some boys, but not to you; I believe in you too much, and have too much confidence in you.

January 18, 1904. Washington
To Cecil Spring Rice

Dear Cecil:

Well, I am very, very sorry, as we all of us are, that you are not coming here. All along I had a feeling that it was too good to be true. I have a strong desire during the period when I am "up," to have the people I am fond of around me, just as there are quite a number of people I should like to have visit me here in the White House—Morley, Trevelyan, and Edward North Buxton, for instance.

I wish those Russian books you sent had been translated. The pictures look fascinating, and I should suppose the stories just the kind you could translate so well. Both Mrs. Roosevelt and I were delighted with your Persian book,—Mrs. Roosevelt more, perhaps, than I was with the actual Persian story itself, because I have what we will euphemistically, and in a vein of strained compliment, call a robustly Occidental type of mind. But I read what you yourself wrote for the foreword and the epilogue again and again, and I could see Persia before my eyes as I read, and the endless, shadowy perspective of its strange and mighty past stretched backward through the ages that have gone.

Their thoughts are not our thoughts! Nothing could be truer; but I am not sure of the reason. It is not merely that they are an Oriental people, or a non-Aryan race. The Finns and Hungarians, although of course much mixed with our own blood, are perhaps less akin to us by race, and certainly far less by speech, than the Persians; yet they do not differ from us a bit more than the Slavonians and Croats do. There have been moments during the past two years when I have felt that the non-Christian and non-Aryan, far-eastern Japanese were in some essentials closer to us than their chief opponents; and I am certain that there is an immense amount we could learn from the Japanese with extreme advantage to us as a nation. Certainly they are less alien to us than, for instance, the Balkan Slavs who have become Mohammedans. Their orientalism is utterly different from that of the Persians. I never know whether to be most astonished at the complete divergence between portions of the same race which have adopted antagonistic creeds and cults, or at the complete change which creed and cult suffer when adopted by a different race.

Here I have been having most interesting times. I have succeeded in accomplishing a certain amount which I think will stand. I believe I shall put through the Panama treaty (my worst foes being those in the Senate and not those outside of the borders of the United States) and begin to dig the canal. It is always difficult for me to reason with those solemn creatures of imperfect aspirations after righteousness, who never take the trouble to go below names. These people scream about the injustice done Colombia when Panama was released from its domination, which is precisely like bemoaning the wrong done to Turkey when Herzegovina was handed over to Austria. It was a good thing for Egypt and the Sudan, and for the world, when England took Egypt and the Sudan. It is a good thing for India that England should control it. And so it is a good thing, a very good thing, for Cuba and for Panama and for the world that the United States has acted as it has actually done during the last six years. The people of the United States and the people of the Isthmus and the rest of mankind will all be the better because we dig the Panama Canal and keep order in its neighborhood. And the politicians and revolutionists at Bogota are entitled to precisely the amount of sympathy we extend to other inefficient bandits.

Always yours

January 25, 1904. Washington
To George Otto Trevelyan

My dear Sir George:

On the whole we have cause to be grateful to Professor Bury for his address inasmuch as it called out your really noble article on history; for the small amount of damage which Bury can do will be infinitely outweighed by the good you have done. Nor will this good be confined to students and scholars, from whichever point they approach the study of history; surely many busy men will feel the gratitude that I feel toward one who says what we know ought to be said but which we lack both the power and the time to say. As for me personally, inasmuch as I have to keep an iron grip on my temper as regards all men who in actual practice at the moment wittingly or unwittingly proceed on false theories of government or upon false applications of good theories, it is fine satisfaction to be able to get angry with Mr. Bury and at the same time have the comfortable feeling that it does no harm either to him or to me!

Of course in your article what you said constructively—where with wealth of illustration you showed what history could do and could mean to statesman, to philosopher, to lover of literature, to the mere private citizen who possesses catholicity of taste,—even outweighs the value of your destructive criticism of Mr. Bury's contentions. In particular I wish to thank you for your emphatic protest against those writers who in endeavoring to be moderate and impartial succeed in leaving the impression that there is really not difference between the good and the evil, the great and the small. True impartiality, true justice, is as far as possible removed from the dreadful habit of painting all character drab-colored. Hamden and Washington are doubtless not puree white, and here and there it might be possible to find touches of gray in the character of Philip of Spain and Louis the XVth of France; but we do violence to the facts, and ethically we sin if in comparing the four men we fail to show that by every canon of the higher life—social, political, spiritual—two are white and shining souls and two stand in that black circle which numbers the meanest and most contemptible and yet sometimes the most dreadful enemies of mankind. The "impartiality" which would only study the flaws in the character of the two great and good men and set forth the occasional tricks of virtue in the two evildoers would be a shame and a mockery.

But aside from your actually showing what history should be, I am exceedingly glad that you spoke so plainly of Mr. Bury's proposition to make it what it should not be. I am sorry to say that I think the Burys are doing much damage to the cause of historic writing. In a very small way I have been waging war with their kind on this side of the water for a number of years. We have a preposterous little organization called I think the American Historical Association, which, when I was just out of Harvard and very ignorant, I joined. Fortunately I had enough good sense, or obstinacy, or something, to retain a subconscious belief that, inasmuch as books were meant to be read, good books ought to be interesting, and the best books capable in addition of giving one a lift upward in some direction. After a while it dawned on me that all of the conscientious, industrious, painstaking little pedants, who would have been useful people in a rather small way if they had understood their own limitations, had become because of their conceit distinctly noxious. They solemnly believed that if there were only enough of them, and that if they only collected enough facts of all kinds and sorts, there would cease to be any need hereafter for great writers, great thinkers. They looked for instance at Justin Winsor's conglomerate narrative history of America— a book which is either literature or science in the sense in which a second-rate cyclopedia is literature and science—as showing an "advance" upon Francis Parkman—Heaven save the mark! Each of them was a goodenough day laborer, trundling his barrowful of bricks and worthy of his hire; as long as they saw themselves as they were they were worthy of all respect; but when they imagined that by their activity they rendered the work of an architect unnecessary they became both absurd and mischievous. Unfortunately with us it is these small men who do most of the historic teaching in the colleges. They have done much real harm in preventing the development of students who might have a large grasp of what history should really be. They represent what is in itself the excellent revolt against superficiality and lack of research, but they have grown into the opposite and equally noxious belief that research is all in all, that accumulation of facts is everything, and that the ideal history of the future will consist not even of the work of one huge pedant but of a multitude of articles by a multitude of small pedants. They are honestly unconscious that all they are doing is to gather bricks and stones, and that whether their work will or will not amount to anything really worthy depends entirely upon whether or not some great master builder hereafter arrives who will be able to go over their material, to reject the immense majority of it, and out of what is left to fashion some edifice of majesty and beauty instinct with the truth that both charms and teaches. A thousand Burys, and two thousand of the corresponding Germans whom he reverentially admires, would not in the aggregate begin to add to the wisdom of mankind what another Macaulay, should one arise, would add. The great historian must of course have the scientific spirit which gives the power of research, which enables one to marshal and weigh the facts; but unless his finished work is literature of a very high type small will be his claim to greatness.

Even in science itself I think we shall see a turning back from the mere dry-as-dust fact-collecting methods after a while. We shall certainly see such turning back along some lines. Take the old faunal naturalists for instance, of whom Audubon is an example. Audubon did not have anything like a sufficient store of facts to enable him to give judgments that could not be reversed, and he was too much of an outdoor's man, too little of a closet man. But for the last thirty or forty years, the period covering the Germanization of our colleges and universities in this country, the tendency has been to produce shoals of little scientific men, who though free from Audubon's shortcomings were also completely free from any touch of his greatness. During these years the scientific college people have as a rule worked on the theory that the highest duty of a would-be naturalist whom, by the way, they call a biologist—is to work in a laboratory with a complex apparatus which will enable him to study for an indefinite period minute infusoria and to write upon sections of tissue. All of this is excellent work if it is understood that it is work merely of preparation, that it represents only the gathering of material for some man of large mind to mould into matter of importance. But as it is treated as the be all and end all, the result has been a lamentable dearth in America of work in the abstract sciences which is of notable and permanent value. I have a friend, Hart Meriam, who is a great mammalogist. He himself suffers a little from this wrong training, and I am afraid he will never be able to produce the work he could, because he cannot see the forest for the trees. He cannot make up his mind to write a great lasting book, inasmuch as there continually turns up some new series of shrews or meadow mice or gophers concerning which he has not quite got all the facts; and he turns industriously aside once more to the impossible task of collecting all these relatively unimportant facts. Still he does understand that we should not leave to story books the vital life histories of our birds and mammals, and he at least has aspirations toward the proper kind of production; but he is almost unable to find among college graduates anyone fit to act as his assistant in the field or to help him find out the facts which should be found out; for the average college graduate of a scientific turn has had all his impulse toward originality carefully taken out of him, and he leaves college a stereotyped well-meaning little creature, only fit for microscopic work in a laboratory. Now such work is good, but it is chiefly good in so far as it gives a wider and deeper foundation of knowledge to the scientific man like Darwin or Huxley; or even to the nature writer like John Burroughs or White of Selborne.

There I have not been able to deny myself the pleasure of writing you this wholly irrelevant letter. Meanwhile I have kept waiting a good friend from whom I am anxious to learn some facts regarding the present political conditions in California, and I must have him up; so goodby and good luck.

Faithfully yours

January 29, 1904. Washington
To Theodore Roosevelt, Jr.

Dear Ted:

Indeed I do understand your interest in all things affecting me, old boy, and I shall write you at length about the political situation. I do not write you such letters all the time because I do not want you to feel that all my correspondence with you is of a stilted and Chesterfield's-letters-to-hisson style.

In politics, as in life generally, the strife is well-nigh unceasing and breathing spots are few. Even if the struggle results in a victory, it usually only opens the way for another struggle. I believe we shall win out in the

Panama business as soon as we can get a vote, for I think we shall confirm the treaty by a three to one majority; but they are filibustering and talking every which way in the vain hope that something will turn up to help them. In the Wood controversy also I think we shall win out, although possibly there will be an ugly fight. The only legislative matter looming up concerning which I feel uncomfortable is the service pension bill,' which I think is on the whole right, but which contains possibilities of mischief on account of the hostility with which it is regarded by many business people, and by lots of good young fellows who do not realize how much the soldiers did in the Civil War, and how much we owe them.

By the way, if I were you I would not discuss the labor-union question from the side that labor unions are harmful. I think they are beneficial if handled as they should be, and that the attack should be made, not upon the principle of association among working people, but upon the abuses in the manifestation of that principle.

As regards myself personally, Senator Hanna and the Wall Street crowd are causing me some worry, but not of a serious kind. I doubt if they can prevent my nomination. Senator Hanna has not kept his promise to me of last June, and has been intoxicated by the thought that perhaps he could either be nominated himself, or at least dictate the nomination, but he will be thwarted completely if he makes the effort, and I think he will grow sullenly conscious of this fact and refuse to make the effort. He has caused me a little worry, but not much. The Wall Street people of a certain stripe—that is, the rich men who do not desire to obey the law and who think that they are entitled to what I regard as improper consideration merely because of their wishes—will do their best to secure the nomination for him, or at least to use him to beat my nomination and secure that of a third person. I think they will fail; and that when they realize that failure is ahead of them they will turn in and support me. But some will try to elect a democrat. A good many of them who are very bitter against me now will come over to my side when the campaign is actually on. I doubt if they can do much against me as far as the nomination is concerned. The election is a different matter. Of course I may be utterly mistaken, but personally I think I have a good deal of strength in the country districts and indeed in the West generally; but in the big cities, and especially in the eastern big cities, the extreme labor-union people and every one of anarchistic or socialist tendencies on the one hand, and the arrogant men of wealth on the other, will probably both combine against me. If the democrats put up a strong candidate upon whom all their factions can unite, I shall have a hard tussle. Nobody can say whether I shall win or lose. In any event, I have done a good many things worth doing while I have been President, and I have had the public service administered with efficiency and integrity.

I am worked very hard at present, and it is only now and then that I can get off in the afternoon for a ride with Mother or a walk with some friend. When the social season is over I think I shall have a little more leeway.

Ever your loving father

P.S. Be careful not to let any of these letters in which I speak of political subjects lie about where they can be seen by anyone.

February 6, 1904. Washington
To Theodore Roosevelt, Jr.

Personal

Dear Ted:

I was glad to hear that you were to be confirmed.

Secretary Root left on Monday and Governor Taft tools his place. I have missed, and shall miss, Root dreadfully. He has been the ablest, most generous and most disinterested friend and adviser that any President could hope to have; and immediately after leaving he rendered me a great service by a speech at the Union League Club in which he said in most effective fashion the very things I should have liked him to say; and his words, moreover, carried weight as the words of no other man at this time addressing such an audience could have done. Taft is a splendid fellow and will be an aid and comfort in every way. But as mother says he is too much like me to be able to give me as good advice as Mr. Root was able to do because of the very differences of character between us.

If after fully thinking the matter over you remain firmly convinced that you want to go into the army well and good. I shall be rather sorry for your decision because I have great confidence in you and I believe that in civil life you could probably win in the end a greater prize than will be open to you if you go into the army—though of course a man can do well in the army. I know perfectly well that you will have hard times in civil life. Probably most young fellows when they have graduated from college, or from their postgraduate course, if they take any, feel pretty dismal for the first few years. In ordinary cases it at first seems as if their efforts were not leading anywhere, as if the pressure around the foot of the ladder was too great to permit of getting up to the top. But I have faith in your energy, your perseverance, your ability, and your power to force yourself to the front when you have once found out and taken your line. However, you and I and mother will talk the whole matter over when you come back here on Easter.

Your loving father

February 8, 1904. Washington
To Jean Jules Jusserand

My dear M. Jusserand:

Herewith I send you back the *Chanson de Roland*. I have enjoyed it particularly because it is the first copy I ever read which had the old French and the modern French interpaged; so that I was able to read the old French, which I could not otherwise have done. There are a dozen points that I want to talk over with you, and as soon as the social season is over I shall get Madame Jusserand arid you to come around to lunch.

Do you regard the Venetian manuscript as being as authentic as the older English manuscript? I hope so, because I particularly like a certain generous side to that description of the Moorish king, Margaris, who "would have been so great a baron if he had only been a Christian," and who seems to me to have more individuality than any of the other characters, after the three great heroes of the epic and Charlemagne.

It seems to me that it is somewhat doubtful to put the poem after the Norman conquest, and by an Anglo-Norman, on so slender a ground as the mention of the conquest of England; for Poland and Byzantium are also mentioned as having been conquered.

With hearty thanks,

Sincerely yours

February 10, 1904. Washington
To Theodore Roosevelt, Jr.

Blessed Ted:

I loved your letter coaxing for one of the six Arabian stallions, and if they had actually come to me I would not have been able to resist keeping one for your use as long as I was in the White House. But alas, it was all a newspaper story! They really went to the St. Louis Exposition, and so you will not be able to disturb your parents by witching the world with feats of horsemanship. Just at the moment what I most earnestly hope is that I shall have any horse whatever for you to ride when you come home at Easter. All three of my saddle horses are absolutely gone in the wind so that I can't ride them at all; and Yagenka is also touched a little. I think it is undoubtedly due to our stable, and I have had them put in another. I hope soon one of mine will get well. Yagenka I think certainly will. So at present I can't ride. When I get any exercise it takes the form of a walk with one of my faithful bodyguard Garfield, Pinchot, Cooley or Fortescue. I have been able to get very little exercise indeed this winter.

I think the opposition to Panama is pretty well over and I shall be surprised if within a week or so we do not have the treaty ratified. Of course, there will be many perplexing problems to face during the actual work of constructing the canal.

Santo Domingo is drifting into chaos, for after a hundred years of freedom it shows itself utterly incompetent for governmental work. Most reluctantly I have been obliged to take the initial step of interference there. I hope it will be a good while before I have to go further. But sooner or later it seems to me inevitable that the United States should assume an attitude of protection and regulation in regard to all these little states in the neighborhood of the Caribbean. I hope it will be deferred as long as possible, but I fear it is inevitable.

I am greatly interested in the Russian and Japanese war. It has certainly opened most disastrously for the Russians, and their supine carelessness is well-nigh incredible. For several years Russia has behaved very badly in the far East, her attitude toward all nations, including us, but especially toward Japan, being grossly overbearing. We had no sufficient cause for war with her. Yet I was apprehensive lest if she at the very outset whipped Japan on the sea she might assume a position well-nigh intolerable toward us. I thought Japan would probably whip her on the sea, but I could not be certain; and between ourselves for you must not breathe it to anybody—I was thoroughly well pleased with the Japanese victory, for Japan is playing our game.

Always yours

February 19, 1904. Washington
To Theodore Roosevelt, Jr.

Dear Ted:

Poor Hanna's death was a tragedy. At the end he wrote me a note, the last he ever wrote, which showed him at his best, and which I much appreciate. His death was very sad for his family and close friends, for he had many large and generous traits, and had made a great success in life by his energy, perseverence and burly strength. As for me personally, the point had been passed where he could either harm or hurt me to any appreciable extent.

Buffalo Bill was at lunch the other day, together with John Willis, my old hunter. Buffalo Bill has always been a great friend of mine. I remember when I was running for Vice-President I struck a Kansas town just when the Wild West show was there. He got upon the rear platform of my car and made a brief speech on my behalf, ending with the statement that "a cyclone from the West had come; no wonder the rats hunted their cellars!"

Roly Fortescue is moving Heaven and earth to get a chance to start for Korea to see the fighting. He is an adventurous, eager little fellow, and I like him.

As for you, I think the West Point education is of course good for any man, but I still think that you have too much in you for me to be glad to see you go into the Army, where in time of peace progress is so much a matter of routine.

Your loving father

[Handwritten] It is curious that though Roly can—as he ought to—easily outlast me at walking and indeed probably at riding, having better wind and being sounder in limb; yet in a bout with the single sticks or broadswords I can wear him down and do him out, so that he loses his wind and his strength.

March 5, 1904. Washington
To Kermit Roosevelt

Dear Kermit:

It does not look as if Renown would ever be worth anything, and I am afraid that Wyoming is gone too. Bleistein probably, and Yagenka almost certainly, will come out all right. Allan is back here now and very cunning, so you will see him on your return.

I am wrestling with two Japanese wrestlers three times a week. I am not the age or the build, one would think, to be whirled lightly over an opponent's head and batted down on a mattress without damage; but they are so skillful that I have not been hurt at all. My throat is a little sore, because once when one of them had a strangle hold I also got hold of his windpipe and thought I could perhaps choke him off before he could choke me. However, he got ahead!

Your loving father

March 19, 1904. Washington
To Cecil Spring Rice

Strictly personal
Dear Cecil:

Your letter about the Russian situation was most interesting. I have been rather surprised at the unexpectedly hysterical side of the Russian nature, which the Japanese success, and the supposed hostility of this country, seem to have brought in evidence. There is much about the Russians which I admire, and I believe in the future of the Slavs if they can only take the right turn. But I do not believe in the future of any race *while it is under a crushing despotism*. The Japanese are non-Aryan and non-Christian, but they are under the weight of no such despotism as the Russians; and so, although the Russians are fundamentally nearer to us, or rather would be if a chance were given them, they are not in actual fact nearer to us at present. People who feel as we do would be happier today living in Japan than living in Russia.

I am entirely sincere in my purpose to keep this Government neutral in the war. And I am no less sincere in my hope that the area of the war will be as limited as possible, and that it will be brought to a close with as little loss to either combatant as is possible. But this country as a whole tends to sympathize with Russia; while the Jews are as violent in their anti-Russian feeling as the Irish in their pro-Russian feeling. I do not think that the country looks forward to, or concerns itself about, the immense possibilities which the war holds for the future. I suppose democracies will always be shortsighted about anything that is not brought roughly home to them. Still, when I feel exasperated by the limitations upon preparedness and forethought which are imposed by democratic conditions, I can comfort myself by the extraordinary example of these very limitations which the autocratic government of Russia has itself furnished in this crisis.

From all I can gather Russia is as angry with America as with England. The Slav is a great and growing race. But if the Japanese win out, not only the Slav, but all of us will have to reckon with a great new force in eastern Asia. The victory will make Japan by itself a formidable power in the Orient, because all the other powers having interests there will have divided interests, divided cares, double burdens, whereas Japan will have but one care, one interest, one burden. If, moreover, Japan seriously starts in to reorganize China and makes any headway, there will result a real shifting of the center of equilibrium as far as the white races are concerned. Personally I believe that Japan will develop herself, and seek to develop China, along paths which will make the first and possibly the second great civilized powers; but the civilization must of course be of a different type from our civilizations. I do not mean that the mere race taken by itself would cause such a tremendous difference. I have met Japanese, and even Chinese, educated in our ways, who in all their emotions and ways of thought were well-nigh identical with us. But the weight of their own ancestral civilization will press upon them, and will prevent their ever coming into exactly our mold. However, all of this is mere speculation. It may be that the two powers will fight until both are fairly well exhausted, and that then peace will come on terms which will not mean the creation of either a yellow peril or a Slav peril. At any rate all that any of us can do is to try to make our several nations fit themselves by the handling of their own affairs, external and internal, so as to be ready for whatever the future may hold. If new nations come to power, if old nations grow to greater power, the attitude of we who speak English should be one of ready recognition of the rights of the new comers, of desire to avoid giving them just offense, and at the same time of preparedness in body and in mind to hold our own if our interests are menaced.

I cannot believe that there will be such a continental coalition against England as that of which you speak. Undoubtedly England is in some immediate, and America in some remote, danger, because each is unmilitary—judged by the standard of continental Europe—and yet both rich and aggressive. Each tends to think itself secure by its own position from the danger of attack at home. We are not so spread out as you are. We are farther away from Europe; therefore, our danger is for the time being less. But we have to a greater degree than you have, although you have it too, the spirit of mere materialism and shortsighted vanity and folly at work for mischief among us. A society of which a bloated trust magnate is accepted quite simply as the ideal is in a rotten condition; and yet this is exactly the condition of no inconsiderable portion of our society. Many people of property admire such a man; many people of no property envy him; and both the admiration and the envy are tributes to which he is not in the least entitled.

However, I cannot write all that I feel. You must come over. Can't you bring Mrs. Spring Rice here as soon as you are married? It will be such fun to have you at the White House.

Ever yours

March 29, 1904. Washington
To Thomas R. Lounsbury

Personal

My dear Mr. Lounsbury:

Good for the split infinitive! Here have I been laboriously trying to avoid using it in a vain desire to look cultured; and now I shall give unbridled rein to my passions in the matter.

Always yours

April 23, 1904. Washington
To Kentaro Kaneko

My dear Baron Kaneko:

I have read your article and like it much. Moreover, I have enjoyed to the full the books which you and Mr. Takahira were kind enough to send me, and two or three others which, on your recommendation, I have secured. Perhaps I was most impressed by the little volume on Bushido.

It seems to me, my dear Baron, that Japan has much to teach the nations of the Occident, just as she has something to learn from them. I have long felt that Japan's entrance into the circle of the great civilized powers was of good omen for all the world. I am not a utopian—at least not for the near future; and I emphatically believe that no nation is worthy of respect unless its sons possess a high and fine national loyalty, and the courage, hardihood and mental and physical address which make this loyalty effective. But I also believe that on the whole it is growing more and more possible, and in the long run it will, I hope, become completely possible for nations to live together in peace and friendship, just as individuals now live together in civilized countries; and in such companionship each nation can teach and each can learn. Certainly I myself hope that I have learned not a little from what I have read of the fine Samurai spirit, and from the way in which that spirit has been and is being transformed to meet the needs of modern life. All of us who sincerely wish well to our several countries, and also to all mankind, have much seriously to think over as we front the great spiritual, social and industrial problems of our age; and each, if he is wise, will, without losing his own self-reliance and capacity for self-help, yet welcome gladly the lessons he can learn and the aid he can get from the men of other countries; for each country can do its special part in the common uplifting of all.

Pray let me know when you next come to Washington. I should like to talk over with you and with Mr. Takahira, more at length, these matters. With regard,

Sincerely yours

May 28, 1904. Washington
To George Otto Trevelyan

My dear Sir George:

My blunder in my last letter brought me a better reward than I deserved, because owing to it I have read your son's *Age of Wycliffe* with great pleasure. Pray congratulate him from me upon all that he is doing.

I find reading a great comfort. People often say to me that they do not see how I find time for it, to which I answer them (much more truthfully than they believe) that to me it is a dissipation, which I have sometimes to try to avoid, instead of an irksome duty. Of course I have been so busy for the last ten years, so absorbed in political work, that I have simply given up reading any book that I do not find interesting. But there are a great many books which ordinarily pass for "dry" which to me do possess much interest—notably history and anthropology; and these give me ease and relaxation that I can get in no other way, not even on horseback!

The Presidential campaign is now opening. Apparently I shall be nominated without opposition at the Republican Convention. Whom the Democrats will put up I do not know, and of course no one can forecast the results of the contest at this time. There is one point of inferiority in our system to yours which has been very little touched on, and that is the way in which the Presidential office tends to put a premium upon a man's keeping out of trouble rather than upon his accomplishing results. If a man has a very decided character, has a strongly accentuated career, it is normally the case of course that he makes ardent friends and bitter enemies; and unfortunately human nature is such that more enemies will leave their party because of enmity to its head than friends will come in from the opposite party because they think well of that same head. In consequence, the dark horse, the neutral-tinted individual, is very apt to win against the man of pronounced views and active life. The electorate is very apt to vote with its back to the future! Now all this does not apply to the same extent with your Prime Minister. It is not possible for the politicians to throw over the real party leader and put up a dummy or some gray-tinted person under your system; or at least, though perhaps it is possible, the opportunity and the temptation are much less.

In my own case, for instance, I believe that most of my policies have commanded the support of a great majority of my fellow-countrymen, but in each case I have made a certain number of determined foes. Thus, on Panama I had an overwhelming majority of the country with me; but whereas I am not at all sure that any Democrat will vote for me because of my attitude on Panama, there are a certain number of mugwumps who will undoubtedly vote against me because of it. So as regards Cuban reciprocity. The country backed me up in the matter, but there is not a Democrat who will vote for me because I got Cuban reciprocity, while there are not a few beet sugar men who will vote against me because of it. In the same way the whole country breathed freer, and felt as if a nightmare had been lifted, when I settled the anthracite coal strike; but the number of votes I shall gain thereby will be small indeed, while the interests to which I gave mortal offense will make their weight felt as of real moment. Thus I could go on indefinitely. However, I certainly would not be willing to hold the Presidency at the cost of failing to do the things which make the real reason why I care to hold it at all. I had much rather be a real President for three years and a half than a figurehead for seven years and a half. I think I can truthfully say that I now have to my credit a sum of substantial achievement—and the rest must take care of itself.

With renewed regard,
Sincerely yours

June 8, 1904. Washington
To Booker T. Washington

Personal

My dear Mr. Washington:

I think that the circular you enclose is simply designed to do mischief to the Republican party. I know that the alleged quotations given in the circular are some of them absolutely false—the alleged interview with Frank Williams for instance. The whole account of the so-called Lily White convention is false. The convention elected four delegates at large who were white men, but the convention which elected them contained a number of negro delegates. A vigorous fight was made to exclude them but they were recognized and the motion to exclude them was defeated by 381 to 43. Negroes had been sent as delegates from district conventions and had not been excluded from any convention. Moreover, I find now that the Cohen faction has put up no candidates for Governor, for Congress, or for other offices of recent years, but has confined itself to antagonizing the Republicans who were put up, and has openly or covertly supported the Democrats. All that the faction represented by Mr. Cohen has done has been to hold a convention once every four years and go through the form of a contest for delegates and to hold offices.

My dear Mr. Washington, you have your troubles just as I have mine and you have to get along with people who are pushing you askew just as I have to. But it seems to me that it is preposterous in Louisiana to back the same old Republican gang which made the Republican party a byword and which certainly failed to accomplish one thing that was good for the negro in the State. I think that the people who are pressing you to take part in the Louisiana fight are blind to the real welfare of both the white man and the colored man in the South. It is out of the question ever to hope to do anything in Louisiana by a party as Mr. Cohen would like to have it, and I say this in spite of the fact that chiefly on your account I have concluded to keep Mr. Cohen in office. The safety for the colored man in Louisiana is to have a white man's party which shall be responsible and honest, in which the colored man shall have representation but in which he shall not be the dominant force—a party in which, as is now the case in the Federal service under me, he shall hold a percentage of the offices but in which a majority of the offices shall be given to white men of high character who will protect the negro before the law. I am convinced that most of the information you get as to the so-called Lily White party in Louisiana is simply slander. I know it is slander about Williams and Clarke and it speaks ill for Cohen that he should have anything to do with such slander. Let me repeat—and I am only saying to you what you have always said to me—that I think it is not to the interest of the negro, and that even if it were to the interest of the negro it would be attempting the impossible, to try to put a negro party in control in Louisiana, and that it is even worse to try to put in control a negro party led by a few whites like Wimberly. The administration has followed exactly and precisely the right course in Louisiana. Have you forgotten that we have the same number of negro federal officeholders in Louisiana now that we had in McKinley's time? There has been no change in the proportion of negro to white officeholders. The change has been in the direction of raising the character of the officeholders—black and white. The Williams and Clarke people feel, as I think with entire propriety, and as I certainly have always understood that you believe, that it is out of the question in this stage of growth in Louisiana for the negroes to be dominant. The effort to bring about such a state of things would be as disastrous for them as for the whites. So far as the Republican party has power, they are given a number of offices, every effort is made to protect them. in all their rights, they attend all the conventions and they go as delegates to national, state and Congressional conventions.

Sincerely yours

June 13, 1904. Washington
To Cecil Spring Rice

Personal—Be very careful that no one gets a chance to see this.
Dear Cecil:

Like everyone else I, of course, continue to be immensely interested in the war in the East. Do you recollect some of the letters I have written you in the past about Russia? I never anticipated in the least such a rise as this of Japan's, but I have never been able to make myself afraid of Russia in the present. I like the Russian people and believe in them. I earnestly hope that after the fiery ordeal through which they are now passing they will come forth faced in the right way for doing well in the future. But I see nothing of permanent good that can come to Russia, either for herself or for the rest of the world, until her people begin to tread the path of orderly freedom, of civil liberty, and of a measure of self-government. Whatever may be the theoretical advantages of a despotism, they are incompatible with the growth of intelligence and individuality in a civilized people. Either there must be stagnation in the Russian people, or there must be what I should hope would be a gradual, but a very real, growth of governmental institutions to meet the growth in, and the capacity and need for, liberty.

The other day the Japanese Minister here and Baron Kaneko, a Harvard graduate, lunched with me and we had a most interesting talk. I told them that I thought their chief danger was lest Japan might get the "big head" and enter into a general career of insolence and aggression; that such a career would undoubtedly be temporarily very unpleasant to the rest of the world, but that it would in the end be still more unpleasant for Japan. I added that though I felt there was a possibility of this happening, I did not think it probable, because I was a firm believer in the Japanese people, and that I most earnestly hoped as well as believed that Japan would simply take her place from now on among the great civilized nations, with, like each of these nations, something to teach others as well as something to learn from them; with, of course, a paramount interest in what surrounds the Yellow Sea, just as the United States has a paramount interest in what surrounds the Caribbean; but with, I hoped, no more desire for conquest of the weak than we had shown ourselves to have in the case of Cuba, and no more desire for a truculent attitude toward the strong than we had shown with reference to the English and French West Indies. Both of them, I found, took exactly my view, excepting that they did not believe there was any danger of Japan's becoming intoxicated with the victory, because they were convinced that the upper and influential class would not let them, and would show the same caution and decision which has made them so formidable in this war. They then both proceeded to inveigh evidently with much feeling, against the talk about the Yellow Terror, explaining that in the 13th century they had had to dread the Yellow Terror of the Mongolians as much as Europe itself, and that as their aspirations were in every way to become part of the circle of civilized mankind, a place to which they were entitled by over two thousand years of civilization of their own, they did not see why they should be classed as barbarians. I told them that I entirely agreed with them; that without question some of my own ancestors in the 10th century had been part of the "white terror" of the Northmen, a terror to which we now look back with romantic satisfaction, but which represented everything hideous and abhorrent and unspeakably dreadful to the people of Ireland, England and France at that time; and that as we had outgrown the position of being a White Terror I thought that in similar fashion such a civilization as they had developed entitled them to laugh at the accusation of being part of the Yellow Terror. Of course they earnestly assured me that all talk of Japan's even thinking of the Philippines was nonsense. I told them that I was quite sure this was true; that I should certainly do all in my power to avoid giving Japan or any other nation an excuse for aggression; that if aggression come I believed we would be quite competent to defend ourselves. I then said that as far as I was concerned I hoped to see China kept together, and would gladly welcome any part played by Japan which would tend to bring China forward along the road which Japan trod, because I thought it for the interest of all the world that each part of the world should be prosperous and well policed; I added that unless everybody was mistaken in the Chinese character I thought they would have their hands full in mastering it—at which they grinned and said that they were quite aware of the difficulty they were going to have even in Korea and were satisfied with that job. They then began to discuss with me the outcome of the war if they were successful in taking Port Arthur and definitely establishing the upper hand in Manchuria over the Russians. They said that they were afraid the Russians would not keep any promises they made, in view of what I was obliged to admit, namely: the fact that the Russians have for the last three years been following out a consistent career of stupendous mendacity, not only with Japan but with ourselves, as regards Manchuria. It was evident from what the Minister said that their hope is to get the Russians completely out of Manchuria and to turn it over to the Chinese, but that he was not sure whether the Chinese would be strong enough to support themselves. I said that of course if we could get a Chinese Viceroy able to keep definite order under the guarantee of the Powers in Manchuria, that would be the best outcome; but that I did not know whether this was possible, or whether the powers would even consider such an idea. The Minister was evidently very anxious that there should be a general international agreement to guarantee the autonomy of China in Manchuria. Some of the things he said I do not wish to put down on paper—which may astonish you in view of what I fear diplomats would regard as the frankness of this letter anyhow.

Well, my troubles will be domestic I suppose for the next few months. By the end of this month I shall probably be nominated for President by the republican convention. How the election will come out I do not know, but in any event I shall feel that I have had a most enjoyable three years and a half in the White House, and that I have accomplished a certain amount of permanent work for the nation.

Give my love to the future Mrs. Spring Rice. Mrs. Roosevelt sends you hers.

Always yours

P. S. Don't understand from the above that I was laying the ground for any kind of interference by this government in the Far East. The Japanese themselves spoke purely hypothetically as to whether circumstances would arise to warrant such interference, even to the extent of the offer of good services to both parties, and I explained that I could not say that so much as this offer could be made. I was immensely interested to find out the way in which their minds were working.

Of course, in many ways the civilization of the Japs is very alien to ours. I told Takahira and Kaneko that I thought we had to learn from them many things, especially as to the misery in our great cities, but that in return they had to learn from us the ideal of the proper way of treating womanhood. Both cordially agreed with me—whether from mere politeness or not I cannot say.

The Japs interest me and I like them. I am perfectly well aware that if they win out it may possibly mean a struggle between them and us in the future; but I hope not and believe not. At any rate, Russia's course during the past three years has made it evident that if she wins she will organize northern China against us and rule us absolute out of all the ground she can control. Therefore, on the score of mere national self-interest, we would not be justified in balancing the certainty of immediate damage against the possibility of future damage. However, this was merely an academic question anyhow, as there was nothing whatever to warrant us going to war on behalf of either side, or doing otherwise than observe a strict neutrality, which we have done. The good will of our people has been with the Japanese, but the government has been scrupulous in its impartiality between the combatants. As I have said before, I like the Russians; but I do not think they can ever take the place they should take until they gain a measure of civil liberty and self-government such as Occidental nations have. I am not much affected by the statement that the Japanese are of an utterly different race from ourselves and that the Russians are of the same race. I suppose we have all outgrown the belief that language and race have anything to do with one another; and the more I see of life the more I feel that while there are some peoples of a very low standard from whom nothing can be expected, yet that there are others, widely different one from the other, which, nevertheless, stand about on an equality in the proportions of bad and good which they contain—and a good man is a good man and a bad man a bad man wherever they are found. I know certain southern Frenchmen like Jusserand, for instance, (the Ambassador here) and certain Scandinavians like Nansen, or for the matter of that, certain Americans like Peary, who in physical habit of body are as far apart as either is from a Japanese gentleman. Yet they are good fellows, with all the essentials in common, because they have the same conscience and the same cultural creed. Of course, the modern Turks are not Mongolians at all. In the eyes of the physiologist they are just as much white people as the Balkan Christians, or as the Russians, and physiologically they do not differ any more from Danes, Englishmen, Swiss, or Italians, than the latter differ among themselves. But they are absolutely alien because of their creed, their culture, their historic associations, and inherited governmental and social tendencies. Therefore, they are a curse to Europe, and the curse is not mitigated in the least by the fact that by blood they do not differ any more from the European peoples who speak an Aryan tongue than do, for instance, those excellent members of the European body politic, the Magyars, Finns and Basques, all of whom likewise speak non-Aryan tongues. The Turks are ethnically closer to us than the Japanese, but they are impossible members of our international society, while I think the Japs may be desirable additions. That there are large classes of the Japanese who will sometimes go wrong, that Japan as a whole will sometimes go wrong, I do not doubt. The same is true of my own beloved country. I do not anticipate that Tokyo will show a superior morality to that which obtains in Berlin, Vienna and Paris, not to speak of London and Washington, or of St. Petersburg. But I see nothing ruinous to civilization in the advent of the Japanese to power among the great nations.

June 20, 1904. Washington
To Charles W. Eliot

Personal
Dear Mr. Eliot:

It seems to me that what is important to cultivate among the Filipinos at present is, not in the least "patriotic national sentiment" (for there would be at least an even chance that they would confound this with Aguinaldoism), but the sober performance of duty. As far as we *Americans* are concerned I would be delighted to say that we should give the Filipinos a national government at the earliest possible moment. The reason I do not think it wise to say so is for the sake of the Filipinos themselves. It is a disadvantage to stimulate and encourage among them at this time those feelings which are usually understood when we allude to "patriotic national sentiment." The Filipino does not need in the least to be taught that he is to aspire to a national government. What he needs is to be taught that he must, first of all, be able to practice justice to himself and to others. The "main object of American statesmanship in the islands" must be discouragement of any feeling among the Filipinos which will make them subordinate the duty of trying to become self-supporting, self-respecting, orderly people, to the cultivation of anything else.

Sincerely yours

June 21, 1904. Washington
To Kermit Roosevelt

Dear Kermit:

We spent Sunday at the Knoxes'. It is a beautiful farm—just such a one as you could run. Phil Knox, as capable and efficient as he is diminutive, amused mother and me greatly by the silent way in which he did in first-rate shape his full share of all the work.

Tomorrow the National Convention meets, and barring a cataclysm I shall be nominated. There is a great deal of sullen grumbling, but it has taken more the form of resentment against what they think is my dictation as to details than against me personally. They don't dare to oppose me for the nomination and I suppose it is hardly likely the attempt will be made to stampede the Convention for anyone. How the election will turn out no one can tell. Of course I hope to be elected but I realize to the full how very lucky I have been, not only to be President but to have been able to accomplish so much while President, and whatever may be the outcome I am not only content but very sincerely thankful for all the good fortune I have had. From Panama down I have been able to accomplish certain things which will be of lasting importance in our history. Incidentally, I don't think that any family has ever enjoyed the White House more than we have. I was thinking about it just this morning when mother and I took breakfast on the portico and afterwards walked about the lovely grounds and looked at the stately historic old house. It is a wonderful privilege to have been here and to have been given the chance to do this work, and I should regard myself as having a small and mean mind if in the event of defeat I felt soured at not having had more, instead of being thankful for having had so much.

Your loving father

July 13, 1904. Oyster Bay
To James R. Garfield

Dear Jim:

I take a sour satisfaction in your having failed by some seconds in your house-climbing feat, because I like to think that there are some among my junior friends who are themselves getting a little old also. I am bound to say I have seen no traces of it in you hitherto.

Our imitation of your point-to-point walk went off splendidly. I had six boys with me, including all of my own except Quentin. We swam the millpond (which proved to be very broad and covered with duckweed), in great shape, with our clothes on; executed an equally long but easier swim in the bay, with our clothes on; and between times had gone in a straight line through the woods, through the marshes, and up and down the bluffs. The whole thing would have been complete if the Garfield family could only have been along. I did not look exactly presidential when I got back from the walk!

It was delightful having Gifford here on the 4th of July. He and I and Mrs. Roosevelt took an all-day picnic in a rowboat.

With warm regards to Mrs. Garfield.

Always yours

[Handwritten] P. S. July 14th. Last night I spent camping with Kermit, Archie and two of their friends. We went in two rowboats, and camped eight or ten miles off down the sound. I fried beefsteak and chicken, and Kermit potatoes; we all decided that the cooking was excellent and the trip a success.

August 11, 1904. Washington
To Henry Cabot Lodge

Personal

Dear Cabot:

Mellen talked most nicely about you, and said he would help you in every way. I gave him your letter, and he said he was going to write you. He said he wished you would write him in person.

One must always keep in mind what Abraham Lincoln pointed out—that all of the people can be fooled for part of the time. It may be that this election will come in that part of the time; but it is as sure as anything in history can be that the democrats, including Parker and their mugwump and capitalistic allies, are playing a bunco game which ought not to take in any but a low order of intelligence. I think Parker's speech is poor. It is a straddle; and all that can be said in its favor is that there is a certain adroitness shown in avoiding difficult positions, and seeking to imply, in order to placate certain interests, what he dare not say, lest others should be offended. I do not think that there has ever been anything more palpable than the effort to show that no protectionist need be afraid of him because the republicans will prevent any harm being done the protective tariff. In the same way he has rather dangerously given the Colorado labor people to understand that in his judgment I ought to interfere, and yet he has not said it in terms which will prevent his denying having said it to the wealthy scoundrels in New York who are his great backers. The trouble is that these wealthy scoundrels instead of being repelled by trickery on his part, chuckle over it. They believe, what is the truth, that he is deliberately fooling the labor men and trying to get their support by giving them the impression of doing what he has no intention of doing, and instead of minding this they uphold it. As for the neurotic or mugwump class, it is hopeless to expect honesty from them. If they had an ounce of honesty in them they would say about the Philippines that he is seeking to dextrously effect the declaration in the platform declaring for independence for the Philippines, by taking a position that they are to be kept exactly as they are being kept for centuries. He is, of course wholly indifferent, and I suppose that dogs like Carl Schurz and his kind are wholly indifferent, to the fact that this would mean conveying to the Filipinos the impression of broken faith. He is deliberately using language, and the democrats are deliberately using language, to be taken by the Filipinos as meaning one thing, and after election explaining to them as something meaning entirely different.

I shall soon send you a rough draft of my letter. I wish I dared go far enough to say the simple truth—that this contest was essentially one between sincerity and trickiness. Will you be able to come on to Oyster Bay during the last ten days of August? If so, which one would be convenient to you? Make it after the 21st.

Ever yours

October 26, 1904. Washington
To George B. Cortelyou

Confidential

My dear Mr. Cortelyou:

I have just been informed that the Standard Oil people have contributed one hundred thousand dollars to our campaign fund. This may be entirely untrue. But if true I must ask you to direct that the money be returned to them forthwith. I appreciate to the full the need of funds to pay the legitimate and necessarily great expenses of the campaign. I appreciate to the full the fact that under no circumstances will we receive half as much as was received by the National Committee in 1900 and 1896. Moreover, it is entirely legitimate to accept contributions, no matter how large they are, from individuals and corporations on the terms on which I happen to know that you have accepted them: that is, with the explicit understanding that they were given and received with no thought of any more obligation on the part of the National Committee or of the National Administration than is implied in the statement that every man shall receive a square deal, no more and no less, and that this I shall guarantee him in any event to the best of my ability. The big business corporations have a tremendous stake in the welfare of this country. They know that this welfare can only be secured through the continuance in power of the republican party; and if they subscribe for the purpose of securing such national welfare, and with no thought of personal favors to them, why they are acting as is entirely proper; but we cannot under any circumstances afford to take a contribution which can be even improperly construed as putting us under an improper obligation, and in view of my past relations with the Standard Oil Company I fear that such a construction will be put upon receiving any aid from them. In returning the money to them I wish it made clear to them that there is not the slightest personal feeling against them, and that they can count upon being treated exactly as well by the Administration, exactly as fairly, as if we had accepted the contribution. They shall not suffer in any way because we refused it, just as they would not have gained in any way if we had accepted it. But I am not willing that it should be accepted, and must ask that you tell Mr. Bliss to return it.[1]

Sincerely yours

November 1, 1904. Washington
To Rudyard Kipling

Personal

Dear Kipling:

That was awfully good of you, and I never dreamed that you would have taken such trouble or I should not have spoken of the matter to Doubleday. I am greatly obliged for the stories. Do not think me altogether a prig if I say that I have been obliged to think so seriously of many things that I am apt to like to have a story contain a moral—provided always that the story has the prime quality of interest.

We are now closing the campaign, and the Lord only knows how it will go. I have done a good many things in the past three years, and the fact that I did them is doubtless due partly to accident and partly to temperament. Naturally, I think that I was right in doing them, for otherwise I would not have done them. It is equally natural that some people should have been alienated by each thing I did, and the aggregate of all that have been alienated may be more than sufficient to overthrow me. Thus, in dealing with the Philippines I have first the jack fools who seriously think that any group of pirates and head-hunters needs nothing but independence in order that it may be turned forthwith into a dark-hued New England town meeting; and then the entirely practical creatures who join with these extremists because I do not intend that the islands shall be exploited for corrupt purposes. So in Panama, I have to encounter the opposition of the vague individuals of serious mind and limited imagination, who think that a corrupt pithecoid community in which the President has obtained his position by the simple process of clapping the former President into a wooden cage and sending him on an ox cart over the mountains (this is literally what was done at Bogota)—is entitled to just the treatment that I would give, say, to Denmark or Switzerland. Then, in addition, I have the representatives of the transcontinental railways, who are under no delusions, but who do not want a competing canal. In the same way I have alienated some of the big representatives of what we call the trusts, and have had a muss with the trades-unions on the other side. So only a merciful providence can tell what the outcome will be. If elected I shall be very glad. If beaten I shall

---

[1]In fact the money was *not* returned, as became evident years later.

be sorry; but in any event I have had a first-class run for my money, and I have accomplished certain definite things. I would consider myself a hundred times over repaid if I had nothing more to my credit than Panama and the coaling stations in Cuba. So you see that my frame of mind is a good deal like that of your old Viceroy when he addressed the new Viceroy!

    With regards to Mrs. Kipling, and renewed thanks, believe me,
    Sincerely yours

November 8, 1904. Washington
To Kermit Roosevelt

(Telegram)

Am elected by overwhelming majority, about as great as that of McKinley four years ago. Our happiness would be complete if only you were here.

November 15, 1904. Washington
To Michael J. Donovan

Personal

Dear Mike:

    Can you send me on three pairs of boxing gloves; and can you tell me some good men here in Washington who, in the winter months, I can have come around two or three times a week to box with me and my son and another young kinsman? I wish sometime you could get on here for a day or two yourself.

    Faithfully yours

November 19, 1904. Washington
To Owen Wister

Personal: Private

Dear Dan:

    Later I want you and Mrs. Dan to spend a night here at Washington with us if you can.

    I value much your letter. You give expression to exactly what I have felt. I have been most abundantly rewarded, far beyond my deserts, by the American people; and I say this with all sincerity and not in any spirit of mock humility. The stars in their courses fought for me. I was forced to try a dozen pieces of doubtful and difficult work in which it was possible to deserve success, but in which it would not have been possible even for Lincoln or Washington to be sure of commanding success. I mean the Panama business, the anthracite coal strike, the Northern Securities suit, the Philippine Church question, the whole Cuban business, the Alaska boundary, the Government open-shop matter, irrigation and forestry work, etc., etc. In each case, partly by hard and intelligent work and partly by good fortune, we won out. Moreover, Parker, who had been most carefully groomed for some years to bring the democracy back into power by uniting the Bryanites and Clevelandites, and who had very strong political and financial interests behind him, when actually tried in the great strain of a struggle for the Presidency, proved a poor type of candidate; so that many outside circumstances, over which I could have exercised but partial control, favored me. Of course it would be foolish for me to say that I did not think that I myself was responsible for part of the victory. I have done a great deal of substantive work. I have never sought trouble, but I have never feared to take the initiative when, after careful thought, I deemed it necessary. Moreover, in Hay, Taft, Root, Knox and one or two others I have had as staunch and able friends and supporters as ever a President had. My relations with these men have been very close and very, very pleasant. If circumstances had been different I would most gladly have served in the Cabinet of any one of the four men I have named; and we have had the most thorough comradeship of feeling now that circumstances have been such that they have all served in my Cabinet.

Moreover, it is a peculiar gratification to me to have owed my election not to the politicians primarily, although of course I have done my best to get on with them; not to the financiers, although I have staunchly upheld the rights of property; but above all to Abraham Lincoln's "plain people"; to the folk who work hard on farm, in shop, or on the railroads, or who own little stores, little businesses which they manage themselves. I would literally, not figuratively, rather cut off my right hand than forfeit by any improper act of mine the trust and regard of these people. I may have to do something of which they will disapprove, because I deem it absolutely right and necessary; but most assuredly I shall endeavor not to merit their disapproval by any act inconsistent with the ideal they have formed of me.

But the gentle folk, the people whom you and I meet at the houses of our friends and at our clubs; the people who went to Harvard as we did, or to other colleges more or less like Harvard: these people have contained many of those who have been most bitter in their opposition to me, and their support on the whole has been much more lukewarm than the support of those whom I have called the plain people. As you say, I do not at all mind what Mr. Baer or Mr. J. J. Hill or Mr. Thomas F. Ryan does in the way of opposing me. Mr. Baer was doing what I thought wrong in the coal strike. Mr. Hill was doing what I thought wrong in the Northern Securities Company. Mr. Ryan was doing what I thought wrong about the franchise tax law in New York. And I upset them all. They are all three big men and very wealthy. They are accustomed to being treated with great consideration, and they have doubtless quite sincerely come to feel that their own wisdom and rightmindedness are such that it is improper to oppose them. I do not wonder that they are bitter towards me.

But the *Evening Post* crowd, the Carl Schutz and Charles Francis Adams crowd, are hypocritical and insincere when they oppose me. They have loudly professed to demand just exactly the kind of government I have given, and yet they have done their futile best to defeat me. They have not been able to do me personally any harm; but they continually do the cause of good government a certain amount of harm by diverting into foolish channels of snarling and critical impotence the energies of fine young fellows who ought to be a power for good. Take Carl Schurz's attack upon me for acting as any gentleman would act with Hanna and Quay when they were on their death beds; or take his statement that because I had seen Addicks and Lou Payn I was to be repudiated, as "the friendship of the wicked has its price." In the first place, I had seen Lou Payn just once, at his request. I have seen Addicks perhaps three times, at his request, of course. I have never since I have been President done for either Addicks or Payn one single act; never made an appointment for either of them or done anything else for either of them. In the next place, I shall continue to see both of them whenever they choose to call, and to see everybody else who chooses to call—unless it be some creature who renders it impossible for me to see him. For instance, if Hearst, while Congressman, calls upon me I shall see him as a matter of course. I continually see "Dry Dollar" Sullivan. If my virtue ever becomes so frail that it will not stand meeting men of whom I thoroughly disapprove, but who are in active official life and whom I must encounter, why I shall go out of politics and become an anchorite. Whether I see these men or do not see them, if I do for them any thing improper then I am legitimately subject to criticism; but only a fool will criticize me because I see them. Moreover, the hypocrisy of Carl Schurz and the *Evening Post* crowd is the more evident because they support Parker, who owes his political existence to Hill, and is the intimate social and political friend of Hill, Sheehan and Tom Taggart, and yet attack me for seeing men not one particle worse than these men whom Parker has seen all the time, and with whom he is on terms of hand-in-glove intimacy. To choose Tom Taggart to run his campaign was precisely as if I had chosen Lou Payn to run mine; and the morality of Hill, his creator, is no more advanced than the morality of Addicks.

Of course in my work I have made certain mistakes, as was

inevitable when I had such countless questions to meet all the time. I do not think that they have been very numerous or very important. Furthermore, there are some decisions I have made where I think I was right, but where doubtless other people with the same state of facts before them would think I was wrong. But in the great majority of the cases for which I am criticized by the people in question, the fact simply is that they have criticized in ignorance of all the circumstances of the case; in ignorance of the conditions which I, being at the center of affairs, must know better than anyone else, and upon which I must act upon my own responsibility.

There—I have written you a long screed!

Goodby and good luck.

Ever yours

[Handwritten] P. S. Take the college bred men of the country as a whole, and I think I have the majority.

January 4, 1905. Washington
To William Howard Taft

The Secretary of War:

I must say that I think that ramrod bayonet about as poor an invention as I ever saw. As you observed, it broke short off as soon as hit with even moderate violence. It would have no moral effect and mighty little physical effect. I think the suggestion of a short triangular bayonet a great improvement. After you have gone over this subject of the bayonet and the sword, do take it up with me.

I wish our officers could carry rifles. If they carry any sword they ought to carry a sword that they can cut or thrust with. Personally I do not see any point in having the cavalry armed with a bayonet, even though the modern cavalryman is nine times out of ten on foot. He might have a sword in his belt, only it ought to be a sword that can do damage.

I am particularly anxious that we should have a thorough test made of the long and the short rifle (that is of the 24-inch and 30-inch rifle) at some place like that in Utah where several companies of men can be employed at firing both weapons at long ranges. This ramrod bayonet business does not make me feel that we can afford to trust too much to theory of the closet variety. I would like to have the opinion of Captain March, and then the opinion of the other military attaches who saw the fighting between the Russians and Japanese, about both the bayonet and the sword. I would also like to have the opinion of any of our officers in the Philippines who have seen the bayonet actually used.

February 6, 1905. Washington
To Andrew Carnegie

My dear Mr. Carnegie:

I do not agree with you about the treaties. I am not willing to go into a farce. We have the power to make special arbitration treaties now, and it is simply nonsense, from my standpoint, to pass a general treaty which says that we can negotiate special treaties if we like, which of course we can do whether the general treaty is or is not passed. But I shall take up the matter with Secretary Hay tomorrow morning and go carefully over it with him.

Sincerely yours

February 20, 1905. Washington
To James Ford Rhodes[1]

My dear Mr. Rhodes:

I thank you for your letter and am very glad you like my speech. But, my dear sir, while I agree with you fully as to the folly of the Congressional scheme of reconstruction based on universal negro suffrage, in writing about it I pray you not to forget that the initial folly lay with the southerners themselves. You say, quite properly, that you do not wonder that much bitterness still remains in the breasts of the southern people about the carpetbag negro regime. So it is not to be wondered at that in the late sixties much bitterness should have remained in the hearts of the northerners over the remembrance of the senseless folly and wickedness of the southerners in the early sixties. Those of us who most heartily agree that it was the presence of the negro which made the problem, and that slavery was merely the worst possible method of solving it, must therefore hold up to reprobation as guilty of doing one of the worst deeds which history records, those men who tried to break up this Union because they were not allowed to bring slavery and the negro into new territory. Every step which followed, from freeing the slave to enfranchising him, was due only to the North being slowly and reluctantly forced to act by the South's persistence in its folly and wickedness.

I would not say these things in public because they tend, when coming from a man in public place, to embitter people. But you are writing what I hope will prove the great permanent history of the period, and it would be a misfortune for the country, and especially a misfortune for the South, if they were allowed to confuse right and wrong in perspective.

My difficulties with the southern people have come not from the

---

[1]Industrialist-turned-historian, at this time working on his multivolume *History of the United States from the Compromise of 1850.*

North but from the South. I have never done one thing that was not for their interest. At present they are, as a whole, speaking well of me. When they will begin again to speak ill I do not know. In either case my duty is equally clear.

Faithfully yours

March 9, 1905. Washington
To George Otto Trevelyan

My dear Sir George:

I liked your son's book much. I am not well read in the period; but it gave me a much clearer idea of the times, a much more vivid picture of them, than I ever before had had. Moreover, in addition to being instructive it had the great merit of being interesting! Having begun the book I read it in all my spare hours until I had finished it.

Well, I have just been inaugurated and have begun my second term. Of course I greatly enjoyed inauguration day, and indeed I have thoroughly enjoyed being President. But I believe I can also say that I am thoroughly alive to the tremendous responsibilities of my position. Life is a long campaign where every victory merely leaves the ground free for another battle, and sooner or later defeat comes to every man, unless death forestalls it. But the final defeat does not and should not cancel the triumphs, if the latter have been substantial and for a cause worth championing.

It has been peculiarly pleasant to me to find that my supporters are to be found in the overwhelming majority among those whom Abraham Lincoln called the plain people. As I suppose you know, Lincoln is my hero. He was a man of the people who always felt with and for the people, but who had not the slightest touch of the demagogue in him. It is probably difficult for his countrymen to get him exactly in the right perspective as compared with the great men of other lands. But to me he does seem to be one of the great figures, who will loom ever larger as the centuries go by. His unfaltering resolution, his quiet, unyielding courage, his infinite patience and gentleness, and the heights of disinterestedness which he attained whenever the crisis called for putting aside self, together with his farsighted, hardheaded common sense, point him out as just the kind of chief who can do most good in a democratic republic like ours.

Having such an admiration for the great railsplitter, it has been a matter of keen pride to me that I have appealed peculiarly to the very men to whom he most appealed and who gave him their heartiest support. I am a college-bred man, belonging to a well-to-do family so that, as I was more than contented to live simply, and was fortunate enough to marry a wife with the same tastes, I have not had to make my own livelihood; though I have always had to add to my private income by work of some kind. But the farmers, lumbermen, mechanics, ranchmen, miners, of the North, East and West, have felt that I was just as much in sympathy with them, just as devoted to their interests, and as proud of them and as representative of them, as if I had sprung from among their own ranks; and I certainly feel that I do understand them and believe in them and feel for them and try to represent them just as much as if I had from earliest childhood made each day's toil pay for that day's existence or achievement. How long this feeling toward me will last I cannot say. It was overwhelming at the time of the election last November, and I judge by the extraordinary turnout for the inauguration it is over-whelming now. Inasmuch as the crest of the wave is invariably suc-ceeded by the hollow, this means that there will be a reaction. But mean-while I shall have accomplished something worth accomplishing, I hope.

I wish you could have been here on inauguration day, for I should think that the ceremonies, if such they can be called, would have inter-ested you. I send you herewith a copy of my inaugural speech. The Sec-retary of State. John Hay, was Lincoln's private secretary, and the night before the inauguration he gave me a ring containing some of Lincoln's hair, cut from his head just after he was assassinated nearly forty years ago; and I wore the ring when I took my oath of office next day. I had thirty members of my old regiment as my special guard of honor, riding to and from the Capitol. And in the parade itself, besides the regular army and navy and the national guard, there was every variety of civic organization, including a delegation of coal miners with a banner recall-ing that I had settled the anthracite coal strike; Porto Ricans and Philip-pine Scouts; old-style Indians, in their war paint and with horses painted green and blue and red and yellow, with their war bonnets of eagles' feathers and their spears and tomahawks, followed by the new Indians, the students of Hampton and Carlisle; sixty or seventy cowboys; farmers clubs; mechanics clubs—everybody and everything. Many of my old friends with whom I had lived on the ranches and worked in the roundups in the early days came on to see me inaugurated.

There, I am half ashamed of having written you about such purely personal matters. Our internal problems are of course much more im-portant than our relations with foreign powers. Somehow or other we shall have to work out methods of controlling the big corporations with-out paralyzing the energies of the business community and of prevent-ing any tyranny on the part of the labor unions while cordially assisting in every proper effort made by the wageworkers to better themselves by combinations. In all these matters I have to do the best I can with the

Congress. I have just as much difficulty in preventing the demagogues from going too far as in making those who arc directly or indirectly responsive to Wall Street go far enough. In foreign affairs I have considerable difficulty in getting the Senate to work genuinely for peace, and also in making it understand, and indeed in making our people understand, that we cannot perpetually assert the Monroe Doctrine on behalf of all American republics, bad and good, without ourselves accepting some responsibility in connection therewith. Of course in the Senate I have to deal with frank enemies like Gorman, and in addition with the entire tribe of fat-witted people, headed by a voluble, pinheaded creature named Bacon from Georgia, a horrid instance of the mischief that can be done by a man of very slender capacity, if only he possesses great loquacity, effrontery, and an entire indifference to the national welfare. However, though there is much that is worrying and exasperating and though there are many checks and though we never get more than a third to a half of what really ought to be gotten, yet on the whole there is progress. This country is, I think, learning to take its position more seriously. I am very proud of what we did with Cuba. I hope that ultimately it will be possible to do much the same kind of thing with the Philippines, though as yet the Philippines have not begun to make enough progress to enable me, even to myself, to formulate this hope with distinctness. As far as I can see this country is on good terms with other countries, and I believe it wishes to act fairly and justly, and yet to keep a sufficient armament to make it evident that the attitude proceeds not from fear, but from the genuine desire to do justice.

Just at present it looks as if Kuropatkin's army was in desperate straits. Six weeks ago I privately and unofficially advised the Russian Government, and afterwards repeated the advice indirectly through the French Government, to make peace, telling them that of course if they were sure their fleet could now beat the Japanese, and if they were sure they could put and keep 600,000 men in Manchuria, I had nothing to say; but that in my own belief the measure of their mistaken judgment for the last year would be the measure of their mistaken judgment for the next if they continued the war, and that they could not count upon as favorable terms of peace as the Japanese were still willing to offer if they refused to come to terms until the Japanese armies were north of Harbin. But the Russian Government has shown a fairly Chinese temper for the last year or two. Their conduct in Manchuria was such as wholly to alienate American sympathy, and to make it evident that they intended to organize China as a step toward the domination of the rest of the world. The Japanese have treated us well. What they will do hereafter, when intoxicated by their victory over Russia, is another question which only the future can decide. Meanwhile, when I realize most keenly the difficulties inherent under a free representative government in dealing with foreign questions, it is rather a comfort to feel that Russia, where freedom has been completely sacrificed, where the darkest and most reactionary tyranny reigns, has as yet been unable to do well in the exercise of those functions, proficiency in which could alone justify in any degree the tyranny. Both from the diplomatic and military standpoints Russia has during the last year or two done as badly as any republic could possibly do; and much worse than either of our governments has ever yet done.

The English-speaking peoples have a wholly different set of evil tendencies to combat. I believe that we shall work through our troubles and ultimately come well out of them; but there are plenty of anxious times ahead, and there are many serious evils to face. In England, in the United States, in Canada, in Australia, and in the English parts of South Africa there is more and more a tendency for the men who speak English to gather into the cities and towns, so that these grow at the expense of the country folk. Now in the past the man on the farm has always proved to be the man who, in the last analysis, did best service in governing himself in times of peace, and also in fighting in times of war. The city-bred folk, and especially where the cities are of enormous size, have not yet shown that they can adequately fill the place left vacant by the dwindling of the country population. Moreover, the diminishing birth rate among our people is an ugly thing. In New England, for instance, the old native stock is not quite holding its own. Here the results are not visible owing to the great immigration, but in Australia the effect is alarming, for the population is increasing slowly and moreover at a constantly diminishing rate, in spite of the fact that the great island continent is very sparsely populated, and in spite of the two or three very large cities.

However, I suppose that almost always and in almost every country there has been cause for anxiety. The most marvelous growth in population and material prosperity, and, I believe, in the average of human happiness, that the world has ever seen in any race, has taken place among the English-peoples since the time when Goldsmith gave poetic expression to the general feeling of gloom which prevailed among educated men at what they were pleased to consider the morbid growth of the cities and the decadence of the men in England. Much good has gone hand in hand with the evil of the tremendous industrial development of the day. I do not think the average American multi-millionaire a very high type, and I do not much admire him. But in his place he is well enough; and I am inclined to think that on the whole our people are, spiritually as well as materially, on the average better and not worse off than they were a hundred years ago.

How I wish I could take advantage of your delightful invitation and visit you! But there is no such luck for me at present.

With warm regards,

Sincerely yours

April 14, 1905. Colorado Springs, Colorado
To Kermit Roosevelt

Blessed Kermit:

I hope you had as successful a trip in Florida as I have had in Texas and Oklahoma. The first six days were of the usual Presidential tour type, but much more pleasant than ordinarily because I, did not have to do quite as much speaking; and there was a certain irresponsibility about it all, due I suppose in part to the fact that I am no longer a candidate and am free from the everlasting suspicion and ill-natured judgment which being a candidate entails. Moreover, both in Kentucky, and especially in Texas, I was received with a warmth and heartiness that surprised me; while the Rough Riders' reunion at San Antonio was delightful in every way.

Then came the five days' wolf hunting in Oklahoma, and this was unalloyed pleasure, except for my uneasiness about Auntie Bye and poor little Sheffield. General Young, Dr. Lambert and Roly Fortescue were each in his own way just the nicest companions imaginable, and my Texas hosts were too kind and friendly and openhearted for anything. I want to have the whole party up at Washington next winter. The party got seventeen wolves, three coons, and any number of rattlesnakes. I was in at the death of eleven wolves. The other six wolves were killed by members of the party who were off with bunches of dogs in some place where I was not. I never took part in a row which ended in the death of a wolf without getting through the run in time to see the death. It was tremendous galloping over cut banks, prairie dog towns, flats, creek bottoms, everything. One run was nine miles long and I was the only man in at the finish except the professional wolf hunter Abernathy, who is a really wonderful fellow, catching the wolves alive by thrusting his gloved hands down between their jaws so that they cannot bite. He has caught one wolf alive, tied up this wolf, and then held it on the saddle, followed his dogs in a seven-mile run, and helped kill another wolf. He has a pretty wife and five cunning children of whom he is very proud, and introduced them to me; and I liked him much. We were in the saddle eight or nine hours every day and I am rather glad to have thirty-six hours rest on the cars before starting on my Colorado bear hunt.

Your loving father

May 6, 1905. Glenwood Springs, Colorado
To George Kennan

Confidential

My dear Kennan:

The general idea conveyed by Barry of my conversation was correct, although of course certain sentences were not correct. Your letter interests me immensely.

You cannot feel as badly as I do over such action as that by the idiots of the California Legislature. The California Legislature would have had an entire right to protest as emphatically as possible against the admission of Japanese laborers, for their very frugality, abstemiousness and clannishness make them formidable to our laboring class, and you may not know that they have begun to offer a serious problem in Hawaii—all the more serious because they keep an entirely distinct and alien mass. Moreover, I understand that the Japanese themselves do not permit any foreigners to own land in Japan, and where they draw one kind of a sharp line against us, they have no right whatever to object to our drawing another kind of a line against them. So as I say, I would not have objected at all to the California Legislature passing a resolution, courteous and proper in its terms, which would really have achieved the object they were after. But I do object to, and feel humiliated by, the foolish offensiveness of the resolution they passed

I agree with all you say about the Japanese. I admire them and respect them. I regard them as a highly civilized people, and their feats of heroism in the present war should be an example to us and to all other nations. I am keenly mortified that any Americans should insult such a people. I am powerless myself to do anything more than I have done; that is, in every possible way, personally and officially, to show the utmost courtesy and consideration to the Japanese. If the courts have decided that the Japanese cannot be naturalized, I am powerless. I shall take the matter up to find out exactly what the situation is. It is deeply exasperating to me to see so many of our countrymen doing just exactly the reverse of what I have made the cardinal doctrine of my foreign policy. That is to say, they talk offensively of foreign powers and yet decline ever to make ready for war. I do not believe we shall ever have trouble with Japan; but my own theory is to keep our navy so strong and so efficient that we shall be able to handle Japan if ever the need arises, and at the same time to treat her with scrupulous courtesy and friendliness so that she shall have no excuse for bearing malice toward us. Too many of our people seem wholly unable to grasp, not merely the wisdom, but the common decency of such a policy.

As to what you say about the alliance, the trouble is, my dear Mr.

Kennan, that you are talking academically. Have you followed some of my experiences in endeavoring to get treaties through the Senate? I might just as well strive for the moon as for such a policy as you indicate. Mind you, I personally entirely agree with you. But if you have followed the difficulty I have had even in getting such obvious things done as those connected with Panama and Santo Domingo, you would get some faint idea of the absolute impossibility of carrying out any such policy as that you indicate in your letter.

I look forward to seeing you.

Sincerely yours

May 31, 1905. Washington
To Kentaro Kaneko

Personal

My dear Baron Kaneko:

No wonder you are happy! Neither Trafalgar nor the defeat of the Spanish Armada was as complete—as overwhelming.[1] If you are coming to Washington in the next three weeks, pray let me see you. As Commander Takeshita left my office this morning, the Secretary of the Navy, looking after him, said, "Well, there goes a happy man. Every Japanese, but perhaps above all every Japanese naval man, must feel as if he was treading on air today."

Sincerely yours

June 11, 1905. Washington
To Kermit Roosevelt

Dear Kermit:

Mother and I have just come home from a lovely trip to "Pine Knot." It is really a perfectly delightful little place; the nicest little place of the kind you could imagine. Mother is a great deal more pleased with it than any child with any toy I ever saw, and is too cunning and pretty, and busy for anything. She went down the day before, Thursday, and I followed on Friday morning. Good Mr. Joe Wilmer met me at the station and we rode on horseback to "Round Top," where we met Mother and Mr. Willie Wilmer. We all had tea there and then drove to "Plain Dealing," where we had dinner. Of course I loved both "Round Top" and "Plain Dealing," and as for the two Mr. Wilmers, they are the most generous, thoughtful, self-effacing friends that anyone could wish to see. After dinner we went over to "Pine Knot," put everything to order and

---

[1] The Japanese had just smashed the Russian fleet in the battle of Tsushima Straits.

went to bed. Next day we spent all by ourselves at "Pine Knot." In the morning I fried bacon and eggs, while Mother boiled the kettle for tea and laid the table. Breakfast was most successful, and then Mother washed the dishes and did most of the work, while I did odd jobs, like emptying the slops, etc. Then we walked about the place, which is fifteen acres in all, saw the lovely spring, admired the pine trees and the oak trees, and then Mother lay in the hammock while I cut away some trees to give us a better view from the piazza. The piazza is the real feature of the house. It is broad and runs along the whole length and the roof is high near the wall, for it is a continuation of the roof of the house. It was lovely to sit there in the rocking chairs and hear all the birds by daytime and at night the whippoorwills and owls and little forest folk. Inside, the house is just a bare wall with one big room below, which is nice now, and will be still nicer when the chimneys are up and there is a fireplace in each end. A rough stairs leads above, where there are two rooms, separated by a passageway. We did everything for ourselves, but all the food we had was sent over to us by the dear Wilmers, together with milk. We cooked it ourselves, so there was no one around the house to bother us at all. As we found that cleaning dishes took up an awful time we only took two meals a day, which was all we wanted. On Saturday evening I fried two chickens for dinner, while mother boiled the tea and we had cherries and wild strawberries, as well as biscuits and cornbread. To my pleasure Mother greatly enjoyed the fried chicken, and admitted that what you children had said of the way I fried chicken was all true. In the evening we sat out a long time on the piazza, and then read indoors and then went to bed. Sunday morning we did not get up until nine. Then I fried Mother some beefsteak and some eggs in two frying pans, and she liked them both very much. We went to church at the dear little church where the Wilmers' father and mother had been married, dined soon after two at "Plain Dealing," and then were driven over to the station to go back to Washington. I rode the big black stallion—Chief—and enjoyed it thoroughly. Altogether we had a very nice holiday.

I was lucky to be able to get it, for during the past fortnight, and indeed for a considerable time before, I have been carrying on negotiations with both Russia and Japan, together with side negotiations with Germany, France and England, to try to get the present war stopped. With infinite labor and by the exercise of a good deal of tact and judgment—if I do say it myself—I have finally gotten the Japanese and Russians to agree to meet to discuss the terms of peace. Whether they will be able to come to an agreement or not I can't say. But it is worth while to have obtained the chance of peace, and the only possible way to get this chance was to secure such an agreement of the two powers that they would meet and discuss the terms direct. Of course Japan will want to ask more than she ought to ask, and Russia to give less than she ought to give. Perhaps both sides will prove impracticable. Perhaps one will. But there is the chance that they will prove sensible and make a peace, which will really be for the interest of each as things are now. At any rate the experiment was worth trying. I have kept the secret very successfully, and my dealings with the Japanese in particular have been known to no one, so that the result is in the nature of a surprise.

I am looking forward to seeing you at Bishop Lawrence's. On receipt of your letter I looked up that piece in *Collier's* and I liked the description. Yes, the men who live much in the desert grow to look like that.

Your loving father

June 16, 1905. Washington
To Cecil Spring Rice

Confidential
Dear Springy:

Well, it seems to me that the Russian bubble has been pretty thoroughly pricked. I thought the Japanese would defeat Rojestvensky; but I had no conception, and no one else had any conception save possibly Admiral Evans and Lord Charles Beresford, that there would be a slaughter rather than a fight, and that the Russians would really make no adequate resistance whatever. I have never been able to persuade myself that Russia was going to conquer the world at any time [indecipherable] justified in considering, and I suppose this particular fear is now at an end everywhere.

What wonderful people the Japanese are! They are quite as remarkable industrially as in warfare. In a dozen years the English, Americans and Germans, who now dread one another as rivals in the trade of the Pacific, will have each to dread the Japanese more than they do any other nation. In the middle of this war they have actually steadily increased their exports to China, and are proceeding in the establishment of new lines of steamers in new points of Japanese trade expansion throughout the Pacific. Their lines of steamers are not allowed to compete with one another, but each competes with some foreign line, and usually the competition is to the advantage of the Japanese. The industrial growth of the nation is as marvellous as its military growth. It is now a great power and will be a greater power. As I have always said, I cannot pretend to prophesy what the results, as they affect the United States, Australia, and the European powers with interests in the Pacific, will ultimately be. I believe that Japan will take its place as a great civilized power of a formidable type, and with motives and ways of thought which are not quite those of the powers of our race. My own policy is perfectly simple, though I have not the slightest idea whether I can get my country to follow it. I wish to see the United States treat the Japanese in a spirit of all possible courtesy, and with generosity and justice. At the same time I wish to see our navy constantly built up and each ship kept at the highest possible point of efficiency as a fighting unit. If we follow this course we shall have no trouble with the Japanese or anyone else. But if we bluster; if we behave rather badly to other nations; if we show that we regard the Japanese as an inferior and alien race, and try to treat them as we have treated the Chinese; and if at the same time we fail to keep our navy at the highest point of efficiency and size—then we shall invite disaster.

You of course have seen all that I have had on hand in the matter of the peace negotiations. It has been rather worse than getting a treaty through the United States Senate! Each side has been so suspicious, and often so unreasonable, and so foolish. I am bound to say that the Kaiser has behaved admirably and has really helped me. I hope that your people are sincerely desirous of peace and will use their influence at the proper time to prevent their asking impossible terms. In this particular case I think that peace will be in the interest of all mankind, including both combatants. If the war goes on for a year Japan will drive Russia out of East Asia. But in such a case she will get no indemnity; she will have the terrific strain of an extra year's loss of blood and money; and she will have acquired a territory which will be of no use to her. On the other hand, Russia will have been pushed out of East Asia and will have suffered a humiliating loss which a century could not repair. If they now make peace, Russia giving up Sakhalin and paying a reasonable indemnity—these being the two chief features of the peace, together with Japan retaining control of what she has already obtained— then we shall have Russia with the territory she possessed in East Asia a dozen years ago still practically intact, so that no unbearable humiliation and loss will have been inflicted upon her. Japan will have gained enormously by the war. At the same time each power will be in a sense the guarantor of the other's good conduct. As I told you, I do not need any such guarantee as far as the United States is concerned. In the first place, I do not believe that Japan would menace the United States in any military way; and in the next place, if the menace comes I believe we could be saved only by our own efforts and not by an alliance with anyone else. And I believe that the peace I am trying to get will not be only a good thing temporarily, but will be a good thing permanently. I earnestly hope that your people take the same view, and that they will not permit any feeling that they would like to see both combatants exhausted to prevent them doing all they can to bring about peace. Germany and France should make their influence felt by making Russia willing to yield what she ought to yield; and England should make her influence felt in making the Japanese terms not so severe that Russia, instead of granting them, would prefer to continue the war.

Give my love to Mrs. Springy.

Ever yours

July 11, 1905. Oyster Bay
To Jean Jules Jusserand

My dear Mr. Ambassador:

I read Cahun's *Turks and Mongols* with such thoroughness and assiduity that at the end it was dangling out of the covers, and I have sent it to Washington to have it bound, with directions to deliver it to you.

I am very much obliged to you for loaning it to me, and I have been immensely interested in it. It is extraordinary how little the average European historian has understood the real significance of the immense Mongol movement of the 13th century and its connection with the previous history of the Turks, Mongols, and similar peoples. Until I read Cahun I never understood the sequence of cause and effect and never appreciated the historic importance of the existence of the vast, loosely bound Turkish power of the 5th and 6th centuries and of its proposition to unite with the Byzantines for the overthrow of the Persians. Moreover it is astounding that military critics have given so little space to, or rather have totally disregarded, the extraordinary Mongol campaigns of the 13th century. I doubt if the average military critic so much as knows of the existence of Subutai, who won sixty victories on pitched fields and went from the Yellow Sea to the Adriatic, trampling Russia into the dust, overrunning Hungary and Poland, and defeating with inferior numbers the picked chivalry of Germany as he had already defeated the Manchus, the Korean, and the Chinese. Moreover the victories were not won by brute superiority of numbers. The armies of the Mongols were not at all what we understand when we speak of hordes. They were marvelously trained bodies wherein the prowess of the individual soldier was only less remarkable than the perfect obedience, precision and effectiveness with which he did his part in carrying out the tactical and strategic schemes of the generals. For a Frenchman, Cahun is dry; but the dryness of writers of your race, if they are good at all, is miles asunder from the hopeless aridity of similar writers among our people. Cahun has a really fine phrase, for instance—a phrase that tells an important truth when he contrasts the purely personal and therefore in the end not very important wars of Timur, with what he calls the great "anonymous" campaigns and victories of the Mongols proper under Ghengis Khan and in the years immediately succeeding his death.

Naturally, this difference in dryness makes an immense difference in interest. Thus I took up de La Gorce's history of the Second Empire because of tile allusions to it in Walpole's history, which covers much the same period; but Walpole's history was only readable in the sense that a guidebook or a cookery book is readable; whereas I found de La Gorce exceedingly interesting and filled with much that was philosophical and much that was picturesque.

I wish you could get down here to see me sometime. Now under no circumstances must you permit Madame Jusserand to take a trip that would be tiresome, but if you and she happen to be passing through New York I shall arrange to have the *Sylph* take you out here for lunch and then back in the afternoon, and you would have an enjoyable sail; while Mrs. Roosevelt and I would have an enjoyable lunch!

Always yours

P. S. Since writing this your telegram has come. I hope you both will enjoy your summer to the full. If you see de la Gorce tell him how much I like his work—and that I read every word, & was at times rather painfully struck by certain essential similarities in political human nature whether in an Empire or a Republic, cis-Atlantic or trans-Atlantic.

July 11, 1905. Oyster Bay
To Henry Cabot Lodge

Dear Cabot:

John Hay's death was very sudden and removes from American public life a man whose position was literally unique. The country was the better because he had lived, for it was a fine thing to have set before our men the example of success contained in the career of a man who had held so many and such important public positions, while there was not in his nature the slightest touch of the demagogue, and who in addition to his great career in political life had also left a deep mark in literature. His *Life of Lincoln* is a monument, and of its kind his *Castilian Days* is perfect. This is all very sad for Mrs. Hay. Personally his loss is very great to me because I was very fond of him, and as you know always stopped at his house after church on Sunday to have an hour's talk with him. From the standpoint of the public business—not from the standpoint of the loss to the public of such a figure—the case is different. Of course, what I am about to say I can only say to a close friend, for it seems almost ungenerous. But for two years his health has been such that he could do very little work of importance. His name, his reputation, his staunch loyalty, all made him a real asset of the administration. But in actual work I had to do the big things myself, and the other things I always feared would be badly done or not done at all. He had grown to hate the Kaiser so that I could not trust him in dealing with Germany. When, for instance, the Kaiser made the excellent proposition about the integrity of China, Hay wished to refuse and pointed out where the Kaiser's proposition as originally made contained what was inadvisable. I took hold of it myself, accepted the Kaiser's offer, but at the same time blandly changed it so as to wholly remove the objectionable feature (that is, I accepted it as applying to all of China outside of Manchuria, whereas he had proposed in effect that we should allow Russia to work her sweet will in all northern China) and had Hay publish it in this form. Even before this time in the British Panama canal negotiations I got the treaty in right shape only by securing the correction of all of the original faults. But all this is only for you and me to talk over together, for it is not of the slightest consequence now, and what is of consequence is that America should be the richer by John Hay's high and fine reputation.

I hesitated a little between Root and Taft, for Taft is as you know very close to me. But as soon as I began seriously to think it over I saw there was really no room for doubt whatever, because it was not a choice as far as the Cabinet was concerned between Root and Taft, but a choice of having both instead of one. I was not at all sure that Root would take it, although from various hints I had received I thought the chances at least even. To my great pleasure he accepted at once and was evidently glad to accept and to be back in public life and in the Cabinet in such a position. He will be a tower of strength to us all. I not only hope but believe that he will get on well with the Senate, and he will at once take a great burden off my mind in connection with various subjects, such as Santo Domingo and Venezuela. For a number of months now I have had to be my own Secretary of State, and while I am very glad to be it so far as the broad outlines of the work are concerned, I of course ought not to have to attend to the details.

At Russia's request I asked Japan for an armistice, but I did not expect that Japan would grant it, although I of course put the request as strongly as possible. Indeed I cannot say that I really blame Japan for not granting it, for she is naturally afraid that magnanimity on her part would be misinterpreted and turned to bad account against her. The Japanese envoys have sailed and the Russians I am informed will be here by August first. I think then they can get an armistice. I received a message of thanks from the German Government for my part in securing a conference between Germany and France with the other Powers on the Morocco question. This is a dead secret. Not a word of it has gotten out into the papers; but I became the intermediary between Germany and

France when they seemed to have gotten into an impasse; and have already been cordially thanked by the French Government through Jusserand. I suggested the final terms by which they could come together. Speck acted merely of course as the mouthpiece of the Emperor; but with Jusserand I was able to go over the whole matter, and we finally worked out a conclusion which I think was entirely satisfactory. Do not let anyone, excepting of course Nannie, know of this. Even Whitelaw Reid does not know it. I had told Taft but not Hay. I shall tell Root.

Taft is a great big fellow. He urged me to bring Root into the Cabinet. Of course the papers with their usual hysteria have for the moment completely dropped Taft whom they were all booming violently up to three weeks ago, and are now occupied with their new toy, Root. They are sure that he has come into the Cabinet for the purpose of making himself President, and the more picturesque among them take the view that he stipulated this before he accepted and that I in effect pledged him the Presidency—omitting the trifling detail that even if I had been idiot enough to feel that way, he would not have been idiot enough to think that I had any power in the matter. As a matter of fact I am inclined to think that Taft's being from the west, together with his attitude on corporations, would for the moment make him the more available man. Of course no one can tell what will be the outcome three years hence.

Will you tell Nannie that I have sent her at Nahant one of the Saint-Gaudens inauguration medals. I am very glad we got Saint-Gaudens to do this work. Edith makes believe that she thinks it is a good likeness, of me, which I regard as most wifely on her part. But of the eagle on the reverse I do approve and also of the Latin rendering for "a square deal."

Ever yours

P. S. About the Morocco business I received the following cablegram from Ambassador Tower:

> The German Minister for Foreign Affairs announces to me that the agreement between Germany and France in regard to Morocco was signed in Paris last Saturday. He asked me to communicate the information to you and say that the Government of Germany recognizes the interest which the President has taken in that subject, and greatly appreciates what he has done to bring about a speedy and peaceful solution of the questions at issue.

and also the following from Ambassador Jusserand:

> I leave greatly comforted by the news concerning Morocco, the agreement arrived at is in substance the one we had considered and the acceptation of which you did so very much to secure. Letters just received by me from Paris show that your beneficent influence at this

grave juncture is deeply and gratefully felt. They confirm also what I
guessed was the case, that is that there was a point where more yielding would have been impossible; everybody in France felt it, and
people, braced up silently in view of the possible greatest events.

I consider it rather extraordinary that my suggestions should apparently have gratefully been received by both sides as well as acted
on. A still more extraordinary thing is that the Emperor should have
sent through Speck a statement that he should instruct his delegate to
vote as the United States delegate does on any point where I consider
it desirable. This is a point, however, about which I shall be very wary
of availing myself of.

August 27, 1905. Oyster Bay
To William II

(Telegram)

Peace can be obtained on the following terms: Russia to pay no indemnity whatever and to receive back north half of Sakhalin for which it is
to pay to Japan whatever amount a mixed commission may determine.
This is my proposition to which the Japanese have assented reluctantly
and only under strong pressure from me. The plan is for each of the con-
tending parties to name an equal number of members of the commission and for them themselves to name the odd member. The Japanese
assert that Witte has in principle agreed that Russia should pay something to get back the north half of Sakhalin and indeed he intimated to
me that they might buy it back at a reasonable figure, something on the
scale of that for which Alaska was sold to the United States.

These terms which strike me as extremely moderate I have not presented in this form to the Russian Emperor. I feel that you have more influence with him than either I or anyone else can have. As the situation
is exceedingly strained and the relations between the plenipotentiaries
critical to a degree, immediate action is necessary. Can you not take the
initiative by presenting these terms at once to him? Your success in the
matter will make the entire civilized world your debtor. This proposition
virtually relegates all the unsettled issues of the war to the arbitration of
a mixed commission as outlined above, and I am unable to see how Russia can refuse your request if in your wisdom you see fit to make it.

August 31, 1905. Oyster Bay
To Nicholas II

(Telegram)

I thank you heartily for your message. I congratulate you upon the outcome and I share the feelings of all other sincere well-wishers to peace

in my gratitude for what has been accomplished. I earnestly hope for every blessing upon you and your great country.

September 2, 1905. Oyster Bay
To Alice Roosevelt

Dear Alice:

I hope you will enjoy your Chinese trip. I am curious to hear of your Philippine experiences.

Well, I have had a pretty vigorous summer myself and by no means a restful one, but I do not care in the least, for it seems now that we have actually been able to get peace between Japan and Russia. I have had all kinds of experiences with the envoys and with their Governments, and to the two latter I finally had to write time after time as a very polite but also very insistent Dutch Uncle. I am amused to see the way in which the Japanese kept silent. Whenever I wrote a letter to the Czar the Russians were sure to divulge it, almost always in twisted form, but the outside world never had so much as a hint of any letter I sent to the Japanese. The Russians became very angry with me during the course of the proceedings because they thought I was only writing to them. But they made the amends in good shape when it was over, and the Czar sent me the following cable of congratulation, which I thought rather nice of him:

> Accept my congratulations and warmest thanks for having brought the peace negotiations to a successful conclusion, owing to your personal energetic efforts. My country will gratefully recognize the great part you have played in the Portsmouth peace conference.

It has been a wearing summer, because I have had no Secretary of State and have had to do all the foreign business myself, and as Taft has been absent I have also had to handle everything connected with Panama myself. For the last three months the chief business I have had has been in connection with the peace business, Panama, Venezuela, and Santo Domingo, and about all of these matters I have had to proceed without any advice or help.

It is enough to give anyone a sense of sardonic amusement to see the way in which the people generally, not only in my own country but elsewhere, gauge the work purely by the fact that it succeeded. If I had not brought about peace I should have been laughed at and condemned. Now I am overpraised. I am credited with being extremely longheaded, etc. As a matter of fact I took the position I finally did not of my own volition but because events so shaped themselves that I would have felt as if I was flinching from a plain duty if I had acted otherwise. I advised the

Russians informally to make peace on several occasions last winter, and to this they paid no heed. I had also consulted with the Japanese, telling them what I had told the Russians. It was undoubtedly due to the Japanese belief that I would act squarely that they themselves came forward after their great naval victory and asked me to bring about the conference, but not to let it be known that they had made the suggestion—so of course this is not to be spoken about. Accordingly I undertook the work and of course got the assent of both Governments before I took any public action. Then neither Government would consent to meet where the other wished and the Japanese would not consent to meet at The Hague, which was the place I desired. The result was that they had to meet in this country, and this necessarily threw me into a position of prominence which I had not sought, and indeed which I had sought to avoid—though I feel now that unless they had met here they would never have made peace. Then they met, and after a while came to a deadlock, and I had to intervene again by getting into direct touch with the Governments themselves. It was touch and go, but things have apparently come out right. I say "apparently," because I shall not feel entirely easy until the terms of peace are actually signed. The Japanese people have been much less wise than the Japanese Government, for I am convinced that the best thing for Japan was to give up trying to get any indemnity. The Russians would not have given it; and if the war had gone on the Japanese would simply have spent—that is wasted and worse than wasted—hundreds of millions of dollars additional without getting back what they had already paid out.

At present we are having a house party for Ted and Ethel. Ted and Ethel count themselves as the two first guests, and then, by way of a total change, Steve and Cornelia Landon, and finally Jack Thayer and Martha Bacon. Today is rainy and I look forward with gloomy foreboding to a play in the barn with the smallest folks this afternoon. Mother and I have had lovely rides and rows together. I chop a good deal and sometimes play tennis. I am still rather better than James Roosevelt and Jack.

Give my regards to all who are with you and thank the Griscoms especially for their hospitality.

Your loving father

September 6, 1905. Oyster Bay
To Hermann Speck von Sternberg

Confidential

Dear Speck:

I have just received your most interesting letter of August 21st. What a wonderful people those Romans were. The Emperor has done a bit of work, as characteristic as it is excellent, in excavating and restoring the fort in question. Is it not astonishing how completely the art of war was lost when the Roman Empire broke up? The empire had been a totally artificial product for a couple of centuries when the break came, and it was its extraordinary organization and administration, especially in military matters, which enabled it to go on. Within its borders population had shrunk and the standard of citizenship lowered so that the descendants of the Old Romans, and those (mostly themselves the descendants of slaves) who were associated with them in citizenship, had become for the most part beneath contempt; and yet their military science and traditions, that enabled them to build such forts as that you describe and to train their soldiers to use such weapons as that you describe, still enabled them to overmatch tumultuous hordes of brave barbarians.

When the crash came these barbarians were not intellectually sufficiently advanced to make any use of the weapons of war which the Romans had through centuries evolved; and even the memory of scientific warfare perished.

I sent you the two notes I had sent the Mikado's Government for I felt that you ought to understand, and that the Emperor ought to understand, the pressure I had brought to bear upon Japan. We were only able to make the Czar yield on one point, but that was the vital point of the southern half of Sakhalin. The Japanese are now having trouble with their own people at home, and Griscom has just cabled us that there is heavy rioting in Tokyo and a tendency to attack all foreigners. Why in the world the Japanese statesmen, usually so astute, permitted their people to think they had to get a large indemnity, I cannot understand. If they had in the beginning blown their trumpets over the immense amount they were getting; if they had shown how Korea was theirs, Manchuria in effect theirs, Port Arthur and Dalny theirs; how they had won a triumph which since the days of Napoleon has only been paralleled by Germany in 1870—if they had done all this I think they could have made their people feel proud instead of humiliated. The governing class in Japan have appeared very well, but the people, at least in Tokyo, are making much such an exhibition of themselves as the Russians have been making in their own homes. I do most earnestly hope that the Czar will turn his attention in good faith to reform at home.

I enclose to the Baroness—to whom I beg you will give our warm regards—that Japanese book for the Princess Ratibor, which I have at last succeeded in obtaining.

I have written Senator Aldrich to see if we cannot arrange for the negotiations on the tariff as you suggest, and I hope it can be done.

I look forward to seeing you in Washington.

Faithfully yours

P.S. Your second letter has just come. I did my best to get Pierpont Morgan and the Hankow concession people to stand to their guns, but they would not do it, stating (and I think with truth) that they could not without improperly disregarding the interest of their stockholders. They said that the price offered them was large—probably much larger than they could get in the way of damages before any arbitral body— and that if the Chinese would not allow the railroad to be built all they could hope for was damages. I am greatly interested in what you tell me about the English Government authorizing a loan for the amount to be paid. I have heard utterly conflicting accounts as to how this money was to be paid. I shall want to talk all this over with you in October.

If you see His Majesty tell him (but only for his own ear) that in Meyer's last audience with the Czar the latter commented upon the fact that whenever Meyer made a visit to him, simultaneously there came a cable from the German Emperor. I think this may amuse the Emperor.

I myself am both amused and interested as to what you say about the interest excited about my trip in the *Plunger*. I went down in it chiefly because I did not like to have the officers and enlisted men think I wanted them to try things I was reluctant to try myself. I believe a good deal can be done with these submarines, although there is always the danger of people getting carried away with the idea and thinking that they can be of more use than they possibly could be.

September 8, 1905. Oyster Bay
To Carl Schurz

Personal

My dear Mr. Schurz:

I thank you for your congratulations. As to what you say about dis- armament—which I suppose is the rough equivalent of "the gradual diminution of the oppressive burdens imposed upon the world by armed peace"—I am not clear either what can be done or what ought to be done. If I had been known as one of the conventional type of peace advocates I could have done nothing whatever in bringing about peace now, I would be powerless in the future to accomplish anything, and I would not have been able to help confer the boons upon Cuba, the Philippines, Porto Rico and Panama, brought about by our action therein. If the Japanese had not armed during the last twenty years, this would indeed be a sorrowful century for Japan. If this country had not fought the Spanish War; if we had failed to take the action we did about Panama; all mankind would have been the loser. While the Turks were butchering the Armenians the European powers kept the peace and thereby added a burden of infamy to the Nineteenth Century, for in keeping that peace a greater number of lives were lost than in any European war since the days of Napoleon, and these lives were those of women and children as well as of men; while the moral degradation, the brutality inflicted and endured, the aggregate of hideous wrong done, surpassed that of any war of which we have record in modern times. Until people get it firmly fixed in their minds that peace is valuable chiefly as a means to righteousness, and that it can only be considered as an end when it also coincides with righteousness, we can do only a limited amount to advance its coming on this earth. There is of course no analogy at present between international law and private or municipal law, because there is no sanction of force for the former while there is for the latter. Inside our own nation the law-abiding man does not have to arm himself against the lawless simply because there is some armed force—the police, the sheriff's posse, the national guard, the regulars—which can be called out to enforce the laws. At present there is no similar international force to call on, and I do not as yet see how it could at present be created. Hitherto peace has often come only because some strong and on the whole just power has by armed force, or the threat of armed force, put a stop to disorder. In a very interesting French book the other day I was reading of how the Mediterranean was freed from pirates only by the "pax Britannica," established by England's naval force. The hopeless and hideous bloodshed and wickedness of Algiers and Turkestan were stopped, and only could be stopped, when civilized nations in the shape of Russia and France took possession of them. The same was true of Burma and the Malay states, as well as Egypt, with regard to England. Peace has come only as the sequel to the armed interference of a civilized power which, relatively to its opponent, was a just and beneficent power. If England had disarmed to the point of being unable to conquer the Sudan and protect Egypt, so that the Mahdists had established their supremacy in northeastern Africa, the result would have been a horrible and bloody calamity to mankind. It was only the growth of the European powers in military efficiency that freed eastern Europe from the dreadful scourge of the Tartar and partially freed it from the dreadful scourge of the Turk. Unjust war is dreadful; a just war may be the highest duty. To have the best nations, the free and civilized nations, disarm and leave the despotisms and barbarisms with great military force, would be a calamity compared to which the calamities caused by all the wars of the Nineteenth Century would be trivial. Yet it is not easy to see how we can by international agreement state exactly which power ceases to be free and civilized and which comes near the line of barbarism or despotism. For example, I suppose it would be very difficult to get Russia and Japan to come to a common agreement on this point; and there are at least some citizens of other nations, not to speak of their governments, whom it would also be hard to get together.

This does not in the least mean that it is hopeless to make the effort. It may be that some scheme will be developed. America, fortunately, can cordially assist in such an effort, for no one in his senses would suggest our disarmament; and though we should continue to perfect our small navy and our minute army, I do not think it necessary to increase the number of our ships—at any rate as things look now—nor the number of our soldiers. Of course our navy must be kept up to the highest point of efficiency, and the replacing of old and worthless vessels by first-class new ones may involve an increase in the personnel; but not enough to interfere with our action along the lines you have suggested. But before I would know how to advocate such action, save in some such way as commending it to the attention of The Hague Tribunal, I would have to have a feasible and rational plan of action presented.

Sincerely yours

[Handwritten] It seems to me that a general stop in the increase of the war navies of the world *might* be a good thing; but I would not like to speak too positively offhand. Of course it is only in continental Europe that the armies are too large; and before advocating action as regards them I should have to weigh matters carefully—including by the way such a matter as the Turkish army. At any rate nothing useful can be done unless with the clear recognition that we put peace second to righteousness.

September 29, 1905. Oyster Bay
To Charles W. Eliot

Personal

My dear President Eliot:

I have been really concerned by the reported outrageous conduct of the newspapers in reference to Ted. I care less than nothing about what they do or say about me, for I am entirely competent to defend myself and I am past the stage where they can do me any material damage; but it is perfectly possible for them to create in the minds of Ted's fellow college boys an opinion about Ted which will go far toward seriously interfering with the enjoyment and the profit of his college career. They published the statement that he had a room in Claverly, thereby giving the impression that he had begun with a splurge. The room is a small one, for which he pays $150; less than I paid for my own when I was in college. I have given him an allowance of $1200. The boy is an ordinary boy, who I believe will study well, who is fond of sports but not especially proficient in them. In addition to the unspeakable vulgarity of the references of the papers to him before he got to Harvard, I see that with a spirit of even grosser offense against good taste, in utter heedlessness of the possible lasting damage they could do him, they have been trying to take kodak pictures of him as he walked about the yard, and I suppose they will make similar attempts if he goes on the football field. I am inclined to tell him, if he sees any man taking a photograph of him, to run up and smash the camera, but I do not like to do this if you would disapprove. Is there no way he can be protected? I do not suppose you could interfere; I don't even suppose it would be possible to tell one or two of the influential college men to put an instant stop to the cameras, and to the newspapermen running around after Ted. I suppose there would not be the slightest use in my writing to the papers. It would only accentuate things.

I must apologize for bothering you about what must seem to you an insignificant matter; but this crass, hideous vulgarity is not merely extremely distasteful, but may have a very damaging effect upon poor Ted, at least in his relation to the other boys, and in the very improbable event of your having any advice to give, I should be glad to get it.

With high regard,

Sincerely yours

October 2, 1905. Washington
To Theodore Roosevelt, Jr.

Blessed old Ted:

You have been having an infernal time through these cursed newspapers. I was so indignant that I wrote to President Eliot about it, and I felt positively warlike. I have been talking it over with Gifford Pinchot[1] and some other college fellows, and we are all agreed that it is just one of the occasions where the big bear cannot help the small bear at all, though he sympathizes awfully with him. The thing to do is to go on just as you have evidently been doing, attract as little attention as possible, do not make a fuss about the newspapermen, camera creatures, and idiots generally, letting it be seen that you do not like them and avoid them, but not letting them betray you into any excessive irritation. I believe they will soon drop you, and it is just an unpleasant thing that you will have to live down. Ted, I have had an enormous number of unpleasant things that I have had to live down in my life at different times, and you have begun to have them now. I saw that you were not out on the football field on Saturday and was rather glad of it, as evidently

---

[1]Head of the Forestry Service and a close Roosevelt friend and ally.

these infernal idiots were eagerly waiting for you; but whenever you do go you will have to make up your mind that they will make it exceedingly unpleasant for you for once or twice, and you will just have to bear it; for you can never in the world afford to let them drive you away from anything you intend to do, whether it is football or anything else, and by going about your own business quietly and pleasantly, doing just what you would do if they were not there, gradually they will get tired of it, and the boys themselves will see that it is not your fault and will feel, if anything, rather a sympathy for you. Meanwhile I want you to know that we are all thinking of you and sympathizing with you the whole time; and it is a great comfort to me to have such confidence in you and to know that though these creatures can cause you a little trouble and make you feel a little downcast, they cannot drive you one way or the other, or make you alter the course you have set out for yourself.

We were all of us, I am almost ashamed to say, rather blue at getting back in the White House, simply because we missed Sagamore Hill so much. But it is very beautiful and we feel very ungrateful at having even a temporary fit of blueness, and we are enjoying it to the full now. I have just seen Archie dragging some fifty foot of hose pipe across the tennis court to play in the sand box. I have been playing tennis with Mr. Pinchot, who beat me three sets to one, the only deuce set being the one I won.

Your loving father

[Handwritten] This is just an occasion to show the stuff there is in you. Do'n't let these newspaper creatures and kindred idiots drive you one hairsbreadth from the line you had marked out, in football or anything else; & avoid any fuss, if possible.

November 20, 1905. Washington
To Ray Stannard Baker

Personal

My dear Mr. Baker:

I have your letter enclosing advance proof of your article. I think you are entirely mistaken in your depreciation of what is accomplished by fixing a maximum rate. Surely you must see that if the Commission has the power to make the maximum rate that which the railroad gives to the most favored shipper, it will speedily become impossible thus to favor any shipper save in altogether exceptional cases. I have gone all over the question of allowing the Commission to condemn the rate instead of fixing it, and am convinced that there is nothing in it. The railroads would eagerly accept such a proposition, because it would really leave the situation untouched. They would put in a new rate differing hardly at all from the old one. Fixing a maximum rate will not do all that is desired; but the power merely to condemn a rate and not to say what rate shall go into effect in its place would, I think, be a sham. I do not think it would accomplish any of the things that we wish. I shall go over your letter with Mr. Moody.

Do remember that while it is above all important to keep in mind the fact that there can be a substantial alleviation of almost every evil, it is of only secondary importance to keep in mind the further fact that no given measure and no given set of measures will work a perfect cure for any serious evil; and the insistence upon having only the perfect cure often results in securing no betterment whatever. I have had a great deal to do with railroads in the West, and a great deal to do with eastern legislatures which were dealing with railroads. I have often been impressed by the swinish indifference to right by certain railroad men in dealing both with the people and with railroads; but I am bound in honor to say that I have seen ten such exhibitions of indifference to the rights of railroads among legislatures and even among communities for one that I have seen among the railroad people themselves. This is doubtless in part due to the fact that there are a great many more people who are not railroad kings than there are people who are railroad kings; but the fact remains that if you would examine the bills introduced in the New York legislature, for instance, about corporations, you would see that there are ten so-called strike bills—blackmail bills, ten bills improperly attacking railroads—for one bill to the improper advantage of railroads, or for one bill against their interests which ought to pass and of which they secure the defeat. Now, no dealing with the railroad problem is going to accomplish anything permanent unless as its main feature it contains insistence upon the fact that the first essential is honesty, and that the public conscience which regards with amused tolerance or approval a blackmailing attempt upon a railroad prepares the way for that railroad itself, by improper methods, getting something it ought not to have at some other time. Moreover, remember that if the management of the railroads was literally ideal there would remain an immense volume of complaint from individuals and localities; some of these complaints being due to simple ignorance, some to the fact that those who are foredoomed to failure like to cast the blame for their failure upon others.

So much for legislatures; now for the people at large. I have lived—not merely sojourned in, but lived—in Western communities where there were not railroads. Until railroads are built there is nothing the community will not promise in order to get them in; and I regret to state that after the railroad has come in the whole community is only too apt to pay attention to the demagogue who tries under one form or another to get them to repudiate their solemn promises to the railroad. They often promise too much; and they often fail to perform anything. Any movement conducted not on the ground of insisting upon justice to the railroads as well as *from* the railroads—any movement which limits itself simply to an attack upon railroads or upon the big corporations, is necessarily carried on in a spirit which invites disaster.

The railroads have been crazy in their hostility to my maximum rate proposition, and evidently do not share in the least your belief that nothing will result from it. I think that their alarm is foolishly overdrawn; and I have not a question that if we get the legislation there will be bitter disappointment among the people who expect, and have been taught to expect, the impossible. That it will accomplish some good I am certain. Moreover, it gives us a definite point of leverage. A single year's experience by the Commission in the enforcement of the maximum rate will show whether or not it fails in its purpose, as you anticipate that it will. If it makes such complete failure I do not believe there will be difficulty in at least trying the experiment in some shape or other of the definite rate. Meanwhile, I am absolutely certain that to adopt your proposal to substitute the power to condemn a rate for what we propose to do, would give not one particle of relief of any kind. I would not regard it as a bad power; I would simply regard it as a wholly ineffective power. I think it probably exists already; but if anyone wants to embody it in the bill, I have not the slightest objection, provided it is put in a separate paragraph so that there is no chance of its destroying the effect of the bill. I do not think it would accomplish any harm. I think it would merely accomplish nothing.

Sincerely yours

November 21, 1905. Washington
To James Brander Matthews

Personal

Dear Brander:

I am hurt and grieved at your evident jealousy of my poetic reputation. Evidently you have not read my notable review of the epic poems of Mr. Robinson,[1] or you would appreciate that, even though I have not written poetry myself, I have yet shown such keen appreciation of the poetry of other great poets that I felt justified in securing the insertion of that advertisement. If you saw my review of Mr. Robinson's poems you

---

[1] Edward Arlington Robinson, Roosevelt's favorite living poet. Roosevelt gave him a federal job that allowed him time to write.

may have noticed that I refrained from calling him "our American Homer." This was simply due to the fact that I hoped some discerning friend would see where the epithet ought to go; less perhaps as an acknowledgment of what I have actually done, than as an inspiration and prophecy concerning the future.

Regretfully and reproachfully yours

[Handwritten] When are you coming on here?

November 24, 1905. Washington
To Walter W. Camp

My dear Mr. Camp:

Ted (who, as you probably know, played on the Harvard freshman eleven) wrote me as follows:

> All that talk about the Yale boys laying for me was a lie. They played a clean, straight game and played no favorites. I met a good many of them whom I knew after the game and we had a friendly drink together. They beat us by simply and plainly outplaying us.

If you happen to see Mr. McClintock, who is said to have been the coach of the Yale freshmen, will you show him this?

Ted evidently thoroughly enjoyed himself. His letter runs on, in part, as follows:

> Well, I am very glad that I made the team anyway. I feel so large in my black sweater with the numerals on. Saturday's game was a hard one, as I knew it was bound to be. I was not seriously hurt at all. Just shaken up and bruised. I broke my nose.

In a letter to his mother he says:

> The report in the paper about Yale directing their interference against me was all bosh. Of course I knew all the rotten talk would come out in the papers, but it could not be helped.

Sutro, formerly of Princeton, tells me that the Yale-Princeton game was as cleanly played as any game could be. I believe your efforts have borne real fruit for good.

Sincerely yours

P.S. I have just received your letter of the 22d, with enclosed clipping. Although not quite accurate, that report has a substantial basis of truth. It was Cotty Peabody who first asked that I should hold the meeting, and certain graduates of Harvard, Yale and Princeton wrote suggesting it. The statement in the papers is inaccurate, but it would have been accurate if it had said instead of "representatives of Harvard, Yale and Princeton," "graduates of Harvard, Yale and Princeton." A very prominent representative of Columbia before the meeting was held suggested that I should have a Columbia man present, and I told him that I did not see how I could do that without having Pennsylvania and Cornell men, and that as the proposition had orginally been made to me by graduates of Harvard, Yale and Princeton I did not think it wise to go beyond those three colleges. My own judgment is that it is not worth while discussing the matter further. The initiative was through me, and college politics had no place in it in any shape or way.

November 27, 1905. Washington
To Gifford Pinchot

My dear Mr. Pinchot:

The great importance I attach to the grazing problem throughout the West has led me to interrupt your work on the Committee on Department Methods, so that you might attend the meeting at Glenwood Springs. In dealing with this problem I should like to have you remember that recent investigations have demonstrated the destructive character of the free range system in the past. A very large proportion of the vacant public lands are valuable at present only for grazing. The grazing value of much of these lands is not now more than half what it once was. It therefore becomes the duty of the Government to see to it that in the future these lands are used in a way that will preserve their grazing value and give them the greatest usefulness to the people.

In the forest reserves the question becomes doubly important, because the future welfare of almost the entire West depends upon the preservation of the water supply, and this in turn upon the wise use of the forests and the range.

It must not be forgotten that the forest reserves belong to all the people, but the grazing privilege can be used only by a few. It is therefore only just and right that those who enjoy the special advantages of a protected range should contribute toward the expense of handling the reserves.

Important progress has been made in the forest reserves in the practical solution of the grazing problems, and I heartily approve the general policy outlined in the new rules and regulations.

Sincerely yours

December 7, 1905. Washington
To David Starr Jordan

My dear President[1] Jordan:

Indeed I shall be very glad to have those fish[2] named after me. Who would not be?

It was such a pleasure to see you here the other day.

Sincerely yours

December 14, 1905. Washington
To Jacob H. Schiff

My dear Mr. Schiff:

I sent your previous letter to Secretary Root. I did not answer it because, my dear Mr. Schiff, I must frankly say that it would be difficult to answer it without hurting your feelings. You made a request for action on my part which if I took it would make the United States Government ridiculous, and so far from helping the condition of the Jews would have hurt them in Russia and would have tended to hurt them here. It is simply nonsense to suppose that when Russia is in the condition that she now is any kind of action on my part would accomplish anything. When the governmental authorities in Russia are wholly unable to protect themselves—when there is revolt in every quarter of the empire among every class of the people—and the bonds of social order everywhere are relaxed, it is idle to suppose that anything can be done by diplomatic representation. The idea of a European coalition in which we should join is of course wholly chimerical. What would such a coalition do: enforce liberty or order—restore the autocracy or install a republic? Therefore it is evident we could do nothing, and where we can do nothing I have a horror of saying anything. We never have taken—and while I am President we never will take—any action which we cannot make good. Why, my dear Mr. Schiff, the case was much simpler as regards the Armenians a few years ago. There the Turkish Government was responsible and was able to enforce whatever was desired. The outrages on the Armenians were exactly the same as those perpetrated upon the Jews of Russia both in character and in extent. But we did not go to war with Turkey. Inasmuch as it was certain that our people would not go into such a war, at least with the determination for the lavish outlay of blood and money necessary to make it effective, it would have been worse than foolish to have threatened it, and not the slightest good would have been or was gained by any agitation which it was known would not be backed up by

---

[1] Of Stanford University.

[2] The Roosevelt golden trout.

arms. I shall take no action until I know that any action I take will do good instead of harm, and I shall announce no position which I may have to abandon at the cost of putting the United States Government in a humiliating and ridiculous attitude. I thoroughly believe that in national affairs we should act in accordance with the plains adage when I was in the ranch business: "Never to draw unless you mean to shoot."

Sincerely yours

P.S. I sympathize thoroughly with your feelings, wrought up as they are and ought to be by the dreadful outrages committed on the Jews in Russia; anything I can do I will do; but I will not threaten aimlessly and thereby do harm.

December 21, 1905. Washington
To James Wilson

My dear Mr. Secretary:

I have received your letter of December 20th. I cordially approve of the policy you are carrying on. Your effort is to keep the grazing lands in the forest reserves for the use of the stockmen, and especially the small stockmen, who actually live in the neighborhood of the reserves. To prevent the waste and destruction of the reserves and to keep them so that they can be permanently used by the stockmen no less than by the public, you have to spend a certain amount of money. Part of this money is to be obtained by charging a small fee for each head of stock pastured on the reserve. Less than a third of the actual value of the grazing is at present charged, and it is of course perfectly obvious that the man who pastures his stock should pay something for the preservation of that pasture. He gets all the benefit of the pasture and he pays for its use but a small fraction of the value that it is to him; and this money is in reality returned to him because it is used in keeping the forest reserve permanently available for use. You this year make a special reduction by which the small ranchmen pay but half rates. This is in accordance with the steady policy of your department as regards the western lands, which is to favor in every way the actual settler, the actual homemaker, the man who himself tills the soil or himself rears and cares for his small herd of cattle. In granting grazing permits you give preference first to the small near-by owners; after that, to all regular occupants of the reserve range; and finally to the owners of transient stock. This is exactly as it should be. The small near-by owners are the homesteaders, the men who are making homes for themselves by the labor of their hands, the men who have entered to possess the land and to bring up their children therein. The other regular occupants of the reserve range—that is, the larger ranch owners—are only entitled to come after the smaller men. If after these have been admitted there still remains an ample pasturage, then the owners of transient stock, the men who drive great tramp herds or tramp flocks hither and thither, should be admitted. These men have no permanent abode, do but very little to build up the land, and are not to be favored at the expense of the regular occupants, large or small. This system prevents the grass from being eaten out by the great herds or flocks of non-residents, for only enough cattle and sheep are admitted upon the reserves to fatten upon the pasturage without damaging it. In other words, under the policy you have adopted the forest reserves are to be used as among the most potent influences in favor of the actual homemaker, of the man with a few dozen or few score head of cattle, which he has gathered by his own industry and is himself caring for. This is the kind of man upon whom the foundations of our citizenship rest, and it is eminently proper to favor him in every way.

Sincerely yours

January 22, 1906. Washington
To Leonard Wood

Dear Leonard:

I regarded your letter as not merely very interesting but very able. I entirely agree with you about fortifying the Sandwich Islands; and wish you had a little experience in the difficulties of getting Congress to agree with me in such matters! Moreover, I entirely agree with you that we can retain the Philippines only so long as we have a first-class fighting navy, superior to the navy of any possible opponent. I do not for a moment agree, however, that Japan has any immediate intention of moving against us in the Philippines. Her eyes for some time to come will be directed toward Korea and southern Manchuria. If she attacked us and met disaster, she would lose everything she has gained in the war with Russia; and if she attacked us and won, she would make this republic her envenomed and resolute foe for all time, and would without question speedily lose the alliance with Great Britain and see a coalition between Russia, the United States, and very possibly Germany and France to destroy her in the Far East. No man can prophesy about the future, but I see not the slightest chance of Japan attacking us in the Philippines for a decade or two, or until the present conditions of international politics change.

I entirely agree with you in what you say about the Chinese situation. Under no circumstances would I ever approve any legislation admitting any form of Chinese labor into the United States; and I agree entirely with your criticism upon the English colonies.

As for what you say about the legislation for the Philippine Islands,

I agree with most of it, but I am amused at your falling into the common mistake of thinking that the United States shipping laws apply to the islands. They do not have any application to the Philippine Islands at all. The shipping regulations of the islands are subject to the Commission, and the American coastwise shipping laws as yet have never been applied to the islands. I am trying to prevent their being applied, and I am also trying to secure the abolition of the Philippine tariff.

With love to Mrs. Wood, believe me,

Faithfully yours

January 24, 1906. Washington
To Jane Addams

My dear Miss Addams:

Good for you! I shall see Mr. Neill, and tell him to keep me informed if there is anything I can do to help out.

Will you let me say a word of very sincere thanks to you for the eminent sanity, good humor and judgment you always display in pushing matters you have at heart? I have such awful times with reformers of the hysterical and sensational stamp, and yet I so thoroughly believe in reform, that I fairly revel in dealing with anyone like you.

With all good wishes, believe me,

Sincerely yours

February 3, 1906. Washington
To Kermit Roosevelt

Dear Kermit:

I agree pretty well with your views of *David Copperfield*. Dora was very cunning and attractive, but I am not sure that the husband would retain enough respect for her to make life quite what it ought to be with her. This is a harsh criticism and I have known plenty of women of the Dora type whom I have felt were a good deal better than the men they married, and I have seen them sometimes make very happy homes. I also feel as you do that if a man had to struggle on and make his way it would be a great deal better to have someone like Sophie. Do you recollect that dinner at which David Copperfield and Traddles were, where they are described as seated at the dinner, one "in the glare of the red velvet lady" and the other "in the gloom of Hamlet's aunt?" I am so glad you like Thackeray. *Pendennis* and *The Newcomes* and *Vanity Fair* I can read over and over again.

Ted blew in today. I think he has been studying pretty well this term and now he is through all his examinations but one. He hopes, and I do, that you will pay what attention you can to athletics. Play hockey for instance, and try to get into shape for the mile run. I know it is too short a distance for you, but if you will try for the hare and hounds running and the mile too, you may be able to try for the two miles when you go to Harvard.

The weather was very mild early in the week. It has turned cold now; but Mother and I had a good ride yesterday, and Ted and I a good ride this afternoon, Ted on Grey Dawn. We have been having a perfect whirl of dinner engagements; but thank heavens they will stop shortly after Sister's wedding.

Your loving father

February 17, 1906. Washington
To Charles J. Bonaparte[1]

My dear Mr. Secretary:

I forgot to bring up one thing with you and Admiral Sands yesterday. I am not satisfied about the giving up of the judo or jujitsu at the Naval Academy. It is not physical exercise so much as it is an extraordinarily successful means of self-defense and training in dexterity and decision. Naturally, elderly men of a routine habit of mind who have known nothing whatever of it are against it; but I know enough of boxing, wrestling, rough-and-tumble fighting, and of the very art in question to be absolutely certain that it is of real and on occasions may be of great use to any man whose duties are such as a naval officer's may at any time become. I should like to have it continued next year at the Naval Academy.

With great regard,
Sincerely yours

To Charles Joseph Bonaparte
Washington, February 21, 1906

The Secretary of the Navy:

In the recent war in the East Admiral Togo took his place among the great sea fighters of all time. His message to the United Squadron which he commanded, on the occasion of its dispersal at the close of the war, is so noteworthy that I deem it proper to have it inserted in a general order of the Department.

The qualities which make a formidable fighting man, on sea or on shore, and which therefore make a formidable army or navy, are the same for all nations. The individual men must have the fighting edge; there must be in them courage, determination, individual initiative, combined

---

[1]Secretary of the Navy.

with willingness to learn and subordination of self, together with physical address, in order that they may form the stuff out of which in the aggregate good armies and navies are made; but in addition to this there
must be preparedness—there must be thorough training in advance.
Every American officer and enlisted man, whether serving in the army or
the navy, should keep ever before his eyes the fact that he will not be fit
thoroughly to do his work in the event of war unless in peace he has thoroughly done the work of preparing for war. If in peace the soldier and the
sailor abandon themselves to ease and sloth, when war comes they will
go down before rivals who have been less self-indulgent. Nor is it only the
men of the army and the navy who should constantly remember these
facts. In a great self-governing republic like ours the army and the navy
can be only so good as the mass of the people wish them to be. The citizens of our country owe it to themselves and to their children and their
children's children that there shall be no chance of having the national
honor tarnished, the national flag stained with aught that is discreditable.
The men of the army and the navy, in any great crisis such as even the
most peaceful nation may at times have to face, will be those upon whom
the especial responsibility will rest of keeping the nation's honor bright
and unsullied. They cannot do this if the nation does not exercise forethought on their behalf. We must have an adequate navy and an adequate
army in point of size; they must be provided with the most effective
mechanism in the form of weapons and other material; above all they
must be given every chance in time of peace to train themselves so that
they may be adepts in handling the mechanism, and be fitted in body and
in mind unflinchingly to endure the tremendous strain and bear the
tremendous responsibility of war.

Omitting certain allusions having no bearing on our conditions,
the address runs as follows:

The war of twenty months' duration is now a thing of the past, and
our United Squadron, having completed its functions, is to be herewith
dispersed. But our duties as naval men are not at all lightened for that
reason. To preserve in perpetuity the fruits of this war, to promote to an
ever greater height of prosperity the fortunes of the country, the Navy,
which, irrespective of peace or war, has to stand between the Empire
and shocks from abroad, must always maintain its strength at sea and
must be prepared to meet any emergency. This strength does not consist solely in ships and armament; it consists also in immaterial ability
to utilize such agents. When we understand that one gun which scores
a hundred per cent of hits is a match for a hundred of the enemy's guns
each of which scores only one per cent, it becomes evident that we
sailors must have recourse before everything to the strength which is

over and above externals. The triumphs recently won by our Navy are largely to be attributed to the habitual training which enabled us to garner the fruits of the fighting. If then we infer the future from the past, we recognize that though war may cease we cannot abandon ourselves to ease and rest. A soldier's whole life is one continuous and unceasing battle, and there is no reason why his responsibilities should vary with the state of the times. In days of crisis he has to display his strength; in days of peace to accumulate it, thus perpetually and uniquely discharging his duties to the full. It was no light task that during the past year and a half we fought with wind and waves, encountered heat and cold, and kept the sea while frequently engaging a stubborn enemy in a death-or-life struggle; yet, when we reflect, this is seen to have been only one in a long series of general maneuvers, wherein we had the happiness to make some discoveries; happiness which throws into comparative insignificance the hardships of war. If men calling themselves sailors grasp at the pleasures of peace, they will learn the lesson that however fine in appearance their engines of war, these, like a house built on the sand, will, fail at the first approach of the storm. From the day when in ancient times we conquered Korea, that country remained for over 400 years under our control, only to be lost immediately so soon as our navy declined. Again when under the sway of the Tokugawa in modern days our armaments were neglected, the coming of a few American ships threw us into distress, and we were unable to offer any resistance to attempts against the Kuriles and Sakhalin. On the other hand, if we turn to the annals of the Occident, we see that at the beginning of the 19th century the British Navy which won the battles of the Nile and of Trafalgar, not only made England as secure as a great mountain but also by thenceforth carefully maintaining its strength and keeping it on a level with the world's progress, has throughout the long interval between that era and the present day safeguarded the country's interests and promoted its fortunes. For such lessons, whether ancient or modern, Occidental or Oriental, though to some extent they are the outcome of political happenings, must be regarded as in the main the natural result of whether the soldier remembers war in the day of peace. We naval men who have survived the war must take these examples deeply to heart, and adding to the training which we have already received our actual experiences in the war, must plan future developments and seek not to fall behind the progress of the time. If, keeping the instructions of our Sovereign ever graven on our hearts, we serve earnestly and diligently, and putting forth our full strength, await what the hour may bring forth, we shall then have discharged our great duty of perpetually guarding our country. Heaven gives the crown of victory to those only who by habitual preparation win without fighting, and at the same time forthwith deprives of that crown those who, content with one success, give themselves up to the case of peace. The ancients well said: "Tighten your helmet strings in the hour of victory."

(Dated) 21st December, 1905.

Togo Heihachiro.

I commend the above address to every man who is or may be a part of the fighting force of the United States, and to every man who believes that, if ever, unhappily, war should come, it should be so conducted as to reflect credit upon the American nation.

March 15, 1906. Washington
To Upton Sinclair[2]

My dear Mr. Sinclair:

I have your letter of the 13th instant. I have now read, if not all, yet a good deal of your book, and if you can come down here during the first week in April I shall be particularly glad to see you.

I do not think very much of your ecclesiastical correspondent. A quarter of a century's hard work over what I may call politico-sociological problems has made me distrust men of hysterical temperament. I think the preacher furnishes his measure when he compares you to Tolstoy, Zola and Gorki, intending thereby to praise you. The abortiveness of the late revolution in Russia sprang precisely from the fact that too much of the leadership was of the Gorki type and therefore the kind of leadership which can never lead anybody anywhere save into a Serbonian bog. Of course the net result of Zola's writings has been evil. Where one man has gained from them a shuddering horror at existing wrong which has impelled him to try to right that wrong, a hundred have simply had the lascivious, the beast side of their natures strengthened and intensified by them. Oliver Wendell Holmes has an excellent paragraph on this in his *Over the Teacups*. As for Tolstoy, his novels are good, but his so-called religious and reformatory writings constitute one of the age-forces which tell seriously for bad. His *Kreutzer Sonata* could only have been written by a man of diseased moral nature, a man in whose person the devotee and debauchee alternately obtain sway, as they sometimes do in successive generations of decadent families or in whole communities of unhealthy social conditions. In the end of your book, among the various characters who preach socialism, almost all betray the pathetic belief that the individual capacity which is unable to

---

[2]Muckraking socialist author of *The Jungle*.

raise itself even in the comparatively simple work of directing the individual how to earn his own livelihood, will, when it becomes the
banded incapacity of all the people, succeed in doing admirably a form
of government work infinitely more complex, infinitely more difficult
than any which the most intelligent and highly developed people has
ever yet successfully tried. Personally I think that one of the chief early
effects of such attempt to put socialism of the kind there preached into
practice, would be the elimination by starvation, and the diseases, moral
and physical, attendant upon starvation, of that same portion of the
community on whose behalf socialism would be invoked. Of course you
have read Wyckoff's account of his experiences as an unskilled laborer
of the lowest class. Probably you know him. He was a Princeton man
wholly without the physique to do manual labor as well as the ordinary
manual laborer can do it, yet in going across the continent his experience was that in every place, sooner or later, and in most places very
soon indeed, a man not very strong physically and working at trades
that did not need intelligence, could raise himself to a position where he
had steady work and where he could save and lead a self-respecting life.
There are doubtless communities where such self-raising is very hard
for the time being; there are unquestionably men who are crippled by
accident (as by being old and having large families dependent on them);
there are many, many men who lack any intelligence or character and
who therefore cannot thus raise themselves. But while I agree with you
that energetic, and, as I believe, in the long run radical, action must be
taken to do away with the effects of arrogant and selfish greed on the
part of the capitalist, yet I am more than ever convinced that the real factor in the elevation of any man or any mass of men must be the development within his or their hearts and heads of the qualities which alone
can make either the individual, the class or the nation permanently useful to themselves and to others.

Sincerely yours

[Handwritten] But all this has nothing to do with the fact that the
specific evils you point out shall, if their existence be proved, and if I
have power, be eradicated.

March 28, 1906. Washington
To Andrew Carnegie

My dear Mr. Carnegie:

I thank you for your letter, received through Secretary Root. I am
delighted that you feel in sympathy with my attitude in the rate legislation. To my mind, the big corporations who are opposing this measure and find their representatives in Senator Aldrich and others, are

making a very serious mistake, not only from their own standpoint but from the standpoint of all those who are against the growth of a hysterical radicalism or socialism in the country.

Sincerely yours

April 27, 1906. Washington
To Owen Wister

Personal
Dear Dan:

That I have read *Lady Baltimore* with interest and that I think it a very considerable book the length of this letter will show. If my wife were to write the letter it would be one of almost undiluted praise, because she looked at it simply as a work of art, simply as a story, and from either standpoint it is entitled to nothing but admiration. The description of the people and of their surroundings will always live in my memory, and will make me continually turn back to read bits of the book here and there. Moreover, (to a man of my possibly priggish way of looking at novels), the general tone of the book is admirable, and to one who does not look at it in any way as a tract of the times it leaves the right impression of sturdy protest against what is sordid, against what is mere spangle-covered baseness, against brutal greed and sensuality and vacuity; it teaches admiration of manliness and womanliness, as both terms must always be understood by those capable of holding a high ideal.

But I am afraid the book cannot but be considered save as in part a tract of the times, and from this standpoint, in spite of my hearty sympathy with your denunciation of the very things that you denounce and your admiration of the very things that you admire, I cannot but think that at the best you will fail to do good, and that at the worst you may do harm, by overstating your case. The longer I have been in public life, and the more zealous I have grown in movements of true reform, the greater the horror I have come to feel for the exaggeration which so often defeats its own object. It is needless to say to you that the exaggeration can be just as surely shown as in any other way by merely omitting or slurring over certain important facts. In your remarkable little sketch of Grant, by reciting with entire truth certain facts of Grant's life and passing over with insufficient notice the remainder you could have drawn a picture of him as a drunken, brutal and corrupt incapable, a picture in which almost every detail in the framework would have been true in itself, but in which the summing up and general effect would have been quite as false as if the whole had been a mere invention. Now, of course, I don't mean that this is true of *Lady Baltimore*. You call attention to some mighty ugly facts and tendencies in our modern American civilization, and it is because I so earnestly wish to see the most effective kind of warfare waged against exactly what you denounce that I regret you did not put your denunciation in a way which would accomplish more good. In the first place, though it may have been all right from the standpoint of the story, from the standpoint of the tract it was a capital error to make your swine-devils practically all northerners and your angels practically all southerners. You speak so sweepingly, moreover, that you clearly leave the impression of intending the swine-devils to be representative not of a small section of the well-to-do North, but of the over-whelming majority of the well-to-do North; indeed, of the North which leads. Now, as a matter of fact (remember I am speaking from the standpoint of the tract) the contrast could have been made with much more real truth between northerners and northerners, for then there would not have been a strong tendency to divert the attention from the difference of quality to the difference of locality, and to confound this difference of quality with difference of locality.

In the next place, I do not regard your sweeping indictment of the northern people as warranted. That there is an immense amount of swinish greed in northern business circles and of vulgarity and vice and vacuity and extravagance in the social life of the North, I freely admit. But I am not prepared to say that these are the dominant notes in either the business life or the social life of the North. I know they are not the only notes. I am struck, whenever I visit a college, whenever I have a chance to meet the people of any city or town, with the number of good, straight, decent people with whom I am brought in contact, with the number of earnest young fellows with high purpose whom I meet, with the sweet young girls whom I see. The men I get together to settle the Anthracite Coal Strike, the men I see when there is a scientific gathering in Washington, the artists like Saint-Gaudens and French and MacMonnies, the writers like Crothers and Hyde, the men of the army whom I meet, the young fellows with whom I am brought in contact in doing political work, the families with whom I am intimate, yours, the Grant La Farges, the Gilders, my cousins, the Bacons, and so I could go on indefinitely—all these go to show that the outlook is in no shape or way one of unrelieved gloom. There is plenty of gloom in it, but there is plenty of light also, and if it is painted as all gloomy, I am afraid the chief effect will be to tend to make people believe that either it is all black or else it is all white; and in its effect one view is just as bad as the other. Smash vacuous, divorce-ridden Newport; but don't forget Saunderstown and Oyster Bay!

You also continually speak as if we have fallen steadily away from the high standard of our past. Now I am unable to say exactly what the proportions of good and evil are in the present, but I have not the slightest doubt that they are quite favorable as in the past. I have studied history a good deal and it is a matter of rather grim amusement to me to listen to the praise bestowed on our national past at the expense of our national present. Have you ever read Lecky's account of the Revolutionary war? It is perhaps a trifle too unfavorable to us, but is more nearly accurate than any other I have seen. Beyond all question we ought to have fought that war; and it was very creditable to Washington and some of his followers and to a goodly portion of the Continental troops; but I cannot say that it was very creditable to the nation as a whole. There were two and a half millions of us then, just ten times as many as there were of the Boers in South Africa, and Great Britain was not a fourth as strong as she was in the Boer war, and yet on the whole I think the Boers made a good deal better showing than we did. My forefathers, northerners and southerners alike, fought in the Revolutionary army and served in the Continental Congress, and one of them was the first Revolutionary governor of Georgia, so that I am not prejudiced against our Revolutionary people. But while they had many excellent qualities I think they were lacking as a whole in just the traits in which we are lacking today; and I do not think they were as fine, on the whole, as we are now. The second greatest Revolutionary figure, Franklin, to my mind embodied just precisely the faults which are most distrusted in the average American of the North today. Coming down to after the Revolution, we have never seen a more pitiful exhibition of weakness at home or a greater mixture of blustering insolence and incapacity in reference to affairs abroad than was shown under Jefferson and Madison. So I could go on indefinitely. But let me take only what I have myself seen; where I can speak as a witness and participator. Thirty years ago politics in this country were distinctly more corrupt than they are now, and I believe that the general tone was a little more sordid and that there was a little less of realizable idealism. The social life in New York was not one bit better than it is now. Gould, Sage, Daniel Drew, the elder Vanderbilt, Jim Fisk and the other financiers of the day of that type were at the very least as bad as the corresponding men of today. No financier at present would dare perpetrate the outrages that Huntington was perpetrating some thirty years ago. Nothing so bad has been done in the insurance companies as was done in the *Chapter of Erie*. The Newport set is wealthier and more conspicuous now, and I think the divorce business is more loathsome, but I would certainly hesitate to say that things were worse now than then, taking it as a whole. The Porcellian Club of the last ten years, for instance, averages at least as well as the Porcellian Club for the ten years before I went into it. Among my own friends and in the little circle in which I live at Oyster Bay I don't see that there is any difference of an essential kind as compared with my father's friends and with the circle in which he lived. In the Civil War our people—a mere democracy—were better than in the Revolution, when they formed in part a provincial aristocracy.

When you come to the South and imply or express comparison between the South and the North, I again think you have overstated it. I am half a southerner myself. I am as proud of the South as I am of the North. The South has retained some barbaric virtues which we have tended to lose in the North, partly owning to a mistaken pseudo-humanitarianism among our ethical creatures, partly owing to persistence in and perhaps the development of those business traits which, however, distinguished New York, New England and Pennsylvania a century ago just as they do today. On the other hand the southerners have developed traits of a very unhealthy kind. They are not as dishonest as, they do not repudiate their debts as frequently as their predecessors did in the good old times from which you think we have deteriorated; but they do not send as valuable men into the national councils as the northerners. They are not on the whole as efficient, and they exaggerate the common American tendency of using bombastic language which is not made good by performance. Your particular heroes, the Charleston aristocrats, offer as melancholy an example as I know of people whose whole life for generations has been warped by their own willful perversity. In the early part of South Carolina's history there was a small federalist party and later a small and dwindling union party within the State, of which I cannot speak too highly. But the South Carolina aristocrats, the Charleston aristocrats and their kinsfolk in the upcountry (let me repeat that I am of their blood, that my ancestors before they came to Georgia were members of these very South Carolina families of whom you write) have never made good their pretentions. They were no more to blame than the rest of the country for the slave trade of colonial days, but when the rest of the country woke up they shut their eyes tight to the horrors, they insisted that the slave trade should be kept, and succeeded in keeping it for a quarter of a century after the Revolutionary war closed, they went into secession partly to reopen it. They drank and dueled and made speeches, but they contributed very, very little toward anything of which we as Americans are now proud. Their life was not as ignoble as that of the Newport people whom you rightly condemn, yet I think it was in reality an ignoble life. South Carolina and Mississippi were very much alike. Their two great men of the deified past were Calhoun and Jefferson Davis, and I confess, I am unable to see wherein any conscienceless financier of the present day is worse than these two slave owners who spent their years in trying to feed their thirst for personal power by leading their followers to the destruction of the Union. Remember that the Charleston aristocrats (under Yancey) wished to reopen the slave trade at the time of the outbreak of the Civil War. Reconstruction was a mistake as it was actually carried out, and there is very much to reprobate in what was done by Sumner and Seward and their followers. But the blame attaching to them is as nothing compared to the blame attaching to the southerners for forty years preceding the war, and for the years immediately succeeding it. There never was another war, so far as I know, where it can be honestly and truthfully said as of this war that the right was wholly on one side, and the wrong wholly on the other. Even the courage and prowess of those South Carolina aristocrats were shown only at the expense of their own country, and only in the effort to tear in sunder their country's flag. In the Revolutionary war, in that remote past which you idealize, as compared to the present, the South Carolinians made as against the British a fight which can only be called respectable. There was little heroism; and Marion and Sumter, in their fight against Tarleton and the other British commanders, show at a striking disadvantage when compared with De Wet and De La Rey and the other Boer leaders. In the war of 1812 South Carolina did nothing. She reserved her strength until she could strike for slavery and against the Union. Her people have good stuff in them, but I do not think they are entitled to overpraise as compared to the North. As for the days of reconstruction, they brought their punishment absolutely on themselves, and are, in my judgment, entitled to not one particle of sympathy. The North blundered, but its blunders were in trying to do right in the impossible circumstances which the South had itself created, and for which the South was solely responsible.

Now as to the Negroes! I entirely agree with you that as a race and in the mass they are altogether inferior to the whites. Your small German scientific friend had probably not heard of the latest scientific theory—doubtless itself to be superseded by others—which is that the Negro and the white man as shown by their skulls, are closely akin, and taken together, differ widely from the round skulled Mongolian. But admitting all that can be truthfully said against the Negro, it also remains true that a great deal that is untrue is said against him; and that much more is untruthfully said in favor of the white man who lives beside and upon him. Your views of the Negro are those expressed by all of your type of Charlestonians. You must forgive my saying that they are only expressed in their entirety to those who don't know the facts. Are you aware that these white men of the South who say that the Negro is unfit to cast a vote, and who by fraud or force prevent his voting, are equally clamorous in insisting that his votes must be counted as cast when it comes to comparing their own representation with the representation of the white men of the North? The present leader of the Democrats in the House of Representatives is John Sharp Williams, a typical southerner of the type you mention. In his district three out of every four men are Negroes; the fourth man, a white man, does not allow any of these Negroes to vote, but insists upon counting their votes, so that his one vote offsets the votes of four white men in New York, Massachusetts or Pennsylvania. During my term as President bills have been introduced to cut down the southern representation so as to have it based in effect only on the white vote. With absolute unanimity the southerners have declared that to deprive them of the right of the extra representation which as white men they get by the fraudulent or violent suppression of the black vote is an outrage. With their usual absurd misuse of nomenclature they inveigh against the effort to prevent them crediting themselves with the votes of which they deprive others as "waving the bloody shirt," or being a plea for "negro domination." Your Charleston friends lead this outcry and are among the chief beneficiaries, politically, of the fraud and violence which they triumphantly defend. The North takes absolutely no interest in any such measure, and so far from having any feeling against the South or giving any justification for the South's statement that it wants to interfere with the South's concerns, it is really altogether too indifferent to what is done in the South.

Now remember, Dan, what I am saying has nothing to do with the right of the Negro to vote, or of his unfitness generally to exercise that right. It has to do simply with the consistent dishonesty championed and gloried in by your special southern friends who will not allow the Negro to vote and will not allow the nation to take notice of the fact that he is not voting; and insist upon his vote counted so as to enable them to overcome the honest white vote. I may add that my own personal belief is that the talk about the Negro having become worse since the Civil war is the veriest nonsense. He has on the whole become better. Among the Negroes of the South when slavery was abolished there was not one who stood as in any shape or way comparable with Booker Washington. Incidentally I may add that I do not know a white man of the South who is as as good a man as Booker Washington today. You say you would not like to take orders from a Negro yourself. If you had played football in Harvard at any time during the last fifteen years you would have had to do so, and you would not have minded it in the least; for during that time Lewis has been field captain and a coach. When I was in Charleston at the exposition the very Charlestonians who had hysterics afterward over Crum's appointment as collector of the port, assured me that Crum was one of the best citizens of Charleston, a very admirable man in every way, and while they protested that Negroes ought not to be appointed as postmasters they said there was no such objection to appointing them in other places, and specifically mentioned the then colored collector of customs in Savannah as a case in point. You cannot be more keenly aware than I am of the fact that our effort to deal with the Negro has not been successful. Whatever I have done with him I have found has often worked badly; but when I have tried to fall in with the views of the very southern people, which in this volume you seem to be upholding, the results have been worse than in any other way. These very people whose views you endorse are those who have tried to reintroduce slavery by the infamous system of peonage; which, however, I think in the last three years we have pretty well broken up. I am not satisfied that I acted wisely in either the Booker Washington dinner or the Crum appointment, though each was absolutely justified from every proper standpoint save that of expediency. But the anger against me was just as great in the communities where I acted exactly as the Charlestonians said I ought to act. I know no people in the North so slavishly conventional, so slavishly afraid of expressing any opinion hostile to or different from that held by their neighbors, as is true of the southerners, and most especially of the Charleston aristocrats, on all vital questions. They shriek in public about miscegenation, but they leer as they talk to me privately of the colored mistresses and colored children of white men whom they know. Twice southern senators who in the Senate yell about the purity of the white blood, deceived me into appointing postmasters whom I found had colored mistresses and colored children. Are you acquainted with the case of the Indianola post office in Mississippi? I found in office there a colored woman as postmaster. She and her husband were well-to-do, and were quite heavy taxpayers. She was a very kindly, humble and respectable colored woman. The best people of the town liked her. The two bankers of the town, one of them the Democratic State senator, were on her bond. I reappointed her, and the Senators from Mississippi moved her confirmation. Afterwards the low whites in the town happened to get stirred up by the arrival of an educated colored doctor. His practice was of course exclusively among the Negroes. He was one of those men who are painfully educating themselves, and whose cases are more pitiful than the cases of any other people in our country, for they not only find it exceedingly difficult to secure a livelihood but are followed with hatred by the very whites who ought to wish them well. Too many southern people and too many northern people, repeat like parrots the statement that these "educated darkies" are "a deal worse than the old darkies." As a matter of fact almost all the Tuskegee students do well. This particular Negro doctor took away the Negro patients from the lowest white doctors of the town. They instigated the mob which held the mass meeting and notified the Negro doctor to leave town at once; which to save his life he did that very night. Not satisfied with this the mob then notified the colored postmistress that she must at once resign her office. The "best citizens" of the town did what throughout the South the "best citizens" of the type you praise almost always do in such emergencies; what your Charleston friends have invariably and at all times done in such emergencies; that is they "deprecated" the conduct of the mob and said it was "not representative of the real southern feeling"; and then added that to save trouble the woman must go! She went. The mayor and the sheriff notified her and me that they could not protect her if she came back. I shut up the office for the remainder of her term. It was all I could do and the least I could do. Now Dan, so far from there being any reprobation of this infamy the entire South, led by your friends in Charleston, screamed for months over the outrage of depriving the citizens of Indianola of their mail simply because they let a mob chase away by threats of murder a worthy, refined, educated and hard-working colored woman whom every reputable citizen of that town had endorsed for the position! This is at present the typical southern attitude toward the best type of colored men or colored women; and absolutely all I have been doing is to ask, not that the average Negro be allowed to vote, not that ninety-five per cent of the Negroes be allowed to vote, not that there be Negro domination in any shape or form, but that these occasionally good, well-educated, intelligent and honest colored men and women be given the pitiful chance to have a little reward, a little respect, a little regard, if they can by earnest useful work succeed in winning it. The best people in the South I firmly believe are with me in what I have done. In Trinity College in North Carolina, in Roanoke College, Virginia, here and there elsewhere, they have stood up manfully for *just what I have done*. The bishops of the Episcopal church have for the most part stood up for it. The best southern judges have stood up for it. In so standing up all of these college professors and students, bishops and occasional businessmen have had to face the violent and angry assaults of the majority; and in *Lady Baltimore* you give what strength you can to those denouncing and opposing the men who are doing their best to bring a little nearer the era of right conduct in the South.

Now Dan, I have written to you as I should only write to a dear friend whose book is a power, and who has written about things as to which I think I know a good deal, and as to which I hold convictions down to the very bottom of my heart.

Can't you get on here soon and spend a night or two? I will get Root and Bob Bacon and Taft to come to dinner and perhaps Moody, and I will tell you in full detail some of the various facts about the North and South on which I base my beliefs.

With love to Mrs. Wister,

Ever yours

P.S. Have you read *Democracy*, a novel published nearly thirty years ago? Of course you have read *Martin Chuzzlewit*, published over sixty years ago. Each deals mainly with the society of the North; each makes any number of statements which are true as isolated facts; and each would go to show worse conditions than those you set forth. I think poorly of the author of *Democracy*, whoever he or she may have been[1]; but Dickens was a great writer, and the American characters in *Martin Chuzzlewit* are types that are true as well as amusing, and the book itself is valuable as a tract even today; yet as a picture of the social life of the United States at the time which you are tempted to idealize, it is false because it suppresses or slurs over so much of the truth. Now in each of these books, as in yours, I eagerly welcome the assault on what is evil; but I think that it hinders instead of helping the effort to secure something like a moral regeneration if we get the picture completely out of perspective by slurring over some facts and overemphasizing others.

David Graham Phillips has written a book called *The Plum Tree*. I only read the first half. In it he portrays all politics as sordid, base and corrupt. Sinclair, the socialist, has written a book called *The Jungle*, about the labor world in Chicago. He portrays the results of the present capitalistic system in Chicago as on one uniform level of hideous horror. Now there is very much which needs merciless attack both in our politics and in our industrial and social life. There is much need for reform; but I do not think the two books in question, though they have been very widely read and are very popular and have produced a great effect, have really produced a healthy effect, simply because, while they set forth many facts which are true, they convey an entirely false impression when they imply that these are the only facts that are true and that the whole life is such as they represent it. Of course *Lady Baltimore* is the work of a master and so cannot be compared with either of these two books; but as a tract on the social life of the North as compared with the North's past and the South's present, it really seems to me to be about as inaccurate as they are; and what is more, it produces the very feeling which makes men followers of David Graham Phillips, the Hearst writer, and of Sinclair, the socialist, and which makes them feel that there is no use of trying to reform anything because everything is so rotten that the whole social structure should either be let alone or destroyed.

---

[1]The anonymous author was Roosevelt's old friend Henry Adams.

May 5, 1906. Washington
To John Burroughs

Dear Oom John:

That warbler I wrote you about yesterday was the Cape May warbler. As soon as I got hold of an ornithological book I identified it. I do not think I ever saw one before, for it is rather a rare bird—at least on Long Island, where most of my bird knowledge was picked up. It was a male, in the brilliant spring plumage; and the orange-brown cheeks, the brilliant yellow sides of the neck just behind the cheeks, and the brilliant yellow under parts with thick black streaks on the breast, made the bird unmistakable. It was in a little pine, and I examined it very closely with the glasses but could not see much of its back. Have you found it a common bird?

Ever yours

May 7, 1906. Washington
To Hannah Kent Schoff

Private & personal

My dear Mrs. Schoff:

I have your letter of the 7th instant. The reason I wired you was that it is my firm belief that the agitation of the Mormon question during the past few years has been an unmitigated misfortune. You quote people as asking you why I do not "settle the Mormon question." What do you mean by "settle" it, and what do they mean? The simple fact is that they do not know. I should be glad to see that constitutional amendment about polygamy adopted. At the same time I am not at all sure that there is any necessity for its adoption. All the evidence that I have seen goes to show me that there is less polygamy among the Mormons—that is, that there have been fewer polygamous marriages among the Mormons for the last dozen years—than there have been bigamous marriages among an equal number of Christians. Nothing helps a creed so much as a foolish and futile persecution. Of course the Mormon has precisely the same right to be a Mormon as the Jew has to be a Jew, or the Catholic and Protestant to be Christians. If there is anything being done in the way of a violation of the law by polygamy, I will take any action I can against it. But there has been a complete failure so far to bring to my attention anything that would require or justify such action. No facts have been given to me on which I could proceed. Now it seems to me that the first thing to do is to try to get these facts. I may add that I am sure that in Idaho the attacks upon the Mormon church during the last few years have merely tended to drive them together and make the Mormons tend to act as a unit and tend to act under the hierarchy; whereas they were disintegrating and tending to act as the people of other sects act until these attacks were made. In Idaho the effort to show any kind of polygamy save of an entirely exceptional character failed completely and signally. I repeat that as far as any proof has been produced, polygamous marriages among Mormons in Idaho have of recent years been relatively no more numerous than bigamous marriages among the Christians.

This letter is for you personally and is not to be circulated. I shall act at once when any evidence of crime is brought before me; but it strikes me that what is needed now on this Mormon question is not loose and foolish declamations, which may only do harm, but a study of the actual facts. If these facts warrant action, no one will take it in quicker or more drastic fashion than I will.

Sincerely yours

June 18, 1906. Washington
To Lyman Abbott

My dear Dr. Abbott:

Just a word in addition to what I last wrote you. At the risk of repetition let me say that I wrote you because I believe so entirely in you and the *Outlook*. *Harper's Weekly* is the frank tool of the corporations. The *Cosmopolitan* is owned by Hearst, and, with articles in it from men like David Graham Phillips, is the friend of disorder, less from principle than from the hope of getting profit out of troubled waters; and there is no element of conscience to appeal to in men who write lies for hire or who hire others to lie. The Norman Hapgoods and the Oswald Villards and the like, and papers like *Collier's Weekly* and the New York *Evening Post*, and still more those who edit and write for the *Herald*, the *World*, the *Times*, the Brooklyn *Eagle*, Hearst's papers, and so forth and so forth, cannot be reached by honest argument, and it is therefore of no use to try to get them to uphold the standard of right. But the *Outlook* can and does hold aloft such a standard.

Now I think it essential that we make it clear that we war on the evil of human nature, whether shown in the labor man or the capitalist, in the tyrant or in the assassin. Therefore we cannot afford by omission or softening to make our assaults tell really only against one side. Just at this moment, for instance, I am having an experience which exactly illustrates what I mean. In my effort to correct the abuses in the packing industry I am met by a most violent opposition, not merely from the packers—not merely from the honest industries which they in part control, and sometimes oppress, but which will undoubtedly suffer more or less when the packers suffer—but also from great bodies of capitalists who are interested mainly through that noxious feeling in which the socialists exult and which they call "class consciousness." The National Manufacturers' Association and the Chicago Board of Trade have written me violent protests in offensive language, stating that the reports of the Government committees are false, that everything is clean and perfect in Packingtown, and that all that is necessary is for the Department of Agriculture to say so—in other words, for the Department of Agriculture to lie. Now these capitalist associations are doing just exactly what the numerous labor organizations have been doing in flying to the defense of Moyer and Haywood and the Western Federation of Miners in connection with the effort to bring to justice the man charged with the murder of ex-Governor Steunenberg. They use the same arguments in each case. One side says that "this is a sensational attack upon capital." The other side speaks of the "effort to coerce labor." Each loudly proclaims that it only wants justice; and each does its level best to create a feeling of public opinion, and by direct and indirect pressure to create an apprehension among public officials, which will frustrate justice. One works through the fear of assassination, joined with the fear of political destruction; the other through the fear of political destruction, and the fear of business damage in addition. There are of course honest men who get misled either by one cry or by the other. There are plenty of cowardly or dishonest men who are only too anxious loudly to champion one or the other side, and to do anything possible in public or private life to prevent justice being done as against that side. But what is necessary and at the same time what is exceedingly difficult, is to steer the straight course, the only proper course, and to hold down each set of would-be wrongdoers with a steady hand.

One point should always be remembered in connection with the beef packers, by the way. I did not wish to make the report public. I had the different Senators informed privately of the facts that would be shown, and stated that if I could get proper legislation I would not make these facts public until I could also make public the fact that the evils had been remedied. The Senate passed the necessary legislation. But the packers, through their tools in the House, held up the legislation, produced a sham bill, and made it evident that the only chance to get a decent law was through an aroused public feeling that could only act on full knowledge. It was the packers themselves and their foolish or wicked friends who rendered imperative the publication of the report, with its undoubted attendant harm to our export business in meat. We can put this export business in meat on a proper footing again only by proper legislation; and if we have this legislation I will guarantee proper administration under it.

Sincerely yours

August 6, 1906. Oyster Bay
To Andrew Carnegie

Personal and private

My dear Mr. Carnegie:

Your letter is most interesting. Do you know, I sometimes wish that we did not have the ironclad custom which forbids a President ever to go abroad. If I could meet the Kaiser and the responsible authorities of France and England, I think I could be of help in this Hague Conference business; which is now utterly impossible, and as facts are unadvisable. In any such matter the violent extremists who favor the matter are to be dreaded almost or quite as much as the Bourbon reactionaries who are against it. This is as true of the cause of international peace as it is of the cause of economic equity as between labor and capital at home. I do not know whether in the French Revolution I have most contempt and abhorrence for the Marat, Hebert, Robespierre and Danton type of revolutionists, or for the aristocratic, bureaucratic and despotic rulers of the old regime; for the former did no good in the revolution, but at the best simply nullified the good that others did and produced a reaction which re-enthroned despotism; while they made the name of liberty a word of shuddering horror for the time being.

I hope to see real progress made at the next Hague Conference. If it is possible in some way to bring about a stop, complete or partial, to the race in adding to armaments, I shall be glad; but I do not yet see my way clear as regards the details of such a plan. We must always remember that it would be a fatal thing for the great free peoples to reduce themselves to impotence and leave the despotisms and barbarisms armed. It would be safe to do so if there was some system of international police; but there is now no such system; if there were, Turkey for instance would be abolished forthwith unless it showed itself capable of working real reform. As things are now it is for the advantage of peace and order that Russia should be in Turkestan, that France should have Algiers, and that England should have Egypt and the Sudan. It would be an advantage to justice if we were able in some way effectively to interfere in the Congo Free State to secure a more righteous government; if we were able effectively to interfere for the Armenians in Turkey, and for the Jews in Russia. But at present I do not see how we can interfere in any of these three matters, and the one thing I won't do is to bluff when I cannot make good; to bluster and threaten and then fail to take the action if my words need to be backed up.

I have always felt that our special peace champions in the United States were guilty of criminal folly in their failure to give me effective support in my contest with the Senate over the arbitration treaties. In this contest I had the support of certain Senators, headed by the very best man in the Senate—O. H. Platt of Connecticut. But the Senate, which has undoubtedly shown itself at certain points not merely an inefficient but often a dangerous body as regards its dealings with foreign affairs, so amended the treaties as to make them absolutely worthless. Yet there were some people—including, for instance, a man named Love or Dove, who is the head of the peace conference that meets at Lake Mohonk—who in their anxiety to get anything, no matter how great a sham, and in their ignorance of the fact that foreign powers would undoubtedly have refused to ratify the amended treaties, declined entirely to give me any support and thereby committed a very serious wrong against the cause of arbitration.

You have doubtless seen how well the Pan-American Conference has gone off. Root's going there was a great stroke. Gradually we are coming to a condition which will insure permanent peace in the Western Hemisphere. If only the Senate will ratify the Santo Domingo treaty, we shall have taken another stride in this direction. At The Hague I hope we can work hand in hand with France and England; but all three nations must be extremely careful not to get led off into vagaries, and not to acquiesce in some propositions such as those I am sorry to say Russia has more than once made in the past—propositions in the name of peace which were really designed to favor military despotisms at the expense of their free neighbors. I believe in peace, but I believe that as things are at present, the cause not only of peace but of what is greater than peace, justice, is favored by having those nations which really stand at the head of civilization show, not merely by words but by action, that they ask peace in the name of justice and not from any weakness.

With warm regards to Mrs. Carnegie, believe me,

Faithfully yours

August 9, 1906. Oyster Bay
To Frederick S. Oliver

My dear Mr. Oliver:

I have so thoroughly enjoyed your book on Hamilton that you must allow me the privilege of writing to tell you so. I have just sent a copy to Lodge. There are naturally one or two points on which you and I would not quite agree; but they are very few, and it is really remarkable that you, an English man of letters, and I, an American politician largely of non-English descent, should be in such entire accord as regards the essentials. I shall inflict upon you a rather cruel punishment for having written the book; for I am sending you a volume of mine. As it deals with New York City most of it will be of no interest whatever to you; but it is possible that pages 104 to 158, in which I touch on some of the very questions you deal with, both as regards the Revolutionary War, the adoption of the Constitution, and Hamilton himself, will appeal to you, because it seems to me that the ideas are substantially like those which you develop.

Thank Heaven, I have never hesitated to criticize Jefferson; he was infinitely below Hamilton; I think the worship of Jefferson a discredit to my country; and I have as small use for the ordinary Jeffersonian as for the ordinary defender of the house of Stuart—and I am delighted to notice that you share this last prejudice with me. I think Jefferson *on the whole* did harm in public life. At the same time, there are two [indecipherable] Jefferson stood at [indecipherable] advantage compared to his Federalist opponents (always excepting Washington). He did thoroughly believe in the people, just as Abraham Lincoln did, just as Chatham and Pitt believed in England; and though this did not blind Lincoln to popular faults and failings any more than it blinded the elder and the younger Pitts to English failings, it was in each case a prerequisite to doing the work well. In the second place, Jefferson believed in the West and in the expansion of our people westward, whereas the northeastern Federalists allowed themselves to get into a position of utter hostility to western expansion. Finally, Jefferson was a politician and Hamilton was not. Hamilton's admirers are apt to speak as if this was really to his credit; but such a position is all nonsense. A politician may be and often is a very base creature, and if he cares only for party success, if he panders to what is evil in the people, and still more if he cares only for his own success, his special abilities merely render him a curse. But among free peoples, and especially among the free peoples who speak English, it is only in very exceptional circumstances that a statesman can be efficient, can be of use to the country, unless he is also (not as a substitute, but in addition) a politician. This is a very rough-and-tumble, workaday world, and the persons, such as our "anti-imperialist" critics over here, who sit in comfortable libraries and construct theories, or even the people who like to do splendid and spectacular feats in public office without undergoing all the necessary preliminary outside drudgery, are and deserve to be at a disadvantage compared to the man who takes the trouble, who takes the pains, to organize victory. Lincoln—who, as you finely put it, unconsciously carried out the Hamiltonian tradition—was superior to Hamilton just because he was a politician and was a genuine democrat and therefore suited to lead a genuine democracy. He was infinitely superior to Jefferson of course; for Jefferson led the people wrong, and followed them when they went wrong; and though he had plenty of imagination and of sentimental aspiration, he had neither courage nor farsighted common sense, where the interests of the nation were at stake.

I have not much sympathy with Hamilton's distrust of the democracy. Nobody knows better than I that a democracy may go very wrong indeed, and I loathe the kind of demagogy which finds expression in such statements as "the voice of the people is the voice of God"; but in my own experience it has certainly been true, and if I read history aright it was true both before and at the time of the Civil War, that the highly cultivated classes, who tend to become either cynically worldly-wise or to develop along the lines of the Eighteenth Century philosophers, and the moneyed classes, especially those of large fortune, whose ideal tends to be mere money, are not fitted for any predominant guidance in a really great nation. I do not dislike, but I certainly have no especial respect or admiration for and no trust in, the typical big moneyed men of my country. I do not regard them as furnishing sound opinion as regards either foreign or domestic policies. Quite as little do I regard as furnishing such opinion the men who especially pride themselves on their cultivation—the men like many of those who graduate from my own college of Harvard, and who find their organs in the New York *Evening Post* and *Nation*. These papers are written especially for cultivated gentlefolk. They have many minor virtues, moral and intellectual; and yet during my twenty-five years in public life I have found them much more often wrong than right on the great and vital public issues. In England they would be howling little Englanders, would be raving against the expense of the navy, and eager to find out something to criticize in Lord Cromer's management of Egypt, not to speak of perpetually insisting upon abandoning the Sudan. Sumner, whose life of Hamilton you quote, is an exact representative of this type. He is a college professor, a cold-blooded creature of a good deal of intellect, but lacking the fighting virtues and all wide patriotism, who has an idea that he can teach statesmen and politicians their duty. Three times out of four he goes as wrong on public questions as any Tammany alderman possibly could go; and he would be quite unable even to understand the lofty ambition which, for instance, makes you desire to treat the tariff as something neither good nor bad in itself, but to be handled in whatever way best contributes to solidifying the British Empire and making it a compact and coherent union.

You speak of your lack of direct familiarity with American politics. Do come over to this side next winter and spend a night or two with me at the White House. I shall have Lodge and various others in to see you, and I think you would enjoy meeting them. By the way, I shall, under those circumstances, try to have you meet one of Hamilton's many

descendants, Miss Louisa Lee Schuyler of whom I am very fond; she is
a dear,—almost an elderly lady now; whenever she comes to dine at
the White House she wears a brooch with Hamilton's hair. I shall also
have you meet my Commissioner of Corporations, Garfield,—his father, the President, was the first of our Presidents who publicly put
Hamilton in the high place where he belongs. By the way, the inkstand
I am using was given me by the Hamilton Club of Chicago when I was
inaugurated Governor of New York.

With regard,

Sincerely yours

**August 18, 1906. Oyster Bay
To George Otto Trevelyan**

Personal

My dear Trevelyan:

It seems to me that the last sessions of the national legislatures alike
of Great Britain, France and the United States have possessed peculiar interest. I have followed the work of your Parliament with entire sympathy
on most points; although there are of course two or three matters as to
which I do not know enough to express any opinion. I was really greatly
impressed and pleased with Clemenceau's speech in answer to the socialist Jaurès when the latter attacked Clemenceau for preserving order at
the time of the riotous demonstration by the workingmen. Clemenceau
must be a very able man, and the program he sketched out as that which
his party should undertake in economic matters is substantially the program to which I should like to see the American people committed. Here
we are greatly hampered in dealing with industrial questions affecting
combinations of capital and combinations of labor both with reference to
one another and with reference to the general public, by the peculiarities
of our Federal Constitution. It is most important that so far as possible
these matters should be entrusted to the Federal Government; and we
made astounding progress during the last session of Congress along the
lines of this desirable policy by greatly increasing the power of the federal
authorities to deal with interstate commerce, both in connection with the
railroads, in connection with the meat-packing industry, and in connection with pure food. We also got a very good employers' liability law
passed, not to speak of the work of the Panama canal and other matters.

I have now been five years President. It is about time for the swinging of the pendulum. I should not be in the least surprised to see the
Congressional elections go against us; but whether this happens or not,
it will remain true that during those five years we have accomplished
a great quantity of substantive work of an important kind. Indeed, I can

hardly recall any other five years since the reconstruction days succeeding the Civil War during which as much important work has been
done. I do not think that this has been undertaken in the least in a demagogic spirit. We have tried, and I think we have succeeded, in making
it evident that while we intend to do all we can in the way of giving the
widest social and economic opportunity to the wageworker and to the
poor man, and while we intend to supervise and control the business
use of wealth so that it shall not be used in an unethical or antisocial
spirit, yet that we intended fearlessly to put down anything in the nature of mob violence, and that we set our faces like flint against the
preachers who appeal to or excite the dark and evil passions of men. I
shall hope later to get action taken along the lines of the graduated income tax and the graduated inheritance tax. Just at present we have
been obliged to make it evident that we will not submit to the tyranny
of the trades-union any more than to the tyranny of the corporation.

Of the absolute propriety of this general course from the standpoint of the nation and of the good that it will ultimately do I am certain. But of course, as inevitably happens in any period of constructive
legislation, we tend to alienate the extremists of both sides. There are
great numbers of radicals who think we have not gone far enough, and
a great number of reactionaries who think we have gone altogether too
far, and we array against ourselves both the sordid beneficiaries of the
evils we assail and the wild-eyed agitators who tend to indiscriminate
assault on everything good and bad alike. This is of course not an experience in any way peculiar to our contest. It is the kind of combination that always appears in every such contest. The consolation is that
even though the alliance is temporarily effective, it is never able wholly
to undo all the good work that has been done.

In your last letter you spoke very bitterly of Balfour. Would you
mind writing me exactly what it is about him that makes you feel so bitterly? With very many of the policies with which Mr. Balfour has been
identified I have not met the slightest sympathy; but I had not supposed he was a man who personally excited much active hostility.

I am interested, of course, in The Hague conference. On the one
hand I am anxious that we shall do something effective toward the sub-
stitution of other agents than war for settling disputes between nations.
On the other hand, I feel very strongly that if we try to go too far—if we
try to do what the preposterous apostles of peace of the type of ex-Secretary of State Foster and, I am sorry to say, Congressman Burton in
this country would desire—we should put ourselves in the position of
having the free peoples rendered helpless in the face of the various military despotisms and barbarisms of the world. For example, if we can

come to an agreement to stop the general increase of the navies of the world, I shall be very glad. But I do not feel that England and the United States should impair the efficiency of their navies if it is permitted to other Powers, which may some day be hostile to them, to go on building up and increasing their military strength.

I shall inflict upon you a copy of my letter on behalf of the Republican candidates for Congress, which I send herewith.

Believe me, with warm regards,

Very sincerely yours

August 24, 1906. Oyster Bay
To Gifford Pinchot

My dear Mr. Pinchot:

Through you let me extend my heartiest congratulations and good wishes to those assembled to forward the cause of reclamation and irrigation.[1]

Operations under the Reclamation Act, which I signed on June 17, 1902, have been carried on energetically during the four years since that date. The Reclamation Service, consisting of over 400 skilled engineers and experts in various lines, has been organized, and it is now handling the work with rapidity and effectiveness. Construction is already well advanced on twenty-three great enterprises in the arid States and Territories. Over 1,000,000 acres of land have been laid out for irrigation, and of this 200,000 acres are now under ditch; 800 miles of canals and ditches and 30,000 feet of tunnel have been completed; and 16,000,000 cubic yards of earth and 3,000,000 cubic yards of rock have been moved. Detailed topographic surveys have been extended over 10,000 square miles of country within which the reclamation work is located and 20,000 miles of level lines have been run. Three hundred buildings, including offices and sleeping quarters for workmen, have been erected by the Reclamation Service, and about an equal number by the contractors. Over 10,000 men and about 5,000 horses are at present employed.

The period of general surveys and examinations for projects is past. Effort is now concentrated on getting the water upon a sufficient area of irrigable land in each project to put it on a revenue-producing basis. To bring all the projects to this point will require upwards of $40,000,000, which amount, it is estimated, will be available from the receipts from the disposal of public lands for the years 1901–1908.

We may well congratulate ourselves upon the rapid progress already

---

[1]Pinchot was representing the Roosevelt administration at an irrigation convention in Idaho.

made, and rejoice that the infancy of the work has been safely passed. But we must not forget that there are dangers and difficulties still ahead, and that only unbroken vigilance, efficiency, integrity, and good sense will suffice to prevent disaster. There is now no question as to where the work shall be done, how it shall be done, or the precise way in which the expenditures shall be made. All that is settled. There remains, however, the critical question of how best to utilize the reclaimed lands by putting them into the hands of actual cultivators and homemakers, who will return the original outlay in annual installments paid back into the reclamation fund; the question of seeing that the lands are used for homes, and not for purposes of speculation or for the building up of large fortunes.

This question is by no means simple. It is easy to make plans and spend money. During the time when the Government is making a great investment like this, the men in charge are praised and the rapid progress is commended. But when the time comes for the Government to demand the refund of the investment under the terms of the law, then the law itself will be put to the test, and the quality of its administration will appear.

The pressing danger just now springs from the desire of nearly every man to get and hold as much land as he can, whether he can handle it profitably or not, and whether or not it is for the interest of the community that he should have it. The prosperity of the present irrigated areas came from the subdivision of the land and the consequent intensive cultivation. With an adequate supply of water, a farm of five acres in some parts of the arid West, or of forty acres elsewhere, is as large as may be successfully tilled by one family. When, therefore, a man attempts to hold 150 acres of land completely irrigated by Government works, he is preventing others from acquiring a home, and is actually keeping down the population of his State.

Speculation in lands reclaimed by the Government must be checked at whatever cost. The object of the Reclamation Act is not to make money, but to make homes. Therefore, the requirement of the Reclamation Act that the size of the farm unit shall be limited in each region to the area which will comfortably support one family must be enforced in letter and in spirit. This does not mean that the farm unit should be sufficient for the present family with its future grown children and grandchildren, but rather that during the ten years of payment the area assigned for each family shall be sufficient to support it. When once the farms have been fully tilled by freeholders, little danger of land monopoly will remain.

This great meeting of practical irrigators should give particular attention to this problem and others of the same kind. You should, and I doubt not that you will, give your effectual support to the officers of the Government in making the Reclamation law successful in all respects, and particularly in getting back the original investment, so that the money may be used again and again in the completion of other projects and thus in the general extension of prosperity in the West. Until it has been proved that this great investment of $40,000,000 in irrigation made by the Government will be returning to the Treasury, it is useless to expect that the people of the country will consider direct appropriations for the work. Let us give the Reclamation Service a chance to utilize the present investment a second time before discussing such increase. I look forward with great confidence to the result.

By the side of the Reclamation Service there has grown up another service of not less interest and value to you of the West. This is the Forest Service, which was created when the charge of the forest reserves was transferred from the Interior Department to the Department of Agriculture. The forest policy of the administration, which the Forest Service is engaged in carrying out, is based, as I have often said, on the vigorous purpose to make every resource of the forest reserves contribute in the highest degree to the permanent prosperity of the people who depend upon them. If ever the time should come when the western forests are destroyed, there will disappear with them the prosperity of the stockman, the miner, the lumberman and the railroads, and, most important of all, the small ranchman who cultivates his own land. I know that you are with me in the intention to preserve the timber, the water, and the grass by using them fully, but wisely and conservatively. We propose to do this through the freest and most cordial co-operation between the Government and every man who is in sympathy with this policy, the wisdom of which no man, who knows the facts can for a moment doubt.

It is now less than two years since the Forest Service was established. It had a great task before it,—to create or reorganize the Service on a hundred forest reserves and to ascertain and meet the very different local conditions and local needs all over the West. This task is not finished, and of course it could not have been finished in so short a time. But the work has been carried forward with energy and intelligence, and enough has been done to show how our forest policy is working out.

The result of first importance to you as irrigators is this: The Forest Service has proved that forest fires can be controlled, by controlling them. Only one-tenth of one per cent of the area of the forest reserves was burned over in 1905. This achievement was due both to the Forest Service and to the effective assistance of settlers and others in and near the reserves. Everything the Government has ever spent upon its forest work is a small price to pay for the knowledge that the streams which make your prosperity can be and are being freed from the ever-present threat of forest fires.

The long-standing and formerly bitter differences between the stockmen and the forest officers are nearly all settled. Those which remain are in process of settlement. Hearty co-operation exists almost everywhere between the officers of the Forest Service and the local associations of stockmen, who are appointing advisory committees which are systematically consulted by the Forest Service on all questions in which they are concerned. This most satisfactory condition of mutual help will be as welcome to you as it is to the Administration and to the stockmen. To the stockmen it means more, and more certain, grass; to you, because of the better protection and wiser use of the range, it means steadier stream-flow and more water.

The sales of forest reserve timber to settlers, miners, lumbermen and other users are increasing very rapidly, and in that way also the reserves are successfully meeting a growing need.

Lands in the forest reserves that are more valuable for agriculture than for forest purposes are being opened to settlement and entry as fast as their agricultural character can be ascertained. There is therefore no longer excuse for saying that the reserves retard the legitimate settlement and development of the country. On the contrary, they promote and sustain that development, and they will do so in no way more powerfully than through their direct contributions to the schools and roads. Ten per cent of all the money received from the forest reserves goes to the States for the use of the counties in which the reserves lie, to be used for schools and roads. The amount of this contribution is nearly $70,000 for the first year. It will grow steadily larger, and will form a certain and permanent source of income, which would not have been the case with the taxes whose place it takes.

Finally, a body of intelligent, practical, well-trained men, citizens of the West, is being built up—men in whose hands the public interests, including your own, are and will be safe.

All these results are good; but they have not been achieved by the Forest Service alone. On the contrary, they represent also the needs and suggestions of the people of the whole West. They embody constant changes and adjustments to meet these suggestions and needs. The forest policy of the Government in the West has now become what the West desired it to be. It is a national policy, wider than the boundaries of any State, and larger than the interests of any single industry. Of course it cannot give any set of men exactly what they would choose. Undoubtedly the irrigator would often like to have less stock on his watersheds, while the stockman wants more. The lumberman would like to cut more timber, the settler and the miner would often like him to cut less. The county authorities want to see more money coming in for schools and roads, while the lumberman and stockman object to the rise in value of timber and grass. But the interests of the people as a whole are, I repeat, safe in the hands of the Forest Service.

By keeping the public forests in the public hands our forest policy substitutes the good of the whole people for the profits of the privileged few. With that result none will quarrel except the men who are losing the chance of personal profit at the public expense.

Our western forest policy is based upon meeting the wishes of the best public sentiment of the whole West. It proposes to create new reserves wherever forest lands still vacant are found in the public domain, and to give the reserves already made the highest possible usefulness to all the people. So far our promises to the people in regard to it have all been made good; and I have faith that this policy will be carried to successful completion, because I believe that the people of the West are behind it.

Sincerely yours

August 27, 1906. Oyster Bay
To Charles A. Stillings

My dear Mr. Stillings:

I enclose herewith copies of certain circulars of the Simplified Spelling Board, which can be obtained free from the Board at No. 1 Madison Avenue, New York City. Please hereafter direct that in all Government publications of the executive departments the three hundred words enumerated in Circular No. 5 shall be spelled as therein set forth. If anyone asks the reason for the action, refer him to Circulars 3, 4 and 6 as issued by the Simplified Spelling Board. Most of the criticism of the proposed step is evidently made in entire ignorance of what the step is, no less than in entire ignorance of the very moderate and common-sense views as to the purposes to be achieved, which views are so excellently set forth in the circulars to which I have referred. There is not the slightest intention to do anything revolutionary or initiate any far-reaching policy. The purpose simply is for the Government, instead of lagging behind popular sentiment, to advance abreast of it and at the same time abreast of the views of the ablest and most practical educators of our time as well as the most profound scholars—men of the stamp of Professor Lounsbury. If the slight changes in the spelling of the three hundred words proposed wholly or partially meet popular approval, then the changes will become permanent without any reference to what public officials or individual private citizens may feel; if they do not ultimately meet with popular approval they will be dropt, and that is all there is about it. They represent nothing in the world but a very slight extension of the unconscious movement which has made agricultural implement makers and farmers write "plow" instead of "plough"; which has made most Americans write "honor" without the somewhat absurd, superfluous "u"; and which is even now making people write "program" without the "me"— just as all people who speak English now write "bat," "set," "dim," "sum," and "fish," instead of the Elizabethan "baste," "sette," "dimme," "summe," and "fysshe"; which makes us write "public," "almanac," "era," "fantasy," and "wagon," instead of the "publick," "almanack," "aera," "phantasy," and "waggon" of our great-grandfathers. It is not an attack on the language of Shakespeare and Milton, because it is in some instances a going back to the forms they used, and in others merely the extension of changes which, as regards other words, have taken place since their time. It is not an attempt to do anything far-reaching or sudden or violent; or indeed anything very great at all. It is merely an attempt to cast what slight weight can properly be cast on the side of the popular forces which are endeavoring to make our spelling a little less foolish and fantastic.

Sincerely yours

October 25, 1906. Washington
To John St. Loe Strachey

Personal & Private
My dear Strachey:

I am always delighted to tell you anything I can. Of course it is a little difficult for me to give you an exact historic judgment about a man whom I so thoroly dislike and despise as I do Hearst. I think that he is a man without any real principle; that tho he is posing as a radical, he is in reality no more a radical than he is a conservative. But when I have said this, after all, I am not at all sure that I am saying much more of Hearst than could probably be said—or which would contain a large element of truth if said—about both Winston Churchill and his father, Lord Randolph. Hearst's private life has been disreputable. He is now married, and as far as I know, entirely respectable. His wife was a chorus girl or something like that on the stage, and it is of course neither necessary nor advisable, in my judgment, to make any allusion to any of the reports about either of them before their marriage. It is not the kind of a family which people who believe that sound home relations form the basis of national citizenship would be glad to see in the Executive Mansion in Albany, and still less in the White House. But I think that only harm comes from any public discussion of, or even allusion to, such a matter.

Hearst has edited a large number of the very worst type of sensational, scandal-mongering newspapers. They have been edited with great ability and with entire unscrupulousness. The editorials are well written, and often appeal for high morality in the abstract. Moreover, being a fearless man, and shrewd and farsighted, Hearst has often been of real use in attacking abuses which benefited great corporations, and in attacking individuals of great wealth who have done what was wrong. In these matters he has often led the way, and honest men who are overconservative have been shocked and surprised to find that they had to follow him. He will never attack any abuse, any wickedness, any corruption, not even if it takes the most horrible form, unless he is satisfied that no votes are to be lost by doing it. He preaches the gospel of envy, hatred and unrest. His actions so far go to show that he is entirely willing to sanction any mob violence if he thinks that for the moment votes are to be gained by so doing. He of course cares nothing whatever as to the results to the nation, in the long run, of embroiling it with any foreign power, if for the moment he can gain any applause for so doing. He cares nothing for the nation, nor for any citizens in it.

Mr. Bryan I regard as being a man of the Thomas Jefferson type, altho of course not as able. I would greatly regret his election and think it detrimental to the nation, just as I think Thomas Jefferson's election meant that the American people were not developed to the standard necessary for the appreciation of Washington, Marshall and Hamilton—a standard which they did not reach until Lincoln came to the front sixty years later; for Lincoln had, in addition to the good qualities of Hamilton and Marshall, also those good qualities which they lacked and which Jefferson possest. So much for Bryan. Hearst, I should think, would represent a distinctly lower level than we have ever sunk to as President. As Governor of New York I should think he would be more dangerous, but perhaps not intrinsically worse, than one or two others we have had.

But all this is the judgment of a man who is himself in the thick of the fight; who knows that we have in Hughes an ideal candidate; who does not see how decent citizens can hesitate between Hughes and Hearst; but who thoroly appreciates the gross iniquity, corruption and selfishness of men in high financial and political places which have given Hearst the chance to take advantage of the reaction; and who also appreciates how seared the conscience of the public has sometimes seemed in the presence of great wrong, and how necessary it is that the conscience should be forcefully awakened. If the circumstances were ripe in America, which they are not, I should think that Hearst would aspire to play the part of some of the least worthy creatures of the French Revolution. As it is, he would, if successful, merely do on a larger scale what was done by some of the men who became populist Governors in the Western States. Those States have now recovered, or partially recovered and are conducting themselves in decent fashion. But the damage done, morally and physically, was real and lasting. So it would be with Hearst. He is the most potent single influence for evil we have in our life.

I should not think that it was advisable for you to make more than very brief comments on the situation. In your place I should show a good deal of self-restraint in handling Hearst, but I should certainly not be led into anything that would even impliedly seem to be praise of him.

Faithfully yours

October 27, 1906. Washington
To Eugene Hale

Private

My dear Senator Hale:

This letter is of course strictly private. I write you because of your position in the Senate, where I *know* you to be one of the two or three men of most influence, and where I *believe* you to be the man of most influence.

You have doubtless seen the trouble we are having in connection with the Japanese in California. This is not due to the possession of the Philippines, for our clash with Japan has come purely from the Japanese in Hawaii and on the Pacific Slope (save in connection with the Japanese seal poachers last summer). Under the lead of the trades unions the San Francisco people, and apparently also the people in certain other California cities, have been indulging in boycotts against Japanese restaurant keepers; have excluded the Japanese children from the public schools, and have in other ways threatened, sometimes by law and sometimes by the action of mobs, the rights secured to Japanese in this country by our solemn treaty engagements with Japan. I am doing everything in my power to secure the righting of these wrongs. Thru the Department of Justice we are seeking such aid as the courts will grant. I have sent Secretary Metcalf out to California to confer with the authorities and with the labor union people, and to point out the grave risk they are forcing the whole country to incur. Probably Root will have to communicate formally with the Governor of California. Exactly how much further I shall go I do not know. It is possible I may have to use the army in connection with boycotting or the suppression of mob violence.

If these troubles merely affected our internal arrangements, I should not bother you with them; but of course they may possibly bring about war with Japan. I do not think that they will bring it about at the moment, but even as to this I am not certain, for the Japanese are proud, sensitive, warlike, are flushed with the glory of their recent triumph, and are in my opinion bent upon establishing themselves as the leading power in the Pacific. As I told you at the time, while my main motive in striving to bring about peace between Japan and Russia was the disinterested one of putting an end to the bloodshed, I was also influenced by the desirability of preventing Japan from driving Russia completely out of East Asia. This object was achieved, and Russia stands face to face with Japan in Manchuria. But the internal condition of Russia is now such that she is no longer in any way a menace to or restraint upon Japan, and probably will not be for a number of years to come. I do not pretend to have the least idea as to Japan's policy or real feeling, whether toward us or toward anyone else. I do not think that she wishes war as such, and I doubt if she will go to war now; but I am very sure that if sufficiently irritated and humiliated by us she will get to accept us instead of Russia as the national enemy whom she will ultimately have to fight; and under such circumstances her concentration and continuity of purpose, and the exceedingly formidable character of her army and navy, make it necessary to reckon very seriously with her. It seems to me that all of this necessitates our having a definite policy with regard to her; a policy of behaving with absolute good faith, courtesy and justice to her on the one hand, and on the other, of keeping our navy in such shape as to make it a risky thing for Japan to go into war with us. The first part of the policy I shall carry out as well as I am able; but our federal form of government, with all its advantages, has very great disadvantages when we come to carrying out a foreign policy, and it would be a most difficult thing to prevent mobs and demagogs in certain parts of the country from doing a succession of acts which will tend to embroil us with the Japanese. This being the case, I most earnestly feel that we cannot afford to let our navy fall behind. The Cuban business this year was managed admirably, alike by the navy and the army; and as a matter of practical experience I am now able to say that the general staff of the army and the general board of the navy were among the most efficient causes in bringing about this result. The improvement in both army and navy over things as they were at the beginning of the Spanish War is marvelous. I do not think we can afford to let the army go back, and I think we must keep building the navy up. I have made a very careful study of the Japanese-Russian War last year, and I am convinced that the advantages of size and speed in battleships, the advantages of having battleships carrying say eight twelve-inch guns, are very, very great. I would be delighted if the Hague Conference would agree that hereafter all battleships should be limited in size; but after sounding France, Germany, England and Italy in the matter, I see no hope of accomplishing this result. In view of this I feel that we ought to go ahead with the steady progress of building this year the ship authorized last year and the ship to be authorized this—that is, two ships the equal of any laid down by any nation.

I very earnestly hope that you will consider this matter especially from the standpoint of our possibly having trouble with Japan because of the peculiar circumstances of our relations.

With great regard, believe me,

Sincerely yours

October 27, 1906. Washington
To Kermit Roosevelt

Dear Kermit:

I have an autograph letter of James Monroe, one of his official letters as Governor of Virginia, which I have given to Mother to keep for you. Mother has taken Ethel and Archie down the river this morning and they are not coming back until tomorrow (Sunday) evening. She thinks Ethel needed the rest, and I think it will be a good thing for Mother herself. Archie went off first to play a game of football and was to overtake them in a motor boat. Archie was tremendously exercised over the shameful shortcoming of two members of the team, a tackle and a half-back who, as he informed me, were "Mohammedan Turks"—this I found to be literally true as they are the sons of the Turkish Minister—and who had kept a previous engagement instead of going to play in the match. I regret to state Archie seemed to think they were rather above the average of the remaining Christians in this play; and he felt that the effect upon the team would be most sinister. Skip loathes the football and when Archie and his team are practicing out on the grounds here always rushes up-stairs to stay with Mademoiselle whereas Rollo acts just like the huge bouncing puppy he is and takes as much part in the game as the players will stand.

I am being horribly bothered about the Japanese business. The infernal fools in California, and especially in San Francisco, insult the Japanese recklessly, and in the event of war it will be the Nation as a whole which will pay the consequences. However I hope to keep things straight. I am perfectly willing that this Nation should fight any nation if it has got to, but I would loathe to see it forced into a war in which it was wrong.

Your loving father

[Handwritten] Sunday. I have just had a delightful long ride with Baron Speck; this afternoon I shall take Quentin out to the open air services at the Cathedral to hear a sermon from our former Rough Rider chaplain.

October 29, 1906. Washington
To Elihu Root

To the Secretary of State:

During my absence in Panama I direct you if necessary to use the armed forces of the United States to protect the Japanese in any portion of this country if they are menaced by mobs or jeoparded in the rights guaranteed them under our solemn treaty obligations.

November, 1906. On board the U.S.S. *Louisiana* en route to Panama
To Kermit Roosevelt

Dear Kermit:

So far the trip has been a great success, and I think Mother has really enjoyed it. As for me I of course feel a little bored as I always do on shipboard, but I have brought on a great variety of books, and am at this moment reading Milton's prose works, Tacitus and a German novel called *Jörn Uhl*. Mother and I walk briskly up and down the deck together or else sit aft under the awning or in the aftercabin, with the gun ports open and read; and I also spend a good deal of time on the forward bridge and sometimes on the aft bridge, and of course have gone over the ship to inspect it with the Captain. It is a splendid thing to see one of these men-of-war, and it does really make one proud of one's country. Both the officers and the enlisted men are as fine a set as one could wish to see.

It is a beautiful sight, these three great war vessels steaming southward in close column, and almost as beautiful at night when we see not only the lights but the loom through the darkness of the ships astern. We are now in the tropics and I have thought a good deal of the time over eight years ago when I was sailing to Santiago in the fleet of warships and transports. It seems a strange thing to think of my now being President, going to visit the work of the Panama Canal which I have made possible.

Mother, very pretty and dainty in white summer clothes, came up on Sunday morning to see inspection and review, or whatever they call it, of the men. I usually spend half an hour on deck before Mother is dressed. Then we breakfast together alone; have also taken lunch alone, but at dinner have two or three officers to dine with us. Doctor Rixey is along and is a perfect dear as always.

November 14th.

The fourth day out was in some respects the most interesting. All the forenoon we had Cuba on our right and most of the forenoon and part of the afternoon Haiti on our left; and in each case green, jungly shores and bold mountains—two great, beautiful, venomous tropic islands. These are historic seas and Mother and I have kept thinking of all that has happened in them since Columbus landed at San Salvador, (which we also saw), the Spanish explorers, the buccaneers, the English and Dutch seadogs and adventurers, the great English and French fleets, the desperate fighting, the triumphs, the pestilences, all the turbulence, the splendor and the wickedness, and the hot, evil, riotous life of the old planters and slave-owners, Spanish, French, English and Dutch; their extermination of the Indians and bringing in of negro slaves, the decay of most of the islands, the turning of Haiti into a land of savage negroes, who have reverted to voodooism and cannibalism; the effort we are now making to bring Cuba and Porto Rico forward.

Today is calm and beautiful as all the days have been on our trip. We have just sighted the highest land of Panama ahead of us, and we shall be at anchor by two o'clock this afternoon; just a little less than six days from the time we left Washington.

Your loving father

November 20. U.S.S. *Louisiana*
To Kermit Roosevelt

Dear Kermit:

Our visit to Panama was most successful as well as most interesting. We were there three days and we worked from morning till night. The second day I was up at a quarter to six and got to bed at a quarter of twelve, and I do not believe that in the intervening time, save when I was dressing, there were ten consecutive minutes when I was not busily at work in some shape or form. For two days there uninterrupted tropic rains without a glimpse of the sun, and the Chagres River rose in a flood higher than any for fifteen years; so that we saw the climate at its worst. It was just what I desired to do.

It certainly adds to one's pleasure to have read history and to appreciate the picturesque. When on Wednesday we approached the coast and the jungle-covered mountains loomed clearer and clearer until we could see the surf beating on the shores, while there was hardly a sign of human habitation, I kept thinking of the four centuries of wild and bloody romance, mixed with abject squalor and suffering, which made up the history of the Isthmus until three years ago. I could see Balboa crossing at Darien, and the wars between the Spaniards and the Indians, and the settlement and the building up of the quaint walled Spanish towns; and the trade, across the seas by galleon, and over land by pack train and river canoe, in gold and silver, in precious stones; and then the advent of the buccaneers, and of the English seamen, of Drake and Frobisher and Morgan, and many, many others, and the wild destruction they wrought. Then I thought of the rebellion against the Spanish dominion, and the uninterrupted and bloody civil wars that followed, the last occurring when I became President; wars, the victorious heroes of which have their pictures frescoed on the quaint rooms of the palace at Panama city, and in similar palaces in all the other capitals of these strange, turbulent little half-caste civilizations. Meanwhile the Panama railroad had been built by Americans over a half a century ago, with appalling loss of life, so that it is said, of course with exaggeration, that every sleeper laid represented the death of a man. Then the French canal company started work, and for two or three years did a good deal until it became evident that the task far exceeded its powers; and then to miscalculation and inefficiency was added the hideous greed of adventurers, trying each to save something from the general wreck, and the company closed with infamy and scandal.

Now we have taken hold of the job. We have difficulties with our own people, of course, I haven't a doubt that it will take a little longer and cost a little more than men now appreciate, but I believe that the work is being done with a very high degree both of efficiency and honesty; and I am immensely struck by the character of American employees who are engaged not merely in superintending the work, but in doing all the jobs that need skill and intelligence. The steam shovels, the dirt trains, the machine shops, and the like are all filled with American engineers, conductors, machinists, boilermakers, carpenters. From the top to the bottom these men are so hardy, so efficient, so energetic, that it is a real pleasure to look at them. Stevens, the head engineer is a big fellow, a man of daring and good sense, and burly power. All of these men are quite as formidable, and would if it were necessary do quite as much in battle as the crews of Drake and Morgan; but as it is they are doing a work of infinitely more lasting consequence. Nothing whatever remains to show what Drake and Morgan did. They produced no real effect down here. But Stevens and his men are changing the face of the continent, are doing the greatest engineering feat of the ages, and the effect of their work will be felt while our civilization lasts. I went over everything that I could possibly go over in the time at my disposal. I examined the quarters of married men and single men, white men and negros. I went over the ground of the Gatun and La Boca dams; went through Panama and Colón, and spent a day in the Culebra cut, where the great work is being done. There the huge steam shovels are hard at it; scooping huge masses of rock and gravel and dirt previously loosened by the drillers and dynamite blasters, loading it on trains which take it away to some dump, either in the jungle or where the dams are to be built. They are eating steadily into the mountain cutting it down and down. Little tracks are laid on the side hills, rocks blasted out, and the great ninety-five ton steam shovels work up like mountain howitzers until they come to where they can with advantage begin their work of eating into and destroying the mountainside. With intense energy men and machines do their task, the white men supervising matters and handling the machines, while the tens of thousands of black men do the rough manual labor where it is not worth while to have machines do it. It is an epic feat, and one of immense significance.

The deluge of rain meant that many of the villages were knee-deep in water, while the flooded rivers tore through the tropic forests. It is a real tropic forest, palms and bananas, breadfruit trees, bamboos, lofty ceibas, and gorgeous butterflies and brilliant colored birds fluttering among the orchids. There are beautiful flowers, too. All my old enthusiasm for natural history seemed to revive, and I would have given a good deal to have stayed and tried to collect specimens. It would be a good hunting country too; deer and now and then jaguars and tapir, and great birds that they call wild turkeys; there are alligators in the rivers. One of the trained nurses from a hospital went to bathe in a pool last August and an alligator grabbed him by the legs and was making off with him, but was fortunately scared away, leaving the man badly injured.

I tramped everywhere through the mud. Mother did not do this roughest work, and had time to see more of the really picturesque and beautiful side of the life, and really enjoyed herself.

Your loving father

P.S. The Gatun dam will make a lake miles long, and the railroad now goes at what will be the bottom of this lake, and it was curious to think that in a few years great ships would be floating in water 100 feet above where we were.

November 21, 1906. Ponce, Puerto Rico
To William Howard Taft

(Telegram)

Discharge is not to be suspended unless there are new facts of such importance as to warrant your cabling me.[1] I care nothing whatever for

---

[1]Reference is to the Brownsville riot involving African-American soldiers and townspeople. On this subject, more below.

the yelling of either the politicians or the sentimentalists. The offense was most heinous and the punishment I inflicted was imposed after due deliberation. All I shall pay heed to is the presentation of facts showing the official reports to be in whole or in part untrue; or clearly exculpating some individual man. If any such facts shall later appear I can act as may be deemed advisable, but nothing has been brought before me to warrant the suspension of the order, and I direct that it be executed.

**November 27, 1906. Washington
To Silas McBee**

Personal

My dear Mr. McBee:

Of course I liked your letter. I have been amazed and indignant at the attitude of the negroes and of shortsighted white sentimentalists as to my action. It has been shown conclusively that some of these troops made a midnight murderous and entirely unprovoked assault upon the citizens of Brownsville—for the fact that some of their number had been slighted by some of the citizens of Brownsville, the warranting criticism upon Brownsville, is not to be considered for a moment as provocation for such a murderous assault. All of the men of the companies concerned, including their veteran noncommissioned officers, instantly banded together to shield the criminals. In other words they took action which cannot be tolerated in any soldiers, black or white, in any policeman, black or white, and which, if taken generally in the army, would mean not merely that the usefulness of the army was at an end but that it had better be disbanded in its entirety at once. Under no conceivable circumstances would I submit to such a condition of things. There has been great pressure not only by sentimentalists but by the northern politicians who wish to keep the negro vote. As you know I believe in practical politics, and, where possible, I always weigh well any action which may cost votes before I consent to take it; but in a case like this, where the issue is not merely one of naked right and wrong but one of vital concern to the whole country, I will not for one moment consider the political effect.

There is another side to this also. In that part of my message about lynching, which you have read, I speak of the grave and evil fact that the negroes too often band together to shelter their own criminals, which action had an undoubted effect in helping to precipitate the hideous Atlanta race riots. I condemn such attitude strongly, for I feel that it is fraught with the gravest danger to both races. Here, where I have power to deal with it, I find this identical attitude displayed among the negro troops. I should be recreant to my duty if I failed by deeds as well as words to emphasize with the utmost severity my disapproval of it.

Sincerely yours

December 5, 1906. Washington
To Kermit Roosevelt

Dear Kermit:

I have written Mr. Fergie. I enclose the program of the entertainment and also the menu of the dinner given us by the Chief Petty Officers' Mess.

As Mother is away, I have been doing what little I could for Archie and Quentin. It has chiefly taken the shape of reading to them in the evening what the absurd little geese call "I" stories. Being translated this term includes all hunting stories I read them, which are naturally told in the first person; the little boys evidently have a vague feeling that being thus told in the first person they all somehow represent the deeds of the same individual. My reading for the last two evenings to them has been a most satisfactorily lurid Man-eating Lion story. After breakfast this morning Ethel started to school in high spirits driving Mollie, her high spirits being due to the fact that she anticipated that Mollie would balk, and thereby furnish excitement.

I have been a little puzzled over the Nobel prize. It appears that there is a large sum of money—they say about $40,000—that goes with it. Now, I hate to do anything foolish or quixotic and above all I hate to do anything that means the refusal of money which would ultimately come to you children. But Mother and I talked it over and came to the conclusion that while I was President at any rate, and perhaps anyhow, I could not accept money given to me for making peace between two nations, especially when I was able to make peace simply because I was President. To receive money for making peace would in any event be a little too much like being given money for rescuing a man from drowning, or for performing a daring feat in war. Of course there was the additional fact that what I did I was able to do because I was President. Altogether Mother and I felt that there was no alternative and that I would have to apply the money to some public purpose. But I hated to have to come to the decision, because I very much wisht for the extra money to leave all you children.

Yes, I saw Robinson's poem, which you had already shown me, and I like it. He certainly has a touch of genius in him.

Your loving father

December 13, 1906. Washington
To Ethan A. Hitchcock[1]

My dear Mr. Secretary:

The more I have thought over the matter the more convinced I am that we need radical action about the public lands. The illegal fencing represents the temporary withdrawal of land from the public, sometimes to the disadvantage and sometimes rather to the advantage of the public, but does not represent any permanent theft of it; altho of course it must be stopt. The obtaining of land under false pretenses, nominally by settlers, but really by absentee owners, corporate or others, represents, however, real theft; that is, the permanent taking possession of the land by people who are not entitled to it. In order to reach the illegal fencing I shall notify Congress that they must pass laws which will enable the Government to handle the public range as it is now handled in the forest reserves, and that otherwise I shall make it my purpose to see that the illegal fencing is put an end to, whether it is harmful or not. In order to reach the fraud in the shape of theft of the public land, I believe it is necessary to have actual examination on the ground, by one of our officers, of each patent before granting it. I accordingly direct that this be hereafter done. I shall notify Congress of this order and ask them for a number of additional land agents, stating that unless this increase is granted either there will be great delay and damage to bona fide settlers, or else a continuance of the fraud.

As for the coal lands, I shall also ask again that we be given power to supervise and control their management and use. The present laws put a premium upon fraud because they forbid individuals and corporations from securing a sufficient quantity of land to warrant their going into the coal mining business, and yet render it easy for them to secure the extra quantity by evasion of the law. I shall call the attention of Congress to this fact. The Chancellor of a certain university has been to me to point out the great damage to the university resulting from the present laws, which render it impossible, or well-nigh impossible, to procure the coal in workable quantities without resorting to practices from which men of a high standard of integrity revolt, while they are comparatively easily carried on with impunity by men with a less high standard of integrity. I of course know nothing about the merits of the claim of this university.

Sincerely yours

---

[1]Secretary of the Interior.

December 16, 1906. Washington
To James Brander Matthews

Dear Brander:

I could not by fighting have kept the new spelling in, and it was evidently worse than useless to go into an undignified contest when I was beaten. Do you know I think that the one word as to which I thought the new spelling was wrong—thru—was more responsible than anything else for our discomfiture? But I am mighty glad I did the thing anyhow. In my own correspondence I shall continue using the new spelling.

Faithfully yours

January 10, 1907. Washington
To Whitelaw Reid

Private

My dear Mr. Ambassador:

There is one not very important thing of which I think you should be informed; altho I do not see that either you or I can do anything about it. Apparently the members of the present British Cabinet talk with extreme freedom to Carnegie. In one instance, at least, this has been most unwise on their part, as is shown by the following incident. Mr. Carnegie recently came first to me and then to Root with a story that he had been told by a member of the Cabinet (whose name he gave me, but which I forget) that the British Ambassador at Berlin had informed the said member of the Cabinet, or else the whole Cabinet, that at a recent conversation with him the Emperor had stated that he was building his navy against America (this was to show that he was not building it against England) and was also hostile to The Hague conference. Carnegie seemed much disturbed over the information, which naturally did not impress me in the least—in the first place, because even if the Emperor had said it I did not regard it as a fact of importance, and in the next place because I could not be at all confident that the conversation coming thru three or four people had, by the time it reached me any resemblance at all to what it originally was. In other words, it was an instance of that international gossip with which one is deluged if one chooses to listen to it.

So far Carnegie had not done any mischief; but what must he then do, of all things in the world, but call on Speck and complain bitterly of the Emperor's hostility to America and to peace, as shown by the conversation in question! Speck of course cabled the news home, and I received a somewhat lurid cable from the Emperor in consequence. I answered it by letter. I enclose you copies of both. It is unnecessary to say how careful you must be that they do not get out; but as I cannot possibly tell whether something about the matter may not get back to London from Berlin I think it well that you should be fully informed.

Give my warm regards to Mrs. Reid. I trust I need not say what a genuine pleasure it has been to see you both.

With all good wishes, believe me,

Faithfully yours

March 16, 1907. Washington
To James Wilson

My dear Mr. Secretary:

I have been going all over the papers you submitted to me together with an argument of Senator McCumber's. I confess I am very much puzzled. It seems to me that your pages 8, 9 and 10 cover the matter. From these it appears that two or more whiskies are sometimes mixt together and the mixture sold as a blended whisky. There is no question, therefore, that the label "blended whisky" should apply to such a mixture. As you say, there ought to be some way of informing the consumer whether he is furnished a mixture of two whiskies, or of whisky and neutral spirit or grain distillate; for the Pure Food law is largely a labeling law, and "misbranding" is to use a false or deceptive label—that is one deceptive to the average consumer. As you point out, if the average consumer receives a mixture of whisky and neutral spirit labeled "blended whisky," he will naturally conclude that two or more whiskies of different ages or distillations have been added together. You state that it may be questioned whether, under the law, if we allow the use of the word "blend" for the mixture of whisky and neutral spirit any additional words can be required; but that the Solicitor thinks they can be required. It seems to me very desirable that the matter should be so determined that the question of our power to add these descriptive words cannot arise. You further say that it is imperatively necessary in order to prevent misbranding that there shall be some difference in the label to permit the consumer to tell at once that a blended whisky consisting of a mixture of two whiskies is different from a mixture of whisky and neutral spirit.

Taking all these considerations together it seems to me that only a mixture of whiskies should be labeled "blended whisky"; and that we should use the words "whisky, compound of grain distillates," or "whisky, compounded with grain distillates" to give notice to the consumer that a mixture of whisky and neutral spirit is not a blend of two whiskies. It has further been suggested to me that this type of label should only apply to a mixture of straight whisky with neutral spirit derived from grain; and that there should be a further label of "whisky, compound with neutral spirit," to characterize a mixture of straight whisky with neutral spirit derived from molasses, sawdust, or any basis except grain. What do you think of this?

I went over this matter very carefully with certain medical men, including a New York physician of note, who has had much experience with straight, blended, and compounded whiskies, and who of course is wholly unprejudiced as regards what action is taken. He says that the whiskies with which we are concerned are certainly compound whiskies, but that they are whiskies preferred by a great many men, and are the only whiskies sold by some leading grocers and the only whiskies to be obtained in some leading hotels and clubs. He believes that the above labels would recognize clearly and accurately the exact facts; and he does not believe that any damage would come to the sellers of the compound whiskies, because in a very few months the customers who prefer them would grow entirely accustomed to the terminology, would pay no more heed to the word "compound" than the word "blend," and would simply take the whisky they prefer.

Sincerely yours

March 25, 1907. Washington
To Jacob H. Schiff

Personal

My dear Mr. Schiff:

I have your letter of the 24th instant, which I have carefully noted. Will you look at pages 12 to 14 of the enclosed copy of my last annual message to Congress? It is difficult for me to understand, in view of this and my many other utterances like it, why there should be this belief in Wall Street that I am a wild-eyed revolutionist. I cannot condone wrong, but I certainly do not intend to do aught save what is beneficial to the man of means who acts squarely and fairly. When I see you I will explain at length why I do not think it advantageous from any standpoint for me to ask any railroad man to call upon me. I can only say to you, as I have said to Mr. Morgan when he suggested that he would like to have certain of them call upon me (a suggestion which they refused to adopt, by the way) that it would be a pleasure to me to see any of them at any time. Sooner or later I think they will realize that in their opposition to me for the last few years they have been utterly mistaken, even from the standpoint of their own interests; and that nothing better for them could be devised than the laws I have striven and am striving to have enacted. I wish to do everything in my power to aid every honest businessman, and the dishonest businessman I wish to punish simply as I would punish the dishonest man of any type. Moreover, I am not desirous of avenging what has been done wrong in the past, especially when the punishment would be apt to fall upon innocent third parties; my prime object is to prevent injustice and work equity for the future.

With great regard, believe me,

Sincerely yours

March 30, 1907. Washington
To Ray Stannard Baker

Personal: Private

My dear Mr. Baker:

I am genuinely imprest with your article on the Atlanta riots. It helped me in more than one way to a clearer understanding of the situation. Sometime I should like to see you. I have been really deprest over this Brownsville (Texas) business—not so much by the attitude of the colored troops themselves, altho that was sufficiently ominous, but by the attitude taken by the enormous majority of the colored people in regard to the matter. I had never really believed there was much justification for the claim of the Southern whites that the decent Negroes would actively or passively shield their own wrongdoers; or at least I had never realized the extent to which the statement was true; but this Brownsville business has given me the most serious concern on this very point. If they were white troops I do not believe that at this moment any human being would be maintaining their innocence, and indeed I doubt very seriously whether the incident could have occurred exactly as it did occur if they had been white troops. But as it is, with a few noted exceptions the colored people have made a fetish of the innocence of the troops and have been supporting in every way the political demagogs and visionary enthusiasts who have struck hands in the matter of their defense.

Foraker, for instance, is an able man, and it is simply not supposable that he seriously questions the guilt of the Negro troops, both of those among them who are actively concerned in the shooting and the attendant murder, and of the others who were accessory before or after the fact. Whether he, as I am personally inclined to believe, championed the cause of the colored troops merely as an incident in his campaign against me because of our fundamental disagreement on the question of the control of corporations, or whether, as is possible, he did it simply as a political move to secure the Negro vote—for it is impossible to admit that he could be sincere in any belief in the troops' innocence—the fact remains that the overwhelming majority of the colored people have stood by him heartily and have been inclined to lose sight of every real movement for the betterment of their race, of every real wrong done their race by peonage or lynching, and to fix their eyes only upon this movement to prevent the punishment of atrociously guilty men of their race.

Senator Clay, Clark Howell and two or three others have given me substantially the view of the Atlanta riot which you give; but you work out features of it as to which I had been entirely ignorant, and I was particularly glad to see them.

Sincerely yours

**April 28, 1907. Washington
To Kogoro Takahira**

Personal

My dear Mr. Ambassador:

I have your letter of April 3d.

Permit me first to congratulate you upon your appointment to your new post, and upon the distinguished honor accorded to you by His Majesty the Emperor of Japan in conferring on you the Grand Cordon of the Imperial Order of the Rising Sun. The news gave me personal pleasure, for, as I think you need not be assured, you won my high regard and esteem while you were Minister at Washington, and in particular during the trying months when we were thrown together so intimately at the time of the peace negotiations.

As for the San Francisco incident, it caused me more concern than you can imagine. But such international incidents are from time to time inevitable as between any nations. The business of statesmen is to try to close them successfully and in a way to leave behind as little hard feeling as possible. You do not need to have me tell you of my high regard and admiration for the people of Japan and my resolute purpose to work in all ways for the friendship and good understanding between the American and Japanese Governments and peoples. All nations have advanced far on the path of international good will and fair dealing in the last few centuries; but we all of us have still a long way to go. Fifty years ago even educated Americans and Japanese would have risked a good deal in going to one another's countries. Now, all gentlemen, all educated men of your country and of mine can visit or stay each in the other's land, as travelers or students, as scientists or artists, as professional men or merchants, and be sure not merely of good treatment but of heartiest welcome; and this whether it is the American who comes to Japan or the Japanese who comes to America. But as yet we are not at the point where it is possible that the classes of citizens of the two countries who are more suspicious and less broad-minded should feel in the same way about one another; and above all is this true when they compete in their labor. This feeling is the same in Japan as in the United States. If tens of thousands of American miners went to Sakhalin to take up the mines; if tens of thousands of American laborers went to Japan itself to compete with the laboring men there, a rivalry would be sure soon to spring up which could not be fortunate in its effect. There would certainly then tend to grow up in Japan the same feeling toward Americans that now influences you in forbidding Chinese laborers to come to Japan. I think it very greatly for the interests of both nations that the laborers of neither should go to the other. As I have said, my dear Mr. Ambassador, while we have all of us traveled far on the road of proper international relations, we have a long distance yet to go, and I feel that it is the part of wise statesmanship to go so carefully as not to jeopardize the future. A couple of centuries ago, when French and Flemish workmen came to England, being driven from their homes by religious persecution, the English workmen, altho of the same creed, violently assailed them and protested against their presence even to the point of mob violence. Now, we have gone so far along that this danger has been past. I firmly believe that in another generation or two the danger of any trouble on any such grounds between Japan and the United States will have past just as now what would have seemed impossible half a century ago has come to pass, and all Japanese and American gentlemen, men of letters, scientists, professional men, and the like, can meet together on terms of the heartiest friendship and good will; but if we should try to hurry things too much there would be risk of disaster. So I think that the laboring people of each country had better not, at this time, go to the other's country.

With high regard, believe me,

Sincerely yours

July 10, 1907. Oyster Bay
To Henry Cabot Lodge

Confidential

Dear Cabot:

The enclosed letter from Cooley shows, I think, that we ought not to except these positions of inspectors under the new naturalization law. I find that there is a universal protest against making the exceptions. They say that in most localities to make the exceptions would work great damage. Of course treat Cooley's letter as confidential and return it to me.

As regards the fleet going to the Pacific, there has been no change, save that the naval board decided sooner than I had expected. I could not entertain any proposition to divide the fleet and send some vessels there, which has been the fool proposition of our own jingoes; but this winter we shall have reached the period when it is advisable to send the whole fleet on a practice cruise around the world. It became evident to me, from talking with the naval authorities, that in the event of war they would have a good deal to find out in the way of sending the fleet to the Pacific. Now, the one thing that I won't run the risk of is to experiment for the first time in a matter of vital importance in time of war. Accordingly I concluded that it was imperative that we should send the fleet on what would practically be a practice voyage. I do not intend to keep it in the Pacific for any length of time; but I want all failures, blunders, and shortcomings to be made apparent in time of peace and not in time of war. Moreover, I think that before matters become more strained we had better make it evident that when it comes to visiting our own coasts on the Pacific or Atlantic and assembling the fleet in our own waters, we cannot submit to any outside protests or interference. Curiously enough, the Japs have seen this more quickly than our own people.

I have the Japanese Ambassador and a Cabinet Minister out here the day after tomorrow. I shall continue to do everything I can by politeness and consideration to the Japs to offset the worse than criminal stupidity of the San Francisco mob, the San Francisco press, and such papers as the New York *Herald*. I do not believe we shall have war; but it is no fault of the yellow press if we do not have it. The Japanese seem to have about the same proportion of prize jingo fools that we have.

Love to Nannie.

Ever yours

July 13, 1907. Oyster Bay
To Elihu Root

Personal

Dear Elihu:

I suppose you have read Wilson's admirable memorandum on the Japanese situation. Incidentally, let me say how well he has justified your choice of him as Assistant Secretary of the Department.

I am more concerned over this Japanese situation than almost any other. Thank Heaven we have the navy in good shape. It is high time, however, that it should go on a cruise around the world. In the first place I think it will have a pacific effect to show that it can be done; and in the next place, after talking thoroly over the situation with the naval board I became convinced that it was absolutely necessary for us to try in time of peace to see just what we could do in the way of putting a big battle fleet in the Pacific, and not make the experiment in time of war. Moreover, the hideous cowardice and stupidity of many of our people, which match the hideous sensationalism and offensiveness of many of the yellow press, are almost as serious a menace to us in our foreign relations. A goodly number of our papers spend their time in insulting the Japanese and in writing articles which, when they are repeated, as they are sure to be, in Japan, cause the greatest irritation against us. An equally large body of people never by any chance comment on or rebuke this action, but confine themselves to action which in its turn tends to convince foreigners that in addition to being blusterers we are cowards. Take Hale,[1] for instance. He is a conscienceless voluptuary, and in his private affairs, both in business and politics, he is as astute as he is unscrupulous. But in addition to being a physical coward without one scrap of patriotism or of understanding what patriotism is, he is also a fool when it comes to dealing with foreign affairs or with the army and navy. Never in the Senate has he uttered one word to rebuke Tillman, for instance, or anyone like Tillman, when language exasperating and provocative to Japan was used. Never has he said a word to support us in our effort to secure good treatment for the Japanese. His consistent theory is not to interfere with our being as offensive and irritating to Japan, as possible, but to try to prevent at all hazards the navy from being either efficient or respected, and to cheerfully incur the risk of being kicked by any foreign power rather than show our ability to fight. Even from his own contemptible standpoint his policy is bad; for he spends his time in increasing the likelihood of the very dangers the thought of which casts him into such spasms of terror.

Aoki and Admiral Yamamoto were out here yesterday at lunch. Aoki is a singularly cool-headed and wise old boy. I am afraid he is much more so than his fellow countrymen. Yamamoto, an ex-Cabinet Minister and a man of importance, evidently had completely misunderstood the situation here and what the possibilities were. I had a long talk with him thru an interpreter. He kept insisting that the Japanese must not be kept out save as we kept out Europeans. I kept explaining to him that what we had to do was to face facts; that if American laboring men came in and cut down the wages of Japanese laboring men they would be shut out of Japan in one moment; and that Japanese laborers must be excluded from the U.S. on economic grounds. I told him emphatically that it was not possible to admit Japanese laborers into the United States. I pointed out to him those rules which Wilson quoted in his memorandum, which show that the Japanese Government has already in force restrictions against American laborers coming into Japan, save in the old treaty ports. I pointed out that under our present treaty we had explicitly reserved the

---

[1] Senator Eugene Hale, chairman of the Naval Affairs Committee.

right to exclude Japanese laborers. I talked freely of the intended trip of the battleship fleet thru the Pacific, mentioning that it would return home very shortly after it had been sent out there; at least in all probability. I also was most complimentary about Japan, and repeated at length the arguments that I had written to Takahira and Kaneko. How much impression I made upon him I cannot say. Meanwhile, I have received, and enclose to you, the disquieting statistics of the Japanese arrivals in the United States for the fiscal year just closed as compared with the fiscal year preceding. There has been a great increase in these arrivals; and for the last two months, during which the new policy has been in effect, while the increase is less marked, it still exists. More Japanese came here during May and June than during the preceding May and June, or than during March and April. I am inclined to think that many of them who come as petty traders are really laborers. In any event I believe we shall have to urge most strongly upon the Japanese Government the need of restricting the total number of passports if we are not to have trouble. If there is not a falling off in the number of Japanese arrivals, I think we can safely count upon at least a very dangerous agitation in Congress next year for their total exclusion by a law modeled after our Chinese exclusion act.

The Newfoundland business and similar matters are mere child's play compared with this Japanese business, from the standpoint of its ultimate importance.

I am not at all sure that later you ought not to come out here and have a talk with me. When you do I hope you will bring Mrs. Root. I do not think she has ever been here.

Bacon is a great comfort, as always, in your absence.

Ever yours

July 24, 1907. Oyster Bay
To William Cowles

Personal

Dear Will:

Is Admiral Manney a lunatic? He has sent me some thoughts on the Japanese and on our fleet going to the Pacific which really would do discredit to an outpatient of Bedlam.

Ever yours

July 26, 1907. Oyster Bay
Willard H. Brownson

My dear Admiral:

Many thanks for your letter. I would like thru you to congratulate Admiral Thomas and especially the officers and crew of the *Georgia* upon the way in which without a moment's delay the ship went back to her work. The whole navy is to be congratulated at the spirit shown by the officers and enlisted men on board the *Georgia* in this instance, and on board the *Missouri* and *Texas* in the other instance to which you refer.

Confidential. Is there any way in which we can hurry up the building of our big battleships? Of course any inquiry about this must be very quiet. Moreover, would it be possible to have an inquiry started by which I should ascertain how soon it would be possible in case of dire emergency to build new battleships? What I want to know is whether, if a war, was started, we could build battleships during the course of a year or eighteen months, so that if the war lasted that length of time we could begin to have ships take the place of those we should lose. In the improbable event of hostilities with Japan, for instance, it might turn out that the difficulty would be to get the Japanese to engage. This might not be the difficulty at all; but the German and English experts evidently believe that in the event of war, which they (as I hope and believe, wrongly) think inevitable, the Japanese would at first avoid a general engagement and trust to torpedo attacks and the like, and the long distance from our base, gradually to wear our fleet down. Under such circumstances I should like to know whether we could not ourselves play a waiting game by taking advantage of the delay and of our enormous wealth to build up the fleet.

I would also like information as to the amount of powder, projectiles, and so forth, we need and have on hand.

Sincerely yours

September 2, 1907. Oyster Bay
To Henry Cabot Lodge

Dear Cabot:

I at once sent your letter to Newberry. I had already told him that the *Constitution* ought not to be disposed of at present. Frankly, I think it ought to be at Annapolis, but it does not seem to me to be of enough consequence to warrant a muss.

As for the campaign of the *Sun, Times* and *World* about the navy going to the Pacific, I do not see much that they can do. My impression is that the people as a whole have been extremely well pleased at my sending the fleet to the Pacific, for a good many different reasons. I need hardly say to alter the decision now would be ruinous. Hale has been writing Newberry a series of bullying letters to which I have told Newberry to pay not the slightest heed. Hale would like to introduce into our naval and military affairs a system of supervision based upon the proceedings of the Aulic Council of Vienna and flavored with the spirit of

Moorfield Storey's Anti-Imperialist League, plus the heroism of the average New York financier.

Give my love to Nannie.

Ever yours

September 16, 1907. Oyster Bay
To John Muir

My dear Mr. Muir:

I gather that Garfield and Pinchot are rather favorable to the Hetch Hetchy plan, but not definitely so. I have sent them your letter with a request for a report upon it. I will do everything in my power to protect not only the Yosemite, which we have already protected, but other similar great natural beauties of this country; but you must remember that it is out of the question permanently to protect them unless we have a certain degree of friendliness toward them on the part of the people of the State in which they are situated; and if they are used so as to interfere with the permanent material development of the State instead of helping the permanent material development, the result will be bad. I would not have any difficulty at all if, as you say, nine tenths of the citizens took ground against the Hetch Hetchy project; but so far everyone [indecipherable] has been for it and I have been in the disagreeable position of seeming to interfere with the development of the State for the sake of keeping a valley, which apparently hardly anyone wanted to have kept, under national control.

I wish I could see you in person; and how I do wish I were again with you camping out under those great sequoias or in the and under the silver firs.

Faithfully yours

October 25, 1907. Washington
To George B. Cortelyou[1]

My dear Mr. Cortelyou:

I congratulate you upon the admirable way in which you have handled the present crisis. I congratulate also those conservative and substantial businessmen who in this crisis have acted with such wisdom and public spirit. By their action they did invaluable service in checking the panic which, beginning as a matter of speculation, was threatening to destroy the confidence and credit necessary to the conduct of legitimate business. No one who considers calmly can question that the underlying conditions which make up our financial and industrial

---

[1]At this time Secretary of the Treasury.

well-being are essentially sound and honest. Dishonest dealing and speculative enterprise are merely the occasional incidents of our real prosperity. The action taken by you and by the businessmen in question has been of the utmost consequence and has secured opportunity for the calm consideration which must inevitably produce entire confidence in our business conditions.

Faithfully yours

November 4, 1907. Washington
To Charles J. Bonaparte

My dear Mr. Attorney General:

Judge E. H. Gary and Mr. H. C. Frick on behalf of the Steel Corporation[1] have just called upon me. They state that there is a certain business firm (the name of which I have not been told, but which is of real importance in New York business circles) which will undoubtedly fail this week if help is not given. Among its assets are a majority of the securities of the Tennessee Coal Company. Application has been urgently made to the Steel Corporation to purchase this stock as the only means of avoiding a failure. Judge Gary and Mr. Frick inform me that as a mere business transaction they do not care to purchase the stock; that under ordinary circumstances they would not consider purchasing the stock because but little benefit will come to the Steel Corporation from the purchase; that they are aware that the purchase will be used as a handle for attack upon them on the ground that they are striving to secure a monopoly of the business and prevent competition—not that this would represent what could honestly be said, but what might recklessly and untruthfully be said. They further inform me that as a matter of fact the policy of the Company has been to decline to acquire more than sixty per cent of the steel properties, and that this purpose has been persevered in for several years past, with the object of preventing these accusations, and as a matter of fact their proportion of steel properties has slightly decreased, so that it is below this sixty per cent, and the acquisition of the property in question will not raise it above sixty per cent. But they feel that it is immensely to their interest, as to the interest of every responsible businessman, to try to prevent a panic and general industrial smashup at this time, and that they are willing to go into this transaction, which they would not otherwise go into, because it seems the opinion of those best fitted to express judgment in New York that it will be an important factor in preventing a break that might be ruinous; and that this has been urged upon them by the combination of the most

---

[1]The United States Steel Corporation.

responsible bankers in New York who are now thus engaged in endeavoring to save the situation. But they asserted they did not wish to do this if I stated that it ought not to be done. I answered that while of course I could not advise them to take the action proposed, I felt it no public duty of mine to interpose any objection.

Sincerely yours

November 11, 1907. Washington
To Roland C. Dryer

Dear Sir:

When the question of the new coinage came up we lookt into the law and found there was no warrant therein for putting "IN GOD WE TRUST" on the coins. As the custom, altho without legal warrant, had grown up, however, I might have felt at liberty to keep the inscription had I approved of its being on the coinage. But as I did not approve of it, I did not direct that it should again be put on. Of course the matter of the law is absolutely in the hands of Congress, and any direction of Congress in the matter will be immediately obeyed. At present, as I have said, there is no warrant in law for the inscription.

My own feeling in the matter is due to my very firm conviction that to put such a motto on coins, or to use it in any kindred manner, not only does no good but does positive harm, and is in effect irreverence which comes dangerously close to sacrilege. A beautiful and solemn sentence such as the one in question should be treated and uttered only with that fine reverence which necessarily implies a certain exaltation of spirit. Any use which tends to cheapen it, and, above all, any use which tends to secure its being treated in a spirit of levity, is from every standpoint profoundly to be regretted. It is a motto which it is indeed well to have inscribed on our great national monuments, in our temples of justice, in our legislative halls, and in buildings such as those at West Point and Annapolis—in short, wherever it will tend to arouse and inspire a lofty emotion in those who look thereon. But it seems to me eminently unwise to cheapen such a motto by use on coins, just as it would be to cheapen it by use on postage stamps, or in advertisements. As regards its use on the coinage we have actual experience by which to go. In all my life I have never heard any human being speak reverently of this motto on the coins or show any sign of its having appealed to any high emotion in him. But I have literally hundreds of times heard it used as an occasion of, and incitement to, the sneering ridicule which it is above all things undesirable that so beautiful and exalted a phrase should excite. For example, thruout the long contest, extending over several decades, on the free coinage question, the existence of this motto on the coins was a constant source of jest and ridicule; and this was unavoidable. Everyone must remember the innumerable cartoons and articles based on phrases like "In God we trust for the other eight cents"; "In God we trust for the short weight"; "In God we trust for the thirty-seven cents we do not pay"; and so forth and so forth. Surely I am well within bounds when I say that a use of the phrase which invites constant levity of this type is most undesirable. If Congress alters the law and directs me to replace on the coins the sentence in question the direction will be immediately put into effect; but I very earnestly trust that the religious sentiment of the country, the spirit of reverence in the country, will prevent any such action being taken.

Sincerely yours

November 12, 1907. Washington
To Thomas E. Watson[1]

My dear Mr. Watson:

Many thanks for your letter. In the first place, my dear sir, I trust I need hardly assure you that I shall not "surrender" to the bankers, or to anyone else, and there will be no "secret midnight conferences" with any big financier, or anyone else. I have not seen Mr. Morgan, but I intend to see him soon, and he will call at the White House just as openly as Mr. Gompers did the other day, just as openly as he has called in the past, and just as openly as Mr. Gompers and his associates have more often called in the past. I know I have your hearty support in the proposition that the doors of the White House swing open with equal readiness to capitalist and wageworkers, to the head of a great corporation or a union, or the man who is neither—all shall have a fair hearing from me, and none shall exert any influence save what their case, openly stated and openly repeated, warrants.

As to the financial situation, I am not yet by any means clear what I ought to do. I shall confer with Secretary Cortelyou very carefully.

I wish I could see you in person to talk over several matters. Are you not to be in Washington sometime in the not too distant future?

Sincerely yours

November 19, 1907. Washington
To Andrew Carnegie

Personal

My dear Mr. Carnegie:

I have your letter of the 18th instant. I shall recommend an increase in the navy. I shall urge it as strongly as I know how. I believe that every farsighted and patriotic man ought to stand by me. I will give sufficient

---

[1]Former populist-minded congressman from Georgia; Populist nominee for president in 1904.

reasons in my message. I cannot state *all* the reasons in my message, and I certainly will not state them in a letter to you or anyone else or state them verbally save in strict confidence, but I shall state in my message reasons which are amply sufficient. You say the question needs my serious attention. It has had it; and, as I say, I cannot imagine how anyone, in view of the known conditions of the world and of the absolute refusal of The Hague conference to limit armaments, can fail to back me up.

Sincerely yours

November 23, 1907. Washington
To Hamlin Garland

Dear Garland:

Thank you for your letter. When hard times come it is inevitable that the President under whom they come should be blamed. There are foolish people who supported me because we had heavy crops; and there are foolish people who now oppose me because extravagant speculations, complicated here and there with dishonesty, have produced the inevitable reaction. It is just the kind of incident upon which one must count. It may produce a temporary setback for my policies in either one of two ways; that is in securing the election as my successor of a reactionary or of some good man who will be the tool of reactionaries; or else thru having the pendulum swing with violence the other way, so that my successor as a wild radical will bring utter discredit on the reforms by attempting to do too much, and especially by doing a number of things that ought not to be done;. thereby ensuring a real reaction. But I am perfectly certain that in the end the Nation will have to come to my policies, or substantially to my policies, simply because the Republic cannot endure unless its governmental actions are founded on these policies, for they represent nothing whatever but aggressive honesty and fair treatment for all—not make-believe fair treatment, but genuine fair treatment. I do not think that my policies had anything to do with producing the conditions which brought on the panic; but I do think that very possibly the assaults and exposures which I made, and which were more or less successfully imitated in the several States, have brought on the panic a year or two sooner than would otherwise have been the case. The panic would have been infinitely worse, however, had it been deferred.

As for the New York financiers, their hangers-on, the innocent men whom they have deceived or who follow them and the newspapers that they own or inspire, why I have to expect that these people will attack me. Their hostility toward me is fundamental. I neither respect nor admire the huge monied men to whom money is the be-all and the end-all of existence; to whom the acquisition of untold millions is the supreme goal of life, and who are too often utterly indifferent as to how these millions are obtained. I thoroly believe that the first duty of every man is to earn his own living, to pull his own weight, to support his own wife and family; but after this has been done, and he is able to keep his family according to his station and according to the tastes that have become a necessity to him, then I despise him if he does not treat other things as of more importance in his scheme of life than mere money getting; if he does not care for art, or literature, of science, or statecraft, or warcraft, or philanthropy— in short, for some form of service to his fellows, for some form of the kind of life which is alone worth living.

With regards to Mrs. Garland,
Sincerely yours

November 27, 1907. Washington
To Henry White

Personal
My dear White:

Many thanks for your interesting letter and the enclosed clipping. I quite agree with you that foreigners as well as ourselves always mistake the evanescent for the permanent, and always forget that they made the very same mistake the last time the same conditions were present. They will get over the effects of this panic in time both at home and abroad, just as they have got over the effects of previous panics; and during the continuance of the panic there will be the same fear, and distrust, and folly, and bitter denunciation of the man most prominent at the moment in public life, that we saw in previous panics. Our fiscal system is not good from the purely fiscal side. I am inclined to think that from this side, a central bank would be a very good thing. Certainly I believe that at least a central bank, with branch banks, in each of the States (I mean national banks, of course) would be good; but I doubt whether our people would support either scheme at present; and there is this grave objection, at least to the first, that the inevitable popular distrust of big financial men might result very dangerously if it were concentrated upon the officials of one huge bank. Sooner or later there would be in that bank some insolent man whose head would be turned by his own power and ability, who would fail to realize other types of ability and the limitations upon his power, and would by his actions awaken the slumbering popular distrust and cause a storm in which he would be as helpless as a child, and which would overwhelm not only him but other men and other things of far more importance. (There! that sentence is as long and involved as if I were a populist Senator; but I hope it conveys my idea.) One difficulty is that on this continent we are as naturally insular, or parochial, as ever the English were in the old days when compared with the rest of Europe. The same feeling that made England believe that it did not have to take part in any European concert of any kind makes this country feel that it can be a law for itself in many different matters. As yet our people do not fully realize the modern interdependence in financial and business relations. I believe that there will be an awakening, but it will be gradual.

Of course as yet it is impossible to say how long this depression will last, or how severe it will be. Naturally and inevitably I shall be held accountable for it, at first by those who wish to hold me accountable for everything, and gradually by honest men who suffer and who cannot be expected while suffering to keep their sanity of judgment. The business community of New York (by which I mean the New York plutocracy and those who are in the pay of or are led by the plutocracy) is a rather preposterous body when judged by anything but its own peculiar, and not always healthy, work. In private conversation these businessmen will themselves tell you how much they suffer from the scoundrelism of the Harrimans and Rockefellers and Morses and Heinzes and Barneys, the insurance crowd, and the rest of those who represent simply a sublimated type of sand-the-sugar deacon in a country store; but the minute that any action is taken to get rid of the rascality, they fall into a perfect panic and say that business conditions must not be jeopardized; and they are blind to the fact that sooner or later the rascality must be found out and that then honest men will suffer for the deeds of the rascals.

In my message I think I have brought out pretty clearly the fundamental soundness of our position.

That must have been a very interesting experience in England. Poor Chamberlain! I suppose his work as a public leader is over. What an extraordinary public career he has had! I suppose he cannot help feeling a sense of incompleteness in the fact that he has never been Prime Minister, altho the ablest man in English politics, with the exception of Gladstone, since the death of Beaconsfield.

With warm regards to Mrs. White, believe me,
Faithfully yours

December 21, 1907. Washington
To Cecil Spring Rice

Dear Cecil:

As usual Mrs. Roosevelt and I were equally pleased and interested with your letter. You speak as if you were to have a little holiday from official life. Cannot you take advantage of it to bring your wife over and spend a few days with us at The White House? Not so very much time remains now, and I do wish we could see you both here. Do not leave the diplomatic service unless you have to. You have worked thru the years of mere drudgery. You have made your reputation. You are at the very time of life when your training and experience will enable you to do your best; and even if the harness galls a little, you will be happier doing steady trace-and-collar work. If you have to get out, well and good. You have done honorably; you have won your spurs, and it is all right. But if you can go on, by all means go on. My own case is peculiar, for I am not very clear that there will be anything possible for me to do after a year from the next fourth of March. But we are all on the knees of the Gods and must await events; the when the opportunity comes we can improve it, and, indeed, can to a certain extent make it.

I do very much wish to talk with you over some of the questions which you raise which I can hardly discuss at length in a letter. Fundamentally my philosophy is yours, tho not so pessimistic. I do not think we know enough about the future to be able to say with certainty how great any given danger is. The things we dread do not occur, and evils which no human being had foreseen or could have foreseen loom portentous. We may have a race conflict such as you dread in the Pacific, but I hope not; and therefore I hope that the ten-year limit that you set is altogether too short. I very much wish that Australia would either encourage European immigration or would see a higher birth rate among its own citizens. It is not pleasant to realize how slowly the scanty population of that island continent increases. But as long as Great Britain retains her naval superiority and Australia is part of the British Empire Australia is safe. On our own Pacific coast British Columbia feels exactly as our Pacific Coast States feel. Both the United States and Canada are increasing so much in population that it is hard to imagine an ethnic conquest by a yellow race here on the mainland; but of course national folly on the part of the United States, both in permitting outrages against the Japanese and in declining to keep the navy up to the highest point of efficiency, might result in a bitterly humiliating and disastrous war which would turn over not only the Philippines but Hawaii to Japan. I do not anticipate any such war, and I think I am taking the best possible measures to prevent it and to get the two races or nations on a footing which will permit a policy of permanent friendliness or at least mutual toleration. Here again all we can say is that the future is dim before our eyes. With the voyages of Columbus and Vasco da Gama, the invention of printing, and the Reformation, began the great modern movement of spreading European civilization and its

influences over the whole world, just as at one time the Greek civilization spread so largely over the Mediterranean world. Tho checked here
and there, and while one European race after another has fallen back,
the movement as a whole has gone on for four centuries, with as one
side of it the spread of the European peoples and their influence over
Asia, Africa, America and Australia, with as the other side, the development within their own limits of a highly complex, highly efficient,
but luxurious and in some respects enervating and demoralizing, industrial civilization. There is as yet no sign of the movement as a whole
being arrested. Industrial inventiveness of all kinds and the exploita-
tion of the world's resources go on with increasing rapidity. Our children and our children's children will see the mechanical agents of this
civilization working with an ever increasing strength and effectiveness.
Gyroscope trains may cross these continents in a day; we may see air-
ships; we may see all kinds of things; on the other hand the century that
has opened may in all probability see something like a timber famine
and also the approaching exhaustion of the iron fields. Even the coal itself cannot last for many centuries. What will come after? Will substitutes be found? Will a simpler and saner civilization, really better, succeed our own; or will it be overwhelmed by barbarism from within or
without? No one can tell. It matters very little whether we are optimists
or pessimists. Our duty is to do our work well and abide the event.

As regards myself, I am at the moment having rather more than my
usual share of difficulties. The panic is bad and it has produced great depression in business, with, as a consequence, laborers thrown out of employment, farmers suffering, and an unhealthy stagnation everywhere.
Inevitably and naturally ignorant good men, under the lead of men who
are neither ignorant nor good, tend to hold me responsible for this condition. As a matter of fact, it is in part the kind of reaction that comes under
any circumstances; it is in part due to unhealthy and dishonest methods
in the field of speculative high finance; and my own share is limited to
having exposed abuses and therefore to bringing on the crisis a little
quicker than it otherwise would have come, but making it less severe. In
large part, however, the movement is world-wide. You have with great
acuteness stated in your letter the exact fact about the newspapers and
any movement on behalf of the fundamental rights of the people as a
whole, such as that in which I think I may fairly say I have taken a considerable part. The movement itself will in the end succeed, but the man
who leads it must necessarily fail or seem to fail for the time being. All I
am fighting for, in the last analysis, is honest methods in business and in
politics, and justice alike for (and on to) capitalist and working man. I
have never hesitated to oppose labor unions when I thought them wrong,

any more than to oppose corporations when I thought them wrong. I am certain that if our Republic is to endure on a healthy basis, it must proceed along the course I have outlined. But the thing that astonishes me is not that I should now be attacked, but that I should have been triumphant for so long a period, for I have awakened the bitter antagonism of very powerful men and very powerful interests whose memory is as long as the memory of the public at large is short, and their attacks on me thru the papers which they subsidize (and these are the big papers of the biggest industrial centers) never cease for a moment. They misrepresent everything I say or do; the wonder is that anyone should have any belief in me at all. But it is all in the day's work. I have had an uncommonly good run for my money; I have been treated mighty well and favored by fortune above my deserts; and whatever comes in the future, I am ahead of the game.

It certainly is curious how the great racial questions are looming up. I was glad to see your agreement with Russia; but of course we are all perfectly ignorant of what Russia's future will be. As for the governing class in England having no real foreign policy, of course our people tend to have even less, and the melancholy fact is that the capitalist and educated classes are those least to be trusted in this matter. It is, as you say, a melancholy fact that the countries which are most humanitarian, which are most interested in internal improvement, tend to grow weaker compared with the other countries which possess a less altruistic civilization. The great countries with strong central government and military instincts do tend to be the dominant ones; and I have fought, not very successfully, to make our people understand that unless freedom shows itself compatible with military strength, with national efficiency, it will ultimately have to go to the wall. For your sins I send you a copy of my message and ask you to look at what I say about the army and navy, pages 45 to 55. It is astounding to see how shortsighted many people in your country and mine and even in France are where war is concerned. Carnegie represents the most objectionable class of these peace advocates. He represents those people who in crude and foolish fashion have imbibed Tolstoi's foolish theory that good men should never make war because, forsooth, when bad men are stronger than good men they make war in evil fashion, and who add a peculiar baseness to this view by championing an industrialism which wrecks far more lives than any ordinary war. The country that loses the capacity to hold its own in actual warfare with other nations, will ultimately show that it has lost everything. I abhor and despise that pseudo-humanitarianism which treats advance in civilization as necessarily and rightfully implying a weakening of the fighting spirit and which therefore invites destruction of the advanced civilization by some less-advanced type.

Good-by, Springy; and do bring Mrs. Springy over to see us sometime this year.

Ever yours

December 21, 1907. Washington
To Thomas E. Watson

My dear Mr. Watson:

Your letter deeply touches me, and the concluding paragraph gave
me grave concern. It is of very little consequence what becomes of me
or of any other one man, but it is of very great consequence that the
people—the plain people—in the country and city shall be relieved
from suffering, from financial panic, and yet that this relief shall in no
wise represent any backing down from our principles in the matter of
corporation controls. I have more difficulty about dealing with the currency than with anything else, for I feel less sure of my ground in the
matter, and at the moment I cannot answer you save by again expressing how touched I am, my dear Sir, by your good opinion. I hope I shall
not forfeit it. I shall certainly try not to deserve to forfeit it.

Sincerely yours

P.S. It seems to me that the trouble about issuing greenbacks as you
suggest is that it is like a man temporarily relieving himself by issuing
notes of indebtedness. He can do it with safety if he exercises severe
self-control; but a government will not permanently exercise such self-
control. I have no doubt that $50,000,000 of greenbacks, if it was ab-
solutely certain that no more would be issued, would achieve something of the purpose that you have in mind; but I also believe that most
people would think that it foretold an indefinite issuance of greenbacks
and that in consequence it would have a frightening effect.

January 2, 1908. Washington
To Charles J. Bonaparte

My dear Bonaparte:

I must congratulate you on your admirable speech at Chicago. You
said the very things it was good to say at this time. What you said bore especial weight because it represented what you had done. You have
shown by what you have actually accomplished that the law is enforced
against the wealthiest corporation, and the richest and most powerful
manager or manipulator of that corporation, just as resolutely and fearlessly as against the humblest citizen. The Department of Justice is now in
very fact the Department of Justice, and justice is meted out with an even
hand to great and small, rich and poor, weak and strong. Those who have
denounced you and the action of the Department of Justice are either mis-

led, or else are the very wrongdoers, and the agents of the very wrong-doers, who have for so many years gone scot-free and flouted the laws with impunity. Above all, you are to be congratulated upon the bitterness felt and exprest towards you by the representatives and agents of the great lawdefying corporations of immense wealth, who, until within the last half dozen years, have treated themselves and have expected others to treat them as being beyond and above all possible check from law.

It was time to say something, for the representatives of predatory wealth, of wealth accumulated on a giant scale by iniquity, by wrong-doing in many forms, by plain swindling, by oppressing wageworkers, by manipulating securities, by unfair and unwholesome competition, and by stockjobbing, in short by conduct abhorrent to every man of or-dinarily decent conscience, have during the last few months made it evident that they are banded together to work for a reaction, to en-deavor to overthrow and discredit all who honestly administer the law, and to secure a return to the days when every unscrupulous wrong-doer could do what he wisht unchecked, provided he had enough money. They attack you because they know your honesty and fearless-ness, and dread them. The enormous sums of money these men have at their control enable them to carry on an effective campaign. They find their tools in a portion of the public press including especially certain of the great New York newspapers. They find their agents in some men in public life—now and then occupying, or having occupied, positions as high as Senator or Governor—in some men in the pulpit, and most melancholy of all, in a few men on the bench. By gifts to colleges and universities they are occasionally able to subsidize in their own inter-est some head of an educational body, who, save only a judge, should of all men be most careful to keep his skirts clear from the taint of such corruption. There are ample material rewards for those who serve with fidelity the Mammon of unrighteousness, but they are dearly paid for by that institution of learning whose head, by example and precept, teaches the scholars who sit under him that there is one law for the rich and another for the poor. The amount of money the representatives of the great monied interests are willing to spend can be gauged by their recent publication broadcast thruout the papers of the country from the Atlantic to the Pacific of huge advertisements, attacking with enven-omed bitterness the Administration's policy of warring against suc-cessful dishonesty, advertisements that must have cost enormous sums of money. This advertisement, as also a pamphlet called "The Roo-sevelt Panic," and one or two similar books and pamphlets, are written especially in the interest of the Standard Oil and Harriman combina-tions, but also defend all the individuals and corporations of great wealth that have been guilty of wrongdoing. From the railroad rate law to the pure food law, every measure for honesty in business that has been pressed during the last six years, has been opposed by these men, on its passage and in its administration, with every resource that bitter and unscrupulous craft could suggest, and the command of almost unlimited money secure. These men do not themselves speak or write; they hire others to do their bidding. Their spirit and purpose are made clear alike by the editorials of the papers owned in, or whose policy is dictated by, Wall Street, and by the speeches of the public men who, as Senators, Governors, or Mayors, have served these their masters to the cost of the plain people. At one time one of their writers or speakers attacks the rate law as the cause of the panic; he is, whether in public life or not, usually a clever corporation lawyer, and he is not so foolish a being as to believe in the truth of what he says; he has too closely represented the railroads not to know well that the Hepburn Rate Bill has helped every honest railroad, and has hurt only the railroads that regarded themselves as above the law. At another time, one of them assails the Administration for not imprisoning people under the Sherman Antitrust Law; for declining to make what he well knows, in view of the actual attitude of juries (as shown in the Tobacco Trust cases and in San Francisco in one or two of the cases brought against corrupt businessmen) would have been the futile endeavor to imprison defendants, whom we are actually able to fine. He raises the usual clamor, raised by all who object to the enforcement of the law, that we are fining corporations instead of putting the heads of the corporations in jail; and he states that this does not really harm the chief offenders. Were this statement true he himself would not be found attacking us. The extraordinary violence of the assault upon our policy contained in speeches like these, in the articles in the subsidized press, in such huge advertisements and pamphlets as those above referred to, and the enormous sums of money spent in these various ways, give a fairly accurate measure of the anger and terror which our actions have caused the corrupt men of vast wealth to feel in the very marrow of their being.

The man thus attacking us is usually, like so many of his fellows, either a great lawyer, or a paid editor who takes his commands from the financiers and his arguments from their attorneys. If the former, he has defended many malefactors and he knows well that, thanks to the advice of lawyers like himself, a certain kind of modern corporation has been turned into an admirable instrument by which to render it well-nigh impossible to get at the really guilty man, so that in most cases the only way of punishing the wrong is by fining the corporation or by proceeding personally against some of the minor agents. These lawyers and their employers are the men mainly responsible for this state of things, and their responsibility is shared with the legislators who ingeniously oppose the passing of just and effective laws, and with those judges whose one aim seems to be to construe such laws so that they cannot be executed. Nothing is sillier than this outcry on behalf of the "innocent stockholders" in the corporations. We are besought to pity the Standard Oil Company for a fine relatively far less great than the fines every day inflicted in the police courts upon multitudes of pushcart peddlers and other petty offenders, whose woes never extort one word from the men whose withers are wrung by the woes of the mighty. The stockholders have the control of the corporation in their own hands. The corporation officials are elected by those holding the majority of the stock and can keep office only by having behind them the good will of these majority stockholders. They are not entitled to the slightest pity if they deliberately choose to resign into the hands of great wrongdoers the control of the corporations in which they own the stock. Of course innocent people have become involved in these big corporations and suffer because of the misdeeds of their criminal associates. Let these innocent people be careful not to invest in corporations where those in control are not men of probity, men who respect the laws; above all let them avoid the men who make it their one effort to evade or defy the laws. But if these honest innocent people are in the majority in any corporation they can immediately resume control and throw out of the directory the men who misrepresent them. Does any man for a moment suppose that the majority stockholders of the Standard Oil are others than Mr. Rockefeller and his associates themselves and the beneficiaries of their wrongdoing? When the stock is watered so that the innocent investors suffer, a grave wrong is indeed done to these innocent investors as well as to the public; but the public men, lawyers and editors, to whom I refer, do not under these circumstances express sympathy for the innocent; on the contrary they are the first to protest with frantic vehemence against our efforts by law to put a stop to overcapitalization and stock-watering. The apologists of successful dishonesty always declaim against any effort to punish or prevent it on the ground that such effort will "unsettle business." It is they who by their acts have unsettled business; and the very men raising this cry spend hundreds of thousands of dollars in securing, by speech, editorial, book or pamphlet, the defense by misstatement of what they have done; and yet when we correct their misstatements by telling the truth, they declaim against us for breaking silence, lest "values be unsettled"! They have hurt honest businessmen, honest workingmen, honest farmers; and now they clamor against the truth being told.

The keynote of all these attacks upon the effort to secure honesty in business and in politics, is exprest in a recent speech in which the speaker stated that prosperity had been checked by the effort for the "moral regeneration of the business world," an effort which he denounced as "unnatural, unwarranted and injurious" and for which he stated the panic was the penalty. The morality of such a plea is precisely as great as if made on behalf of the men caught in a gambling establishment when that gambling establishment is raided by the police. If such words mean anything they mean that those sentiments they represent stand against the effort to bring about a moral regeneration of business which will prevent a repetition of the insurance, banking and street railroad scandals in New York; repetition of the Chicago and Alton deal; a repetition of the combination between certain professional politicians, certain professional labor leaders and certain big financiers from the disgrace of which San Francisco has just been rescued; a repetition of the successful efforts by the Standard Oil people to crush out every competitor, to overawe the common carriers, and to establish a monopoly which treats the public with the contempt which the public deserves so long as it permits men like the public men of whom I speak to represent it in politics, men like the heads of colleges to whom I refer to educate its youth. The outcry against stopping dishonest practices among the very wealthy is precisely similar to the outcry raised against every effort for cleanliness and decency in city government because, forsooth, it will "hurt business." The same outcry is made against the Department of Justice for prosecuting the heads of colossal corporations that is made against the men who in San Francisco are prosecuting with impartial severity the wrongdoers among businessmen, public officials, and labor leaders alike. The principle is the same in the two cases. Just as the blackmailer and the bribe-giver stand on the same evil eminence of infamy, so the man who makes an enormous fortune by corrupting Legislatures and municipalities and fleecing his stockholders and the public stands on a level with the creature who fattens on the blood money of the gambling house, the saloon and the brothel. Moreover both kinds of corruption in the last analysis are far more intimately connected than would at first sight appear; the wrongdoing is at bottom the same. Corrupt business and corrupt politics act and react, with ever increasing debasement, one on the other; the rebate-taker, the franchise-trafficker, the manipulator of securities, the purveyor and protector of vice, the blackmailing ward boss, the ballot-box-stuffer, the demagogue, the mob leader, the hired bully and man-killer, all alike work at the same web of corruption, and all alike should be abhorred by honest men.

The "business" which is hurt by the movement for honesty is the kind of business which, in the long run, it pays the country to have hurt.

It is the kind of business which has tended to make the very name "high finance" a term of scandal to which all honest American men of business should join in putting an end. One of the special pleaders for business dishonesty, in a recent speech, in denouncing the Administration for enforcing the law against the huge and corrupt corporations which have defied the law, also denounced it for endeavoring to secure a far-reaching law making employers liable for injuries to their employees. It is meet and fit that the apologists for corrupt wealth should oppose every effort to relieve weak and helpless people from crushing misfortune brought upon them by injury in the business from which they gain a bare livelihood and their employers fortunes. It is hypocritical baseness to speak of a girl who works in a factory where the dangerous machinery is unprotected as having the "right" freely to contract to expose herself to dangers to life and limb. She has no alternative but to suffer want or else to expose herself to such dangers, and when she loses a hand or is otherwise maimed or disfigured for life it is a moral wrong that the burden of the risk necessarily incidental to the business should be placed with crushing weight upon her weak shoulders and the man who has profited by her work escape scot-free. This is what our opponents advocate, and it is proper that they should advocate it, for it rounds out their advocacy of those most dangerous members of the criminal class, the criminals of vast wealth, the men who can afford best to pay for such championship in the press and on the stump.

It is difficult to speak about the judges, for it behooves us all to treat with the utmost respect the high office of judge; and our judges as a whole are brave and upright men. But there is need that those who go wrong should not be allowed to feel that there is no condemnation of their wrongdoing. A judge who on the bench either truckles to the mob or bows down before a corporation; or who, having left the bench to become a corporation lawyer, seeks to aid his clients by denouncing as enemies of property all those who seek to stop the abuses of the criminal rich; such a man performs an even worse service to the body politic than the Legislator or Executive who goes wrong. In no way can respect for the courts be so quickly undermined as by teaching the public thru the action of a judge himself that there is reason for the loss of such respect. The judge who by word or deed makes it plain that the corrupt corporation, the law-defying corporation, the law-defying rich man, has in him a sure and trustworthy ally, the judge who by misuse of the process of injunction makes it plain that in him the wageworker has a determined and unscrupulous enemy, the judge who when he decides in an employer's liability or a tenement house factory case shows that he has neither sympathy for nor understanding of those fellow citizens of his who most need his sympathy and understanding; these judges work as much evil as if they pandered to the mob, as if they shrank from sternly repressing violence and disorder. The judge who does his full duty well stands higher, and renders a better service to the people, than any other public servant; he is entitled to greater respect; and if he is a true servant of the people, if he is upright, wise and fearless he will unhesitatingly disregard even the wishes of the people if they conflict with the eternal principles of right as against wrong. He must serve the people; but he must serve his conscience first. All honor to such a judge; and all honor cannot be rendered him if it is rendered equally to his brethren who fall immeasurably below the high ideals for which he stands. There should be a sharp discrimination against such judges. They claim immunity from criticism, and the claim is heatedly advanced by men and newspapers like those of whom I speak. Most certainly they can claim immunity from untruthful criticism; and their champions, the newspapers and the public men I have mentioned, exquisitely illustrate by their own actions mendacious criticism in its most flagrant and iniquitous form.

But no servant of the people has a right to expect to be free from just and honest criticism. It is the newspapers and the public men whose thoughts and deeds show them to be most alien to honesty and truth who themselves loudly object to truthful and honest criticism of their fellow servants of the great monied interests.

We have no quarrel with the individuals, whether public men, lawyers or editors, to whom I refer. These men derive their sole power from the great, sinister offenders who stand behind them. They are but puppets who move as the strings are pulled by those who control the enormous masses of corporate wealth which if itself left uncontrolled threatens dire evil to the Republic. It is, not the puppets, but the strong, cunning men and the mighty forces working for evil behind, and to a certain extent thru, the puppets, with whom we have to deal. We seek to control law-defying wealth, in the first place to prevent its doing evil, and in the next place to avoid the vindictive and dreadful radicalism which if left uncontrolled it is certain in the end to arouse. Sweeping attacks upon all property, upon all men of means, without regard to whether they do well or ill, would sound the death knell of the Republic; and such attacks become inevitable if decent citizens permit rich men whose lives are corrupt and evil to domineer in swollen pride, unchecked and unhindered, over the destinies of this country. We act in no vindictive spirit, and we are no respecters of persons. If a labor union does what is wrong we oppose it as fearlessly as we oppose a corporation that does wrong; and we stand with equal stoutness for the rights of the man of wealth and for the rights of the wageworkers; just as much so for one as for the other. We seek to stop wrongdoing; and we desire to punish the wrongdoer only so far as is necessary in order to achieve this end. We are the staunch upholders of every honest man, whether businessman or wageworker.

I do not for a moment believe that our actions have brought on business distress; so far as this is due to local and not world-wide causes, and to the actions of any particular individuals, it is due to the speculative folly and flagrant dishonesty of a few men of great wealth, who now seek to shield themselves from the effects of their own wrongdoings by ascribing its results to the actions of those who have sought to put a stop to the wrongdoing. But if it were true that to cut out rottenness from the body politic meant a momentary check to an unhealthy-seeming prosperity, I should not for one moment hesitate to put the knife to the cancer. On behalf of all our people, on behalf no less of the honest man of means than of the honest man who earns each day's livelihood by that day's sweat of his brow, it is necessary to insist upon honesty in business and politics alike, in all walks of life, in big things and in little things; upon just and fair dealing as between man and man. We are striving for the right in the spirit of Abraham Lincoln when he said:

Fondly do we hope—fervently do we pray—that this mighty scourge [of war] may speedily pass away. Yet, if God wills that it continue until all the wealth piled by the bondsmen's two hundred and fifty years of unrequited toil shall be sunk, and until every drop of blood drawn with the lash shall be paid by another drawn with the sword, as was said three thousand years ago, so still it must be said, "The judgments of the Lord are true and righteous altogether."

With malice toward none; with charity for all; with firmness in the right, as God gives us to see the right, let us strive on to finish the work we are in.

Sincerely yours

January 6, 1908. Washington
To William Howard Taft

Dear Will:

Do you want any action about those Federal officials? I will break their necks with the utmost cheerfulness if you say the word!

Ever yours

January 12, 1908. Washington
To George B. Cortelyou

Dear Mr. Cortelyou:

Will you glance at the enclosed? I do not know quite how to answer it, and I should like a little information which would enable me to do so. As far as I can make out, the chief objection (outside of New York) to our course is the allegation that money is loaned to bankers without interest which they loan for speculative purposes to the stock brokers at a high rate of interest. I do wish we could tax stock speculation out of existence. The purchase and sale of stocks on a margin is gambling, pure and simple. I know how difficult it is to do anything effective to stop such practices, but I do wish that it were possible to devise some scheme to effect the object.

Sincerely yours

[Handwritten] Will you go over the enclosed papers from Root; and return them with your comments and suggestions?

January 27, 1908. Washington
To Kermit Roosevelt

Dear Kermit:

The campaign for Taft seems to be getting along well. Of course the statements that I am trying to dictate his nomination are ludicrous falsehoods, and the statements that I am using the offices to force his nomination are wicked falsehoods. But I believe with all my soul that Taft, far more than any other public man of prominence, represents the principles for which I stand; and, furthermore, I believe in these principles with all my soul; and I should hold myself false to my duty if I sat supine and let the men who have taken such joy in my refusal to run again select some candidate whose success would mean the undoing of what I have sought to achieve. The men most hostile to me show a tendency to gather around Hughes.[1] Hughes is a fairly good man (but not a big man) and an inordinately conceited one. He is therefore jealous of me, and the men who are backing him believe that they could count upon his jealousy of me to make him take action which would amount in effect to undoing what I had done, altho that might not be Hughes' conscious purpose. Hughes is not knee-high to Taft in any way, but he has the kind of quality which is apt to win out in conventions as against a man of bold, generous type like Taft, who looks out too little for his own interests. But this year I believe we shall be able to awaken people to what the real situation is. I am confident that if the convention was held at once Taft would be nominated. It is always unsafe to prophesy in politics, and all that can be said is that if we can hold things as they are we shall be all right. Whether we can so hold them I cannot tell, and nobody can.

We are at the height of the social season, and as formal social entertainments are rather a nightmare to me, I look forward eagerly to its

---

[1]Charles Evans Hughes, governor of New York.

ending. I am worked up to my limit, having just been carefully preparing a message to Congress in which I intend to draw the issue as sharply as I well can between the men of predatory wealth and the administration. As I also try to get some exercise riding or walking every day this means that going to entertainments in the evening makes a serious tax upon me.

Your loving father

February 2, 1908. Washington
To Kermit Roosevelt

Dear Kermit:

On January 31st everything was frozen hard and this put the tennis court in fair condition, so the Tennis Cabinet had what I think will really be its last session until spring. Gifford Pinchot and I played six sets against the French Ambassador and Alford Cooley, breaking even. It was bitterly cold but we thoroly enjoyed it. I had been riding with mother the two or three previous days, but February opened with a snowstorm and then freezing weather, and I think walking will be good enough as a form of exercise for some little time to come.

On Friday I sent in my message on the trusts and labor, and incidentally on corporations. I am well satisfied with the message and I think it was time to send it in. Of course it caused a great flutter in the dovecote. As we approach nearer the convention more and more people will pay heed to what the candidates will say rather than to what the President may say, and this is well-nigh the last occasion I shall have to speak when all men, however unwilling, must listen, and I wanted to put my deep and earnest convictions into the message. All of my advisers were naturally enough against my sending it in, for councils of war never fight; but Mother really likes the message, and I am sure that it is on the right track and that it says what ought to be said and that the ultimate effect will be good.

Your loving father

[Handwritten] 7:30 now I have just come in from a brisk three hours walk over the frozen snow out to Chevy Chase and back by Rock Creek. Meyer and Winthrop went with me.

February 13, 1908. Washington
To Florence Lockwood La Farge

Dear Florence:

I have read Miss Addams' book and I am greatly disappointed in it. Hull House has done admirable work which means that Miss Addams has done admirable work; just as Dr. Rainsford in his parish did admirable work which I am not sure was not even better in its ultimate results upon the people affected. But evidently Miss Addams is one of those confused thinkers whose thought cannot be accepted for the guidance of others. In certain of the chapters of her book she states facts and conditions that are interesting and once or twice develops theories which have in them an element of good. But there is always in what she says an element both of the fantastic and of the obscure; and this is absolutely inevitable when the book is written with an *idée fixe*—the theory that antimilitarism is the solvent for all troubles. Of course she might just as well say that vegetarianism or antivaccination would solve our industrial problems as to say that militarism has anything of the kind, sort or description to do with any of either the social or industrial troubles with which this country is confronted. Her idea on militarism is itself preposterous; but granting that it were right the fact would remain that militarism has no more to do with the crisis of American society than, say, eating horseflesh in honor of Thor. The benefits and abuses of militarism are very real in the social and industrial life of the nations of continental Europe; but militarism has been a practically imponderable element in producing the social and industrial conditions of England during the last ninety years, and has not been any element at all in the United States for the past forty years.

The trouble evidently is that Miss Addams is a striking example of the mischievous effect produced by the teachings of a man like Tolstoi upon a mind without the strength, training and natural ability to withstand them. Tolstoi is a great novelist, and his novels like *Anna Karenina, War and Peace, The Cossacks,* and *Sevastopol* can be read with advantage if we read them just as we read the novels of medieval Poland by Sienkiewicz; but the minute that Tolstoi is accepted as a moral teacher he can benefit only the very small fraction of mankind which can differentiate the good he teaches from the mass of fantastic and unhealthy absurdity in which it is embodied. As it happens, I have never yet met any human being who had been morally benefited by Tolstoi; but I have met hundreds of well-meaning, crude creatures who have been seriously damaged by him. He preaches against war, for instance, just as he preaches against marriage. His *Kreutzer Sonata* is treated by his admirers as if it were a melancholy and unnatural production of his. It is melancholy, but it is not unnatural in the least. The same law of action and reaction which tended under the old regime in France to make the debauchee and the devotee alternate in the same family and sometimes in the same individual, makes it natural that a filthy and repulsive book like the *Kreutzer Sonata* should be written by a man in whom a fantastic theory of race annihilation by abstention from marriage is fitly and inevitably supplemented by gross and criminal aberrations of the sexual passion. No really good pure-minded and healthy man or woman could have written or approved of the *Kreutzer Sonata;* and just as little would any such man or woman be capable of approving either the unnatural asceticism which Tolstoi preaches or the gross and unnatural debauchery which such asceti-cism in its turn inevitably breeds.

Now all this applies in principle just as much to his assault on all war—which foolish Jane Addams, like still more foolish justice Brewer, enthusiastically applauds. Of course Tolstoi himself is logical in his folly. He is against all industrialism just as he is against all war; and he wants the whole race to die out immediately. Industrialism under any circum-stances means the loss of thousands of lives. Industrialism in the United States has to its credit probably a hundred times the number of men and women killed and crippled that have been killed and crippled since the foundation of the Republic in all our wars. We must make every effort to lighten the suffering that this killing and crippling entails; but to declare that because lives are lost in mines, on railways and in factories, we should abandon all work in or on them, would be not one bit better and not one bit worse than declaring that righteous people must not be pre-pared to defend their rights because scoundrels often do wrong by vio-lence. There is no possible theory by which the existence of a policeman can be justified that does not also justify the existence of a soldier. Russia, Tolstoi's own country, suffers primarily because for two centuries and a half she was under the hideous Tartar yoke, and she endured this slavery because her people could not fight successfully. If the Russians of the 13th, 14th and 15th centuries had been able to fight as the Swiss fought at the same period, I very firmly believe that Russia would today be as pros-perous and progressive as Switzerland. There is misery and suffering in Switzerland, but nothing like what there is in Russia. The doctrine of non-resistance is old, and its results have always been evil. The same fantastic morality on this point which Tolstoi now develops was rife in the later ages of Byzantium, and that decadent people disbelieved in militarism as heartily as Miss Jane Addams. Up to the very last, with the Turk at their gates, there were plenty of priests and laymen in Constantinople who de-clared it unlawful to shed blood, even that of an enemy; and such an atti-tude had no small part in producing the condition which has subjected southwestern Europe for four centuries to the unspeakable horror of Turkish rule. In our own country the most sordid political corruption has, as Owen Wister recently pointed out, existed in the regions where the English and German nonresistant and antimilitary sects had supreme control. What the distant future holds in store, no man can tell; but today it is just as wicked to preach unrighteous peace as to preach unrighteous war, and it is even more foolish.

 With love to Grant,

 Ever yours

March 15, 1908. Washington
To Clinton H. Merriam

Personal

Dear Merriam:

 Is there any kind of air gun which you would recommend which I could use for killing English sparrows around my Long Island place? I would like to do as little damage as possible to our other birds, and so I suppose the less noise I make the better.

 Faithfully yours

March 20, 1908. Washington
To John H. Patterson

Private

My dear Colonel Patterson:

 A year hence I shall leave the Presidency, and, while I cannot now decide what I shall do, it is possible that I might be able to make a trip to Africa. Would you be willing to give me some advice about it? I shall be fifty years old, and for ten years I have led a busy, sedentary life, and so it is unnecessary to say that I shall be in no trim for the hardest kind of explorers' work. But I am fairly healthy, and willing to work in order to get into a game country where I could do some shooting. I should suppose I could be absent a year on the trip. Now, is it imposing too much on your good nature to tell me when and where I ought to go to get some really good shooting, such as you and your friends had last Christmas day, for instance. Would it be possible for me to go in from Mozambique or some such place and come out down the Nile? How much time should I allow in order to give ample opportunity for hunting? Would it be possible for you to give me any idea of the expense, and to tell me how I should make my preparations; whom to write to in advance, etc.? Is there anyone who outfits for a trip like that to whom I could turn to know what I was to take?

 I trust you will excuse me if I am trespassing too much on your good nature. It may be that I shall not be able to go at all; but I should like mightily to see the great African fauna, and to kill one or two rhino or buffalo and some of the big antelopes, with the chance of a shot at a lion.

 Sincerely yours

[Handwritten] I suppose that in a year's trip I could get into a really good game country; I am no butcher, but I would like to *see* plenty of game, and kill a few head.

March 21, 1908. Washington
To Charles S. Sperry

My dear Admiral Sperry:

You are to take the fleet back, and it will be an even more responsible voyage than the outward one, for you are to visit Australia and Japan, as well as coming home thru Suez. I need not tell you that you should exercise the most careful watch thruout the time that you are in Oriental waters—for you will naturally exercise the most careful watch at all times both before and after you leave the Orient. I wish to impress upon you, what I do not suppose is necessary, to see to it that none of our men does anything out of the way while in Japan. If you give the enlisted men leave while at Tokyo or anywhere else in Japan be careful to choose only those upon whom you can absolutely depend. There must be no suspicion of insolence or rudeness on our part. Of course the most important thing is to guard our ships against possible attack by fanatics; but next to this in importance is to prevent there being any kind of action by any one of our men which would give an excuse for the feeling that we had been in any way guilty of misconduct. Aside from the loss of a ship I had far rather that we were insulted than that we insult anybody under these peculiar conditions. I firmly believe that the Japanese Government will use every effort to see that the highest consideration and courtesy are accorded to our people, and you of course will do everything in your power to show the utmost consideration and courtesy to the Japanese with whom you are brought in contact, not only in Japan but elsewhere. We want to take peculiar care in this matter. I am delighted with your letter to Secretary Metcalf; so much so that I want parts of it published. I have just seen your letter to Pillsbury. We will try to get you a proper ship.

With regard, believe me,
Sincerely yours

March 30, 1908. Washington
To Albert J. Beveridge

My dear Senator Beveridge:

I very earnestly hope that you will not offer your general child labor bill as an amendment to any measure that may come up affecting child labor in the District of Columbia. I find that some people feel that the failure to have a good child labor law for the District of Columbia is due, as they claim, to your announced intention last year and this year of insisting on offering your measure as an amendment to the District child labor bill. I have told my informants that I was sure this was a mistake, but that in any event I would write you and say that I very earnestly hoped you would not do anything that would mix up the two measures. There is no question whatever that we should have a model child labor law for the District, whereas many excellent people, whether misguided or not, did not favor as yet the proposed Federal law—I mean the one to get at the products of child labor everywhere thruout the Union. Under such circumstances the wise thing is to get what is imperatively needed and can be had, and not to throw it away in making what is certain to be an unsuccessful effort to get something else in addition.

I am confident that this is your own view, but my informants were so positive that I write you anyhow.

Sincerely yours

April 11, 1908. Washington
To Cecil Spring Rice

Dear Cecil:

I was delighted with the Mazzini, and with no part of it quite so much as with the poem on the title page. How I wish that you and Mrs. Springy were to be here! There is such an infinity of things to talk over and I cannot begin to write about them all. Mrs. Roosevelt and I were thinking just the other day, in connection with the recent fuss over the American Ambassador to Berlin, about a remark in your last letter in which you spoke of the growing materialism of the Germans. The ambassadorial incident emphasized this. Tower is a good fellow, of great wealth, & of rather cultivated tastes. Hill is a somewhat better man—in fact I think a decidedly better man—but without the wealth. In consequence, to my surprise, I found that not only the American sojourners abroad who belong to the class of the vulgar rich, but all of the vulgar rich in Berlin, and especially those who are connected with the court circle, were violently against the change. Not a few both in the court circle and among the traveling Americans stated with obvious sincerity that under Tower the American Embassy stood easily foremost in Berlin as compared with all the other Embassies, and it evidently never entered their heads that in the question of standing foremost there was anything to be considered save wealth combined with social aptitude. As a matter of fact I am anxious to have it understood that it is not necessary to be a multimillionaire in order to reach the highest positions in the American diplomatic service. The trouble was entirely unexpected to me. I am simply unable to understand the value placed by so many people upon great wealth. I very thoroly understand the need of sufficient means to enable the man or woman to be comfortable; I also entirely understand the pleasure of having enough more than this so as to add certain luxuries, and above all, that greatest of all luxuries, the escape from the need of considering at every turn whether it is possible to spend a dollar or two extra; but when the last limit has been reached, then increase in wealth means but little, certainly as compared with all kinds of other things. In consequence, I am simply unable to make myself take the attitude of respect toward the very wealthy men which such an enormous multitude of people evidently really feel. I am delighted to show any courtesy to Pierpont Morgan or Andrew Carnegie or James J. Hill; but as for regarding any one of them as, for instance, I regard Professor Bury, or Peary, the Arctic explorer, or Admiral Evans, or Rhodes, the historian, or Selous, the big game hunter (to mention at random guests who have been at the White House not long ago)—why, I could not force myself to do it even if I wanted to, which I do not. The very luxurious, grossly material life of the average multimillionaire whom I know, does not appeal to me in the least, and nothing would hire me to lead it. It is an exceedingly nice thing to have enough money to be able to take a hunting trip in Africa after big game (if you are not able to make it pay for itself in some other way). It is an exceedingly nice thing, if you are young, to have one or two good jumping horses and to be able to occasionally hunt—altho Heaven forfend that anyone for whom I care should treat riding to hounds as the serious business of life! It is an exceedingly nice thing to have a good house and to be able to purchase good books and good pictures, and especially to have that house isolated from others. But I wholly fail to see where any real enjoyment comes from a dozen automobiles, a couple of hundred horses, and a good many different homes luxuriously upholstered. From the standpoint of real pleasure I should selfishly prefer my old-time ranch on the Little Missouri to anything in Newport.

There! I did not intend to go into a statement of my own views. I merely got interested in trying to explain why it is that I have been quite unable either to get on with the typical multimillionaire, or to understand the attitude of admiration toward him assumed by a good many different persons, from sovereigns down.

Give my love to Mrs. Springy.

Faithfully yours

April 11, 1908. Washington
To Archibald Roosevelt

Dearest Archie:

Ethel has bought on trial an eight-months' bulldog pup. He is very cunning, very friendly, and wriggles all over in a frantic desire to be petted.

Quentin really seems to be getting on pretty well with his baseball. In each of the last two games he made a base hit and a run. I have just had to give him and three of his associates a dressing down—one of the three being Charlie Taft. Yesterday afternoon was rainy, and the four of them played five hours inside the White House. They were very boisterous and were all the time on the verge of mischief, and finally they made spitballs and deliberately put them on the portraits. I did not discover it until after dinner, and then pulled Quentin out of bed and had him take them all off the portraits, and this morning required him to bring in the three other culprits before me. I explained to them that they had acted like boors; that it would have been a disgrace to have behaved so in any gentleman's house, but that it was a double disgrace in the house of the Nation; that Quentin could have no friend to see him, and the other three could not come inside the White House, until I felt that a sufficient time had elapsed to serve as a punishment. They were four very sheepish small boys when I got thru with them!

Your loving father

April 19, 1908. Washington
To Kermit Roosevelt

Dearest Kermit:

Ted turned up Thursday morning with a very sore throat, the doctor having sent him home. Being home with Mother and Ethel, and the rest and good food, speedily set him all right, and by Friday afternoon he was able to play tennis with great vigor, and Saturday he and Fitz went out riding. Mother and I also rode, going up the new bridle trail beside Rock Creek just beyond the other end of the Park. It is in low ground, and the flowers were too beautiful for anything, especially the Virginia cowslips and the dogtooth violets.

I made a hard fight to get Congress to give me four battleships, but they wouldn't do it. Most of them mean well enough, but do not know much, and the leaders are narrow-minded and selfish, and some of them, like Senator Hale, profoundly unpatriotic, and others, like McCall and Burton, if not unpatriotic, at least utterly indifferent to the honor and interest of the country when compared with their own advancement. I cannot give in public my reasons for being apprehensive about Japan, for of course to do so might bring on grave trouble; but I said enough to put Congress thoroly on its guard, if it cared to be on its guard. I do not believe there will be war with Japan, but I do believe that there is enough chance of war to make it eminently wise to insure against it by building such a navy as to forbid Japan's hoping for success. I happen to know that the Japanese military party is inclined for war with us and is not only confident of success, but confident that they could land a large expeditionary force in California and conquer all of the United States west of the Rockies. I fully believe that they would in the end pay dearly for this, but meantime we would have been set back at least a generation by the loss of life, the humiliation, and the material damage.

Your loving father

[Handwritten] I enclose another poem of Phil's; good, but not as good, or as original, as the first.

May 18, 1908. Washington
To De Alva Stanwood Alexander

Dear Mr. Alexander:

I do hope you will succeed in getting the compensation act for government employees amended in the Senate along more liberal lines than were followed in the House.

The compensation in case of death, at the best, will ordinarily be very small, and in the event that an injured man died after ten or eleven months, the amount that would be paid to his wife and children would be so pitifully small as to be almost a mockery.

There ought certainly to be some provision for permanent disability. Where a man is not killed but his earning power is entirely and permanently destroyed, his family is really in a more pitiable condition economically than if it had actually lost its breadwinner thru death, for it has not only lost his earning power, but has to carry the burden of an invalid member.

We are probably the richest nation in the world, yet we are doing less, far less, for those injured or killed in the service of the Government than even the poorest of the European countries have done.

On the other hand, I think very careful consideration should be given to the suggestion that some time should elapse between the injury and the payment of benefits. We do not want to put a premium upon malingering nor to destroy the spirit of self-reliance or self-help. It seems to me that the bill in its present form goes too far in relieving cases where the burden upon the injured man and his family would be slight, and leaves without adequate relief cases where the burden would be severe and crushing.

I think, too, the bill ought to be extended to cover any civilian employee who is injured or killed while protecting the property of the United States or while enforcing its laws.

I hope that before the bill is reported by the Senate Committee you will go over it with Mr. Neill, as I have before suggested, and see if we cannot secure a little more satisfactory bill than the present one.

Sincerely yours

May 23, 1908. Washington
To Theodore Roosevelt, Jr.

Dear Ted:

It gave me quite a pang to receive your letter and feel that you are really making up your mind to what you are going to do next fall. Of course I feel sad to think of the little bear going out into the world at last with a good many troubles and hard times before him. But you will be twenty-one, Ted; you want to make your own way, and I have the utmost confidence and belief in you, and indeed, am very proud of you; and I am sure you will succeed. It will be hard at first; especially when you are working your utmost, while Kermit and I, eaten alive with ticks, horseflies, jiggers, and the like, are enjoying ourselves in Africa. The only thing will be to remember that you have had first-rate fun as a boy up to the time you were twenty-one; and that the man who is to succeed must buckle to real work during the early and most important years of his manhood.

Yes, that is an interesting book of Winston Churchill's about his father; but I can't help feeling about both of them that the older one *was* a rather cheap character, and the younger one *is* a rather cheap character. Recently I have been reading my usual odd variety of books, including for the last three or four nights Creasy's *History of the Ottoman Turks*, which gave me much comfort. I had a very nice note from the Brothers in acknowledgment of the volumes I sent on.

David Gray was here this week. Both Roswell and Audrey are laid up, much to my disappointment; but good Bob Bacon gave David Gray a horse, and good George Meyer gave me another, and the four of us had a first-class ride. I was on George Meyer's crack jumper, and really I think he is the best heavyweight carrier I have ever been on, unless, perhaps, it was one horse of Austin Wadsworth's up in the Geneseo Valley. Sagamore, in the old days, did not have to carry my present weight. This horse is a good deal better than Roswell, being both a more powerful and more willing jumper. Still Roswell is a mighty good horse.

Your loving father

May 29, 1908. Washington
To Lyman Abbott

My dear Dr. Abbott:

As to the matter of my renomination, it seems to me that the proper ground to take is that any man who supposes that I have been scheming for it, is not merely a fool, but shows himself to be a man of low morality. He reflects upon himself, not upon me. There has never been a moment when I could not have had the Republican nomination with practical unanimity by simply raising one finger. At this moment I am still actively engaged in getting delegates for Taft—as in Texas, for instance, to mention something that occurred a week ago; or in preventing delegates who have been instructed for Taft from declaring that they would go for me anyhow—to cite action which I took yesterday as regards two delegates in West Virginia. Any man competent to express any opinion whatever knows this perfectly well. He knows that not merely the far West but that, for instance, the conventions of New York, New Jersey, Massachusetts and Vermont would have gone for me with the wildest enthusiasm if I had merely said I was willing to abide by the judgment of the party as to whether or not it was expedient that I should run. Under such circumstances, when I could without the slightest difficulty have made each State convention declare for me with infinitely greater enthusiasm than any State convention has shown about anything yet, it is simply silly to suppose that I would go into some intrigue even more futile than tortuous—an intrigue that would have to be kept secret from all my best friends, including, for instance, Senator Lodge, and Loeb, and all my family—an intrigue which would be entirely pointless, and almost certainly of no avail. Moreover, be it remembered that the same people who speak of this as my secret intention are at other times the ones who are loudest in denouncing me for trying to bring about Taft's nomination. The real fact is, as most of them know perfectly well, that nothing could have prevented my renomination excepting the most resolute effort on my part to get someone else accepted as representing me and nominated in my place; and I had this object partly in view in endeavoring to get Taft nominated, altho I was of course mainly actuated by the fact that I think that of all men in this country Taft is the best fitted at this time to be President and to carry on the work upon which we have entered during the past six years.

The facts about the third-term agitation are that it does not come from any men high in public life, but from plain people who take no very great part in politics, and who seem to have been puzzled at my attitude in declining to run. The politicians, like the big-business men, all cordially agree with me that I ought not to run again. A few weeks ago there was an article published in *Success* which you ought to see if you have any desire to know where the third-term talk comes from; it isn't "inspired" from above at all. Yesterday, for instance, Vorys, Taft's campaign manager in Ohio, suddenly told me that he had difficulty in Ohio in preventing the ordinary voters, the men whom he would meet at the drugstores or in the cars, or in similar places, from insisting upon my being renominated. Under such circumstances I would be exasperated, if I were not amused, at so much as anybody talking about the supposition that I was engaged in an effort to have the renomination forced upon me. As a matter of fact I doubt if Taft himself could be more anxious than I am that Taft be nominated, and that any stampede to me be prevented. I wish it on every account, personal and public, and I am lending every energy now to prevent the possibility of such a stampede; because if the convention were stampeded and I were nominated an exceedingly ugly situation would be created, a situation very difficult to meet at all, and (probably difficult) impossible to meet satisfactorily; whereas, if as I have every reason to believe, Taft is nominated almost by acclamation, certainly on the first ballot, everything is as it should be.

Do tell your Mr. Steiner how I like his articles on the immigrant. I grow extremely indignant at the attitude of coarse hostility to the immigrant taken by so many natives of the type he describes. I have never had much chance to deal with the Slav, Magyar, or Italian; but wherever I have had the chance I have tried to do with them as with the German and the Irishman, the Catholic and the Jew, and that is, treat them so as to appeal to their self-respect and make it easy for them to become enthusiastically loyal Americans as well as good citizens. I have one Catholic in my Cabinet and have had another, and I now have a Jew in the Cabinet; and part of my object in each appointment was to implant in the minds of our fellow-Americans of Catholic or of Jewish faith, or of foreign ancestry or birth, the knowledge that they have in this country just the same rights and opportunities as everyone else, just the same chance of reward for doing the highest kind of service; and therefore just the same ideals as a standard toward which to strive. I want the Jewish young man who is born in this country to feel that Straus stands for his ideal of the successful man rather than some crooked Jew moneymaker. I want the young Catholic of Irish or French descent to feel that if he acts as a good American should, he can become a Cabinet minister like Bonaparte or Wynne; a Governor of the Philippines, like Smith; a judge, like Tracey; in short, that the right chance is open to him and the right ideals before him. In my Cabinet there sit together Meyer, whose granduncle was a colonel under Blucher at Waterloo; and Bonaparte, whose great grandfather was Napoleon's brother and a king whom Meyer's granduncle helped to overthrow. That they are both good Americans and nothing else is all that we think of; (and it is not considered) nobody asks whether any member of my Cabinet is of English, or Scotch, or Dutch, or German, or Irish descent; whether he is Protestant, Catholic or Jew. In short, we have acted on principles of straight Americanism; and I am glad that before I end my term I shall have in my Cabinet Luke Wright, a representative of the South, a man who fought in the Confederate service, and who is just as loyal an American today as the best veterans of the Grand Army. It was the one thing which I felt was wanted to emphasize the entire Americanism of the Cabinet, to give it from the national standpoint an absolutely representative character.

So give my regards to Steiner. I wish I could help in some striking fashion to do justice to, and get justice for, the Slav!—and our other recent immigrants just as has finally been done for the sons of those who came here a generation ago.

Faithfully yours

June 15, 1908. Washington
To Joel Chandler Harris

Dear Uncle Remus:

Here is something in which I would like to get the assistance of Mr. Billy Sanders, the sage of Shady Dale, and of all the readers of the *Home Magazine* and of all who think as the editors of the *Home Magazine* evidently do think.

Last Saturday, in the late afternoon, when it had grown a little cool, I was riding with two of my aides, Captain Fitzhugh Lee, and Captain Archie Butt of your own State and my Mother's State of Georgia. The mare I was on by the way was named Georgia, and a good mare she is, too, well-behaved, and a good jumper. We were taking our horses out to exercise them over some jumps. We had just been listening to the really superb singing of the men's chorus of the Arion Singing Society, an organization of citizens of German birth or parentage, who were about to go abroad to appear at certain courts and elsewhere in Europe, and who had wish to sing in the White House as a farewell before starting on their foreign journey. Among other things they had, at my request, sung "Dixie" (as well as the Old Kentucky Home and the Suwanee River). While riding we were talking over the fact that "Dixie" was far and away the best tune (and the best military tune, that we knew, not even excepting Garry Owen), and that it had won its way until it was the tune which would bring everybody to his feet with a yell in any audience in any part of the country; and we were bemoaning the fact that there never had been any words which were in any way adequate to the tune, and dwelling on the further fact that it was such a fine battle tune—the best battle tune of our army. Captain Butt then added that just as "Dixie" stood alone among tunes, so we had in Julia Ward Howe's great "Battle Hymn of the Republic" the very finest and noblest battle hymn possest by any Nation of the world, a hymn that in loftiness of thought and expression, in both words and tune, lent itself to choral singing as no other battle hymn did in any country; and he added that there was not a sectional line in the hymn, not a word that could awaken a single un-pleasant thought in the mind of any American, no matter where he lived and no matter on which side he or his father had fought in the great war. I told him I entirely agreed with him, and that, just as "Dixie" was be-coming the tune which when played excited most enthusiasm among Americans everywhere, so I hoped that sooner or later all Americans would grow to realize that in this "Battle Hymn of the Republic" we had what really ought to be a great National treasure, something that all Americans would grow to know intimately, so that in any audience any-where in the land when the tune was started most of the audience should be able to join in singing the words. We then grew to wondering if this good result would ever be achieved, and we thought it would be worth while to write to you. We know that any such movement can come, if at all, only because of a genuine popular feeling, and with small regard to the opinion of any one man or any particular set of men; and it can only come slowly in any event; but we thought it might be helped on a little if what we had to say was published in your magazine. I append a copy of the Battle Hymn.

Faithfully yours

June 17, 1908. Washington
To Hermann H. Kohlsaat

Dear Kohlsaat:

Taft is reading the letter of yours now and chuckling over it heartily. We are going to elect him with a swoop; but we must all work on the assumption that it is a very hard contest!

Faithfully yours

June 19, 1908. Washington
To George Otto Trevelyan

My dear Trevelyan:

Well, the convention is over and Taft is nominated on a platform which I heartily approve. No one can prophesy in politics, and so I can-not be sure that we shall elect him, but the chances I believe favor it, and most certainly it will show [indecipherable] in the country if he is not elected. For, always excepting Washington and Lincoln, I believe that Taft as President will rank with any other man who has ever been in the White House.

It has been a curious contest, for I have had to fight tooth and nail against being nominated myself, and in the last three weeks it has needed very resolute effort on my part to prevent a break among the delegations, which would have meant a stampede for me and my nomination. I could not have prevented it at all unless I had thrown myself heart and soul into the business of nominating Taft and had shown to the country that he stood for exactly the same principles and policies that I did, and that I believed with all my heart and soul that under him we should progress steadily along the road this administration has traveled. He and I view public questions exactly alike. In fact, I think it has been very rare that two public men have ever been so much at one in all the essentials of their beliefs and practices.

When I made my announcement three years ago last November, just after the election, that I would under no circumstances again be a candidate, I of course acted on a carefully thought-out and considered theory. Having made it and having given my word to the people at large as to what I would do, and other men, including Taft, having entered the field on the strength of this statement of mine, I never felt the slightest hesitancy, the slightest wavering, as to the proper course to follow. But the developments of the last year or two have been so out of the common that at times I have felt a little uncomfortable as to whether my announced decision had been wise. But I think it was wise; and now I want to give you my reasons in full.

In the first place, I will freely admit what there is to say against it. I have a good deal of contempt for the type which Mirabeau condemned in Lafayette as the "Cromwell-Grandison" type, for those who, like Dante's Pope, are guilty of "il gran refuito" (I am a trifle uncertain as to the correctness of the Italian.) I do not like any man who flinches from work, and I like him none the better if he covers his flinching under the title of self-abnegation or renunciation or any other phrase, which may mean merely weakness, or else that he is willing to subordinate great and real public interests to a meticulous and fantastic morality in which he is concerned chiefly for the sake of his own shriveled soul. There is very much to be said in favor of the theory that the public has a right to demand as long service from any man who is doing good service as it thinks will be useful; and during the last year or two I have been rendered extremely uncomfortable both by the exultation of my foes over my announced intention to retire, and by the real uneasiness and chagrin felt by many good men because, as they believed, they were losing quite needlessly the leader in whom they trusted, and who they believed could bring to a successful conclusion certain struggles which they regarded as of vital concern to the national welfare. Moreover, it was of course impossible to foresee, and I did not foresee, when I made my public announcement of my intention, that the then leadership I possest would continue (as far as I am able to tell) unbroken, as has actually been the case; and that the people who believed in me and trusted me and followed me would three or four years later still feel that I was the man of all others whom they wisht to see President. Yet such I think has been the case; and therefore, when I felt obliged to insist on retiring and abandoning the leadership, now and then I felt ugly qualms as to whether I was not refusing to do what I ought to do, and abandoning great work on a mere fantastic point of honor.

These are strong reasons why my course should be condemned; yet I think that the countervailing reasons are still stronger. Of course when I spoke I had in view the precedent set by Washington and continued ever since, the precedent which recognizes the fact that, as there inheres in the Presidency more power than in any other office in any great republic or constitutional monarchy of modern times, it can only be saved from abuse by having the people as a whole accept as axiomatic the position that one man can hold it for no more than a limited time. I don't think that any harm comes from the concentration of powers in one man's hands, provided the holder does not keep it for more than a certain, definite time, and then returns to the people from whom he sprang. In the great days of the Roman Republic no harm whatever came from the dictatorship, because great tho the power of the dictator was, after a comparatively short period he surrendered it back to those from whom he gained it. On the other hand, the history of the first and second French Republics, not to speak of the Spanish-American Republics, not to speak of the Commonwealth, in Seventeenth-Century England, has shown that the strong man, and even the strong man who is good, may very readily subvert free institutions if he and the people at large grow to accept his continued possession of vast power as being necessary to good government. It is a very unhealthy thing that any man should be considered necessary to the people as a whole, save in the way of meeting some given crisis. Moreover, in a republic like ours the vital need is that there shall be a general recognition of the moral law, of the law which, as regards public men, means belief in efficient and disinterested service for the public rendered without thought of personal gain, and above all without the thought of self-perpetuation in office. I regard the memories of Washington and Lincoln as priceless heritages for our people, just because they are the memories of strong men, of men who cannot be accused of weakness or timidity, of men who I believe were quite as strong for instance as Cromwell or Bismarck, and very much stronger than the Louis Napoleon type, who, nevertheless, led careers marked by disinterestedness just as much as by strength; who, like Timoleon and Hampden, in very deed, and not as a mere matter of oratory or fine writing, put the public good, the good of the people as a whole, as the first of all considerations.

Now, my ambition is that, in however small a way, the work I do shall be along the Washington and Lincoln lines. While President I have *been* President, emphatically; I have used every ounce of power there was in the office and I have not cared a rap for the criticisms of those who spoke of my "usurpation of power"; for I knew that the talk was all nonsense and that there was no usurpation. I believe that the efficiency of this Government depends upon its possessing a strong central executive, and wherever I could establish a precedent for strength in the executive, as I did for instance as regards external affairs in the case of sending the fleet around the world, taking Panama, settling affairs of Santo Domingo and Cuba; or as I did in internal affairs in settling the anthracite coal strike, in keeping order in Nevada this year when the Federation of Miners threatened anarchy, or as I have done in bringing the big corporations to book—why, in all these cases I have felt not merely that my action was right in itself, but that in showing the strength of, or in giving strength to, the executive, I was establishing a precedent of value. I believe in a strong executive; I believe in power; but I believe that responsibility should go with power, and that it is not well that the strong executive should be a perpetual executive. Above all and beyond all I believe as I have said before that the salvation of this country depends upon Washington and Lincoln representing the type of leader to which we are true. I hope that in my acts I have been a good President, a President who has deserved well of the Republic; but most of all, I believe that whatever value my service may have comes even more from what I *am* than from what I *do*. I may be mistaken, but it is my belief that the bulk of my countrymen, the men whom Abraham Lincoln called "the plain people"—the farmers, mechanics, small tradesmen, hard-working professional men—feel that I am in a peculiar sense their President, that I represent the democracy in somewhat the fashion that Lincoln did, that is, not in any demagogic way but with the sincere effort to stand for a government by the people and for the people. Now the chief service I can render these plain people who believe in me is, not to destroy their ideal of me. They have followed me for the past six or seven years, indeed for some years previously, because they thought they recognized in me certain qualities in which they believed, because they regarded me as honest and disinterested, as having courage and common sense. Now I wouldn't for anything in the world shatter this belief of theirs in me, unless it were necessary to do so because they had embarked on a wrong course, and I could only be really true to them by forfeiting their good will. For instance, if they made up their minds that they would repudiate their debts, or under a gust of emotion decided to follow any course that was wrong, I could show loyalty to them only by opposing them tooth and nail, without the slightest regard to any amount of unpopularity or obloquy. But this of course isn't what I mean when I say I do not want to shatter their belief in me. What I mean is that I do not want to make them think that after all I am actuated by selfish motives, by motives of self-interest, that my championship of their cause, that my opposition to the plutocracy, is simply due to the usual demagog's desire to pander to the mob, or to the no more dangerous, but even more sinister, desire to secure self-advancement under the cloak of championship of popular rights. Of course I may be wrong in my belief, but my belief is that a great many honest people in this country who lead hard lives are helped in their efforts to keep straight and avoid envy and hatred and despair by their faith in me and in the principles I preach and in my practice of these principles. I would not for anything do the moral damage to these people that might come from shattering their faith in my personal disinterestedness. A few months ago three old back-country farmers turned up in Washington and after a while managed to get in to see me. They were rugged old fellows, as hairy as Boers and a good deal of the Boer type. They hadn't a black coat among them, and two of them wore no cravats; that, is, they just had on their working clothes, but all cleaned and brushed. When they finally got to see me they explained that they hadn't anything whatever to ask, but that they believed in me, believed that I stood for what they regarded as the American ideal, and as one rugged old fellow put it, "We want to shake that honest hand." Now this anecdote seems rather sentimental as I tell it, and I do not know that I can convey to you the effect that incident produced on me; but it was one of the very many incidents which have occurred, and they have made me feel that I am under a big debt of obligation to the good people of this country, and that I am bound not, by any unnecessary action of mine to forfeit their respect, not to hurt them by taking away any part of what they have built up as their ideal of me. It is just as I would not be willing to hurt my soldiers, to destroy my influence among men who look up to me as leader, by needlessly doing anything in battle which would give the idea that I was not personally brave; even tho some given risk might seem a little unnecessary to an outsider. However certain I might be that in seeking or accepting a third term I was actuated by a sincere desire to serve my fellow countrymen, I am very much afraid that multitudes of thoroly honest men who have believed deeply in me, (and some of whom, by the way, until I consented to run might think that they wisht me to run) would nevertheless have a feeling of disappointment if I did try to occupy the Presidency for three consecutive terms, to hold it longer than it was deemed wise that Washington should hold it.

I would have felt very differently, and very much more doubtful about what to do, if my leaving the Presidency had meant that there was no chance to continue the work in which I am engaged and which I deem vital to the welfare of the people. But in Taft there was ready to hand a man whose theory of public and private duty is my own, and whose practice of this theory is what I hope mine is; and if we can elect him President we achieve all that could be achieved by continuing me in the office, and yet we avoid all the objections, all the risk of creating a bad precedent.

There, my dear Sir George! I am afraid there is a good deal of ego in this letter, but I wanted you to feel just what it was that actuated me in the course I have followed, and I think you will understand me.

When I get thru the Presidency next year I am going for ten months or a year to Africa, and I am already in consultation with Edward North Buxton and Selous about the details of my trip. As I wrote to Selous, my aim is to visit the Pleistocene and the world "as it lay in sunshine unworn of the plow"; to see the great beasts whose like our forefathers saw when they lived in caves and smote one another with stone-headed axes. I do not want to do any butchering, but I would like to get a few trophies. Probably all to be put in the National Museum here at Washington. My second son will go with me, and if I come out by the Nile the following spring I shall hope to meet Mrs. Roosevelt and my younger daughter there. I should then greatly like to spend a few weeks in North Italy, France and England; but I shall not try to if I find I have to be presented at the various courts, & meet the sovereigns, prime ministers, and others. When I am thru with the Presidency I am thru with it, definitely and once and for all. The second my successor takes the oath of office I become a private citizen, and then I wish to go downstream among the earthen pots and not among the brazen pots. For instance, I should be delighted to meet the Kaiser if I could meet him now and talk with him and consult with him as the head of one great country can and ought to talk and consult with the head of another, but I have not the slightest desire to meet him when I am thru with the Presidency. On the contrary I should very much object to doing so. I should think it would bore him, and I know it would bore me. In fact, I should go nearly crazy if I were obliged to make numbers of formal visits to people of merely titular interest; and I should mind even more the fact that they, poor creatures, were suffering because from a mistaken sense of duty they thought they ought to see me. If I can visit England without having my own ambassador or anyone else call on me, without being expected to see anybody I didn't already know, I should love to come. I should love to meet you and Selous and Buxton and Arthur Lee, and to see the English lanes in spring, and stop at English country inns, and see a cathedral here and there; and if just before, provided it were not too hot, I could have seen some of the hill towns of Italy and seen some Provençal towns and some of the French cathedrals, and have gotten to Paris for a day in the Louvre—why this is what I should like most of all to do. But if all thus is impossible, and I have to go thru the dreary farce of unspeakably foolish formal entertainment at the cost of people in whom I take not the slightest real interest, why I shall come straight back from Africa to the United States.

Faithfully yours

August 18, 1908. Oyster Bay
To George C. Buell

Private

My dear Mr. Buell:

I have received your letter and the enclosures in reference to the winners in the Olympic games. You say that it seems to you "that before congratulations are extended to the team by me the public should know the truth in reference to the running of Carpenter in the 400 meters race," and you state that you have seen that he has said that he has "no recollection of having touched Lieutenant Halswelle at all," and that you feel that the American sportsmen should not be given praise where praise is not due.

I entirely agree with you as to the desirability of the public's knowing the truth and of no praise being given where praise is not due; but it seems to me that you do not fully understand the bearing of the extract from the American in London which your letter contains nor the clippings from English papers which you enclose. You apparently accept without question the statement of your correspondent as to the disgraceful conduct of the Americans and endorse her remark that the English people are justified in thinking Americans unprincipled, dishonest and unsportsmanlike. Your correspondent speaks of a photograph of the footmarks which show how one man was crowded from the track. You enclose a print from a sporting English paper called *The Daily Mirror* which contains what I suppose is this photograph. Immediately above it is the print of the same race with Carpenter finishing, and if you would simply glance at the two prints you would see that the footmarks in the lower have been put in in the engraving, or in some way altered in the engraving, for there are no such footprints which appear in the upper one; and if you have ever taken photos of footprints on the track you would know that it would be in the highest degree unlikely for them to appear as they appear in this picture. Your correspondent states how at dinner an English lady told her that no American barristers were honest, and she also states that at the finish of the Marathon race there was very bitter feeling and no enthusiasm that the American won. It seems to me that these two statements of hers offer conclusive proof of a bitterness of hostile feeling on the part of English people of her acquaintance that would render them utterly unfit to pass judgment upon whether or not Carpenter had been guilty of fouling, a bitterness so discreditable to them that it deprives them of all right to criticize others.

You enclose me a paper called *The Sportsman* containing an account of this fouling which apparently you wish accepted as the truth. This paper opens by saying that in advance of the race it had announced that it believed there would be foul tactics on the part of the three Americans, and, in a tone which is even more hysterically foolish than offensive, the paper continues that what occurred in this race casts a slur upon American sportsmanship in the eyes of all Europe which can never be eradicated, and it uses language which, even if the offense really occurred as alleged, nevertheless shows that this British sporting paper was guilty of a far more serious offense itself. I am astonished that you or whoever sent you this paper should not perceive this fact. Let me repeat that if Carpenter was guilty of the offense the comments of this British paper itself deliberately inviting attention the day before to the probability of what it now says actually happened (and thereby of course giving the excuse to everybody who so desired, and who wisht to make believe that it happened, to pretend that it did actually happen) make its offense worse than that which it condemns. This is so evident that it ought not to be necessary to point it out. There are papers in this country whose utterances make one feel heartily ashamed, but I have yet to see an American paper writing on this Olympic matter whose utterances should be condemned as unstintedly as those of thus paper, *The Sportsman*, which you enclose and apparently approve.*

This unmeasured vituperation by the English press, and above all this fact that English sporting authorities, apparently considered in England as reputable, deliberately invited the trouble by saying in advance that they expected the foul, thus taking exactly the attitude that would have been taken by anyone who intended to claim a foul in any event if his candidate did not win, shows so unworthy a spirit as inevitably to cast doubt upon the justice of the decision. Moreover, you seemingly completely fail to understand what is shown by the article from the *Morning Post* which you enclose. This states that when the

Italian came on the track at the Stadium he fell; that he was stimulated by the cheers of the spectators and officials *and by other forms of encouragement,* and proceeded. This British paper which you send me as an authority evidently lacks the honesty to state that the other forms of encouragement were stimulants administered to the Italian in utter disregard of every principle of fair play, and because of which, if the officials who were then cheering him had themselves possest the slightest sense of their duty, they would have ordered him removed from the track. The paper then goes on to say that after going a little further the Italian then fell, but was helped to his feet again, and, fell once more. This English paper thus shows that for the second time he was illegally and improperly helped and that the English officials took no notice and did not order him from the track. It then goes on to say that after fifty yards more he "falls once more and with much difficulty is got to his feet." But again the British officials decline to take the action which they are bound to take, their conduct being in scandalous contrast to the way in which the day before they broke the tape and crowded onto the track in advance of any decision as to the fouling by Carpenter. This paper, the paper you quote as authority, goes on to say that the Italian once more falls but that by vigorous chafing of his limbs and in other ways he is got to his feet and helped onwards. It seems literally incredible that even at this time the British officials did not order him off the track but permitted him to finish and to have his name go up as winner. The judges, who had waited for no protest to permit the people to rush on the track the day before and to declare Carpenter's race no race, now with all this happening before their eyes, refused to take any action until the Americans on behalf of the man who had really won entered a protest. This showing from this British paper which you enclose is such as to make it evident that the judges four times declined to do their duty; that they again and again connived at improper assistance being rendered to the one man on the track who they thought might beat the American champion, and that they showed a scandalous partiality which ought to cause you very grave doubts before accepting their verdict in the case of Carpenter.

I re-enclose you these papers as you request.

Carpenter is a Cornell man. He has contested again and again in intercollegiate and other contests here. A young cousin of mine, George Roosevelt, who won his "H" for Harvard in the high jumping contest, once in the intercollegiates and in another year in the dual games with Yale, has repeatedly been on teams where Carpenter has been on the opposing team, and he says that he is a good, straight fellow and that there has never been a suspicion of crookedness about him. In all his contests here there has never been so much as a hint raised by any of his competitors to the effect that he has misbehaved himself. Now it is of course possible that he did misbehave himself; but the extraordinary misconduct of the English officials at the close of the Marathon race as set forth in the papers you send me, and the outrageous attitude of certain other sporting papers and of certain high social people as portrayed by the papers you send me and by your correspondent, show a bitterness of prejudice on their part and a willingness to believe evil in advance and to announce possible fouls in advance which puts their conduct under the gravest suspicion. If *The Sportsman*, for instance, copy of which you enclose, had been deliberately preparing for a successful conspiracy to steal the victory away from the American if he won, by claiming foul play, it would have acted precisely as it did in announcing in advance that it believed there would be foul play and that precautions were being taken to prevent it. If under similar circumstances here any American paper so behaved it would be accepted everywhere in England as proof positive of such a conspiracy. Moreover, it is very difficult to understand the conduct of the British officials in refusing to hear Carpenter or his side, deciding the case without permitting any statement to be made on that side, and in permitting officials and others to swarm in over the track when the American was ahead and before any official decision had been rendered in the matter. When with such overzealousness against the American one day coupled such blind in-difference to misconduct of the grossest kind when practiced against the American the next day at the close of the Marathon race, it is hard not to draw an uncharitable conclusion.

Now, I never should have stated my views at all, even privately, except in answer to a letter such as yours, and I state them to you for your private information merely. Fouls continually occur in races, both rowing and running, where there is no intentional misconduct at all. Thirty years ago I was in a foot race in which I was beaten, where my antagonist and I touched, and each of us firmly believed that the other had fouled him. Neither of us made the claim and neither for a moment supposed that the other had fouled him intentionally. When the Groton eight (with one son of mine rowing, and another cox) rowed the Harvard freshmen this year it fouled them, but nobody for a moment dreamed that the foul was intentional. Carpenter is a gentleman of good character. The judges, who were not of his nationality but of the nationality of his opponent, held him guilty of fouling. The wise thing to do was to accept their decision as being honestly given on the one hand, and on the other not to attack Carpenter as having been guilty of disgraceful conduct. The action of the judges and the crowd, however, seems to have shown a very violent and malignant spirit. On the other hand, I think that the Americans by the protest they made in the papers and by their bitter complaints of English unfairness behaved as badly themselves. Carpenter alone behaved well, for he has never said anything excepting that he does not remember having touched his competitor and that he thinks that there ought to be no more talk about it. When the next day the British competitor, who had thus been handed the race as a gift, ran over the course alone and tried to make record time, he failed to come up to Carpenter's time. But it is well to remember that the conduct of the British judges at the end of the Marathon race, on the statement of the English authorities themselves, showed impropriety at least as gross as that of which Carpenter is alleged by his most malignant critics to have been guilty; and whereas, altho it may have been entirely proper to rule Carpenter out, there is no sufficient proof that he was guilty of turpitude, the misconduct of the British officials in this instance is perfectly clear. Now, it would be improper, ungenerous, unwise and tend to no good purpose to make any such statement as this in public. Entirely honorable men when prejudiced and under great excitement are capable of doing deeds which seem very improper to others, and which indeed are improper. I should deprecate in the strongest way any kind of public criticism of the British judges for the Marathon race, any criticism of or impugning of the motives of the judges who decided against Carpenter in his race; but it is nonsense to talk about "the public knowing the truth about the running of Carpenter," by which you apparently mean that the public should accept as gospel the blackguardly article of that English paper, *The Sportsman;* and as for "not giving American sportsmen praise where praise is not due," I think that man is a mighty poor American and a mighty poor sportsman who fails in the heartiest way to give praise to our men who went abroad and won out so gallantly in those Olympic contests. I do not suppose that if I have anything to do with it there will be any effort to discriminate among the members of the team, save perhaps in bringing before me the victors; and as Carpenter was not adjudged a victor he, of course, won't come before me in any such special class—that is, if the team comes to see me at all, of which I know nothing.

Understand me. If I am convinced of the moral turpitude of any American and I have any duty in the matter I will condemn him unhesitatingly. But to condemn him on such clippings as you enclose would be even more silly than wicked, especially where these same clippings conclusively prove that the British judges, the officials who above all others should be held to the highest standard of rectitude, had been culpably remiss in the matter of the Marathon race.

My idea is to refrain from every statement which will tend to cause international bitterness, and simply to congratulate the American team, which, as your correspondent shows, before an unfriendly audience and with unfriendly surroundings nevertheless scored so signal a triumph.

Yours truly

*Remember also that the conduct of the judges in the Carpenter race in breaking the tape, crowding on the track and declaring the race off on a foul, before any investigation could possibly have been held, was itself in the highest degree improper and unsportsmanlike.

P.S. Your correspondent and the papers you enclose omit all mention of the fact that after requiring our team in the tug of war to wear only ordinary shoes, the British officials permitted their team to appear with hobnails and steel plates. They permitted this upon the ground that they were policemen and that these were ordinary policemen's shoes. Here is a case where there is far greater justification than in the Carpenter case for the accusation of bad faith; nevertheless I should not for one moment make it. It is perfectly possible that our men understood the prohibition in one way and lived up to it strictly, whereas the British did not desire that it should be so strictly lived up to, and that therefore it was an honest misunderstanding. But papers like *The Sportsman* and people such as those with whom your correspondent comes in contact would have exhausted their vocabulary of vituperation in screaming against Yankee trickery and foul play and lack of good sportsmanship if it had been the American team that wore those shoes when the British team did not; and you might just as well protest against the Englishmen giving any credit to any of their people in view of this tug of war incident as to protest, as you seemingly do, against the American team receiving credit for its remarkable aggregate of victories because, forsooth, in one case possibly prejudiced judges alleged a foul.

September 5, 1908. Oyster Bay
To William Howard Taft

Strictly private

Dear Will:

I do not want this letter to be seen by anyone but you and Mrs. Taft. It does not seem to me that the National Committee is accomplishing quite as much as it should. Du Pont's connection with the speakers' committee has done far-reaching harm, especially in the West. It may be that it is too late to do anything about this, but if he should retire now I cannot help feeling that some of the damage would be undone.

I believe you are entirely right about the wisdom of making a few speeches on just the terms you mention. You should put yourself prominently and emphatically into this campaign. Also I hope to see everything done henceforth to give the impression that you are working steadily in the campaign. It seems absurd, but I am convinced that the prominence that has been given to your golf playing has not been wise, and from now on I hope your people will do everything they can to prevent one word being sent out about either your fishing or your playing golf. The American people regard the campaign as a very serious business, and we want to be careful that your opponents do not get the chance to misrepresent you as not taking it with sufficient seriousness. I wish you could keep your hand on Hitchcock a little. I don't want to see him travel around the country, but I think he ought now and then to visit you and that you should impress upon him the desirability of prompt access to him by the people of importance. I know that complaints are always made of the manager of any campaign, and many of the complaints of Hitchcock simply represent this general tendency; but there is a pretty widespread feeling that things are not quite as lively as they should be at headquarters. Brooker and Ward, for instance, have mentioned the fact that they do not know what their duties are or what is expected of them.

I am doing everything I can to force the nomination of Hughes, but it is a much more difficult job than I anticipated. Hughes has succeeded in arousing a very bitter feeling against him. Here in my own county I am having difficulty in forcing his endorsement. The workers are bitter against him.

Ever yours

September 9, 1908. Oyster Bay
To Mark Sullivan

Personal and Private

My dear Sullivan:

I have been looking over the last number of *Collier's*, and sometime or other I wish you and Hapgood could either come out here to lunch or take lunch with me at the White House, for I would like to say one or two things in connection with Hapgood's political articles in that number. But in the present letter I want to discuss the article you published by Jack London, and especially the headlines of the article—my position being that of the South Carolina lawyer who, in the dark days shortly after the Civil War, finally protested to a reconstruction judge that he could live under bad law but that he could not live under bad Latin. In the headlines (to this article by Jack London) for which I suppose *Collier's* itself is responsible, he is described as "locating the President in the Ananias Club[1]." Now neither you nor I regard falsehood as

---

[1]Roosevelt's label for those who told untruths about him.

a jest, and therefore we neither of us regard an accusation of falsehood as a jest. If that headline were correct, Collier's would not be justified in making the effort it did to get me to write for it. Moreover, there is, as far as I am able to see, in Jack London's article not a line in which London says anything on which such a headline could be based. If there is I should be glad to have you point it out to me.

Now as for Jack London himself; and here again I want to speak to Collier's rather than to Jack London, altho of course you are perfectly welcome to show him this letter, with the distinct understanding, however, that I am not entering into a controversy with him but with Collier's; and that of a purely private, not public, nature. In my Presidential speeches and messages which Collier published, in Volume VI on pages 1333 to 1345, you will find what I said on nature faking and nature fakers, including London, and my concluding words were that my quarrel was not with these nature fakers "but with those who give them their chance"—"who, holding a position which entitles them to respect, yet condone and encourage such untruth." In the first place, read thru this article of mine and anything else that I have written and you will see at once that when London says that I state that animals do not reason, that all animals below man are automatons and perform actions only of two sorts, mechanical and reflex, and that in such actions no reasoning enters at all, and that man is the only animal that is capable of reasoning or ever does reason—when London says this he deliberately invents statements which I have never made and in which I do not believe. As a matter of fact, on this point I disagree with John Burroughs, my points of agreement with John Burroughs being my admiration for his accuracy of observation, and the way he can report his observations, and for his abhorrence of untruth. As a matter of fact, I believe that the higher mammals and birds have reasoning powers, which differ in degree rather than in kind from the lower reasoning powers of, for instance, the lower savages. London's statement as to my attitude on this point—a statement to which you give currency—is wholly without basis; and he cannot find, and nobody else can find, anything that I have written which forms a basis for it.

But this is not his only invention or misstatement. In my article I stated and proved (see page 1325) that London knew nothing whatever about wolves or lynxes; that his story White Fang would be excellent if it was avowedly put forth as a fable, but as realism it was nonsense, and mischievous nonsense to boot. I attributed his making misstatements simply to ignorance; but in this article in Collier's his misstatements are deliberate. They are not due to ignorance at all. Get his book White Fang to which I am about to refer, and open it at the pages I shall mention, comparing them with my article on the page I have given you, and with his article in *Collier's*. In the first place he says that I tried and condemned him because a big fighting bulldog whipped a wolf dog. I did not. I condemned him because his wolf (for the amount of dog in it, or indeed in its mother, is so small that Jack London continually alludes to both as wolves and not wolf dogs) and his bulldog fought in impossible fashion. He describes this huge wolf which kills all other wolves against which it is pitted and all other dogs—a wolf that can hamstring a horse or gut a steer—as ripping and slashing with long tearing strokes a score of times a bulldog a third its size without inflicting any serious injury upon the bulldog. Now this is simply nonsense. Two or three such bites would mean the death of the bulldog. I will make a comparison which will bring it home. It is possible, altho very improbable, that a feather-weight professional boxer, or say the champion heavyweight amateur boxer of a college or a theological institute, could knock out Jim Jeffries or John L. Sullivan when they were in full training. But it is not possible that the knockout could take place after Jeffries or Sullivan had a score of times knocked down said featherweight, or amateur heavyweight from a college or theological seminary, with blows striking them full on the point of the chin or over the heart. Such a description of a prize fight would be a purely fake description.

But this is small compared to Mr. London's second offense. He says that I claimed he was guilty of allowing a lynx to kill a wolf dog in a pitched battle, and that this was not true; that he never made such a statement in his story. Now turn to what I wrote on page 1325. What I say is that "London describes a great dog wolf being torn in pieces by a lucivee, a northern lynx." London denies this. Now turn to his book *White Fang*, page 83. He describes the she-wolf following a day-old trail of her mate, the great dog wolf. He goes on—"And she found him, or what remained of him, at the end of the trail. There were many signs of the battle that had been fought, and of the lynx's withdrawal to her lair after having won the victory." Mr. London should take the trouble to read what he himself has written before he again makes a denial of this type. A real nature observer, not a nature faker, James Sheldon, has just passed the winter in northern Alaska, and he caught or shot and weighed various lynxes, practically from the region London is supposed to discuss. The female lynx up there weighs barely twenty pounds; and London describes such an animal as tearing to pieces the huge fighting wolf six or seven times its weight. As a matter of fact, any capable fighting bull terrier would be an overmatch for such a lynx. I do not wonder that London did not like to admit having made such a statement, but I am rather surprised at his having the effrontery to make such a denial in *Collier's*.

Now mind you, I have not the slightest intention of entering into any controversy on this subject with London. I would as soon think of discussing seriously with him any social or political reform. But it does seem to me that *Collier's* should be rather careful about admitting such an article, into its columns, and of giving it such a headline as that I have above quoted.

Sincerely yours

September 10, 1908. Oyster Bay
To A. H. Fox

My dear Mr. Fox:

When I wrote you I did not intend to take a shotgun to Africa. I find, however, that I would like to take such a gun, provided that at close quarters I could use it with ball also. In other words, I should like in case of an emergency to have it loaded with ball and use it as a spare gun for a lion. Now I have rather a pride in taking American rifles on this trip, and in the same way I should like to take an American gun; but of course you may have by this time decided that you do not care to repeat your very kind offer; in that event will you tell me what the cost of such a gun as I have described, twelve-bore and plain finish, would be?

Sincerely yours

September 11, 1908. Oyster Bay
To William Howard Taft

Dear Will:

Henry Beach Needham, who of course is now a wild supporter of yours, sends me some suggestions about your speech-making which I enclose to you. Hit them hard, old man! Why not call attention to Bryan's[1] insincerity in saying he was my heir when without any protest he practically made as his own Clayton's speech at the Denver convention, which was full of the foulest assault upon me. Let the audience see you smile always, because I feel that your nature shines out so transparently when you do smile—you big, generous, high-minded fellow. Moreover let them realize the truth, which is that for all your gentleness and kindliness and generous good nature, there never existed a man who was a better fighter when the need arose. The trouble is that you would always rather fight for a principle or for a friend then for yourself. Now hit at them; challenge Bryan on his record. Ask that you be judged by your record, and dare Bryan to stand on his.

Good luck to you, and love to dear Mrs. Taft.

Ever yours

---

[1]Taft's Democratic opponent was William Jennings Bryan.

October 3, 1908. Washington
To Kermit Roosevelt

Dear Kermit:

This is such a nice letter that I thought I would send it to you. By the way, I wrote Wells that I hoped you would keep up on your own account your reading of Greek. I was extremely pleased to find you reading Homer last summer, just as I am glad that Ted reads Latin. I never got so that I could with any real pleasure read either Greek or Latin. It was a labor. You may be amused that both Mr. Loeb and I feel that you have chosen the exact six courses that we ourselves would have chosen!

Ever your loving father

November 6, 1908. Washington
To George Otto Trevelyan

My dear Sir George:

Well, the election is over and to say that I am pleased with the result is to express it mildly. I can hardly express my satisfaction. If the result of my "renunciation" had been either the nomination of a reactionary in the place of Taft, or the turning over of the Government to Bryan, I should have felt a very uncomfortable apprehension as to whether I did not deserve a place beside Dante's pope who was guilty of *il gran refiuto*. Renunciation is so often the act of a weak nature, or the term by which a weak nature seeks to cover up its lack of strength, that I suppose that every man who feels that he ought to renounce something, also tends to feel a little uncomfortable as to whether he is really acting in accordance with the dictates of a sound morality or from weakness. Yet, feeling as I do about this people and about the proper standard for its chosen leaders, I could not have acted otherwise than as I did; and naturally the relief is very great to have the event justify me. Taft will carry on the work substantially as I have carried it on. His policies, principles, purposes and ideals are the same as mine and he is a strong, forceful, efficient man, absolutely upright, absolutely disinterested and fearless. In leaving I have the profound satisfaction of knowing that he will do all in his power to further every one of the great causes for which I have fought and that he will persevere in every one of the great governmental policies in which I most firmly believe. Therefore nothing whatever is lost by my having refused to run for a third term, and much is gained. Washington and Lincoln set the standard of conduct for the public servants of this people. They showed how men of the strongest type could also possess all the disinterested, all the unselfish, devotion to duty and to the interests of their fellow countrymen that we have a right to expect, but can only hope to see in the very highest type of public servant. At however great a distance I have been anxious to follow in their footsteps, and anxious that, however great the difference in degree, my service to the Nation should be approximately the same *in kind* as theirs.

Of course if I had conscientiously felt at liberty to run again and try once more to hold this great office, I should greatly have liked to do so and to continue to keep my hands on the levers of this mighty machine. I do not believe that my President has ever had as thoroly good a time as I have had, or has ever enjoyed himself as much. Moreover I have achieved a far greater proportion than I had dared to think possible of the things I most desired to achieve. In fact I do not know any man of my age who has had as good a time as I have had during my life! Whatever comes hereafter I have had far more than the normal share of human happiness, far more happiness than any but a very, very few men ever have. But I am bound to say in addition that I cannot help looking forward to much enjoyment in the future. In fact, I am almost ashamed to say that while I would have been glad to remain as President, I am wholly unable to feel the slightest regret, the slightest sorrow, at leaving the office. I love the White House; I greatly enjoy the exercise of power; but I shall leave the White House without a pang, and, indeed, on the contrary, I am looking forward eagerly and keenly to being a private citizen again, without anybody being able to make a fuss over me or hamper my movements. I am as interested as I can be in the thought of getting back in my own home at Sagamore Hill, in the thought of the African trip, and of various things I intend to do when that is over. Indeed I have been, and am, very fortunate, and I trust I am duly thankful for it.

In May, 1910, after getting out of Africa I am to be in England to deliver the Romanes Lecture at Oxford. Will you be in England then, and if so where? I must see you if you are where it is possible for me to reach you.

Your new edition of the *Life of Macaulay* came and I have reread the whole volume with the delight it always gives me. But oh, my dear Sir George, why do you quote Rosebery's comment on Macaulay's marginal notes, to the effect that he was a "sublime guide to sublime things?" Don't you think that this is open to just the good-natured raillery with which Macaulay himself spoke of the "Yankee" who stared that to "see Macaulay at the grave of Wordsworth" would be a "sublime spectacle?" Rosebery has a slight tendency anyhow to overemphasis; as witness the way in which he speaks of Winston Churchill's clever, forceful, rather cheap and vulgar life of that clever, forceful, rather cheap and vulgar egoist, his father, as if it was one of the very greatest biographies in the world; instead of being one of the smart, bright, amusing books of a given season. "Sublime" is a word that should be reserved for certain things in nature, and for a very few of the loftiest feelings, emotions and actions of mankind. There is only an occasional cathedral, an occasional great poem, to which the word could rightly be applied; and not to marginal notes by anybody about anything.

I have made up my mind that I will have to take some books on my African trip, and the special piece of resistance is to be Macaulay's complete works—to which I may have to add your *American Revolution*. My son Kermit, by the way, I was rather pleased to find, among his books for the voyage has included Homer in the original. He and my elder boy, Ted, have both rather chuckled over your inability to tell me the best translations of the Greek tragic poets on the ground that you were old-fashioned enough to read them in the original; for I am much pleased to find that Ted, for instance, who is now hard at work in a carpet factory, quite spontaneously reads Virgil and Horace for his own amusement before going to bed. I never got so that reading any Greek or Latin author in the original represented to me anything except dreary labor.

With regard,

Faithfully yours

[Handwritten] I am extremely pleased at the way our battle fleet has done on its trip around the world; and at its reception both in Australia and Japan.

November 22, 1908. Washington
To Kermit Roosevelt

Dearest Kermit:

Three cheers for the football match! It must have been simply fine seeing it. How I wish I could have been there! I have never yet seen Harvard win against Yale at football, altho I saw one draw.

Col. Patterson, the man who killed the man-eating lions of Tsavo, spent Friday night with us, and was most interesting. Next day I had Carl Akeley, the Chicago man who has also hunted elephant & rhino in Africa, at lunch, and it was interesting to hear the two. I think I got some valuable advice from both. There is no question that you and I must be extremely careful in dealing with lion, elephant, buffalo, and rhino; they are dangerous game. Both of us must be extremely cautious, and of course I shall want some first-class man with you until you grow accustomed to what is being done. All our arrangements are made; the stores have been sent to Africa, etc. etc. Both Patterson and Akeley were very much pleased at my having engaged Cuninghame, and said that with a caravan the size of ours I would have been unable to have done much hunting if I had been obliged to manage the caravan myself.

It is not in the least like Buxton's trips, which are merely for a few days at a time away from the railroad. You and I want to go up into the really wild country such as Patterson described in that letter of his, if it is a possible thing.

The Kaiser has come an awful cropper. He has been a perfect fool, and the German people after standing his folly and bumptiousness for years finally exploded over something which was of course bad, but was no worse than scores of similar things he had done before.

I have finished both my Romanes lecture and my Sorbonne address. I wanted to get them off my hands before the Congress met, as I shall have in all probability a good deal of irritating work while Congress is in session, for the outgoing President hasn't very much power. They tell me Foraker is preparing a violent attack on me. I can imagine nothing to which I should be more indifferent.

Your loving father

[Handwritten] This morning when mother and I walked around the grounds as usual, she was still able to pick a rose for my buttonhole, from the rose beds in the garden. It was a misty morning; and the trees with their leafless branches, and the monument, were very beautiful.

December 9, 1908. Washington
To Henry L. Stimson[1]

My dear Stimson:

I do not know anything about the law of criminal libel, but I should dearly like to have it invoked about Pulitzer, of the *World*. Usually, papers in making charges do not ascribe improper motives of financial interest, but the *World* made the mistake of doing it in this instance. Pulitzer is one of these creatures of the gutter of such unspeakable degradation that to him even eminence on a dunghill seems enviable, and he evidently hopes I will place him there beside Laffan and Delavan Smith. Heaven knows that they occupy a sufficiently low stratum of infamy, but Pulitzer has plumbed depths even lower and I do not wish to put him beside them unless it is necessary; this aside from the fact that when I was Police Commissioner I once for all summed him up by quoting the close of Macaulay's article about Barère as applying to him. But if he can be reached by a proceeding on the part of the Government for criminal libel in connection with his assertions about the Panama Canal, I should like to do it. Would you have his various utterances for the last three or four months on this subject look up, and let me know?

Faithfully yours

---

[1]At that time federal attorney for New York City.

January 10, 1909. Washington
To Kermit Roosevelt

Dearest Kermit:

Since you left, Ethel has continued in the whirl. On Friday night we had a dinner and dance for her; but there were also many older people present. The Speaker, for instance, was at the dinner; and all the Ambassadors and their wives came to the dance. I think it was one of the very pleasantest dances that has ever taken place in The White House. I danced myself two or three times, and persuaded Mother to dance with me. She lookt so pretty and shy, tho she finally accepted; and evidently had much the same feeling that she would have had if we had been secretly engaged and she was afraid that such a public attention might compromise her! Poor, blessed Mother; the dance coming on top of the rest of the week's activities was the final straw, and tho she thoroly enjoyed it, the next morning she had one of her worst headaches and it is only now, twenty-fours later, that she has recovered. I have gotten her to promise that she will now try taking breakfast in bed and I will have my breakfast up in the room with her.

Congress has been having a brainstorm—a brainstorm in its belly, so to speak; both Houses have held a can-can over the secret service. Personally I doubt if they have gained very much. I think I have knocked the paint off of Tillman, who is one of the foulest and rottenest demagogs in the whole country; and I do not see how the House can get away from what I have said about it.*

John Jay White, that African hunter who struck us as being a little nervous, to judge by his letters, was on here to lunch. He was very interesting and gave me one or two points. He was also very kind; he has left his double-barreled .450 cordite in Nairobi. He says it is in fine trim and that he will give it to us. Accordingly I wrote to Newland, Tarlton & Company, our agents in Nairobi, who have the gun, to get it all ready and get cartridges for it. If necessary either you or I can take this gun and the other take the double-barreled Holland, and therefore we now have each a type of the hard-hitting double-barreled English gun which they say is necessary. Personally I cannot help feeling that the Winchester will be our ordinary weapon, but of course I may be utterly mistaken. Moreover, nice George Meyer has given me his little Manlicher rifle, which has a telescopic sight. The weapon is a perfect beauty; and with the telescopic sight one certainly does see marvelously up to say 300 yards. I have made up my mind not to take out my 45.70 rifle, and shall take this little Manlicher in place of it. The more I have thought over the matter the more convinced I have become that I would prefer the .405 Winchester for any purpose for which I desired to take the 45.70, and as long as I now have an extra .405 it is not worth while taking the 45.70 at all. My Holland double barrel is on the way here for me to try.

Give my regards to Randy and to all the other boys, including Charlie Emory. I hope he goes to the sailors' union with you. I felt that we had just about the most satisfactory Christmas and Christmas holiday from the stand-point of the entire family as it was possible to have.

Taft told me with a chuckle, when he was last here, that one of his friends in New York had said to him that he supposed that between the election and his inauguration there would be a period of stagnation at Washington. I have felt like wiring him that the period of stagnation continues to rage with uninterrupted violence.

Your loving father

[Handwritten] I enclose the list of the English donors of my rifle.

Quentin has left school without permission, and told untruths about it; I had to give him a severe whipping. Mother and I are worried about him.

[Handwritten] *Still, it won't hurt the House, and this they know. Election is over 18 months off; this will be forgotten then; I will no longer count, appreciably, for Taft will be President, and the fight will have to be, and ought to be, on Taft's record only.

January 14, 1909. Washington
To Kermit Roosevelt

Dearest Kermit:

There has been a good deal of talk in Congress and in the papers and among the grumblers in the army and navy about my physical exercise order, which as a matter of fact was very moderate. So I concluded, on the suggestion of Dr. Rixey, to ride ninety miles in one day myself, which would put a stop to any grumbling because I required other people to ride ninety miles in three days. Accordingly yesterday Dr. Rixey, Dr. Grayson, Archie Butt and I rode out to Warrenton and back from and to the White House. It was just ninety-eight miles, altho the people at Warrenton claim it was 104. We left the White House a few minutes after half past three in the morning and got back there a few minutes after half past eight in the evening, lunching at Warrenton, where I had to shake hands with prominent citizens, say a word to the school children, &c. We had sent out relays of horses, and each rode four horses, riding each horse twice as the journey back was over the same ground. I began and ended the day on old Roswell, who is really a perfect trump. The last fifteen miles in were done in pitch darkness and with a blizzard of sleet blowing in our faces. But we got thru safely, and altho we are a little stiff and tired nobody is laid up.

Congress of course feels that I will never again have to be reckoned with and that it is safe to be ugly with me. Accordingly, in one way I am not having an easy time, and I shall have additional fights over certain veto messages I shall send. But I am pretty philosophical about it. I did not expect any legislation this winter, and I don't see that Congress can really do very much to harm me. I have gotten the men I went after, Foraker and Tillman, and I shall soon start the libel suits against the *World* and the Indianapolis *News*.

I have had a great run for my money, and I should have liked to stay in as President if I had felt it was right for me to do so; but there are many compensations about going, and Mother and I are in the curious and very pleasant position of having enjoyed the White House more than any other President and his wife whom I recall, and yet being entirely willing to leave it, and looking forward to a life of interest and happiness after we leave.

I enclose a copy of the list of the men who have given me my gun, with annotations put on by E. N. Buxton. Will you send it back to me?

Your loving father

February 8, 1909. Washington
To Philander C. Knox

My dear Senator Knox:

You are soon to become Secretary of State under Mr. Taft. At the outset both he and you will be overwhelmed with every kind of work; but there is one matter of foreign policy of such great and permanent importance that I wish to lay it before the President-to-be and yourself. I speak of the relations of the United States and Japan.

It is utterly impossible to foretell as regards either foreign or domestic policy what particular questions may appear as at the moment of most engrossing interest. It may be that there will be no ripple of trouble between Japan and the United States during your term of service. It may very well be that you will have acute trouble about Cuba, or with Venezuela or in Central America, or with some European power; but it is not likely that grave international complications—that is, complications which can possibly lead to serious war—can come from any such troubles. If we have to interfere again in Cuba, or take possession of the Island, it will be exasperating, and we may in consequence have to repeat our Philippine experiences by putting down an annoying but unimportant guerrilla outbreak. But this would represent merely annoyance. The same would be true of anything in Central America or Venezuela. I do not believe that Germany has any designs that would bring her in conflict with the Monroe Doctrine. The last seven years have tended steadily toward a better understanding of Germany on our part, and a more thoro understanding on the part of Germany that she must not expect colonial expansion in South America. As for England, I cannot imagine serious trouble with her. The settlement of the Alaskan boundary removed the one grave danger. The treaties now before the Senate are excellent, and all we have to fear is some annoying, but hardly grave, friction, in the event of the failure of the Senate to ratify them.

But with Japan the case is different. She is a most formidable military power. Her people have peculiar fighting capacity. They are very proud, very warlike, very sensitive, and are influenced by two contradictory feelings, namely, a great self-confidence, both ferocious and conceited, due to their victory over the mighty empire of Russia; and a great touchiness because they would like to be considered as on a full equality with, as one of the brotherhood of, Occidental nations, and have been bitterly humiliated to find that even their allies, the English, and their friends, the Americans, won't admit them to association and citizenship, as they admit the least advanced or most decadent European peoples. Moreover, Japan's population is increasing rapidly and demands an outlet, and the Japanese laborers, small farmers, and petty traders would, if permitted, flock by the hundred thousand into the United States, Canada, and Australia.

Now for our side. The events of the last three years have forced me to the clear understanding that our people will not permit the Japanese to come in large numbers among them; will not accept them as citizens; will not tolerate their presence as large bodies of permanent settlers. This is just as true in Australia and Columbia as in our Rocky Mountain and Pacific States; but at present the problem is more acute with us because the desire of the Japanese to come here has grown. The opposition to the presence of the Japanese, I have reluctantly come to feel, is entirely warranted, and not only must be, but ought to be, heeded by the national Government in the interest of our people and our civilization; and this in spite of the fact that many of the manifestations of the opposition are unwise and improper to the highest degree. To permit the Japanese to come in large numbers into this country would be to cause a race problem and invite and insure a race contest. It is necessary to keep them out. But it is almost equally necessary that we should both show all possible courtesy and consideration in carrying out this necessarily disagreeable policy of exclusion,* and that we should be thoroly armed, so as to prevent the Japanese from feeling safe in attacking us. Unfortunately, great masses of our people show a foolish indifference to arming, and at the same time a foolish willingness to be offensive to the Japanese. Labor unions pass violent resolutions against the Japanese and almost at the same moment protest against strengthening our military resources on land or sea. Big corporations seek to introduce Japanese coolies, so as to get cheap labor, and thereby invite agitation which they are powerless to quell. The peace societies, and Senators and Congressmen like Burton of Ohio, Perkins of California, Perkins of New York, Tawney of Minnesota, McCall of Massachusetts, and Bartholdt of Missouri, blatantly or furtively oppose the navy and hamper its upbuilding, while doing nothing whatever to prevent insult to Japan. The California Legislature is threatening to pass the most offensive kind of legislation aimed at the Japanese, and yet it reelects a wretched creature like Perkins to the Senate altho he has opposed, with his usual feeble timidity and so far as he dared, the upbuilding of the navy, following Hale's lead.

We are therefore faced by the fact that our people will not tolerate and ought not to tolerate, the presence among them of large bodies of Japanese and that so long as they are here in large bodies there is always chance either of violence on the part of mobs or of indiscreet and improper action by the legislative bodies of the Western States under demagogic influence. Furthermore, in Hawaii the Japanese already many times outnumber the whites, and have shown on more than one recent occasion a spirit both truculent and insolent.

In Hawaii the trouble is primarily due to the shortsighted greed of the sugar planters and of the great employers generally, who showed themselves incapable of thinking of the future of their children and anxious only to make fortunes from estates tilled by coolie labor. Accordingly they imported, first, masses of Chinese laborers, and then masses of Japanese laborers. Thruout my term as President I have so far as possible conducted our policy against this desire of the sugar planters, against the theory of turning Hawaii into an island of coolie-tilled plantations, and in favor of making it so far as possible the abode of small settlers. With this purpose, I have done everything I could to encourage the immigration of Southern Europeans to the islands, and have endeavored so far as I could in the absence of legislation to restrict the entrance of Asiatic coolies. So far as possible our aim should be to diminish the number of Japanese in the islands without any regard to the fortunes of the sugar planters, and to bring in Europeans, no matter of what ancestry, in order that the islands may be filled with a white population of our general civilization and culture.

As regards the mainland, our policy should have three sides, and should be shaped not to meet the exigencies of this year or next, but to meet what may occur for the next few decades. Japan is poor and is therefore reluctant to go to war. Moreover, Japan is vitally interested in China and on the Asiatic mainland and her wiser statesmen will if possible prevent her getting entangled in a war with us, because whatever its result it would hamper and possibly ruin Japan when she came to deal again with affairs in China. But with so proud and sensitive a people neither lack of money nor possible future complications will prevent a war if once they get sufficiently hurt and angry; and there is always danger of a mob outbreak there just as there is danger of a mob outbreak here. Our task therefore is on the one hand to meet the demands which our own people make and which cannot permanently be resisted and on the other to treat Japan so courteously that she will not be offended more than is necessary; and at the same time to prepare our fleet in such shape that she will feel very cautious about attacking us. Disturbances like those going on at present are certain to occur unless the Japanese immigration, so far as it is an immigration for settlement, stops. For the last six months under our agreement with Japan it has been stopped to the extent that more Japanese have left the country than have come into it. But the Japanese should be made clearly to understand that this process must continue and if there is relaxation it will be impossible to prevent our people from enacting drastic exclusion laws; and that in such case all of us would favor such drastic legislation. Hand in hand with insistence on the stopping of Japanese immigration should go insistence as regards our own people that they be courteous and considerate, that they treat the Japanese who are here well; and above all that they go on with the building of the navy, keep it at the highest point of efficiency, securing not merely battleships but an ample supply of colliers and other auxiliary vessels of every kind. Much of the necessary expense would be met by closing the useless navy yards. By the way, the fighting navy should not be divided; it should be kept either in the Pacific or in the Atlantic, merely a squadron being left in the other ocean and this in such shape that in the event of war it could avoid attack and at once join the main body of fighting ships.

All this is so obvious that it ought not to be necessary to dwell upon it. But our people are shortsighted and have short memories—I suppose all peoples are shortsighted and have short memories. The minute we arrange matters so that for the moment everything is smooth and pleasant, the more foolish peace societies, led by men like ex-Secretary of State Foster and ex-Secretary of the Navy Long, clamor for a stoppage in the building up of the navy. On the other hand, at the very moment when we are actually keeping out the Japanese and reducing the number of Japanese here, demagogs and agitators like those who have recently appeared in the California and Nevada Legislatures work for the passage of laws which are humiliating and irritating to the Japanese and yet of no avail so far as keeping out immigrants is concerned; for this can be done effectively only by the National Government. The defenselessness of the coast, the fact that we have no army to hold or reconquer the Philippines and Hawaii, the fact that we have not enough battleships nor enough auxiliaries in the navy—all these facts are ignored and forgotten. On the other hand, the Japanese, if we do not keep pressure upon them will let up in their effort to control the emigration from Japan to this country, and they must be continually reminded that unless they themselves stop it, in the end this country is certain to stop it, and ought to stop it, no matter what the consequences may be.

There is no more important continuing feature of our foreign policy than this in reference to our dealing with Japan; the whole question of our dealings with the Orient is certain to grow in importance. I do not believe that there will be war, but there is always the chance that war will come, and if it did come, the calamity would be very great, and while I believe we would win, there is at least a chance of disaster. We should therefore do everything in our power to guard against the possibility of war by preventing the occurrence of conditions which would invite war and by keeping our navy so strong that war may not come or that we may be successful if it does come.

Sincerely yours

[Handwritten] P.S. I enclose a copy of my telegram to the Speaker of the California Lower House; this was really meant almost as much for Japan as for California, and sets forth, seemingly as incidental, what our future policy must be.

[Handwritten] *If possible, the Japanese should be shown, what is the truth, that our keeping them out means not that they are inferior to us—in some ways they are superior—but that they are *different;* so different that, whatever the future may hold, at present the two races ought not to come together in masses.

February 25, 1909. Washington
To Jean Jules Jusserand

My dear Mr. Jusserand:

A Texas professor is doing some really good work in collecting frontier ballads in the cow-country of Texas. They are of course for the most part mere doggerel, (as I believe to be true with the majority of all ballads as they were originally written); but these are interesting because they are genuine. The deification of Jesse James is precisely like the deification of Robin Hood; and the cowboy is a hero exactly as the hunter of the greenwood was a hero. Also, the view taken of women seems to be much the same as that taken in many of the medieval ballads! I will talk to you about them when I see you.

Faithfully yours

March 3, 1909. Washington
To William Howard Taft

Dear Will:

One closing legacy. Under no circumstances divide the battleship fleet between the Atlantic and Pacific Oceans prior to the finishing of the Panama Canal. Malevolent enemies of the navy, like Hale; timid fools, like Perkins; and conscienceless scoundrels, like Tillman, will try to lead public opinion in a matter like this without regard to the dreadful harm they may do the country; and good, but entirely ignorant, men may be thus misled. I should obey no direction of Congress and pay heed to no popular sentiment, no matter how strong, if it went wrong in such a vital matter as this. When I sent the fleet around the world there was a wild clamor that some of it should be sent to the Pacific, and an equally mad clamor that some of it should be left in the Atlantic. I disregarded both. At first it seemed as if popular feeling was nearly a unit against me. It is now nearly a unit in favor of what I did.

It is now nearly four years since the close of the Russian-Japanese war. There were various factors that brought about Russia's defeat; but most important by all odds was her having divided her fleet between the Baltic and the Pacific, and, furthermore, splitting up her Pacific fleet into three utterly unequal divisions. The entire Japanese force was always used to smash some fraction of the Russian force. The knaves and fools who advise the separation of our fleet nowadays and the honest, misguided creatures who think so little that they are misled by such advice, ought to take into account this striking lesson furnished by actual experience in a great war but four years ago. Keep the battle fleet either in one ocean or the other and have the armed cruisers always in trim, as they are now, so that they can be at once sent to join the battle fleet if the need should arise.

Faithfully yours

PART SIX

The Most Famous Man in the World

1909–1919

*U*pon leaving the White House, Roosevelt sailed off to Africa where, for nearly a year, he engaged in a grand safari. The expedition was partly scientific (and underwritten by Andrew Carnegie), and indeed it produced hundreds of specimens for the Smithsonian museum. But it was also the great hunt of Roosevelt's life, and he enjoyed every minute.

En route home he toured the capitals and courts of Europe. The former president cut a wide swath, reviewing the German troops with Kaiser Wilhelm II, attending the funeral of Britain's Edward VII, accepting his Nobel Peace Prize from 1906, addressing academic audiences at Oxford and Cambridge universities.

Yet even while accepting the plaudits of the princes and people of Europe, Roosevelt received unsettling news from America. President Taft appeared to have fallen under the spell of Republican reactionaries. The firing of forester Gifford Pinchot yielded an early indication that Roosevelt's reforms were at peril; additional reports fed further suspicions. Roosevelt was greeted uproariously at dockside in New York City and treated to a ticker tape parade; as the most potent vote-getter in living memory, he was immediately approached by reformers, reporters, and others as to whether he would reenter politics. He resisted for a time, but in early 1912 allowed himself to be persuaded that the national interest required another run for the White House.

He fought Taft vigorously—and eventually bitterly—for the Republican nomination. Although Roosevelt carried most of the primaries, Taft maintained control of the party machinery, and at the national convention in Chicago the president secured the nomination.

Roosevelt thereupon bolted. At the head of the Progressive ("Bull Moose") Party he mounted the most successful third-party challenge in American history. He never underestimated the odds against him—privately predicting a victory by Democrat Woodrow Wilson—but he felt obliged by principle to carry the reform fight forward. The dramatic climax of the contest occurred three weeks before the election when a would-be assassin put a bullet in Roosevelt's chest. Bleeding, he gave the most rousing speech of his career before being sped to the hospital.

After Wilson did indeed win, Roosevelt was left to ponder his own future and that of the Progressives. While weighing his options he embarked on a voyage of exploration down an uncharted river in Brazil—the aptly named Rio da Dúvida, or River of Doubt. The journey nearly killed him when an injury suffered trying to rescue a canoe from a rapid poisoned his blood. If not for the determination of son Kermit—his partner in Africa, and now again in Amazonia—he probably would have been buried in the wilds of Brazil.

Although he likely wouldn't have objected to such a final resting place, he preferred France. Roosevelt returned to America in the summer of 1914 just in *time for Europe to erupt into war. Almost at once he criticized the Wilson administration for insufficient resolve in resisting German aggression. As both a public platform and a way of gaining money—his inheritance having long since vanished—Roosevelt wrote opinion pieces for the* Outlook *magazine and the* Kansas City Star; *in these columns and especially in private letters he raked Wilson unmercifully. When finally Wilson took America to war, Roosevelt requested permission to raise a division for service in France. But Wilson rejected the offer, leaving Roosevelt to gnash his teeth in fury at the president.*

Yet at the same time he helped send his sons off to war. And as they marched—in the case of Quentin, flew—into battle, he expressed simultaneously his pride in their courage and his fear for their safety. News that Quentin had been killed raised both emotions to an exquisite, excruciating pitch.

Figuratively heart-broken, Roosevelt died of an actual heart attack six months later.

May 12, 1909. On safari in British East Africa
To Robert Bridges

Dear Bridges,

Here is my first article. I have had great luck; the game has come quicker than I thought. Indeed it has been almost too quick; I have had no time to write. Please say frankly if you do'n't like the articles; omit any, & cut out any parts you please; and throw any two of them in together if you desire, as I think they will only be 7 or 8000 words apiece. My next three, which I shall send within a fortnight, will *probably* be;

II.   On an East African ranch.
III. Lion hunting on the Kapiti Plains
IV.   On Safari; Rhino and Giraffe.

Kermit has already sent you some pictures for this first article or chapter. I wish I could do better work; it is hard, out on the wilderness.

Ever yours

May 23rd

At last I send you, herewith, the two first chapters. I shall try to send you within a month chapters III, IV, V, & VI—the last two, being named: "On Juja Farm; Hippo and Rhino" and "A buffalo hunt on the Kamiti." I have had great luck; I have the material for six chapters now; if I can only write them. Of course tell me perfectly frankly if you do'n't like the work. Kermit, in addition to the pictures he has already sent you chapter I, is sending you a large number of others, each marked for the appropriate chapter. Use what you wish; & you can distribute them around without regard to the chapters, if you desire; altho I hope you will not find it necessary to do this.

I also enclose photos by J. A. Loring & Edmund Heller, each marked for the appropriate chapter; use all you wish, crediting them. This means that you will receive herewith, not only the photos for these two chapters, but also some for the next three or four. (I marked each with the man's initials)

May 17, 1909. Juja Farm, British East Africa
To Theodore Roosevelt, Jr.

Dear Ted:

Just a line to say that everything is going on well. I am really proud of Kermit. It is hard to realize that the rather timid boy of four years ago has turned out a perfectly cool and daring fellow. Indeed he is a little too reckless and keeps my heart in my throat, for I worry about him all the time: he is not a good shot, not even as good as I am, and Heaven knows I am poor enough; but he is a bold rider, always cool and fearless, and eager to work all day long. He ran down and killed a Giraffe, alone, and a Hyena also, and the day before yesterday he stopped a charging Leopard within six yards of him, after it had mauled one of our porters. I have had very good luck. I have killed four good Lions in addition to two cubs; it was exciting, and you would have loved it. I also killed two Rhinos both of which charged, a Hippo and two Bull Giraffes, and various Antelopes, Zebras and so forth. So far we have been in the settled districts, and I have lived most comfortably, at the moment being at Juja Farm which is really luxurious.

Naturally I am specially interested to know of every new development in your own affairs. Do let me know as soon as anything definite is decided on.

Your loving father

June 1, 1909. Juja Farm
To Andrew Carnegie

My dear Mr. Carnegie:

I am sending this letter in duplicate to New York and Skibo Castle. I write you because I know you were one of those who helped Dr. Walcott to send out this expedition. The expense of the expedition is very much greater than we had foreseen, because the condition of doing the excellent work that the three naturalists have done, is that they shall take an immense amount of scientific impedimenta with them. As one item I may mention that there are four tons of salt—which when carried on the backs of porters makes a heavy showing. On our last trip we needed a number of porters simply to carry the paper and the cotton batting for the specimens. We need special skinning tents, special tents for storing the skins, and of course the skins of the big animals have to be carried along by numbers of additional porters. All this will serve simply to show by example why the expedition is necessarily far more expensive than an ordinary hunting trip of the same size. So far the naturalists have done excellent work; I am inclined to think better work than has ever before been done here by naturalists in the same length of time. We have collected and are shipping home to the National Museum over a thousand specimens already, including some seventy skins of big game. Now that the expedition is here, I feel that it would be a real misfortune for it to be unable to finish the trip as intended, because some of the best work of the naturalists will be done in Uganda and down the Nile. But enough funds have not been provided, and even now I am paying the expenses myself. This I cannot afford to do, for as you know I am a man of small means. Understand me; I of course pay every penny for Kermit and myself, and what I am speaking about is purely the expense of the scientific part of the expedition and of the three naturalists. As the simple way of managing, we divide the expenses into five parts, that being the number of persons in the expedition, and the National Museum is supposed to pay three parts for the three naturalists while I pay two for my son and myself. (At the moment I am paying everything.) As they of course from the nature of the case need to use more porters and the like than we do, this is a little more than just to them. Moreover, they get the skins of the big game I shoot, many of which are of very great value; and in fact, their being able to make the trip at all depends upon me.

I have written to Walcott that if by August 1st he cannot make arrangements for the extra money needed, the scientific people will have to go home and the scientific expedition to come to an end, though of course my son and I will continue the trip on our own account. Now I feel that it would be a real misfortune to have this happen, from the standpoint of science in America. It may be that Dr. Walcott can raise the money or can agree with Fairfield Osborn of the American Museum in New York to have the trip continue on joint account. But I would greatly like to make sure. In my judgment it would not be safe to count on less than thirty thousand dollars as being needed to enable the scientific expedition to continue until we reach Khartoum next March.

Now my dear Sir, I know the multitude of demands made upon you, and it may very well be that it is out of the question for you to give such a sum—and of course out here it is impossible for me to take any steps towards raising it, and, aside from Walcott, you are the only man I have written to in the matter. If you feel that you can give it I shall of course be greatly relieved and I believe that you will be rendering a great service to science. Of course I shall return whatever is not actually used, and I shall account to you for everything. And let me repeat that not one penny will go directly or indirectly for any personal expenses of either myself or my son. It will be used purely on account of the National Muscurn, where the results of this trip will constitute a permanent memorial.

You may not receive this until late in July, and as it is necessary for me to know by the First of August, and if possible before, so that I can shape my plans, I should be greatly obliged if you would cable me in the event that you are able to adopt my suggestion. If you do not so feel, I need hardly say, my dear Mr. Carnegie, that I shall absolutely understand and shall be entirely content with your decision.

Give my regards to Mrs. Carnegie. Is there any chance of your being in London when I am there next May? Or in Berlin, where I shall be shortly before?

Very sincerely yours

July 26, 1909. Juja Farm
To Henry Cabot Lodge

Dear Cabot:

Your letter of June 21st has just arrived. Indeed I do realize that for the first time in twenty-five years I am out of touch with you—out of touch in a physical way only, I mean.

Tell Root that I don't at all like his hardened skepticism about the lions. If this kind of thing goes on, I shall have to head an insurrection to put Tom Platt back in Root's seat when the latter's term expires—if as I anticipate the worthy Platt at that period still continues to exist in a condition of wicked and malevolent mummification. As for what Aldrich said as to my remarks about the tariff, I was really pleased by it; it was praise from Sir Hubert.

Of course I shan't make a prediction of any kind about my future. I shall not discuss with any human being anything so absurd as the question as to whether I shall ever return to political life in any shape or form. And any interview or statement on the subject purporting to come from me you can set down at once as a pure invention. The chances are infinitesimal that I shall ever go back into public life, but it would be the height of folly even to talk of the subject in any way. My destiny at present is to shoot rhino and lions, and I hope ultimately elephant. I haven't thought of politics or opened a newspaper since I left New York, and I know nothing save what you and Edith have told me. I believed the Cabinet would do well and am pleased but not surprised to know that it is doing well. As for George Meyer, he will surely make a great Secretary of the Navy. I am extremely sorry about Harry White. It is a grave misfortune for the public service that he should be removed. If he had to be removed, there could be no better man for the place than Bob Bacon. I can't understand why North was taken out. All that you say about the tariff is extremely interesting and just about what I expected. As you know, I believe we should have a Federal Inheritance Tax, aimed only at the very large fortunes, which cannot be adequately reached by State Inheritance taxes, if they are sufficiently high and the graduation sufficiently marked. Offhand, it would seem to me that a tax on the net receipts of corporations would be the best way out on the Income Tax business.

Well, we have had a most successful trip and are back in Nairobi to ship our second lot of specimens. We shall bring back to the Smithsonian an exceptionally fine series of scientific collections, and the best series of big game specimens that has ever gone out from Africa or any other continent as the result of a single trip. I shan't try to tell you about my hunting experiences. If you feel in robust health, you shall read about them when in October or November they begin to appear in *Scribner's*. In any event, when they appear in book form you shall have a copy—You may like to look at the outside, and Nannie will doubtless find it as interesting as she once found the American Statesman Series.

You would have been amused if you could have seen one incident the other day. Kermit and I were after hippo in a rowboat manned by natives. I wounded one in a shallow bay covered with waterlilies, and it came straight for the boat with open jaws. I used my entire magazine in stopping it, while Kermit industriously took its photograph during the process. I have sent *Scribner's* eight articles already and for the rest of the trip shall not write more than from four to six. I think they are good, but of course I can't judge, and it may be a subject in which nobody will take any interest, especially in view of the particular way in which I have tried to handle it. I think Kermit's photos really excellent.

With dearest love to Nannie and all the children and grandchildren.

Ever yours

September 10, 1909. Mount Kenya
To Henry Cabot Lodge and Anna Lodge

Dear Cabot and Nannie:

This letter is to both of you, because I miss you both so very much, and look forward so eagerly to seeing you, and to telling you as much about the trip as your patience will bear. I have to write in pencil because we are far out in the wilderness. But the extraordinary thing has been the comfort in which we have traveled. We have had no period of hardships lasting more than two or three days. The sun is, naturally, very hot at noon; but there has not been one hot night, not a night when I have not slept under at least one blanket. This camp, on the slopes of the mountain, is as cool and pleasant as possible. To reach here we traveled, higher up the slopes, east for a couple of days, almost exactly on the equator, and each night there was a heavy frost. We have been in excellent health; Kermit, bar a couple of days with tick fever, has never been sick at all; and though I have had one or two slight touches of fever, it has never been for more than two or three days.

First a word to Cabot, on matters that will interest Nannie about as much as Vest and the lucifer matches did once. Apparently you have come out as well as we could hope on the tariff question. I regard your success in putting on the corporation tax as most important; from the permanent and most important standpoint, as establishing the principle of national supervision; from the temporary standpoint, as scoring a triumph which the west will appreciate, and which may take the sting out of some of the inevitable grumbling about the tariff, by diverting attention to what is really of far greater moment. I am not in the least surprised at what you tell me about Cannon's shortsightedness. He is a strong, hard, narrow old Boeotian. Still less am I surprised about Aldrich; my intercourse with Aldrich gave me a steadily higher opinion of him. Least of all am I surprised at what you tell me of the unfairness of the newspapers. If, as I am confident, business steadily improves, the grumbling will have no permanent effect—unless indeed the spirit of unrest in the West grows strong. The Constitutional Amendment about the income tax is all right; but an income tax must always have in it elements of gross inequality and must always be to a certain extent a tax on honesty. A heavily progressive inheritance tax—national (and heavy) only on really great fortunes going to single individuals—would be far preferable to a national income tax. But whether we can persuade the people to adopt this view I don't know.

I am greatly concerned at what you tell me about Moody. He is one of the ablest and most valuable men in public life. How I wish he were Chief Justice! I feel for him not only a lively regard and affection, but the highest esteem. I do hope he is now all right. Whenever you see him give him my warmest greetings.

Of course George Meyer is doing well in the Navy. You showed mighty good judgment in the men you especially championed for my Cabinet!

Needless to say I entirely agree with you and Loeb about the Mayoralty. There are moments when I feel that I could be of help to you and Root and could render service there, in the Senate; but on the whole I am inclined to believe that as things are now I can do more outside—that is, on the supposition that I can do anything, for people easily grow tired of the advice of a man whose day is past. The last statement sounds melancholy, but it really isn't; I know no other man who has had as good a time as I have had in life; no other President ever enjoyed the Presidency as I did; no other ex-President ever enjoyed himself as I am now enjoying myself, and as I think it likely I shall enjoy myself in the future. The American people have left me heavily in their debt; and I appreciate the fact.

Now for what may appeal to Nannie also. You will both be amused to hear that at last, when fifty years old, I have come into my inheritance in Shakespeare. I never before really cared for more than one or two of his plays; but for some inexplicable reason the sealed book was suddenly opened to me on this trip. I suppose that when a man fond of reading is for long periods in the wilderness with but few books he inevitably grows into a true appreciation of the books that are good. I still balk at three or four of Shakespeare's plays; but most of them I have read or am reading over and over again. The pigskin library has been of great comfort; and ditto the fact that I am writing my book, and must finish it before I reach Khartoum, for I am now too old to be able contentedly to spend a year living only as a hunter and with my brain lying fallow. I have all of Lowell with me; I care more and more for his Biglow Papers, especially the second series; I like his literary essays; but what a real mugwump he gradually became, as he let his fastidiousness, his love of ease and luxury, and his shrinking from the necessary roughness of contact with the world, grow upon him! I think his sudden painting of Dante as a mugwump is deliciously funny. I suppose that his character was not really strong, and that he was permanently injured by association with the Charles Eliot Norton type, and above all by following that impossible creature, Godkin.

Edith sent me ex-President Eliot's list of books. It is all right as *a* list of books which a cultivated man would like to read; but as *the* list it strikes me as slightly absurd. I have never heard of Woolman's journal, but to include it and Penn's "Fruits of Solitude," while leaving out Cervantes and Montaigne, seems odd. To put in Emerson's "English Traits," and leave out Herodotus, Tacitus and Thucydides; to put in Tennyson's "Becket," Middleton's "Changeling" and Dryden's "All for Love" and entirely leave out Æschylus, Sophocles, Molière and Calderon; to put in a translation of the Aeneid and to leave out Homer; in short to put in half the books he has put in, while leaving out scores of really great masters, of every description, from Aristotle to Chaucer and Pascal and Gibbon, not to speak of all poetry and novels—why I think that such things done and left undone make the list ridiculous as *the* list of books to "give a man the essentials of a liberal education"; although excellent if avowedly only one of a hundred possible lists of excellent books, any one of which lists would furnish good reading. Personally, I do not have much patience with serious people going into such business as preparing the "twenty-five best books" of the world. There are so many thousand good books, in so many languages, suited for so many different moods, and needs, and individuals, that all a man ought to do is to say that a given number of books proved of interest and use to him personally at a given time under given conditions.

We have had a great hunt; and the big game here offer plenty of chances for healthy excitement. Three days ago I killed my second bull elephant, and at this moment its tusks and skin are being brought into camp; and yesterday Kermit killed his first elephant. While I was hunting my first elephant he went off on the plains for three weeks, and was very successful, getting among other things, five lions and three buffalo. He is as hardy as a moose, and can outrun, when after a wounded beast, or outlast, in a day's or week's tramp, any man, black or white, in the outfit. He is a very good rider, and will ride at anything, over any ground—he has had some frightful tumbles. He is a fair shot, now, and utterly cool and fearless. But he is so reckless that he keeps me when I am with him, or whichever hunter, Cunningham or Tarlton, I send with him, rather on edge. Both he and I have had some interesting experiences with charging lion, elephant and rhino. We shall send and bring home the most noteworthy collections of big animals that has ever come out of Africa, and the trip will have permanent scientific value. You and I were wise when we determined that this was the thing for me to do. I have been thoroly interested in writing my book, the chapters of which will be for the most part substantially the articles that appear in *Scribner's*. I only hope I have been able in some degree to put on paper what I have seen as I have seen it; the country, the great game, the lions as they charged, the gray bulk of the elephants as we peered at them close at hand in the matted jungle, the hippos round the boat, the rhinos, truculent and stupid, standing in the bright sunlight on the open plains. Then these absolutely wild savages; they are Matthew Arnold's "vigorous, primitive tribes," sure enough; but they, and especially their women kind, differ markedly from those the worthy Arnold evolved from his inner consciousness.

All the English officials, and the settlers, have been most kind. The day is past when an American was regarded as a poor relation; and if we remain self reliant and powerful it will never return. I am interested to see how extensive American influence is, and in how many directions it is felt. Among the novels I see in the houses no English ones are more common than, for instance, David Harum, or Winston Churchill's—I mean, of course, our Winston Churchill, Winston Churchill the gentleman. When we dined with the officers of the local regiment, and they played and sang, I found that they had no knowledge of Garry Owen, but they all knew Marching through Georgia, John Brown's Body and Hampton Racetrack. Tarlton, the hunter, is an Australian, and fond of books; Oliver Wendell Holmes, Longfellow, Bret Harte and Mark Twain are evidently those that he has read as his favorites, and he feels towards the United States just about as he feels towards England—if anything, more warmly.

I really like the men I have met; and many are exactly such as Kipling describes.

Give my love to all the children and grandchildren. This was one of the rare days when I had the chance to write, and I have taken advantage of it. I have been greatly concerned to hear of Sturgis Bigelow's sickness; give him my love; I suppose he is now all well.

Ever yours

October 16, 1909. En route Nairobi
To Andrew Carnegie

Dear Mr. Carnegie:

I heartily thank you for your two letters. I am now entirely easy as to the expense of the scientific Smithsonian part of the trip—the only part as to which there was anything to worry about. I have read your two pamphlets with real interest and with entire agreement as to the general policy—of course could not speak of details. The increase of naval armaments is becoming a well-nigh intolerable burden. You are characteristically kind about our London arrangements for next June; but we have already agreed to stay with Arthur Lee, a very old friend.

When I see the Kaiser I will go over the matter at length with him, telling him I wish to repeat our whole conversation to you; then I'll tell it all to you when I am in London. I shall be in London about May 1st. I regard the proposed quiet conference as most important. I leave absolutely with you the arrangements to be made through Morley, as you suggest. Any day *about* the second week in May would do. Can't he find out from the Chancellor of Oxford just what day I speak there, and then arrange for the conference accordingly? I only fear, my dear Mr. Carnegie, that you do not realize how unimportant a man I now am, and how little weight I shall have in the matter.

With hearty regards to Mrs. Carnegie, I am,

Ever faithfully yours

January 17, 1910. In the Lado Enclave
To Gifford Pinchot

Dear Gifford:

We have just heard by special runner that you have been removed. I cannot believe it. I do not know any man in public life who has rendered quite the service you have rendered; and it seems to me absolutely impossible that there can be any truth in this statement. But of course it makes me very uneasy. Do write me, care of the American Embassy at Paris, just what the real situation is. I have only been able to follow things very imperfectly while out here.

We have had a great hunt, and shall bring home the best scientific collection ever brought out of Africa. Kermit has been a trump.

Give my love to your dear mother; and to Florence and Grant; and of course to Jim and Mrs. Jim. He is doing well, is he not?

Yours ever

January 17, 1910. In the Lado Enclave
To Henry Cabot Lodge

Dear Cabot:

Here we are, camped on the banks of the White Nile, about two degrees north of the equator. It is the heart of the African wilderness. Last night a hippo came almost into camp; lions were roaring and elephants trumpeting within a mile; and yesterday I shot two white rhinoceroses. Tell Raynor that they are not as white as they are painted. Ever since we reached Lake Albert Nyanza the heat has been intense. The mosquitoes are rather bad in the evenings, but we have headnets and gauntlets; and at night we sleep comfortably under our nettings—although usually with nothing on, on account of the heat. Kermit is really a first class hunter now, and as hard as nails. We both continue in excellent health; and while of course we shall probably have fever, we are about past the spirillum tick and sleeping sickness districts.

The Press Agency sent in a runner with a cable to say that Pinchot had been removed, and asking for a statement. Of course I said nothing. I most earnestly hope it is not true.

I am not very sure when you will get this; the postman is a wild savage who runs stark naked with the mail.

Love to dearest Nannie,

Ever yours

March 4, 1910. On the White Nile
To Henry Cabot Lodge

Dear Cabot:

Your two letters of December 27th and February 15th were handed me from the steamer we met at Gondokoro.

I intend to follow absolutely the course you suggest; keep absolutely still about home politics, refusing to say anything about any phase of the situation; and come home towards the end of June. But if Gifford Pinchot comes abroad I shall certainly see him as intimately as if nothing had happened (by the way, he writes me that Wilson saw and assented to his letter before he sent it; of course in any event he ought not to have sent it).

I have written Root urging him to meet me in Berlin and be in London with me.

It seems to me that we shall probably find that we must fight the campaign on Taft's administration, and therefore must renominate him; but I know nothing of the situation, and I may be all wrong; I am absolutely free to act as I deem wise for the country, in any way, and shall keep my freedom, exactly as you urge. At present it does not seem to me that it would be wise, from any side, for me to be a candidate. But all this can wait.

Indeed, my very dear friend—whose letters have touched me inexpressibly—I should be more than glad to write of Bay as you suggest. I hope it can be in some more permanent way than a mere review. Have you thought of any way? Could I write a foreword or something of the kind for an edition of his works? Love to dearest Nannie.

Ever yours

I like Mrs. Wharton's appreciation of him.

(I have just come in from a successful hunt after a rare kind of water antelope, "Mrs. Grays.")

March 21, 1910. Aswan
To Theodore Roosevelt, Jr.

Dear old Ted,

Your letter delighted me. I have already written darling Eleanor[1]; and give my love to her dear mother. Mother and Ethel have told me just the very nicest things about Eleanor; if I had wished to choose an ideal wife for my son, it would have been exactly the sweet, wise, charming girl that she is. I only hope my other boys and girl, when the time comes, will be anything like as fortunate.

Cunning Mother, looking very pretty and triumphant and mischievous, told me that she had advised Eleanor, with me as an awful example—but would not tell me what she had said! She was so charming, and felt so much that she had both been wise and scored off me that I had to keep kissing her while she told me. So now, through you, I wish to give Eleanor a word of advice myself. Please show her this. Greatly tho I loved Mother I was at times thoughtless and selfish, and if Mother had been a mere unhealthy Patient Griselda, I might have grown set in selfish and inconsiderate ways. Mother, always tender, gentle and considerate, and always loving, yet when necessary pointed out where I was thoughtless and therefore inconsiderate and selfish, instead of submitting to it. Had she not done this it would in the end have made her life very much harder, and mine very much less happy. It is the girl who has the hardest time in marriage; a man, even a good and loving man, is often thoughtless; and the wisest and most loving wife is she who will,

---

[1]Eleanor Alexander, Ted's fiancée.

with gentleness and tenderness, prevent his letting thoughtfulness "set" into selfishness.

Your letter is in other ways most interesting; you raise certain points about which I want to talk with you before you go to California; I can't write it.

We sail for N.Y on the 10th, (I am hurrying things, to sail on this date) & ought to reach there the 16th; I suppose there will be a public reception for me on that day or the next; so that if the wedding is the 18th you are cutting things very fine.

Your loving father

April 6, 1910. Rome
To Henry Cabot Lodge

Dear Cabot:

Cannot you and Nannie come over to England, meet us there, and come back with us? I believe the sea voyage would be an excellent thing for Nannie, and for you too. You do not need to be told how dearly we should love to see you. Do come, both of you, if you can.

Ever since striking Khartoum I have been in almost as much of a whirl as if I were on a Presidential tour at home. In the Soudan and Egypt, much to my amusement, everybody turned to me precisely as if I were in my own country. They were hoping and praying for leadership, and I shall show you the letters of curiously intense gratitude which the Sirdar of the Soudan, and Eldon Gorst, as Governor in Egypt, wrote me because of what I had said. The English Government is showing an uncomfortable flabbiness in Egyptian matters.

At Rome I had an elegant row, the details of which you have doubtless seen in the papers. The Pope imposed conditions upon my reception, requiring a pledge—secret or open—that I would not visit and speak to the Methodist Mission. Of course I declined absolutely to assent to any conditions whatever, and the reception did not take place. Then with a folly as incredible as that of the Vatican itself, the Methodist missionaries, whose game was perfectly simple because the Pope had played it for them, and who had nothing to do but sit quiet, promptly issued an address of exultation which can only be called scurrilous, and with equal promptness I cancelled the arrangements I had made for seeing them. Our clerical brother is capable of showing extraordinarily little sense when he gets into public affairs. The only satisfaction I had out of the affair, and it was a very great satisfaction, was that on the one hand I administered a needed lesson to the Vatican, and on the other hand I made it understood that I feared the most powerful Protestant Church just as little as I feared the Roman Catholics. If I were in politics, or intended to run for any public office, I should regard the incident as gravely compromising my usefulness as a candidate, but inasmuch as I have no idea that I shall ever again be a candidate for anything, I can take unalloyed satisfaction in having rendered what I regard as a small service to the cause of right-thinking in America.

Then I became involved in a queer little affair with the Kaiser, which fortunately came to nothing. He notified our Embassy that he wished me to be his guest for three days at the Schloss in Berlin; but he said nothing about Edith. I accordingly wrote to our Ambassador at Berlin, and told the German representative in Egypt, Hatzveldt, that while I deeply appreciated the Emperor's courtesy and would eagerly endeavor to meet his wishes wherever I could, I must respectfully ask to be excused from going to the castle, and be permitted to stay at the Embassy with Mrs. Roosevelt. I wrote this to our Ambassador by letter, but Hatzveldt evidently communicated by cable, for simultaneously with my letter there arrived at our Berlin Embassy another note from the Kaiser including Edith in the invitation, which I accordingly accepted.

I thoroughly enjoyed meeting the King and Queen here, and their children. They are as nice a family as I have come across anywhere, thoroughly good citizens in every way, very cultivated, very intelligent, very simple and upright and straightforward. I should greatly like to have them as neighbors, and the King would make a first-class United States Senator, or Cabinet Minister, and, with a little change, a first-class President!

Physically, I am really having too much to do, as every day is passed in a perfect whirl, and I can only keep up with my mail with the utmost difficulty. I shall not try to speak about politics with you, and shall rigidly follow your advice to keep absolutely clear from any possible statement one way or the other, and listen pleasantly to all that is said on both sides. I am very much afraid we are in for a wash-out, and that nothing can stop it.

Just as I had finished writing the above your letter came. Now, Cabot, it seems to me that you have changed ground. In your previous letters you have said most strongly that you wished me to keep out of politics, and specifically that you did not see how I could help the Congressional Committee with speeches or a letter. In this letter you seem to think that I ought so to help. It is unnecessary to say that whatever I can do for you in Mass. will be done; but to make a general appeal for Congress it seems to me would be impossible. I don't think it would do any good, and it would simply eliminate me as a possible factor of usefulness thereafter. From the scanty information I had, I was at first inclined to think that as much had been done with the tariff as was possible. The

Outlook people wrote me this, and even if they had not I was more than content with your statement. It does seem to me, with what little additional knowledge I have now, that the tariff issue was not met as it was necessary to meet it; that certain things that ought to have been done were left undone, and that the whole was done in a way that caused trouble. I am not at all sure that it was possible under the old methods to get any other result. I am very much afraid that the trouble was fundamental; in other words, that it is not possible, as Congress is actually constituted, to expect the tariff to be well handled by *representatives of localities*. I am beginning to believe in the truth of what Root continually said while he was in the Cabinet; that it was useless to hope to do good work on the tariff if we adhered to the way which Cannon, Payne, Dalzell, and even as able a man as Aldrich, declared to be the only way, and that a complete change, into the details of which I need not go, ought to have been made in the methods of achieving the result. Now this may not be the right impression at all. I shall read through your memorandum most carefully; but with my present information I should be excessively uncomfortable going on the stump and trying to defend the tariff, and in addition, as an offhand judgment, I am inclined to doubt whether any good whatever would come from such a course.

I don't agree with you about not seeing Pinchot. I am delighted to see him. The only man I invited to see me was Root, and Root said he could not come; but when Pinchot said he wanted to see me I said I should be more than delighted. I shall listen to all he has to say, I shall not commit myself, and, in short, I shall do just as you have been advising me. I shall not come to any conclusion as to any of these things until I see you. I should suppose this Catholic-Methodist business would eliminate me anyhow as a factor of much usefulness in the party. I am very uncomfortable about all I hear from home. There is no use of my writing, for I should have to talk it over for forty-eight hours with you. I have answered to everyone that I am saying nothing whatever for or against anyone, or any policy, and am not to be quoted in any possible way. I am anything but happy over the prospect of being at home. You can be sure that if I had the slightest idea of being a candidate I should not have come home until after the Congressional elections. I entirely agree with you that under no circumstances should I accept either the Governorship or the Senatorship. As for what you say about the American people looking to me for leadership, it is unfortunately preposterous, and makes me more uncomfortable than ever. That is why I got out of the country, and apparently I ought to have stayed out of the country even longer.

Ever yours

April 11, 1910. Porto Maurizio
To Henry Cabot Lodge

Dear Cabot:

I want to explain what I meant in my last letter, though I think you will understand it without explanation. I have not said as much, or implied as much, to any human being as in that letter. I don't want you to think that I have the slightest feeling of personal chagrin about Taft. The Presidency of the United States, the success of the Republican Party, above all the welfare of the country—matters like these cannot possibly be considered from any standpoint but that of the broadest public interest. I am sincere when I say that I am not yet sure whether Taft could with wisdom have followed any course save the one he did. The qualities shown by a thoroughly able and trustworthy lieutenant are totally different, or at least may be totally different, from those needed by the leader, the commander. Very possibly if Taft had tried to work in my spirit, and along my lines, he would have failed; that he has conscientiously tried to work for the objects I had in view, so far as he could approve them, I have no doubt. I wish, in my own mind, and to you, to give Taft the benefit of every doubt, and to think and say the very utmost that can be said and thought in his favor. Probably the only course open was not to do as he originally told me before the nomination he intended to do, and as he even sometimes said he intended to do between nomination and election, but to do as he actually has done. Moreover, it seems to me, there is at least a good chance that a reaction will come in his favor. Everyone believes him to be honest, and most believe him to be doing the best he knows how. I have noticed very little real personal abuse of him, or indeed attack upon him. Such being the case, it is entirely possible that there will be a revulsion of feeling in his favor, a revulsion of feeling which may put him all right not only as the head of the party but as able to make the party continue in control of the country.

But it puzzles me to see how I can help him or Congress to victory; it must be on the ground that they are approved by the nation for having on many important points completely twisted round the policies I advocated and acted upon. In 1904 Congress had done admirably. I stood as strongly for it as I knew how. In 1906 Congress had shown very marked signs of falling back; still it had in some respects behaved fairly. The leaders called on me at Oyster Bay, had a perfectly frank talk with me, expressed regret at their shortcomings, said that my help was vital, and that if I would give it they would back me up in every possible way. I made as strong an appeal for them as I knew how. When the new Congress, elected, as they themselves at the time told me, explicitly on this appeal, assembled in Washington, the leaders had come to the conclusion that I really meant what I said when I took myself out of the position of a possible candidate for the Presidency. The change in their attitude was instantaneous. They had a feeling of great relief so obvious that everyone could note it; a feeling that it was no longer necessary to pay very much heed to me; that it would not be the outgoing President, but the possible incoming President, whose words and record would count in the approaching election. When the election arrived they felt differently and came to me not once, but again and again, begging me to endorse their work, and make an appeal for them. I told them that it was very difficult to do so, that I would not say anything that I did not truthfully believe and that I could not truthfully say they had done well; but, finally, on their explicit and repeated assurances that they did intend to stand by my policies, that they would not only support Taft in carrying out those policies, but would heartily support me during the remaining four months of my term, I wrote an appeal for them on the ground of the good conduct of the party, and of Congress as part of the party, during the preceding seven years. The instant the election was over they turned round with the utmost hilarity, frankly saying that now I was dead and it was of no consequence what I did one way or the other, and they proposed to show their real feelings of animosity and dislike. Nothing but the fact that I showed them that they could not possibly run over me, even during the last four months of my time, prevented their putting their will into action. Now twice I have asked the American people to elect a Republican Congress, in one case in spite of an indifferent record, in the other case in spite of a poor record, and in each case on their explicit promises and assurances. In each case the leaders of Congress have promptly gone back on their promises and have put me in the position of having promised what there was no intention of performing. I don't see how I can put myself in such a position again. I think that the people who ask me to promise things must first bring forth fruit meet for repentance. Now for Taft. You do not need to be told that Taft was nominated solely on my assurance to the Western people especially, but almost as much to the people of the East, that he would carry out my work unbroken; not (as he has done) merely for somewhat the same objects in a totally different spirit, and with a totally different result, but exactly along my lines, with all his heart and strength. Of course you know that among my heartiest supporters, especially in the West, and, curiously enough, also, in Eastern states like New York and New Jersey, there has been any amount of criticism of me because I got them to take a man on my word who they now find understood his own promise in a totally different sense from that in which both I and the men who acted on my word understood it. There is only a little harsh criticism either of my sincerity or of his, but there is a very widespread feeling that, quite unintentionally, I have deceived them, and that however much they may still believe in my professions when I say what I myself will do, they do not intend again to accept any statements of mine as to what anyone else will do.

Now, under these circumstances, for me to go into a wholehearted campaign, battling for the Administration through thick and thin, upholding Congress, making such appeals as I did in 1906 and 1908, would be, as far as I can now see, out of the question. The party leaders have shown with the utmost possible distinctness that while they welcome and are anxious for my help in carrying an election, they are cynically indifferent, or rather cynically and contemptuously hostile to doing themselves anything after election which shall show the slightest regard to what I have promised. Now when I left the Presidency I was prepared, and of course am now prepared, not to be a leader at all; I don't see how an outsider can be a leader; that is the business of the President and the party leaders who hold office; but it is folly to try to be a leader when all that those who appeal to you really desire is that your leadership shall count in getting them elected, but shall be instantly thrown aside when it comes to dealing with party policy after once they have been elected, and no longer need your assistance. I don't believe that any such appeal as I might make would be heeded; on the contrary, I think it would help no one else, and would discredit me, because people would believe that I was either insincere or a fool.

The trouble, as it looks to me, is that much of what has been called leadership in the Republican Party consists of leadership which has no following. Now I may be utterly mistaken, and I write with a full knowledge that I may thus be mistaken, but my impression is that even as strong and able a man as Aldrich, a man whom I have been obliged to oppose on many fundamental points, but whose good qualities I cordially recognize, has no real following whatever among the people at large, not even in his own state. Cannon has had a much greater personal following, but he also excites even more hostility. The trouble is that the Cannon-Aldrich type of leadership down at bottom represents not more than, say, ten per cent. of the rank and file of the party's voting strength. This ten per cent. or whatever it may be, includes the bulk of the big business men, the big professional politicians, the big lawyers who carry on their work in connection with the leaders of high finance, and of the political machine, their representatives among the great papers, and so forth and so forth. All this makes a body of exceedingly influential people, but if the great mass—the ninety per cent. of the party,—the men who stand for it as their fathers stood for it in the days of Lincoln, get convinced that the ten per cent. are not leading them right, a revolt is sure to ensue. If politicians of sufficient ability lead that revolt, as in the Western States, they get control of the organization. If, as in Massachusetts, it is merely men like Foss who can thus lead the revolt, while opposed to them are such men as you and Draper, they cannot control the party, but they can cause infinite damage. Of course it is hard for me to tell how things are from this distance, but Foss's election to Congress makes it look as if the discontent in Massachusetts were almost as formidable as the discontent in Iowa and Ohio, except for the fact that the quality of its leadership is totally different, and also the quality of the opposition to it in the regular organization. Now in Massachusetts I will hoist the black flag and fight for you without either giving or taking quarter, and elsewhere in the country, here and there, I can fight in the same shape, but I certainly could not at the moment say that I can do it everywhere, and we have to consider just what limitations this imposes upon me outside of the fights like that for you into which I can go wholeheartedly. Cabot, they will believe me when I speak for you, largely because I am not insincere enough to speak in the same terms for other people in whom I don't believe.

I entirely appreciate the distinction you draw between the Insurgents in the Senate and in the House, although I should suppose that a man like Dolliver in the Senate really came in the House class.

Well, so much for politics, about which I as yet know very little, my views as to which may be totally changed after I have been at home. Here we continue to have an interesting but an excessively fatiguing time. The Italians have the Southern enthusiasm, and really on my trip through Italy I have been received almost as I would have been if I had been at home, with crowds at the stations, the city officials down to greet me wherever I have gone, and so forth and so forth. Edith and I had a thoroughly pleasant two days' trip in a carriage, marred only by the hideous vulgarity of the press of all shades—American, Italian, and French—in alluding to it, till toward the end of the two days, when everybody had become advised by telephone and telegraph of where we were going, it became out of the question to continue. We were simply swamped with people, Italians in all the little Italian towns, Americans wherever we came near a winter hotel, and others, all of them with great good nature and friendliness joining to make it impossible for us to go out of our rooms unless we cared to be accompanied by increasing crowds; and wherever we wanted to admire anything, from a view to a picture, having local officials start amiably in to help us in our admiration!

Give my love to Nannie, and do both of you come abroad to meet us in England if you possibly can, and go back with us on the steamer.

Ever yours

P. S.—I could send you a number of very significant letters which I have received, but it is not worth while.

Infinitely more important is the fact that I myself cannot help feeling that even though there has been a certain adherence to the objects of the policies which I deemed essential to the National welfare, these objects have been pursued by the present Administration in a spirit and with methods which have rendered the effort almost nugatory. I don't think that under the Taft-Aldrich-Cannon régime there has been a real appreciation of the needs of the country, and I am certain that there has been no real appreciation of the way the country felt. Now, I am well aware that a man with strong convictions is always apt to feel overintensely the difference between himself and others with slighter convictions, and throughout most of my political career I have been in the position of adhering to one side because, after a general balancing, in spite of my discontent with my own people, I was infinitely more discontented with the other side. But I do think we had the Republican Party in a shape that warranted the practical continuance of just what we were doing. To announce allegiance to what had been done, and to abandon the only methods by which it was possible to continue to get it done, was not satisfactory from my standpoint. I have played my part, and I have the very strongest objection to having to play any further part; I very earnestly hope that Taft will retrieve himself yet, and if, from whatever causes, the present condition of the party is hopeless, I most emphatically desire that I shall not be put in the position of having to run for the Presidency, staggering under a load which I cannot carry, and which has been put on my shoulders through no fault of my own. Therefore my present feeling is that Taft should be the next nominee, because, if the people approve of what he has done, they will elect him, and if they don't approve of what he has done, it is unfair to me to have me suffer for the distrust which others have earned, and for which I am in no way responsible. This represents not a settled conviction on my part, but my guess as to the situation from this distance. Of course things may entirely change, and my attitude change with them. But I don't see how, at present, anyone can expect me to stand whole-heartedly for those responsible for what has been done which, according to my view, is not much more like real Republicanism than the creed of the Cotton Whigs in '56 resembled the creed of the Republican party of Lincoln. I shall speak as little as possible when I get home, and yet when I do speak, I shall have to exercise the most extreme care, because I cannot, without stultifying myself, avoid saying things which, no matter how impersonal and general I keep them, shall seem to stand in contrast with what has been done in the past year. It is a very unpleasant situation. I wish I could have come back after the Congressional elections, for, on the one hand, I will not be put into the attitude of antagonizing my friends, or criticizing my successor, and, on the other hand, I will not be put into the attitude of failing to stand for the great principles which I regard as essential. I may add that it looks to me as if the people were bound to have certain policies carried out, and that if they do not get the right type of aggressive leadership—leadership which a Cabinet of lawyers, or an Administration which is primarily a lawyers' Administration, is totally unfit to give—they will turn to the wrong kind of leadership. I might be able to *guide* this movement, but I should be wholly unable to *stop* it, even if I were to try. There is not a greater delusion than the belief that a lawyer is, *per se*, also a statesman. On the contrary, the mere lawyer is rather more unfit than, say, the mere dentist, or mere bricklayer, or mere banker, to be a public man. The ablest lawyer often has had public experience of one type or another which makes him more apt than the ordinary business man to be able to excel in public life; but it is not because he is a lawyer at all; it is because he has great ability and a certain knowledge of public affairs. I could go still further and say that to be a great lawyer is, while a good thing in a judge, very far from being the most important thing. Taney was probably as good a lawyer as Marshall; the abysmal difference between the two men came because one was a statesman and the other was not. We now need on the Supreme Court not better lawyers, but broad-minded, far-seeing statesmen, utterly out of sympathy with higgling technicalities.

June 4, 1910. London
To Henry Cabot Lodge

Dear Cabot:

I shall see you soon; this is only a line to say how glad I was to get your last letter. I thought your Navy speech first rate of course, and was both amused and interested by Hale's.

I have had a most amusing and interesting time here, but, literally, there hasn't been a five minutes free. I suppose you have seen the Guildhall speech, and you will have seen my Romanes lecture before this reaches you.

I have refused to meet Winston Churchill, being able to avoid causing any scandal by doing so. All the other public men, on both sides, I was glad to meet, and everybody—from the King and Queen to the Irish Members—has been more than kind. I have had a thoroughly good time—but how homesick I am!

Ever yours

July 19, 1910. New York
To Arthur H. Lee

Dear Arthur:

Of course we all of us enjoyed your letter, Mrs. Roosevelt quite as much as I did, while Ethel, in Kermit's absence, chuckled heartily over the advice to her and Kermit to treat their somewhat irresponsible father as gently as circumstances would permit. I also much enjoyed the magazines you sent me—perhaps most of all, the wholly unconscious humor of the *Nation's* rage.

Here I have been in a position of inconceivable difficulty. The ultra-Taft people have been bent on making me come out for Taft in a way which would, in the first place, represent insincerity on my part, and in the next place, would simply cause me to lose all my hold on my own supporters, and therefore deprive me of all power of helping Taft. On the other hand, the extremists have been wild to have me break with Taft. I have resolutely declined to follow either course. The way I can best help Taft and most probably secure his renomination so as to make it worth having is to secure a Republican victory this Fall, for such a victory would strengthen his hands and redound to his credit. I have done my best, and shall do my best, to achieve such a victory. You see, even more clearly than my best friends here like Lodge (although they also rather reluctantly see it) that it is to my personal interest that Taft should succeed himself; and all that I can conscientiously do to effect this will be done. I am not satisfied with him, but you and I who have been in practical politics and have actually tried public life, know that it is not often that one is able to be thoroughly satisfied; and when we cannot do the best, then, as Abraham Lincoln said, we have to do the best possible. Taft has come far short of doing what he ought to have done, but after all he has done well enough to make me feel justified in supporting him; and if he will go on as he has for the last two months, I shall be able to support him with entirely good grace, and what is far more important, the people will accept him, and will not insist upon my nomination. The really awkward situation has been the possibility of such action on their part.

Well, I am glad you enjoyed having us, for our stay with you, both in London and even more at Chequers, was a practically unalloyed delight. I shall never forget it. We were very fond already of you and your dear wife, but of course now we are even fonder, and feel that we know you even better. Give her our warmest love.

Let me know if the Rough Rider medals do not come. They were posted a few days later than the letter, and were sent by registered post.

Ever yours

November 11, 1910. Oyster Bay
To William Allen White

Dear White:

I thank you for your telegram. Speaking generally, I feel as you do, but of course the Tower of Siloam is very apt to fall upon the just as well as upon the unjust when there is an earthquake such as that through which we have just been. Almost as many Congressmen who voted against Cannon were beaten as Congressmen who voted for him. In New York and New Jersey, for instance, every Congressman who had so voted was defeated. Moreover, there was a big sag even in such progressive States as Iowa and Kansas, the vote for Governor in both States showing an infinitely greater falling off than we did here in New York, in proportion. Moreover, in New York and Indiana, the Democrats won fair and square against progressive policies, against the New Nationalism. In New York the victory was won on an ultrareactionary basis, as was also the case in Connecticut and in Ohio—the fight in Ohio being between two bodies of reactionaries. However, in the main, I think you are entirely right, and of one thing at any rate I am certain; while the Republican Party may be beaten even if it stands for progressive policies, it will surely be beaten, and what is more, deserve to be beaten, if it does not. I have never been one of those men who has to use hope to supply the defect of courage, and win or lose, I am in this fight to a finish. I can give you no idea of the frightful odds we have had to contend with in New York. Of course, personally, I think that if it had not been for what we did at Saratoga, the Republican ticket would have been beaten by 300,000 majority; in other words, that there would not have been any real fight at all. But this I shall not say in public, because nobody cares a rap what might have been, and it is a poor business for the defeated side to begin making excuses. A more barefaced alliance for evil than that between Tammany Hall and the powerful and crooked section of Wall Street has never before triumphed in this country to the extent that it triumphed here in New York on Tuesday last; but I do not think it could have won if it had not been for the general sweep against us. One thing always to remember in politics is that it takes a long time to overcome inertia, and that, when it has been overcome, it takes all equally long time to overcome momentum. All kinds of things continue to occur which make people angry with a given political party, just as they have occurred in Washington for the past eighteen months. For some time no great effect is visible. Finally, the people become thoroughly angry and decide to punish the party. If at that time the reformers within the party get hold of it, as we did here in New York, and purge it of its wickedness, they are able to remove some of the disaffection, but a good deal is simply transferred to the new men in control; a section of the public taking a dull satisfaction in punishing the new managers for the very faults which have been corrected. I hope soon to see you.

Sincerely yours

February 2, 1911. New York
To Charles A. Kofoid

My dear Mr. Kofoid:

I have read Mr. Tracy's pamphlet with great interest. He seems to me to have made his case very clear. (I am not certain about "sky pattern." My experience is that colors show almost as conspicuously against the sky as against any other background. A white gull or pigeon is quite visible against the sky.) There is one point, however, which I would like to suggest to you and to him. This is where he speaks of the dark colors of the crows, saying that such coloration "can exist largely because of their size and aggressiveness and therefore of their immunity from raptatorial birds," and added that seed-eating birds of delicate flesh and harmless disposition could not have developed black plumage like that of the raven, because they would have become extinct for lack of protective coloration. Now it seems to me that this is negatived by the fact that cow buntings are numerous. Indeed, I might go farther and say that the abundance of purple and rusty grackles, yellow-headed grackles and red-winged blackbirds, not to speak of bobolinks, is proof to the contrary. With some of these birds, the black plumage only exists in the male during the breeding season; but the grackles are always quite as conspicuous except in point of size as are ravens, and the cow buntings which are very plentiful are almost as conspicuous—the cocks quite as much, and the hens not much less. From my piazza here in the Summer I can watch close by both grasshopper sparrows and cow buntings. The grasshopper sparrows behave just as Mr. Tracy describes. They try to hide, and I have not a doubt that their coloration has a concealing or protective value both when they crouch and when they skulk through the grass. But the cow buntings, as they stalk over the grass, make not the slightest effort to hide, and they are just as conspicuous as little crows or ravens would be. Their coloration has not the smallest protective or concealing quality. They are not big; they are not aggressive; their flesh is delicate; and yet they are very common, and are striking examples of an instance where the concealing coloration theory completely breaks down.

In my criticisms of Mr. Thayer's article, I have been very careful not to criticize the general theory of concealing or protective coloration.

That it applies in multitudes of cases, I have no question. There are multitudes of other cases where I do not think that, as yet, we are able to say with definiteness one way or the other as to its application. There remain very large numbers of cases where his theory is certainly without even the smallest foundation of fact. (In the immense class of humming birds there is not one species in a score to which his theory, as he states it, can apply. See what Hudson says about them. It does not apply to swallows; the brilliantly colored species, wholly without concealing coloration are infinitely more numerous than those to which the theory could by any possibility apply—the bank swallows (& swifts).) The comparison I made with Agassiz and some of the other ultraglacialists is applicable. In the Northern continents the discovery of the effects of glacial action was of enormous importance, but it was a simple absurdity to try to explain phenomena in South America, and in Africa—in the Amazon Valley, for instance—on the theory that the land had been subjected to glacial action. It is similarly a wild absurdity for Mr. Thayer to make such sweeping announcements as he does where he says, in speaking of the nuptial dress of birds, that even this dress is protective. But we can go much further than this. There are unquestionably large numbers of species of both mammals and birds as to which Mr. Thayer's theory has not the smallest particle of justification. Indeed merely reading his own book shows such a fantastic quality of mind on his part that it is a matter of very real surprise to me that any scientific observer, in commenting on the book, no matter how much credit he may give to Mr. Thayer for certain discoveries and theories, should fail to enter the most emphatic protest against the utter looseness and wildness of his theorizing. Think of being required seriously to consider the theory that flamingos are colored red so that fishes (or oysters for that matter—there is no absurdity of which Mr. Thayer could not be capable) would mistake them for the sunset! This is only an extreme example of the literally countless follies of which Mr. Thayer is guilty. I think that serious scientific men, when they come to discuss Mr. Thayer, should first of all and in the most emphatic way repudiate the ludicrous part of his theory, the part in which he pushes it to extremes. (To discuss the effects of glacial action, for instance, would be absurd without the statement that it was potent only in boreal realms or at high elevations.) There then will remain much matter for serious discussion. But there can be no serious discussion of the theory as a whole until such eliminations have been made. Our first business is to see whether, as he says, the law is one of universal and practically inclusive potency, or whether it is one of many laws, all of which are limited by others, and act with various effects. Of course you are familiar with Allen's pamphlet on *The Influence of Physical Conditions in the Genesis of Species,* and also of course you are familiar with Nelson's very interesting discussion on Directive Coloration in the Southern Jack Rabbit Group.

What I would like to get is a serious study by a competent scientific man who will first of all try to distinguish between cases where the coloration is concealing, or protective, and the cases where it is not. At this moment here on the Sound there are two kinds of ducks found in far greater abundance than any others. These are the surf ducks or scoters, and the long-tailed ducks or old squaws. The former are black, or in the case of young birds so dark a brown that the effect at a distance is the same. They are as conspicuous as ravens. They can be seen on the water as far as it is possible to see anything. Their coloration is not only not concealing or protective, but it is in the highest degree advertising. The old squaws have a broken pattern of coloration, and while they are conspicuous birds they are very much less conspicuous in coloration than the scoters; but they are the most noisy and restless of any ducks. They can be heard long before they are seen, and they are almost always moving. I do not believe that they ever escape observation from any possible foe, owing to their color. Now as to these ducks—the most numerous ducks around here, the most successful in other words—Mr. Thayer's theory certainly does not apply. It is just the same with land birds. The soaring hen hawks and the bigger true falcons alike are always conspicuous even to human eyes. It simply is not possible, as far as I can see, that they are helped by their coloration in catching prey. If they are, the fact must certainly be shown by a totally different series of experiments from anything that Mr. Thayer has even attempted.

So with a number of our smaller birds. Bluebirds, Baltimore orioles, scarlet tanagers, red-winged blackbirds, grackles, swallows, indigo buntings, towhees, and many many others are either all the time, or at certain important seasons, colored in a manner most calculated to strike the attention. (This is true of thousands of kinds of large birds (like all the white egrets and glossy or dark ibises, pied storks, coots, water hens &c) as of brilliantly colored birds in the tropics.) Even as regards warblers, I think that the nuptial coloration of certain species must have an advertising rather than a concealing value; and with some I should say that this would apply at other seasons also. The mourning warbler, the Kentucky warbler, the Maryland yellowthroat, the Blackburnian, the black-throated green, the blue-winged yellow—I might almost indefinitely extend the list—are colored so that at certain seasons, or at all seasons, they attract the eye under normal conditions. The only reason that they do not attract the eye here is that their size and the leafy cover in which they

dwell offset the effect of their brilliant and highly nonprotective noncon-
cealing special coloration.

The utter breakdown of the theory as regards most big game I have
elsewhere discussed. Giraffes, zebras, buffalos, oryx, gnu, hartebeests
owe nothing whatever to concealing coloration; they have none. Moreover, where a number of different species utterly differently colored
exist with equal success, two things are sure; first, that if one of them is
protectively colored, the others are not; and second, that this protective
coloration must be of very small consequence compared with other features in enabling the animal to thrive. If a chipmunk's stripes are concealing, then the uniform tint of a weasel or a red squirrel is not concealing; or vice versa. In fact, as regards a great multitude of mammals,
large and small, I think there is need of far more thorough examination
than has yet been made before we can say just how far countershading,
for instance, is of real protective value. It is an interesting discovery
about color; but its value in effecting concealment as regards many
mammals, snakes, birds &c, is enormously exaggerated.

I look forward to seeing your museum. As you know, I have presented it an elephant.

Sincerely yours

[Handwritten] In Egypt, on the edge of the desert, there are sand
chats which are protectively colored above and which try to escape notice by crowding; and there are black and white chats, whose coloration
is advertising; they never try to escape notice, and are as conspicuous as
if they were little crows.

February 10, 1911. New York
To James E. West

My dear Sir:

It is unfortunately out of the question for me to accept your invitation to speak at the Boy Scout banquet of the National Council at Washington on the evening of February 14th. I am very sorry. I earnestly believe in the Boy Scout Movement, because I see the national possibility
of this Movement among boys. There are several things which we
should see in the lives of our American boys. They should grow up
strong and alert, able to stand the strain of an honest day's hard work,
and of an honest attempt to help forward the material and moral
progress of our nation.

American boyhood should be resourceful and inventive so that the
American man of the future may be ever ready to help in the hour of the
nation's need. American boys should always show good manners, and
the desire to help all who are in trouble or difficulty, and indeed to help

the weak at all times. Courtesy is as much the mark of a gentleman as truthfulness and courage, and every American boy should be a gentleman, fearless in defending his own rights and the rights of the weak, and scrupulous to inflict no wrong on others. The boy who is to grow into the right kind of man should scorn lying as he scorns cowardice, and he should remember that the right kind of strong man is always considerate of and courteous towards others. In this nation of ours, the ideal of everyone should be to help in the work of all. Therefore let each boy try to render service to others, and try to do well every task that comes to his hands, big or little. The boys of America should understand our institutions and their history; they should know of the lives of the great men that have blazed the trail for our national greatness, and of the mighty deeds that they wrought; they should feel a high pride of country and a real spirit of patriotism, which will make them emulate these careers of gallant and efficient service and of willingness to make sacrifices for the sake of a lofty ideal. American boys should grow up understanding the life of the community about them, and appreciating the privileges and the duties of citizenship, so that they may face the great questions of national life with the ability and resolute purpose to help in solving them aright. Each boy should make up his mind that when a man he will be able to earn his own living and care for all those dependent upon him, and that in addition he will do his part in serving the nation as a whole.

I believe heartily in the work your Association is doing. You seek to supply the necessary stimulus to alert and strong manhood. You insist on the doing of a good turn daily to somebody without reward, and thus furnish the elements of a national, widespread American courtesy. You try to teach boys to do things for themselves and so make them resourceful. You stand for true patriotism, true citizenship, true Americanism. I wish all success to a movement fraught with such good purposes.

Faithfully yours

March 2, 1911. Oyster Bay
To Quentin Roosevelt

Dearest Quentin:

I do not remember what Archie said to me about White, but surely he could not have told White that I could get him a Springfield rifle. Those are not sold to outsiders. Even Kermit did not have a Springfield rifle in Africa. He used the 30–40 Winchester, which carries the same ammunition and is a very good rifle. It is not quite as strong shooting, but for target work and for any American game it is just as good as the Springfield. I should advise your friend to get one of those.

I have sent you a copy of my European and other addresses, and
you will find my speech on Egypt in it. I need not say how proud I have
been over your standing in school. It is simply fine! Heavens! to think
of one of our family standing as high as that! It is almost paralyzing!
Kermit wrote what a nice time he had had at Groton.

The poor motorcar is showing the results of the hard work this
Winter. Next Winter I do not think I shall try to use it as much. I will
much more often take the regular cars in and out. If a big thaw comes I
do not believe we will be able to use it at all, for the other day when
there was a thaw the back road literally looked as if it had been plowed,
and Arthur was barely able to get up it. Now it is frozen again and the
roads are awful, but still it is possible for Arthur to get the car along.
Well! I will see you in San Francisco.

Your loving father

March 14, 1911. En route El Paso, Texas
To William Howard Taft

Personal and private

Dear Mr. President:

I don't suppose that there is anything in this war talk, and I most
earnestly hope that we will not have to intervene even to do temporary
police duty in Mexico.[1] But just because there is, I suppose, one chance
in a thousand of serious trouble such as would occur if Japan or some
other big power were to back Mexico, I write. Of course I would not
wish to take any part in a mere war with Mexico—it would not be my
business to do peculiarly irksome and disagreeable and profitless police duty of the kind any occupation of Mexico would entail. But if by
any remote chance—and I know how remote it is—there should be a
serious war, a war in which Mexico was backed by Japan or some other
big power, then I would wish immediately to apply for permission to
raise a division of cavalry, such as the regiment I commanded in Cuba.
The division would consist of three brigades of three regiments each. If
given a free hand, I could render it, I am certain, as formidable a body
of horse riflemen, that is, of soldiers such as those of Sheridan, Forrest
and Stuart, as has ever been seen. In order to make it efficient and formidable, and to prepare it in the shortest possible time, I would need to
choose my own officers. To follow any other course would be to risk
losing half, or possibly all, of the efficiency of the force. I have my
brigade commanders, colonels, and in many cases majors and captains

---

[1] The Mexican revolution was beginning. Before it was over, the United
States would send troops—but not yet.

already in mind, and they would be men under whom organization could be pushed to very rapid completion, while the ranks would be immediately filled to overflowing with men, every one of whom would be already a good horseman and rifleman, able to live in the open and take care of himself. My brigade commanders would be Howze and Boughton of the regular army, and Cecil Lyon of Texas. My nine colonels would include men like Fitzhugh Lee and Gordon Johnston of the regular army, and among others John Greenway, Seth Bullock, Harry Stimson and John McIlhenny. I need not bother you with the names of the majors and captains whom I have already picked out because I understand that I am writing in view of an exceedingly remote possibility. Nevertheless I would like you to know what my intention is. To let volunteer regiments as the rule elect their own officers is to insure very many of the regiments being utterly incompetent. There were three rough rider regiments in the Spanish War, but you have never heard of more than one, simply because the other two, although composed of just as good material, did not have at the head of either a man in any way comparable to Wood. If I am allowed to raise a cavalry division, choosing my own upper officers as above outlined, and many or most of the lower officers, the organization will proceed with the utmost speed, and I will guarantee the efficiency of the division. I ask, Sir, that instead of treating this as a boast, you will remember that in the war with Spain our regiment was raised, armed, equipped, mounted, dismounted, drilled, kept two weeks on transports, and put through two victorious aggressive fights in which it lost nearly a quarter of the men engaged, and over one third of the officers, a loss greater than that suffered by any but two of the twenty-four regular regiments in the same army corps; and all this within sixty days. Each regiment would consist of from 1,200 to 1,400 men all told, the division being 10,000 to 12,000 strong. I know just where I would raise these men, some of them coming from the East, most from the West and South.

Very respectfully yours

**May 31, 1911. Oyster Bay
To Oscar K. Davis**

Dear O.K.:

I am certain that nothing you say in any article will be unsatisfactory, and for the first time I shall now read an article in *Hampton's*. But as far as I can now see, no situation could arise which would make it possible for me to accept a nomination next year. However, it is academic, for I think we have taken steps to prevent all agitation on the subject. I have explained that every friend of mine will show his friendship by seeing that there is no movement started to have me nominated.

What an awful tangle things are in at Washington! I get almost as much disgusted with most of the progressives as with the standpat crowd. Judge Madison of Kansas seems to me to be about straight. You will like Harry Stimson. I enclose the note.

Very sincerely yours

June 27, 1911. New York
To Henry Wallace[1]

Dear Mr. Wallace:

It is not possible for me to go into any other speechmaking. Do you know, my dear sir, that I have had to refuse between 3600 and 4000 requests to speak in the last year? If I accepted even a small fraction of the requests made to me to speak for admirable causes, I should spend my whole time in speaking; and I should utterly destroy any moral power for usefulness which I may possess. I have spoken now on conservation again and again. Everyone knows where I stand, and I sincerely believe it is not an advantage to the cause, and a detriment to my own influence, to have to speak on the subject again unless there is some specific issue which it is vital for me to deal with. I hate not to do anything you ask but it just won't do for me to come out again. Incidentally, if I came out, I should be speaking all the way out and all the way back. For the next year, as far as I know, I have only one engagement to speak; and I feel very strongly that what is needed for me is to follow the advice given by the New Bedford whaling captain to his mate when he told him that all he wanted from him was silence and damned little of that.

Faithfully yours

August 22, 1911. New York
To Cecil Spring Rice

Dear Cecil:

How are you and Lady Springy? Give her our warmest love. I would also send love to the children, but fear they would treat the message coldly. I write with the especial purpose of telling you that Ted has a daughter, and of course Edith and I are very proud and happy as grandparents. Ted has really been doing very well out in San Francisco,

---

[1]Iowa editor, father of Henry C. Wallace, Republican Secretary of Agriculture during the 1920s, and grandfather of Henry A. Wallace, Democratic Secretary of Agriculture in the 1930s and 1940s (and subsequently Vice President and Secretary of Commerce).

working hard at his business, and taking a very nice stand in politics. To my immense amusement, a couple of months ago he made his debut as a public orator by speaking one Sunday evening in a church on the subject of "Our Civic Duties," his wife and mother-in-law and an intimate Grotonian classmate being present, as his devoted and admiring backers. It immensely amused me, for he is just the age I was when I first went to the New York Legislature. He has the dearest wife that ever was, and a very dear mother-in-law. Kermit went down to Silver City to stay with Bob Ferguson and Isabella. Kermit is a loyal soul and devoted to his friends with singlehearted devotion. Once down there he could not resist going on into the Mexican desert south of Arizona, nominally on a hunt for mountain sheep. He is there at the present moment, and his mother is slightly uneasy about him. I take a more philosophical view, partly because I have great confidence in his hardihood, and partly because I feel that he has got to take risks, and that there is no use worrying about it. Ethel is on the Maine coast. She is twenty years old now, has had three summers out, and is becoming quite a staid young lady— within moderate and reasonable limits. Archie and Quentin are here with us, and Alice is coming to see us this week on the adjournment of Congress. Edith and I ride a great deal together, and go for long rows, and I play tennis with those of my offspring who play sufficiently badly.

Countries go through stages when their politics are interesting. At the moment yours are and ours are not. Personally I think it is a good thing that there has been the reform of the House of Lords, and I hope that the Conservatives will not undertake to upset it when they come into power. I feel about the House of Lords just as I feel about the American judiciary in constitutional matters. It is all right to make the people think and prevent them from passing snap judgments, but it is wrong to have an irresponsible body able to block their set purpose when they have deliberately thought out a matter and decided what they want. I do not think there is a chance that I shall ever again be back in political life, but if I ever did have power, much though I admire our judicial system, I should certainly do anything I could to bring about a condition in which it would be possible, as it is not now possible, after due deliberations to carry into effect the legislation necessary to meet changing social and industrial conditions. I am always amused at the queer mistake that Macaulay made when fifty-odd years ago he said that the American Constitution was all sail and no ballast or anchor. Our trouble has been that we have tended to permit one set of people to hoist sails for their own amusement, and another set of people to put down anchors for their own purposes; and the result from the standpoint of progress has not been happy. I have been much disappointed in Taft. He is a well-meaning, honest man, and I hope we can re-elect him. But like many another man, though a most admirable lieutenant, he is not particularly wise or efficient as a leader. As was probably inevitable, he permitted his wife and brother, and a number of less disinterested advisers, to make him very jealous of me, and very anxious to emphasize the contrast between our administrations by sundering himself from my especial friends and followers, and appearing hereafter as the great, wise conservative. In consequence he has frequently taken a reactionary attitude, and the progressives and radicals in the party, being left without any progressive leadership at all, have gone every which way, and have often been both violent and foolish. Their violence and folly have redounded to Taft's advantage, and he is considerably stronger than he was last December; but it has been a real misfortune to have the Republican Party taken back from the path of progress and once more aligned with the influences in it which were represented by Hanna rather than the influences which were represented by Abraham Lincoln. The Democratic Party I really do believe pretty hopeless. Taft will be renominated, and I hope will be re-elected. I shall not interfere in the nomination, except to see that no movement looking toward me takes place, but I shall do whatever I can for his re-election. I have no sympathy with his arbitration treaty business. If we were avowedly to limit it to a treaty between Great Britain and ourselves I should say Yes with all heartiness, and indeed I should cheerfully advocate an even closer arrangement. But as a model for world treaties, for treaties between us or you and every other nation, I think it is absurd. I do not think it would do great damage simply because the purpose which the worthy peace disciple of the Carnegie type has embodied in it would not be carried out in practice. But this would mean hypocrisy, and hypocrisy is not nice. If the purpose nominally contained in this treaty were lived up to, and arbitration had been resorted to for the last thirty years, England would not now be in Egypt, and would be out of South Africa, to the great detriment not merely of England, but of Egypt, South Africa and civilization; and Cuba would still be Spanish, and the Isthmus of Panama would belong to Colombia, and the canal would not be even begun or anywhere near the time of beginning. The whole business is tainted by that noxious form of silliness which always accompanies the sentimental refusal to look facts in the face. The sentimentalist, by the way, is by no means always a decent creature to deal with; if Andrew Carnegie had employed his fortune and his time in doing justice to the steelworkers who gave him his fortune, he would have accomplished a thousand times what he has accomplished or ever can accomplish in connection with international peace.

Our life here is very happy. I almost feel as if it was a confession of weakness on my part to be as thoroughly contented as I am. There are moments when I see things, as I think, going wrong, or when I very earnestly desire to champion a cause; and then I should like to be back in public life; but they are fleeting moments, and I am thoroughly enjoying myself. Twenty years ago, or ten years ago, I should not have been at all happy living as I now am living, because I should have felt that I had no business to have quit the arena, that it was ignoble to be merely an onlooker instead of doing my part in the strife. But as it is I have no such feeling. I have worked very hard along many different lines, my work has been decent and honorable and moderately efficient; and to me it has been interesting and on the whole satisfactory. I have thoroughly enjoyed it all—being President, being colonel in the Spanish War, my African trip, my ranch life in the West, my work and association with the men in our great cities who are trying to help better our civic and social and economic conditions. I have toiled and fought with men! Not only am I no longer a young man, but I am really an old man, and I could not do the physical things which I used to like doing, so that I do not feel restless and discontented by being deprived of the opportunity to do them. As for other work, if it came I should of course do it and feel ashamed of not doing it; but I no longer feel that I ought to be ashamed unless I can make work for myself to do. It is not desirable that I should try to make work for myself. Indeed if I had plenty of money I should be inclined not to do anything at all, for our habits and ways of thought here in America are such that it is very hard for an ex-President to do anything that shall really tell for good causes. But as it is, while of course I could get along without doing anything, I prefer, from the standpoint of the family, to be able to continue working until Quentin finishes college eight years hence. Then all the children will have been launched in life, and I shall be sixty years old, and I shall feel that I have a right to draw out of work entirely. Meanwhile I thoroughly enjoy my associations at *The Outlook*. My fellow editors have the same high purpose and sanity that, for instance, the members of the Tennis Cabinet had! I can work with them in complete sympathy, and as long as they continue to think me valuable I shall continue to work with them because I feel that, though there probably is not much effect from what I am doing, yet whatever effect there is is good and wholesome; and it is an honorable thing to cast even a little weight on the side of decency and fair and honest dealing.

Good-by and good luck to you and yours!

Ever your friend

August 22, 1911. New York
To Theodore Roosevelt, Jr.

Dearest Ted:

Having written about the really important matter—Grace—to you and to Eleanor and to the "little mother," I shall now send you this letter, mainly dealing with matters of less importance. First, however, just a word to say that we are all continually planning and talking about the baby. Mother fairly longs for her; she looks too pretty as she tells how the baby must look in Eleanor's arms, and when you gingerly take it up, and when its grandmother carries it; she wishes she were living alongside it. Everyone I meet congratulates me on being a grandfather, and really I am more proud than I can say. Incidentally, I feel that it justifies my preaching, so to speak; I have always had a horror of preaching what I did not practice, whether in the matter of work, or of doing one's duty in public life, or in going to war, or above all in family life, and I feel that you and Eleanor by your life, in every way, have given me the right to preach wholesome conduct, and not feel that it is a case of "Physician, heal thyself." I only hope the other children will be anything like as fortunate, or half as fortunate, as you have been in getting Eleanor. I wish that the next couple of years would see Kermit and Ethel married. I would like to stay with *The Outlook* and continue work for eight years, until Quentin gets through college, and by that time I should hope that all the children would be making their way, and I would be very pleased if all except Quentin, who will hardly be old enough, were married; and as I shall be sixty, I shall feel as if I had a right to retire and not try to earn any more money or do anything. From *The Outlook* I get $12,000, which it is very important for me to have as long as the family are being brought up and four of them have to be supported entirely by me. Of course I cannot tell when *The Outlook* will find me no longer useful, for an ex-President's field of usefulness is very limited, and I would like more and more to substitute writing on general subjects for writing on political subjects; and if it does not find me useful, fortunately there is absolutely no vital need of my working; but if I can continue to work until I am sixty I shall be glad.

I think Taft is considerably stronger than he was last November. The Insurgents have played into his hands because they have not been coherent, and they have tended to go to extremes. Gifford Pinchot is a dear, but he is a fanatic, with an element of hardness and narrowness in his temperament, and an extremist. La Follette has lost ground very much. There is no use in saying "I told you so," but if the Insurgents a year ago had followed my lead, they would have been infinitely better off. The one vital contest last year was that here in New York, because that contest and only that contest would have determined the control of the Republican Party, if successful. Yet the Insurgents in the country at large had so completely lost their heads and sense of proportion, and had surrendered themselves with such lack of reserve to the leadership of the extremists, and to the guidance, partly of the magazine muckrakers and partly of the visionary writers in the magazines, that they gave me much less help than I was entitled to.

I send you, by the way, my *Outlook* article giving my dealings with the Tennessee Coal and Iron Company. I do not think that the Committee ought to have called me, for I think that an ex-President should only be brought before a Congressional Committee under exceptional conditions; but; as they called me, there was no question about my going. Thank heavens! I have succeeded in stopping all speechmaking. In October I shall have to make one speech to please Albert Shaw and the Civic Forum people, who have been my staunch and good friends, and who put the request in such a way as to make it evident that I would seriously offend them by refusing. But thus is the only speech I am to make.

Taft will be nominated, and as things are now I am not at all sure that La Follette will make a fight against him, although I think that having gone so far he would be foolish not to make the fight, simply as a point of honor. My present intention is to make a couple of speeches for Taft, but not to go actively into the campaign. Woodrow Wilson still remains the strongest as Democratic Candidate, but he has lost and not gained during the last few months. There is a good chance of Harmon's being nominated. I hope we can carry Taft through, and there would be a fair chance against Harmon, although much less of a chance against Wilson. But I do not care for Taft, indeed I think less of him as time goes on, in spite of the fact that I believe he is improving his position before the people. He is a flubdub with a streak of the second-rate and the common in him, and he has not the slightest idea of what is necessary if this country is to make social and industrial progress. He does not even know what the problems are that confront our civilization, not to speak of realizing their seriousness. However, during my thirty years in politics, for nine tenths of the time I have been accustomed to make the best I could out of the second-best and the second-rate. I think Taft a better President than McKinley or Harrison, and I thoroughly distrust the Democratic Party. But it is an awful pity that when Taft had such a chance as he had, and when the progressives were in control of the Republican Party and moving along the path of rational progress, he should have thrown over his chance and hurt the party and the country by so acting as to identify conservatism with reaction, and to deprive the progressives of leadership and permit them to run every which way to destruction.

Ever your father

September 8, 1911. New York
To James Bryce

Dear Mr. Ambassador:

I am really pleased that you liked my Dante article. Like you, I have always been fond of Dante, and this particular point never seemed to me to have been clearly brought forward. I suppose, as you say, that it is the very simplicity of the great poet that has so much charm for us moderns. He realized the past so vividly, and—quite a distinct gift—he also realized the present so vividly, that there seemed nothing incongruous to him in bringing both into close juxtaposition. Unfortunately nowadays the man who does this is usually of the type of your newspaper friend who couples Julius Caesar and Lloyd George. He possesses Dante's attitude, with the unfortunate difference that Dante's greatness is left out.

I must say I should thoroughly enjoy having a Dante write of a number of our present-day politicians, labor leaders, and Wall Street people! When he came to deal with the worst offenders among our newspaper editors and magazine writers, I hope he would not dignify them by putting them in a circle of flame, but leave them in the circles of pitch and of filth. Having dictated this statement, it sounds to me as if it had all of Dante's own revengefulness in it—but I shall leave it.

Give my warm regards to Mrs. Bryce. I wish I could see you both again.

Very sincerely yours

September 29, 1911. Oyster Bay
To Robert M. La Follette

Dear Senator La Follette:

I must send you just a line to say how greatly interested I have been in your first article in the *American*. It is capital! I was especially pleased, by the way, with the sentence in which you said that what fundamentally counts most is having the right attitude toward public questions. Like you, when I left college, I had no particular governmental convictions beyond the very strong and vital conviction that we were a nation and must act nationally; I had not thought out, or been given the opportunity to think out, a great many questions which I have since recognized as vital; but from various causes I had been given fundamentally the right attitude in looking at public questions, and I hope at private questions too. It is half amusing and half pathetic to see so many good people convinced that the world can be reformed without difficulty merely by reforming the machinery of government. At the moment many of the New Jersey reformers, for instance, are much cast down because they find that open primaries do not work automatically for independence and against the machine. Of course open primaries can only give the chance to the majority to have good government if they choose to take the trouble to get it; and if they do not take the trouble, the boss will run the open primary exactly as he ran politics before the open primary was adopted. Good machinery is indispensable in order to produce the best results, but the best machinery will be of no use unless, as you say, men have the right attitude on public questions—and of course the right attitude must include not merely a right understanding of what is needed by the people, but the right spirit and the necessary courage and capacity to make this spirit effective.

Sincerely yours

October 2, 1911. Oyster Bay
To Theodore Roosevelt, Jr.

Dear Ted:

On Saturday, while Archie and I were riding with her, Mother's horse Pine Knot suddenly performed a trick of his by making a tremendous swerve or shy, and threw Mother off into the middle of the road. She landed with terrific force on the hard macadam in front of the Cove school-house. She was knocked senseless, and did not really regain consciousness for some thirty-six hours. Fortunately your old schoolmate, Benny Voris, a very good fellow, soon afterwards passed by with his delivery automobile, and I brought mother up to the house in that, while Archie rode the Sirdar and led his horse and Mother's. Until Dr. Faller came, we had no idea how serious the injuries were. The doctor, after an examination, said that she had broken no bones, and that there was no real concussion of the brain. But the shock was frightful, and since regaining consciousness she has had a really terrible headache, a headache of the kind that is literally agony. She does not know that she was riding or had a fall, and still thinks it is merely one of her ordinary headaches. Archie has put off his departure for a couple of days. We tried to get Dr. Lambert, but he is away, and now we are going to get Dr. Rixey. When you receive, this letter, I believe she will be all right. Ethel and Archie behaved like trumps.

Ted Douglas made an extraordinary fight in his county and really carried it, but they counted him out by the grossest fraud in two towns and nominated his opponent.

Give my warmest love to Eleanor and Grace and Grace's grandmother.

Ever your father

November 22, 1911. Oyster Bay
To Learned Hand[1]

Dear Judge:

Evidently I must try to make my expression more clear. I absolutely agree with you as to bringing pressure to bear on the judges, but in Constitutional cases the alternative must be to have the right of appeal from the judges. Take the New York cases to which I refer. My idea would be to have the Constitutional Convention provide that the people shall have the right to vote as to whether or not the judges' interpretation of the law in such a case is correct, and that their vote shall be decisive.

Evidently I have got to get you to come out again and talk this matter over with me. I am sincerely obliged to you for your article.

Faithfully yours

December 2, 1911. Oyster Bay
To James Kennedy

My dear Mr. Kennedy:

I don't wonder at your anger toward the muckraking press. As I have said repeatedly, I think the muckrakers stand on a level of infamy with the corruptionists in politics. After all there is no great difference between violation of the eighth and ninth commandments, and to sell one's vote for money is morally, I believe, hardly as reprehensible as to practice slanderous mendacity for hire. As regards the Presidency, what I have said has been consistently that I did not intend to take part in the nomination, but of course I intended to support the nominee, and the only thing I do ask of my friends is that they shall see to it that no movement of any kind is made to nominate me. It would be a real pleasure to see you in New York.

Sincerely yours

January 9, 1912. New York
To William L. Ward

Private & Confidential
Dear Ward:

I have asked to see Hayward and I have asked to see McHarg. I have also communicated with Tim along the lines you mention.

In your letter you state the case just exactly as it is, and as it must remain. If my nomination should come as the result of artificial stimulus, I do not want it, and I will not take it. If it comes at all, it must be as the result of an honest widespread desire of the people, and not

---

[1] Most eminent American jurist never to sit on the Supreme Court.

as the result of the slightest manipulation on the part of any individual or set of individuals. I do not want for one moment believe that any such widespread desire will be manifested, and so far from being disappointed I shall be most heartily relieved if there is no such movement, and if there is not even the slightest talk of nominating me. The nomination is the very last thing I desire, and I would consider it at all only from the standpoint of the public interest and without the slightest regard to my own wishes.

With hearty thanks,

Always yours

P.S. I like the last long paragraph so much that I have had it copied out and have sent it to several friends.

February 24, 1912. New York
To William E. Glasscock and others

Gentlemen:

I deeply appreciate your letter, and I realize to the full the heavy responsibility it puts upon me, expressing as it does the carefully considered convictions of the men elected by popular vote to stand as the heads of government in their several States.

I absolutely agree with you that this matter is not one to be decided with any reference to the personal preferences or interests of any man, but purely from the standpoint of the interests of the people as a whole. I will accept the nomination for President if it is tendered to me, and I will adhere to this decision until the convention has expressed its preference.

One of the chief principles for which I have stood, and for which I now stand, and which I have always endeavored and always shall endeavor to reduce to action, is the genuine rule of the people, and therefore I hope that so far as possible the people may be given the chance, through direct primaries, to express their preference as to who shall be the nominee of the Republican Presidential Convention.

Very truly yours

February 29, 1912. New York
To Herbert S. Hadley

Dear Governor:

My hat is in the ring and the fight is on! It was just fine to hear from you! The amusing thing is that in the Dakotas I am being opposed on the ground that I am being a Conservative and in the East on the ground that I am a radical.

Faithfully yours

**March 8, 1912. New York
To Joseph M. Dixon**

My dear Senator Dixon:

I have received your letter of March 6th, stating that in your opinion it is of vital importance to the success of the Republican Party in the November elections that the National Republican Convention shall nominate the candidate whom the mass of the Republican voters wish nominated and that, therefore, this sentiment should be given expression through presidential preferential primaries in the several States in order that the wishes of the voters may be ascertained before, instead of after, the nomination.

I have also seen your correspondence with Mr. McKinley. You proposed to him that as far as possible the selection of the Republican candidate for the presidency should be determined by the voters of the party in preferential presidential primaries. Mr. McKinley's answer is contained practically in one sentence in the letter sent you: "I do not favor changes in the rules of the game while the game is in progress."

The point of view expressed in that sentence contains the issue within the Republican Party at this time. We who stand for the progressive cause, for the cause of honest and genuine democracy, genuine representative government, hold that a public contest between parties or within parties is not carried on as a game, is not carried on for the purpose of winning prizes for the contestants or with a view to the personal wishes or welfare of any one man. We hold that it should be carried on for the purpose of ascertaining and putting into effect the will of the people so that the people may jointly do for themselves what no man can do so well for them. We hold that the laws that govern elections and govern party organizations should not be treated as rules which are fit subjects for trickery manipulation by contestants for a prize. We hold that as far as possible these laws should be treated as rules to ascertain the will of those whom the public officials and party officials are supposed to represent. In sum, therefore, we hold that the object of this contest is not to secure rewards for individuals but to secure the more effective government of the people, by the people, and for the people.

Our opponents, on the contrary, take Mr. McKinley's view that we are engaged in a game in which the interests of the people, it is true, are at stake but in which the people themselves are not to have their voice. Mr. McKinley's position was stated with frank cynicism by Congressman Campbell on behalf of the reactionary element in the Republican Party when, in a recent speech in New Hampshire, he is quoted as "rousing the greatest enthusiasm by declaring that the Republican Party does not believe in an appeal from the umpire to the bleachers." Mr. Campbell has simply stated more frankly the view held (as is evident by Mr. McKinley's statement) generally among our opponents. Their feeling is that politics is a game, that the people should simply sit on the bleachers as spectators, and that no appeal lies to the people from the men who, for their own profit, are playing the game. It is astounding that men should venture to take a position; and it shows that these men and those for whom they speak and whom they represent have wandered far indeed from the ground held by Abraham Lincoln when he declared this to be a government dedicated to the welfare of the common people and to be managed justly and honorably by these plain people for their own welfare in accordance with the immutable laws of righteousness.

Our opponents take the view that this contest is merely a game, that the object of the contest is to win prizes for the contestants, and that public office is the reward that goes to the winners of the game and that, therefore, it is a piece of allowable smartness to refuse to make changes in the laws during the progress of the contest, if these changes would deprive the led captains of the political world of the advantage they now hold over the plain people.

In short, the issue may be stated as follows: Should election laws be framed with a view to the interests of politicians or should election laws be framed with a view to carrying out the popular will? We have, on the one hand, Mr. McKinley and Mr. Campbell and the reactionary element for whom they stand, an element which has made it evident that they prefer to see the Republican Party ruined rather than to see it made again what it was in the days of Lincoln; and, on the other hand, those who believe that the Republican Party can and shall be made now what it was made under Lincoln—a great instrument for the achievement of righteousness through the rule of the plain people. We regard the present contest not as a contest between individuals—for we are not concerned with the welfare of any particular individual, neither with mine nor with that of any other man—but as a contest between these two radically different views of the function of politics in a great democracy.

Therefore, we demand that States like Illinois, Michigan, New York, Massachusetts, be given the chance to express their preference in presidential primaries as to whom they wish for President. Practically the entire body of professional politicians are pitted against us in this contest and in every State and in every Congressional district they are led by the officeholders who, with the example before them of what was done in connection with the nominations for local offices in North Carolina, are working as we have rarely seen them work in American political life. Against such forces it is in any event difficult enough for the ordinary plain citizens, who have only the general welfare at heart, to win. But it becomes well-nigh impossible for these plain citizens to give expression to the popular will when there is no popular primary. The convention system in our party was founded on the theory that it would represent and not thwart the popular will. When, as is too often now the case, it is turned into an instrument to be used for the direct overthrow of the popular will, then it is not representative but thoroughly and mischievously misrepresentative of the party and of the people. Here in New York, for instance, the machines of the two parties have cooperated to draw up a primary law which imposes on the people a system so cumbrous, so involved, as to make it impossible to get a fair expression of public sentiment, and very difficult to get any expression of public sentiment at all. The present primary law in New York is admirably adapted to achieve its purpose; for its purpose is to prevent the people's controlling party organizations or having their say in party nominations, and to preserve such control and such domination purely for the class of professional politicians.

It is idle to say that it is too late to make the change we ask. Our opponents are themselves to blame for the fact that the demand has not been sooner granted. For a long time—for over eighteen months in the State of New York, for instance—every Progressive, every friend of really popular government, has been demanding a system of genuine direct primaries. Wherever we have failed to get this system, such failure is due to the action of the reactionaries whose one aim is to prevent the people from controlling party organizations to which they belong, who thoroughly distrust the people and do not believe in their right to rule. And now these men, who have thus prevented the people from getting direct primaries, demand that they be allowed to remain the beneficiaries of their own wrong and ask to be excused from granting the demand for direct primaries now just because they have contemptuously refused to grant that demand in the past.

There never was a straighter fight waged for the principle of popular rule than that which we are now waging. We are fighting against intrenched privilege, both political privilege and financial privilege. We believe that if given a fair chance the people will declare against both political and financial privilege. Therefore, we demand that they be given that fair chance.

If the people decide against us, we will bow cheerfully to the decision, confident that they will in the end see that the cause for which we fight is indeed the cause of human rights and human welfare. But we very emphatically object, here in this democracy and within the confines of the party which claims Abraham Lincoln as its national founder, to having the issue decided against us not by the people, but by the spoils politicians and patronage-mongers who are engaged in defrauding the American people out of their first and most elemental right—the right to self-government.

Faithfully yours

May 11, 1912. Oyster Bay
To George H. Payne

Dear Mr. Payne:

I never drink whisky at all, and on none of these trips have I even drunk any wine. But I am told that on several trips other members of the party have drunk whisky and that bills have been submitted and paid for showing that whisky was drunk. In view of the absolute scoundrelishness of our political foes, it would be quite possible that they would obtain possession of these bills in order to show that I had drunk the whisky in question. Under the circumstances, therefore, I shall ask you to see that no whisky, in fact no liquor of any kind, and no wine is carried on the trip by the pullman people. Of course I do not mean that you should search each individual's luggage to see if he carries whisky! I merely mean that no whisky is to be carried or used at the expense of the Committee, or paid for by the Committee, or by any person directly or indirectly responsible for my campaign. I do not drink it myself and I do not intend that any scoundrel of the type of some of our opponents shall be able to assert that I do drink or have drunk it.

Faithfully yours

June 22, 1912. Chicago
To the Republican National Convention

A clear majority of the delegates honestly elected to this convention were chosen by the people to nominate me. Under the direction, and with the encouragement, of Mr. Taft, the majority of the National Committee, by the so-called "steam-roller" methods, and with scandalous disregard of every principle of elementary honesty and decency stole eighty or ninety delegates, putting on the temporary roll call a sufficient number of fraudulent delegates to defeat the legally expressed will of the people, and to substitute a dishonest for an honest majority.

The Convention has now declined to purge the roll of the fraudulent delegates placed thereon by the defunct National Committee; and the majority which thus endorsed fraud was made a majority only because it included the fraudulent delegates themselves, who all sat as judges on one another's cases. If their fraudulent votes had not thus been cast and counted, the convention would have been purged of their presence. This action makes the convention in no proper sense any longer a Republican convention, representing the real Republican party, therefore I hope that the men elected as Roosevelt delegates will now decline to vote on any matter before the Convention. I do not release any delegate from his honorable obligation to vote for me if he votes at all; but under the actual conditions I hope that he will not vote at all. The Convention as now composed has no claim to represent the voters of the Republican Party. It represents nothing but successful fraud in overriding the will of the rank and file of the party. Any man nominated by the Convention as now constituted would be merely the beneficiary of this successful fraud, it would be deeply discreditable to any man to accept the Convention's nomination under these circumstances; and any man thus accepting it would have no claim to the support of any Republican on party grounds, and would have forfeited the right to ask the support of any honest man of any party on moral grounds.

July 1, 1912. Oyster Bay
To William D. Foulke

Dear Foulke:

That is awfully nice. In strict confidence, my feeling is that the Democrats will probably win if they nominate a progressive. But of course there is no use of my getting into a fight in a halfhearted fashion and I could not expect Republicans to follow me out if they were merely to endorse the Democratic Convention. So I hoisted the flag and will win or fall under it.

That was a fine call to arms and a fine meeting. What an awful set of crooks they were at Chicago!

Faithfully yours

August 3, 1912. Oyster Bay
To Horace Plunkett

My dear Plunkett:

It is good to hear from you. I send you under separate cover three pieces I wrote in The Outlook, "Mr. Taft's Majority," "Thou Shalt Not Steal," and "The 'Steam Roller'" and after. The third piece contains an allusion to the Democratic platform and the reasons why it would be utterly impossible for me to support a man standing on such a platform. I am also sending you a copy of my speech before the National Progressive Convention. Let me add a word to you in your capacity of Devil's Advocate! I do not quite understand those among our friends the enemy who, as you say, were shocked at the general conduct of the convention, and seemed to hold me a little responsible for it. Personally I was very much more than shocked at the general conduct of the Convention, but

I can say quite sincerely that no members of any convention in any country have ever behaved with higher and more patriotic purpose and more real dignity in facing a genuine crisis than was the case of the Roosevelt men at that convention. There was of course much guying of Root and the machine leaders, but it did not go to anything like the extreme that is common in Great Britain in the course of heckling would-be Members of Parliament.

Now as to the second point,—the supposition that Wilson and his platform and his independence of the party machine so nearly resemble me that they do not see how I can expect the people of the United States to prefer me to him. As a matter of fact, and of course not for publication, I do not expect the people of the United States to prefer me to him. As you say, I would have had a good sporting chance if the Democrats had put up a reactionary candidate. As it is, I think there are enough Americans who think just as you say the English in question think, to elect him. But from my standpoint they are all wrong in this, and my answer would be practically the same as the answer you have already made, that only a third party will relieve the honest and farsighted man of the necessity of voting either for the puppet of the machine Republicans, or for the highly undesirable Democratic Party. So far from the Baltimore platform nearly resembling mine, it is the exact reverse. It is, to my mind, one of the worst platforms that any party has put out for over forty years, and certainly worse than any, with the possible exception of the Democratic platform of '96. It is not progressive at all. It represents partly an unintelligent rural toryism, and partly an utterly insincere willingness to promise the impossible, with cynical indifference to perform anything whatever. I am also sending you my article in The Outlook on "Platform Insincerity." How any human being who believes in any shape or way in the principles for which I stand can expect me to support any candidate on such a platform, I cannot understand. Wilson is a good man who has in no way shown that he possesses any special fitness for the Presidency. Until he was fifty years old, as college professor and college president he advocated with skill, intelligence and good breeding the outworn doctrines which were responsible for four fifths of the political troubles of the United States. He posed as, and believed himself to be, a strong conservative, and was being groomed by a section of Wall Street as the special conservative champion against me and my ideas. Then he ran as Governor of New Jersey, and during the last eighteen months discovered that he could get nowhere advocating the doctrines he had advocated, and instantly turned an absolute somersault so far as at least half of these doctrines was concerned. He still clings to the other half, and he has shown not the slightest understanding of the really great problems of our present industrial situation, the very problems, for instance, with which you have been particularly concerned—in other words, all of the problems of our industrial and agricultural life. He is an able man, and I have no doubt could speedily acquaint himself with these problems, and would not show Taft's muddleheaded inability to try to understand them when left by himself. But he is not a Nationalist, he has no real and deep-seated convictions on the things that I regard as most vital, and he is in the position where he can only win by standing on a platform which he must afterwards repudiate under penalty of himself becoming a grotesque disaster to the community, and furthermore, he can only win by the help of the worst bosses in this country, and by perpetuating their control of their several States in return for their aid.

You say that you hope that our platform will avoid the impression of merely going one better than the extremely able and clear-thinking Democratic candidate. I hardly understand this because the said candidate has not yet spoken. Is it possible that you refer to the Democratic platform? I do not think that that platform shows either clearheadedness or ability; I think it shows a combination of complete muddleheadedness, with great insincerity, and so far from wishing to go it one better, I shall endeavor on every vital point, from the Navy and the Philippines, to the trusts, the tariff, the welfare of the farmer, and the welfare of the workingmen, either to take exactly the opposite position from, or else to take a position upon which it has not even touched, probably because the makers of the platform were either afraid, or are dismally ignorant of the things that are most vital in American political life of today. If you do, however, mean the utterances of Wilson himself, I at once agree with you about his ability. Moreover, I think that he is generally clearheaded, but I think that he is very wrongheaded on many issues, and that on other issues he has not thought at all. As for going him one better, that I certainly shall not try to do, for on the various points where I think he is right, he has merely taken the same position I have taken some time after I had taken it.

For your private information I will say again that I think it probable at present that Wilson will win. There are plenty of well-meaning progressives who do not think deeply or fundamentally who will go to him. He will take the majority of the progressive Democrats, and he will not only keep all the reactionary Democrats, but he will take some reactionary Republicans when they find, as I believe they will find, that Taft cannot be elected. Among the Republicans I shall only get the progressive Republicans, of course, and while I think these make up the great majority of the party, yet I shall not get any but those of strong convictions, for the weaker and more timid men, and those with least imagination, will tend to vote the straight party ticket. Among the independents I shall get a considerable number of the students of social science, of such men and women as those who attended the recent Charities Conference, for instance, including the active workers for social betterment in our big cities. I shall also get a considerable number of Democratic workingmen and farmers. It is possible that as the campaign develops my strength will grow, and I shall be able to show that Taft means reaction in its extreme form, that there is no real hope of coherent progress in Wilson, and that we should have a new party for practically the same reasons that in '56 it became necessary to break up the old Whig Party and ultimately beat the Democratic Party with the Republican organization. But I do not think this probable. However, win or lose, the fight had to be made, and it happened that no human being could make it except myself. I shall make it on clean-cut issues, and will make a standard in my speeches and in our platform such as never before has been made, and which will, I think, have a considerable influence for good in our future political history. If you see Arthur Lee, give him my warm regards.

Always yours

[August 8, 1912] En route to Oyster Bay
To Jane Addams

(Telegram)

Dear Miss Addams:

I wished to see you in person to thank you for seconding me. I do it now instead. I prized your action not only because of what you are and stand for, but because of what it symbolized for the new movement. In this great National Convention starting the new party women have thereby been shown to have their place to fill precisely as men have, and on an absolute equality. It is idle now to argue whether women can play their part in politics, because in this convention we saw the accomplished fact, and moreover the women who have actively participated in this work of launching the new party represent all that we are most proud to associate with American womanhood. My earnest hope is to see the Progressive Party movement in all its State and local divisions recognize this fact, precisely as it has been recognized at the National Convention. Our party stands for social and industrial justice, and we have a right to expect that women and men will work within the party for the cause with the same high sincerity of purpose and with like efficiency. I therefore earnestly hope that in the campaign now opened we shall see women active members of the various State and County committees. Four women are to be put on the National Committee, and I trust that there will be a full representation of them on every State and County committee. While I am now addressing you I desire that this shall be taken as the expression of my personal hope and desire by all members of such State and County Committees, and I believe that I express the feelings of the great majority of progressives in making this request. I have Judge Hotchkiss's assurance that it will be done in the State of New York, and I very much hope that it will be done in the other States. With great esteem, I am,

Faithfully yours

October 14, 1912. Milwaukee
To Edith Carow Roosevelt

(Telegram)
Am in excellent shape. Made an hour and a half speech. The wound is a trivial one. I think they will find that it merely glanced on a rib and went somewhere into a cavity of the body; it certainly did not touch a lung and isn't a particle more serious than one of the injuries any of the boys used continually to be having. Am at the Emergency Hospital at the moment, but anticipate going right on with my engagements. My voice seems to be in good shape. Best love to Ethel.

October 19, 1912. Chicago
To Anna Roosevelt Cowles

Dearest Bye:
I am dictating this in bed, and it will have to be signed for me by Edith. It is just a line to tell you I am in great shape. Really the time in the hospital, with Edith and the children on here, has been a positive spree, and I have enjoyed it. Of course, I would like to have been in the campaign, but it can't be helped and there is no use in crying over what can't be helped! Do tell Joe Alsop and Herbert Knox Smith from me how immensely I appreciate the wonderful work they have done. I hate not being in Connecticut to speak for them. Joe especially has been a tower of strength throughout all this contest. I love Will's letter, and I am very proud of the praise he gave me, for I know no man who is gamer and cooler than Will in time of danger, or shows to better advantage in a crisis.

Your loving brother

November 5, 1912. Oyster Bay
To Arthur H. Lee

Dear Arthur:
I am profoundly touched and pleased by your letter. My dear fellow, I doubt if you know how much your friendship means to me. Mrs. Roo-

sevelt and I are particularly pleased at the news about your wife. She is just one of the sweetest women I ever knew and I cannot bear to think of her as suffering.

I sent the part of your letter referring to Jane Addams direct to her, and, when I get an answer from her, I will send it to you. I have deeply prized her support. There were points where I had to drag her forward, notably as regards our battleship program, for she is a disciple of Tolstoi; but she is a really good woman who has done really practical work for the betterment of social conditions.

I am immensely pleased that you so clearly grasp just what we have been doing in this Progressive fight. It would be more accurate to say what we have been *trying* to do, for there is no use disguising the fact that the defeat at the polls is overwhelming. I had expected defeat, but I had expected that we would make a better showing. For instance, I thought that in New York and Massachusetts we would come second to Wilson, whereas Taft beat us. But I suppose that I ought not to expect that in three months we could form a new Party that would do as well as we have actually done. We had all the money, all the newspapers and all the political machinery against us and, above all, we had the habit of thought of the immense mass of dull unimaginative men who simply vote according to the party symbol. Whether the Progressive Party itself will disappear or not, I do not know; but the Progressive movement must and will go forward even though its progress is fitful. It is essential for this country that it should go forward. The alternative is oscillation between the greedy arrogance of a party directed by conscienceless millionaires and the greedy envy of a party directed by reckless and unscrupulous demagogues.

As things were this year, there was no human being who could have made any fight or have saved the whole movement from collapse if I had not been willing to step in and take the hammering. But it doesn't seem to me as if I ever could make up my mind to repeat the experiment. Not only do I shrink from it personally but at present it seems to me that I cannot accomplish enough to warrant the damage that another candidacy of mine would do. I try not to think of the damage to myself personally; but I feel torn in two ways from the public standpoint; for while the fight could only have been made under my leadership, yet it is also true that an infinitely stronger attack was made upon me than would have been made upon any other Progressive leader, and that there is a strong tendency, among even, respectable people, to feel that it is only my own personal ambition which I am desirous of gratifying.

Well, my dear Arthur, I do wish there was a chance of seeing you both over here. I should like to go at great length into the political and social conditions both in England and here.

With warmest love to your dear wife, I am
Faithfully yours

November 8, 1912. Oyster Bay
To James R. Garfield

Dear Jim:

We have fought the good fight, we have kept the faith, and we have nothing to regret. Probably we have put the ideal a little higher than we can expect the people as a whole to take offhand.

Always yours

December 3, 1912. New York
To Frances Parsons

Dear Fanny,

Indeed I am quite ashamed that you should mislead Russell in such fashion! It seems rather egotistical to say even what I am about to say:— but if there is any lesson to teach a boy from my life (aside from the avoidance of my blunders and shortcomings) it is that a man of commonplace and ordinary attributes can achieve a measure of success *if he will only use to the utmost, and develop to their limit,* these ordinary qualities, so that they become reasonably good instruments for his purpose. Then he may do the work of the half-gods, and until the gods appear, or if they never appear, the work of the half-gods is useful.

I enjoyed to the full the delightful evening.

Ever your friend

December 16, 1912. Oyster Bay
To John St. Loe Strachey

My dear Strachey:

In your editorial, and now in your letter, you show as usual your thorough understanding of what I was trying to do. We succeeded to even a greater extent than I had hoped.

Just one word about the madman who shot me. He was not really a madman at all; he was a man of the same disordered brain which most criminals, and a great many noncriminals, have. I very gravely question if he has a more unsound brain than Senator La Follette or Eugene Debs. He simply represents a different stratum of life and of temperament, which if not more violent is yet more accustomed to brutal physical expression. He had quite enough sense to avoid shooting me in any Southern State, where he would have been lynched, and he waited until he got into a State where there was no death penalty. I have not the slightest feeling against him; I have a very strong feeling against the people who, by their ceaseless and intemperate abuse, excited him to the action, and against the mushy people who would excuse him and all other criminals once the crime has been committed.

I wish there were a chance of seeing you on this side.

Sincerely yours

March 18, 1913. Oyster Bay
To Franklin Delano Roosevelt

Dear Franklin:

I was very much pleased that you were appointed as Assistant Secretary of the Navy. It is interesting to see that you are in another place which I myself once held. I am sure you will enjoy yourself to the full as Assistant Secretary of the Navy, and that you will do capital work. When I see Eleanor[1] I shall say to her that I do hope she will be particularly nice to the naval officers' wives. They have a pretty hard time, with very little money to get along on, and yet a position to keep up, and everything that can properly be done to make things pleasant for them should be done. When I see you and Eleanor I will speak to you more at length about this.

Yours aff.

April 2, 1913. Oyster Bay
To the Progressives in Congress

To the Progressives in Congress:

I greet you, the men of stout heart and firm faith who dare to stand up to your colors and fight the people's contest. In Congress you will find the odds against you very great, but among the people at large I firmly believe that the changes are steadily in your favor. We cannot amalgamate with either of the old boss-ridden, privilege-controlled parties. We stand for the rights of the people. Where the rights of the people can only be secured through the exercise of the National power, then we are committed to the doctrine of using the National power to any extent that the rights of the people demand. This of itself sunders us from the Democratic Party, for the Democratic Party must either be false to its pledges—and you can trust no party that is false to its pledges—or else it is irrevocably committed to the doctrine of some fifty separate sovereignties, a doctrine which in practice means that the powers of privilege can nullify every effort of the plain people to take possession of their own government. As for the Republicans, their present position is the exact negation of the attitude of Abraham Lincoln and the men in Lincoln's days.

---

[1]Eleanor Roosevelt Roosevelt, Theodore Roosevelt's niece and Franklin Roosevelt's wife.

Lincoln declared that the people were masters over both Congress and the Courts, not, as he phrased it, to destroy the Constitution, but to overthrow those who perverted the Constitution. We stand for the right of the people to have their well-determined wish become part of the fundamental law of the land without permitting either court, legislature or executive to debar them from this right. In short, our two essential principles are:

(1) That this government belongs to the people of all the United States, and that every governmental agency is to be responsive to their will; and

(2) That when they obtain, as they shall obtain, full control over all the powers of government, those powers shall be used primarily to increase the moral and economic well-being of the average man and average woman of this nation.

Yours sincerely

January 16, 1914. Tapirapuan, Mato Grosso, Brazil
To Quentin Roosevelt

Dearest Quentin:

As I wrote Archie, I am sending these few lines to you and to him as the only ones of the family except Mother, because I feel as though this trip with Kermit was more or less an extension of the trip I took with you two and Nick last summer. We had pretty good fun, didn't we? So far there have been no hardships on this trip, although of course there has been some fatigue and some discomfort, and naturally I have had to work a good deal harder than when I was with you. It is very interesting. We see all kinds of queer birds, and we now and then collect very queer beasts. The queerest of all was the giant anteater. It was the size of a bear, with a tail like an enormous skunk, and a head that looks more like that of a long-billed bird than of any normal quadruped. The most dangerous things I hunted were the white-lipped peccaries, because they are such savage little beasts which make a kind of moaning noise of defiance and clatter their teeth like castanets. It was also very interesting to hunt the jaguar. Kermit is, however, by this time a far better hunter than I am. I think Archie would be almost as good a hunter, and probably quite as good with a little experience, but I don't think he would really care for it as much, and I am really glad of this, for hunting should never be anything but a pastime. However I am glad that Kermit, evidently from the bottom of his heart, does not care for this hunting as he did in Africa. He is getting to take a serious interest in life, and is anxious to get back to his work. Of course the thing he is most anxious to do is to get out of the wilderness and marry Belle, but he would not let me leave him behind, and he has been a great help and comfort, although I was utterly miserable with worry about him during the four or five days he had the fever and could with difficulty be persuaded to take any care of himself. This is the last letter you will receive from me, for I think it will take six weeks to two months in getting to you, and I hope that not long after that time I will be able to send a telegram to Mother announcing that I have gotten out of the wilderness and am about to sail for home. Before I get home I think Mr. Harper will have reached home and will be able to tell Mother the latest news about me.

Give my love to the Rector and to dear Mrs. Peabody,

Your loving father

One of the naturalists, Miller, has a dear little owl as a pet. Moses is his name. He spends most of the time in a basket, but some of it at large; and he croons and chuckles with pleasure when he is taken up and petted.

April 30, 1914. Manaus, Brazil
To Lauro Severiano Müller

(Telegram)

My dear General Lauro Müller:

I wish first to express my profound acknowledgements to you personally and to the other members of the Brazilian Government whose generous courtesy alone rendered possible the Expediçao Scientifica Roosevelt-Rondon. I wish also to express my high admiration and regard for Colonel Rondon and his associates who have been my colleagues in this work of exploration. In the third place I wish to point out that what we have just done was rendered possible only by the hard and perilous labor of the Brazilian Telegraphic Commission in the unexplored western Wilderness of Mato Grosso during the last seven years. We have merely put the cap on the pyramid of which they had previously laid deep and broad the foundations. We have had a hard and somewhat dangerous but very successful trip. No less than six weeks were spent in slowly and with peril and exhausting labor forcing our way down through what seemed a literally endless succession of rapids and cataracts. For forty-eight days we saw no human being. In passing these rapids we lost five of the seven canoes with which we started and had to build others. One of our best men lost his life in the rapids. Under the strain one of the men went completely bad, shirked all his work, stole his comrades' food and when punished by the sergeant he with cold-blooded deliberation murdered the sergeant and fled into the wilderness. Col. Rondon's dog, running ahead of him while hunting, was shot by two Indians; by his death he in all probability saved the life of his master. We have put on the map a river about 1500 kilometers in length running from just south of the 13th degree to north of the 5th degree and the biggest affluent of the Madeira. Until now its upper course has been utterly unknown to everyone, and its lower course altho known for years to the rubber-men utterly unknown to all cartographers. Its source is between the 12th and 13th parallels of latitude South, and between longitude 59° and longitude 60° west from Greenwich. We embarked on it about at latitude 12° 1' south and longitude 60° 18' west. After that its entire course was between the 60° and 61st degrees of longitude, approaching the latter most closely about in latitude 8° 15'. The first rapids were at Navaité in 11° 44', and after that they were continuous and very difficult and dangerous until the rapids named after the murdered sergeant Paishon in 11° 12'. At 11° 23' it received the Rio Kermit from the left. At 11° 22' the Marciano Carlo entered it from the right. At 11° 18' the Taunay entered from the left. At 10 58' the Cardozo entered from the right. At 10° 24' we encountered the first rubber-men. The Rio Branco entered from the left at 9° 38'. We camped at 8° 49' on approximately the boundary line between Mato Grosso and Amazonas. The confluence with the Amazonas, which entered from the left was in 7° 34'. The mouth, where it entered the Madeira was in 5° 30'. The stream we have followed down is that which rises farthest away from the mouth, and its general course is almost due north.

My dear Sir, I thank you from my heart for the chance to take part in this great work of exploration.

With high regard and respect, believe me,

Very sincerely yours

July 6, 1914. Oyster Bay
To William Allen White

Dear White:

I am very pleased that Mrs. White likes the jaguar skin. But, my dear fellow, I think it would be very unwise for us to go into government ownership of railways, or national prohibition. It is possible that government ownership of railways may come, but I shall feel it is a real misfortune if this becomes necessary. I have just come from England, where they have government ownership of telephones, and the service is not to be compared with the service in this country where telephones are privately owned. It is a mere matter of expediency whether a given thing should be run by private individuals or by the Government. I believe our railroads are run better than the State-owned railroads of Germany and France. I believe that wise regulation is the proper method of getting at them.

As for prohibition nationally, it would merely mean free rum and utter lawlessness in our big cities. Worthy people sometimes say that liquor is responsible for nine tenths of all crime. As a matter of fact foreigners of the races that furnish most crime in New York at the present time do not drink at all. I think that in Maine local option for the last fifty years would have been infinitely better than the State prohibition which they have had. I will favor prohibition wherever the sentiment is strong enough actively and locally to support it, but I do not believe that the American people can be dragooned into being good by any outside influence, whether it is a king or the majority in some other locality. I wish I could see you and talk with you at length about Perkins. It is my deliberate judgment that the party in the East would have gone out of existence if it had not been for Perkins, and most assuredly it would go out of existence if the people in the party got any idea that we were standing for men like Amos Pinchot and Record as against Perkins.

I do wish I could see you. With warm love to Mrs. White,
Faithfully yours

August 22, 1914. Oyster Bay
To Arthur H. Lee

Dear Arthur:

I cannot forbear writing you just a word of affectionate sympathy in the very hard time you are having in England. Thank Heaven! at least you do not have to suffer what the continental nations are suffering. I thought England behaved exactly as she ought to behave, and with very great dignity. It was a fine thing. In this country the feeling is overwhelmingly anti-German. It is emphatically in favor of England, France and Belgium; yet curiously enough it is very lukewarm as regards Russia and Serbia. They feel that Germany's course on her Western frontier is a menace to civilization, whereas they are very doubtful when it comes to an issue between the Slav and the German. Our own preposterous little fools have thought this a happy time to pass universal arbitration treaties. In international affairs Wilson is almost as much of a prize jackass as Bryan. The arbitration treaties won't do us any serious harm, because they would be contemptuously disregarded if it was ever proposed to apply them in a way that would damage us in face of Germany or Japan, the only two nations from whom we have to fear aggression in the New World, at least so far as we can see now. But they do do us a certain amount of damage, and it seems incredible that at the moment when the experience of Luxembourg and Belgium shows the utter worthlessness of treaties of this kind, our sapient jacks should officially proclaim to the world their belief in the unlimited power of bits of paper with names put on them.

Belle and Kermit are in the house. Belle has recovered from her typhoid fever, as it was only a slight attack. My own parochial affairs are of no earthly consequence at a time like this, and so I do not write you about them. I hope you are entirely over your sickness. One good result of the war, so far as England is concerned, seems to be the absolute sweeping away of danger from the Home Rule question.

With dearest love to Ruth,

Ever yours

P.S. After dictating the above, and when it was brought up for my signature, I received your welcome letter. It was most thoughtful to send it to me. By the time this reaches you I believe you will have practically regained your health and will be doing all you can in this grave crisis. I read your letter aloud at the table, and it gave the utmost satisfaction to all of us. I have never liked Winston Churchill, but in view of what you tell me as to his admirable conduct and nerve in mobilizing the fleet, I do wish that if it comes in your way you would extend to him my congratulations on his action. It must be strictly confidential, of course. It seems to me that Edward Grey[1] behaved very well. All that you say about the conduct of England is true. I doubt if she has ever shown to more advantage. The great seriousness of the crisis seems to have brought out everything that is best in the national character. I am bound to say substantially the same thing about both France and Belgium. As for the Germans, I have a very real and sincere liking and respect for them individually. In all essentials they are like ourselves—indeed so far as Americans are concerned they are largely ourselves, for we have an immense German strain in our blood, and I for instance number among my ancestors Germans as well as Englishmen, although they are outnumbered by my Dutch and Scotch ancestors. I can honestly say that I have not one particle of feeling except of respect and kindly regard for the German people as such. But the Government of Prussianized Germany for the last forty-three years has behaved in such fashion as inevitably to make almost every nation with which it came in contact its foe, because it has convinced everybody except Austria that it has no regard for anything except its own interest, and that it will enter instantly on any career of aggression with cynical brutality and bad faith if it thinks its interest requires such action. I do not know whether I would be acting right if I were President or not, but it seems to me that if I were President I should register a very emphatic protest, a protest that would mean something, against the levy of the huge war contributions on Belgium. As regards Belgium, there is not even room for an argument. The Germans, to suit

---

[1]British Foreign Secretary.

their own purposes, trampled on their solemn obligations to Belgium and on Belgium's rights. The Belgians have fought for their hearthstones and homes and for the elemental rights without which it is not worth while to exist. To visit them with grinding punishment because of such action is proof positive that any power which now or hereafter may be put at the mercy of Germany will suffer in similar shape—and this whether the power were the United States, or England, or France, or Russia. I agree with you that if Germany is beaten, England will in self-defense be obliged utterly to destroy her colonial empire, and to take the sharpest measures in restriction of her navy. There is no alternative. For the last forty-three years Germany has spread out everywhere, and has menaced every nation where she thought it was to her advantage to do so. Her share in doing injury to Japan has now been promptly avenged by that nation, which has bided its time for nineteen years with quiet politeness, and struck at once when it was safe to do so. Of course Japan was not influenced in the least by any loyalty to England in thus striking; she simply took the opportunity when she could with safety deliver a smash at Germany, just as she would deliver a smash at us if ever she thought it safe and easy to do so. With the Japanese in the Pacific we can avoid war permanently only if we keep our navy at the highest state of efficiency. Without an efficient navy we would be as helpless before Japan as you would be before Germany if you had a useless navy. Italy has really been quite as much menaced by her ally Germany as by France, and I should not be a bit surprised to see her throw her forces into the scale against the two Germanic powers.

You are a little more ready to prophesy than I am, although the action of the Germans in Belgium has from a military standpoint exactly borne out the beliefs you gained from what occurred at the German maneuvers. It does, however, seem to me an impossibility that Germany can conquer in any complete sense. She will certainly lose all she has beyond the seas. At any time now I should expect to hear that the Australians had taken possession of the German islands and ports in the Pacific, and that the African possessions of Germany had gone; while of course Japan will gobble up what she has in Asia. Even from the standpoint of brutal self-interest, I think Germany's invasion of Belgium was a mistake. The Germans, as I happen to know, counted confidently upon being mobilized within ten days, and at the end of that time having an army which had marched through Belgium break up the French before their mobilization was complete. As it is, three weeks have gone by and no German troops are yet on French soil, while great loss has been experienced by the Germans in forcing their way into Southern Belgium, and hitherto they have not succeeded in taking the most important forts that the Belgians hold. If the Franco-British armies hold their own against the Germans, whether they win a victory or whether the result is a draw, it is in my judgment all up with Germany. Even if the Germans win against the Franco-British armies, my belief is that they cannot win sufficiently soon or in such crushing manner as to enable them to complete the conquest of France and the driving of the British Army from the continent before with enfeebled forces they turn to meet the tremendous advance of the Russian armies. Evidently Montenegro and Serbia now hold in check the Austrian armies which Austria is obliged to keep on her Southern frontiers instead of using them against either France or Russia. If Germany is mastered, she will be reduced to international impotence. If she wins, which I regard as possible but improbable, she will not be able to reduce Russia to impotence, she will not materially have harmed England, but will have turned it into a great military power, and in all probability will have excited in the United States a feeling of active hostility. Our people have never forgotten the attitude taken by Germany in the Spanish War, and since then threatened by Germany in South America. It was decades before we got over the remembrance of England's attitude during the Civil War, but England's friendliness for the last few decades, and Germany's hostile attitude for the last fifteen or twenty years, have worked an extraordinary change in public sentiment here.

At the same time I do not agree with you when you speak of this as being the last war for civilization. I see no reason for believing that Russia is more advanced than Germany as regards international ethics, and Japan with all her politeness and her veneer of western civilization is at heart delighted to attack any and every western nation whenever the chance comes and there is an opportunity for Japan to gain what she desires with reasonable safety. If Germany is smashed it is perfectly possible that later she will have to be supported as a bulwark against the Slav by the nations of Western Europe, and while as regards the United States there can be little chance of hostility between us and Russia, there is always the chance of hostility between us and Japan, or Oriental Asia under the lead of Japan.

It seems to me that the attitude of the Irish in this business has been fine, and of good omen to the British Empire; and I am also immensely impressed with the fine attitude of the warlike peoples of India.

You may remember that after my visit to Germany four years ago I told you that I was impressed that Germany might very possibly—whether probably or not I could not say—strike at England if she thought the chance favorable. You say you think that for ten years the Emperor and his advisers have been leading a pipe-dream type of existence. I should make it forty years. When Germany took Alsace and Lorraine from France she of course made France forever her bitter foe. It may be that at the time Germany was right in feeling that the course she took was the only one possible. But if so she should then have made up her mind that France would always be her foe, and that she must do everything in her power to isolate that foe and convince the other nations that Germany was no menace to them. She should not have tried for a colonial empire, or in any way have made England a foe, and should have made it evident to England that she was bent upon safeguarding the independence of both Holland and Belgium. She should have avoided giving mortal offense to Japan, and making the United States feel that she was antagonistic. She should have grappled Italy as well as Austria to her with hoops of steel and have exhausted every expedient to prevent that Austrian attitude which rendered a clash with Russia inevitable. Surely the directors of German policy must by this time realize the damage they have done.

Give my dearest love to Ruth. I am very glad at what you are doing around Chequers, and at what you propose to do with Chequers itself. Edith sends her love to both of you.

[Handwritten] Of course this letter is only for you and Ruth. I am an ex-President; and my public attitude must be one of entire impartiality—and above all no verbal or paper "on to Berlin" business.

September 4, 1914. Oyster Bay
To Arthur H. Lee

Dear Arthur:

I cannot refrain from sending you a line of affection and sympathy in these terrible and trying hours. It is very difficult to gain a clear idea of what has happened. It seems, however, to have been shown that the British Army has fought admirably. There is no use of my commenting in any way on the military situation, because it will doubtless have changed completely by the time you receive this. The attitude of the English people seems to be on the whole admirable. I have been greatly impressed by everything that Kitchener has said and done. He is indeed a strong man. I have also been immensely pleased with all that Lord Roberts has done. How completely this war seems to have justified his teachings for the past few years! I was particularly pleased at his severe comment on people who persist in making a fetish of sports and pastimes in this moment of the nation's need. Of course you have some creatures who represent types with which we over here are only too familiar—the unhung traitor Keir Hardie, the blue-rumped ape Bernard Shaw, and the assemblage of clever and venomous but essentially foolish and physically timid creatures of the type of the editors of the *Nation*.

If it is any comfort to you to know that there are others who in minor degree have cause for suffering, we on this side of the water can give you that comfort. With all your suffering you are playing a heroic part, and whatever Germany's successes or failures on the continent, England is as certain to win now as she was to win against Napoleon a century ago if only she will be true to herself; and so far she has given every proof that she intends to be true to herself. On this side of the water at the moment there is no opportunity for the display of heroic qualities, and not the slightest indication that there will be a desire to display them if the need arose. Wilson and Bryan leave the navy scattered, and slightly but steadily deteriorating because not assembled for maneuvers. They have passed a procession of idiotic universal arbitration treaties with Paraguay and similar world powers, and all the apostles of the utterly inane scream joyfully that this shows that the United States does not need any battleships, and that if Europe had only had these treaties there never would have been any war! One curious feature of the professional pacificists, the peace-at-any-price men, is that in the crisis they always tend to support the apostles of brutal violence. Most of them now have a sneaking admiration for Germany. I think this admiration proceeds primarily from fear, for the great bulk of them are physically timid men, and at bottom are only concerned in covering their own abjectness with high-sounding phrases. Therefore their tendency is to lick the hand which they fear may strike them, and to confine their assaults upon honest men who fight for right.

It seems to me that Edward Grey has borne himself peculiarly well in these trying and difficult times. He showed clearly that he was a statesman of the Timoleon and John Hampden, the Washington and Lincoln school; that nothing could persuade him to do wrong to any other nation, weak or strong, or to be a party to such wrongdoing; but that on the other hand, no menace of danger could make him shrink from insisting upon right being done in return; and he has not hesitated to draw the sword rather than submit to wrongdoing.

Give my dearest love to Ruth, and remember me to any friend who you think would care to have such remembrance from me.

Faithfully yours

October 3, 1914. Oyster Bay
To Cecil Spring Rice

Dear Cecil:

I have received your letters. I am glad you liked the *Outlook* article and the others. I see the Cologne *Gazette* has attacked me. With this I am pleased, because, while I wished to be scrupulously fair and not in the least bitter toward Germany, I yet wished to make my position as clear as a bell. As a matter of fact, it has been very hard for me to keep myself in. If I had been President, I should have acted on the thirtieth or thirty-first of July, as head of a signatory power of the Hague treaties, calling attention to the guaranty of Belgium's neutrality and saying that I accepted the treaties as imposing a serious obligation which I expected not only the United States but all other neutral nations to join in enforcing. Of course I would not have made such a statement unless I was willing to back it up. I believe that if I had been President the American people would have followed me. But whether I am mistaken or not as regards this, I am certain that the majority are now following Wilson. Only a limited number of people could or ought to be expected to make up their minds for themselves in a crisis like this; and they tend, and ought to tend, to support the President in such a crisis. It would be worse than folly for me to clamor now about what ought to be done or ought to have been done, when it would be mere clamor and nothing else.

The above is only for yourself. It is a freer expression of opinion than I have permitted myself in any letter hitherto.

Of course, I only acted in the Japanese-Russian affair when I had received explicit assurances, verbally from the Russians and in writing from the Japanese, that my action would be welcome; and three or four months of talk and negotiation had preceded this action on my part.

As for the people who clamor for peace now, I shall take the opportunity of reminding them that there were in the northern United States in 1864 several hundred thousand men who in the loudest terms declared their extreme devotion to peace and that these to a man voted against Abraham Lincoln; and if in that year England and France had joined, as certain of their public men wished them to join, in offering mediation so as to bring about "peace," we should have treated it as an unfriendly act.

I believe that you will put the war through. I am glad the opinion of our country is on your side. It is perfectly possible that Russia may in its turn become a great military danger in the future, but it is also possible that this war may see the dawn of the reaction against militarism and that Russia may tend to grow more civilized and more liberal. At any rate there is no question as to where the interests of civilization lie at this moment.

Faithfully yours

November 4, 1914. Oyster Bay
To Ethel Roosevelt Derby[1]

Darling Ethel,

Of course we think of you and Dick all the time. I know you are having a hard time, of wearing anxiety and sorrow and effort; but I am very

---

[1]Ethel had married Richard Derby; the couple had a son, also Richard.

proud of you both and very glad that you have been able to go over to do your part—and a portion of this nation's part—in helping those who suffer in this terrible cataclysm. I am utterly sick of the spiritless "neutrality" of the Administration; and I have at last said so, in emphatic language, in an article that appears next Sunday; I shall send it to you.

Richard is the dearest, merriest little fellow that ever was. He is always smiling, and is such a cuddly baby. He adores his grandmother's amber beads, puts them in his mouth, and then the string hangs out of each corner of his mouth like the moustache of a Chinese mandarin. His grandmother calls him Littlejohn Bottlejohn; and he sits up in his chair and hugs his bottle with both hands. His grandmother read aloud to me the enclosed piece from the Atlantic Monthly about merry souls that "waggle," like nice bow wows; and we send it to you because Littlejohn Bottlejohn is always so cheerful and friendly. My drawings are only good for grownups who can be caricatured! I can't draw the blessed baby. He is a great comfort; and we most earnestly hope that in another month or so you will be starting back to him.

November has opened with beautiful weather. Mother and I have had two lovely rows, and a good walk. Somehow this always seems to me one of the loveliest seasons of the year; I like the wintry sunsets, and the tang in the air, and the wood fires in the North Room and Library.

As of course I expected the Progressives went down to utter and hopeless defeat; I do'n't think they can much longer be kept as a party. They are way ahead of the country as a whole in morality, and the country will need too long a time to catch up with them. It will be, from the selfish standpoint, a great relief to me personally when and if they do disband. But it is rather pathetic for the remnant who stood fast. Well, they really have shoved a good many reforms quite a distance forward.

We are somewhat concerned about Kermit and Belle, in view of the harrying of English ships by the Germans; we can only hope that the too-newly-weds managed to show efficiency enough to get on the very earliest ship that went.

Good bye, darling; I wish I could stroke your neck and hair. Give my dearest love to Dick.

Your loving father

November 30, 1914. Oyster Bay
To Henry Ford

My dear Mr. Ford:

There are a great many things that you are doing that interest me peculiarly. I am not only desirous of knowing how you handle your workingmen from the purely industrial and social side but also I want to know your method of dealing with the immigrant workingmen. I have heard a great deal about you both from Mr. Pope and through Mr. Edison, and Judge Lindsey has been very anxious that I should know at firsthand some of the things you have to say. When you next come to New York will you not give me the pleasure of taking lunch or dinner with me? I should like to ask Miss Kellor at the same time.

Faithfully yours

December 8, 1914. Oyster Bay
To Henry Cabot Lodge

Dear Cabot:

I am much pleased that you liked my Mexican article. I should particularly like to write a second article showing the outrages committed on American citizens. I have general statements of these outrages but nothing specific, whereas I was given the specific and detailed statements of the outrages committed upon the priests and nuns. Of course, however, incidentally in that article we have the clearest and most specific charge of the worst kind of outrage; and this charge is cheerfully made by Mr. Bryan against himself. I refer to his statement to Father Tierney about the two American women from Iowa. I see that both he and Wilson have announced that they will not reply to my article. If he does not, then he admits that this statement is true and unless he makes a denial speedily he is stopped from denying it at all, and when I come to deal with the outrages on American citizens I shall head my article with this outrage testified to by Bryan himself.

Your speech was an admirable one.

Nothing irritated me more last summer than the attitude of my own friends and also of the Republicans toward Wilson's foreign policy, especially in Mexico. My own friends and supporters besought me not to touch him, and whatever they said themselves was really in his favor. The Republicans took just the same ground. They criticised him about the tariff, but fell over themselves to say that they supported him for his noble and humanitarian peace policy. They took this ground over and over again here in New York, vieing with the Democrats in saying how splendid it was that Wilson had kept us out of war with Mexico and had preserved such absolute neutrality in the European war. I told my own friends that as I was doing what I could for them this fall I should not make an attack which they thought would hurt them but that after election I should smite the administration with a heavy hand.

I see that Wilson is against any investigation into our unpreparedness. Upon my word, Wilson and Bryan are the very worst men we have ever had in their positions. It would not hurt them to say publicly what is nevertheless historically true, namely, that they are worse then Jefferson and Madison. I really believe that I would rather have Murphy, Penrose or Barnes as the standard-bearer of this nation in the face of international wrong-doing.

I have accepted an offer from the *Metropolitan Magazine* to write for it anything I have to say on questions of this kind. My first article will appear in mid-January, dealing with the Panama-Colombian business. I also have an article on our unpreparedness for war in this month's *Everbody's Magazine*

With dearest love to Nannie.

Always yours

December 22, 1914. Oyster Bay
To Mrs. Ralph Sanger

My dear Mrs. Sanger:

I am very sorry; but I cannot sign that appeal. I do not approve of it. You are asking Americans to proclaim themselves Anglo-Americans and to sympathize with England on the ground that England is the motherland and in order to make what you call "hands across the sea" a matter of living policy. I do not believe that this is the right attitude for Americans to take. England is not my motherland any more than Germany is my fatherland. My motherland and fatherland and my own land are all three of them the United States. I am among those Americans whose ancestors include men and women from many different European countries. The proportion of Americans of this type will steadily increase. I do not believe in hyphenated Americans. I do not believe in German-Americans or Irish-Americans; and I believe just as little in English-Americans. I do not approve of American citizens of German descent forming organizations to force the United States into practical alliance with Germany because their ancestors came from Germany. Just as little do I believe in American citizens of English descent forming leagues to force the United States into an alliance with England because their ancestors came from England. We Americans are a separate people. We are separated from, although akin to, many European peoples. The old Revolutionary stock was predominantly English, but by no means exclusively so; for many of the descendants of the Revolutionary New Yorkers, Pennsylvanians and Georgians have, like myself, strains of Dutch, French, Scotch, Irish, Welsh and German blood in their veins. During the century and a quarter that has elapsed since we became a nation there has been far more immigration from Germany and Ireland and perhaps even from Scandinavia than there has been from England. We have a right to ask all of these immigrants and the sons of these immigrants that they become Americans and nothing else; but we have no right to ask that they become transplanted or second-rate Englishmen. Most emphatically I myself am not an Englishman once removed! I am straight United States!

In international matters we should treat each nation on its conduct and without the slightest reference to the fact that a larger or smaller proportion of its blood flows in the veins of our own citizens. I have publicly and emphatically taken ground for Belgium and I wish that the United States would take ground for Belgium, because I hold that this is our duty, and that Germany's conduct toward Belgium demands that we antagonize her in this matter so far as Belgium is concerned, and that we emphatically and in practical shape try to see that Belgium's wrongs are redressed. Because of the British attitude toward Belgium I have publicly and emphatically approved of this attitude and of Great Britain's conduct in living up to her obligations, by defending Belgium, even at the cost of war. But I am not doing this on any ground that there is any "hands across the sea" alliance, explicit or implicit, with England. I have never used in peace or in war any such expression as "hands across the sea"; and I emphatically disapprove of what it signifies save in so far as it means cordial friendship between us and any other nation that acts in accordance with the standards that we deem just and right. On this ground, all Americans, no matter what their race origins, ought to stand together. It is not just that they should be asked to stand with any foreign power on the ground of community of origin between some of them and the citizens of that foreign power.

Sincerely yours

January 6, 1915. Oyster Bay
To Rómulo Sebastian Naón

My dear Mr. Ambassador:

I take very great pleasure in presenting to you Mr. Walter Lippmann,[1] one of the editors of *The New Republic*. Mr. Lippmann is a personal friend of mine and is, I think, on the whole the most brilliant young man of his age in all the United States. He is a great writer and economist. He has real international sense; and I am very anxious that he should understand something about South America. What I especially desire is that he shall understand that Argentina, Chile and Brazil are in no shape or way to be considered from the same standpoint from which we consider certain of the States along the Caribbean Sea and the Gulf of Mexico. You may possibly have noticed that in my recent articles I have

---

[1]The famous journalist was just beginning his career.

been holding up Argentina as a military model for the United States and as entitled to go into any world league of peace on the footing of a nation of the first rank and on an equality with the United States, Germany, Russia and the other powers.

Sincerely yours

January 22, 1915. Oyster Bay
To Edward Grey

My dear Grey:

Through Spring Rice I am sending you this letter. If you choose to show it to your colleagues in the Cabinet, you are welcome to do so. But I need hardly say that outside of such action, it is strictly confidential— not from reasons personal to you or me, but because of what I have at heart in writing.

You probably know my general attitude toward this war, as set forth in the little volume I have just published. (It would be entirely unnecessary for you to read this volume. It is addressed to and intended for my own countrymen.)

To me the crux of the situation has been Belgium. If England or France had acted toward Belgium as Germany has acted I should have opposed them, exactly as I now oppose Germany. I have emphatically approved your action as a model for what should be done by those who believe that treaties should be observed in good faith and that there is such a thing as international morality. I take this position as an American who is no more an Englishman than he is a German, who endeavors loyally to serve the interests of his own country, but who also endeavors to do what he can for justice and decency as regards mankind at large, and who therefore feels obliged to judge all other nations by their conduct on any given occasion.

I do not think you need to have me show a precedent for writing you; but, if you do, I shall ask you to turn to young Trevelyan's *Life of John Bright*, pages 314 to 316. Bright was writing to Sumner at the time, when the bulk of the leading English politicians, from Palmerston and Derby to Gladstone and the editor of the *Times*, were more or less openly hostile to the cause of the American Union and of the freeing of the slaves. Bright's letters were written to Sumner in order that they could be read aloud by Lincoln to his Cabinet, which was actually done. He was afraid the United States would drift into war with England. His letters run in part as follows:

"You know that I write to you with as much earnest wish for your national welfare as if I were a native and resident of your country. I need not tell you, who are much better acquainted with modern history than I am, that nations drift into wars. I fervently hope that you may act firmly and courteously (towards England). Any moderate course you may take will meet with great support here. I have no doubt you will be able to produce strong cases from English practice in support of your actions but I doubt if any number of these will change opinion here. You must put the matter in such a shape as to save your honor and to put our government in the wrong if they refuse your propositions. *At all hazards you must not let this matter grow to a war with England, even if you are right and we are wrong.*" The italics are mine. I am as little in sympathy with Wilson and Bryan in their attitude now, as Bright was in sympathy with the Palmerston-Derby view of our civil war in '61–65. "War will be fatal to your idea of restoring the Union. I am not now considering its effects here; but I am looking alone to your great country and I implore you, not on any feeling that nothing can be conceded and that England is arrogant and seeking a quarrel, not to play the game of every enemy of your country. Nations in great crises and difficulties have often done that which in their prosperous and powerful hour they would not have done; and they have done it without humiliation and disgrace. You may disappoint your enemies by the moderation and reasonableness of your conduct; and every honest and good man in England will applaud your wisdom. If you are resolved to succeed against the South, have no war with England. Make every concession that can be made. Do not hesitate to tell the world that you will even consider what two years ago no power would have asked of you rather than give another nation a pretense for assisting your enemies. It is your interest to baffle your enemies even by any concession which is not disgraceful."

America then acted along the lines John Bright advised. I do not know whether his advice carried any weight. I have not the slightest idea whether you may not resent my giving advice; but I assure you that it is given with as much friendliness and disinterestedness as fifty-odd years ago John Bright gave his to Sumner and Lincoln, and with as sincere a purpose to serve what I believe to be the cause of justice and morality; and with reversal of names the advice I am giving is the same as John Bright gave; and my reasons are the same.

There have been fluctuations in American opinion about the war. The actions of the German Zeppelins have revived the feeling in favor of the Allies. But I believe that for a couple of months preceding this action there had been a distinct lessening of the feeling for the Allies and a growth of pro-German feeling. I do not think that this was the case among the people who are best informed; but I do think it was the case among the mass of not very well-informed people, who have little to go

upon except what they read in the newspapers or see at Cinemato-
graph shows. There were several causes for this change. There has been
a very striking contrast between the lavish attentions showered on
American war correspondents by the German military authorities and
the blank refusal to have anything whatever to do with them by the
British and French governments. Our best war correspondent, on the
whole, is probably Frederick Palmer. He is favorable to the Allies. But
it was the Germans and not the allies who did everything for him. They
did not change his attitude; but they unquestionably did change the attitude of many other good men. The only real war news written by
Americans who are known to and trusted by the American public
comes from the German side; as a result of this, the sympathizers with
the cause of the Allies can hear nothing whatever about the trials and
achievements of the British and French armies. These correspondents
inform me that it is not the generals at the front who raise the objections
but the Home Governments; and in consequence they get the chance to
write for their fellow countrymen what happens from the German side
and they are not given a chance from the side of the Allies. I do not find
that the permission granted them by the Germans has interfered with
the efficiency of German military operations; and it has certainly
helped the Germans in American public opinion. It may be that your
people do not believe that American public opinion is of sufficient
value to be taken into account; but, if you think that it should be taken
into account, then it is worth your while considering whether much of
your censorship work and much of your refusal to allow correspondents at the front has not been damaging to your cause from the standpoint of the effect on public opinion, without any corresponding military gain. I realize perfectly that it would be criminal to permit
correspondents to act as they acted as late as our own Spanish War; but,
as a layman, I feel sure that there has been a good deal of work of the
kind of which I have spoken in the way of censorship and refusing the
correspondents permission to go to the front which has not been of the
slightest military service to you and which has had a very real effect in
preventing any rallying of public opinion to you.

I have also just written to Spring Rice a letter of which I shall ask
him to send you a copy, which I should like you to consider in connection with this letter I am writing to you and as part of it.

Now, as to the question of contraband. You know that I am as little in sympathy with President Wilson and Secretary Bryan as regards
their attitude in international matters as John Bright was in sympathy
with Lords Palmerston and Derby and Mr. Gladstone in their attitude
toward the American Republic when it was at war fifty years ago. But

they speak for the country; and I have no influence whatever in shaping public action and, as I have reason to believe, very little influence indeed in shaping public opinion. My advice therefore must be taken or rejected by you purely with reference to what you think it is worth.

President Wilson is a pacificist, with apparently no adequate understanding of any military problem—at least his action on our own affairs seems to show this. He is certainly not desirous of war with anybody. But he is very obstinate, very anxious to be president again, and he takes the professorial views of international matters. I need not point out to you that it is often pacificists who, halting and stumbling and not knowing whither they are going, finally drift helplessly into a war, which they have rendered inevitable, without the slightest idea that they were doing so. A century ago this was what happened to the United States under Presidents Jefferson and Madison—although at that time the attitude of both England and France rendered war with one of them, and ought to have rendered war with both of them, inevitable on our part. I do not know if you have seen the letter I wrote to Spring Rice on this question a couple of weeks ago I presume he has sent it to you, or, if not, that he will send it together with this letter. I regard the proposed purchase by the Administration of German ships as entirely improper. I am supporting the Republicans in their opposition to the measure. I regard some of the actions of the Administration, in, for instance, refusing to make public the manifests in advance and the like, as improper. I think Great Britain is now showing great courtesy and forbearance. I believe that she has done things to our ships that ought not to have been done; but I am not aware that she is now doing them. I am not discussing this question from the standpoint of right. I am discussing it from the standpoint of expediency, in the interest of Great Britain. Our trade, under existing circumstances, is of vastly more service to you and France than to Germany. I think I underestimate the case when I say that it is ten times as valuable to the allies as to Germany. There are circumstances under which it might become not merely valuable but vital. I am not a naval man. I do not know what the possibilities of the submarine are. But they have accomplished some notable feats; and if they should now begin to destroy ships carrying foodstuffs to Great Britain, the effect might be not merely serious but appalling. Under such conditions, it would be of the utmost consequence to England to have accepted the most extreme view the United States could advance as to her right to ship cargoes unmolested. Even although this possibility, which I do not regard as more than a very remote possibility, is in reality wholly impossible, it yet remains true that the trade in contraband is overwhelmingly to the advantage of England, France and Russia, because of your command of the seas. You assume that this command gives you the right to make the advantage still more overwhelming. I ask you merely to take careful thought, so that you shall not excite our government, even wrongfully, to act in such a way that it would diminish or altogether abolish the great advantage you now have. I do not question that there are in Mr. Wilson's Cabinet men who will protest against improper action being taken to favor Germany at England's expense. But they are in the minority in the Administration, and the majority see that the political advantage will unquestionably lie with those who try to placate the German-American vote and the professional pacificist vote. It would be extraordinary, were it not characteristic of the professional pacificist mind, that the pacificists applaud action which would be to the advantage of the power whose invasion of Belgium has been the greatest blow to peace and international morality that has been struck during the lifetime of the present generation. The German-Americans wish to put a stop to all exportation of contraband because such action would result to the benefit of Germany. The pacificists are inclined to fall in with the suggestion, because they feebly believe it would be in the interest of "Peace"—just as they are inclined heartily to favor any peace proposal, even though it should leave Belgium in Germany's hands and pave the way for certain renewal of the war.

Now, in all this I cannot advise you in detail. Many different cases come up; and the circumstances vary completely from case to case. I very earnestly hope that you will ostentatiously show every possible consideration to the American Flag and the American position and that, wherever possible, you will yield the point, even though you think you are right, rather than increase friction with this country and make our well-meaning but not well-informed people feel a sense of irritation and grow to regard England as trying to wrong America and being with difficulty prevented by the patriotic activities of the American Administration, the American government. Exactly how far you can go in any given case, I cannot say. But where it is so very important for you that there should be no American hostility, I hope you will not only avoid doubtful action but will not insist on your rights, even when these rights are clear, unless you are convinced that the gain to you will more than offset causing an irritation in this country which might have effects that I will not even contemplate, because they would cause me real horror.

I have publicly taken the position that, inasmuch as we did not stand up for Belgium's rights, it is a base and ignoble thing to take any action for our own moneyed interests as regards neutral affairs which may bring us into collision with the warring power; but I need not say to you that in countries like England and the United States, although in times when there is no strain everybody is willing to applaud the most foolish pacificist utterance, yet under strain there is always a tendency to assert the overwhelmingly superior claim of pure self-interest, untinged by any regard for international morality. I am as wholly hostile to the one tendency as to the other; but it is the part of wisdom to recognize that these tendencies exist.

I make no apology to you for writing; for I am certain that you understand the spirit in which I write and the reason for my doing so; and you are under no obligation to pay a moment's heed to what I have written or to answer the letter.

Yours very truly

February 5, 1915. Oyster Bay
To Cecil Spring Rice

Dear Cecil:

Just after sending you another letter to Grey, I received one from him dated December 18th. I don't know why it took six weeks to reach me.

Since I wrote the long letter to Grey, the success of German submarines against merchant vessels has given me a very uneasy feeling lest what I hinted at may come to pass, and the submarines may make effective war against the merchant vessels going into England. This would be a very serious business and might mean that your whole chance of going on with the war at all depended upon American merchantmen bringing you in food. This is something, of course, that your own people ought to consider when they make protests about neutrality rights or confiscate cargoes. However, I assume they know their own interests and their own capabilities. I have felt that if they choose to protest against our Government purchasing German interned ships, they had a right to do so; and accordingly I have done all I could to prevent the passage of this bill of the Administration, a bill which is pushed by the German interests here and by the Jewish bankers who are doing Germany's business. Now, my dear Cecil, I hope your people will remember that it is they who must determine what their own interest is and that if they find afterwards that they were mistaken, the responsibility will be upon them and not upon those who have tried to help them.

Moreover, do let me say as strongly as I know how that I hope that at all costs your people will avoid a clash with us, *where we are right*. On grounds of expediency, as you know, I hope you will not have a clash with us if it can possibly be avoided, even although we are wrong—just as it was expedient for the United States to avoid a clash with Great Britain or France during the Civil War, even although they were wrong. For it would be a veritable calamity for you to put yourselves in a position where you were wrong and where America had to stand against you or else herself abandon the right. In such a case I and those who think as I do would, however reluctantly, be obliged to take a stand against you, because we would be obliged to do the thing that was right. Your government evidently feels a great contempt for the Wilson-Bryan Administration; and I don't wonder. They are truckling to the German vote; they are utterly selfish and insincere; and they are timid to the last degree. Doubtless your people feel that they could not be kicked into a war. But it is just weak and timid but shifty creatures of the Wilson-Bryan type who are most apt to be responsible for a country drifting into war. I would regard it as an unspeakable calamity if a war should come between the United States and Great Britain. You do not need to be told that everything I can do I am doing, have done and shall do to prevent wrong conduct, offensive conduct, by this administration and to make your path smooth; I feel that the case of Belgium alone ought to put us absolutely on the side of the Allies. It is for this very reason that I so earnestly hope that you will under no circumstances yourselves do something wrong, something evil, as regards which I and the men like me will have to clearly take the stand on the other side.

By the way, if the Allies have to act against us on some point, where they are clearly right and we clearly wrong, I wish it could be a French and not a British ship that took the action.

Faithfully yours

May 19, 1915. Syracuse, New York
To Archibald Roosevelt

Dear Archie:

There is a chance of our going to war; but I don't think it is very much of a chance. Wilson and Bryan are cordially supported by all the hyphenated Americans, by the solid flubdub and pacifist vote. Every soft creature, every coward and weakling, every man who can't look more than six inches ahead, every man whose god is money, or pleasure, or ease, and every man who has not got in him both the sterner virtues and the power of seeking after an ideal, is enthusiastically in favor of Wilson; and at present the good citizens, as a whole, are puzzled and don't understand the situation, and so a majority of them also tend to be with him. This is not pardonable; but it is natural. As a nation, we have thought very little about foreign affairs; we don't realize that the murder of the thousand men, women and children on the *Lusitania* is due, solely, to Wilson's abject cowardice and weakness in failing to take energetic action when the *Gulflight* was sunk but a few days previously. He and Bryan are morally responsible for the loss of the lives of those American women and children—and for the lives lost in Mexico, no less than for the lives lost on the high seas. They are both of them abject creatures and they won't go to war unless they are kicked into it, and they will consider nothing whatever but their own personal advantage in the matter. Nevertheless, there is a chance that Germany may behave in such fashion that they will have to go to war. Of course, I will notify you at once if war is declared; but I hope in any event, that it won't be until you and Quentin have had your month in camp. Probably, as you suggest, in the event of war, I would send you out at once to get under Jack Greenway.

As for the libel suit here[1], the rulings of the Judge have been such that he has refused to let the jury take into account all my most important evidence, evidence which, to my mind, showed Barnes' guilt beyond a shadow of doubt. The rulings are quite incomprehensible from the standpoint of common sense. But whether they will appeal to the legalistic mind as proper, I do not know.

I am much interested in what you tell me about the incident that led up to your conversation with good Mr. Branding, and I grinned over the incident. I need not say I accept absolutely your statement—that goes without saying; I think you are very right, under all the circumstances, not to drink anything more.

Ever yours

June 17, 1915. Oyster Bay
To Arthur H. Lee

Dear Arthur:

Your long and most interesting letter of June 2nd has just come; and I am so glad to get it. Yes, I received your other letter. I have written you quite often and have sent you the different public statements I have made. I do not know whether they have reached you or not. I have not written you as fully as I otherwise would, just because I am so sick at heart over affairs in the world at large at this moment and particularly over the course of my own government and my own people. One has to be a philosopher; one has to remember that there come long periods when you agree with the bulk of your fellow countrymen and long periods when you don't and that at times the world as a whole seems to go very wrong and at times very right; and that one's duty is to struggle for the right and not get cast down, and to remember that all things pass, and that through the centuries good and evil have been mixed, sometimes one predominating and sometimes the other. But after all, such type of philosophy is not very much consolation to a man who believes

---

[1]Roosevelt was being sued for libel by New York Republican boss William Barnes.

in right, a man who wants to see his own country do what is right, when, as is the case just at present, the forces of evil have on the whole shown to advantage as compared to the forces of good during the past eleven months, and when the free countries, above all America, have shown qualities that are very ominous for the future when contrasted with the brutal and ruthless efficiency with which Germany is handled.

Now, my dear fellow, I was half amused and half ashamed at the part of your letter where you said that you hoped you had not unwittingly offended me by your comments. There is no man closer to me than you are. I have never had a more devoted friend; and, what is more, my country has never had a more devoted friend in England or in any other country than you have shown yourself to be. You have the right to say to me anything that you desire and, as a matter of fact, you are always so careful in what you say that no human being of the least sense could ever take offense.

There is no use disguising the fact that Germany has shown an extraordinary efficiency during the last eleven months. Her submarine warfare makes it proper to say that this efficiency has been shown at sea no less than on land. The way she has organized her industry is no less remarkable than the way she has organized her fighting force. For fifty years Germany has been trained by an intelligent and despotic upper class with an eye single to efficiency of a purely militaristic kind. In both peace and war, in both industrial and military matters the result is astounding. The only democracy that has shown similar efficiency is little Switzerland. France comes next, although far from equaling Germany. To our shame be it said, we of the English-speaking peoples have acted precisely in the spirit set forth and condemned in Kipling's famous poem about "the flannelled fool at the wicket, the muddied oaf in the goals." England has done this; even Australia and Canada have done this. But America has been infinitely worse than any of the other English-speaking peoples in this matter. The sad and irritating thing is that it is so much a matter of leadership. When I left office in 1909, I greeted the battle fleet on its return from its trip around the world. Our fleet was then second to that of England in fighting efficiency. Our diplomacy was courteous, respectful to others, self-respecting and absolutely firm. Our word as a nation carried great weight. We were working cordially with England for the common good of the British Empire and the United States—and I think I may say without cant for the common good of humanity as a whole. I had brought both Germany and Japan to a sharp account and made them instantly back water when we came into conflict with them, and especially with Germany, on points where I thought they were wrong. But I suppose that even then the flabby peace propaganda was gaining weight. I was not myself at all awake to the need that America should have universal military service. I can hardly blame myself in this matter for no one was awake to it; and hardly any of our people are now awake to it. Very few people backed up Lord Roberts, even in England. The trouble is that England, thanks to the Channel, has believed that she need not do the things that were necessary to the continental powers of Europe; and this country is in this respect worse than England by just about the proportion of the ocean to the Channel. The same reasons that have made England blind and slothful compared to France and Switzerland in the way of preparedness against hideous disaster have made us blind and slothful compared to England.

You have seen my public utterances. I would from the beginning, if I had been President, have taken a stand which would have made the Germans either absolutely alter all their conduct or else put them into war with us. If the United States had taken this stand, in my judgment we would now have been fighting beside you. Most emphatically, if we had done what we ought to have done after the sinking of the *Lusitania*, I and my four boys would now be in an army getting ready to serve with you in Flanders or else to serve against Constantinople. But our people lack imagination; they do not understand the conditions abroad; and above all they have been misled by the screaming and shrieking and bleating of the peace people until really good men and women have gotten so puzzle-headed that they advocate a course of national infamy. I have spoken out as strongly and as clearly as possible; and I do not think it has had any effect beyond making people think that I am a truculent and bloodthirsty person, endeavoring futilely to thwart able, dignified, humane Mr. Wilson in his noble plan to bring peace everywhere by excellently written letters sent to persons who care nothing whatever for any letter that is not backed up by force!

Bryan has now split with Wilson. For a moment I thought that this meant that Wilson had waked up to the national needs, national duty. But when his note came out, I was utterly unable to see that he had changed in the least. He and Bryan apparently agree with cordiality that our policy should be one of milk and water. They only disagree as to the precise quantity of dilution in the mixture; and this does not seem to me to be important enough to warrant a quarrel.

Naturally I sympathize entirely with your views as to your Home Government; and I do not wonder that you feel that you are breathing a cleaner and manlier air now that you are again a soldier and not in politics. Messrs. Asquith and Morley, while able men, impressed me as being "able" only in the sense that Wilson and Taft are able. Five years ago I felt that they were both doctrinaires; that they were both utterly unfit to deal with the Imperial interests; and that their real concern was, in the case of Morley with literary work, setting forth lofty and humane ideals which could not be reduced to practice, and in the case of Asquith in the ordinary party success achieved in the ordinary political way. I did not believe that either of them was fit to care for the future interests of the Empire. I do not think so now. On the other hand, I liked Edward Grey and believed in him thoroughly; and I liked Lloyd George, in spite of all his vagaries. Of course in England, what should have been done was at the outset to put the whole population under conscription on the German plan, to put the whole population at the service of the state. All workingmen should have been made work in the different factories, if they were not sent to the front, on the basis that their work was the work of soldiers. Any man that went into a strike should have been promptly shipped to the front and put in the trenches nearest the German lines. On the other hand, the same thing should have been done to the employers. There has been a good deal of profit-making by certain employers in England as compared to Germany during this war. The employer and capitalist should have been informed that during the war they were as much under the Government as the soldiers, or the workingmen; that they were entitled to live just as the workingmen were entitled to live; but that their whole activities beyond this point were to be employed by the Government and as the Government chose to direct; they were not to make profit for themselves until the nation had won the war.

Of course, this kind of action would have been denounced in your country by every tomfool sentimentalist and fake Liberal. In my own country it would have been denounced even more strongly; there would be even less chance of getting it. But our peoples have got to make up their minds that with the world as it now is either the men who believe in freedom must submit themselves to organization and use their whole power in defense of the state, as in Switzerland the whole power of the people is used; or else that disaster awaits them at the hands of Germany or of Japan or of some other well-organized despotism, whether the despotism be that of a single man, of an oligarchy or of a bureaucracy.

The antics of the peace people here pass belief. President Wilson's delightful statement about the nation being "too proud to fight" seemed to me to reach the nadir of cowardly infamy. But as a whole our people did not especially resent it. Taft, Nicholas Murray Butler, Andrew Carnegie and the rest of the crowd are at the moment engaged in holding a grand Peace Conference to insist that everything shall be arbitrated everywhere. The Californians for the most part cordially join in the cry. They applaud the movement with enthusiasm and say how splendid it is. Then when they pause for breath for a moment they proceed to insult the Japanese and thereby invite future war with that power. It is the literal fact that not a few of these Pacific Slope leaders are delighted to promise to arbitrate everything at the very moment when they would repudiate with utter horror any proposal to arbitrate under any conditions the question whether or not there shall he unlimited Asiatic immigration to these shores. Wilson passes thirty all-inclusive arbitration commission treaties with various nations, in which it is agreed that there shall be a commission to investigate for a year any matter before war is resorted to. Under these treaties the sinking of the *Lusitania,* as Bryan pointed out, would necessitate a year's investigation before war could be thought of. Now, (to their discredit be it said, although their discredit is much less than ours) England, France and Russia have actually entered into these treaties with us. In this respect Germany was more straightforward and declined to enter into them. But she asked that we apply the principle to the case of the *Lusitania.* Fortunately even Wilson's cold and tepid soul revolted at that proposal, whereas nothing could revolt Bryan's ignoble soul—no, as my secretary, by birth a Newfoundlander, with kinsfolk in our army, has just pointed out, Wilson's soul did *not* revolt, but he knew that our people, in spite of all their timidity and ignorance and folly, would not sanction such a proceeding and so he blandly repudiated the policies to which he was solemnly pledged and declined to do as Bryan wished. But his policy of interchanging at considerable intervals notes couched in vigorous English which means nothing will achieve the same result, I am very much afraid. I have tried not to denounce him; but it is extremely hard effectively to attack crime without attacking the criminal. This country has behaved very badly because there has been no popular revolt against what Wilson has done; and it is a very difficult thing to arouse our people to a knowledge of how badly they have done except by pointing out the shortcomings of those who are responsible.

From time to time I shall send you anything I say in public. I put the case as strongly as I can. I speak as often as I think will do good. If I speak too often and too strongly no good comes. I enclose you a copy of a communication I have recently sent to Hudson Maxim, and of a letter I have recently sent to a Pacific Slope Editor. Both explain themselves.

The winning of my libel suit was a big personal victory for me and was a big thing for clean politics. But I really lost interest in it, because my interest was so much greater in the things that were going on abroad. There were a couple of Germans on the jury. When the *Lusitania* business occurred, I made a public statement which you may perhaps have seen; I think I sent it to you. I then went to my lawyers, who of course were almost as much concerned in my success as I was, and told them I was very sorry, for I feared they would disapprove of my making the statement, but that I did not feel there was any alternative, no matter what the effect might be on the case. They are both of them trumps and they answered at once that I was entirely right; that they would not have had me act differently; that though the libel suit was important the interests of the nation and of humanity were more important and that it was my duty to disregard everything but the public interest, and that they were extremely glad I had made the statement I did make.

As I have said before, the efficiency of the Germans is as wonderful as their ruthlessness and brutality; and I only wish I and my boys were beside you in the trenches. I am already planning to raise a division of mounted riflemen such as our old regiment. (It will fight in the trenches or anywhere else.) I have the brigade commanders and regimental commanders picked; but I do not believe Wilson can be kicked into war.

Archie and Quentin are going to the summer camp of instruction which General Wood has started at Plattsburg. I am very sorry that your force was deflected to the Dardanelles, for it seems to me you have need of all the men you can get in Flanders. The Russians have come a fearful cropper. I am glad that the Italians have shown more manliness than we have shown and have gone into the war. Of course, I cannot help feeling that there must be more strain on Germany and Austria than we believe; but I am not prophesying, and, thank the Lord, I have not been prophesying about this war.

I thoroughly agree with you about the submarine menace. It has been the one thing that has caused me real alarm. It is because of my feeling about the submarines that I have felt that England should have had universal military service and that by now she should have had on the Continent of Europe an army as large as that of France, so that the growth of the submarine fleet of Germany would have been too late. Curiously enough, I had myself worked out just the conclusion to which you have come as to what the United States could do. I felt that if war came what we ought to do was to send over all our light craft and destroyers to keep the submarines as much as possible in check around England, to hasten the output of ammunition to the allies, to get thirty or forty thousand men as soon as possible in Flanders or at Constantinople, as you desired, and to keep these thirty or forty thousand men up to their full fighting strength; and meanwhile to put half a million men or perhaps a million into training, and prepare equipment for them. However, with Wilson nothing whatever can be done. He is now sending an occasional ultimatum, or penultimatum or antepenultimatum to Mexico. He is not sending one to the Kaiser and he is not preparing one single soldier to make any of his ultimatums of the slightest possible consequence. He sends a few marines to Mexico!

As for the breaking of my ribs, I am practically over the effects of the accident. Of course, they were a little painful for two or three weeks. The simple fact is that I tried to ride a horse that was too good for me. I might just as well admit that I am old and stiff; and while I can sit on a horse fairly well, I cannot mount him if he misbehaves. This horse threw me before I got my right foot into the stirrup, and I struck the ground a good deal as if I had been a walrus, and broke a couple of ribs in consequence.

Mrs. Roosevelt had a rather serious operation at the hospital but it was absolutely necessary and now she is better than she has been for a long time. Ethel is only fairly well but is really enjoying life; and she and Dick and the baby make a very dear household. They are all coming out the end of next week to us. Ted and Eleanor and the two babies have just left here. Kermit and Belle are having a lovely time in South America.

May all good come to you and yours, my dear Arthur, and every success attend your country in its great struggle for its own life and for the best interests of mankind!

Faithfully your friend

July 6, 1915. Oyster Bay
To John Pierpont Morgan, Jr.
My dear Mr. Morgan:

I saw Springy yesterday. He told me all about the attempted murder,[1] about the heroism of Mrs. Morgan, and the instant decision and efficiency of your action, action to which you undoubtedly owed your life.

Well, at a period when the pacificist, the flubdub and the mollycoddle seem to engross the popular approval, it is very comforting to know that there is now and then an American left who has not lost the virile virtues. I congratulate you with all my heart; and I beg to present my warmest regards to Mrs. Morgan.

Sincerely yours

July 10, 1915. Oyster Bay
To William R. Thayer
Dear Billy:

You are welcome to use my simile of the currant jelly and the accompanying remark that the Colombians were like Calabrian bandits.

Now, as for what you say as to the "superior people" assumption. My answer must be that each case must be judged on its merits, for the excellent reason that there is not any international tribunal to which we

---

[1]Morgan was the object of an assassination attempt by an apparently unbalanced German sympathizer.

can apply for judgment as to whether a given nation is or is not a public nuisance. Within our own boundaries we can apply to the courts, if a man murders his wife or gets drunk and shoots up a neighborhood or merely sits down and blocks a highway. But in international matters we can do nothing of the kind. If we fail to act on the "superior people" theory *when we ought to* barbarism and savagery and squalid obstruction will prevail over most of the globe. If we act on it improperly, *when we ought not to* frightful injustice will be done as regards the rest of the globe. England took the Sudan. At that time I knew a Frenchman, the Marquis de Morès, whose admiration for the Mahdi was such that he started across the Sahara to join him and fight the English. Unfortunately the Tuaregs, not being able to appreciate the fine frenzy of his altruism, killed him before he got anywhere near the Mahdi. A Tolstoyite New Yorker, a son of a clergyman, named Ernest Crosby, used to write little sonnets on behalf of the Sudan as against England. These sonnets were admirable examples of pacificist logic. The Sudanese insisted upon keeping their liberty in order that they might kill all outsiders and two thirds of their own number; and they depopulated the Sudan with torture and murder; and this pacificist gentleman sincerely felt that he was serving the cause of peace when he protested against putting a stop to such iniquity. At the present day there are plenty of Germans who say that it is hypocritical for the English, after having taken the Sudan, to object to what they did in Belgium. Now, what I did in Panama was substantially what the British had done in the Sudan and certainly was on a par with what they did in Egypt, both of which feats were very useful to mankind. In the same way the Germans were right to expel the slave-raiding Arabs of East Africa and the French right to take Algiers, and the Russians to take Turkistan. Frankly, I do not think that any of these cases, and least of all Panama, has anything in common with the German attitude towards Belgium. Before there was law in California and Montana, and indeed as a requisite for bringing the law there, the Vigilantes had to be organized and had to hang people. Technically this was murder; practically, it was the removal of murderers. It seems to me both absurd and immoral not to acknowledge the righteousness of such actions as those in Egypt, the Sudan, Panama, Algiers & Turkistan; and immoral not to protest against such action as the German action towards Belgium.

Now, as to your other two questions. You cannot quote me on either. In 1902 Balfour and the Conservatives were still laboriously endeavoring to placate Germany and act with her, under the impression that this was the proper international attitude for England to take, because at the time England still regarded Russia as her great foe and France as an ally of Russia. British diplomacy has been a pretty foolish thing for the last fifteen years. As you say, Venezuela was merely an incident in a course of conduct which among other things resulted in Germany's securing Helgoland.

In the Holleben business, I did not warn England for two reasons: 1. England was *not* formidable. I had not the least fear of England and knew that there was no danger from England; Germany *was* formidable. I also knew that English public opinion was already very hostile to the action of the English Government and that Germany alone offered the problem with which I had to deal. If you write about this business you had better let me go over it after you have written it so as to be sure that you get it perfectly straight. Then, it may be that I can have you quote me.

Faithfully yours

August 28, 1915. Oyster Bay
To Kermit Roosevelt

Dearest Kermit:

The enclosed letter from old Heller explains itself. I thought you would enjoy reading it. I am glad the leisurely Bwano got the spectacled bear.

Quentin is home from the camp, having received [a] very good certificate from the regular officer over him, Captain Van Horn. In these certificates the regular officers are required to state exactly their opinion as it would be if they were to have the man about whom they write under them in a volunteer regiment. Quentin's certificate read that he had done good work and that with more age and experience he would make an excellent Second Lieutenant. Archie did really very well indeed. He was given a Battalion Second Lieutenancy at the close of the Students' Camp and stayed a fortnight longer with the Businessmen. Rather to my delight he was put over Ted! One Sunday the two regular officers over them, together with Archie and Ted, went to Montreal to look at some of the military preparations there. Archie with glee mentioned to me the fact that at the Club the two regular officers were both always addressed as "Major," he (Archie) as "Captain," and Ted as "Mr. Roosevelt." I shall tactfully and sympathetically question Ted about the matter day after tomorrow when I see him in camp. Archie's recommendation read in the highest terms, stating that he was fit to be Captain in a volunteer regiment now; and if this infernal skunk in the White House can be kicked into war a Captain Archie shall be. Ted has already been promoted to be a Sergeant. When he comes back a supplementary camp is to be held, to which Mac will go, so that I shall have had three sons and a private secretary in the camps. The camps have been very successful. They are starting others in various parts of the country. But of course they represent nothing whatever but makeshifts.

We ought to have universal military service. I enclose you a copy of the address I shall make at the camp and also a statement I have just given to the paper about the sinking of the *Arabic*.

I agree with all that you say about the German brutality and ruthlessness. But after all a brute is not any worse than a coward. Wilson is at heart an abject coward; or else he has a heart so cold and selfish that he is entirely willing to sacrifice the honor and the interest of the country to his own political advancement. Think of President Eliot and Lawrence Lowell and Cleve Dodge and men like that supporting Wilson! Well, I am making as stout a fight as I know how; but the old proverb applies: there are no bad regiments but there are plenty of bad colonels. The United States would stand like a unit if we had in the Presidency a man of the stamp of Andrew Jackson. Think of Old Hickory letting our citizens be constantly murdered on the high seas by the Germans and in Mexico by the Greasers! But men are easily puzzled; and it is easy to mislead them, if one chooses to give them high-sounding names to excuse ignoble deeds. This is the evil service that President Wilson has rendered and is now rendering the American nation. Still, the Germans may kick us into war. He has acted in Mexico in simply ludicrous fashion. In order to seem to do something and yet to do nothing he got a number of the South American powers into consultation and of course what they have told him is that America ought not to intervene at all. Naturally if we have not the manhood ourselves to intervene, we cannot expect Bolivia and Guatemala to lead us along the path of manful duty.

Give my darling Belle many kisses for me. Ethel and her baby have gone off to visit Dorothy Straight. Willard Straight, by the way, is in camp and has been made a Lieutenant. The two Bob Bacons, father and son, are also in camp. Mother and I have had some lovely rows recently.

Your loving father

October 4, 1915. Oyster Bay
To James Brander Matthews

Dear Brander,

Can you give me the name of the editor of Harper's Monthly who passes on contributions? I have written an article on "Prehistoric Man; and the Horse, the Lion and the Elephant" (yes, it *does* remind one of the "Parrot who talked in his Sleep"). It is too long—16,000 words—and I can't compress it, and am doubtful about dividing it; Fair Osborn is the only human being to whom it might appeal, and to him only that he might pull it in pieces; even the long suffering Scribners does'n't want it. But it is possible the Harper's editor may not be quite sober, or something, and may take it; and as I am not conscientious I wish to give him the chance.[1]

Love to Mrs. Brander and all the descendants. I must see you soon. Ever yours

October 15, 1915. Oyster Bay
To Ethel E. V. Dreier

My dear Mrs. Dreier:

It gives me great pleasure to send through you this letter on behalf of the Suffrage amendment in New York State; and of course what I write applies no less to Massachusetts and New Jersey and to all the other states which vote this year on the proposition to give women the right to vote.

There has always been to me an element of great absurdity in the arguments advanced against Woman Suffrage when we consider the fact that from time immemorial in monarchies women have been deemed fit to hold the very highest place of governmental power, that is, the position of sovereign. For example, this continent was discovered by Columbus under the patronage of King Ferdinand and Queen Isabella of Spain; and he owed more to the Queen than to the King. The oldest state in the Union, Virginia, derives its name from the fact that the first effort at colonization from England on our shores was in the reign of Queen Elizabeth; and during the last four centuries Queen Elizabeth was certainly the greatest sovereign who sat on the English throne. When Frederick the Great was King of Prussia the only two European sovereigns who in any shape or way compared with him were two women—Catherine of Russia and Maria Theresa of Austria.

I have thus mentioned four queens who were great sovereigns, four queens who would by all capable historians be given leading places among the sovereigns of their times. If a woman is deemed fit to be the head of a mighty monarchy, surely no adequate reason can be advanced against allowing her to exercise the rights of sovereignty in a democracy, that is, to be one of the free citizens who vote so as to decide how their own intimate concerns shall be managed.

The opponents of woman suffrage say that this will take women away from the home. If this were so, I should certainly not favor it, just as if giving man the suffrage took him away from his business, I should not favor it; for making and keeping the home must always be the chief work for both man and woman. There is, however, in my opinion, nothing

---

[1]*Harper's* declined, but *National Geographic* published it.

whatever in this objection. Undoubtedly some foolish women may believe that getting the vote will excuse them from the performance of home
duties just as in every democratic extension of the suffrage some foolish
men have believed that getting the vote somehow entitled them to live
without working. But it is no more possible to base action on an argument
of this kind in one case than in the other. There are of course exceptional
women who will do work outside of the home just as there are exceptional men who do work outside of their business—and by business I
mean not only what is commonly called business but any of the professions and handicrafts, so that I am speaking of businessman, professional
man, farmer, skilled mechanic, clerk, laborer. The average man has to
work hard at his business or profession or trade or occupation and does
not do much work outside of this. In just the same way the average
woman will find that her time is largely occupied in dealing with her
household duties; but this is no more an argument against giving suffrage
to the one than to the other. Moreover, where the woman does have the
ability to work outside the home, it no more means that she will neglect
the home than the fact that the man is an artist or a poet or a musician
means that he will neglect the home. The other day I was pleased, as I am
sure many of us were, to see the charming photograph of Madame
Homer and all her children in some of the Sunday papers. It is evident in
her case that to be mistress of her profession has not interfered with her
being a fine type of mother and mistress of her own house.

I emphatically do not believe that between men and women there
ever can be identity of function but this has nothing to do with giving
them equality of right. This they are entitled to and this they ought to
have.

Faithfully yours

November 30, 1915. Oyster Bay
To James E. West

Private

My dear Mr. West:

I have received your letter of November 29th. It is not possible for me
to make a speech on such short notice. In addition to this, until I have one
or two things made clearer to my mind, I would not be willing to make
the speech anyhow. I have been in communication with General Wood
over the matter of the Boy Scouts. It is my understanding that as part of
the wicked and degrading pacificist agitation of the last few years certain
leaders therein, including Messrs. Carnegie, Jordan and others, have used
the Boy Scouts organization as a medium for the dissemination of
pacificist literature and have done everything they could to use the

organization as a propaganda for interfering with the training of our boys to a standard of military efficiency. Now, I believe that the professional pacificists by their activities during the last half-dozen years have done more damage to this country and to humanity than all the political and business crooks combined. The effort to prevent the boys of this country, of the kind who naturally should be gathered into the Boy Scouts, from being trained to arms so that they could serve the country in time of need, and the effort to prevent their acquiring the spirit of self-respect which will make them eager and ready to fight for the right both as individuals and as members of the nation—these efforts from my point of view represent treason to the country and treason to the cause of humanity. A Boy Scout who is not trained actively and affirmatively that it is his duty to bear arms for the country in time of need is at least negatively trained to be a sissy; and there cannot be anything worse for this country than to have an organization of boys brought up to accept the mushy milk and water which is the stock in trade of the apostles of pacificism. The Boy Scouts of England and Belgium have shown themselves real patriots in the present war. I am heartily in favor of an organization of boys which shall teach them as these boys, for example, in England have been taught, that is: that shall teach them the duties of gentleness and chivalry toward the weak, of good citizenship in internal affairs, and, as no less important, the duty of fitting themselves in mind and body so that they shall regard cowardice as the unpardonable sin and physical and moral flabbiness as disgraceful and shall be eager and willing to bear their part in any war that this country feels it necessary to engage in.

Sincerely yours

February 8, 1916. New York
To Hugo Münsterberg

Private not for publication

My dear Professor Münsterberg:

That is such a kind and friendly letter of yours that I wish I had time to answer it more at length.

Yes, I understand entirely how absolutely sincere men may be on exactly opposite sides of every question. Furthermore, I understand entirely, what, my dear Professor, you do not set forth, and that is that thoroughly good men may be thoroughly wrong at some vital moment of history.

I am half a Southerner. I am very proud of my Southern blood. My mother was an unreconstructed rebel to the day of her death. Both of her brothers, my two uncles, fought in the Confederate service. They were as valiant and high-minded men as I ever met. I do not think that there ever

PART SIX

existed men and women who were more sincere and more self-sacrificing, more devoted to duty, as they saw it, than the Confederates. Yet, I believe with all my heart that their victory would not only have spelled death to this nation, but the direst calamity to mankind.

I assure you I hold no brief for England, nor yet for France. I hope you saw the letter I wrote when I was asked to join the Anglo-American Alliance. Privately, it is not improper for me to tell you that, while I was President, I had to take with England, over the Alaska boundary, much the same kind of drastic action that I had to take with Germany over the question of her acquiring territory (nominally temporarily, but really permanently) that would control the approach to the Panama Canal. In each case I did everything possible to save the other nation's face and in each case I only insisted upon the other nation doing what I would have been entirely willing to do under reversed circumstances. You, of course, know that the voyage of the battle fleet around the world was really an answer to the very ugly war talk that had begun to spring up in Japan; and it was the best example that I know of, "of speaking softly and carrying a big stick."

Now, as for what you say about the Americans of German descent. With most of what you say I entirely agree. I do not for a moment believe that the Americanism of today should be a mere submission to the American ideals of the period of the Declaration of Independence. Such action would be not only to stand still, but to go back. American democracy, of course, must mean an opportunity for everyone to contribute his own ideas to the working out of the future. But I will go further than you have done. I have actively fought in favor of grafting on our social life, no less than on our industrial life, many of the German ideals. For instance, I like the German type of club much more than I like the American type of club. In the German clubs in this country women were admitted long before that was the case in American clubs. Of course, I suppose I shall never again be received in the Milwaukee clubs; but of all the clubs I have ever been in, that Milwaukee German Club is the one where I really enjoyed myself most! It has often puzzled me to find out why it has been impossible to spread these clubs and have them the recognized type of American club, just as much as of German-American club. I think that one explanation lies in the fact that they have been unconsciously used to keep their members away from American life. If with entire frankness, those handling them had treated them as American clubs, to develop every kind of ideal that was found good, including those that they had brought over from Germany, I think most of the difficulty would have been averted and that they would have spread everywhere. This is only an example; I am certain I have tried to graft German ideals and habits a dozen times, for every single English ideal or habit, on American life. One word about preparedness! The Illinois *Staats-Zeitung* is an example. It is fighting preparedness tooth and nail. It is backing up David Starr Jordan and people like him; and I think this pretty bad. Many of the Milwaukee German-Americans have been advocating the same pacifist position for America, at the same time that they defend German militarism.

    With real thanks for your letter,

    Faithfully yours

[June 10, 1916]. Oyster Bay
To the Progressive National Convention

(Telegram)

To the Progressive Convention:

    I am very grateful for the honor you confer upon me by nominating me as President. I cannot accept it at this time. I do not know the attitude of the candidate of the Republican Party toward the vital questions of the day. Therefore, if you desire an immediate decision, I must decline the nomination. But if you prefer it, I suggest that my conditional refusal to run be placed in the hands of the Progressive National Committee.

    If Mr. Hughes's[1] statements, when he makes them, shall satisfy the committee that it is for the interest of the country that he be elected, they can act accordingly and treat my refusal as definitely accepted. If they are not satisfied they can so notify the Progressive Party, and at the same time then can confer with me and then determine on whatever action we may severally deem appropriate to meet the needs of the country.

June 16, 1916. New York
To William R. Thayer

Dear Billy:

    I agree entirely with you. I shall do all I can for Mr. Hughes. But don't forget that Mr. Hughes alone can make it possible for me to be efficient in his behalf. If he merely speaks like Mr. Wilson, only a little more weakly, he will rob my support of its effectiveness. Speeches such as those of mine to which you kindly allude, have their merit only if delivered for a man who is himself speaking uncompromisingly and without equivocation. I have just sent word to Hughes through one of our big New York financiers to make a smashing attack on Wilson for his actions, and to do it immediately, in connection with this Democratic Nominating Convention.

---

[1]Charles Evans Hughes.

Wilson was afraid of me. He never dared answer me; but if Hughes lets him, he will proceed to take the offensive against Hughes.

I shall do everything I can for him, but don't forget that the efficiency of what I do must largely depend upon Hughes.

Always yours

P.S. Please return editorial when you are through with it.

[Handwritten] I have from Callizon permission to use the Buenz matter; and of course the Dewy letter. You can use both.

July 3, 1916. Oyster Bay
To Henry Cabot Lodge

Dear Cabot:

I am very much obliged to you for the letter. It was just about what I supposed, but as Wood had backed up Belmont I hardly felt at liberty to refuse to make the inquiry.

I was very much pleased with my talk with Hughes, and with both his letters. I believe as you do that he will make a straight-out fight for preparedness and national defense. He told me he personally believed in universal service, but was doubtful as to the expediency of coming out for it at this time.

Of course, I am simply unable to understand how the American people can tolerate Wilson; but then in retrospect I am simply unable to understand how they could have tolerated Jefferson and Madison in the beginning of the Nineteenth Century. Andrew Jackson had his faults, but at least he was a fighting man, and had some idea of the proper correspondence between words and deeds. This creature is not of the Jackson, but the Jefferson and Buchanan type.

Sending the National Guard down to the border, and leaving their wives and children helpless is one of the most wicked things that has ever been done.

Always yours

July 9, 1916. Oyster Bay
To Frank R. McCoy

Dear Mac,

It was good to hear from you; and those enclosures were interesting and instructive.

Whether our people, or rather our Administration, can be kicked into war with Mexico I do not know; but it is difficult to see how it can be avoided. The difficulty I shall have with my division will be persuading men of the right type that they will not be put in a ridiculous position if they enlist; for all fighting men despise the present Adminis-

tration so, and distrust it so deeply, that they believe it is equally powerless to do well in keeping peace or making war. But I shall get them;
and I explain to all that we are simply facing the usual conditions in
American history; for at least three times out of war [four?] the people
and its civil leaders behave so badly in war, and above all in preparing
for war, that a few men must individually make good, at their own risk,
the shortcomings of the majority.

The one man for whom I shall ask ahead of all others is yourself, as
Divisional Chief of Staff. Harry Stimson will be associated with you as
Divisional Quartermaster General. You and he will be my right and left
bowers. My son-in-law Dick Derby is handling the medical end; I have
asked Surgeon-Major Page to come in as head.

I have informed the War Department that I should like to be em-
powered to raise either a cavalry division, or (which would be preferable
if we seriously go to war and attack Mexico City via Vera Cruz) a division of infantry, with one or two of the three brigades mounted infantry,
and a divisional brigade instead of a divisional regiment of cavalry—this
would really mean three brigades of cavalry, for my mounted infantry
would be the same thing, and yet we would not be held up if there were
a shortage of horses for the entire division. Instead of a brigade of artillery, I should ask for a regiment, and in addition a regiment of motor
cycle machine gun men. I should ask to assemble at Fort Sill, Oklahoma.
I should ask for Henry T. Allen as my Senior Brigade commander; Rear
Admiral Cameron Winslow would be another; Howze and Harbord two
others. Fitz Lee, Lincoln Andrews, Phil Sheridan, Hugh Wise, Collins,
Roscoe, White, Parker would be among the others for whom I should
ask—also Chaffee, Wainwright, Christian, Conger, &c. Dan Moore
would take the artillery; Smedberg the machine guns. I should endeavor
to get some of our American aviators back from France for our aero-
squadron.

If they'll give me a show, such an outfit will do something!

Always yours

You can show this letter to any of the above-named men whom you
meet.

August 21, 1916. Oyster Bay
To William R. Thayer

My dear Mr. Thayer,

There is now no reason why I should not speak of the facts connected with the disagreement between the United States and Germany
over the Venezuela matter, in the early part of my administration as
President, and of the final amicable settlement of the disagreement.

At that time Venezuelan Dictator-President Castro had committed various offences against different European nations, including Germany and England. The English Government was then endeavoring to keep on good terms with Germany, and on this occasion acted jointly with her. Germany sent a squadron of war vessels to the Venezuelan. coast, and they were accompanied by some English war vessels. I had no objection whatever to Castro's being punished, as long as the punishment did not take the form of seizure of territory and its more or less permanent occupation by some old-world power. At this particular point such seizure of territory would have been a direct menace to the United States because it would have threatened or partially controlled the approach to the projected Isthmian Canal.

I speedily became convinced that Germany was the leader, and the really formidable party, in the transaction; and that England was merely following Germany's lead in rather half hearted fashion. I became convinced that England would not back Germany in the event of a clash over the matter between Germany and the United States, but would remain neutral; I did not desire that she should do more than remain neutral. I also became convinced that Germany intended to seize some Venezuela harbor and turn it into a strongly fortified place of arms, on the model of Kiauchau, with a view to exercising some measure of control over the future Isthmian Canal, and over South American affairs generally.

For some time the usual methods of diplomatic intercourse were tried. Germany declined to agree to arbitrate the question at issue between her and Venezuela, and declined to say that she would not take possession of Venezuelan territory, merely saying that such possession would be "temporary"—which might mean anything. I finally decided that no useful purpose would be served by further delay, and I took action accordingly. I assembled our battle fleet, under Admiral Dewey, near Porto Rico, for "maneuvers," with instructions that the fleet should be kept in hand and in fighting trim and should be ready to sail at an hour's notice. The fact that the fleet was in West Indian waters was of course generally known; but I believe that the Secretary of the Navy, and Admiral Dewey, and perhaps his chief of staff, and the Secretary of State, John Hay, were the only persons who knew about the order for the fleet to be ready to sail at an hour's notice. I told John Hay that I would now see the German Ambassador, Herr von Holleben, myself and that I intended to bring matters to an early conclusion. Our navy was in very efficient condition, being superior to the German navy.

I saw the Ambassador, and explained that in view of the presence of the German Squadron on the Venezuelan coast I could not permit longer delay in answering my request for an arbitration, and that I could not acquiesce in any seizure of Venezuelan territory. The Ambassador responded that his Government could not agree to arbitrate, and that there was no intention to take "permanent" possession of Venezuelan territory. I answered that Kiauchau was not a "permanent" possession of Germany's—that I understood that it was merely held by a ninety nine years lease; and that I did not intend to have another Kiauchau, held by similar tenure, on the approach to the Isthmian Canal. The Ambassador repeated that his Government would not agree to arbitrate. I then asked him to inform his government that if no notification for arbitration came during the next ten days I would be obliged to order Dewey to take his fleet to the Venezuelan coast and see that the German forces did not take possession of any territory. He expressed very grave concern, and asked me if I realized the serious consequences that would follow such action; consequences so serious to both countries that he dreaded to give them a name. I answered that I had thoroughly counted the cost before I decided on the step, and asked him to look at the map, as a glance would show him that there was no spot in the world where Germany in the event of conflict with the United States would be at a greater disadvantage than in the Caribbean sea.

A week later the Ambassador came to see me, talked pleasantly on several subjects, and rose to go. I asked him if he had any answer to make from his Government to my request, and when he said no, I informed him that in such event it was useless to wait as long as I had intended, and that Dewey would be ordered to sail twenty four hours in advance of the time I had set. He expressed deep apprehension, and said that his Government would not arbitrate. However, less than twenty four hours before the time I had appointed for cabling the order to Dewey, the Ambassador notified me that His Imperial Majesty the German Emperor had directed him to request me to undertake the arbitration myself. I felt, and publicly expressed, great gratification at this outcome, and great appreciation of the course the German Government had finally agreed to take. Later I secured the consent of the German Government to have the arbitration undertaken by the Hague Tribunal, and not by me.

At that time there was in New York as German Consul-General a very able and agreeable man, Dr. Buenz, a native of Holstein. He was intimate with a friend and then neighbor of mine, Mr. A. W. Callisen—whose father was born in Schleswig, and who, incidentally, was and is exactly as straight an American as I am. Mr. Callisen introduced Dr. Buenz to me; and I found the Doctor an exceptionally well informed man about American matters and indeed about world affairs generally. He was at my house on several occasions, and I discussed many things with him, in-

cluding the German and American navies. I had, however, no idea that
he had any knowledge whatever of the Venezuelan affair until after your
book appeared. Mr. Callisen happened to read it, was much interested in
the part referring to Venezuela, and wrote to a friend of his, Mr. Ambrose
C. Richardson, of Buffalo, a letter running in part as follows:—

"'A Chapter of Diplomacy' interested me greatly, all the more as I
knew Dr. Holleben personally, and what is still more to the purpose his
most intimate friend, Dr. Buenz, at that time German Consul-General
at New York. The story is absolutely true, and here is the sequel.

The German and British Governments firmly counted on our well-
established jellyfish squashiness and felt sure they had a free hand. The
Kaiser and Junker party especially had everything cut and dried, and
counted the affair as accomplished. The first time, Holleben informed
his government that probably Roosevelt's attitude was a bluff; but on
second thought went to his friend Buenz for advice as B. knew the
American people better than any German living, and was a close friend
of Roosevelt's (I introduced him) and hence a good judge of the situation. Buenz at once assured him that Roosevelt was not bluffing, and
that he could count on his doing as threatened; and that in a conversation Roosevelt had shown that he had an intimate knowledge of the
strength and condition of the German fleet which was . . . . (then) no
match for ours.

Holleben was obliged to eat his own words and telegraph in hot
haste to Berlin, where his message fell like a bomb shell. You know the
rest. This resulted in Holleben's being recalled and dismissed from the
diplomatic service . . . . . . When he sailed from Hoboken not a single
member of the diplomatic corps or German official dared to see him off.
Only Buenz (and I) dared to brave official disapproval, and went on
board to bid him farewell. I went at Buenz's request. I have this story
first in hand."

A copy of this letter came into my possession and I showed it to Mr.
Callisen when he was here, at my house, on May 7th last. He wrote
alongside the part I have quoted:—"The above is absolutely accurate.
(signed) A. W. Callisen." Mr. Callisen informed me that he had not intended the letter for publication, but that as the copy had been shown
to several people I was at liberty to make whatever use of it I desired.

After your book appeared some person wrote a letter to the press
stating that at the time of the Venezuela incident the American fleet
was not mobilized under Admiral Dewey in the West Indies. The letter
was sent to Mr. Henry A. Wise Wood, of the National Security League,
who thereupon wrote to Admiral Dewey for information on the subject. Admiral Dewey answered him as follows:

"Office of
The Admiral of the Navy
Washington

May 23d 1916

Mr. Henry A. Wise Wood
25 Madison Avenue
New York City
My dear Mr. Wood,

I beg to acknowledge the receipt of your letter of May 22d, asking me to set you right respecting certain facts regarding Colonel Roosevelt's action over Venezuela.

I was at Culebra, Puerto Rico, at the time in command of a fleet consisting of over fifty ships, including every battle ship and every torpedo boat that we had, with orders from Washington to hold the fleet in hand and be ready to move at a moment's notice. Fortunately however the whole matter was amicably adjusted and there was no need for action.

Hoping the above statement is exactly what you want, and thanking you for the compliments you pay me, I am

very truly yours
George Dewey."

This letter was published in the press; and Mr. Wood then sent me copies of the correspondence. Your biography of Hay is a really great piece of historical writing; and I am glad to be of any service in connection with it.

Sincerely yours

November 10, 1916. Oyster Bay
To Arthur H. Lee

Dear Arthur:

I have carefully considered your letter (no letter from Grey has come). My dear fellow, I hate not to do anything you ask. But my judgment is most strongly and unqualifiedly that it would be a grave error for me to do so in this case. I have consulted Whitridge and Bacon, both of whom at this moment are more interested in the success of the Allies than in any internal American questions, and they agree with me—Whitridge feeling at least as strongly as I do in the matter. Wilson has probably been elected, and if Hughes were elected it would only slightly alter the case so far as this particular proposal is concerned. For a number of months to come the American public would positively resent any conduct on my part which could be construed as indicating my presuming to give advice about, or an expression of, American opinion. Wilson would certainly endeavor to do exactly the opposite to what he thought I had indicated; even Hughes if elected would resent any seeming desire of the British and French to consult me; and my coming over would give every greedy sensation-monger in the Yellow press and even in the pale saffron press, the cue to advertize the fact, with statements and inferences grotesquely false but very mischievous. Moreover, those whom I spoke to on your side of the water could not but feel that my words carried weight, and to this extent I cannot be guilty of deception towards them, for my words carry no weight and it would be unwise to pay any heed to what I said as representing the American people. At the moment I am as completely out of sympathy with the American people as I would have been out of sympathy with the English people in 1910 or the French people in 1904. The Wilson "policies" are those of the Democrats, who have just polled a bare plurality of the popular vote. Mr. Wilson would like to antagonize every proposition I make. The Republicans by an overwhelming majority nominated Hughes precisely because he did *not* represent my views; they thought it wise to dodge the issues I thought it vital to raise. No other man of national importance (for Root really exerted not the slightest weight in the campaign and only spoke once to a half-empty hall) took the stand I took—which I took in every speech. I was the only man who raised my voice about Wilson's iniquity in suffering the German submarines to do as they did on our coast.

If I went abroad I could give you no advice of even the slightest worth. I would diminish my already almost imperceptible influence here at home. I would expose myself to bitter mortifications—no matter how much one condemns one's own country, one cannot stand condemnation of it by promiscuous outsiders (*you* may say *anything* and I will say ditto to it!). I would like to visit the Front at the head of an American Division of 12 Regiments like my Rough Riders—but not otherwise.

Always yours

P.S. The amiable Bryce steadily exerts what influence he has here on behalf of the Pacifist crowd, who are really the tepid enemies of the Allies.

January 10, 1917. Oyster Bay
To Stanwood Menken

My dear Mr. Menken:

As it is unfortunately impossible for me to be present in person, I desire in this letter to express my heartiest good wishes for the success of your meeting and my belief that the movement, in which you are engaged, is one of the really vital movements—indeed at the moment it is I think the really vital movement—for the ultimate honor and welfare of this country.

We need, more than anything else in this country, thoroughgoing Americanism,—for unless we are Americans and nothing else, we are not a nation at all—and thoroughgoing preparedness in time of peace against war,—for if we are not thus prepared, we shall remain a nation only until some more virile nation finds it worth while to conquer us.

The work of preparedness—spiritual and material, civic, industrial, and military—and the work of Americanization are simply the two paramount phases or elements of the work of constructive patriotism which your Congress has gathered to foster. There can be no real preparedness in this country unless this country is thoroughly Americanized; for only a patriotic people will prepare; and there can be no deep national feeling for America, until we are all of us Americans through and through.

Americanism means many things. It means equality of rights and therefore equality of duty and of obligation. It means service to our common country. It means loyalty to one flag, to our flag, the flag of all of us. It means on the part of each of us respect for the rights of the rest of us. It means that all of us guarantee the rights of each of us. It means free education, genuinely representative government, freedom of speech and thought, equality before the law for all men, genuine political and religious freedom, and the democratizing of industry so as to give at least a measurable quality of opportunity for all, and so as to place before us, as our ideal in all industries where this ideal is possible of attainment, the system of co-operative ownership and management, in order that the tool users may, so far as possible, become the tool owners. Everything is un-American that tends either to government by a plutocracy, or government by a mob. To divide along the lines of section or caste or creed is un-American. All privilege based on wealth, and all enmity to honest men merely because they are wealthy, are un-American—both of them equally so. Americanism means the virtues of courage, honor, justice, truth, sincerity, and hardihood—the virtues that made America. The things that will destroy America are prosperity-at-any-price, peace-at-any-price, safety-first instead of duty-first, the love of soft living, and the get-rich-quick theory of life.

Preparedness must be of the soul no less than of the body. We must keep lofty ideals steadily before us, and must train ourselves in practical fashion so that we may realize these ideals. Throughout our whole land we must have fundamental common purposes, to be achieved through education, through intelligent organization, and through the recognition of the great vital standards of life and living. We must make Americanism and Americanization mean the same thing to the native born and to the foreign born; to the men and to the women; to the rich and to the poor; to the employer and to the wage-worker. If we believe in American standards, we shall insist that all privileges springing from them be extended to immigrants, and that they in return accept these standards with wholehearted and entire loyalty. Either we must stand absolutely by our ideals and conceptions of duty, or else we are against them. There is no middle course, and if we attempt to find one, we insure for ourselves defeat and disaster.

Citizenship must mean an undivided loyalty to America; there can be no citizenship on the 50–50 basis; there can be no loyalty half to America and half to Germany, or England, or France, or Ireland, or any other country. Our citizens must be Americans, and nothing else, and if they try to be something else in addition, then they should be sent out of this country and back to the other country to which, in their hearts, they pay allegiance. We must have one American language; the language of the Declaration of Independence and the Constitution, of Lincoln's Gettysburg speech and Second Inaugural, and of Washington's farewell address. The American standard of living conditions, and the American standard of working conditions, both must be high. We must insist upon them for immigrants, as well as for the native born. We must insist that the people who work here, live here; that they are not mere birds of passage from abroad. We must insist upon industrial justice, and we cannot get it if we let ignorance and need be preyed upon either by vulpine cunning or by wolfish brutality, and if we do not train the ignorant and the needy up to self-reliance and efficiency.

Preparedness does not mean merely a man with a gun. It means that too; but it means a great deal more. It means that in this country we must secure conditions which will make the farmer and the workingman understand that it is in a special sense their country; that the work of preparedness is entered into for the defense of the country which belongs to them, to all of us, and the government of which is administered in their interest, in the interest of all of us. At this moment, Lloyd George is able to do more than any other man in rallying the people of Great Britain to the defense of that Empire, because the workingmen, the men who actually do the manual labor, know that he has their welfare at heart, that the national ideal for which he is fighting is that which will give them the best chance for self-developing, and for that happiness which comes to the man who achieves his rights at the same time that he performs his duties. He is followed by the people as a whole because they know that he stands for the people as a whole. We in America who are striving for preparedness must make it evident that the preparedness is to serve the people as a whole. The war on the other side has shown that there can be no efficient army in the field unless the men behind are trained and efficient, and unless they are wholeheartedly loyal in their patriotic devotion to their country. Here in America we must do justice to the workers, or they will not feel that this is the country to which their devotion is due; and we must exact patriotic devotion to the flag from them, for if they fail to render it they are unfit to live in this country at all. I appeal to all Americans to join in the common effort for the common good. Any man who holds back, and refuses to serve his country with wholehearted devotion, on the ground that enough has not been done for him, will do well to remember that any such holding back, or lukewarmness of patriotism, is itself an admission of inferiority, an admission of personal unfitness for citizenship in a democracy, and ought to deprive him of the rights of citizenship. As for the men of means, from whom we have the right to expect a special quality of leadership, let them remember that as much has been given to them, so much will be expected of them, and that they have no moral right whatsoever to the enjoyment of the ease and the comforts of life beyond that their fellows enjoy, unless they render service beyond what their fellows render.

I advocate military preparedness not for the sake of war, but for the sake of safeguarding this nation against war, so long as that is possible, and of guaranteeing its honor and safety if war should nevertheless come. We hope ultimately the day will come on this earth when wars will cease. But at present the realization of that hope seems as far in the future as the realization of that other hope, that some day in the future all crime shall cease. By wise action, based equally on observed good faith and on thoroughly prepared strength—the precise characteristics which during the last few years we have failed to show—we may hope to limit the probable field of wars; but at present it is as certain as anything can be that every great nation will at some time or other, as generations follow generations, have to face war, and that ours will be no exception to the rule. It is therefore not merely folly, but criminal and unpatriotic folly, to fail to prepare, or to preach the ignoble cult of the professional pacifist, the peace-at-any-price man.

We need first and foremost a thoroughly efficient and large Navy; a navy kept under professional guidance; a navy trained at every point with the sole purpose of making it the most formidable possible instrument of war the moment that war comes; a navy, the mismanagement of which shall be treated as a capital offense against the nation. In the next place, we need a small but highly efficient regular army, of say a quarter million men; an army where provision is made for a certain proportion of the promotions to be by merit, instead of merely seniority; an army of short-term soldiers, better paid than at present; and an army which, like the navy, shall be under the guidance of a general staff. Moreover, every year there should be at one time field maneuvers of from fifty to one hundred thousand men, so that the Army Commander, the Corps Commanders, the Division, Brigade, and Regimental Commanders, who would have to face a foe at the outbreak of war, would all have had experience in performing their duties, under actual field conditions, in time of peace.

The events of the last summer have shown that the Hay bill was as foolish and unpatriotic a bit of flintlock legislation as was ever put on the statute book. I have the greatest admiration and respect for the individual militiamen who went to the border. But the system under which they were sent worked rank injustice to most of them, rank favoritism for some of them, and was worse than ineffective from the national standpoint. It is folly, and worse than folly, to pretend that the National Guard is an efficient second line of defense. Remember also that the laws passed nominally for the betterment of the regular army and navy are producing almost no result. The delays in building the ships are extraordinary. The shortage of enlisted men in the navy and army is appalling, nor is it being made good. It cannot wholly be made good under the volunteer system. But much could be done. Our first care should be to make the navy and the regular army thoroughly efficient.

But this is not enough. To trust only to the Navy and the regular Army amounts merely to preparing to let the other men do it. If we ordinary citizens are fit to be citizens of this country, we shall fit ourselves to defend this country. No man has a right to citizenship in a democracy, if, for any cause whatsoever, he is unwilling to fight, or is morally or mentally incapable of fighting, for the defense of that democracy against a powerful alien aggressor. If a man is physically unfit but is right in his soul and in his head, then he can render high service to the nation, although incapable of bearing arms. But, if from any moral or mental causes he is unwilling to train himself to bear arms, and to bear them if necessary in his country's cause, then he has no moral right to vote.

Be it remembered that such a national armed force as that for which I ask, while very powerful for defense, would be almost useless for aggression. I wish to see our Navy second only to that of Great Britain, because Great Britain is the only power whose naval needs are greater than ours. I do not ask that our Army become second, or anywhere near second, to Germany's because Germany's military needs are far greater than ours; but merely that relatively to our size our army be made to correspond to that of Switzerland.

This would mean that for the last two or three years of school, our boys would have some military training, substantially such as is given in the Swiss and Australian schools; and that at about the age of nineteen they would spend six months in actual service in the field (or at sea with the fleet) with the colors, and would thereafter for three or four years be required to spend a couple of weeks each year with the colors. Each year, among those who had served well for the six months, a number could be chosen to be trained as officers. These would then be given by the nation for two years, free, a training somewhat like that at West Point, although not as rigid or as thorough. They would be required to pay for this training by, for a certain number of months during each of the few following years doing their part in drilling the recruits of that year. It would probably be necessary to pay the recruits a small minimum wage so as to be sure that the poorest family would not suffer hardship because of the absence of the young man for six months. No man would be allowed to purchase exemption. The sons of the richest men in the land would have to serve exactly like anyone else, and do exactly the same work—which incidently would be a bit of uncommon good fortune for them.

Side by side with this preparation of the manhood of the country must go the preparation of its resources. The Government should keep a record of every factory, or workshop, of any kind which would be called upon to render service in war, and of all the railroads. All the workers in such factories and railroads should be tabulated so that in the event of war they would not be sent to the front if they could do better service where they were—although as far as possible every strong man should be sent to the front, to the position of danger, while work done in safety should be done by women and old men. The transportation system should receive special study. Factories which would be needed in time of war should be encouraged by the Government to keep themselves properly prepared in time of peace, and should be required to fill specimen orders, so that there would be no chance of their breaking down in the event of a sudden call at the outbreak of war. Industrial preparedness must go hand in hand with military preparedness.

Indeed, this military preparedness and the acceptance by the nation of the principle of universal, obligatory, military training in time of peace, as a basis of universal, obligatory service in time of war, would do more than anything else to help us solve our most pressing social and industrial problems in time of peace. It would Americanize and nationalize our people as nothing else could possibly do. It would teach our young men that there are other ideals besides making money. It would render them alert, energetic, self-reliant, capable of command, and willing to obey; respectful to others, and demanding respect from others for themselves. It would be the best possible way to teach us how to use our collective strength in order to accomplish those social and industrial tasks which must be done by all of us collectively if we are to do them well.

Just before this war began the male and female apostles of folly and
fatuity were at their highest pitch of denunciation of preparedness, and
were announcing at the tops of their voices that never again would
there be a great war. These preachers of professional pacifism, of peace-
at-any-price, of peace put before righteousness and honor and duty,
temporarily lead astray many good and earnest men and women.
These good, honest intelligent men and women can be shown the facts
and when shown the facts will ultimately see the profound immorality
as well as the utter folly of the professional pacifist or peace-at-any-
price position. There is, however, little to hope for as regards the professional pacifists themselves. The antics of their brethren in England
have shown that even although brayed in a mortar their folly shall not
depart from them. At the moment their clamor is drowned by the thunder of the great war. But when this war comes to an end, their voices
will be as loud as ever on behalf of folly and wickedness, and their
brazen effrontery will be proof against all shame, as well as against all
wisdom. They will unblushingly repeat every prophecy that has just
been falsified by the merciless march of events; they will reiterate all
the promises that have always been broken in the past and will always
be broken in the future. They are in the majority of cases primarily concerned for the safety of their own wretched bodies; and they are physically safe in the course they follow, for if, the disaster they court
should come upon this nation, they would themselves instantly flee to
safety, while their folly and wrongdoing would be atoned for by the
blood of better and braver men.

It is useless to appeal to these persons. But it is necessary to warn our
people against them. If our people fail to prepare, whatever the real reason may be, and whatever the reason is which they allege, their fate in
the end will be the same. Sooner or later, in such case, either we ourselves
or our children will tread the stony path of disaster, and eat the bitter
bread of shame.

Faithfully yours

February 2, 1917. New York
To Newton D. Baker[1]

Sir:

I have already on file in your Department, my application to be
permitted to raise a Division of Infantry, with a divisional brigade of
cavalry in the event of war (possibly with the permission to make one
or two of the brigades of infantry, mounted infantry). In view of the re-

---

[1]Secretary of War.

cent German note,[1] and of the fact that my wife and I are booked to sail next week for a month in Jamaica, I respectfully write you as follows.

If you believe that there will be war, and a call for volunteers to go to war, immediately, I respectfully and earnestly request that you notify me at once, so that I may not sail. Otherwise, I shall sail, and in such case I respectfully request that if or when it becomes certain that we will have war, and that there will be a call for volunteers to go to war, you will direct that a telegram be sent to me, at the *Metropolitan Magazine* office, New York, from whence a cable will be sent me to Jamaica, and I shall immediately return. I have prepared the skeleton outline of what I have desired the Division to be, and what men I should recommend to the Department, for brigade and regimental commanders, Chief of Staff, Chief Surgeon, Quartermaster general, etc. etc. etc. The men whom I would desire for officers and enlisted men are, for the most part, men earning their living in the active business of life, who would be glad to go to war at their country's call, but who could not be expected, and who would probably refuse, to drop their business and see their families embarrassed, unless there is war, and the intention to send them to war. So it is not possible for me to do much more in the way of preliminary action, than I have already done, until I have official directions.

Very respectfully

February 16, 1917. Oyster Bay
To Jean Jules Jusserand

My dear M. Jusserand:

I cannot tell whether we shall have war or not; yet it seems to me almost impossible to avoid it. I have already applied for permission to raise a division. It may be that the Government will not intend to send an expeditionary force; it may be that if they do they will not permit me to go with it. In such event, what I should like to do is to raise a division of Americans, who would fight in co-operation with the allies, either under the orders of France or of England. I might be able to make the place of raising it Canada. Of course, I would not attempt to raise it so far as I can now see, unless this country went to war, because I gravely doubt the propriety of an ex-President of the United States attempting to go to war, unless his country is at war. But if we were at war, I should be profoundly unhappy unless I got into the fighting line, and I believe I should raise a division of 20,000 men, even if the Government declined to hold out the promise of an expeditionary force, of which I should form part,

---

[1]Germany had just announced a policy of submarine warfare against American and other shipping.

to go at the earliest moment. I believe that in six months I could get this division ready for the trenches. Now, I don't want to be a nuisance instead of a help to France and England, but it is barely possible that inasmuch as they want men, it would be an object to them to have these 20,000 men, and that it would be worth their while to have an ex-President with his division in the trenches—and I need hardly tell you that I would not be a political general, and that I would expect no favors of any kind, except the great favor of being sent to the front. Do you care to inquire confidentially of your Government, whether, under the conditions above outlined, it would be likely that they would care to call upon me, and whether I should raise my troops in Canada, and take them over there for final training in France; or, whether it would be better that I should be under the command of English or French Generals? I shall make some inquiry of England also.

Faithfully yours

March 18, 1917. Oyster Bay
To Henry Cabot Lodge

Dear Cabot:

Johnson wired me his regret at not being present; I have now written him in full. Here in this country we are paralleled by England's experience, where Lloyd George was the only man who was an imperialistic radical, so to speak, that is who understood that there had to be sweeping internal reforms but that the questions connected with the maintenance and defence of the Empire came ahead of all others. The ordinary liberal or radical in Great Britain became an utterly hopeless nuisance because of his incredible silliness in foreign affairs; and our own progressives and near-progressives and progressive Republicans have tended to travel the same gait. Kellogg, and apparently Poindexter, are pretty sound.

I am so utterly sick of the gush about "supporting the President" that I shall write a brief and courteous, but unequivocal statement of our present condition in face of Germany to the Thursday evening meeting in Madison Square Garden. I have kept silent for seven weeks. Whatever the effect on myself, I think that the situation now calls for some statement by me. Taft, Hughes and even Root take part in the general idiot cry which aligns us behind the President, right or wrong—and he is 99 per cent wrong. As I wrote to one of his supporters, he is entitled to "support" in his foreign policy, exactly to the extent that Buchanan was entitled to "support" in his policies about slavery and secession. Buchanan's policy was better than Jefferson Davis'—and that is about all the praise to which he is entitled.

I intend to go to Florida for some shark and devil-fish harpooning.

I can do absolutely nothing here. Wilson evidently does not intend to do anything until Congress meets; and I can return within forty-eight hours; if there is need to, wire me.

Ever yours

March 22, 1917. Oyster Bay
To Henry Cabot Lodge

Dear Cabot:

On Monday, when the news of the sinking of our three ships came, I sent the enclosed telegram to the War Department. Baker answered, declining the offer, and stating that general officers would be appointed for the regulars and militia. I shall answer respectfully pointing out that I am the retired Commander-in-Chief of the whole Army, and that towards the close of the Santiago expedition I actually commanded a brigade—I am a retired volunteer officer also. Will you tell some of my friends in the Senate and House about the matter, and if legislation is passed, try to have it made proper to employ an ex-President—a retired Commander-in-Chief—in such fashion?

Meanwhile I have notified Jusserand of the facts, and told him that if either Congress or the Administration declares that a state of war exists, I shall take an expeditionary infantry division to France (under the American flag) on my own account if his Government thinks it worth while to pay for us. If his Government does not, I shall try whether Canada would like to pay for an American division (under our flag)— I understand that they need more men.

I am sure you liked what I have said during the last two days. I have kept silent since the break; I felt that it would not do for me to fail to speak at this moment. I am of course being pestered every hour to answer questions and make statements; I have done all the preliminary work of the division; there is absolutely nothing I can do until Congress meets; and I am going for a ten days' devil-fishing trip to Florida (it was to have been a month). I shall be back by April 2nd.

Give my warmest regards to Brandegee, Borah and all the men who go straight in this crisis.

Ever yours

March 23, 1917. Oyster Bay
To Newton D. Baker

Sir:

I have the honor to acknowledge the receipt of your telegram in answer to my telegram of the 19th, and will govern myself accordingly.

I understood, Sir, that there would be a far larger force than a division called out; I merely wished to be permitted to get ready a division for immediate use in the first expeditionary force sent over.

In reference to your concluding sentence, I wish respectfully to point out that I am a retired Commander in Chief of the United States Army, and eligible to any position of command over American troops to which I may be appointed. As for my fitness for command of troops, I respectfully refer you to my three immediate superiors in the field, Lieutenant General S. B. M. Young (retired), Major General Samuel Sumner (retired), and Major General Leonard Wood. In the Santiago Campaign I served in the first fight as commander first of the right wing and then of the left wing of the regiment; in the next, the big, fight, as Colonel of the Regiment; and I ended the campaign in command of the brigade.

The regiment, 1st United States Volunteer Cavalry, in which I first served as Lieutenant Colonel, and which I then commanded as Colonel, was raised, armed, equipped, drilled, mounted, dismounted, kept for two weeks on a transport, and then put through two victorious aggressive fights, in which we lost a third of the officers, and a fifth of the enlisted men, all within little over fifty days.

I have the honor to be,

Very respectfully

April 13, 1917. New York
To John Callan O'Laughlin

Dear Cal:

I found that it was advisable to send my letters at once as people were inquiring about them from the committees.

Now, a word as to my interview the other day. Of course, strictly for your private information, I had to choose my words rather carefully, in private and in public. Everything I have said in criticism of Mr. Wilson was not only true and justified and necessary to say, but has been proved to be such by Mr. Wilson's message the other day. His message bears out all I have said for the past two and a half years, and condemns all he has said and done for those two and a half years. Therefore, I am not going to, directly or by inference, take back one thing. But I am more than willing to let it all drift into oblivion, if he will now go into the war with all his heart, and with single-minded patriotism serve this country. I care nothing for his future, and nothing for my own. But I care immensely for this country, and I wish to have it a land of which my grandchildren will be proud to be citizens.

I put before the President my proposals and the reasons therefor, substantially as I have put them in public. He evidently felt pleased that I was going to support his bill and to ask for action supplementary to it, and not contradictory to it. He suddenly entered into a defense of his past conduct, saying that he had for a long time felt what he now said in his speech to Congress, but that the American people were not awake to the need, and that he had to bide his time; and he added that many people had misunderstood him (hastily interpolating, with obvious insincerity, that he did not mean me). I answered in substance, and almost in words, as follows: "Mr. President, what I have said and thought, and what others have said and thought, is all dust in a windy street, if now we can make your message good. Of course, it amounts to nothing, if we cannot make it good. But, if we can translate it into fact, then it will rank as a great state paper, with the great state papers of Washington and Lincoln. Now, all that I ask is that I be allowed to do all that in me is to help make good this speech of yours—to help get the nation to act, so as to justify and live up to the speech, and the declaration of war that followed." I added that I felt that the situation was as if Jefferson, after the *Leopard* attacked *Chesapeake,* had gone to war with Great Britain, in which case it would have been Light-Horse Harry Lee's duty instantly to support to the best of his power and ability such action; and that I wished to act toward him as in such case I would have felt it the duty of Light-Horse Harry Lee to act toward Jefferson.

Faithfully yours

P.S. Of course I am hampered by the folly of the Administration's war proposals. As I told Wilson & Baker, we need the universal military service, or conscription, system to reach people who ought *not* to be exempt from service; but it is nonsense to use it to prevent men from serving; and therefore it is criminal not to supplement it by providing at once for the hundreds of thousands of volunteers which it would not touch, and who could be used for the first expeditionary force.

May 17, 1917. Oyster Bay
To Henry Cabot Lodge

Dear Cabot:

I am exceedingly glad that you fearlessly told the truth about the Administration; it was a great and sorely needed service. Some members of the Senate and House have done badly; these should be unsparingly condemned; on one or two points the Administration has done well; here it has deserved support—and you have always given such support; but as a whole the blame for our grave and numerous shortcomings rests purely on the Administration, and those who support it generally stand on an exact level with those who supported Buchanan. The one real arch offender is Wilson. If our people were really awake he would be impeached tomorrow; Daniels, and Baker, and the General Staff are merely his tools. (Taft's two Chiefs of Staff, Wood and Witherspoon, feel even more strongly about the present General Staff than I do.)

The *Boston Herald* has been doing splendid work; if you see O'Brien thank him for me.

I congratulate you and the Republicans and the anti-Administration Democrats on what you have now done.

Of course be very careful never to antagonize Wilson on any point where he is right. But it is imperatively necessary to expose his hypocrisy, his inefficiency, his rancorous partisanship, and his selfish eagerness to sacrifice all patriotic considerations to whatever he thinks will be of benefit to himself politically.

Ever yours

May 20, 1917. Oyster Bay
To John J. Pershing

My dear General Pershing:

I very heartily congratulate you, and especially the people of the United States, upon your selection to lead the expeditionary force to the front. When I was endeavoring to persuade the Secretary of War to permit me to raise a division or two of volunteers I stated that if you or some man like you were to command the expeditionary force I could raise the divisions without trouble.

I write you now to request that my two sons, Theodore Roosevelt, Jr., aged 27, and Archibald B. Roosevelt, aged 23, both of Harvard, be allowed to enlist as privates under you, to go over with the first troops. The former is a Major, and the latter a Captain in the Officers' Reserve Corps. They are at Plattsburg for their third summer. My own belief is that competent men of their standing and rank can gain very little from a third summer at Plattsburg, and that they should be utilized, as officers, even if only as second lieutenants. But they are keenly desirous to see service; and if they serve under you at the front, and are not killed, they will be far better able to instruct the draft army next fall, or next winter, or whenever they are sent home, than they will be after spending the summer at Plattsburg. The President has announced that only regular officers are to go with you; and if this is to be the invariable rule then I apply on behalf of my two sons that they may serve under you as enlisted men, to go to the front with the first troops sent over.

Trusting to hear that this request has been granted, I am, with great respect,

Very sincerely yours

P.S. If I were physically fit, instead of old and heavy and stiff, I should myself ask to go under you in any capacity down to and including a sergeant; but at my age, and condition, I suppose that I could not do work you would consider worth while in the fighting line (my only line) in a lower grade than brigade commander.

July 27, 1917. Oyster Bay
To Augustus Post

My dear Mr. Post:

I heartily congratulate the Aero Club of America on its efforts to secure a great aerial government program here in America. It should be one of the most important features in that work of adequate preparedness in advance which depends for its success primarily upon the adoption of the principle of universal obligatory military training for all our young men. I believe that the peculiar American characteristics especially fit us for success in developing and using the airplane on land, and the hydro-airplane on sea; yet this country, which gave birth to aviation, has so far lagged behind that now, three years after the great war began, and six months after we were dragged into it, we still have not a single machine competent to fight the war machines of our enemies. We have to trust entirely to the machines of our Allies. I am not prepared to speak as to the sufficiency of airplanes to do some of the tasks which you have in view; but that they will be a very great factor in the accomplishment of these tasks, I am sure. As you well say, this should be the fifth arm of our Army; and it should be made a long-reaching weapon, to use effectively, if conditions at any time arise that will enable it to strike the deciding blow.

It may be utterly impossible to strike that blow without a thoroughly effective air force; and it is utterly impossible to improvise such a force. It has been unpardonable folly on our part as a nation that for three years, with this great war staring us in the face, we have absolutely failed to prepare for it; and our folly has been at least as marked as regards aviation as in any other field. No one can tell how long this war will last. If we are true to ourselves, we will make it last just as long as is necessary in order to secure the complete overthrow of the Prussianized Germany of the Hohenzollerns. Therefore, we should at once begin to prepare on the largest scale for warfare in the air, as one of the great features of the warfare of the future. In all probability such preparation will be of the utmost consequence in this war. I am absolutely certain it will be of the utmost consequence in preventing us from being overwhelmed by disaster in some future war.

Faithfully yours

August 3, 1917. New York
To William Allen White

Dear W. A.:

I never see the *Atlantic*, but in view of your statement I shall look up the August number and read Kellogg's piece.

I enclose two letters, one to Jusserand, and one to Bunau-Varilla in Paris, who speaks English admirably and is a journalist; and I think he is the man who would be most useful to you. He is the man with whom I was thrown in close contact through and about the Panama Canal; he can tell you about that also. I know slightly a great many public men in France, but I have never given anyone a letter to them, for I do not know them well enough.

Now, as to what you say about Wilson. I entirely agree with you that we should stand for whatever good things he does. I stand by him in these matters and stand most actively by him against the La Follette-German-socialism-pacifism combination. But I regard it as the gravest possible moral offense against this country to stand by him *as a whole,* or to use language about him which will mislead people into the belief that on the whole he has done well and ought to be backed. Fundamentally our whole trouble in this country is due more to Wilson than any other one man, and his foes of the stamp you mention are able to attack him now only because of the weapons he himself forged for their use. Everything he has said since April 2nd can be justified only if we not merely unstintedly condemn, but treat with abhorrence what he had done before; and he has *done* badly. As Raymond Robins said to me, "Wilson has spent two and one half years dulling the conscience of our people and weakening their moral fiber, and then without any change in circumstances he reversed himself while running full speed; and naturally the machinery stops and an immense number of people are completely puzzled and find themselves wholly unable to get up any moral enthusiasm." He won the election on the "He kept us out of war" issue. He had no convictions in the matter. He has no convictions at all; although he has opinions and coldly malicious hatreds. He thought, and thought rightly, that this was a good campaign cry until after election. Hughes did not meet the issues squarely, and the bulk of the Republican leaders were but very little better than the Democrats. But the fact remains that it was Wilson who was the great offender, and that the damage he did to our people morally and materially during the last three years will bear evil fruit for a generation to come. Moreover his attitude since the declaration of war has been one of intolerable hypocrisy. It was possible to make some kind of a defense for our going to war on the ground that we were fighting purely for our own interests and rights, and because after two years Germany still adhered to the position about which we had sent her an ultimatum two years previous. Mind you, I say it was *possible* to take this attitude; but it would not have been a *proper* attitude, for there was more justification for going to war immediately after the sinking of the *Lusitania* than there was for going to war last Spring. But what is perfectly impossible, what represent really nauseous hypocrisy, is to say that we have gone to war to make the work safe for democracy, in April, when sixty days previously we had been announcing that we wished a "Peace without victory," and had no concern with the "causes or objects" of the war. I do not regard any speech as a great speech when it is obviously hypocritical and in bad faith; nor do I regard the making of such a speech of service to the world. I regard it as damage to the cause of morality and decency.

So far as concerns that Wilson has done in the past few months, I think on the whole it has been badly done; and, what is more, that it has been badly done because of very evil traits on his part. He was emphatically right about the draft. He was emphatically wrong about the militia and about turning down the volunteer system as a vitally necessary stopgap. He took these attitudes because he was much more anxious to spite Leonard Wood and myself than he was to save the country. He has permitted seven months to go by without making an effective move in the vital matter of shipping, because for political reasons he was not willing to back Goethals. To have appointed Daniels and Baker originally was evil enough; to have kept them on during a great war was a criminal thing.

The greatest damage that can be done to the cause of decency in this country is to stand by Wilson in such a way as to imply that we approve or condone his utterly cynical disregard of considerations of patriotism and national efficiency and his eagerness to sacrifice anything if to do so will advance his own political interests. He has just one kind of ability; a most sinister and adroit power of appealing in his own interest to all that is foolish and base in our people. He not only appeals to base and foolish men; he appeals also to the Mr. Hyde who, even in many good and honorable men, lurks behind the Dr. Jekyl in their souls.

Faithfully yours

September 1, 1917. Oyster Bay
To Quentin Roosevelt

Dearest Quentin,

We were immensely pleased to get a note from Miss Emily Tuckerman saying that you, and the blessed Harrahs, were all in Paris together. I hope you saw Eleanor.

Miss Giren Wilson is just leaving for six months in France with the Red Cross; she is immensely pleased. The other evening she and darling Flora came over to dinner. Really, we are inexpressibly touched by Flora's attitude towards [?]; she is the dearest girl; and the way that pretty, charming pleasure-loving young girl has risen to the heights as soon as the need came is one of the finest things I have seen. By George, you *are* fortunate.

I suppose you are now hard at work learning the new type of air-game. My disappointment at not going myself was down at bottom chiefly reluctance to see you four, in whom my heart was wrapped, exposed to danger while I stayed at home in do-nothing ease and safety. But the feeling has now been completely swallowed in my immense pride in all four of you. I feel that *Mother,* and all of *you* children, have by your deeds justified *my* words!!

I hope to continue earning a good salary until all of you come home, so that I can start Archie and you all right. Then I intend to retire. An elderly male Cassandra has-been can do a little, a very little, towards waking the people now and then; but undue persistency in issuing Jeremiads does no real good and makes the Jeremiah an awful nuisance.

I am just publishing a book, for which Mother gave me the title:— "The Foes of our own Household"; I dedicate it on behalf of both of us to our sons and daughters—the latter to include daughters in law, and Flora shall have her copy with a special inscription to show that she is included among those of whom I am most proud.

I make a few speeches; I loathe making them; among other reasons because I always fear to back up the Administration too strongly lest it turn another somersault. At the moment New York City, having seen the National Guard, fresh from gathering at the Armories parade, believes that Germany is already conquered!

Your loving father

December 24, 1917. Oyster Bay
To Quentin Roosevelt

Dearest Quentin,

Mother, the adamantine, has stopped writing to you because you have not written to her—or to any of us—for a long time. That will make no permanent difference to you; but I write about something that may make a permanent difference. Flora spoke to Ethel yesterday of the fact that you only wrote rarely to her. She made no complaint whatever. But she knows that some of her friends receive three or four letters a week from their lovers or husbands (Archie writes Gracie rather more often than this—exceedingly interesting letters).

Now of course you may not keep Flora anyhow. But if you wish to lose her, continue to be an infrequent correspondent. If however you wish to keep her write her letters—interesting letters, and love letters—at least three times a week. Write no matter how tired you are, no matter how inconvenient it is; write if you're smashed up in a hospital; write when you are doing your most dangerous stunts; write when your work is most irksome and disheartening; write all the time! Write enough letters to allow for half being lost.

Affectionately

A hardened and wary old father

February 2, 1918. Oyster Bay
To Archibald Roosevelt

Dearest Archie,

If you want shoes or other things for your men and can order them abroad, get them and tell the Farmers Loan & Trust Company to pay for them and at once send the bill to me; or I will put to your credit any money you wish; and cable me if you wish me to send anything from here. I have told you that thanks to my pen I am making money; I have no object in doing so unless I spend it in this crisis for you and Gracie and your brothers and for your comrades if I can relieve their grinding needs.

I suppose you are now in the trenches. Whether the great German drive will materialize or not I have no idea. The revolt in Germany is evidently serious and shows that the economic strain and social unrest are very serious.

I am not in sympathy with the bulk of my fellow countrymen, and therefore am no longer fit to lead the public men or politicians. The Republicans have on the whole behaved far better than the Democrats; but even among them there are any number of pacifists and shortsighted reactionary materialists; and I see very evident, altho furtive, tendencies to deal with the pro-Germans—chiefly among the Democrats but also among the Republicans. I do not now possess the power of appealing in convincing manner to our easy going, shortsighted, fairly well-meaning countrymen; probably I am too extreme. Well, all I now care for is to keep on with my work until the war is over and all of you get back; while the war lasts I serve a very limited public usefulness by telling truths which nobody else will tell; and my real usefulness is helping to keep things going until the soldiers return to their wives and children and sweethearts! I am to see darling Gracie next week.

The only thing they have caught me on so far is my statement—on your say so!—that thousands of coffins have been sent to France. Of course I do'n't bring you in in any way; but can you without trouble put me in the way of getting at the facts? My Y.M.C.A. controversy still rages fitfully!

Mother looks too pretty for anything.
Your loving father

February 18, 1918. Roosevelt Hospital, New York
To Kermit Roosevelt

Dearest Kermit:

Four of your letters written in the last two weeks of November have just come. They are delightful. Of course in a way I sympathize with you in your feeling that you would liked to have been at the taking of Jerusalem, but after all the essential thing is to get at the battle front and there do your duty, and this essential thing has been accomplished. Moreover, it would be very hard after all to have a more interesting experience than you have had with Indian as well as English troops in a campaign through the strange country that saw one of the two earliest and greatest of civilizations, and that they saw this succeeded by other and wholly distinct civilizations until they died away into a barbarism not really more advanced than the barbarism from which the first of these civilizations had sprung five thousand years previously.

It would be delightful if you could get in that light-armored-car battery. It would be the modern equivalent of the most efficient form of fighting light cavalry. If by the end of the cold season your superiors are willing to have you come to France and you find you can do it and wish to do it, I cannot see any possible objection. If you got back on the French front I should write to Pershing and try to get you transferred to our army, and I think I would succeed, although of course I cannot guarantee it. Most of the fighting Generals of our army would like to do for me anything they dare. But of course the War Department would hail the chance in so far as they dare to do me or those near me an injury. Fortunately, they have a wholesome respect for my fighting powers. Here we have finished the first year of the war and have accomplished, in a military sense, absolutely nothing. We have never had a more incompetent Administration than the present one and it is most incompetent in everything connected with the war. The frightful mishandling of the machine-gun situation alone ought to have meant the impeachment not merely of the Secretary of War but of the President. However, our army in France is now reasonably well supplied—at last has plenty of shoes and clothing and has obtained airplanes, field artillery, machine guns and auto-rifles from the French. But it is sickening to feel that this army including Ted and Archie, may be sacrificed without any adequate reinforcement, because of tile folly, and worse than folly, of our high civilians at home, and of the fuddled elderly fools of the regular army who were kept in high position by these same civilians during the first year of the war. Congress has behaved infinitely better than the President and the Senate investigating committee has forced the worst of the swivel-chair War Department Generals out of office. I think there will be a slight improvement and of course in the end even though the incompetence of the Administration prevents our exerting more than one quarter of our strength, yet even the expression of this quarter will accomplish a great deal.

It is the greatest relief and delight to us to think of Belle, darling Belle, and blessed Kim and the blessed new baby. Our anxiety now is for Gracie. I have just been over selections from Archie's letters, which he sent me and which she will see whether the *Atlantic Monthly* would like to publish, of course anonymously. They are well worth publishing but that does not in the least mean that the *Atlantic Monthly* will accept them.

I am writing from the Roosevelt Hospital where I have been for nearly a fortnight and shall be for a fortnight more. My old Brazilian trouble, both the fever and the abscesses recurred and I had to go under the knife. It was entirely trivial. I think mother has written you about it. I can quite honestly say that my only feeling was the deepest gratitude that it was not one of you boys, and a very earnest wish that it were possible for me to play my small part by taking it, instead of having some similar thing happen to one of you boys. I of course have had the best of care from the Doctors and nurses. I am in clean, pleasant surroundings. Mother is staying in the hospital and Ethel and Alice are in every day and any number of friends—many more than I can as yet see (Miss Stricker to whom I am dictating this letter ejaculates "many more than you could ever see"). I have taken a somewhat sardonic amusement in the real panic that affected a great many people when for a moment it looked as if I might not pull through. They have been bitterly against me for the last three and a half years and have denounced me beyond measure.

But when they thought I might die they suddenly had an awful feeling that maybe I represented what down at the bottom of their hearts they really believed to be right, and that although they have followed Wilson they knew also, down at the bottom of their hearts, that they did so only because he pandered to the basest side of their natures, and gave them an excuse for following the easy path that led away from effort and hardship and risk and unpleasantness of every kind, and also incidentally from honor and duty.

Well, old side partner, your letters are perfectly delightful and surely you must know how my heart thrills with pride whenever I think of you. I don't believe in all the United States there is any father who has quite the same right that I have to be proud of his four sons.

Your loving father

March 12, 1918. Oyster Bay
To George V of Britain

Your Majesty,

It was exceedingly kind and thoughtful of you, Sir, to cable when I was in the hospital. I am now on the highroad to recovery. The trouble was the aftermath of my Brazilian exploring trip of four years ago; and I really felt ashamed that any one should be concerned now over such a trivial matter as my sickness when we have to think of all the dreadful suffering of the men at the front.

I need hardly say how immensely I admire England's attitude and all that she has done. She has paid and is paying a terrible price; but her achievement has been wonderful; and bitter altho her experience has been, I believe that she has immensely strengthened herself thereby.

The chief reason I wished to get well was in order to resume my work of endeavoring to get my country to exert her great, but lazy and unprepared, strength as speedily and effectively as possible. For the last three years and a half I have been preaching to my fellow countrymen their duty as I saw it; they finally saw it the same way but always two years behind-time as regards each phase of the duty; and nine tenths of wisdom is being wise in time. It is maddening to see Russia break and Germany stride nearer triumph because my country failed to prepare, and failed to act decisively when the Lusitania was sunk—the moment when all our people would have responded without wavering to the call for action, if only such call had been made. Germany's power, energy, determination, resourcefulness, have been extraordinary; and the abhorrent quality of her conduct even more so. There is just one thing to do, and that is to beat her to her knees. If our two peoples have the right stuff in them, this is what we shall do. If the Lansdownes on your side of the water, and their rather more noxious representatives on this side of the water, are sufficiently numerous and influential, we shall fail; and in such case we shall speedily have to sink to the position of Holland or else fight the war over again under greater disadvantages.

One of my sons, Kermit, is a Captain in your army in Mesopotamia. My other three sons are with Pershing in France; one in aviation, two in the infantry; one of the latter has just received from a French general the croix de guerre for gallantry in action.* My son in law Dick Derby is also with Pershing.

We now have eight grandchildren.

I am, Sir, with great respect, very faithfully yours

*His name is Archibald; he is a Captain; he was wounded in the leg, and his arm broken.

March 17, 1918. Oyster Bay
To Quentin Roosevelt

Dearest Quentin,

In a Rochester paper appeared a note from one Whaley, a superintendent of a post office "somewhere in France," who writes "Young Quentin Roosevelt is as modest as a school girl, but as game as they make 'em in aviation. Keep tabs on this game young chap."

Early in the week we were greatly depressed to learn that gallant young Tommy Hitchcock had been captured by the Germans; it is said that he was not hurt. Then came the excitement about Archie. The first news—whether true or not we do not know—was that he had been given the croix de guerre by a French General "under dramatic circumstances"; then the War Dept notified us that he was slightly wounded; then Ted cabled that he had been hit in the leg, and his arm broken, by shrapnel, but that he was in no danger, and that Eleanor would take care of him. Our pride and our anxiety are equal—as indeed they are about all of you.

Why do'n't you write to Flora, and to her father and mother, asking if she wo'n't come abroad and marry you? As for your getting killed, or ordinarily crippled, afterwards, why she would a thousand times rather have married you than not have married you under those conditions; and as for the extraordinary kinds of crippling, they are rare, and anyway we have to take certain chances in life. You and she have now passed your period of probation; you have been tried; you are absolutely sure of yourselves; and I would most heartily approve of your getting married at the earliest possible moment.

Mr. Beebe is out here; he has just come from France; on the French front he was allowed to do some flying and bombing—not fighting the German war-planes.

Your loving father

March 22, 1918. Oyster Bay
To Georges Clemenceau[1]

My dear M. Clemenceau:

The most influential and malignant foe of the Allies, and most powerful supporter and friend of the Germans, in this country is Hearst, the newspaper editor. He is far more dangerous than any organization or newspaper of the German-Americans because he has far wider influence of a very base kind, and far more astuteness. He ardently served Germany up to the period when we went into the war. Since that time he has continued to serve her less openly but quite as effectively. He renders the service in many different ways. He ardently champions negotiations

---

[1] French premier.

which would lead to the complete triumph of Germany, under cover of supporting the Pope's appeal for peace, or under cover of supporting the Russian Bolshevists' appeal for peace, or under cover of supporting efforts to find out if Austria wouldn't like to make peace. He ardently champions our proposing a peace on the basis of the status quo ante bellum. He strongly supports every proposal that means delay in sending troops or munitions and war instruments abroad, or any refusal to declare war on Germany's allies. He continually seeks to create prejudice against, and to embroil us with, England or Japan, as the occasion offers. In short he is as sinister and efficient a friend of Germany as is to be found in all the world. In order to cover up his activities he makes a great pretense of patriotism, or of devotion to the Allies' cause on points where no possible damage to Germany is involved. The feeling in this country for France is very strong and he does not venture to go against it, (although he expressed the greatest disapproval of, and strongly protested against, the demand that France receive back Alsace and Lorraine; and he loudly backs the Russian Bolshevists and their no-annexation and no-indemnities proposal). As part of his campaign he has conducted an advertising scheme for a fund to help "rebuild France." If he can get the French Government. Oh Lord, how I wish you were President of the United States!

April 21, 1918. Oyster Bay
To Quentin Roosevelt

Dearest Quentin,

We are all at sea as to where you are and what you are doing; and in this crisis the possibilities are such that we know not what conditions may have become when our letters reach you. I think that our people really are somewhat aroused by the fact that we are of so little weight in the terrible battle now going on; and accordingly, one year after the event, the Administration is endeavoring in earnest to speed up certain matters. But it is very late; and the Administration's inveterate habit of boasting and of treating roseate forecasts as an offset to insufficient performance makes it difficult to tell what the probabilities for the future really are. For example, a layman like myself is utterly unable to make out what our airplane situation is. We all know now that you have no American battle planes and apparently no American bombing planes (I am doubtless using the wrong terms) on the other side; but we can not tell how soon you will have them, and in what proportion you will get them from the French or be utilized among the French fliers. Therefore I have no idea whether there is any possibility of your getting to the front; I simply have no idea what you are doing—whether you are fighting, or raging because you can't get to the fighting line. Phil wrote me an awfully nice letter; he has been completely disillusioned, I should suppose, by his experiences in France, as he relates them.

Here, spring is now well under way, altho the weather is cold and gray. The woods are showing a green foam; the gay yellow of the forsythia has appeared; the blood root spangles with brilliant white the brown dead leaves of the hill side across the wet hollow by the frog spring. Mother is well, and so charming; and very brave. I have ceased to fret at my impotence to do anything in this great crisis; I rejoice that my four sons, and Dick, are playing the great part; and I putter round like Alty Morgan and the other old frumps, trying to help with the Liberty Loan & Red Cross and such like.

Your loving father

July 1, 1918. Oyster Bay
To Richard Derby

Dear Dick,

Much to my sorrow Ethel and her little brood leave today for Islesboro, and I write to tell you that they are all well. Ethel has improved wonderfully; really, now she only suffers from the strain of your absence and of the war. The children are the dearest small persons imaginable. Richard is so manly and friendly, and amuses himself, and is adored both in the house and in the stable! In the case of Shady the adoration is accompanied by some reserves, as Richard makes his life haggard by busy and officious affection. Edie is about the dearest one year old baby I have ever known. She loves me *very* much if there is no one more attractive round! At any rate I offer an agreeable relief from the monotony of the crib or of the little pen on the floor, and she hails me with little soft outstretched arms, and of course my heart is like water and I can't resist taking her up. Now she generally comes down to breakfast and crawls actively round the floor; and Richard as soon as he has finished his breakfast also drops hastily on all fours and joins in the all-fours scamper, to Edie's intense delight; and Shady, no matter what his desires, is included in the game. Already Edie is a real amusement to Richard, and in a sense gives him some companionship.

Your last letters to Ethel have been absorbingly interesting; in them you gave so vivid a picture of your life and work, and of the fine fighting men of your division and their self-reliant gallantry, that I could see it all before my eyes. That was a close call you had from the shell. Well, you are all of you leading lives which are uninterrupted series of close calls. It is dreadful; but it would be worse if you were'n't leading them, in this great world crisis. In days such as these the only men about whom one can feel joy and pride are the men about whom one must also feel deep anxiety. The pride and the anxiety go hand in hand.

Thank Heavens, we now have an army about; some 600,000 fighting soldiers, with a few airplanes, and what cannon we get from the

French; and I am sure that the units, up to the regiments, are first class. I do not know what the average quality of our generals, our high command and staff, is.

Here, I speak occasionally and write occasionally, and render what small help I can in speeding up the war. It amounts to very little; deeds, not words, are all that count now; and the justification for my existence is furnished by you and Ethel, by the three elder boys and their wives, by Quentin and Flora.

Well, Quentin too is at least at the front; and his part is one of peculiar honor and peril.

Ever yours

July 25, 1918. Oyster Bay
To Georges Clemenceau

My dear M. Clemenceau:

I have received many messages from rulers of nations and leaders of peoples; but among these there is none I have valued quite as much as yours, because I have a peculiar admiration for you and feel that you have played a greater part than any man not a soldier has played, and a greater part than any soldier, except one or two, has played in this great world war. It is a very sad thing to see the young die when the old who are doing nothing, as I am doing nothing, are left alive. Therefore it is very bitter to me that I was not allowed to face the danger with my sons. But whatever may be their fate, I am glad and proud that my sons have done their part in this mighty war against despotism and barbarism. Of my four boys Quentin, as you know, has been killed, and two of the other three wounded and all three of these have been decorated for gallantry and efficiency in action.

Thank Heaven, it begins to look as if at last Germany had spent her strength, and I thank Heaven also that we now have at least a few hundred thousand Americans to fight beside the French.

Faithfully yours

August 11, 1918. Dark Harbor, Maine
To Belle Willard Roosevelt

Darling Belle,

I have written you many times, sometimes like this, direct to the Embassy at Madrid, sometimes, as I am going to do in two or three days, through Mr. Love. If you receive either of these letters (for I shall make the same request in both) will you let me know which address to use hereafter?

Your delightful letter to Mother about your trip with Kermit and blessed Willard from Rome to Madrid has just come. It was even more interesting than Kermit's on the same subject. Aunt Emily also wrote us a most enthusiastic letter about you, and the baby, whom she worships. She immensely admires Kermit, but, quite properly, it is *you* to whom her heart especially goes out. I could not overstate, dearest Belle, how very deeply Mother and I appreciate all that your thoughtfulness and sweetness have meant to and have done for Aunt Emily.

Well, Kermit's extraordinary combination of gentleness, of dauntless courage and energy, and of possession of that elusive but most real quality of being extremely interested in matters and interesting to people, has never been more evident than at the present time; and you, darling girl, have shown that the very sweetest traits of the old-style lovely girl can be joined with the finest heroism and capacity. But I am exactly as proud of the wives of my sons, and of Ethel, as I am of my boys and of Dick.

It is no use pretending that Quentin's death is not very terrible. It is most so for poor Flora who is staying here with Ethel, as we are. But it is almost as hard for Mother. They have both been very brave. There is nothing to comfort Flora at the moment; but she is young; I most earnestly hope that time will be very merciful to her, and that in a few years she will keep Quentin only as a loving memory of her golden youth, as the lover of her golden dawn, and that she will find happiness with another good and fine man. But of course it would be all wrong for me to tell her this *now*. As for Mother, her heart will ache for Quentin until she dies. I would not for all the world have had him fail fearlessly to do his duty, and to tread his allotted path, high of heart, even altho it led to the gates of death. But it is useless for me to pretend that it is not very bitter to see that good, gallant, tenderhearted boy, leave life at its crest, when it held Flora, and such happiness, and certainly an honorable and perhaps a distinguished career.

Evidently Archie is crippled, at least for many months to come, and I wish he would come home. Hitherto the rascal has refused. I would'n't suggest it if he could render any service with the army, but to spend months of pain and idleness in Paris, instead of at least being with his wife and baby and his mother does'n't seem worth while.

Ted has apparently recovered from the gassing, and will soon recover from the bullet wounds in his leg; I am so glad he is with Eleanor.

I do'n't yet know just what Kermit is doing, for I have had no letter from him since he got to France.

Your birthday cable to Mother has just come; it was dear of you to remember.

Kim and Willard must be the most adorable small persons! We have been greatly comforted by Richard and little Edie; the former loves Mother, and the latter lets me love her! (There is a somewhat nice distinction between the two). In time of trouble the unconsciousness of children is often a great comfort.

Tell your father how deeply we appreciated the trouble he took, and the information he got for us from Germany; and give our love to all your dear family.

Ever affectionately yours
Kermit's father

August 11, 1918. Oyster Bay
To Belle Willard Roosevelt

Darling Belle,

Day before yesterday I wrote you from Dark Harbor, Maine, where we had been for a fortnight with Ethel and the babies; I addressed it direct to the American Embassy, Madrid; this, which is a sketchy note, is being sent through Mr. Love; do write me which gets to you first, as a guide to my future correspondence.

When we reached here we found Quentin's last letters; he was at the fighting front, very proud and happy—and singularly modest, with all his pride, and his pleasure at showing his metal. Of course that was a wonderful company of men, flying in the swift battle planes—not the ordinary observation or bombing planes—at the front; they were bound together in the close ties of men who know that most of them are to die, and who face their fate high of heart and with a gallant defiance; and Quentin wrote that he would not for any consideration have been any where else. Two days before he was killed he was with Eleanor in Paris; and she was so proud of him, and took him round as the young hero. He had his crowded hour of glorious life.

Yet I do not pretend that it is not very dreadful that his young life, of such promise, should be darkened at dawn. And for Flora and his mother the pain is great. When we reached home yesterday afternoon Alice was waiting us; a real comfort.

Mrs. Tom Page wrote Belle James a dear letter about you and the adorable baby and Kermit in Rome; such a nice letter. Will you write Kipling and tell him about things? He wrote that he had never heard from Kermit; and he is evidently really fond of you both.

Love to your father, mother and Elizabeth.

Devotedly
Kermit's father

I enclose the photo of a preposterous elderly creature, the father of *real* soldiers in a *real* war, at a time when he went to the only war there was in his time!

November 19, 1918. Roosevelt Hospital, New York
To Arthur H. Lee

Dear Arthur:

Well, we have seen the mighty days and you, at least, have done your full share in them. We have lived through the most tremendous tragedy in the history of civilization. We should be sternly thankful that the tragedy ended with a grim appropriateness, too often lacking. All the people directly or indirectly responsible for the tragedy, all those who have preached and practiced the cynical treachery, brutality and barbarism and the conscienceless worshipping of revolting cunning and brute force which made the German people what it was in 1914 (and what, except that it is defeated, it now is)—all these people have come down in the crash. When the war first broke out I did not think the Kaiser was really to blame. I thought he was simply the tool; gradually I was forced to realize that he was one of the leading conspirators, plotters and wrongdoers. The last fortnight has shown that he was not even a valorous barbarian—he was unwilling to pay, with his body when his hopes were wrecked. Think of the Kaiser and his six sons saving their own worthless carcasses at the end, leaving their women, like their honor, behind them. If ever there was a case where on the last day of the fighting the leaders should have died, this was the case.

I was able to render substantial service to the allies during the last month by being probably the chief factor in preventing Wilson from doing what he fully intended to do, namely, double-cross the allies, appear as an umpire between them and the Central Powers and act a negotiated peace which would put him personally on a pinnacle of glory in the sight of every sinister pro-German and every vapid and fatuous doctrinaire sentimentalist throughout the world. I knew in advance what Wilson's intentions were. The probably necessary kowtowing performed in front of him by almost all the British leaders, and by the great majority of the French leaders, had made him certain that they would accept whatever he did. His success in fooling and browbeating our own people, the terror which he had impressed on the newspapers, the immense political funds which he used nominally for national, but really for party, purposes, and the natural tendency of good people to stand by the President in wartime made him convinced that he could induce the nation to follow him in another somersault. Accordingly he entered into negotiations with Germany on the basis of a peace, conditioned upon his famous fourteen points. Germany agreed eagerly and absolutely to his demands. The Fourteen Points were thoroughly mischievous and would have meant a negotiated peace with Germany. Moreover, last January when the Fourteen Points were promulgated our people knew so little of the matter and were so accustomed to loose rhetoric that they did not show any discontent with them. But by the first of October when the Wilson-Germany negotiations were on, our people had waked up. They wished unconditional surrender, and there was an outburst of popular feeling such as I have very rarely seen in America. The President was repudiated and threatened by people who had been his slavish adherents. Wilson is utterly shameless and as soon as he became convinced that the people would upset him, he promptly double-crossed Germany instead of the allies, and appeared again as the lofty opponent of the German Government. But the incident caused him to lose his temper, and he thought he would provide himself with a rubber-stamp Congress in the elections that were about to take place. Accordingly he made an appeal for a Democratic Senate and House, saying that although the Republicans were prowar they were anti-Administration and that he would not regard his policies as sustained if either the House or the Senate were Republican. This gave me my chance, and in the last week of the campaign we did the seemingly impossible,—carried the House by a substantial and the Senate by a bare majority. Wilson explicitly stated that he made no test excepting that of support of his administration, by which he meant support of himself at any point where his personal comfort or personal administration was involved. He appealed just as strongly for antiwar Democrats as for prowar Democrats and his whole argument was against prowar Republicans.

The German people thoroughly understood what the issue was and after election thoroughly understood what had happened. The *Berliner Tageblatt* stated with refreshing frankness that the election of a Republican Congress rendered it impossible for Germany to hope that Mr. Wilson would be able to give them the kind of peace that was "reasonable"—in other words, pro-German.

The comparison between Foch's Twenty-three Points which were actually adopted in the armistice and Wilson's Fourteen show the difference between the shifty rhetorician who wants an indecisive peace and the resolute soldier who will accept only the peace of overwhelming victory. By the way, you will be amused to know that in Canada and Australia I am regarded with hearty sympathy in my views as to the retention by the British Empire of all the German Colonies, etc. etc. I have made the Canadians and Australians feel that my utterances do not need a key to explain them!

As regards England, I end the war more convinced than ever that there should be the closest alliance between the British Empire and the United States; and also I am more convinced than ever that neither one can afford for one moment to rely on the other in a sufficiently tight place. There would always of course be the chance that the other, in such event, would wake up to the needs of the situation; but there would also be the chance that its own political tricksters and doctrinaires and sentimental charlatans and base materialists would make it false to its duty. There are just two Englishmen, of the civilian class, with whom I now feel in entire sympathy, namely Kipling and yourself—I am not speaking of dear Trevelyan and the other persons to whom I am attached on mere social and literary grounds.

However, all this is of little account. In spite of our pacifists and sentimentalists and tricky politicians at home, and in spite of the aid given to the worst American foes of England by so many well-meaning foolish Englishmen, America did finally play a real part in the war and played it manfully. England of course has suffered and achieved more than ever before in her whole history. The victory is tremendous, the overthrow of Germany complete.

Ted and Kermit have taken part in the last fighting, and I believe they are now walking toward the Rhine. Archie, pretty badly crippled, is back with us. I doubt if his arm will ever be quite right again, but he will be able to do a great many things with it. Ted has been made Lieutenant Colonel, and commanded his regiment in the final fighting. Dick Derby has done exceedingly well and has been promoted to be Lieutenant Colonel. This is Quentin's birthday. With dearest love to Ruth and Faith,

Always yours

Index

ABOUT THE EDITOR

H. W. Brands is Distinguished Professor of History and Ralph R. Thomas '21 Professor of Liberal Arts at Texas A&M University. He is the author of *T. R.: The Last Romantic; The First American: The Life and Times of Benjamin Franklin; The Devil We Knew: Americans and the Cold War;* and several other books of American history. He lives in Austin, Texas.

OTHER COOPER SQUARE PRESS
TITLES OF INTEREST

THROUGH THE BRAZILIAN WILDERNESS
Theodore Roosevelt
New introduction by H. W. Brands
448 pp., 9 b/w photos, 2 maps
0-8154-1095-6
$19.95

AFRICAN GAME TRAILS
**An Account of the African Wanderings of an American Hunter-
   Naturalist**
Theodore Roosevelt
New introduction by H. W. Brands
616 pp., 210 b/w photos
0-8154-1132-4
$22.95

THE NORTH POLE
Robert Peary
Foreword by Theodore Roosevelt
New introduction by Robert M. Bryce
480 pp., 109 b/w illustrations, 1 map
0-8154-1138-3
$22.95

MY ATTAINMENT OF THE POLE
Frederick A. Cook
New introduction by Robert M. Bryce
680 pp., 45 b/w illustrations
0-8154-1137-5
$22.95

THE SOUTH POLE
**An Account of the Norwegian Antarctic Expedition in the *Fram*,
  1910–1912**
Captain Roald Amundsen
Foreword by Fridtjof Nansen
New introduction by Roland Huntford
1008 pp., 155 b/w illustrations
0-8154-1127-8
$29.95

THE *KARLUK'S* LAST VOYAGE
An Epic of Death and Survival in the Arctic, 1913–1916
Captain Robert A. Bartlett
New introduction by Edward E. Leslie
378 pp., 23 b/w photos, 3 maps
0-8154-1124-3
$18.95

LIFE AS I FIND IT
A Treasury of Mark Twain Rarities
Edited by Charles Neider
with a new foreword
343 pp., 1 b/w photo
0-8154-1027-1
$17.95

THE TRAVELS OF MARK TWAIN
Edited by Charles Neider
448 pp., 6 b/w line drawings
0-8154-1039-5
$19.95

THE SELECTED LETTERS OF MARK TWAIN
Edited by Charles Neider
352 pp., 1 b/w photo
0-8154-1011-5
$16.95

MARK TWAIN: PLYMOUTH ROCK AND THE PILGRIMS
and Other Essays
Edited by Charles Neider
368 pp.
0-8154-1104-9
$18.95

ESSAYS OF THE MASTERS
Edited by Charles Neider
480 pp.
0-8154-1097-2
$17.95

GREAT SHIPWRECKS AND CASTAWAYS
Firsthand Accounts of Disasters at Sea
Edited by Charles Neider
256 pp.
0-8154-1094-8
$16.95

T. E. LAWRENCE
A Biography
Michael Yardley
308 pp., 71 b/w photos., 5 b/w maps
0-8154-1054-9
$17.95

THE WAR OF 1812
Henry Adams
New introduction by Col. John R. Elting
377 pp., 27 b/w maps & sketches
0-8154-1013-1
$18.95